AMERICAN
FOREIGN
POLICY

Past, Present, Future

AMERICAN FOREIGN POLICY

Past, Present, Future

Sixth Edition

GLENN P. HASTEDT

James Madison University

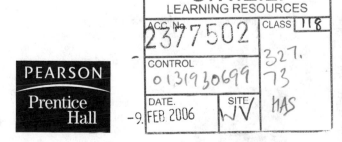

PEARSON
Prentice
Hall

Upper Saddle River, New Jersey 07458

Library of Congress Cataloging-in-Publication Data

Hastedt, Glenn P.
  American foreign policy : past, present, future / Glenn P. Hastedt.—6th ed.
    p. cm.
  Includes bibliographical references.
  ISBN 0-13-193069-9
  1. United States—Foreign relations. 2. United States—Foreign relations—1945-1989
3. United States–Foreign relations—1989– 4. United States—Foreign relations administration.
I. Title.
  E183.7.H27 2005
  327.73′009–dc22

                                                                    2005008360

Editorial Director: Charlyce Jones-Owen
Editorial Assistant: Suzanne Remore
Marketing Manager: Kara Kindstrom
Marketing Assistant: Jennifer Lang
Managing Editor: Lisa Iarkowski
Production Editor: Fran Russello
Manufacturing Buyer: Sherry Lewis

Cover Design: Bruce Kenselaar
Cover Director: Jayne Conte
Composition/Full-Service Project Management:
  Jan Pushard/Pine Tree Composition, Inc.
Printer/Binder: R.R. Donnelley & Sons, Inc.
Cover Printer: R.R.Donnelley & Sons, Inc.

Pearson Education LTD., London
Pearson Education Singapore, Pte. Ltd
Pearson Education, Canada, Ltd
Pearson Education—Japan
Pearson Education Australia PTY, Limited

Pearson Education North Asia Ltd
Pearson Educación de Mexico, S.A. de C.V.
Pearson Education Malaysia, Pte. Ltd
Pearson Education, Upper Saddle River, New Jersey

10 9 8 7 6 5 4 3 2 1
ISBN 0-13-193069-9

To Cathy,
Sarah,
and Matthew

CONTENTS

Chapter 7:   The Constitution and Foreign Affairs   160

✳ Chapter 8:   The Presidency   182

Chapter 9:   Congress and Foreign Policy   200

Chapter 10:   The Foreign Affairs Bureaucracy   218

Chapter 11:   Models of Policy Making: Overview   246

Chapter 12:   Decision Making: Case Studies   261

Chapter 13:   Diplomacy   283

Chapter 14:   Covert Action   303

Chapter 15:   The Economic Instruments   326

Chapter 16:   Military Power   347

Chapter 17:   Arms Control and Missile Defense   373

— PREFACE —

The terrorist attacks on the World Trade Center and the Pentagon on September 11, 2001 marked a turning point in American foreign policy. For more than a decade, American foreign policy seemed to be adrift. While the cold war had ended, the post–cold war era had yet to take on a defining characteristic. This period brought forward a host of suggestions from academics and practitioners as to what direction American foreign policy ought to take. The American public, however, was not very engaged in this debate. Domestic issues rather than foreign policy problems commanded their attention.

With the attacks of 9/11, Americans rediscovered the world. For at least a moment, the shape of the post–cold war era became clear to most Americans, and the time for debate had passed. The terrorist attacks demanded unity of purpose. It was not long, however, before expressions of doubt and caution were being raised about the feasibility of the original set of goals set forward by President George W. Bush, the language used to frame the challenges facing the United States, and the proper American response. These doubts and concerns intensified as the United States moved toward war with Iraq and then came face-to-face with the challenges of occupation and reconstruction.

The events of 9/11 are a turning point, not because they ended debate over American foreign policy but because they provide a new point of reference for an ongoing debate over its content and conduct. Choices continue to exist. We continue to need to understand where we have been, where we are today, and where we want to go.

Conceptually and organizationally, the sixth edition of *American Foreign Policy: Past, Present, Future* remains the same. Part I examines the global context of American foreign policy. Part II examines the historical context of American foreign policy. Part III examines the domestic setting of American foreign policy and the foreign affairs government. Part IV looks at the process by which American foreign policy is made. Part V presents an overview of the foreign policy tools at the disposal of policy makers. Part VI concludes the discussion of American foreign policy with a survey of alternative futures.

Material in each of the chapters has been updated to include recent events in American foreign policy. Those who have used previous editions will also find some additional changes in how the same chapters are structured. Chapter 1 now contains a discussion of "American Hegemony" and "What the World Wants from the United States" Chapter 2 has been reorganized to end with extended discussion of terrorism. The discussion in Chapter 4 has been refocused around a theme of grand strategies with much of the international economic material removed. A summary section looks at the George W. Bush administration and the war on terrorism. Chapter 6 contains a discussion of the media and the Iraq War. The major change is the inclusion of a lengthy example of how intelligence was used to build support for the Iraq War. Chapter 7 contains a section on "Civil Liberties" under War Powers. A discussion of the role of Vice President and Chief of Staff as influences on decision making has been added to Chapter 8. In Chapter 9, the discussion of the changing relationship between Congress and the president has been rewritten and tightened. A discussion of the Department of Homeland Security has been added to Chapter 10. A major change takes place in Chapter 12: Two case studies have been removed and one added on pre–9/11 intelligence policy and the war on terrorism. Chapter 13 now has a section on public diplomacy and an expanded discussion on deterrence that brings in material that had been in Chapter 16. In Chapter 15, the section on economic sanctions was reorganized and updated. There is a short case study on sanctions against Libya. Preemption is discussed in Chapter 16. Chapter 17 has been tightened, shortened, and updated. Finally, in Chapter 18, there has been a general updating of material. The discussion of each alternative future now ends with a paragraph relating it to terrorism.

Glenn P. Hastedt

AMERICAN FOREIGN POLICY

Past, Present, Future

— *1* —

THE GLOBAL SETTING
OF AMERICAN FOREIGN POLICY

Why the International System Matters

The terrorist attacks of 9/11 and subsequent events drive home two important points about why the international system matters to the United States.
First, it is simultaneously a source of threats and opportunities. President
George W. Bush spoke to both when he identified a Saddam Hussein–led
Iraq as a threat to American security and portrayed a democratic Iraq as key
to the future stability and prosperity of the Middle East. Second, and often
less appreciated, the international system is capable of exerting a powerful
influence on American domestic politics. In the case of the 9/11 attacks, we
can see this most clearly in the creation of a Department of Homeland Security and the passage of the USA Patriot Act that was passed in October
2001, forty-five days after those deadly attacks. Its provisions allowed federal
investigators to monitor individuals who have been identified as suspects
and search their homes and offices without prior notice. Noncitizens may
be jailed on suspicion of involvement in terrorist acts and detained indefinitely in six-month intervals without meaningful judicial review. Less visible
are changes mandated by membership in the World Trade Organization.
For example, it ruled that tax breaks given to exporters that amount to $5
billion annually are an unfair subsidy. In order to avoid a $4 billion annual
penalty, Congress has had to rewrite tax laws for U.S. exporters. Taking a
broader perspective, scholars have argued that through America's participation in war and trade, the international system has refashioned the make-up
of the American population through immigration, promoted a sense of

civic volunteerism in the American public, and altered the power of political institutions.[1]

Two much commented upon features of the contemporary international system provide us with a window on the scope of the over America's relationship to the world. They are globalization and American hegemony.

GLOBALIZATION

Globalization is the most frequent term used to characterize the structure of the international economic system today.[2] It is a summary term that speaks to the "intrusive and intense economic interaction" currently taking place in the international economy among "a large and growing number of entities outside government control." It has been brought on by rapid advances in communication and information technologies and government policies designed to reduce barriers to the free flow of goods and capital across national boundaries. Globalization is, at the same time, credited with promoting prosperity and growth for the U.S. economy while it is held accountable for the loss of jobs and increasing income disparities.

Richard Haass and Robert Litan assert that "globalization is a reality, not a choice."[3] The problem facing the United States is not whether to participate in a globalized economy but how to participate. Focusing on the economic costs and benefits of globalization, they argue against erecting economic barriers whose purpose it would be to insulate the American economy from the forces of globalization. Instead, they urge that ways be found to better manage America's participation in a globalized economy.

Security specialists also see dangers in globalization. They note that "with this advent of this burgeoning free trade in technical ideas and the people who think about them, we have entered a new era in the history of [nuclear] proliferation." These dangers extend beyond the domain of highly sophisticated weapons technologies. Michael Klare notes that small arms and light weapons now play a central role in many ethnic and sectarian conflicts.[4] In fact, they have become weapons of choice. These weapons are easily produced and readily obtained in the global marketplace. The Israeli Uzi submachine gun is in the inventory of thirty-nine states, and the Belgian FAL assault rifle has been manufactured in such diverse states as Argentina, Australia, Canada, Mexico, Israel, and South Africa.

The potential impact of globalization extends far beyond realms of military security and economic prosperity. Benjamin Barber fears that the emerging global consumer culture that is accompanying economic globalization is indifferent to the existence of democracy in the United States and around the world.[5] Alan Tonelson is also fearful of the noneconomic consequences of globalization.[6] He sees the globalization of production as threatening America's future as a cohesive and successful society. David Rieff summarizes many of these concerns in worrying that "globalization is an extremely unfavorable environment for the exercise of great power duties and prerogatives, at least as traditionally understood."[7]

AMERICAN HEGEMONY

In the early 1990s, in the first years after the end of the cold war, a great debate raged over the direction in which the international system would evolve. Few questioned the assertion that the United States had won the cold war, but many doubted that it could remain the sole remaining superpower for very long. The logic of world politics seemed to dictate that other states would try to balance its military power and that, as a result, we would soon see the emergence of a bipolar or, more likely, a multipolar system. Today there is little life in this debate. Virtually all observers speak of unchallenged American military hegemony. The international military system is solidly unipolar. Some go so far as to argue that the United States is so strong that it cannot be balanced in the foreseeable future.[8]

The implications and dynamics of American hegemony, however, are unclear. Consider first the question of implications. American hegemony means that the United States is without military peers. The terrorist attacks of 9/11 and concerns over weapons of mass destruction in the hands of rogue states suggest that it does not mean that the United States operates in a threat-free world. It is now the power of the weak that poses dangers and not the power of equals, such as was the case with the Soviet Union during the cold war. New strategies and forms of military power may be needed to deal with these asymmetric threats.[9] President George W. Bush has asserted as much by advocating that a policy of preemption replace the cold war strategies of deterrence and containment. The violence and instability that have characterized the occupation and reconstruction of Iraq suggests that American hegemony may not mean that the United States can do without the help of other states and the international community more broadly in pursuing its foreign policy goals. It also needs to be recognized that allies may pay a price in supporting the United States. Fouad Ajami observed of the United States' role in the Middle East shortly after 9/11, "a foreign power that stands sentry in that world cannot spare its local allies the retribution of those who brand them 'collaborators' and betrayers of the faith."[10] Overwhelming military power thus might not allow the United States to have its way on all issues.

Similar uncertainties exist over the dynamics of American hegemony. A debate persists over how long it can endure.[11] Pessimists continue to assert that balancing by other major powers is to be expected and the end of American hegemony is inevitable. Optimists hold that so long as the United States acts with restraint and pursues limited objectives, other states will remain on the American bandwagon indefinitely. A parallel debate exists over the location of the primary threat to American hegemony. Is it external, to be found in the actions of other states, or will hegemony pass because of the unwillingness of Americans to bear the economic and political burdens of being the world's only superpower. Finally, there is the question of whether American hegemony is worth the price. Is it desirable? In a manner of speaking, President George W. Bush touched on this question when in his address to the American people following the 9/11 attacks he asked, "Why do they hate us?"

WHAT THE WORLD WANTS FROM THE UNITED STATES

Efforts to answer the president's question have produced a multilay-ered picture of how the world sees the United States.[12] A sampling of these views is presented in Table 1.1. To begin with there is much about the United States that is viewed in a positive light. This is especially true for those who have visited the United States or are in regular communication with Americans. It is still the indispensable power, and broad support exists for the general goal of combating terrorism. Few people around the world are interested in seeing a second superpower emerge. American technology is widely admired, but American democracy receives mixed reviews around the world. The American model is seen in a positive light in many parts of the developing world and in Eastern Europe. West Europe and Russia hold more negative views as do the people of the Middle East. There is also much with which the world finds fault. For many in the Arab world America's greatest sins are careless acts of omission. They point to failures in American foreign policy to produce a meaningful peace settlement between Israel and the Palestinians, its support of conservative and anti-democratic oil-rich regimes, and its willingness to use military and economic force against the Iraqi people in its effort to remove Saddam Hussein from power. More gen-erally in the world, concern is expressed for America's unpredictability in conducting its foreign policy, its unwillingness to show respect for and give consideration to the feelings of others; they also fear the "Americanization" of their societies, and are critical of the American unwillingness to treat ad-vanced science and technology as a common public good to which all states can have access.

For Fouad Ajami, the reasons for these competing positive and negative views of the United States can be traced back to its hegemonic position.[13] Be-cause of the unrivaled scope of its power, any foreign policy position is bound to be praised by some and offend others. He notes, "for the crowds in Karachi, Cairo, and Amman, [the United States] could never get it right . . . the more pro-American the regime, the more anti-American the political class." But the world's simultaneous attraction to the United States and its re-sentment of it springs from even deeper sources. The United States comes to the far corners of the world bringing with it modernity and has done so for many years. Approached from this perspective, the current wave of global anti-Americanism predates the Bush administration and its unilateral foreign policy. It is neither new nor to be worried about.

While it is a striking feature of the contemporary international system, globalization is not its sole defining characteristic. Some observers stress the continued importance of underlying structural constants in assessing the ways in which the international system provides opportunities and challenges to policy makers. Others emphasize the importance of post–World War II trends. More recently some scholars have begun to catalog the emerging characteristics of the post–cold war era. In the remainder of this chapter, we examine each of these aspects of the contemporary international system in order to clarify the global setting of American foreign policy.

TABLE 1.1 Global Opinion of the United States, 2002

Country	% Favorable	% Unfavorable	%DK/refused to answer
Canada	72	27	3
Great Britain	75	16	9
France	63	35	2
Poland	79	11	2
Russia	61	33	6
Pakistan	10	69	20
Egypt	6	69	25
Mexico	64	25	11
Japan	72	26	2
South Korea	53	44	3
South Africa	65	28	8

Global Opinion on U.S. Foreign Policy and the War on Terror, 2002

Country	U.S. Foreign Policy Considers Others		U.S.-led War on Terror	
	Yes	No	Favor	Oppose
Canada	25	75	68	27
Great Britain	44	52	69	23
France	21	76	75	23
Poland	29	59	81	11
Russia	21	70	73	16
Pakistan	23	36	20	45
Egypt	17	66	5	79
Mexico	42	52	52	37
Japan	36	59	61	32
South Korea	23	73	24	72
South Africa	51	35	55	32

Global Opinion on Spread of American Ideas and Customs, 2002

Country	Good	Bad	DK/refused to answer
Canada	37	54	8
Great Britain	39	50	11
France	25	71	4
Poland	31	55	14
Russia	16	68	15
Pakistan	2	81	17
Egypt	6	84	10
Mexico	22	65	13
Japan	49	35	15
South Korea	30	62	8
South Africa	43	45	12

Source: "What the World Thinks in 2002"; Report of the Pew Global Attitudes Project, www.people-press.org.

The International System: Structural Constants

DECENTRALIZATION

The first enduring feature of the international system is its decentralized nature. Unlike in highly developed domestic political systems, there exist no central political institutions to make laws or see to their enforcement. In addition, there is no common political culture in which to anchor an agreed-upon set of norms governing the behavior of states. The combined result is a highly competitive international system in which there is a constant expectation of violence and very little expectation that either international law or appeals to moral principles will greatly influence the resolution of an issue.

Decentralization does not mean that the international system operates in a state of anarchy. Ordered anarchy would be a more apt characterization. For while enforceable laws and common values are absent, rules do exist that lend a measure of predictability and certainty to international transactions. They do so by indicating the limits of permissible behavior and the directions to follow in settling disputes. Rules are less permanent than laws, are more general in nature, and tend to be normative statements rather than commands. Different international systems operate according to different rules and therefore place different opportunities and challenges before policy makers. Neutrality, for example, is generally held to be permissible according to the rules of loose bipolarity but impossible under the rules of tight bipolarity.

SELF-HELP SYSTEM

The second structural constant grows out of the first: The international system is a self-help system. States must rely on only themselves to accomplish their foreign policy goals. To do otherwise runs the risk of manipulation or betrayal at the hands of another state. It is important to stress that great powers as well as smaller powers need to heed the admonition to avoid excessive dependence on others. One of the points stressed by opponents within the Reagan administration to using Israel as a go-between in its plan to sell weapons to Iran in hopes of gaining the release of American hostages in Lebanon was that Israeli and U.S. national interests were not identical and that in some cases they were in direct conflict.[14]

The self-help principle challenges policy makers to bring goals and power resources into balance. Pursuing more goals than one has the resources to accomplish or squandering resources on secondary objectives saps the vitality of the state and makes it unable to respond effectively to future challenges. Vietnam is argued by many to be a classic example of the inability to balance goals and resources and its crippling consequences. American policy makers entered into the Vietnam conflict with little understanding of the history of the region or of the Vietnamese struggle for independence. Once involved, U.S. policy produced steady increases in the level of the U.S. commitment to the war, but it did not bring the United States any closer to victory. Instead the reverse occurred. The longer the United States was there and the greater the level of this commitment, the more elusive victory became. Perhaps most frustrating was the inability to devise a workable exit scenario. The Vietnam experience continues to cast a long shadow over U.S. foreign policy. Many conservatives agree that the Vietnam syndrome has prevented the United States from acquiring either the capability or the will to protect its vital interests in the Persian Gulf, Angola, or Central America.

A STRATIFIED SYSTEM

The third structural constant is the stratified nature of the international system. The equality of states embedded in the concept of sovereignty is a legal myth. The principle of sovereignty dates back to the Treaty of Westphalia and the beginnings of the modern state system in 1648. It holds that no legal authority exists above the state except that which the state voluntarily accepts. The reality of international politics is quite different, and sovereignty is a matter of degree rather than an absolute condition. States are "born unequal."[15] The resources they draw on for their power are distributed unequally across the globe. As such, the ability of states to accomplish their foreign policy objectives (as well as their very choice of objectives) will vary from state to state.

Two key areas of disagreement among recent administrations have been over how great a degree of power inequality exists in the international system and the identity of the power centers. Reagan's foreign policy was based on the assumption that the international system is essentially bipolar. The Soviet Union and the United States were held to be the two central actors involved in a global power struggle. Furthermore, it was a struggle in which incompatible ideologies were a powerful force in affecting foreign policy decisions. The Carter, Ford, and Nixon administrations all saw power distributed more broadly, and ideology was seen as less of an important factor for the operation of the international system. The Nixon and Ford foreign policies stressed the ability to coexist with Russia (the policy of détente) and alluded to using other powers as counterweights to Russia (the "China card"). The early Carter administration also felt that the United States could coexist with the Soviet Union. Its foreign policy differed from its predecessors' in its emphasis on human rights and economic issues. This switch in concerns brought with it a shift in the identification of power centers away from the Soviet Union and toward Western Europe, Japan, and key third world states. With the invasion of Afghanistan, Carter's priorities changed, and once again the Soviet threat became the primary foreign policy problem for the United States.

The dramatic easing of cold war hostilities that took place early in the Bush administration left unchanged the stratified nature of world politics. What it did was change the identity of the key world powers and the likely arenas of conflict; consequently, the Soviet military threat is being replaced by Japanese and German economic power.

The International System: Postwar Trends

DIFFUSION OF POWER

Although the basic structure of the international system has endured over time, the system itself is not unchanging. Four post–World War II trends are especially notable: a diffusion of power, issue proliferation, actor proliferation, and regional diversity. Power is the ability to achieve objectives. It is typically viewed as something one possesses, a commodity to be acquired, stored, and manipulated. But power must also be viewed as a relational concept. What is ultimately at issue is not how much power a state has, but how much power it has in a specific issue compared to those it is dealing with.

The postwar era has seen a steady diffusion of power. This in turn has created a frustrating gap between the ends and means of U.S. foreign policy. It is not so much that the quantity of power possessed by the United States has declined. U.S. dominance in the field of nuclear weapons remains unchallenged. The same holds true for conventional weapons. What has changed is the utility of certain types of power, the issues being contested, and the ability of other states to exploit points of sensitivity and vulnerability. The international distribution of power no longer resembles a steep pyramid. It now is one with a bulge in the middle made up of states that possess sufficient power resources to block or resist American initiatives. A prime example is the 1999 expansion of the Group of Eight (G-8), made up of the leading economic powers in the world, into the Group of 20. As a consequence, bargaining and negotiation have replaced command and domination as a key feature of the relationship between the United States and other states.

The causes for the diffusion of power can be found both in the specifics of American foreign policy and in the more universal cycles of hegemonic decline. Robert Gilpin, after examining the decline of empires throughout history, asserts that we can identify a cycle of hegemonic decline.[16] As the cycle progresses, a combination of the burdens of imperial leadership, increased emphasis on the consumption of goods and services, and the international diffusion of technology conspire to sap the strength of the imperial state and bring about its decline.

The specific successes and failures of postwar American foreign policy have also contributed to this diffusion of power. The impact of foreign policy failures is relatively easy to anticipate. In the wake of defeat follows the search for scapegoats, a disillusionment with the task undertaken, and a desire to avoid similar situations. Vietnam stands out as the most significant military failure, and it is held by many to have been responsible for destroying the postwar domestic consensus on the purpose of American power.

Economic failures have also contributed to the diffusion of power. Economic sanctions directed against Castro in the 1960s failed to bring down his regime and only made him more dependent on Soviet support. Repeated efforts at bringing about economic and social development in the third world, such as Truman's Point Four Program and Kennedy's Alliance for Progress, have also failed. The continued existence of widespread poverty has proven to be a fertile breeding ground for anti-U.S. nationalist and revolutionary forces.

Even American foreign policy successes have hastened the decline of U.S. dominance. The reconstruction of the Japanese and Western European economies ranks as two truly remarkable achievements. In a sense U.S. foreign policy has almost been too successful here. These economies are now major economic rivals of the U.S. economy and often outperform it. The North Atlantic Treaty Organization (NATO) is another success that has had a dual impact. Its creation in 1949 did succeed in erecting a military shield for Western Europe and in stopping any further Soviet expansion into Europe. At the same time NATO offered U.S. European allies, most notably the French, the opportunity to pursue their own foreign policy objectives, often at the expense of U.S. interests.

ISSUE PROLIFERATION

The second area of evolutionary change is issue proliferation. More is involved here than simply an increase in the number of issues on the foreign policy agenda. Their character has also changed as the line between foreign and domestic policy has become increasingly blurred. Not long ago one could speak of a clear-cut foreign affairs issue hierarchy. At the top were a relatively small number of high-politics problems involving questions of national security, territorial integrity, and political independence. At the bottom were the numerically more prevalent low-politics issues of commerce, energy, environment, and so on. Although largely intuitive, the line between high and low politics was well established. The positions occupied by issues in this hierarchy were also relatively fixed. This allowed policy makers to develop a familiarity with the issues before them and the options open to them. Today this is no longer the case.

The high-politics category has become crowded. The oil crisis and fear of resource scarcity elevated economic issues to the status of national security issues. Economic recession and high unemployment have made the existence of an open international system a question of high politics. There is now also a great deal of movement within the high–low ranking system. Under Carter human rights for a time became a pivotal concern for the United States. Under the Reagan administration it returned to a low-politics position when the emphasis shifted to international terrorism.

The high–low politics distinction was implicitly based on the existence of a prior distinction between foreign and domestic policy. This distinction has become increasingly difficult to maintain. How, for example, do we classify attempts to get Japan to agree to export restrictions on goods shipped to the United States or the negotiations over the damage done in Canada by acid rain originating in U.S.-based industries? The term increasingly used to characterize these and other issues that contain significant domestic and international dimensions is *intermestic* (*inter* from international and *mestic* from domestic).[17] Issue proliferation has thus brought with it added complexity. Policy makers must judge not only the ranking of an issue but also the extent of its domestic impact. They then must be prepared to constantly reevaluate their thinking in light of changing circumstances. Tables 1.2 and 1.3 illustrate

TABLE 1.2 Illustrative Distribution of Issues in Late 1960s

FOREIGN POLICY "IMPORTANCE"	100% Domestic	50/50 Intermestic	100% Foreign Policy
High		Vietnam War	Nuclear strategy Arms control
		Recognizing China	Covert actions Foreign aid
			Test Ban Treaty Tariffs Energy Grain sales Routine diplomatic negotiations
Low	Interest rates Environmental standards		

RELATIVE IMPORTANCE OF FOREIGN
AND DOMESTIC CONSIDERATIONS
TO RESOLUTION OF ISSUE

TABLE 1.3 Illustrative Distribution of Issues in Early 1980s

FOREIGN POLICY "IMPORTANCE"	100% Domestic	50/50 Intermestic	100% Foreign Policy
High	Arms control/ Nuclear freeze	MX	
	Panama Canal Treaty	Covert action	Human rights— Carter
	Energy policy Tariffs/Quotas	Foreign aid	International terrorism— Reagan
	Grain sales		
		China/Taiwan	
	Interest rates		Human rights— Reagan
	Environmental standards		Routine diplomatic negotiations
Low			

RELATIVE IMPORTANCE OF FOREIGN
AND DOMESTIC CONSIDERATIONS
TO RESOLUTION OF ISSUE

how the high–low scale and the foreign–domestic scale can be used to classify issues and show how issues have changed position over time.

ACTOR PROLIFERATION

The third evolutionary feature of the international system is actor proliferation. On the one hand, actor proliferation has taken the form of an expansion in the number of states. In 1982, the United States had diplomatic relations with 150 states. This compares to 130 in 1970, 74 in 1950, and 58 in 1930. This expansion in the number of states has brought with it a corresponding expansion in the number of views that can be found on any given problem. Quite often these views are based on different starting premises and assumptions from those held by the United States. The Law of the Sea Conference illustrates the impact that the proliferation of states has had on U.S. foreign policy. The very number of states participating presented great obstacles to achieving an agreement. So too did the diversity of views expressed, as well as the intensity with which they were held. The decision-making rules for the proposed International Seabed Authority that would oversee seabed mineral exploration emerged as a major point of contention. The United States insisted on some form of weighted voting. It refused to participate in a system where it could be outvoted by an alliance of small states. In the end, these problems produced a situation where on April 30, 1982, the United States was the only Western industrialized state that refused to sign the treaty. One hundred and thirty states voted to sign it and thereby concluded a process of negotiation and discussion begun in 1967.

Although the growth in the number of states has nearly run its course, continued growth is taking place in a second area, nonstate actors. States have never been the only actors in world politics. Yet it is only comparatively recently that nonstate actors have appeared in sufficient numbers and possessed control over enough resources to be significant actors in world politics. Three categories of nonstate actors may be identified. They are intergovernmental organizations (IGOs) such as the United Nations, NATO, and the Organization of American States; nongovernmental organizations (NGOs) such as General Motors, the International Red Cross, the Catholic Church, and the Palestine Liberation Organization; and subnational actors such as the Central Intelligence Agency (CIA), Defense Department, New York City, and Texas.

Statistically, the growth in the number of nonstate actors has been explosive.[18] On the eve of World War I, there were only forty-nine IGOs and 170 NGOs. In 1940, the numbers had grown to over eighty IGOs and about 500 NGOs. By the mid-1970s, there were approximately 300 IGOs and 2,400 NGOs. Of the NGOs existing in 1966, 501 were founded after 1950 and 251 after 1960. The emergence of nonstate actors as a significant force in world politics is generally tied to the inability of the state to adequately respond to the demands citizens place on it. In some cases, they have emerged as by-products of state efforts to meet these demands. In others, they have emerged as challenges to the state for the loyalties of its citizens.

Actor proliferation has also altered in three ways the context within which American foreign policy decisions are made. First, the presence and actions of nonstate actors have altered the language used in thinking about foreign policy problems. The language of the cold war now competes with the imagery of interdependence for the attention of policy makers. Second, nonstate actors often serve as potential instruments of foreign policy. There are major advantages to using a nonstate actor to advance state objectives. By not being identified as part of a state, their actions may be better received by other actors. Decisions made by the International Monetary Fund or World Bank tend to be more readily accepted by third world states than if they had come directly from the United States. The third impact nonstate actors have on U.S. foreign policy is that they often limit the options open to policy makers. Their ability to resist and frustrate state initiatives necessitates that policy makers consider courses of action that they otherwise would likely reject. The Palestine Liberation Organization serves as just such a complicating and limiting factor in attempts to construct a viable Middle East peace plan.

REGIONAL DIVERSITY

As a superpower, the United States is concerned not only with the structure and operation of the international system as a whole but also with the operation of its subsystems. Three subsystems are especially important to the United States. Each presents the United States with different management problems and thus requires a different solution.[19] It should be stressed that U.S. policy makers have not always viewed the world from this perspective, nor do they uniformly do so today. For much of the cold war era, the international system was viewed as an undifferentiated whole in which competition with the Soviet Union was the key management problem. The first is the Western system, which is made up of the advanced industrial states of the United States, Canada, Western Europe, and Japan. The principal problem in the Western system is managing interdependence. At issue is the distribution of costs and benefits. U.S. leadership and initiative once so eagerly sought by its allies is now often resisted. For its part the United States has begun to question the costs of leadership and seeks to have its allies pick up a larger share of the defense burden. A similar situation holds for economic relations. Many in the United States are no longer willing to underwrite a free trade system or to accept economic discrimination in the name of alliance unity, whereas U.S. allies have become increasingly disenchanted with U.S. economic policies.

The second subsystem is the North–South system. A quite different set of perspectives governs interactions in this system from that in the Western system. In place of expectations of sharing and mutual gain, the South perceives exploitation. The fundamental management problem in the North–South system is coping with military and economic dependence. Whereas solutions to the problems of interdependence lie in the fine-tuning of existing international organizations and practices, solutions to the problems of dependence require constructing a new system that the South is willing to accept as legitimate and in which it is treated as an equal.

The third subsystem of concern to the United States is the East–West system. The fundamental management problem here is one of reintegration. The cold war divided the East and West into two largely self-contained, competing military and economic parts. Détente brought about a limited reintegration of the East and West in the 1970s through arms control and trade agreements. The demise of communism in the Soviet Union and Eastern Europe along with the collapse of the Soviet Union has greatly complicated this task and lent an aura of urgency to it. The task is now seen as urgent because of fears for what a Russian economic collapse could mean for the global economy and its ability to control its remaining nuclear forces. The task is complicated by the fact that there still exists a great military and economic power in the "East" (China), whose reintegration into a Western-centered international military and economic system appears fraught with domestic and international difficulties.

The International System: Emerging Characteristics of the Post–Cold War World

Up until the terrorist attacks of 9/11, the contemporary international system lacked a defining identity. Just as the late 1940s were referred to as the "post–World War II" period, so the 1990s were the "post–cold war" period. It may be that in the future we will come to see the terrorist attacks of that day as inaugurating a new era of world politics with its own temperament. Because much is still uncertain for now, it is better to try and look beyond terrorism in order to more clearly recognize the full range of forces that are currently shaping the international system.

John Lewis Gaddis suggests that we might think about the current international system as being composed of a struggle between two underlying sets of forces tugging in opposite directions.[20] On the one hand are forces of integration that act to bring together peoples and countries. Opposed to it are the forces of fragmentation that work to resurrect old sources of friction and rivalry as well as create new ones. Gaddis notes that it is unclear which set of forces the United States ought to embrace in its foreign policy. Integrationist forces, he cautions, can be disruptive and do not offer automatic protection against unwanted events and trends. In fact, they may help bring them about and thus be part of the problem. Gaddis offers the AIDS pandemic as an example. The freer movement of peoples across international borders is certainly one of the most integrative forces at work in the world today. Yet it also is a major obstacle to dealing with AIDS and a source of friction among states.

Forces of integration and fragmentation are not new to the post–cold war era. Their potential for changing the landscape of world politics in fundamental ways is suggested by another metaphor employed by Gaddis. Borrowing from the field of geology, Gaddis asserts that we might think in terms of "tectonic motion." Geologists describe the earth's crust as composed of giant tectonic plates that press up against one another and are subject to tremendous pressures. Normally these pressures produce only the slightest amount of movement. However, under certain circumstances they can result in large-scale movements (that is, earthquakes, volcanic explosions) that literally reshape continents and alter their climates. From this perspective the challenge facing policy makers is to better understand the nature of tectonic motion so that they will not be as surprised by the end of the post-cold war era as they were by the end of the cold war.

Just what are these potentially volatile integrative and/or fragmenting forces? An extensive list of candidates exists to choose from. While the listing and importance attached to each varies from commentator to commentator, it is possible to identify seven forces that are receiving special attention.

The Proliferation of Weapons of Mass Destruction. A fundamental reality of the nuclear age is that the knowledge needed to build a nuclear weapon is readily available to those who want it. Two trends now merge with this reality to create a scenario in which a large number of states may soon possess an "at-the-ready" nuclear arsenal, one that can be assembled in a matter of hours or days.[21] One of these trends is the increasing ease with which nuclear weapons facilities can be constructed due to advances in technology. "Every year . . . the size of key facilities is getting smaller, as is the required number of scientists and technicians . . . the amount of electrical power consumed . . . and the time for each step in the nuclear weapons development process." The second trend is the diffusion of long-range delivery systems and advances in mobile tactical ballistic missile systems. On the one hand, this represents an extension of the ongoing process of power diffusion that was discussed above. On the other hand, it appears to hold the potential for radically transforming the basic structure of world politics that makes it an unprecedented occurrence. Morton Kaplan first spoke to the international system-transforming capabilities inherent in the widespread proliferation of such weapons in the late 1960s in his pioneering work on international systems theory.[22] He argued that each international system operated according to a unique set of rules determined by the distribution of power. Kaplan continued that the range of possible international systems that might come into existence was not limited by those which we had already experienced (that is, bipolar and multipolar). One such new international system was a unit veto system that could result from ten to twenty countries having a usable nuclear capability. The result would be a situation in which the great powers pursued largely isolationist foreign policies and where there were few alliances, as each state relied on the threat of nuclear retaliation to protect its interests.

The Emergence of New Forms of Power. Historically, the debate over how best to realize one's foreign policy objectives has been cast in terms of the relative utility of military power versus economic power. This debate continues in the post–cold war era, with many arguing that military power now has been supplanted once and for all by economic power as the instrument of choice by policy makers. This is not the first time that an obituary has been written for military power. Similar assessments about the lessened value of military power and the increased importance of economic power were made after Vietnam and during the OPEC-led oil price hikes of the early 1970s. What is new is that commentators are beginning to talk about a new form of power. Joseph Nye refers to it as "soft power." Soft power is not rooted in control of land, an abundance of natural resources, large populations, or inventories of weapons. It draws its strength primarily from human resources.[23] These are resources that the United States is rich in; they provide it with the ability to exert a leadership role in world affairs at a time when its other power resources may be in decline compared to other states. The system-transforming potential of soft power stems from the fact that in order to use it effectively policy makers must embrace a new view of leadership and think about power relationships differently. Soft power is not power that can be used to command or force other states to act in a prescribed fashion. Rather, it is power to lead by example and to foster cooperation. "It is the ability to structure a situation so that other countries develop preferences consistent with our goals."

Advances in Communication Technology. Writing in 1971, Swedish scholar Johan Galtung argued that in the future the advanced states of the world would no longer continue to exert their imperialistic control over less developed areas through the physical presence of troops as they did in the past or through the use of economic instruments such as multinational corporations and international financial and trade bodies as they were currently doing.[24] Instead, they would rely on instant communications where "parties who want to communicate with each other will set up ad hoc communication networks . . . guided by enormous data-banks and idea-banks that permit participants to find their opposite numbers." Live-time coverage of the 1991 attempted Soviet coup, the 1989 student demonstrations on Tiananmen Square, and the Persian Gulf War are testimony to Galtung's insight into the direction in which communications technologies were moving. What is still unclear is the exact role modern communication technologies will play in world politics. Will they allow leaders in one country to shape events abroad (as they did during the Soviet coup attempt and the Gulf War when U.S. leaders were able to judge for themselves what was happening and shape their policies accordingly)? Or will they exert an independent force pushing leaders into action where they otherwise might have remained silent (such as in the Tiananmen Square demonstrations when Chinese student protesters held up English language signs to television cameras)? Will policy be improved by the added information that this revolution in communication technology brings to the policy process, or will policy suffer as officials struggle to have an answer ready for an aroused public on the six o'clock news?

The Ethnicization of International Relations. During the cold war, scholars and practitioners developed a vocabulary to organize their thinking about world politics: East versus West; North versus South; client state; buffer state; and neutral state.[25] Often these terms obscured reality as much as they highlighted its vital characteristics. Still, they provided a point of departure for making policy. With the end of the cold war these concepts have lost much of their relevance. They no longer identify the major fault lines of international relations. A new vocabulary must be created. By the mid-1990s, a consensus had developed that at the center of this new vocabulary must be ethnic conflict. Not only are ethnic conflicts becoming internationalized but an eth-nicization of international relations is taking place. Increasingly states and in-ternational organizations are defining their foreign policies in terms of ethnic sympathies or finding that ethnic considerations weigh heavily in the choices before them. The choices themselves are changing as new forms of conflict management develop. Cold war peacekeeping efforts have been re-placed by peacemaking; UN trusteeship of colonial territories has been re-placed by UN efforts to save failed or failing states; deterrence, it is argued by some, must be replaced by a strategy of reassurance.

Political Fission. The most visible political fault line during the cold war was that separating communist and democratic states. The most signifi-cant political fault line, however, was that intensifying within communist states that led to the emergence of pro-democracy movements. Today three political fault lines are visible. The first separates status quo–oriented states and rogue states. Rogue states are those such as Syria, North Korea, Iran, Iraq under Saddam Hussein, and until recently Libya, which have been labeled as renegades by the United States. Individually and collectively, they are seen as failing to obey fundamental international agreements because of their sup-port for terrorism and often their interest in acquiring weapons of mass de-struction. The second fault line separates successful states from failed states. Failed states are those where the government no longer exists or is incapable of securing minimum levels of public order and services for its citizens.[26] These states do not so much support terrorism as they become the breeding grounds for terrorism and the countries from which terrorists operate. The third fault line separates social movements that seek political, social, and eco-nomic reform within societies and movements of rage.[27] These latter move-ments are groups that seek not only to overthrow societies rather than reform them, but they bring a conspiratorial and global perspective to their cause. Together they have brought an added element of "incoherence" to world pol-itics, as neither state nor international organizations appear to possess the necessary resources or political will to address the problems they create. Speaking in particular to the problems presented by movements of rage, one commentator observes, "policy can never speak to wrath."[28]

Shifting International Norms of State Behavior. Who is responsible for ending genocide in Rwanda or Sudan? Should all states have joined the coali-tion of the willing against Saddam Hussein? Can states reserve for themselves the right to continue to use landmines as the United States has done in the face of a global consensus to ban their use? The answers given to these ques-tions turn in large measure on one's point of reference for deciding proper state behavior. This is not as much a matter of international law as it is inter-national norms. Historically, nationalist norms framed these answers. A state's only responsibility was to further its own national interest. It mattered little what others thought was the proper course of action. Today this nationalist norm competes with three others for primacy in determining what is ex-pected of states.[29] A regional norm exists asserting that a state's behavior must be consistent with the expectations of states around it and that all states in a region share a special responsibility for maintaining peace and order both within states in the region and between them. An international norm expands the reference point for state behavior even further. It is not just the expectation of other states in the region that must be met in deciding on a course of action but all states. The scope of responsibility is now global. Finally we see a cosmopolitan norm emerging that suggests it is not the expectations of other states that matter but the expectations of people around the world who share a common sense of humanity. The presence of competing norms does more than create confusion and conflict over how states react when confronted with a foreign policy challenge. It also calls into question the fundamental nature of the relationship between states and the place of the state in world politics.

Global Resource Scarcity.   A two-front international struggle is emerging in the area of natural resources. The first involves a struggle for control over these resources along with the transit routes through which they must pass.[30] In some respects, this is nothing new. Control over coal and oil has long been an important building block for economic and military power. Globalization, however, has given new impetus to the need to control natural resources. Fueled in large part by technological breakthroughs and rising consumer expectations around the world, globalization has resulted in rapid economic growth and a significant increase in the demand for raw materials. Consider what is happening in China. In 1985, less than one in five urban Chinese households owned a color television. By 1998, the average urban household had more than one. A Department of Energy study predicts that between 1997 and 2020 China's consumption of energy will increase about four times that of the United States and Europe. If correct, this translates into a 150 percent increase in oil consumption, a 158 percent increase in coal consumption, and a 1,100 percent increase in natural gas consumption. Oil (Caspian Sea, South China Sea, Persian Gulf), water (Jordan, Nile, Tigris-Euphrates, Indus Rivers), and minerals and timber (Borneo, Liberia, Philippines, Sierra Leone, Angola, Brazil, Congo) are among the natural resources likely to be most contested through economic, diplomatic, and military means.

The second front in the struggle for control over natural resources is environmental in nature.[31] It involves efforts to preserve and protect natural resources and endangered species from extinction and to improve the quality of air, water, and other shared resources. The situation confronting rain forests provides a vivid illustration of the resource war from this perspective. Only one fifth of the world's original forest cover remains intact. In South America, as much as 645,000 square kilometers of forest were lost to resettlements, agriculture, and logging activities between 1980 and 1990. This struggle is almost entirely diplomatic. At the multilateral level, it has played out in international conferences such as the one that produced the 1997 Kyoto Protocol and that met in Rio de Janeiro in 1992 for the Earth Summit. At the bilateral level, it has taken the form of debt relief legislation such as that signed in 1998 by Bill Clinton that forgave some debts in return for undertaking conservation initiatives.

Plan of the Text

In this chapter, we have examined the ways in which the international system affects U.S. foreign policy and how policy makers have struggled with defining the American national interest. The global setting is one of four influences that serve as background factors in the making of U.S. foreign policy. The other three are past foreign policy undertakings, the American national style, and our ability to learn from the past. Understanding U.S. foreign policy requires us to be sensitive to these more general influences as well as to be aware of how U.S. foreign policy is made and the instruments available to policy makers. The discussion of the foreign policy process begins with an examination of the domestic context within which policy makers operate and then proceeds to examine the major institutional actors in the making of American foreign policy. Next, we turn our attention to policy-making models and case studies to help us better understand how these political forces interact. The following section introduces us to five policy instruments that are of special importance for understanding U.S. foreign policy: diplomacy, economics, covert action, military power, and arms control. The text concludes by presenting eight alternative future paths that American foreign policy might travel down. Within this broad framework of broad-based background factors and more narrowly focused process- and instrument-oriented constraints, no attempt is made to identify a correct interpretation of events or course of action. Instead, a balanced discussion of alternative viewpoints is presented and questions are put forward in the hope of challenging readers to think critically about how U.S. foreign policy can build on its past and present in order to better confront the future. Before completing our overview of the background factors that influence American foreign policy we turn our attention in the next chapter to a discussion of the concepts of foreign policy and the national interest.

Notes

1. Ira Katznelson and Martin Shefter (eds.), *Shaped by War and Trade* (Princeton, NJ: Princeton University Press, 2002).
2. See the annual report on measuring globalization that appears in *Foreign Policy,* Frank Lehner and John Boli (eds.), *The Globalization Reader* (Malden, MA: Blackwell, 2000); and Manfred Steger (ed.), *Rethinking Globalism* (Lanham, MD: Rowman and Littlefield, 2004).
3. Richard Haass and Robert Litan, "Globalization and Its Discontents: Navigating the Dangers of an Entangled World," *Foreign Affairs,* 77 (1998), 2–6.
4. Michael Klare, "The New Arms Race," *Current History,* 96 (April 1997), 173–78.
5. Benjamin Barber, "Democracy at Risk," *World Policy Journal,* 15 (1998), 29–41.
6. Alan Tonelson, "Globalization: The Great American Non-Debate," *Current History,* 96 (November 1997), 353–59.
7. David Rieff, "A Second American Century? The Paradoxes of Power," *World Policy Journal,* 16 (1999/2000), 7–14.
8. William Wohlforth, "U.S. Strategy in a Unipolar World," in G. John Ikenberry (ed.), *America Unrivaled* (Ithaca, NY: Cornell University Press, 2002), 98–118.
9. On the need for a new grand strategy for the United States, see Robert Art, *A Grand Strategy for America* (Ithaca, NY: Cornell University Press, 2003); Joseph Nye, Jr., *The Paradox of American Power*

(New York: Oxford University Press, 2002); and Charles Kupchan, *The End of the American Era* (New York: Knopf, 2002).

10. Fouad Ajami, "The Sentry's Solitude," *Foreign Affairs,* 80 (2001), 15.

11. See Ethan Kapstein and Michael Mastanduno (eds.), *Unipolar Politics* (New York: Columbia University Press, 1999); Christopher Layne, "The Unipolar Illusion," *International Security,* 17 (1993), 5–51; and Robert Kagan and William Kristol (eds.), *Present Dangers* (San Francisco: Encounter Books, 200).

12. See Alexander Lennon (ed.), *What Does the World Want from America* (Cambridge, MA: MIT Press, 2002); and reports by the Pew Global Attitudes Project available online at www.people-press.org.

13. Fouad Ajami, "The Sentry's Solitude," *Foreign Affairs,* 80 (2001), 2–16; and "The Falseness of Anti-Americanism," *Foreign Policy,* 138 (2003), 52–62.

14. *The New York Times, The Tower Commission Report* (New York: Bantam, 1987), p. 137.

15. Robert Tucker, *The Inequality of Nations* (New York: Basic Books, 1977).

16. Robert Gilpin, *War and Change in World Politics* (New York: Cambridge University Press, 1981). For a dissenting view on the decline of U.S. power, see Bruce Russett, "The Mysterious Case of Vanishing Hegemony; or, Is Mark Twain Really Dead?" *International Organization,* 39 (1985). 207–32.

17. Bayliss Manning, "The Congress, the Executive and Intermestic Affairs: Three Proposals," *Foreign Affairs,* 56 (1977), 306–24.

18. For discussions of the growth of nonstate actors, see Werner Feld, *International Relations, A Transnational Approach* (Sherman Oaks, Calif.: Alfred, 1979); and Harold K. Jacobson, *Networks of Interdependence* (New York: Knopf, 1979).

19. The three subsystems as well as the management problems they present are taken from Joan Edleman Spero, *The Politics of International Economic Relations,* 3rd ed. (New York: St. Martin's, 1985), pp. 13–19.

20. John Lewis Gaddis, "Toward the Post–Cold War World," *Foreign Affairs,* 70 (1991), 102–22; and "Tectonics, History, and the End of the Cold War," in John Lewis Gaddis, *The United States and the End of the Cold War: Implications, Reconsiderations, Provocations* (New York: Oxford University Press, 1992), pp. 155–67.

21. Roger C. Molander and Peter A. Wilson, "On Dealing with the Prospect of Nuclear Chaos," *Washington Quarterly,* 17 (1994), 19–39.

22. Morton A. Kaplan, "The Systems Approach to International Relations," in Morton A. Kaplan (ed.), *New Approaches to International Relations* (New York: St. Martin's: 1968).

23. Joseph S. Nye Jr., "Soft Power," *Foreign Policy,* 80 (1990).

24. Johan Galtung, "A Structural Theory of Imperialism," *Journal of Peace Research,* 2 (1971), 91–98.

25. See Stephen P. Cohen, "U.S. Security in a Separatist Season," *Bulletin of Atomic Scientists* (July/August 1992), pp. 28–32; and Rodolfo Stavenhagen, "Ethnic Conflicts and Their Impact on International Society," *International Social Science Journal,* 127 (1991), 117–32.

26. On the problems associated with this see Gerald Helman and Steven Ratner, "Saving Failed States," *Foreign Policy,* 89 (1992/93), 3–20; and Morton H. Halperin and David J. Scheffer, *Self Determination in the New World Order,* (Washington, D.C.: Carnegie Endowment for International Peace, 1992).

27. The term is used by Kenneth Jowitt, "Rage, Hubris, and Regime Change," *Policy Review,* 118 (2003), 33–44.

28. Ajami, "The Sentry's Solitude," p. 10.

29. Coral Bell, "Normative Shift," *The National Interest,* 70 (2002), 44–55.

30. Michael Klare, *Resource Wars,* (New York: Owl Books, 2001).

31. Robert Paarlberg, "Ecodipomacy," in Kenneth Oye, Robert Lieber, and Donald Rothchild (eds.), *Eagle in a New World,* (New York: HarperCollins, 1992), 207–32.

— 2 —

THE EMERGING FOREIGN
POLICY AGENDA

Foreign Policy Problems

Foreign policy is about choices. It is about the goals and values people want to realize and the types of threats they wish to be protected against. Foreign policy is also about costs. It is about how much people are willing to pay in order to achieve their goals and what types of sacrifices they are willing to make. For over forty years, questions of values, threats, costs, and sacrifice were framed with reference to one overriding problem: the Soviet threat. The American people saw the Soviet Union as a global challenger that threatened virtually all aspects of American society. The appropriate response was containment. Over time, the Soviet Union became an enemy that most Americans felt quite comfortable dealing with. By and large, it acted in predictable ways that made the task of containment seem quite manageable.

For a little more than a decade all of that changed. With the breakup of the Soviet Union and the end of the cold war, American foreign policy had lost its "magnetic north pole."[1] An aura of uncertainty hung over its content and conduct.

Threats seemed few in number, and much energy was expended on what some call "C" list foreign policy problems such as Kosovo, Haiti, Bosnia, and Somalia. These are "contingencies that indirectly affect U.S. security but do not directly threaten U.S. interests."[2]

Clarity and focus returned to American foreign policy on September 11, 2001. The attacks on the World Trade Center and the Pentagon elevated terrorism to the top of the "A" list. For a short time, it was the only problem in that category as the United States brought all of its resources to bear on pursuing Osama bin Laden and his al-Qaeda forces, and removing his primary sponsor, the Taliban, from power in Afghanistan. With victory in Afghanistan came renewed uncertainty. Presidential assertions that Iran, Iraq, and North Korea constituted an axis of evil were met with skepticism. Doubts were voiced over the wisdom of replacing deterrence and containment with preemption as the core strategy for dealing with terrorist groups and rogue states. Much debate occurred over the wisdom of moving against Iraq without United Nations support. The military success of the Iraq War temporarily silenced these doubts, but they resurfaced and were reinforced by mounting American casualties, political stalemate, and images of torture and other abuses by American military personnel at the Abu Ghraib prison in post-war Iraq.

The outcome of the current debate is uncertain. It is unclear what goals Americans will want to pursue in their foreign policy in the twenty-first century. It is unclear how they will define and rank threats to the American national interest or what level of protection they will desire. In addition, no one can tell with certainty how much they will be willing to pay or what sacrifices they will be willing to endure in order to realize these goals or to be protected from these threats.

A starting point for thinking about goals, threats, costs, and sacrifice is the realization that there is no such thing as a standard or typical foreign policy problem. Presidents discover two truths very quickly. First, foreign policy problems come in many shapes and sizes and they often defy simple categorization. At a minimum, most foreign policy problems contain within them a bundle of distinct policy problems or issues that intersect in complicated ways. This makes deciding on how to approach a problem difficult because of uncertainty over just what the problem is or how attacking one aspect of the problem will affect its other dimensions. Second, foreign policy problems are seldom ever "solved." As George Shultz, President Ronald Reagan's secretary of state, noted, policy making does not involve confronting "one damn thing after another . . . it involves confronting the same damn thing over and over."[3]

The problem of AIDS (acquired immunodeficiency syndrome) illustrates both these points.[4] Because there is currently no cure for AIDS the great temptation is to treat it as a health problem. For all of the human suffering associated with AIDS, at least from a foreign policy perspective, it is much more. AIDS is an economic problem. The World Bank asserts that the spread of AIDS is in part responsible for the slowed growth rate experienced by the economies of sub-Saharan states. AIDS is also a multifaceted security problem. Large numbers of HIV-infected personnel within a military establishment reduce its ability to carry out assigned tasks. The presence of large numbers of HIV-infected individuals in neighboring states is a potential source of tension as leaders seek to shield their states from its spread or export the AIDS problem to other states through forced deportation programs. Finally, AIDS can be viewed as a human rights problem. Fears exist that cultural norms and public laws will place women and children who have contracted AIDS in a disadvantaged position in seeking help or treatment.

THINKING ABOUT FOREIGN POLICY PROBLEMS

In addition to recognizing that foreign policy problems often represent bundles of issues rather than discrete policy areas, it is important to realize that foreign policy problems also differ in terms of their history and origin. Some foreign policy problems are inherited from previous administrations. The key dilemma faced by presidents is whether to continue the course of action and endorse the policy line of their predecessor or move in a new direction. George W. Bush decided to reverse course on the Kyoto Protocol and end U.S. participation in this international effort to reduce environmental problems. He also decided to go ahead with deployment of the ballistic missile defense system, a "stop-go" decision that Clinton had left to his successor. Clinton inherited a military presence in Somalia from Bush's father and a NAFTA agreement that had yet to be ratified by the Senate.

Some foreign policy problems are new, the product of unfolding events beyond U.S. borders that earlier administrations never had to confront. With no track record of successes and failures against which to weigh their choices, presidents are left only with the informed judgment of their advisers and their own political instincts to guide them in selecting policy options. The most significant event of this type in recent times was the collapse of communism and the breakup of the Soviet Union that confronted the administration of George Bush in 1989. Other than in the Eisenhower administration when calls for "rolling back the iron curtain" were commonplace (but never really acted upon), it is difficult to remember when the United States even had a foreign policy toward Eastern Europe. Certainly, American foreign policy never contemplated the dissolution of its major cold war rival. A similarly momentous new problem faces George W. Bush in the war against global terrorism following the attacks of September 11, 2001.

Other foreign policy problems can largely be attributed to perceived or actual failings in an administration's own foreign policy. The problem here can be either a specific policy or the administration's handling of foreign policy issues in general. At the heart of many of the critiques of Clinton's foreign policies are their inconsistency and his lack of decisiveness. The Reagan administration suffered more from critiques of specific foreign policy intiatives such as the Iran–Contra affair or "Star Wars." In his first months in office, George W. Bush's foreign policy was attacked on both grounds. His unilateralism upset allies as did his handling of specific foreign policy issues, such as his promise to come to the defense of Taiwan in the wake of the Chinese downing of an American spy plane and his plan to grant amnesty to as many as three million illegal Mexican immigrants. The move was supported by Republican strategists who saw this as a way to get a greater portion of the Hispanic vote but opposed by conservatives who saw it as rewarding illegal behavior and by those who feared it would encourage an even greater exodus from Mexico.

A fourth category of foreign policy problems consists of issues considered solved by previous administrations and forgotten about because they were considered solved. Large-scale refugee flows into the United States from Cuba and elsewhere in the Carribbean are one such problem. Clinton was forced to deal with an ominous solved problem in 1998 when India and Pakistan detonated nuclear weapons, thereby reintroducing the problem of nuclear proliferation onto the foreign policy agenda. More recently, Clinton and George W. Bush have both had to confront the possibility of sharply rising energy prices.[5]

A last type of foreign policy problem consists of problems rooted in long-term structural features of the international system. One such problem is found in the area of weapons development. Over the past two decades the Army has spent $15 billion to make the Apache helicopter the most lethal and least vulnerable aircraft of its kind. The dilemma confronting policy makers is the existence of a trade-off between the national security benefits of producing weapons entirely within the United States and by U.S. firms and the economic benefits gained by spreading these costs out through coproduction schemes and jointly undertaken research and development projects. The Apache dilemma is not unique. Earlier the United States confronted the need to involve Japan in the development of a new fighter, the FSX.

The general problem of economic growth being hampered by high levels of military spending is discussed by Paul Kennedy in his *The Rise and Fall of the Great Powers*.[6] He argues that economic growth is the foundation of state power and that funds spent on the military invariably produce lower rates of economic growth. Yet, historically, Great Powers continually overspend on the military. They succumb to "imperial overreach," a perceived need to protect their Great Power status through the possession of a dominant military establishment. By failing to curb their military spending they do not address the long-term needs of their economic base. Thus, they begin their "fall" from Great Power status.

To repeat a point made earlier, foreign policy problems do not come in neat packages. They also do not have neat histories. Some foreign policy problems may contain elements from several of the above categories as they make their way to the White House. For the Clinton administration, Bosnia was one such problem. Dubbed "the problem from Hell" by Secretary of State Warren Christopher, fighting between the Serbs, Croats, and Bosnians in what once was Yugoslavia has its roots in what may be one of the most intractable problems in world politics: the incompatibility between ethnic boundaries and political boundaries and the desire of peoples to bring them into line—something only done at the expense of other peoples. Bosnia was also an inherited problem for the Clinton administration, one it drew attention to in the 1992 presidential campaign when candidate Bill Clinton attacked George H. W. Bush's largely passive policy as unwise and immoral. It became a problem for President Clinton when his administration was unable to convince NATO allies of the wisdom of the U.S. position or even to clearly articulate a consistent position. Finally, Bosnia represents the rebirth of a problem long forgotten. Ethnic tensions are nothing new to this part of Europe. They played important roles in the onset of World War I and the history of World War II. They faded from view with the establishment of communist rule and the emergence of Tito as a strong ruler. Never far beneath the surface, these ethnic tensions reemerged after Tito's death and the subsequent fall of communism in Russia and Eastern Europe.

The National Interest

One unifying thread that runs through these and other types of foreign policy problems is a common vocabulary and set of symbols. The first challenge facing a student of American foreign policy is to become comfortable with its terminology. The experience is often a frustrating one because authors using the same term frequently attach different meanings to it. For example, take the calls from commentators positioned all across the political spectrum for the United States to pursue a foreign policy of "maturity." This plea is based both on a reading of the past and on expectations about the future. Looking to the future, they see problems confronting U.S. foreign policy makers that are not likely to lend themselves to clear-cut alternatives or easy choices. Looking to the past, there is the feeling that U.S. foreign policy has not been all that it could be, that its content has fallen short of our needs and expectations. Commentators are in far less agreement on what constitutes a mature foreign policy. For some *maturity* means greater consistency, for others it means coming to terms with the nature of world politics, and for still others it means a greater attachment to principle.

Debates such as the one over the meaning of *maturity* involve far more than just disagreements over facts and details. They are struggles to control the language of U.S. foreign policy, to set its reference points, assumptions, and symbolism. By looking at the way in which terms are being used, we can learn much about the nature of American foreign policy and the process by which it is made and implemented.[7] The key term whose definition must be controlled if U.S. foreign policy is to be moved in one direction or another is *the national interest.* The problem of defining the national interest is not unique to the George W. Bush administration. The Reagan administration put forward a series of conflicting rationales for sending U.S. Marines to Lebanon in the early 1980s as did the Clinton administration a decade later in justifying sending American forces to Bosnia.

The range of goals and values policy makers may choose to pursue is virtually endless. The same is not true for the resources at their disposal. The limits here are quite real and specific. And since all goals are costly, decisions must constantly be made about what goals and values to emphasize and which ones to neglect. The lack of fit between goals and resources results in the concept of national interest being used in two quite different ways. Some employ the concept to describe the goals and values being pursued in a state's foreign policy. No a priori definition of national interest is assumed to exist, and the U.S. national interest is whatever U.S. policy makers are willing to make sacrifices to achieve. Others use the concept in a normative sense, seeking to have added emphasis given to values and goals that in their view are currently being slighted by policy makers.

Keeping in mind the distinction between normative and descriptive uses of national interest is the first step in understanding the language and nature of the debate about American foreign policy. The second step is to realize that definitions of national interest can be made at varying levels of ab-

[handwritten note:] 7 DISTINCTION BETWEEN NORMATIVE AND DESCRIPTIVE USES OF NATIONAL INTEREST

straction. At a high level of abstraction, national interest is employed with reference to questions of national purpose, national identity, and national survival. At a medium level of abstraction, it is used in relation to matters of priorities and broad policy assumptions. The concept of national interest used at the lowest level of abstraction centers on day-to-day problem-solving concerns: strategies, tactics, and operational assumptions. Table 2.1 presents three foreign policy problem areas for the United States (international economic policy, terrorism, and U.S.–Latin American relations) and illustrates how keeping track of levels of abstraction helps to order and relate competing conceptualizations of national interest to one another.

The Evolving Foreign Policy Agenda

The varied nature of foreign policy problems guarantees that the foreign policy agenda of today and tomorrow will consist of a combination of well established issues, evolving ones, and new ones. Many of the new problems are rooted in one way or another in the globalization and American hegemony. In this section, we will highlight the problem of terrorism because of its overriding importance to American foreign policy today.

TABLE 2.1   Definitions of National Interest at Three Levels of Abstraction

Level of Abstraction	International Economic Policy	Terrorism	U.S.-Latin American Relations
High	U.S. liberal principles prosper in an International economic order.	First war of 21st century	Manifest destiny: U.S. has special responsibility to lead in region.
Medium	Protectionism must remain an exception to the rule.	Preemption Unilateralism Democratization	U.S. (capitalist) pattern of development is most appropriate for Latin America.
	MNC produce growth and development for all states in the international system.		U.S. has special defense responsibilities in region.
Low	Participate in WTO.	Invasion of Afghanistan Invasion of Iraq	Caribbean Basin Initiative
	Reject Kyoto Protocol. Tie foreign aid to state's willingness to adopt procapitalist economic strategies.	Coalitions of the willing Foreign aid to key allies	Isolate Cuba. Invade Grenada when request for help is received. NAFTA

TERRORISM

Used in its most value-free and politically neutral sense, terrorism is violence for purposes of political intimidation. Terrorism is a difficult enemy. It does not specify an organizational form. Governments may engage in terrorism but so too can nongovernmental organizations like al-Qaeda. Post 9/11, we are witnessing yet another organizational change as tightly knit and centrally controlled terrorist groups are giving way to more loosely structured networks of individuals who engage in terrorism. Terrorism rarely exists in unqualified form. We speak of international terrorism, state terrorism, cyberterrorism, and state-sponsored terrorism. Moreover, its presence does not tell us the political cause involved in the conflict. Terrorism is used to protect the environment, stop abortions, preserve racial supremacy, defeat imperialism, and enrich drug traffickers. Terrorism is also a tool of the weak and for that reason often brings forward negative images of those who engage in it (successful terrorists become founding fathers and freedom fighters). For all of these reasons, many commentators are unsure that terrorism will be an enemy that provides American foreign policy with the same type of clear moral focus that communism did.

The Contemporary Context.   In 2002 and 2003, seven countries were designated as state sponsors of terrorism—Cuba, Iran, Iraq, Libya, North Korea, Syria, and Sudan. In 2003, the State Department identified 208 acts of terrorism that killed 625 individuals and wounded 3,646.[8] Thirty-five of those killed were Americans (the State Department report did not count uniformed military personnel as victims of terrorism). In 2002, there were fewer attacks (198). The number of dead was larger (725), but the number of people wounded was less (2,013). The corresponding numbers for 2001 were 355 attacks, 3,295 dead, and 2,283 wounded.

The Historical Context.   Terrorism is not a new phenomenon, but it is also not rigid or incapable of taking on new forms. Today's brand of terrorism dates from 1979 and is the fourth wave of terrorism that has existed since the 1880s. The proceeding three waves each lasted a generation.[9] There is no reason to expect this to be the last wave when it loses its energy in around 2025.

The first anarchist wave of terrorism began in Russia and was set in motion by the political and economic reform efforts of the Czars. Disappointment with the fruits of these policies led to a systematic policy of assassination that swept through Russia, the Balkans, and the West that culminated in the assassination of Archduke Ferdinand and set off World War I.

The second anti-colonial wave of terrorism began in the 1920s and ended in the 1960s. Defining themselves as freedom fighters, these terrorists sought to obtain the independence for those parts of the European empires where the ruling colonial power would not leave on its own, such as Israel, Ireland, Cyprus, and Algeria. Hit-and-run tactics in urban areas and guerrilla warfare in rural areas became defining features of this second wave of terrorism.

The third New Left wave of terrorism contained elements of each of the proceeding waves. It was set in motion by the Vietnam War. One part of this wave was comprised of Marxist groups such as the Weather Underground United States, the Red Brigade (Italy), and the Red Army Faction (West Germany) that directed their terrorism at the center of capitalism in hopes of spurring its demise. The second part of this wave was made of up separatist groups that sought self-determination for minority groups trapped inside of larger states. Prominent examples included the Palestine Liberation Organization (PLO), the Irish Republican Army (IRA), and the Euskadi Ta Askatasuna, (ETA). This wave lost much of its energy in the 1980s as the revolution failed to occur and separatist groups met with military defeat.

The defining features of the current wave of terrorism are twofold. First is its religious base, and Islam is at its core. Its initial energy was drawn from three events in 1979: the start of a new Moslem century, the ouster of the Shah in Iran, and the Soviet invasion of Afghanistan. The United States is the special target of this religious wave of terrorism. Iranian leaders referred to it from the beginning as the "Great Satan," and the common goal shared by Islamic terrorist groups was to drive the United States out of the Middle East. Before 9/11, this wave had produced a steady flow of terrorist attacks on the United States. Marine barracks were attacked in Lebanon in 1983, the World Trade Center was struck in 1993, American embassies were attacked in Kenya and Tanzania in 1998, and the USS *Cole* was attacked in 2000. The second feature of contemporary terrorism is the specter of mass casualties. Where early waves of terror focused on assassinating key individuals or the symbolic killing of relatively small numbers of individuals (capitalist businesspeople, citizens of a specific state against which grievances were held) today in addition to these forms of violence we see terrorist attacks occurring in large numbers of deaths.

COMBATING TERRORISM

The *National Strategy for Combating Terrorism* released in February 1993 defined victory over terrorism in terms of a world where terrorism does not define the daily lives of Americans.[10] To that end, it put forward a "4D" strategy. The United States will: 1) *defeat* terrorist organizations, 2) *deny* them support from rogue states, 3) work to *diminish* the conditions that give rise to terrorism, and 4) *defend* the United States, its citizens and foreign interests from attack.

Realizing these goals and implementing this 4D program of action requires marshalling all available resources and integrating them into an effective antiterrorism strategy that addresses terrorism both as a tactic and the goals it is trying to achieve if it is to avoid the twin dangers of entrapping the United States in local grievances and having its policy become morally ambiguous and inconsistent in its application. Below we will highlight some of the choices and considerations that policy makers will confront in selecting policy tools for this purpose. In Chapter 13–17, we will take a more in-depth view of these instruments and their role in American foreign policy.

Before proceeding to look at specific policy instruments it is important to note that inherent in the use of any of them is one of the fundamental realities of foreign policy making: policies have unintended consequences. "Blowback" is the term commonly used to capture the essence of this phenomenon.[11] It was first used by the CIA to characterize problems that came about as a result of covert action programs. In the eyes of some, we have already seen blowback in the war against terrorism. They see the 1988 bombing of Pan Am 103 over Lockerbie, Scotland, killed 270 people as retaliation for President Ronald Reagan's bombing of Libya in 1986 that killed President Qaddafi's stepdaughter. Others see blowback in the surge of terrorism in Iraq following the ouster of Saddam Hussein. Rather than further weaken international terrorism, it made Iraq a lightning rod attracting terrorists to it.

Diplomacy. The essence of the diplomatic challenge is to leverage other states into assisting the United States in countering terrorism. This requires getting them to cooperate not only in defeating terrorists beyond their own borders but to take on terrorist groups and their sympathizers within their country.[12] Three separate but reinforcing lines of action have been suggested. The first is to strengthen international and national laws that can be used to identify and capture terrorists. A post–9/11 example is United Nations Resolution 1373. It obliges all members to prevent and suppress the financing of terrorist acts, criminalizes providing or collecting funds by their nationals for terrorism, and urges members to freeze any financial assets that might be used by terrorists. To help realize these objectives the resolution sets up a number of information-sharing and cooperative agreements among key international agencies such as Interpol and the Finance Action Task Force.

The second line of diplomatic action is to provide assistance and incentives to states that will lead them to cooperate in countering terrorism. A variety of programs exist that will further this aim. The State Department's Anti-Terrorism Assistance Program provides funding for countries to aid them in improving their civilian and military security services. By 2000, 20,000 law enforcement and airport security personnel from over 100 countries had received training. Military assistance programs can also be used. In spring 2002, these programs were used to send $100 million and 1,200 soldiers to the Philippines, 100 soldiers to Yemen, and 150 military trainers to Georgia.

The third line of diplomatic activity is public diplomacy. Whereas traditional diplomacy is conducted on a government-to-government basis, public diplomacy involves efforts by a government to influence the public in another state. This parallel area of diplomatic activity is needed because defeating terrorism requires gaining foreign support both "on the street" and among the elite. Crafting an effective public diplomacy campaign requires addressing two issues. The first involves means. What medium should be used? Possibilities include through radio or television broadcasts, the print media, or through educational exchange programs. The second involves the selection of a message. Is it better to "stick to the facts" as uncomfortable they may be on occasion, or should the emphasis be on presenting the American side of the story or the American interpretation of events? The problem with choosing the first course of action is determining what the facts are (and who is responsible for making this decision) since events are rarely subject to just one interpretation. The danger of the second course of action is that it easily blends into propaganda activity with the result that the message is rejected.

Military Power.   Prior to declaring war on terrorism after 9/11, the United States responded with military force against terrorism three times between 1983 and 2000. The Reagan administration struck against Libya in 1986 in retaliation for the bombing of the La Belle discotheque in Berlin. President Bill Clinton ordered cruise missile strikes against Iraqi intelligence agencies in 1993 after an attempted assassination of former President George H. W. Bush. Lastly, in 1998 Clinton approved cruise missile attacks on al-Qaeda targets in Afghanistan after the attacks on the U.S. embassies in Kenya and Tanzania.

Three sets of constraints must be taken into consideration in using military power to counter terrorism. The first are legal constraints. They operate at both the international and national level. At the national level, this requires that any use of force by the United States must be authorized in a constitutionally proscribed manner and in accordance with American law. The best-known example of this last requirement is the Posse Comitatus Act's prohibition of using military forces within the United States. At the international level, there is the proscription that any use of force must be consistent with the commonly accepted understanding of a just war. In particular, the use of force must respect the distinction between combatants and innocent civilians, and it must be proportional to the threat faced. The second set of constraints is political in nature. The use of military force, even when carried out in retaliation for terrorist acts already committed, instead of in a preemptive mode, carries with it political consequences. Put simply, in war things often go tragically wrong. Victory on the battlefield may be negated by the political forces it sets in motion. These political consequences may appear in the state against which military action is being taken, allies, neutrals, or within the United States itself. From the American perspective, 9/11 may have loosened these legal and political constraints, but it did not remove them completely.

The third set of constraints is operational in nature. How can military power be employed effectively against terrorists? How do terrorists fight? Modern warfare is sequential in nature. It is a series of separate and discreet steps that build upon one another in order to destroy the opponent's "center of gravity" and in the process degrade the effectiveness of its forces. Terrorists, in contrast, fight cumulative wars. No single military action lays the foundation for the next nor must military undertakings occur in a given sequence. Terrorism attacks the enemy through a series of largely individual and independent episodic actions that when added together have an impact that is greater than the sum of the individual military actions. There is no center of gravity to attack and destroy. Terrorist organizations may be destroyed but terrorism may not be defeated.

This does not mean that military power cannot be used effectively against terrorism. Timothy Hoyt asserts that there are four different strategic situations in which the United States might use conventional military forces against terrorism.[13] The first is to oppose terrorist governments such as the Taliban in Afghanistan. The second is against states that are not friendly to the United States and support terrorist groups or allow them to operate on their territory. President George W. Bush made this part of his rationale for the Iraq War. The third situation is when terrorist groups operate in a country that is friendly to the United States. Pakistan and Saudi Arabia present possible examples of such a situation. Finally, military force might be used against states that are only "tangentially" related to terrorist groups but are actively engaged in anti-American policies. Hoyt gives North Korea and Iran as examples.

Homeland Security. A truism of early cold war nuclear strategy was that there existed no defense against nuclear weapons. Civil defense dealt largely with damage limitation in the event of a Soviet attack. Gradually this view came to be challenged and the belief that defense against nuclear attacks was possible gained currency. The George W. Bush administration's plan for constructing a national ballistic missile defense system represents an endorsement of the idea that defense is possible.

The security challenge to the American homeland presented by terrorists extends beyond constructing a protective shield.[14] As with the civil defense programs, it entails a consequence management component (what to do if an attack happens and how to minimize those consequences). The magnitude of this task can be brought home simply by listing the number of potential targets terrorists might strike in the United States: They include any one of 100 nuclear power plants, 300 oil refineries, 450 major airports, and tens of thousands of miles of electric power lines and natural gas lines. To this list, we can add the challenge of cybersecurity. Defending the homeland also includes two other activities. The first, and most basic, is securing America's borders. The task is daunting. The U.S. borders with Mexico and Canada are 7,500 miles long. In 2002, 9,500 Immigration and Naturalization Service agents patrolled the Mexican border while about 300 guarded the Canadian border. Annually, 11 million trucks, 2.2 million train cars, 964,000 aircraft and 7,500 ships under foreign flags will cross the U.S. border. The second additional activity is intrusion detection and response. In 1999, more than 31 million non–U.S. citizens entered the United States. This number was up from 17.7 million in 1990 and 7.0 million in 1975. In the period preceding 9/11, 13 of the 189 terrorists connected with the attacks of that day entered the United States legally. On September 11, the second hijacked airplane struck the World Trace Center at 9:02 A.M. At 9:00 A.M. there were 4,205 planes in the air over the United States. American skies that day were protected by 14 planes stationed at 7 air bases.

Economics. The United States can consider using its economic power in two very different ways in trying to defeat terrorism. First, it could use it to coerce state supporters of terrorism through the imposition of economic sanctions. The logic here is to affect a hostile government's decision making by imposing economic hardship on the society. The assumption is that subjected to sanctions for a long enough period of time, society will demand a policy change as a condition of continuing to support the rulers. The use of sanctions to combat terrorism raises several issues, not the least of which are that their impact on society is often slow to surface and that sanctions are often more effective against friends then foes. Additionally there is the moral question of it is permissible to inflict harm on common citizens when they are not the enemy. There is also the blowback danger that sanctions may create additional public support for the terrorists.

The second use of economic power in the war against terrorism is as a device for alleviating the social, economic, and political conditions that may give rise to terrorism.[15] As intuitively appealing as it is to use foreign aid to combat terrorism, much uncertainty exists here. Where some see foreign aid as a first line of defense and one that can potentially remove the need for using military force, others argue that the link between poverty and terrorism is weak and superficial. Long-time proponents of foreign aid also worry that the use of foreign aid to enhance national security will divert attention and resources from what they see as its primary purpose of eliminating poverty, hunger, and hopelessness.

Covert Action.   Always controversial, covert action is advocated by some as ideally suited for the war against terrorism.[16] Cited as support for this view is the CIA's successful covert support for the Northern Alliance against the Taliban in Afghanistan. More generally the nonstate nature of the terrorist threat, the prominent role played by charismatic leaders, and the difficulty of finding traditional military targets in the war against terrorism are seen as requiring a robust covert action response. Skeptics question the cost effectiveness of programs in which millions of dollars can be spent with little accountability. And while the success of the Northern Alliance was real, other programs have not been as successful. Beyond questions of financial and personal accountability there are also issues about the long-term efficacy of covert actions designed to neutralize specific individuals or groups. Before he resigned, Director of Central Intelligence George Tenet noted that even if we had killed Osama bin Laden earlier, we probably could not have stopped a 9/11 type attack.

Paramilitary operations are only one aspect of covert action that by definition cover all secret attempts to influence public affairs including bribery, giving advice, and financially supporting individuals, groups, and media outlets. Increasingly these activities are becoming more overt in nature with government corporations or publicly announced programs being tasked for these purposes.

Summary and the Future

There is nothing simple about foreign policy problems. They arrive on the policy agenda from quite varied routes. They constitute bundles of issues that can be separated in any number of ways. And their presence may prove to be short-lived or become a permanent fixture. How foreign policy problems are dealt with is also not a simple matter. There is nothing automatic about how the "communist challenge" is defined or what "promoting democracy" means. Problem definition is heavily influenced by the language of the political debate over the purposes of American foreign policy. The most powerful weapon in this debate is the concept of "the national interest." We can learn much about who controls the policy-making process by studying efforts to give content and direction to this phrase. The George W. Bush administration recognized this truth as it moved quickly to define the terrorist attacks on the World Trade Center and Pentagon as acts of war rather than criminal acts.

Terrorism will not be the only issue on the foreign policy agenda of the United States in the years to come. We can expect this agenda to continue to evolve, for issues to be added and subtracted, to disappear and reappear. We close by presenting two potential major foreign policy problems that are quite different from terrorism.

The first involves the challenges presented by infectious diseases.[17] In 1999, the National Intelligence Council released an unclassified report stating that infectious diseases were responsible for one-fourth to one-third of all deaths globally. It identified twenty diseases that had been on the decline but were now reasserting themselves including drug-resistant strains of malaria, tuberculosis, and cholera. Moreover, in the period 1973 to 1999, twenty-nine previously unknown diseases for which there is no cure were identified, including HIV/AIDS and Ebola. After the study was released, Severe Acute Respiratory Syndrome (SARS), a thirtieth new infectious disease, surfaced. It first appeared in China in fall 2002. By mid-June 2003, SARS had sickened over eighty-four hundred people and killed almost eight hundred in thirty-two countries. On average it killed 15 percent of those infected. SARS was spread worldwide by travelers to Asia returning to their home countries. For heavily infected countries, SARS was more than a health crisis. It was also an economic crisis. Tourism to China and the export of goods abroad plummeted. Hong Kong, Singapore, and Taiwan experienced similar problems. Retail sales in Hong Kong fell 5 percent as people stayed home and stayed away from their jobs. In Toronto, Canada, hotel occupancy rates fell to 20 percent capacity after SARS was reported in that city.

No deaths occurred in the United States, but seventy-three were sickened in twenty-five states during this initial global outbreak of SARS. In an effort to stop its spread, President George W. Bush signed an executive order allowing Immigration and Naturalization Service agents to detail anyone appearing to have SARS symptoms. Federal and state law enforcement officials were authorized to quarantine suspected SARS carriers trying to enter the United States.

The second issue involves human trafficking.[18] In 2000, an estimated 150 million people lived outside of the country where they were born. This number is twice what it was in 1965. Economics and politics play major roles in their process of global migration as individuals search for jobs and freedom. There is also a dark side to these numbers. The global trafficking in people has become a $12 billion a year industry in which 800,000 to 900,000 individuals, many of whom are women and children, are transported across borders as sex workers. Human trafficking is now the third-largest illegal business following drug and arms trafficking. Up to 20,000 people are trafficked to the United States each year, and as many as 750,000 were transported here in the 1990s. Under the federal antiracketeering law (RICO) American authorities can arrest human traffickers. From 2000 to 2003, 111 individuals were charged with human trafficking under this law.

Since the passage of the little noticed Trafficking Victims Protection Act in 2000, the United States is required to cut off most nonhumanitarian foreign aid to states judged not trying hard enough to eliminate human trafficking for three consecutive years. In 2003, fifteen countries were identified as Tier 3 states that fell into this category. They include the Dominican Republic, Cuba, Georgia, Greece, Haiti, Turkey, Kazakhstan, and North Korea. Another seventy-five states were listed as Tier 2 states. These are countries judged to be making some progress. Japan, Saudi Arabia, and Indonesia, and Russia are found here. Only twenty-five states were judged to be actively fighting human trafficking.

The pull of the past, how Americans think about foreign policy problems, and how policy makers have dealt with previous problems will play an important role in determining how these and other foreign policy problems are addressed. It is to the past that we turn for such insights in the next chapters.

Notes

1. James Schlesinger, "Quest for a Post–Cold War Foreign Policy," *Foreign Affairs*, 72 (1992/93), 17–28.

2. Ashton Carter and William Perry, *A New Security Strategy for America* (Washington, D.C.: Brookings, 1999), 9–11.

3. Jim Hoagland, "Why Clinton Improvises," *Washington Post*, September 25, 1994.

4. This section draws from Dennis C. Weeks, "The AIDS Pandemic in Africa," *Current History* (May 1992), 208–13; and Kimberly A. Hamilton, "The HIV and AIDS Pandemic as a Foreign Policy Concern," *Washington Quarterly*, 17 (1993), 201–15. See also the CIA intelligence report on HIV/AIDS, "*The Global Infectious Disease Threat and its Implications for the United States*," available online at www.odci.gov/cia/reports/nie/report/nie99-17d.

5. For a contrasting view of the energy situation as a policy problem, see Amy Myers Jaffe and Robert Manning, "The Shocks of a World of Cheap Oil," *Foreign Affairs*, 79 (2000), 16–29.

6. Paul Kennedy, *The Rise and Fall of the Great Powers* (New York: Random House, 1987).

7. John P. Lovell, "The Idiom of National Security," *JPMS*, 11 (1983), 35–51.

8. For data on terrorism see the State Department's annual report, *Patterns of Global Terrorism*. It is available online at state.gov/s/ct/rls/pgtrpt.

9. David C. Rapoport, "The Four Waves of Modern Terrorism," Audrey Kurth Cronin, "The Sources of Contemporary Terrorism," in Audrey Kurth Cronin and James Ludes (eds.), *Attacking Terrorism* (Washington, D.C.: Georgetown University Press, 2004).

10. Martha Crenshaw, "Terrorism, Strategies, and Grand Strategies," in Cronin and Ludes (ed.), *Attacking Terrorism*, 74–93.

11. Chalmers Johnson, *Blowback* (New York: Owl Books, 2000).

12. Michael Sheehan, "Diplomacy," in Cronin and Ludes (eds.), *Attacking Terrorism*, 97–114; and Alexander Lennon (ed.), *The Battle for Hearts and Minds* (Cambridge, MA: MIT Press, 2003).

13. Timothy Hoyt, "Military Force," in Cronin and Ludes (eds.), *Attacking Terrorism*, 162–185.

14. Daniel Goure, "Homeland Security," in Cronin and Ludes (eds.), *Attacking Terrorism,* 361–84; also Patrick Marshall, "Policing the Borders," *The CQ Researcher,* 12 (February 22, 2002), 145–68.

15. Patrick Cronin, "Foreign Aid," in Cronin and Ludes (eds.), *Attacking Terrorism,* 238–260; and Mary Cooper, "Foreign Aid After September 11," *The CQ Researcher,* 12 (April 26, 2002), 361–92.

16. Jennifer Kibbe, "The Rise of the Shadow Warriors, *Foreign Affairs,* 83 (2004), 102–15.

17. Mary Cooper, "Fighting SARS," *The CQ Researcher,* 13 (June 20, 2003), 569–92.

18. David Masci, "Human Trafficking and Slavery," *The CQ Researcher,* 14 (March 26, 2004), 273–96.

— *3* —

THE AMERICAN NATIONAL STYLE

To the casual observer, one of the most startling qualities of U.S. foreign policy is how suddenly it can change direction. Equally startling can be the depth of the change. In 1976 détente went from being the foreign policy trademark of two administrations to a nonterm in Ford's failed bid to be elected president. Human rights arrived on the scene as the centerpiece of U.S. foreign policy during the Carter administration. Four years later it too was gone, replaced by anticommunist rhetoric reminiscent of the 1950s and 1960s. Or consider Nixon's stunning announcement of July 15, 1971, that he would visit the People's Republic of China. For over two decades the United States had refused to recognize the existence of the mainland communist government. Without warning foreign policy changed, surprising both U.S. friends and enemies in the process. American policy makers now spoke of "playing the China card" instead of trying to promote China's international isolation. Close observers of U.S. foreign policy see a different picture. Looking beyond these and other sudden changes in direction, they see a high degree of continuity in the attitudes toward world affairs and methods of acting that have guided the making of U.S. foreign policy.

The importance of ideas as a force in foreign policy decision making stems from both their immediate and long-term impacts.[1] In the short run, shared ideas help policy makers and citizens cope with the inherent uncertainty involved in selecting between competing policy lines. Consistency with the principles of free trade or isolationism may not produce the "correct" policy, but these criteria do provide a basis for the selection or rejection of one. Ideas also become institutionalized as organizations and laws are designed around them. Because organizations and laws are slow to change, they become an anchor for any future reform debate. Once in place, political constituencies will coalesce around policies rooted in these ideas and lobby for their continued existence. As a result, ideas continue to exert an influence on policy long after they have lost their vitality and after those who espoused them have passed from the scene. Viewed over the long term, the result of this interplay of policies and ideas is a layering pattern in which policies reflecting different sets of ideas and pulling in different directions are combined, with little overall coherence.

This pattern is very much evident in the area of American commercial policy. Judith Goldstein observes that conventional attempts to explain American trade policies by reference to the weight of societal interest groups or the demands of the international system fail to account for their actual evolution.[2] Only by looking at the "political salience of economic theories" can one explain America's movement from a protectionist cycle that began in the early nineteenth century and culminated in the highly protective tariffs of the 1930s to a free trade cycle that now contains elements of free trade and fair trade.

The national security policy arena provides an even clearer picture of the influence of the impact of shared ideas and ways of acting on American foreign policy. Throughout most of the cold war period, these ideas and actions were embodied in the concept of containment. The first public statement of containment came in an article in *Foreign Affairs* authored by George Kennan. In it he argued:

> Soviet pressure against the free institutions of the western world is something that can be contained by the adroit and vigilant application of counter-force at a series of constantly shifting geographical and political points, corresponding to the shifts and maneuvers of Soviet policy but which cannot be charmed or talked out of existence.[3]

The logic of containment became embodied in a wide range of U.S. foreign policy initiatives. The Truman Doctrine, which pledged U.S. support to all states coming under pressure from international communism, was faithful to it. So too were early U.S. foreign aid programs intended to rebuild the economies of Western Europe (the Marshall Plan) and bring economic development to the third world (the Point Four Program). It was U.S. military policy, however, that became the primary vehicle for implementing containment in the form of a series of encircling alliances around the Soviet perimeter: NATO, the Southeast Asia Treaty Organization (SEATO), and the Central Treaty Organization (CENTO). What disagreements existed within policy-making circles were largely over the tactics and strategies to be used and not the ends of U.S. foreign policy. Such disputes were possible in part because in his article Kennan did not specify the means of containment. He would later become a critic of containment, arguing that his ideas had been misinterpreted and misapplied. Kennan specifically objected to the heavy reliance on military force and the perceived need to practice containment everywhere and anywhere that communist expansion was encountered.

Even the Nixon administration's much heralded shift to a policy of détente could be comfortably fit into the larger strategy of containment. Détente was designed to protect U.S. influence as much as possible in an era of lessened power abroad and increased isolationist feeling at home. Confrontation and crisis management were now too expensive to be the primary means for stopping Soviet expansion. Détente sought to accomplish this end by creating a framework of limited cooperation within the context of an international order that recognized the legitimacy of both U.S. and Soviet core security goals.[4]

This long-term continuity in U.S. foreign policy goes back beyond the period of containment. It stretches back to the very beginnings of the United States. In this chapter we examine the foundations of the American national style of foreign policy. First, we look at the tendency for U.S. foreign policy to fluctuate between isolationism and internationalism. Second, we examine the patterns of thought and action that provide the building blocks for both of these general foreign policy orientations. Finally, we look to the post–cold war era.

Isolationism versus Internationalism

U.S. foreign policy is frequently discussed in terms of a tension between two opposing general foreign policy orientations: isolationism and internationalism. From the isolationist perspective American national interests are best served by "quitting the world" or at a minimum maintaining a healthy sense of detachment from events elsewhere. It draws its inspiration from Washington's farewell address in which he urged Americans to "steer clear of permanent alliances with any portion of the foreign world" and asserted that "Europe has a set of primary interests which to us have none or very remote relations."[5] Among the major foreign policy decisions rooted in the principles of isolationism are the Monroe Doctrine, the refusal to join the League of Nations, the neutrality legislation of the 1930s, and, more loosely, the fear of future Vietnams. The internationalist perspective sees protecting and promoting American national interests as requiring an activist foreign policy. Internationalists hold that the United States cannot escape the world. Events abroad inevitably impinge upon U.S. interests and any policy based on the denial of their relevance is self-defeating. The global depression of the 1930s, Hitler's rise to power, the outbreak of World War II, and the constant outward thrust of post–World War II communism are proof to the internationalists that Washington's advice is no longer relevant.]Such widely divergent undertakings as membership in the United Nations and NATO, the Marshall Plan, the Alliance for Progress, CIA covert action, the Helsinki Human Rights Agreement, and involvement in Korea and Vietnam can be traced to the internationalist perspective on world affairs.

The oscillation between isolationism and internationalism has not been haphazard. An underlying logic appears to guide the movement from one to the other. Frank Klingberg identifies five periods of U.S. foreign policy of twenty-thirty years' duration.[6] Each combines an introvert (isolationist) and extrovert (internationalist) phase. According to Klingberg's analysis, the United States is currently in an internationalist phase with the next isolationist phase set to begin around 2014.

	Introvert	Extrovert
1.	1776–1798	1798–1824
2.	1824–1844	1844–1871
3.	1871–1891	1891–1918
4.	1918–1940	1940–1967
5.	1967–1987	1987–2014

Klingberg suggests that in each period U.S. policy makers were forced to confront a major foreign policy problem. In period 1, it was independence; in period 2, issues involving manifest destiny were dominant; in period 3, it was the process of becoming an industrial power. The crisis of world democracy dominated period 4, and today the need to create a stable world order lies at the heart of the challenges facing U.S. foreign policy. In each period, the dominant cycle (introversion or extroversion) imposes limits on the types of solutions that can be considered by policy makers and predisposes the public to accept certain courses of action. Klingberg also sees the cyclical movement between isolationism and internationalism as being spiral in nature. Each movement toward internationalism is deeper than the one before it, and each reversal to isolationism is less complete than the one preceding it.

Disagreement exists over the mechanism triggering a shift from one phase to the next. Klingberg suggests a number of possibilities: the failure of a long-term policy, the arrival of a new generation of policy makers, the onset of a critical problem requiring a solution incompatible with the dominant mood, and the corruption or distortion of an ongoing line of action. Dexter Perkins suggests that shifts in foreign policy orientations may be tied to the business cycle.[7] He finds that in periods of economic recovery after a period of stagnation and decline, U.S. foreign policy takes on a belligerent tone. The more stable the economy, the more moderate is U.S. foreign policy. In a similar vein Robert Dallek sees the periodic outward thrust of U.S. foreign policy as a product of domestic frustrations and disappointments.[8] Foreign policy successes are sought as a sign that the American dream is still valid and capable of producing victories.

Whatever the specific trigger, the movement from isolationism to internationalism and back again is made possible because both general foreign policy orientations are very much a part of the American national style. One does not represent the American approach to world affairs, and the other its denial. They are two different ways in which the patterns of American foreign policy, its fundamental building blocks, come together.[9] Both are united in the conviction that the institutions and ideals brought forward by the American experience need protection. The approaches differ on how best to provide for their continued growth and development. Isolationism seeks to accomplish this end by insulating the American experience from corrupting foreign influences. Internationalism seeks to protect them by creating a more hospitable global environment. For both, world affairs gain meaning and importance (or irrelevance) primarily in terms of how they affect the American historical experience and American ideals.

Sources of the American National Style

The sources of the American national style are found in the conditions under which earlier generations of American policy makers operated and the ideas that guided their thinking.[10] Few nations can look back on as favorable a set of conditions in which to grow and develop. The vast size of the United States brought with it an abundance of natural resources on which to build a prosperous economy. Between the mid-1600s and the mid-1800s, America grew from a series of isolated settlements into an economic power rivaling its European counterparts. Just as important for the development of the American national style is the fact that this growth took place without any master plan. Individual self-reliance, flexibility, and improvisation were the cardinal virtues in developing America. Guided by these principles, the United States has become a "how-to-do-it" society whose energies are largely directed to the problem at hand and whose long-range concerns receive scant attention.[11]

It also needs to be noted that this growth occurred in an era of unparalleled global harmony. With the exception of the Crimean War, from the Congress of Vienna in 1815 until the outbreak of World War I in 1914, the Great Powers of Europe were largely at peace with one another. Closer to home, the defense of its continental borders never required the creation of a large standing army or navy. For more than a century, America's peace and security required very little effort on its part. Peace and security seemed to come naturally, and they were widely accepted as the normal condition of world affairs. The links between American security and developments abroad went unnoticed. Democracy, rather than the strength of the British navy or the European balance of power, was seen as the source of American security.

The faith in the power of democracy reflects the extent to which American political thought is rooted in the eighteenth-century view of human nature. Most important to the development of the ideas that have guided U.S. policy makers is the work of John Locke, who argued that people are rational beings capable of determining their own best interests. The best government was held to be that which governed least. To Locke the historical record indicated that the exercise of power inevitably led to its abuse and corrupted the natural harmony existing among individuals. Conflicts between individuals could be settled without the application of concentrated state power. The wastefulness and destructiveness of war disqualified it as a means of conflict resolution. Negotiation, reason, and discussion are sufficient to overcome misperceptions and reconcile conflicting interests.

In contrast to war, trade is seen as a force promoting the peaceful settlement of disputes. The dynamics of the marketplace bind individuals together in mutually profitable exchanges. The power of the marketplace and the power of governments are seen as being in direct competition with one another. The greater the power of one over society, the less the power of the other. Since commerce creates a vested interest in peace, logic again points to limiting government powers. The American historical experience seemed to offer vivid proof of the correctness of the liberal outlook on human affairs. Had not the United States been largely at peace with the world? When it went to war had it not been provoked? Had it not enjoyed an unprecedented record of economic growth and prosperity? Was not its past free of the class conflicts that had rocked European society?

It is only a short step from answering yes to these questions to a belief in the uniqueness of the American experience and the existence of an American mission. It is a step Americans traditionally have taken. American "exceptionalism"[12] is taken to demand a leadership role in world affairs. During isolationist periods leadership takes the form of standing apart from international politics and leading by example. In internationalist periods it is revealed in attempts to transform the international system. Defending the Clinton administration's use of cruise missiles against Iraq in 1998, Secretary of State Madeline Albright asserted "if we use force, it is because we are America. We are the indispensable nation. We stand tall. We see farther into the future." Vice President Dick Cheney spoke in equally expansive terms in 2002 stating, "America has friends and allies in this cause, but only we can lead it . . . The responsibility did not come to us by chance. We are in a unique position because of our unique assets, because of the character of our people, the strength of our ideals. . . ."

Before proceeding, a caveat is in order. This is not the only way to characterize the American historical experience, value system, or national style.[13] For some, the United States has been antirevolutionary, seeking to prevent social change and third world revolutionary movements that might threaten its dominant position in world affairs. This view is often found in the writings of revisionist historians who find U.S. foreign policy to be imperial in nature and rooted in the expansionist needs of capitalism. Others see U.S. foreign policy as racist, as evidenced by its immigration policy that systematically discriminated against the Chinese and other non-Western Europeans; its hesitancy to support international human rights conventions; and its attitude toward the suitability of Hawaii, Puerto Rico, and the Philippines for either statehood or independence. Finally, some would argue that what we have called internationalism is better defined as interventionism: a tendency to intervene in the affairs of other states to a degree far beyond that which is required by any reasonable definition of U.S. national interest. In this view there is no competing theme of isolationism but only an opposition to specific cases of intervention (such as Vietnam) on pragmatic or tactical grounds.

Patterns

UNILATERALISM

Three patterns of thought and action provide the building blocks from which the American national style emerges. The first pattern is unilateralism, or a predisposition to act alone in addressing foreign policy problems.[14] Unilateralism does not dictate a specific course of action. Isolationism, neutrality, activism, and interventionism are all consistent with its basic orientation to world affairs. The unilateralist thrust of U.S. foreign policy represents a rejection of the balance-of-power approach for providing national security. This approach, second nature to European diplomats, is alien to the American experience. Security could largely be taken for granted, and collaborative efforts were unnecessary. The willingness to apply the American approach to security on a global basis also reflects the American sense of exceptionalism and is often perceived by others to be an insensitive and egoistic nationalism.

The best-known statement of the unilateralist position is the Monroe Doctrine. With the end of the Napoleonic Wars, concern arose that Spain might attempt to reestablish its control over the newly independent Latin American republics. Great Britain approached the United States over the possibility of a joint declaration to prevent this from happening. The United States rejected the British proposal, only to turn around and make a unilateral declaration to the same end: The United States would not tolerate European intervention in the Western Hemisphere, and in return it pledged not to interfere in European affairs. In 1904, the Roosevelt Corollary to the Monroe Doctrine was put forward. Spurred into action by the inability of the Dominican Republic to pay its foreign lenders, President Theodore Roosevelt sent in U.S. forces. The Roosevelt Corollary established the United States as the self-proclaimed policeman of the Western Hemisphere. It would play that role many times. The years 1904 to 1934 saw the United States send eight expeditionary forces to Latin America, conduct five military occupations ranging in duration from a few months to nineteen years, and take over customs collections duties twice. The legacy of the Monroe Doctrine continues into the post–World War II era. The CIA-sponsored overthrows of the Arbenz government in Guatemala and the Allende government in Chile, U.S. behavior in the Bay of Pigs and the Cuban missile crisis, the 1965 invasion of the Dominican Republic, the 1983 invasion of Grenada, and the 1989 invasion of Panama testify to the continued influence of unilateralism on U.S. behavior in the Western Hemisphere.

The nature of the American participation in World War I and the subsequent U.S. refusal to join the League of Nations also reflect the unilateralist impulse. Official World War I documents identify the victors as the Allied and Associated Powers. The only Associated Power of note was the United States. For U.S. policy makers this was more than just a mere symbolic separation from its European allies. Woodrow Wilson engaged in personal negotiations with Germany over ending the war without consulting the allies over the terms of a possible truce. The United States was also the only major victorious power not to join the League of Nations. While this abstention is often attributed to isolationism, Robert Tucker argues that the U.S. refusal represented a triumph of unilateralism.[15] Membership would have committed the United States to a collective security system that could have obliged it to undertake multilateral military action in the name of stopping international aggression.

The impact of unilateralist thinking also comes through clearly in the neutrality legislation of the 1930s. These acts placed an embargo on the sale of arms to warring states. Because arms sales were seen as the most likely method of U.S. entry into a war, they had to be prohibited regardless of the consequences that the embargo might have on events elsewhere. The post–World War II shift from isolationism to internationalism did not bring about an abandonment of unilateralism; it only placed a multilateral façade over it. Control over NATO's nuclear forces remains firmly in the hands of the United States. The presence of the UN flag in Korea and references to SEATO treaty commitments in Vietnam could scarcely conceal the totally U.S. nature of these two wars. Within the United Nations the veto power protects U.S. vital interests from the intrusion of other powers, and the system of weighted voting used in international financial organizations guarantees the United States a preponderant voice in their deliberations.

The American penchant for unilateralism was never far beneath the surface in its dealings with allies during the later years of the cold war. Nowhere was this perhaps more evident than in the Reagan administration's secret effort to sell arms to Iran in return for the freedom of American hostages in Lebanon at a time when its public stance was one of pressuring allies not to negotiate with terrorists. Unilateralism was also evident in its approach to summitry. James Schlesinger argues that at the Reykjavik summit meeting with Mikhail Gorbachev, "The administration suddenly jettisoned 25 years of deterrence doctrine . . . without warning, consultation with Congress or its allies."[16]

Unilateralism continued to characterize U.S. foreign policy in the post–cold war era. President George H. W. Bush embraced unilateralism in assembling a global coalition against Saddam Hussein. It was the United States that decided when to launch air strikes; it was the United States that decided when to begin ground operations; it was the United States that ended the ground war; and it was the United States that declared the coalition's objectives to have been met. A vivid reminder of the continued pull of unilateralist thinking in the post–cold war era came early in the Clinton administration when as a price for congressional approval of the GATT agreement, Clinton agreed to insert an "escape hatch" into the treaty that would allow the United States to withdraw if the World Trade Organization's arbitration process consistently violated U.S. rights. President George W. Bush acted unilaterally several times in the first months of his presidency. The most notable examples included his decision not to participate in the Kyoto Protocol or the international criminal court and to proceed with the ballistic missile defense system. Both decisions were made in face of protests by U.S. allies. The global war against terrorism did not change this unilateralist impulse. In December 2001, Bush unilaterally gave notice that the United States was withdrawing from the 1972 Anti-Ballistic Missile Treaty. In his State of the Union address the following month, he gave notice to the world that he was prepared to act unilaterally against terrorism. "Some governments will be timid in the face of terror . . . If they do not act, America will."

MORAL PRAGMATISM

The second pattern to American foreign policy is moral pragmatism.[17] The American sense of morality involves two elements. The first is that state behavior can be judged by moral standards. The second is that American morality provides the universal standard for making those judgments. By definition American actions are taken to be morally correct and justifiable. Justifying the invasion of Panama as necessary to protect democracy is a case in point. Flawed policy initiatives are routinely attributed to leadership deficiencies or breakdowns in organizational behavior and not to the values that guided that action. In the aftermath of World War I, the Nye Committee investigated charges that the United States had been led into war by banking interests, and the McCarthy investigations followed the "loss of China."

American pragmatism takes the form of an engineering approach to foreign policy problem solving.[18] U.S. involvement is typically put in terms of "setting things right." It is assumed that a right answer does exist and that it is the American answer. Moreover, the answer to the problem (be it Lebanon, Nicaragua, the defense of Europe, economic growth in the third world, arms control) is seen as being permanent in nature. Problems arise when others do not see the problem in similar terms. To some this has been especially evident in U.S.–Soviet arms control talks. According to Freeman Dyson, the American approach to strategic thinking "treats nuclear war as a mathematical exercise," and its basic concepts (deterrence, sufficiency, and retaliation) are supposed to "guarantee" continued U.S. security.[19] Operating on the basis of a very different historical experience, the Soviets have developed concepts (victory, superiority, and offensive action) that "are goals to be striven for, not conditions to be guaranteed." To the Soviets, uncertainty remained inherent in the nature of warfare, for which no engineering solution exists.

The preferred American method for uncovering the solution is to break the problem into smaller ones the same way an engineer would take a blueprint and break it down into smaller tasks. An organizational or mechanical solution is then devised for each of the subproblems. In the process, it is not unusual to lose sight of the political context of the larger problem being addressed. When this happens, the result can be the substitution of means for ends, improvisation, or the reliance on canned formulas to solve the problem.

Both the Monroe Doctrine and its Roosevelt Corollary show the influence of moral pragmatism. Cecil Crabb argues that "the major purpose of the Monroe Doctrine was to preserve the fundamental distinction between old and new world political systems."[20] This goal and its premises went unquestioned. Attention instead focused on how to accomplish this end. The option seized did not reflect the realities of international politics. The Monroe Doctrine was a success because it reflected both British and American interests and because of the power of the British navy. It did not succeed because of American power. Roosevelt justified his corollary to the Monroe Doctrine on the grounds that if nations near the United States could not keep order within their own borders, then the United States had a moral obligation to intervene. Once again the question was largely defined as an engineering problem, how best to intervene.

The neutrality legislation of the 1930s provides an example of moral pragmatism at work in a quite different setting. Here the concern was not with asserting U.S. influence but with detaching the United States from world affairs. As first put forward, the legislation was easy to implement but paid little attention to the political realities of the day. Weapons were not to be sold side. Yet refusing to sell weapons to either participant guaranteed the stronger side and invited its aggression. The neutrality legislation was repeatedly amended in an effort to close the gap between technique and political reality. In 1937 the president was given the authority to distinguish between civil strife and war. In 1939 it permitted the cash-and-carry purchase of weapons by belligerents. This allowed the United States to sell weapons to Great Britain but made a mockery of the neutrality principle.

The overreliance on formulas by the United States in the post–World War II era has frequently been commented on. Among the most prominent have been (1) opposition to aggression, (2) containment of communism, and (3) defense of free nations. All three have been criticized for being moral abstractions, failing to provide concrete guidance on how to tailor goals to the situation at hand, select the proper approach to solve the problem, or weigh the costs and benefits of a course of action.[21] One author argues that the anticommunist impulse in particular has been used to sanction almost any course of action no matter how immoral if it brings about the greater goal of stopping communism.[22] Right-wing dictators have been supported as the lesser of two evils, governments overthrown, states invaded, international law violated, and the rights of American citizens compromised in the pursuit of this end.

The potential dangers of rooting U.S. foreign policy on a foundation of moral pragmatism came through quite clearly in the Iran–Contra fiasco. Convinced of the moral correctness of the goal of freeing American hostages in Lebanon, the Reagan administration proceeded to sell arms to Iran and then diverted monies gained through these sales to the U.S.-backed Contras fighting the Sandinista government in Nicaragua. The reliance on engineering solutions and formulas to solve problems also reached excess here, as witnessed by National Security Council (NSC) staffer Lieutenant Colonel Oliver North's equation for achieving the release of the American hostages, part of which read: 1 707 w/300 TOWs = 1 AMCIT (American citizen).

In carrying out his most ambitious foreign policy initiative, the war against Iraq, George H. W. Bush demonstrated a penchant for moral pragmatism. Saddam Hussein was defined as the embodiment of evil and a threat to American national interests. The justness of the American cause was unquestioned. Attention focused solely on how to accomplish the stated goal of bringing about a removal of Iraqi forces from Kuwait with a minimum loss of American lives. The centerpiece of the chosen solution was air power and, as Elliot Cohen observes, "reliance on air power has set the American way of war apart from all others . . . it plays to the machine-mindedness of American civilization."[23] George W. Bush has continued in this tradition. The classic expressions of moral pragmatism in his administration have come in the war against terrorism. In his address to the American people following the 9/11 attacks, he declared "either you are with the U.S. or you are with the terrorists." He would go on to call for Osama bin Laden's capture "dead or alive." Others find evidence of it not in his language that often invoked images of the American frontier but in his administration's shifting rationales for the Iraq War. The failure to find weapons of mass destruction or links between

Iraq and al-Qaeda did not bring about a admissions of error. Rather it brought forward new rationales for why the war was necessary.

LEGALISM

The third pattern to U.S. foreign policy is legalism. It grows out of the rejection of the balance of power as a means for preserving national security and the liberal view that people are rational beings who abhor war and favor the peaceful settlement of disputes.[24] A central task of U.S. foreign policy, therefore, is to create a global system of institutions and rules that will allow states to settle their disputes without recourse to war. The primary institutional embodiments of the legalist perspective are the League of Nations and the United Nations. Also relevant are the host of post–World War II international economic organizations that the United States joined (that is, the World Bank, International Monetary Fund, and General Agreement on Tariffs and Trade). Just as commerce between individuals binds them together, international trade is assumed to bind states together and reduce the likelihood of war.

The rule-making thrust to legalism is found in the repeated use of the pledge system as an instrument of foreign policy.[25] In creating a pledge system, the United States puts forward a statement of principle and then asks other states to adhere to it either by signing a treaty or by pledging their support for the principle. Noticeably absent is any meaningful enforcement mechanism. The Open Door Notes exemplify this strategy for world affairs problem solving. In the Notes the United States unilaterally proclaimed its opposition to spheres of influence in China and asked other powers to do likewise, but it did not specify any sanctions against a state that reneged on its pledge. The Washington Naval Disarmament Conference of 1922 and the 1928 Kellogg–Briand Pact are also part of the pledge system. The Washington Naval Disarmament Conference sought to prevent war by establishing a fixed power ratio for certain categories of warships. The agreement failed to include inspection or enforcement provisions. Its restraining qualities were soon overtaken by a naval arms race in areas left uncovered by the agreement and by a general heightening of international tensions. The Kellogg–Briand Pact sought to outlaw war as an instrument of foreign policy. Yet true to its unilateralist impulse, the United States stated that signing the pact would not prevent it from enforcing the Monroe Doctrine or obligate it to participate in sanctions against other states. The SALT I and SALT II agreements follow in the tradition of the pledge system. They specify in broad terms the nuclear inventories that the Soviet Union and the United States are permitted to have without creating any enforcement provisions.

A variation of the pledge system has become a prominent feature of U.S. bilateral and multilateral trade policy. Confronted with an intransigent Japan in 1993, U.S. negotiators settled for a "framework" agreement that specified how future agreements would seek to resolve issues of trade imbalances and barriers to trade without detailing the particulars of the agreement. On the multilateral level, agreements were signed in 1994 that pledged the United States and thirty-three other Western Hemisphere states to create a free trade zone by 2005 and that pledged the United States and seventeen Pacific Basin countries to create their own free trade zone by 2020. In neither case were organizational blueprints or detailed schedules for creating these free trade areas presented.

Legalism has also placed a heavy burden on U.S. foreign policy. In rejecting power politics as an approach for providing for U.S. national security, policy makers have denied themselves use of the "reasons-of-state" argument as a justification for their actions. Instead, they have sought to clothe their actions in terms of legal principles. Post–World War II examples include fighting the Korean War under the UN flag, seeking the Organization of American States' approval for a blockade during the Cuban missile crisis, and citing a request by the Organization of Eastern Caribbean States as part of the justification for going into Grenada. This pattern has continued in the post–cold war era. George H. W. Bush obtained UN endorsement for his military campaign against Iraq, and Clinton did the same for his use of force in Haiti. George W. Bush continued this reliance on legalism even though he acted without UN support. His administration argued that no new UN resolution was necessary because Saddam Hussein had violated previous UN resolutions and was thus in violation of an international agreement. In Bush's words, Iraq "had answered a decade of UN demands with a decade of defiance. . . . We want the resolutions of the world's most important multilateral body to be enforced."

Consequences of the American National Style

As we suggested earlier, these three patterns come together to support both isolationism and internationalism. They also produce four consequences for the overall conduct of U.S. foreign policy regardless of which general foreign policy orientation is dominant. The first consequence is a tendency to "win the war and lose the peace." As Robert Osgood wrote in 1957:

> The United States has demonstrated an impressive ability to defeat the enemy. Yet . . . it has been unable to deter war; it has been unprepared to fight war; it has failed to gain the objectives it fought for; and its settlements have not brought satisfactory peace.[26]

This condition stems from the American tendency to see war and peace as polar opposites. War is a social aberration while peace is the normal state of affairs. Strategies and tactics appropriate for one arena have no place in the other. The two categories must be kept separate to prevent the calculations of war from corrupting the principles of peace. In times of peace reason, discussion, and trade are relied on to accomplish foreign policy objectives. In times of war, power is the appropriate tool. The absence of a conceptual link between war and peace means that war cannot serve as an instrument of statecraft and that war plans will be drawn up in a political vacuum. The objective of war is to defeat the enemy as swiftly as possible. Only when that is accomplished can one return to the concerns of peace. The closing stages of World War II illustrate the problem inherent in the war–peace dichotomy. Should U.S. forces have pushed as far as possible eastward for the political purpose of denying the Red Army control over as much territory as possible, or should they have stopped as soon as the purely military objectives of the offensive were realized and not risked the lives of U.S. soldiers on nonmilitary goals? The latter course of action was selected, and the cold war East–West boundary in Europe reflects this choice.

The second consequence is the existence of a double standard in judging the behavior of states. Convinced of its righteousness and the universality of its values, and predisposed to act unilaterally, the United States has often engaged in actions that it condemns when practiced by other states. The United States can be trusted with testing and developing nuclear weapons, but other states, especially third world states, cannot. Soviet interventions into Afghanistan and Czechoslovakia are condemned as imperialism while U.S. interventions into the Dominican Republic, Grenada, and Panama are held to be morally defensible. The United States urges its allies not to sell weapons to terrorists or those who support them while at the same time the United States is selling weapons to Iran in the hopes of securing the release of U.S. hostages in Lebanon. The reverse condition also holds. Activities considered by most states to be a normal part of world affairs have been highly controversial in the United States. The clandestine collection of information and covert attempts to influence developments in other states are cases in point. Both are long-standing instruments of foreign policy. Yet the United States has always exhibited a reluctance to employ them for fear of their potentially corrupting effect on American freedoms.

The third consequence is an ambivalence toward diplomacy. In the abstract, diplomacy is valued as part of the process by which states peacefully resolve their disputes. Along with international law and international organizations, diplomacy occupies a central place in liberal thinking about the proper forums for conducting foreign relations. The product of diplomacy, however, is viewed with great skepticism. If the U.S. position is the morally correct one, how can it compromise (something vital to the success of diplomacy) without rejecting its own sense of mission and the principles it stands for? As John Spanier notes, under these conditions compromise is indistinguishable from appeasement.[27] It does not matter whether the other party to the negotiations is a twentieth-century communist state or an eighteenth- or nineteenth-century European state. In either case, the fruits of diplomacy have been looked upon with suspicion. For the George W. Bush administration, this skepticism over the value of negotiating with the enemy was evident in its dealings with North Korea over its violation of the Agreed Framework it negotiated with the Clinton administration and its open pursuit of a nuclear capability. "Talking" with North Korea was seen as tantamount to "caving in" to a government that the administration had labeled as being part of an "axis of evil."

The fourth consequence is impatience. Optimistic at the start of an undertaking and convinced of the correctness of its position in both a moral and a technical sense, Americans tend to want quick results. They become impatient when positive results are not soon forthcoming. A common reaction is to turn away in frustration. The next time a similar situation presents itself and U.S. action is needed, none may be taken. Calls for no more Vietnams reflect this sense of frustration. So, too, did the demand to get U.S. Marines out of Lebanon following the terrorist attacks on the U.S. compound. The desire for quick and visible results is seen by many as creating a bias for the use of the military as an instrument of foreign policy. Neither diplomacy nor economic power offers quick results. Both are slow working and work best when used out of the public eye. A vicious circle thus can be created. The demand for quick results leads to a reliance on military power, but the rigid distinction between war and peace makes it difficult to use that power effectively. Its use may be marked by a double standard or, as Osgood observed, may simply fail to meet its political objectives. If that is the case, then diplomacy may be turned to. Yet here again the results are likely to be slow in coming, and the settlement will be looked upon with skepticism. Frustration will set in and dominate U.S. foreign policy until a consensus exists supporting new foreign policy initiatives.

All four of these consequences have already shown themselves in the build-up to the Iraq War and its aftermath. This is most evident in the growing sense that while the United States won the war it was losing the peace. Rather than being greeted as liberators as the Bush administration stated they would be, American forces and their Iraqi allies became branded as unwelcomed occupiers and were the targets of deadly attacks by insurgents. In late June 2004, just before the transfer of power to an interim Iraqi government, and just over one year after President Bush proclaimed an end to major combat, 55 percent of Americans believed that the Iraq War had increased U.S. vulnerability to terrorism.[28] The notion that different rules might apply to the United States than to other states surfaced after revelations of widespread abuse by American interrogators at Abu Ghraib prison led to the release of internal memos by the administration (since disavowed) that the Justice Department had asserted and the president agreed that he has the power to sanction torture, suspend the application of international protections for detainees, and that those acting on his authority would be immune from prosecution. An ambivalence to diplomacy was evident in the reluctance of the administration first go to the United Nations and obtain its support for the use of force against Saddam Hussein, and then in its unwillingness to back continued weapons inspections or make the compromises necessary to obtain its support. Finally, there is impatience. That same June 2004 poll found that 54 percent of Americans polled stated that the war had been a mistake. This was the first time that a majority of Americans had answered this way to a war question since Vietnam.

A Revival of Wilsonianism?

What then of American foreign policy in an age of terrorism? Will it move forward on new foundations or continue to build on the traditions of the past? During the 2000 presidential campaign, candidate George W. Bush spoke of the need to adopt a humble foreign policy suggesting a change might be in the offing (although as we shall see in the next section he would not be the first American statesperson to call for such a policy). After 9/11, his foreign policy was anything but modest and unassuming. In fact, George W. Bush began to sound very much like Woodrow Wilson. In his 2002 State of the Union Address, Bush stated, "American will lead by defending liberty and justice because they are right and true and unchanging for people everywhere . . . We have no intention of imposing our culture. But American will always stand firm for the nonnegotiable demands of human dignity." Speaking at West Point later that year, he spoke of the "time of opportunity for America" and how "we will work to translate this moment of influence into decades of peace, prosperity, and liberty." And, in his 2005 Inauguration Day address he spoke of "ending tyranny in our world." This embrace of Wilsonianism is reflective of a broader rediscovery and admiration for Wilson's foreign policy that has taken place since the end of the cold war. A standard ingredient in post mortems of Wilson's foreign policy was that it was naively idealistic. The implication was that it was a fundamentally flawed vision that offered little guidance to future generations of American foreign policy makers. This is no longer the case. Many now concede that the Wilsonian vision was ill-suited to the first decades of the twentieth century but assert that it is quite relevant to the conditions of the post–cold war era. Rather than characterizing Wilson as an idealist, many see him as a vindicated visionary.[29]

Proponents of neo-Wilsonianism as the basis for post–cold war American foreign policy center their attention on his Fourteen Points. Presented in a speech Wilson delivered before Congress in 1918, the Fourteen Points constituted an outline for constructing a new world order. The first five points would lay the foundation for a new, "open" era of international politics. Points 6 through 13 addressed the problems of national self-determination and drawing national boundaries in Europe. Point 14 asserted that "a general association of nations must be formed under specific covenants for the purpose of affording mutual guarantees of political independence and territorial integrity to great and small states alike." Looking beyond the Fourteen Points themselves, the Wilsonian vision of world politics rested on four elements.[30] First, promoting democracy. Second, encouraging free trade. Third, controlling weapons. Together, these three would place restraints on the exercise of power by governments and provide space for the development of individual liberty. The fourth element was the League of Nations. It would provide an alternative to balance-of-power politics as a means of providing for national security.

That Wilson's proposals did not fare well at the Paris Peace Conference and that the United States did not vote to join the League of Nations are acknowledged as great failures but are no longer treated uniformly as signs that the ideas Wilson espoused were defective. Many now echo historian and Wilson biographer Arthur S. Link's conclusion that Wilson possessed a "higher realism" in his handling of foreign affairs.[31] Link characterizes Wilson as a quick learner in foreign policy matters who took personal control over foreign policy making because of the incompetence of those in high-ranking

State Department positions. He was a man who recognized the need for give-and-take in treaty negotiations. He was all of this while remaining loyal to his fundamental Christian principles and belief in democracy.

Those advocating a neo-Wilsonian foreign policy have not gone unchallenged. Some opponents have reexamined the Wilsonian legacy and asked: "Are we all not Wilsonians?" while others have asserted that advocates of a neo-Wilsonian foreign policy have drawn too narrow a picture of Wilsonianism.

Robert Tucker asks the first question.[32] Rare is the modern president, he observes, who does not claim to be a Wilsonian. Some argue that the Reagan Doctrine could be seen as the ultimate embodiment of the Wilsonian legacy, given its commitment to expand democracy, and that Reagan was the "most Wilsonian of presidents since Wilson's time."[33] This overextension of the Wilsonian label leads Tucker to reexamine the roots of Wilsonian thought. He concludes that Wilson's approach to foreign policy shares much in common with Jefferson, who is cited by many as an early advocate of isolationism. They both rejected amoral European-style diplomacy and sought to replace it with a new diplomacy that rested on the will of the people. They were united in the belief that American interests could only be safeguarded by a reformed international system. Tucker asserts that only force could bring this condition about. Rejecting this course of action led Jefferson to embrace isolationism. For Wilson, it came to mean creating a global concert of powers that would bring such a reformed international system into existence. Where the Wilsonian vision encountered problems was in the relationship between ends and means. Could a reformed international system be created with only limited costs and demands being placed on the United States? If not, then the Wilsonian vision of a democratic world could only be purchased at an excessive price and one that threatened to undermine the very American values it was designed to foster. It is these questions of the relationship between means and ends and force and peace that Tucker sees as representing the core challenge facing the Wilsonian vision today.

David Fromkin raises the second question posed above: What is Wilsonianism?[34] He concludes that it is a mistake to equate Wilsonianism with collective security. At a minimum, attention must be given to several other aspects of Wilson's thinking. Foremost among these is his belief in a strong presidency. Wilson saw the president's control of foreign policy as "very absolute." He believed that the Senate had no choice but to ratify any treaty submitted to it by the president regardless of any doubts about its wisdom or the secrecy with which it may have been negotiated. Also critical to any definition of Wilsonianism, Fromkin argues, is a close examination of the relationship between words and deeds in Wilson's decision making. Fromkin sees a pattern in which Wilsonian principles followed his actions rather than preceding them. As a consequence, Wilsonian principles served to rationalize policy made for very different reasons, rather than direct it. He freely changed sides on an issue or applied standards unevenly. Fromkin concludes that Wilsonianism can only be taken to mean "a certain way of talking and thinking about international relations in terms of concepts that are inspiring and high minded but impractical application provides no guidance."

OTHER VOICES FROM THE PAST

Woodrow Wilson's is not the only voice from the past being rediscovered as the United States searches to define its place in the world today. Isolationists point to the writings of John Adams. According to Adams, American foreign policy should be based on the principle that the United States was "the well-wisher to the freedom and independence of all" but "the champion and vindicator only of her own."[35] Adams was putting forward an argument for nonintervention into the affairs of others and advocating a foreign policy that was to be based on the "power of example." To go further, he warns, would involve the United States in "wars of interest and intrigue, of individual avarice, envy, and ambition." Conservative internationalists point to Theodore Roosevelt's writings.[36] They would replace liberal internationalism's conception of humanitarian intervention as a philanthropic exercise with one rooted in a sense of nationalistic patriotism. Writing prior to the Spanish-American War, Roosevelt wrote that "the useful member of a community is the man who first and foremost attends to his own rights and duties . . . the useful member of the brotherhood of nations is that nation which is most thoroughly saturated with the national ideal." Adam Wolfson updates Roosevelt's admonition by asserting that "humanity's cause is likely to have a future with us on the day when more American's come to believe that upholding this cause is a matter of special national honor."

In addition to these two, other voices from the past continue to exert an influence on the present.[37] Alexander Hamilton speaks to those who see the primary purpose of American foreign policy as being the promotion of American economic strength at home and abroad. After World War II, this required an American foreign policy that worked with other states to promote and protect an open international economic order. Andrew Jackson's writings and actions provide a foundation for those who stress the populist principles of courage, honor, and self-reliance in the conduct of American foreign policy. Suspicious of outsiders and their values, Jacksonians champion a foreign policy of constant vigilance backed by overwhelming might that is employed with few if any constraints.

Summary and the Future

What of the future? Will the American national style remain the same, or will it change? Can it be allowed to remain the same, or must it change? The American national style is not frozen in place. In the eyes of one observer, legalism has already lost much of its influence.[38] Change might come about as a result of the increased presence of women, blacks, and Hispanics in the policy-making process.[39] Their histories read quite differently from those presented in the standardized accounts of the American past, and they may bring to the policy process a very different style of acting and thinking about solutions of foreign policy problems. Change might also come about as the result of major crises in the operation of the international or domestic order. The onset of such crises increases societal receptivity to new ideas and creates a window of opportunity for these ideas to seize a place on the political agenda.[40]

In a sense, this is exactly what happened after the end of the cold war. Realism, the dominant paradigm for practicing world politics during the cold war, seemed ill-suited for the emerging conditions of post–cold war international relations. This stimulated a search for an alternative worldview and a renewed interest in Wilsonianism.

By definition the American national style is neither good nor bad.[41] It is simply a descriptive statement about how policy makers tend to think about foreign policy problems. The historical record suggests that the American national style has been a source of strength and weakness. Its impact is often largely determined by the context within which policy makers operate. The very aspect of the American national style, which is a source of strength in one case, has proven to be a source of weakness in another. The Truman administration experienced the success of the Marshall Plan and the failure of the Point Four Program. The Kennedy administration successfully managed the Cuban missile crisis and precipitated the Bay of Pigs fiasco. The fit between American national style and future policy problems is thus uncertain. Much rests on both the nature of those problems and the ability of U.S. policy makers to learn from the past.

A degree of caution must be employed in relying on a national style approach to foreign policy analysis. The patterns we have discussed cannot be seen as dictating the details of U.S. foreign policy. Too many other factors are at work for this to be the case. What they do appear capable of doing is placing boundaries on what type of action will be considered permissible or appropriate for the United States to undertake. Foreign policy initiatives that do not build on these policies (détente) or that are seen as excessive applications of them (the Iran–Contra policy) are unlikely to receive sustained support by the American public.

Notes

1. Judith Goldstein, *Ideas, Interests, and American Trade Policy* (Ithaca, N.Y.: Cornell University Press, 1993), pp. 1–18.
2. Ibid.
3. George Kennan, "The Sources of Soviet Conduct," *Foreign Affairs*, 25 (1947), 576.
4. For convenient discussions of containment and détente, see John Spanier, *American Foreign Policy Since WW II,* 10th ed. (New York: Holt, Rinehart & Winston, 1985), pp. 23–29, 189–200, 304–06, and 316–21; Charles W. Kegley Jr., and Eugene R. Wittkopf, *American Foreign Policy: Pattern and Process,* 2nd ed. (New York: St. Martin's, 1982), pp. 48–69; and Henry T. Nash, *American Foreign Policy: A Search for Security,* 3rd ed. (Homewood, Ill.: Dorsey, 1985), pp. 44–48 and 249–50.
5. Quoted in Howard Bliss and M. Glen Johnson, *Beyond the Water's Edge: American Foreign Policy* (Philadelphia: Lippincott, 1975), pp. 52–53.
6. Frank Klingberg, *Positive Expectation's of America's World Role* (Lanham, MD: University Press of America, 1996).
7. Dexter Perkins, *The American Approach to Foreign Policy* (Cambridge, Mass.: Harvard University Press, 1962), p. 154.

8. Robert Dallek, *The American Style of Foreign Policy, Cultural Politics and Foreign Affairs* (New York: New American Library, 1983).

9. Max Lerner, cited in Cecil Crabb Jr., *American Foreign Policy in the Nuclear Age*, 4th ed. (New York: Harper & Row, 1983), p. 47; and Richard Ullman, "The 'Foreign World' and Ourselves: Washington, Wilson and the Democratic Dilemma," *Foreign Policy*, 21 (1975/76), 97–125.

10. For a discussion of these points, see Stanley Hoffmann, *Gulliver's Troubles, or the Setting of American Foreign Policy* (New York: McGraw-Hill, 1968); John Spanier, *American Foreign Policy Since WW II*, 9th ed. (New York: Holt, Rinehart & Winston, 1983); Perkins, *The American Approach to Foreign Policy;* and Amos Jordan and William J. Taylor, Jr., *American National Security, Policy and Process* (Baltimore, Md.: Johns Hopkins University Press, 1981).

11. Kenneth Keniston, quoted in Bliss and Johnson, *Beyond the Water's Edge*, p. 110.

12. Stanley Hoffmann, "Foreign Policy Transition: Requiem," *Foreign Policy*, 42 (1980/81), 3–26.

13. For a discussion of alternative interpretations of U.S. foreign policy and national style, see Kegley and Wittkopf, *American Foreign Policy*, pp. 69–81.

14. For a discussion of unilateralism, see Gene Rainey, *Patterns of American Foreign Policy* (Boston: Allyn & Bacon, 1975), pp. 19–43.

15. Robert Tucker, *The Radical Left and American Foreign Policy* (Baltimore, Md.: Johns Hopkins University Press, 1971), p. 34.

16. James Schlesinger, "Reykjavik and Revelations: A Turn of the Tide?" *Foreign Affairs*, 65 (1987), 431.

17. For a discussion of American foreign policy highlighting these themes, see Arthur Schlesinger Jr., "Foreign Policy and the American Character," *Foreign Affairs*, 62 (1983), 1–16.

18. Hoffmann, *Gulliver's Troubles*, p. 150.

19. Freeman Dyson, "On Russians and Their Views of Nuclear Strategy," in Charles W. Kegley, Jr., and Eugene R. Wittkopf (eds.), *The Nuclear Reader: Strategy, Weapons, War* (New York: St. Martin's, 1985), pp. 97–99.

20. Crabb, *American Foreign Policy*, pp. 36–37.

21. Hoffmann, *Gulliver's Troubles*, pp. 141–43; and Frederick Hartmann, *The Relations Among Nations*, 6th ed. (New York: Macmillan, 1983), pp. 421–26.

22. David Watt, "As a European Saw It," *Foreign Affairs*, 62 (1983), 530–31.

23. Elliot A. Cohen, "The Mystique of U.S. Air Power," *Foreign Affairs*, 73 (1994), 109–24.

24. For a critical discussion of the impact of legalism, see George Kennan, *American Diplomacy, 1900–1950* (New York: Mentor, 1951).

25. Rainey, *Patterns of American Foreign Policy*, p. 36.

26. Robert E. Osgood, *Limited War: The Challenge to American Strategy* (Chicago: University of Chicago Press, 1957), p. 29.

27. Spanier, *American Foreign Policy Since WW II*, 10th ed., p. 11.

28. USA Today/CNN/Gallup Poll, *USA Today*, June 25, 2004, p.1.

29. See Charles W. Kegley Jr., "The Neoidealist Moment in International Studies? Realist Myths and the New International Realities," *International Studies Quarterly*, 37 (1993), 131–46.

30. Michael Mandlebaum, "Bad Statesman, Good Prophet: Woodrow Wilson and the Post–Cold War Order." *National Interest*, 64 (2001), 31–41.

31. Arthur S. Link, *The Higher Realism of Woodrow Wilson* (Nashville, Tenn.: Vanderbilt University Press, 1971).

32. Robert W. Tucker, "The Triumph of Wilsonianism?" *World Policy Journal*, 10 (1993), 83–100.

33. Ibid.; and Tony Smith, "Making the World Safe for Democracy," *Washington Quarterly*, 16 (1993), 92–102.

34. David Fromkin, "What Is Wilsonianism?" *World Policy Journal*, 11 (1994), 100–12.

35. George Kennan, "On American Principles," *Foreign Affairs*, 74 (1995), 116–26.

36. The material and quotation in this section are found in Adam Wolfson, "How to Think about Humanitarian War," *Commentary*, 110 (July/August 2000), 44–48.

37. Walter Russell Mead, *Special Providence* (New York: Routledge, 2002). Mead also identifies two other American traditions. One is associated with Wilson and the other with Jefferson.

38. Rainey, *Patterns of American Foreign Policy*, p. 386.

39. Kenneth Longmyer, "Black American Demands," *Foreign Policy*, 60 (1985), 3–16; and Bill Richardson, "Hispanic Concerns," *Foreign Policy*, 60 (1985), 30–39.

40. Goldstein, *Ideas, Interests, and American Trade Policy*.

41. Two arguments that do suggest we can judge the American national style as good or bad are provided by Mead, *Special Providence*, who looks upon it favorably, and Colin Dueck, "Hegemony on the Cheap," *World Policy Journal* (Winter 2003/2004), 1–11, who is critical of internationalism.

— 4 —

THE SEARCH FOR GRAND STRATEGY: POST-VIETNAM U.S. FOREIGN POLICY

On September 17, 2002, President George W. Bush released his administration's *"National Security Strategy of the United States of America."*[1] He was required to do so by the 1986 Goldwater–Nichols Act. It sought to strengthen civilian control over military decision making by reorganizing the defense department and mandating that every four years the administration provide Congress with a detailed statement of its national security strategy (NSS). On the whole, the results have not met the expectations of those who directed that an NSS be produced. The content was often vague, overtaken by events, and self-congratulatory in tone. Deadlines were missed. Both Bill Clinton and George. W. Bush did not produce their first NSS on time (Bush's was due June 15, 2001). Bush's NSS drew worldwide attention. He used it as an opportunity to redirect American grand strategy away from containment and deterrence to a policy of preemption based on American hegemony, with the ultimate purpose of transforming the international system through the spread of democracy. None of these elements are without controversy, nor, for that matter, were containment and deterrence.

In this chapter, we focus on the search for a grand strategy to replace them. We pick up the search as the United States is ending its involvement in the Vietnam War. It is a search that continues today and has proceeded in three stages. First, there was an effort to find a new cold war grand strategy. Détente was the first successor concept put forward. It gave way to a reinvigorated and assertive version of containment. This stage ended with the fall of communism and the disintegration of the Soviet Union. Second, there was an effort to find a grand strategy suitable for the immediate post–cold war period. The problem as James Woolsey, President Bill Clinton's first Director of Central Intelligence, noted was that "we have slain the dragon" and now found ourselves living "in a jungle filled with a bewildering variety of poisonous snakes." Cold war strategic principles were ill-suited for such a world. The terrorist attacks of September 11, 2001 brought an end to this stage and launched a third stage. In it, the challenge is to devise a grand strategy that will allow the United States to conduct a successful foreign policy in an age of terrorism.

The Logic and Purpose of Grand Strategy

Before beginning this historical overview, we need to look at what is meant by grand strategy.[2] Strategy is about linking means and ends. Much like the concept of national interest, it operates on many levels. At the broadest level exists grand strategy. It seeks to harness a state's power so that it achieves a state's most pressing political goals. Grand strategy at this level establishes a state's fundamental relationship with other states, identifying enemies and allies and how to interact with them. Without that linkage, the application of military power degenerates into mindless killing, economic sanctions do little more than starve innocent civilians, and spreading one's values becomes indistinguishable from spreading propaganda. When this happens, grand strategy is reduced to a hollow slogan. It ceases to frame policy decisions and instead becomes a cover for the pursuit of organizational or personal goals.

Constructing an effective grand strategy is no easy task. In fact, some believe it cannot be done. Several different problems contribute to this pessimistic view.[3] One limitation on the effectiveness of strategy is our incomplete knowledge of cause and effect in understanding and lack of control over key variables in trying to manipulate the course of international events. A second limitation is found in the organizational and political barriers one encounters in trying to implement grand strategy. Because of this, grand strategy on paper always seems to fall short of grand strategy as put into practice. Third, there are perceptual and psychological barriers to how accurately policy makers see the world and understand their own motives. Still, most believe that there is little choice but to try and craft grand strategies.

The Nixon (and Ford) Administrations: Leaving Vietnam and Entering Détente

During the cold war, one grand strategy—containment—played a prominent role in shaping specific foreign policy actions undertaken by the United States. Although cold war presidents repeatedly invoked this concept, much tactical variation took place. For example, containment as proposed by its originator George Kennan emphasized "strong point defense" in which the United States needed to stop Soviet aggression in only certain portions of the globe. Containment as reinterpreted by NSC-68 supported a "perimeter defense" posture that sought to encircle the Soviet Union and hold its expansion in check everywhere.

The merits of containment as the fundamental framing concept for American foreign policy came under attack from both the political left and right during the Vietnam War. In 1971, four years before the Vietnam War ended with the surrender of the U.S.-backed South Vietnamese government in 1975, President Richard Nixon proclaimed the need for a "new and stable framework for international relations" to replace containment.[4]

The centerpiece of President Nixon's new strategy was a policy of détente with America's two cold war adversaries, Russia and China, and a more balanced partnership with American allies. Gerald Ford did little to change that in his term in office other than to ban the word "détente" from the Republican political vocabulary during his 1976 bid for the presidency.

Much of the intellectual energy behind Nixon's strategy came from Henry Kissinger, who first served as Nixon's National Security Adviser and then became his Secretary of State. To Kissinger, a principal source of unrest in world politics came from the presence of revolutionary states whose interests lay in overturning the status quo rather than working to protect it. Détente was intended to bring about a relaxation of tensions between the United States and its major cold war adversaries so that they might enter into the management of the international system as copartners. Only when the legitimacy of the international system was accepted by all the major powers could there be stability. The decline in American military power necessitated that the economic power be used as a carrot and stick to induce the desired Soviet behavior in the political-military arena. Finally, the central feature to the management of a stable international system was the successful operation of a balance of power. For Nixon and Kissinger that entailed an ability and willingness to play off China and Russia against each other as well as practice "linkage politics."

The basis for U.S.–Soviet détente was laid at the May 1972 Moscow Summit conference between Nixon and Soviet President Leonid Brezhnev. This summit is best known for the Strategic Arms Limitation Agreement (SALT I), which sought to slow the arms race and stabilize the U.S.–Soviet nuclear balance by placing qualitative and quantitative limits on the offensive strategic weapons.

Establishing a basis for détente with China was complicated by the lack of diplomatic relations between the two states. Ever since 1949 when Mao Zedong's forces had driven the pro-Western forces of Jiang Jieshi (Chiang Kaishek) out of China on to the island of Taiwan, the United States had steadfastly refused to recognize Mao's government as the official government of China. Nixon moved to break through the decades of formal silence by announcing to a surprised American people that he would be going to China. The major document emerging from that historic trip was the 1972 Shanghai Communiqué. It pledged both the United States and China to normalize relations and pursue antihegemonic policies in the Asia-Pacific region.

These foundations proved to be too weak to support a new international framework. Détente with the Soviet Union floundered because the two countries never understood it to mean the same thing. For the Soviet Union détente was a means to break out of containment and place U.S.–Soviet competition on a different—more equal—basis. For the United States, détente was a necessary concession intended to preserve America's global influence at lessened cost. Matters quickly came to a head in the third world. Much to Russia's dismay, the United States intervened in the 1973 Arab–Israeli War in a way that all but eliminated Russian influence in the region for a decade. American leaders soon felt betrayed by continued Russian assistance to African Marxist movements in Angola, Mozambique, and the Horn of Africa. Normalization of Chinese–American relations never moved far beyond the symbolic stage. Domestic politics restricted both Nixon and Ford's ability to make the necessary political compromises. During the last part of Nixon's administration, Watergate dominated his political attention. President Ford found himself in a tough primary campaign against the more conservative Ronald Reagan.

Still another part of Nixon's new and stable political framework involved a change in relations between the United States and its allies. The Nixon Doctrine, officially announced in 1969 while the United States was still very much involved in the Vietnam War, stated that America's allies could no longer count on the United States to send troops abroad to defend them. American aid would be restricted to the transfer of money, equipment, and technology. Saudi Arabia and Iran were two prime beneficiaries of the Nixon Doctrine. The United States funneled large amounts of military equipment in their direction in an effort to create surrogate powers whom the United States could count upon to resist the spread of Soviet influence to the Middle East.

Like détente, the Nixon Doctrine proved to be less than an effective foundation for a new world order. The perceived need for loyal allies in the third world blinded American policy makers to the scale of human rights abuses in these countries and the growing isolation of their rulers from the larger society. Nowhere would this become more visible than in Iran, where between 1973 and 1978 the Shah had purchased some $19 billion worth of American-made weapons. The Nixon Doctrine also failed because of the inability of the Nixon administration to exercise the required degree of self-restraint. Faced with the prospect of communist governments in Chile and Angola, the Nixon administration neither left these states to fend for themselves nor turned to surrogate powers to prevent this from happening. Instead, it turned to covert action.

NIXON'S FOREIGN POLICY EVALUATED

Both conservatives and liberals criticized Nixon's foreign policy. Each objected to the status quo–oriented nature of détente and its lack of a clear overriding moral purpose. Liberal critics argued that Nixon's foreign policy was anachronistic. It was irrelevant to the conditions of the post-Vietnam era. The main issues on the international agenda were questions of hunger, poverty, and global inequalities of wealth. These were issues that cried out for policy innovation and international cooperation. To these critics, Vietnam had proven the futility of trying to hold back demands for political and social reform with military power. They were equally skeptical of the ability of American economic power as manifested in foreign aid and the overseas operation of American companies to move international society forward. What was required was a fundamental reorientation of American foreign policy and a recommitment to traditional American values.

Conservative critics took exception to Nixon's willingness to accept the Soviet Union as a full partner in the family of nations. To them, the Soviet Union was still the enemy. To enter into a working relationship with it was tantamount to ideological surrender, implying that fundamental similarities existed between the two states that made cooperation possible. This denied the uniquely revolutionary nature of communist systems and the ultimate objectives of their foreign policy. Nothing about the behavior of the Soviet Union (or China) had changed. What had changed was the American perception of their actions.

A third line of criticism directed at détente focused on its lack of intellectual rigor and problems in its execution. Robert Tucker identified several flaws.[5] First, there was a contradiction between the recognition of the limits of power implied by détente and the overall continuity in roles and interests in American foreign policy. Second, Tucker asked, was there any reason to assume, as détente did, that America's allies would be relatively passive, its adversaries reasonably restrained, and the third world stable and undemanding? Détente required that all of these conditions be met in order to succeed. Third, the Nixon administration's obsession with secret methods undermined the domestic base of support for its policy. Fourth, there was little evidence to suggest that economic carrots and sticks had influenced Soviet foreign policy in the past. Why was it assumed that this would be the case now? Tucker concludes that despite public rhetoric to the contrary, détente was more of a "holding operation than a settled strategy."

The Carter Administration: American Foreign Policy with a Purpose: Promoting Human Rights

In a pattern that was to be repeated four years later, President Jimmy Carter entered office pledging to lay the basis for a new American foreign policy. Where the Nixon–Ford–Kissinger foreign policy had stressed realpolitik and balance-of-power considerations, Carter promised a foreign policy that was "democratic, . . . based on fundamental values, and that uses power and influence . . . for humane purposes." This was to be done by focusing American foreign policy on promoting human rights and solving regional problems rather than on simply countering the Soviet Union's every move.

At the very onset of his administration, Carter proclaimed that "our commitment to human rights must be absolute."[6] Carter did not venture into completely uncharted territory in advocating that human rights be a central element in American foreign policy. As Arthur Schlesinger, Jr., has noted, "Americans have agreed since 1776 that the United States must be the beacon of human rights to an unregenerate world."[7] There also existed a political base on which to build such a policy because Congress had begun to force the human rights issue on reluctant presidents. Congress began requiring the State Department to attest to the acceptability of a country's human rights record as a precondition for the granting of foreign aid. Amendments, such as the Jackson–Vanik Amendment, which made the granting of "most favored nation" status to the Soviet Union dependent on changes in its emigration policy for Soviet Jews, were attached to bills sharply curtailing the president's freedom to make foreign policy. Eventually even the Nixon administration moved to embrace human rights by its participation in the Conference on Security and Cooperation in Europe which produced the Helsinki Accords in August 1975. This agreement made Soviet and Eastern European human rights practices a permanent item on the diplomatic agenda. Carter did, however, move American human rights policy forward. His vision of human rights was more expansive than that held by previous administrations. Where traditionally the United States had thought about human rights in terms of civil and political rights, the Carter administration added a concern for economic and social rights.

Looking back four years later, it was evident that this commitment, however genuine, was not always translated into policy. For every act taken in the name of promoting human rights, there seemed to be a counterexample where human rights concerns were sacrificed in the interests of protecting American economic and strategic interests. The Carter administration sought to portray these lapses as indicative of its willingness to be flexible and take a case-by-case approach in deciding upon what course of action to take. To his critics it translated into inconsistency.

In Latin America, the first regional issue addressed by Carter was the status of the Panama Canal. The United States and Panama had been involved in difficult negotiations over the future of the Panama Canal for over two decades. Carter moved quickly to bring these negotiations to a conclusion, and in September 1977 two treaties were signed. The Panama Canal Treaty immediately voided all existing treaty arrangements and gave the United States the right to run the Panama Canal until December 31, 1999. At that time, control over the Panama Canal would be transferred to Panama. The terms of the second treaty, the Treaty Concerning the Permanent Neutrality and Operation of the Panama Canal, would come into effect in 2000. It authorized the United States and Panama to take "whatever action it deems necessary" to ensure that the canal would "remain secure and open to peaceful transit by vessels of all nations on the terms of entire equality." These treaties provoked intense debate in Congress. It was only after a major lobbying campaign and the acceptance of congressionally authored amendments that the treaties were approved by the Senate and then only by the slimmest of margins.

Carter was less successful in engineering a successful endgame to the political unrest brewing in Central America. In Nicaragua, a long-time U.S. ally, Anastasio Somoza, was under increasing pressure from a broad-based group of opposition forces led by the Sandinista National Liberation Front. In a marked departure from policies followed by previous administrations, Carter chose not to support the besieged dictator. He sought to convince Somoza to enter into negotiations with his opponents. Unwilling to do so, Somoza fled the country in 1979. The Carter administration recognized the new Sandinista government and provided it with economic aid in order to "create stability out of revolution." Relations between the United States and the Sandinistas soon soured, and the final installment of this $75 million aid package was suspended by Carter in his final days in office due to reports of rising Soviet influence there. Carter also authorized a secret intelligence finding that permitted the CIA to support anti-Sandinista forces within Nicaragua. Concerns now grew about Sandinista support for Marxist insurgents in neighboring El Salvador.

Further from home, Carter's regionalist approach scored a major diplomatic triumph when in September 1978 he played host to a meeting between Egyptian President Anwar Sadat and Israeli Prime Minister Menachem Begin at the presidential retreat at Camp David. After decades of war between the Arabs and Israelis, an unexpected peace opening had occurred in November 1977. Sadat announced that he would be willing to go to Israel to discuss a peace agreement. That trip and months of follow-up negotiations made little headway. In a bold move to break this deadlock, Carter invited both leaders to Camp David where they agreed upon a framework for a "just, comprehensive, and durable settlement of the Middle East conflict." The Camp David Accords were not without controversy. First, it was silent on the question of a Palestinian homeland. Second, it brought with it a hefty price tag in terms of U.S. foreign aid that would now begin to flow to Egypt and Israel. Economic and military aid was seen as necessary in order to ensure that these "islands of stability" in the Middle East did not deviate from the path toward peace.

Lessening the central role that the Soviet Union played in American foreign policy deliberations proved to be easier said than done. In large measure this was due to the fact that the Carter administration needed Soviet cooperation in order to realize some of its more ambitious foreign policy goals. Arms control was a case in point. Carter inherited from Ford a virtually completed strategic arms control proposal, the 1974 Vladivostok Accords.

Carter chose not to take the Vladivostok agreement as a starting point for a SALT II treaty. Instead he proposed a treaty that would make radical reductions in each side's strategic arsenal and would limit their ability to modernize strategic weapons systems. Already resenting the implication that the Soviet Union should not be the central focal point of U.S. foreign policy, and distrustful of Carter for his human rights rhetoric and criticism of its treatment of political dissidents, the Soviet Union balked. It saw Carter's proposal as an attempt to restore American nuclear superiority and demanded that negotiations proceed on the basis of the Vladivostok Accords. It would take two and one-half years of difficult negotiations before a SALT II agreement would be reached. Signed by Carter and Brezhnev in Vienna in 1979, and submitted to the Senate for ratification that summer, SALT II was never voted on. It became a victim of the Soviet invasion of Afghanistan and the subsequent hardening of U.S.–Soviet relations.

It was support for pro-Russian Marxist forces in Afghanistan that brought about a return to cold war relations between the United States and the Soviet Union. The roots of the 1979 Soviet invasion can be traced back to a 1973 coup d'état in which the king of Afghanistan was deposed. Within a short period of time the new government came under attack from the Maoist and pro-Soviet factions of the Marxist People's Democratic Party. In April 1978 the Maoist Khalq faction led a successful coup that ended in the signing of a twenty-year treaty of friendship between the two countries. The new government sought to impose a radical series of economic and social reforms on the Afghan people. The government ignored Soviet recommendations to slow down the pace of reform. Unwilling to see an ally fall, the Soviet Union stepped up its shipment of military equipment and sent in combat personnel. In September 1979, a rival Maoist faction seized power. It, too, refused to heed Moscow's advice and followed an even more radical reform program. Once again the Soviet Union increased its military presence in Afghanistan. In December, confronted with an increasingly chaotic situation and the pending triumph of Islamic rebel forces, Russia sent an invasion force of more than fifty thousand soldiers into Afghanistan and brought Babrak Karmal, head of the pro-Soviet Parcham faction, back from exile to serve as the new president.

Carter denounced the Soviet invasion. He halted the SALT II ratification process, suspended the sale of high technology to the Soviet Union, imposed a grain embargo, and called for the establishment of a Rapid Deployment Force. Carter also issued a warning, which came to be referred to as the Carter Doctrine, in his 1980 State of the Union address. He stated that any "attempt by outside force to gain control of the Persian Gulf region will be quickly repelled by any means necessary including military force."

The harsh tone of Carter's response reflected more than just his disillusionment with the Soviet Union. It also reflected his administration's frustrations in dealing with the new rulers of Iran, who one month before the Soviet invasion of Afghanistan had seized the American embassy and taken American hostages. With only a slight period of interruption, Iran had been ruled from 1941 until 1979 by one of America's most loyal third world allies, Mohammed Reza Shah Pahlavi. That interruption came in 1953 when the Shah was forced into exile as Iranian nationalists seized power. He was restored to the throne largely through the efforts of a CIA-inspired coup. Over time the corruption and repression of the Shah's rule reached the point where he became dependent upon the military and his ruthless secret police, the SAVAK, to stay in power. Even this proved to be insufficient as the 1970s drew to a close and Iranians took to the streets demanding reform.

The Carter administration was caught off guard by the Shah's rapidly mounting political troubles. It had become an article of faith that the Shah would remain in power and that Iran would be pro-West. After first backing the Shah, the Carter administration unsuccessfully urged him to negotiate with his opponents. The most important opposition leader was the Ayatollah Khomeini, who was in exile in France and returned to Iran on January 31, 1980, to take over the reins of government. The Shah had left Iran in the middle of the month. The Carter administration first weighed letting him come to the United States but reconsidered due to fear of the reaction it might provoke in Iran. In October, at the urging of Kissinger, Brzezinski, and David Rockefeller, who headed Chase Manhattan Bank, and over the objection of the U.S. embassy in Iran, Carter agreed to let the Shah come to the United States in order to receive potentially life-saving medical care. Two weeks later, the embassy was seized and demands were issued for the return of the Shah to Iran to stand trial.

Carter's response to the hostage crisis was to apply economic sanctions in the hope of securing the hostages' release. This strategy failed to bring about their quick release. Neither did a military rescue mission conducted in April 1980. Instead, Carter's handling of the crisis fed a fervent election-year debate both about his stewardship of American foreign policy and the overall direction that it should take. The hostages would be released on Ronald Reagan's inauguration day after spending 444 days in captivity.

CARTER'S FOREIGN POLICY EVALUATED

Echoing a familiar theme, Stanley Hoffmann characterized Carter's foreign policy as "the hell of good intentions." It suffered, he concluded, from "an almost total addiction to erratic tactics."[8] The Carter administration changed course repeatedly on a constant stream of issues: the status of U.S. troops in South Korea, the neutron bomb, the transfer of high technology to the Soviet Union, relations with Somalia, and the Middle East. According to Hoffmann, while personal and institutional factors contributed to these inconsistencies, the critical factor was his administration's strategic incoherence. Most notable here was the mistaken belief that it could package world affairs into two categories: one involving military relations with the Soviet Union, the other involving everything else. Still, Hoffmann found much good in Carter's foreign policy. It addressed long-term problems ignored by previous administrations, such as conventional arms control and the law of the seas; its human rights policy increased American prestige in the world; and it understood that the conditions for American influence over world affairs were changing. Robert Tucker was less kind in his critique. Labeling it a failure, Tucker asserts that the root cause of Carter's problems lay in his administration's vision of the world, a vision that was futuristic to the point of being irrelevant for policy. Only near the end did his administration face up to the central problem confronting American foreign policy: the rapid growth in Soviet military power. Moreover, it was a vision that Tucker found to be "immoderately optimistic." Citing human rights as a prime example, he asserts that the Carter administration had little sense that its policy departures might come with a hefty price tag. Given this flawed, "immature" view of the world, Tucker argues that the Carter administration had no right to be either surprised or outraged by the Soviet Union's invasion of Afghanistan. Surprise was unwarranted because evidence of increased Soviet aggressiveness and the American unwillingness to use its military power to counter it were clear in the mid-1970s. Outrage was unwarranted because the Soviet Union never promised to play by the American interpretation of détente.

Jeane Kirkpatrick, who would serve as ambassador to the United Nations in the Reagan administration, put forward a critique that resonated well with conservative Republicans.[9] She argued that Carter's human rights policy was fundamentally flawed because it did not recognize the differences between right-wing governments and left-wing totalitarian ones such as in the Soviet Union. Right-wing governments could make a transition to democracy, and their violations of human rights generally were done in the name of national security and stopped short of depriving citizens of their basic freedoms. Totalitarian governments could not make the transition to democracy, she argued. Their violations of human rights were far more destructive and carried out on principle.

A final perspective on the Carter administration's foreign policy is provided by David Skidmore.[10] He argued that Carter's initial foreign policy was neither confused nor incoherent. It was also not a product of his personal moralism. Rather, Carter's troubles stemmed from the domestic response to his strategy of adjustment. By maximizing his political flexibility, Carter had severely limited his ability to draw on the doctrines and symbols that presidents traditionally relied upon to build a foreign policy consensus. In the end, Carter was forced to turn back to such well-established techniques of gaining public support as relying upon anticommunist symbols, overstating threats and overselling solutions, and developing "doctrines" to provide a unifying focus for his foreign policy. He did so too late to save his presidency and further postponed the time at which the aims of American foreign policy are adjusted to correspond with its decline in power.

The Reagan Administration: A Renewed Cold War

Reagan and his foreign policy team possessed a worldview that was fundamentally at odds with the thrust of Carter's foreign policy. Early in his first term, Reagan characterized the Soviet Union as an "evil empire," charging that "the only morality they recognize is what [which] will further their cause: meaning they reserve unto themselves the right to commit any crime; to lie; to cheat." This language was intended to convey to the Soviet Union and the rest of the world that where Nixon and Carter had sought to establish a working relationship with Soviet leaders by using "carrots and sticks" (and then mostly carrots), his administration would rely primarily on the stick.

From the Reagan administration's perspective, a prerequisite for such a policy shift was to rebuild America's military power. To that end, Reagan called for spending $1.6 trillion over five years to revamp the American military establishment. Among the projects to be funded were the construction of one hundred B-1 bombers, development of a neutron bomb, renewing the production of poison gas for use in chemical warfare, the deployment of the MX missile, and an upgrading of the Rapid Deployment Force. Modernizing America's strategic forces (those forces capable of carrying nuclear weapons to the Soviet Union, that is, nuclear submarines, intercontinental ballistic missiles, and the manned bomber) was held to be particularly important because "a window of vulnerability" had opened in the U.S.–Soviet strategic balance. Without these new weapons, the Reagan administration charged that Soviet nuclear forces could threaten and intimidate the United States and its allies.

Consistent with its new hard-line approach, the Reagan administration also changed the tone of U.S. arms control policy. Where Nixon and Carter had voiced their suspicions regarding Soviet violations of SALT II and the

Anti-Ballistic Missile (ABM) Treaty in diplomatic channels, the Reagan administration went public with its misgivings. These highly public accusations of cheating were coupled with a toughening in the language used to characterize the U.S.–Soviet strategic relationship. References to nuclear warfighting capabilities and the ability to prevail in a protracted nuclear conflict were frequently voiced by Reagan administration officials.

Perhaps the most visible symbolic stick employed by the Reagan administration against the Soviet Union was the Strategic Defense Initiative (SDI) or "Star Wars." Announced as a long-term research plan in a speech in March 1983, President Reagan called upon the scientific community to devise a system that would allow the United States to "intercept and destroy their [Soviet] strategic missiles before they reach our soil or that of our allies." To its supporters, Reagan's SDI program offered hope of finding a way out of the uncomfortable reality of the nuclear age: that one's security was dependent upon the ability to carry out a retaliatory nuclear strike because there was no way to prevent that strike from taking place. To its opponents, SDI was dangerous because it promised to unleash a new arms race between the United States and the Soviet Union as each sought to develop offensive weapons capable of penetrating a Star Wars shield.

The Reagan administration's willingness to engage in a strategy of verbal confrontation with the Soviet Union created a great deal of unease among Europe's American allies. An early sign of difficulties came when his administration sought to block a deal that would have given European states access to Soviet natural gas reserves. Further problems surrounded the negotiation of an Intermediate Nuclear Forces (INF) Treaty. The Soviet Union had deployed a new generation of these missiles, and a countermove was necessary given the logic of cold war arms competition. Many in Europe and the United States, however, preferred a new arms control agreement over new weapons. In the end a compromise "dual track" strategy was agreed upon. NATO would begin deployment of Pershing II missiles and cruise missiles in 1983 if no arms control agreement was reached. Movement on the negotiation front was slow. They broke off in 1983 and did not begin again until Mikhail Gorbachev came to power in the Soviet Union. To the surprise of the Reagan administration, Gorbachev embraced the "zero option" proposed by Reagan in which all intermediate nuclear weapons would be removed from Europe by both sides. An INF Treaty was signed in 1987.

Reagan and Gorbachev became regular partners at summit conferences, meeting five times in the last four years of the Reagan administration. The nature of these meetings and their outcomes were quite varied, ranging from working sessions with no formal agenda to ones characterized by serious arms control negotiations. It was their second summit meeting in Reykjavik, Iceland, that provoked the most controversy. Approached with insufficient preparation, the Reagan administration was caught off guard by Gorbachev's proposal that both the United States and the Soviet Union eliminate all offensive strategic weapons. Reagan accepted the proposal only to back off later. The proposal—and its acceptance—were controversial because had the deal gone through it would have meant abandoning twenty-five years of deterrence doctrine without any consultation with Congress or allies.

Moreover, it was only Reagan's personal attachment to a weapons system most believed could never work that prevented this from happening.

The Reagan administration also brought about a reorientation of American foreign policy toward third world states. Where Carter had sought to deal with these issues largely within a regional context, Reagan placed them squarely within the context of expansionist Soviet foreign policy. The initial focal point of attention was Central America where a civil war in El Salvador quickly was cited as a "textbook case" of communist aggression. Large-scale fighting had begun in 1979 when reform-minded elements of the military seized power and installed José Duarte as president. This set off a wave of right-wing violence that targeted radical and reformist political groups. Centrist and leftist forces then united to form the Revolutionary Democratic Front to oppose Duarte, who was unable to control this rising tide of violence. The Reagan administration contended that a large part of the problem in El Salvador was due to Russian and Cuban military support for leftist rebel forces that was being funneled through Nicaragua. In a move to cut off the supply of weapons, Reagan signed a presidential finding in March 1981 authorizing the CIA to organize and fund moderate opponents of the Sandinistas. These forces became known as the Contras, and the administration's staunch support for them became one of the most controversial elements of Reagan's foreign policy.

That controversy had many dimensions and would culminate in a 1984 congressional budget resolution cutting off all funding for the Contras. One issue involved how to judge the activities of the Contras. Human rights groups complained at length about their brutality. Noting that this "after all, was war," CIA officials acknowledged in congressional testimony that the Contras had assassinated judges, doctors, and other supporters of the Sandinista regime. Reagan in a 1983 address stated that the Contras were "freedom fighters" and the "moral equivalent of the founding fathers." Congress was far less enthusiastic in its support for the Contras. It was also suspicious of their ultimate motives and passed legislation forbidding the use of U.S. funds to overthrow the Sandinista government.

The Reagan administration's unwillingness to drop its support for the Contras in spite of military failures and in the face of congressional opposition became one of the driving forces in the Iran–Contra scandal that would engulf the Reagan administration in its second term. The other driving force was the continued specter of Middle East terrorism. An ill-fated attempt by the Israelis to rid Lebanon of terrorists in 1982 led to the establishment of a multinational peacekeeping force in that country. U.S. Marines formed a significant part of that force. At first their presence was welcomed, but gradually the Marines became identified with the pro-Israeli side of the civil war that was taking place in Lebanon. This led to a steady wave of terrorist attacks directed against Americans: In 1983, 241 Marines were killed when terrorists attacked their barracks in Beirut; in 1984 three Americans, one of whom was the CIA station chief, were abducted; and in 1985 four more Americans were taken hostage.

In the Reagan administration's view, the central force behind these anti-American terrorist activities was the Iranian government of Ayatollah

Khomeini. Bringing about a change in this government was seen as a key to ending Middle East terrorism. The standing Reagan administration policy for dealing with terrorists was one of nonnegotiation. However, in this case Reagan's personal obsession with the fate of the American hostages led those around him to explore alternative means for bringing about their release. One proposal put forward was to aid the political stature of Iranian moderates by lifting the arms embargo against Iran and selling it weapons. It was hoped that Iran would respond to this move by arranging for the release of the American hostages.

The two concerns were combined into one policy when the decision was made to take the monies raised by the sale of these weapons and use it to support the Contras. The operation was run from the White House by Lieutenant Colonel Oliver North. President Reagan denied any knowledge of the link between the transfer of weapons, the release of the hostages, and funding for the Contras. A total profit of $16 million was realized from the arms sales, but the Contras only received about $3.8 million. Congress had been kept in the dark about the operation, in violation of existing laws, and when it became public a major confrontation ensued between the two branches.

The Reagan administration's support for the Contras was part of a larger strategy known as the Reagan Doctrine. It was designed to move the United States beyond a policy of containment to one where support would also be given to groups trying to overthrow ruling communist governments. In addition to Central America, the Reagan Doctrine was very much evident in U.S. foreign policy toward Afghanistan. The original Soviet military plan called for the Afghan army to pacify the Afghan population following the 1979 invasion. Wholesale defections negated this strategy and required the introduction of large numbers of Soviet forces who now had to bear the primary responsibility for fighting the guerrillas or Mujahadin.

An important factor standing in the way of any negotiated exit from their "Vietnam" was the military support being received by the Mujahadin from the United States. In 1984, the Reagan administration was underwriting the Mujahadin to the tune of $120 million. In 1987, this figure had increased to $630 million, bringing the total value of U.S. military aid to that point to $2.1 billion. It would be 1988 before a negotiated end to the Soviet presence in Afghanistan was agreed upon through a series of bilateral agreements reached between Afghanistan and Pakistan, and between the United States and the Soviet Union.

REAGAN'S FOREIGN POLICY EVALUATED

As one might expect, Reagan's handling of foreign policy brought forward a wide range of opinion. Michael Mandelbaum argued that in the final analysis Reagan was a "lucky president."[11] He stated that Reagan's success in managing U.S. foreign policy had little to do with his own efforts. The primary reasons for success were "the result of forces and trends outside the control of the United States and of measures undertaken by others and occasionally even opposed by Mr. Reagan." Foremost among these others was Jimmy Carter. According to Mandelbaum, the essence of luck is timing, and good timing was evident all around him: The Soviet Union was gripped by a leadership crisis for most of his term in office; its economy was experiencing a severe downturn; arms control agreements restrained it militarily; the Middle East was quiet politically because of Carter's Camp David agreement; international oil markets were favorable to the West. This combination of circumstances minimized his missteps and allowed Reagan to pursue a status quo foreign policy that experienced few geopolitical setbacks.

Many critics on the political right were dismayed by the final resting place of Reagan's foreign policy. It looked suspiciously like "Carterism without Carter." The radical reorientation of American foreign policy that had been promised did not come about. Gone was much of the combative rhetoric and distrust of communists that marked his first years in office. Gone too was the willingness to stand by America's third world allies. Arms control was once again a fixture on the agenda. President Reagan had traveled to China. With U.S. blessing, President Marcos of the Philippines was removed from office in large measure because of his human rights violations and anti-democratic policies. And, in its last days in office, the Reagan administration had taken steps toward establishing a formal diplomatic dialogue with the Palestine Liberation Organization.

Robert Tucker suggests that all these critics overstate their case and miss the mark.[12] While Reagan may have been lucky, he also skillfully realized his primary foreign policy goals: reversing the decline in American power, restoring the credibility of its power as a force in world politics, and stopping the expansion of Soviet influence. Tucker acknowledged the essential continuity of the Carter and Reagan administrations. But to him, it was not a matter of a Reagan about-face. Instead, it reflected the underlying influence of cultural and geopolitical factors on the selection of policy. Tucker sees Reagan's failure as residing in his inability or unwillingness to make a sustained effort to rebuild the domestic foreign policy consensus that was shattered by Vietnam. Most critically, Reagan failed to get the American people to understand that the pursuit of foreign policy goals deemed to be in the national interest requires sacrifice. "From the very outset, the great appeal of the president's policies was that they demanded so little of the public while promising so much." The defense buildup was paid for with a budget deficit. The invasion of Grenada was swift. Retaliatory strikes against Qaddafi for his support of international terrorism brought no retaliation. When costs were encountered, such as the attack on the Marines in Lebanon, the policy initiative was quickly terminated. Tucker feared that future presidents would find this new consensus with its emphasis on low-cost successes to be too fragile a foundation on which to build a foreign policy.

The George H. W. Bush Administration: Leaving the Cold War and Entering a New World

By temperament and experience, George H. W. Bush was the polar opposite of Ronald Reagan. Where Reagan was an ideologue with little personal experience in world affairs, Bush was a pragmatist who had served as director of

Central Intelligence, ambassador to China, and ambassador to the United Nations. What Bush promised the American people in his 1988 election campaign was continuity in overall policy without the excesses and missteps that hounded the Reagan administration.

Bush first moved to tie up two loose ends of Reagan's Central American foreign policy. He terminated the controversy over Nicaragua by entering into an agreement with Congress over funding for the Contras. Congress would approve nonmilitary aid for the Contras through the elections scheduled for 1990 and the Bush administration would not request any lethal aid. The Bush plan was put forward fully expecting a Sandinista victory. To its surprise, the Sandinistas were voted out of office as the anti-Sandinista candidate, Violeta Barrios de Chamorro, won by an impressive margin.

Panama presented Bush with a very different problem. Rather than dealing with "the enemy," Bush was confronted with a former ally who once had served as a CIA agent and was now a liability openly defying the United States. During the Reagan administration, officials increasingly became concerned with the flow of drugs from Latin America to the United States. Panamanian ruler General Manuel Noriega was a major player in this game. As early as 1985 the Reagan administration had warned Noriega about its concerns over the political situation in Panama and reports about his involvement in drug trafficking and money laundering. Little was done to change the situation until 1988 when, after being unable to agree on the wisdom of using military force against Panama, the Reagan administration imposed economic sanctions.

Matters came to a head in 1989. First, in May, Noriega annulled the Panamanian election won by his opponent, leading Bush to recall the U.S. ambassador. Then, in October, a failed U.S.-supported coup attempt led to strong criticism of Bush's handling of his Noriega problem. Finally, in December, less than one week after the Panamanian National Assembly unanimously voted Noriega to be "maximum leader" and declared Panama to be in a "state of war" with the United States, thirteen thousand U.S. troops were committed to removing Noriega and his forces from power. The invasion was condemned by the Organization of American States but justified by Bush as consistent with American rights under the Panama Canal treaties and as necessary to protect American lives.

Reagan also left Bush unfinished business in the area of strategic arms control. During his campaign against Carter, Reagan had characterized the SALT framework as fatally flawed. In 1981, when the Reagan administration moved to reopen arms control talks with the Soviet Union, they were rechristened the Strategic Arms Reduction Talks (START). No headway was made in these negotiations until the 1986 Reykjavik Summit when an agreement in principle was reached to reduce all strategic nuclear weapons by 50 percent over a five-year period. This breakthrough proved to be somewhat illusory, for it was not until July 1991 that Bush and Gorbachev signed the START I Treaty. START I was submitted to the Senate for ratification in November of that year.

Unforeseen political developments in the Soviet Union stalled the START process. The forces unleased by Gorbachev in his reform drive had succeeded in doing far more than transform the Soviet political system. They also altered its political borders and dispersed its nuclear arsenal. Where the United States once faced one nuclear enemy, it now faced four: Russia, Belarus, Kazakhstan, and Ukraine. Several months of negotiations produced a Protocol to the START I Treaty signed in May 1992 wherein all three new nuclear states pledged to destroy their nuclear arsenals by 1999. With this completed, the U.S. Senate ratified START I in October 1992.

The foreign policy challenges emanating from Gorbachev's reform efforts affected more than just Bush's arms control agenda. They also required the development of a new East Europe policy. In 1989, Solidarity, the independent trade union that had earlier challenged communist rule in Poland, won an election in 1989. The year 1990 brought a series of shocks to the region as communist rule ended in Hungary, East and West Germany were reunited into one country, and Lithuania declared its independence from the Soviet Union. In 1991, the collapse of the Soviet Union was complete, and the unraveling of Yugoslavia had begun.

The Bush administration followed a "wait and see" policy in responding to most of these developments. At the Paris Economic Summit in July 1989 Bush made it clear that he was willing to allow Western European states to play the lead role in promoting peaceful change in Eastern Europe. With the United States preoccupied with the Persian Gulf War, Western Europe also assumed the lead role in responding to the dissolution of Yugoslavia two years later. Although the Bush administration did not try to stop German reunification, it did not play a major role in the endgame. Final details were worked out between Kohl and Gorbachev. Torn by doubts about Gorbachev's true agenda and the long-term prospects for his political survival, the administration responded cautiously to calls for economic assistance. It postponed action to make agricultural credits available to Russia and moved slowly on the question of giving it most favored nation (MFN) status. Early in the administration National Security Adviser Brent Scowcroft wondered publicly about whether the true purpose behind Gorbachev's policies was to weaken the NATO alliance by causing dissension among its members.[13] Yet at the same time the administration was hesitant to abandon Gorbachev as his political difficulties mounted. For example, it refused to impose economic sanctions on Russia for attempting to stop Lithuania from becoming independent.

The Bush administration's indecision in how to respond to the unprecedented also characterized its policy toward China. Following the death of former communist party leader Hu Yaobang in April 1989, thousands of student protesters took to the streets in Shanghai, Beijing, and other cities demanding prodemocracy reforms and calling for the current party leadership to resign. Over the next months the protests escalated, with as many as one million demonstrators crowding on to Beijing's Tiananmen Square. On June 4, Chinese troops attacked the demonstrators on Tiananmen Square, killing hundreds. Martial law was declared. Before it was lifted in January 1990 an often violent crackdown on prodemocracy forces inside and outside the government was carried out.

President George H. W. Bush responded to the Tiananmen Square massacre by imposing economic sanctions against China, including suspending arms sales. In the weeks that followed, the Bush administration suspended all high-level contacts between the two governments and called for international organizations to postpone consideration of Chinese loan applications. By the end of the year, however, the administration had lost much of its enthusiasm for punishing China for its human rights violations. Concern shifted to protecting what it saw as American long-term strategic and economic interests in the region, interests that might be damaged if it were unable to carry out normal diplomatic relations with China. Accordingly, the Bush administration vetoed a bill that would permit Chinese citizens to prolong their legal stay in the United States, lifted a congressional ban on loans to firms doing business with China, and announced the sale of three communication satellites to it.

The defining moment of the Bush administration's foreign policy was the Persian Gulf War.[14] Convinced that Saddam Hussein was engaged in nothing but saber-rattling bravado, George Bush and other world leaders were stunned by the successful August 2, 1990, Iraqi invasion of Kuwait. Charging that Hussein's act was one of "blatant aggression," Bush issued an executive order freezing Iraqi and Kuwaiti assets in the United States and cutting off trade with Iraq. He stated that U.S. military intervention was not under consideration, but he soon backed off from the statement. The administration's attention quickly turned to Saudi Arabia, which it feared might be Iraq's next target. Four days after the invasion, in response to a request from Saudi King Fahd, Bush ordered 2,300 U.S. paratroopers, AWACS, and B-52 and F-11 aircraft to guard Saudi oil fields as part of Operation Desert Shield. The number of U.S. forces sent to Saudi Arabia reached 100,000 before the end of August and climbed over the 200,000 mark in November with predictions of up to 400,000 by early 1991.

Iraq's conquest of Kuwait was declared "null and void" by the UN Security Council. That body also imposed mandatory economic sanctions on Iraq and authorized the United States to use its ships in the region to uphold the embargo. On November 29, it authorized states "to use all means necessary" to end Iraq's occupation of Kuwait. The UN resolution gave Iraq until January 15, 1991, to do so. The Bush administration conducted a major diplomatic campaign to put together a global coalition and make such a resolution possible. In addition to addressing the UN General Assembly, Bush met with Gorbachev in Helsinki and went to the Middle East to meet with King Fahd and Egyptian President Mubarak. He met with Syrian President Assad in Geneva. Secretary of State James Baker traveled to Europe, the Middle East, and the Soviet Union. He also met with Chinese leaders in Cairo.

The year 1991 began with talks between Baker and Iraqi Foreign Minister Tariq Aziz. Since the invasion, Iraq had alternated between issuing bellicose warnings about its resolve and willingness to fight a holy war and more peaceful gestures that indicated a possible willingness to seek a peaceful solution (or divide the alliance), such as releasing hostages and offering to consider a partial withdrawal. The talks produced no headway and Iraq again adopted a hostile posture, indicating that it would strike Israel if attacked. In the United States, Congress began debate over whether to authorize Bush to use force against Iraq or require him to give economic sanctions more time to work. On January 12, both houses voted to give Bush that power. Three days later Bush ordered coalition forces to attack Iraq if the UN deadline was not met and the following day, January 16, Operation Desert Storm was launched to liberate Kuwait.

Amid around-the-clock allied bombing of Iraqi military targets, Iraq made good its threat to attack Israel. Iraqi troops also invaded Saudi Arabia and briefly took possession of a town before being forced to retreat. On February 23, allied forces invaded Iraq and one hundred hours later President Bush declared that Kuwait was liberated. At a joint session of Congress on March 6, Bush announced that the war was over.

Tension in the region did not end, however. Saddam Hussein turned his remaining forces against Kurdish forces in northern Iraq and Shiite Muslims in the south. Although the United Nations condemned Hussein's actions, it took no steps to protect his targets and Bush announced that the United States would not act to either support them or bring down his government. Instead, the United States turned its attention to establishing a new security framework in the region and tried to restart the Arab–Israeli peace process. A new problem came into focus by summer. As part of its surrender, Iraq agreed to allow the United Nations to supervise the destruction of its chemical and biological weapons and its ballistic missiles. Not only was Iraq interfering with UN inspection teams, but mounting evidence pointed to the existence of a larger-than-expected Iraqi nuclear capability.

When he was defeated by Bill Clinton in the 1992 election, Bush's post-election foreign policy was expected to be quiet. It was anything but that. Just days after the election, the Bush administration announced that it was imposing a 200 percent tariff on EC exports to the United States in retaliation for EC's refusal to reduce agricultural subsidies that hampered U.S. trade opportunities in Europe. In early December, the United States began consulting with its European allies over ways of stopping Serbian flights over Bosnia-Herzegovina. In early January, Bush and Yeltsin signed the START II Treaty. And, of utmost significance to the incoming Clinton administration, on December 4, following a UN vote authorizing the action, Bush ordered U.S. troops to move into Somalia to help deliver food and humanitarian assistance. Operation Restore Hope began with three ships carrying eighteen hundred troops. U.S. Marines encountered little resistance upon going ashore, but fighting soon broke out and UN Secretary-General Boutros-Ghali called upon the United States to disarm Somali rebel forces.

GEORGE H. W. BUSH'S FOREIGN POLICY EVALUATED

The hallmark of the George Bush administration was its pragmatism. It is not surprising, therefore, that evaluations of it differ largely over the relative value placed on pragmatism versus "vision." In surveying the scene after the Persian Gulf War, David Gergen wrote that the Bush administration was "far more adept at cleaning up the debris of an old world than building the framework of the new."[15] The problem, according to Gergen, was Bush's concentration on short-term goals and a planning horizon that seemed to extend only a year into the future. The cost of Bush's pragmatism was a series of missed opportunities: an opportunity to build a bipartisan consensus for the post–cold war era similar to that which had been put into place after World

War II and an opportunity to use the afterglow of victory as a springboard to realize other foreign policy goals. Michael Mandelbaum agreed with Gergen.[16] He argued that while the American national interest was well served when Bush kept the United States in the background as the events in Russia and Eastern Europe played themselves out, the same was not true for the post–cold war agenda. What was needed now was a president with vision and one able to master the intricacies of international economics.

Pragmatism was not without its defenders. William Hyland asserted that it was highly desirable because for the remainder of the twentieth century the international system was likely to be in a state of transition.[17] Under such conditions "no overriding principle articulated in advance will be sufficient to handle the burgeoning diversity of the new international agenda." He continued that one of the most difficult lessons Americans would have to learn was that for many of these emerging issues the United States would be on the sidelines rather than in the center of the fray. Thus, both in terms of its restraint and its style the Bush administration's foreign policy was well suited for its time.

Not all commentators focused their attention on the relative merits of pragmatism. Writing after the Gulf War, Owen Harries presented a different critique.[18] Once an admirer of how Bush handled this crisis, he came to believe that the administration's policy was deeply flawed in three respects. The first mistake was "the immediate, unqualified, and unilateral commitment of American power to achieving the complete, unconditional withdrawal of Iraq from Kuwait." Harries maintains that in doing so the Bush administration lost a great deal of leverage it might have had over other countries in the area of burden sharing. Only after commitments from U.S. allies were secured should Bush have made any commitments. The second mistake was "the opportunistic importance it has attached to the role of the United Nations as the authorizer of policy." Harries sees the short-term benefits of this policy as being outweighed by the long-term consequences of fostering the belief that UN approval is needed for the legitimate use of force. The most serious mistake made by Bush was the "disproportion" of its response. "The very size of the reaction . . . ensures that it cannot be a convincing precedent. This kind of behavior is simply not replicable on a regular basis. . . ." As such, he feared that future aggressors would not be deterred by Iraq's defeat because they would realize that the United States was unlikely to respond in a similar manner.

The Clinton Administration: The First Post–Cold War Presidency

Candidate Bill Clinton won the presidency largely on the basis of domestic issues. As president, Clinton planned to continue that emphasis but was prevented from doing so by a series of rapidly unfolding events abroad. American foreign policy in the first months of the Clinton administration was largely reactive in nature. "Damage control" was the order of the day. Efforts at exercising global leadership, either unilaterally or in a collective setting, were sporadic and when undertaken met with little success. Even worse, the vacillation in words and deeds that characterized them reinforced the image of a United States uncertain about its role in the post–cold war international system.

The major international peace initiative under way to end the fighting in Bosnia when Clinton took office was the Vance–Owens plan, which would have split Bosnia into ten semiautonomous provinces united only by a loose central authority. Within the first two months the Clinton administration (1) declared the plan to be "fatally flawed," (2) promised to become actively engaged in its negotiations, and (3) through a policy review indicated a willingness to develop a policy different from that endorsed by Bush. A change in policy would have been consistent with Clinton's campaign promises to lift the UN embargo on weapons to Bosnia and to use American air power. When Clinton's plan was announced in February 1993, it proved to be markedly similar to the Vance–Owens formula. Very quickly, the Clinton administration seemed overwhelmed by the complexity of organizing relief efforts, obtaining allied consent on the use of force, and bringing the warring parties together for peace talks.

Barely two months later, after putting forward his plan, Clinton was proposing a new, stronger policy, one that might involve the use of force. The next day, Secretary of State Warren Christopher assured Congress that the United States would use force only if an exit strategy existed, the public supported such a policy, and it held out the prospect of stabilizing the situation. These were conditions that all recognized would not be easily met. May brought more talk of a united U.S.–Western European position, but negotiations again failed to produce an agreement on U.S. proposals to use force. By July, the Clinton administration was blaming the Europeans for the growing crisis and said it did not have plans for further action. August brought another change in direction, with the Clinton administration outlining conditions for the use of troops in Bosnia to enforce a peace settlement. It also saw three resignations by State Department officials critical of what one termed a "misguided, vacillating, and dangerous" policy.

Delivering humanitarian relief in Somalia also proved to be a complex undertaking. General Colin Powell, chairman of the Joint Chiefs of Staff under Bush, had estimated that the operation would last two to three months. Other Bush administration officials hoped to have the troops home by the end of Bush's term in January 1993. Both forecasts were wide of the mark. The goal was to be humanitarian relief and not nation-building, but once in place U.S. forces found themselves inexorably drawn into the middle of a civil war among rival warlords. The chief U.S. protagonist was General Mohammed Farah Aidid. The United Nations had taken over command of the relief effort in May and Aidid came to view the UN presence (which continued to include U.S. troops) and its efforts to disarm his forces as a direct threat to his political future in Somalia. A June 1993 attack by his forces killed twenty-four Pakistani peacekeeping soldiers and led to a UN Security Council Resolution calling for the apprehension of those responsible. Shortly thereafter UN authorities in Somalia issued an order for Aidid's arrest. However, after that UN forces rarely ventured out of their compounds, and control of Mogadishu increasingly passed into the hands of Somali fighters.

Closer to home, Haiti presented the Clinton administration with still another set of policy challenges. During his presidential campaign Clinton had criticized Bush for his policy of refusing to allow Haitian boat people to enter the United States without a hearing and promised to change that policy. Fearing that thousands or perhaps hundreds of thousands of Haitians might attempt to come to the United States after Clinton's inauguration, however, the president-elect made it known that he would continue George H. W. Bush's policy of interdiction and forced return. Clinton quickly came under attack for breaking yet another campaign promise he had made regarding Haiti. Critics asserted that he was not doing enough to restore exiled Haitian President Jean-Bertrand Aristide to power. The democratically elected Aristide had been forced out of office in a September 1991 coup. A resolution to the crisis seemed at hand in July when, under the increasing weight of UN and U.S. economic sanctions, an agreement was reached setting the terms under which Aristide was to reclaim the presidency.

Stung by the mounting criticism of the content and conduct of its foreign policy, the Clinton administration sought to regain conceptual control over the direction of American foreign policy by having high-ranking administration members present an orchestrated series of high-profile public speeches in September 1993. Anthony Lake, Assistant to the President for National Security Affairs, presented the second speech. In it he identified democracy and market economics as its core concepts and argued that the successor doctrine to containment should be that of "enlargement." Lake argued that as a strategy, enlargement had four component parts: (1) the strengthening of the community of major market democracies, (2) fostering and consolidating new democracies and market economies, (3) countering aggression by "backlash" states hostile to democracy and markets as well as supporting their liberalization, and (4) working to help democracy and market economics take root in regions of greatest humanitarian concern. Lake argued that many of the current foreign policy debates were overdrawn and that although Bosnia and Somalia were important issues, they were not problems whose handling served to define American foreign policy. The more fundamental issue is the age-old question of whether the United States should be significantly engaged abroad at all.

The situation in Bosnia continued to worsen for the Muslim population. This brought renewed cries from Congress in 1994 to lift the arms embargo against the Bosnians so that they might better defend themselves. Clinton resisted these pressures, citing the damage it would do to America's role as a world leader and its ability to convince allies to back the U.S.-supported embargo against Iraq. It also exposed the deep rift that existed between the United States and its European allies over how to respond to the crisis as they wrestled throughout 1994 over the question of using military force against the Serbian separatists in Bosnia. At year's end, the Clinton administration all but admitted defeat and abandoned its two-year effort to get the Europeans to accept the use of air power. On the eve of a NATO summit, it agreed to back the European-favored policy of seeking a diplomatically engineered cease-fire followed by a peace treaty.

Matters took a decided turn for the worse in Somalia. Attacks on U.S. and UN forces continued, casualties mounted, and Aidid eluded capture. The June attack on the Pakistanis had led to the creation of a special American military unit that would be sent to Somalia to capture Aidid or, failing that, to capture a number of his high-ranking aides. This unit was dispatched to Somalia after four U.S. soldiers were killed in an August ambush. The strike took place on October 3, 1994 and resulted in the capture of several of Aidid's aides. However, a U.S. helicopter was shot down in the raid and a rescue effort was mounted. In the fifteen-hour battle that followed, eighteen U.S. soldiers were killed and eighty-four were wounded.

Coming quickly on the heels of the debacle in Somalia was an embarrassment in Haiti. According to the terms of the July agreement, Aristide was to return to power on October 31. In preparation for this transfer of power, the USS *Harlan County* arrived in Haiti carrying American and Canadian trainers whose job it was to reform the Haitian security services. They were met by a mob that threatened to attack the troops. At the request of the Pentagon, which said that the U.S. forces were not combat-ready, Clinton ordered the USS *Harlan County* to leave Haiti. In the wake of this failure, the United States and the United Nations once again turned to economic sanctions in an effort to force the Haitian military to accept Aristide back. Tensions also began to rise between Aristide and the Clinton administration over the content and timing of plans for returning him to power.

By summer 1994, the rising number of Haitians fleeing to the United States and congressional calls for action led the Clinton administration to once again rethink its Haitian policy. Instead of returning fleeing Haitians, they would now send them to "safe havens." There was also open talk about the use of force to end the Haitian crisis. In late July the UN Security Council authorized the use of force in Haiti, and by early September this use of force was referred to by Clinton administration officials as "a certainty." The threatened invasion seemed about to become a reality when an invasion task force was put in place off the Haitian coast on September 18. Then, at the last minute, Clinton dispatched former president Jimmy Carter, Senator Sam Nunn, and General Powell to Haiti to secure a peaceful settlement of the conflict by negotiating the departure of Haitian ruler Lieutenant General Raoul Cedras and his key aides. After receiving a three-hour extension past its original deadline, thirty minutes before the final deadline an agreement was reached. U.S. troops would now land unopposed. The agreement was viewed as a major foreign policy success in Washington, but it did not come without its costs. The Clinton administration succeeded only by accepting Carter's view that Cedras was not a "thug" who had created a "nightmare of bloodshed" but a misunderstood military leader "concerned with his country."

The Clinton administration had barely put the Haitian crisis behind it when it became involved in highly controversial negotiations with North Korea over the fate of that country's nuclear program. In June 1994 North Korea withdrew from the International Atomic Energy Association (IAEA).

Its actions marked the sharpest turn yet in an ongoing international dispute over North Korea's widely rumored efforts to develop nuclear weapons. Concerned not only for what the impact of a North Korean nuclear weapons program would have on the security of neighboring states in Asia but also for Israel and Europe should North Korea begin exporting its nuclear weapons, the United States moved in the United Nations to organize international political and economic sanctions against it. At the same time the Clinton administration sought to negotiate an agreement with North Korea that would place international controls over its nuclear program. Under terms of the agreement reached in October 1994, North Korea agreed to freeze its capacity to make nuclear arms and allow international inspections, but it did not have to dismantle its current facilities. For its part, the United States committed itself to ease trade restrictions and make available advanced nuclear technologies. The major gain from Washington's perspective was North Korea's agreement to do more than was necessary according to the Nonproliferation Treaty (NPT) including the ultimate dismantling of all nuclear facilities built over the past twenty years. The problem as others saw it was that Washington had agreed to give North Korea special status, allowing it to put off for five years meeting full compliance with the provisions of the NPT. This might encourage other renegade nuclear states to bargain for concessions in return for placing limits on, or accepting international inspection of, their nuclear facilities.

Little respite for the Clinton administration in foreign policy matters appeared in 1995. The year began well with the administration negotiating an unlimited extension of the Nonproliferation Treaty (NPT). In its twenty-fifth year, the NPT was the centerpiece of international efforts to stop the spread of nuclear weapons. The end of the cold war had drawn renewed attention to the dangers posed by nuclear proliferation, and many feared that if the NPT agreement was not extended the number of nuclear states might grow rapidly. Because several states objected, the prospects for obtaining international consent to an unlimited extension had been considered problematic. Overcoming their opposition through a combination of behind-the-scenes arm twisting and a public pledge to halt all U.S. nuclear testing (itself a controversial move within the administration), Clinton was able to create a broad-based international consensus behind the treaty's indefinite extension.

By Clinton's second term, fighting in the Balkans had once more erupted. This time it was in Kosovo and came at the very time that Clinton was embroiled in the Monica Lewinsky affair and faced the threat of impeachment. In March 1998 Serbian authorities launched a violent attack against the separatist Albanian Kosovo Liberation Army. NATO threatened but did not launch air strikes against Serbian forces. In December, fighting began again and new evidence of massacres conducted by Serbs against ethnic Albanians was uncovered. Under threat of a NATO attack, Yugoslav President Slobodan Milosevic agreed to participate at peace talks with ethnic Albanians. Held at Rambouillet in February 1999, these talks collapsed when Milosevic refused to permit a NATO peacekeeping force to enter Kosovo. A second effort to broker an agreement failed in March. At that point the Serbian army, which had been largely confined to its barracks since October 1998, went on what amounted to a "scorched earth" military offensive against the Albanians that included a policy of "ethnic cleansing" whereby large numbers of Albanians were killed or forced to flee.

On March 24, NATO began air strikes against Serbian forces. The bombing continued for eleven weeks into mid-June before Milosevic agreed to withdraw all Serbian forces from Kosovo and permit NATO peacekeeping troops to enter. The war produced massive refugee flows in both directions. Approximately 150,000 Serbs and Montenegrins had fled Kosovo in June and July while some 650,000 ethnic Albanians returned. By the end of 1999, approximately 50,000 NATO forces had taken up positions in Kosovo.

Clinton's last major foreign policy initiative came late in his administration and was directed at reenergizing the stalled Middle East peace process. In July 2000 Clinton brought together Arab and Israeli leaders for a summit conference at Camp David. That meeting failed to end the growing violence in the region but was followed by a new round of meetings in September. These too failed, but Clinton was able to get both sides to agree to resume talks in early January. As with the other efforts, they adjourned without any substantive agreement being reached.

CLINTON'S FOREIGN POLICY EVALUATED

Early evaluations of Clinton's foreign policy were almost uniformly negative. The harshest commentary came from isolationists who argued that America's national interest did not extend beyond safeguarding the immediate physical security of the United States and preserving its system of government.[19] Conservative and liberal internationalist critiques centered their complaints on Clinton's inexperience and repeated policy zig-zags. Inexperience was seen as responsible for overly embracing multilateralism and an expansive definition of American national interests. The frequent and abrupt policy changes were seen as the product of Clinton's personality and managerial style. Together they produced qualities that conservatives found troubling. Paul Wolfowitz, who served in the Reagan and Bush administrations, urged the administration to be more cautious in its support of peacekeeping and more forthcoming in its efforts to build an international consensus that supports basic American interests.[20] He compared the challenge facing Clinton to that encountered by Warren Harding and Harry Truman and raised the question of which Clinton would most come to resemble. Both took office after great historic struggles had been completed and faced the challenge of leading the United States into a new era of world politics. History, notes Wolfowitz, judges their foreign policies very differently. Truman's is applauded while Harding's is cited as a major contributing factor to the collapse of the interwar system.

Evaluations presented by American commentators around the conclusion of the first Clinton administration were hardly more supportive. Incoherent, indecisive, inconsistent, and lacking a clear focus continued to be the most frequently heard characterizations of its foreign policy, with one commentator, Michael Mandelbaum, going so far as to summarize Clinton's first-term foreign policy as being akin to a "supermarket shopping spree, grabbing whatever it takes a fancy to, without worrying about the costs or whether the product is the right brand or is genuinely needed."[21]

The neo-Wilsonian orientation of Clinton's foreign policy also continued to attract criticism. Mandelbaum asserted that what united its flawed policies toward Haiti, Bosnia, and Somalia was a mistaken focus on the social, political, and economic conditions within these states. These three foreign policy problems were not inherited, he maintains, but were the product of the Clinton administration's inability to focus its foreign policy on questions of true national interest.

Foreign evaluations of Clinton's foreign policy during his first term were mixed and often more charitable. *Foreign Policy*, a leading academic journal that focuses on problems in American foreign policy and world politics, asked its regional editors to evaluate Clinton's record from their region's perspective.[22] Those aspects of foreign policy on which the Clinton administration rated highest centered on the conduct of diplomacy: sustaining American hegemony, attracting quality people to the foreign policy bureaucracy, and conducting personal diplomacy. Its lowest grades were received on questions dealing with vision: the ability to make tough choices, balancing rhetoric and action, and developing a coherent strategic outlook. Summary regional rankings were quite consistent, with all respondents grading the Clinton administration at between five and six on a ten-point scale. In a telling commentary on Clinton's foreign policy agenda, no editor was asked to provide an African perspective.

By the end of Clinton's second term a more balanced assessment had emerged. Conservatives continued to find much to fault in his foreign policy. Robert Kagan identified four major failings: (1) the failure to contain China, (2) the failure to remove Saddam Hussein, (3) the failure to maintain adequate American military strength, and (4) the failure to deploy a missile defense system.[23] The editors of *Foreign Policy* provided a middle-ground evaluation. Rejecting the argument that Clinton lacked vision, they noted that a more telling critique was that he lacked attention to foreign policy matters. This theme was echoed by others who noted that Clinton overrelied upon his capacity for personal diplomacy and neglected the underlying forces that propelled political events.[24] Critics asserted that this was particularly true in his last-minute efforts to arrange an Arab–Israeli peace agreement.

Stephen Walt presents a much more positive evaluation. Acknowledging mistakes, he identified four foreign policy goals that Clinton advanced: (1) to dampen security competition and reduce the risk of war, (2) to reduce the threat from weapons of mass destruction, (3) to foster an open world economy, and (4) to build a world order compatible with American values. He argues that Clinton's foreign policy was "well suited to an era where there is little to gain in foreign policy and much to lose. The American people recognize this and have made it clear they want neither isolationism nor costly international crusades."[25]

The George W. Bush Administration: Into the War on Terrorism

When he became president, the world that George W. Bush faced was essentially the same that his two immediate predecessors, George H. W. Bush and Bill Clinton, tried to influence through their foreign policies. All of this changed with the terrorist attacks of September 11, 2001. A new grand strategy, preemption, was deemed necessary. Just as the Japanese attack on Pearl Harbor had discredited isolationism as a grand strategy for advancing and protecting the American national interest, so it argued had 9/11 discredited deterrence as the cornerstone of American foreign policy. The Bush administration did not embrace preemption until its second year in office. It already had encountered one foreign policy crisis by then.

Not even one hundred days into his presidency, on March 31, 2001, a U.S. Navy surveillance plane collided with a Chinese fighter in international airspace over the South China Sea. The U.S plane and its crew of twenty-four landed safely on Chinese territory. China blamed the incident on the United States and demanded a formal apology for the collision and the death of a Chinese pilot. The Bush administration refused to apologize, blamed the incident on China, and demanded the release of the U.S. crew and damaged plane. Mindful of how the Carter administration became entrapped in the Iranian hostage crisis George W. Bush adopted a low-keyed public stance. The crisis ended with little more than a whimper. It did, however, set the tone for later U.S.–Chinese relations. The administration walked a thin and difficult line in which it needed Chinese support for the war against terrorism and dealing with North Korea yet was concerned with its growing economic strength and the continuing conflict with Taiwan. Symbolic of the uneasy state of U.S. relations with China was a series of military maneuvers that took place in July 2004, well after the incident described above. Some eighteen-thousand Chinese troops, using advanced weapons, staged an invasion of Dongsham an island that resembles Taiwan in many respects. About the same time, Taiwanese military pilots practiced emergency landings on closed highways, something they would do if China attacked and destroyed its air bases. Meanwhile, the U.S. Navy staged a global readiness drill with seven aircraft carrier groups to demonstrate its ability to move quickly and forcefully anywhere around the world.

Other than the encounter with China, the early initiatives of the George W. Bush administration largely amounted to distancing itself from Clinton's foreign policy and saying "no." The Kyoto Protocol was rejected as flawed, a national ballistic missile system was embraced, it withdrew from participating in the international criminal court, and the ABM treaty was abandoned.

September 11 ushered in a new phase in Bush's foreign policy. He was transformed from a reluctant internationalist with strong unilateralist leanings to a fervent internationalist who embraced the rhetoric of multilateralism without embracing its fundamental assumptions.

After the terrorist attacks President George W. Bush demanded that the Taliban government of Afghanistan expel Osama bin Laden and al-Qaeda and sever its ties with international terrorism in general. When this did not happen, on October 7, 2001, twenty-six days after the attacks on the Pentagon and World Trade Center, the United States and its allies began aerial strikes against terrorist facilities and Taliban military targets inside Afghanistan. Ground forces were supplied largely by the Northern Alliance, a coalition group that had opposed Taliban rule. Their efforts were aided and guided by the CIA. The first U.S. Special Forces entered Afghanistan on October 19. It was the first such commando operation since 1993 in Somalia. Conventional forces arrived on November 25. The last Taliban stronghold fell on December 16. Oasma bin Laden, who was one of the major targets of the military campaign from the outset, remained at large. Parallel to the military campaign to defeat the Taliban, diplomatic negotiations were taking place as to the shape of the future Afghan government. In late November, the United Nations sponsored a meeting of Afghanistan's four main anti-Taliban political groups. On December 5, they agreed to create a multiethnic interim government. Hamid Karazi was selected to head this body that would take power on December 22 as the Afghan Interim Authority. Elections were to be held within two years. It was also agreed that an international peacekeeping force would be sent to Kabul.

In his January 2002 State of the Union address, George W. Bush identified North Korea, Iraq, and Iran as an "axis of evil" that threatened American security interests. In the months that followed, the United States and North Korea entered into a verbal sparring match over the legitimacy of this charge. The conflict took on an entirely new dimension in October when North Korea did not challenge a U.S. assertion that it had a secret uranium enrichment program. In December, North Korea ordered international inspectors out of the country and the next month withdrew from the Non-Proliferation Treaty. In April 2003, North Korea acknowledged it had developed nuclear weapons.

The Bush administration's response consisted of 1) terminating the 1994 Agreed Framework signed during the Clinton administration, 2) not holding bilateral talks with North Korea, 3) assembling an international coalition to pressure North Korea through the denial of foreign aid and other measures, 4) professing a willingness to hold multilateral talks with North Korea, 5) warning of and planning future economic sanctions, and 6) stressing that "all options are open." Russia, China, and South Korea all criticized the Bush administration for its failure to hold bilateral talks, and neither China nor South Korea, North Korea's main sources of foreign aid, were willing to cut off aid. North Korea sought bilateral talks and a formal pledge on the part of the Bush administration not to attack it.

After several diplomatic false starts and internal disagreements within the Bush administration, multilateral talks began in late summer 2003 with North Korea, Russia, China, South Korea, Japan, and the United States in attendance. A June 2004 meeting produced an offer by the United States to grant diplomatic recognition and support multilateral aid for North Korea if it first committed to an internationally verifiable process of dismantling its nuclear weapons. In putting forward the proposal, it urged North Korea to follow Libya's example of voluntarily renouncing weapons of mass destruction.

In July, North Korea officially rejected the offer as a sham. Days later it called upon the United Nations to dissolve the UN Command that continues to operate in South Korea. This demand came after the United States announced it was pulling 37,500 troops out of South Korea and was upgrading South Korea's military technology.

The 37,500 troops were not going home but were needed to help meet American military commitments elsewhere, most notably the occupation of Iraq. The Bush administration began to consider war against Iraq almost immediately after the 9/11 terrorist attacks but postponed action until after the war in Afghanistan was concluded. Signs of movement toward war began in 2002 with Bush's State of the Union address. Activity quickened in the fall. In September, Bush addressed the opening session of the United Nations and challenged it to confront the "grave and gathering danger" of Iraq or become irrelevant. Five days later, on September 17 the administration released its national security strategy that replaced deterrence with preemption. In October, Congress authorized the use of force against Iraq. By the end of the year, Bush had approved the deployment of U.S. forces to the Persian Gulf.

Diplomatic efforts dominated the agenda in spring 2003. In February, UN Weapons Inspector Hans Blix asserted that progress had been made in Iraq. Shortly after this the United States, Great Britain, and Spain introduce a resolution at the Security Council authorizing the use of military force against Iraq. France, Germany, and Russia opposed the resolution. No such resolution was obtained and on March 17, 2003, George W. Bush presented Saddam Hussein with a forty-eight-hour ultimatum to leave Iraq.

Operation Iraq Freedom began on March 19, 2003, with a decapitation strike aimed at Iraqi leadership targets in Baghdad. Major fighting began on March 21 and on April 9 Baghdad fell. On May 1, President George W. Bush declared an end to major combat operations. If, in the final analysis, the war had been as easy as Secretary of Defense Donald Rumsfeld and his key aides had maintained all along, the occupation supported the case made by the critics of the war. In May, thousands in Baghdad peacefully protested the U.S. presence. The protests did not remain peaceful for long. In July, Rumsfeld admitted the cost of the war had been underestimated by one-half. He now placed it at $3.9 billion/month and acknowledged that far more troops than anticipated would be needed for the occupation. Later that month, U.S. combat deaths in Iraq reach the level of the Persian Gulf War.

The year 2003 ended with a major success for the administration as Saddam Hussein was captured. However, 2004 began badly as terrorist attacks and uprisings continued. In April, photos surfaced documenting the torture and mistreatment of Iraqi prisoners by U.S. personnel at the Abu Ghraib prison. In June, search for an exit strategy intensified. On June 8, the United States went back to the United Nations and obtained its support for a resolution ending the American occupation and outlining a role for the United Nations in post-transition Iraq. Then on June 28, two days ahead of schedule, the United States transferred power to a new Iraqi government.

While these events were unfolding in Iraq, the Bush administration found political support for the war waning at home. Its rationales for going to war were publicly questioned, and the performance of its intelligence agency under attack. The administration was also unable to stop congressional committees and an independent commission from holding public hearings and investigating its antiterrorism policies prior to 9/11.

GEORGE W. BUSH'S FOREIGN POLICY EVALUATED

Evaluations of George W. Bush's foreign policy are characterized by both underlying constants and a series of more time-specific concerns. One constant point of criticism has been his administration's unilateralist approach to foreign policy. Neo-liberalists argue his actions are undermining the key international institutions on which the post–World War II security order has been built—NATO and the UN. Realists are not as troubled by the demise of these institutions as they are by the administration's failure to build and sustain meaningful alliance relations with major regional powers. For some realists, sustaining America's position of unipolar dominance is only possible if these states bandwagon with the United States and do not begin to balance against it. These realists fear Bush's aggressive unilateralism will bring this later occurrence about prematurely.

A second constant theme focuses on the administration's excessive reliance on coercive diplomacy and military power as the means for realizing foreign policy objectives. Having divided the world into good and evil states, it has difficulty talking with those whose views it rejects. Diplomatic initiatives such as Middle East peace plans and negotiations with North Korea over its nuclear ambitions are entered into reluctantly, marked by contradictory statements and moves, and interspersed with long periods of neglect. Economic sanctions are seen as having been abandoned too quickly (Iraq) and not given the credit they deserve (Libya).[26] Joseph Nye adds that the administration has neglected and even weakened America's considerable soft power capabilities through its overreliance on military power.[27]

Other critiques have been more sharply focused on specific actions and come from across the political spectrum. For example, on the political right, Mark Helprin was highly critical of the war against the Taliban in Afghanistan.[28] He labeled it a "phony war" and faulted the Bush administration for failing to pursue an across-the-board build-up of American military power that would allow it to act unilaterally against terrorism. Craig Eisendrath presented a liberal critique of that war asserting that a more effective strategy against terrorism would be based on advocating human rights, economic and social development, and supporting international institutions such as the International Criminal Court.[29] Neo-isolationists have long been skeptical of nation building and consider Bosnia, Haiti, Kosovo, and Somalia all to be failures.[30] They see little reason to be optimistic about Iraq. A final critique of note is not so much about Bush's foreign policy as it is the Wilsonian tradition in general. Colin Dueck writes that the problems Bush is facing in Iraq are not caused by his unilateralist approach but the repeated failure of those pursuing a Wilsonian agenda of global transformation to allocate sufficient resources to it. Wilsonians have sought to achieve "hegemony on the cheap" and because of it repeatedly failed to accomplish their objectives.[31]

Summary and Future

As this brief overview of U.S. foreign policy illustrates, constructing a grand strategy and then implementing it is a daunting task. Conceptually, these grand strategies have often been found wanting, either riddled by inconsistencies or at odds with the prevailing conditions of world politics. On occasion, they have bordered on irrelevant as events beyond America's borders either conspired to frustrate policy makers or allowed them the luxury of space to operate in without significant challenges. More often than not, tactical considerations of the moment drove American foreign policy forward as much as did an all-encompassing strategic vision. And finally, domestic political considerations were ever present with changes in strategic outlook frequently coming with the arrival of a new administration from a different party.

What then is the future of the war on terrorism and preemption? Clearly it is too early to tell but the analysis of containment presented by John Lewis Gaddis in the early 1980s does provide us with a starting point for anticipating its fate.[32] At base, Gaddis argues that the United States alternated between two grand strategies of containment. The first was symmetrical containment. In it, the United States met the communist challenge where it was happening and with a corresponding amount of force. The second strategy was asymmetrical containment. Here, the United States responded at places of its own choosing and with a level of force of its own choosing. Both had their advantages and limitations. Symmetrical containment offers protection against incremental threats since now challenge is ignored or allowed to grow out of control. It is also expensive because the enemy has the advantage in terms of time, place, scope, and duration of the challenge. Responding everywhere makes foreign policy appear immature and unable to differentiate between core and secondary interests. Asymmetrical containment gives the initiative back to the United States. It is less costly since not all challenges have to be met and one can deal from strength in meeting them. On the negative side of the ledger, it requires picking and choosing what positions to defend and which not to. Without clear-cut criteria for making these decisions, the asymmetrical containment risks being perceived as unprincipled, weak, and inviting challenges.

More than any other single factor, Gaddis attributes the shifts from symmetrical to asymmetrical containment to be the result of economic considerations. The "tyranny of means" drove policy makers away from symmetrical containment when the budgetary implications of large-scale defense spending became dangerous and allowed them to embrace it when the costs could be borne without setting off an inflationary spiral, raising the deficit, or requiring new taxes.

George W. Bush's initial response to 9/11 was symmetrical. The war against terrorism was global. The United States not only brought down the Taliban government but sent antiterrorist military aid to fight terrorist groups in Indonesia, the Philippines, Georgia, and Central Asia. Preemption was announced without qualification as to target. The Iraq War was a logical extension of a symmetrical response to terrorism and an application of preemption given the administration's twin arguments that links existed between Iraq and al-Qaeda and that Iraq possessed weapons of mass destruction. Questions about the wisdom of a symmetrical response to terrorism are consistent with those expressed about symmetrical containment. Not all terrorist threats are alike, not all responses need be military in nature, and in the final analysis even preemption leaves the initiative to the adversary. Most significantly for the future of a symmetrical response to terrorism and preemption, this strategy has begun to raise questions about its cost foreshadowing a movement toward an asymmetrical response to terrorism. Members of Congress from both parties expressed support for the idea of loans rather than grants to help rebuild Iraq, local communities complained about the costs of having National Guard units activated for long periods of time, and voices were heard calling for repealing tax cuts to help pay for the war effort. Irrespective of how it may be conducted, Gaddis is convinced that there is no turning back from the strategy of preemption and a return to deterrence. Others are not convinced of preemption's staying power.[33]

Notes

1. This document is available at http://www.whitehouse.gov/nsc/nss.html.
2. Martha Crenshaw, "Terrorism, Strategies, and Grand Strategies," in Audrey Cronin and James Ludes (eds.), *Attacking Terrorism* (Washington, D.C.: Georgetown University Press), 74–93.
3. Richard Betts, "Is Strategy an Illusion?" *International Security,* 25 (2000), 5–50.
4. Richard Nixon, *U.S. Foreign Policy for the 1970s: Building for Peace* (Washington, D.C.: U.S. Government Printing Office, 1971), p. 6.
5. Robert Tucker, "America in Decline: The Foreign Policy of Maturity," *Foreign Affairs,* 58 (1980), 449–84.
6. A. Glenn Mower Jr., *Human Rights and American Foreign Policy: The Carter and Reagan Experiences* (New York: Greenwood Press, 1987).
7. Arthur Schlesinger Jr., "Human Rights and the American Tradition," *Foreign Affairs,* 57 (1979), 513.
8. Stanley Hoffmann, "Requiem," *Foreign Policy,* 42 (1981), 3–26.
9. Jeane Kirkpatrick, "Human Rights and American Foreign Policy: A Symposium," *Commentary* (November 1981), 42–45.
10. David Skidmore, "Carter and the Failure of Foreign Policy Reform," *Political Science Quarterly,* 104 (1993/94), 699–729.
11. Michael Mandelbaum, "The Luck of the President," *Foreign Affairs,* 64 (1986), 393–413.
12. Robert W. Tucker, "Reagan's Foreign Policy," *Foreign Affairs,* 68 (1989), 1–27.
13. Arnold Horelick, "U.S.-Soviet Relations: Threshold of a New Era," *Foreign Affairs,* 69 (1990), 51–69.
14. In the next chapter, we will look more closely at the debate over the lessons this event holds for American foreign policy. Here we will concentrate on presenting an overview of the conflict.
15. David Gergen, "Missed Opportunities," *Foreign Affairs,* 71 (1992), 1–20.
16. Michael Mandelbaum, "The Bush Foreign Policy," *Foreign Affairs,* 70 (1991), 5–22.
17. William G. Hyland, "The Case for Pragmatism," *Foreign Affairs,* 71 (1992), 38–52.
18. Owen Harries, "Drift and Mastery, Bush Style," *National Interest,* 23 (1991) 1–7.
19. Doug Bandow, "Keeping the Troops and Money at Home," *Current History,* 579 (1994), 8–13.
20. Paul Wolfowitz, "Clinton's First Year," *Foreign Affairs,* 73 (1994), 28–43.
21. Michael Mandelbaum, "Foreign Policy as Social Work," *Foreign Affairs,* 75 (1996), 16–32.
22. "Grading the President," *Foreign Policy,* 109 (1997/98), 34–69.

23. Robert Kagan, "The Clinton Legacy Abroad: His Sins of Omission in Foreign and Defense Policy," *Weekly Standard,* January 15, 2001.

24. "Clinton's Foreign Policy," *Foreign Policy,* 121 (2000), 18–28.

25. Stephen Walt, "Two Cheers for Clinton's Foreign Policy," *Foreign Affairs,* 79 (2000), 63–79.

26. George Lopez and David Cortright, "Containing Iraq: Sanctions Worked," *Foreign Affairs,* 83 (2004), 90–103; and George Joffe, "Libya: Who Blinked and Why," *Current History,* 103 (May 2004), 221–5.

27. Joseph Nye, Jr., *The Paradox of American Power* (New York: Oxford, 2002).

28. Mark Helprin, "Phony War," *National Review,* 54 (April 22, 2002), 29–34.

29. Craig Eisendrath, "U.S. Foreign Policy After September 11," *USA Today Magazine* (May 2002), 12–14.

30. Gary Dempsey, *Fool's Errands* (Washington, D.C: CATO Institute, 2001).

31. Colin Dueck, "Hegemony on the Cheap," *World Policy Journal,* 20 (2003/2004), 1–11.

32. John Lewis Gaddis, *Strategies of Containment* (New York: Oxford, 1982).

33. John Lewis Gaddis, "Grand Strategy in the Second Term," *Foreign Affairs,* 84 (2005), 2; the other essays in this volume also provide an assessment of Bush's foreign policy in his first term.

— 5 —

LEARNING FROM THE PAST

If there are to be no more Vietnams (or Munichs, Pearl Harbors, Koreas, Irans), policy makers must learn from past foreign policy failures. Yet, as Richard Betts notes in commenting on the problem of strategic surprise, remarkably little learning from the past takes place.[1] The same mistakes occur over and over. Since the beginning of World War II, "there have been few if any examples of failures by major powers attempting to inflict effective shock in the initiation of war."

We begin this chapter by treating the problem of learning from the past as a generic one and asking how and what policy makers learn: the types of events they learn from, the types of calculations they make, and the lessons they learn. The bulk of the chapter presents three case studies drawing on post–World War II U.S. foreign policy to illustrate these points. The cold war illustrates the problem of learning from the past when interpretations vary greatly. Vietnam shows how policy makers relied on historical analogies in making decisions. Finally, the Persian Gulf War is examined to uncover lessons about the effectiveness of U.S. military strategy in the post–cold war era.

How Do Policy Makers Learn from the Past?

Policy makers learn by matching the known with the unknown.[2] This is not a passive act. They do not sit back and simply accept data as a given, but actively interact with it.[3] Much of the foreign policy debate in the Clinton presidency was over what to do about the military and humanitarian crisis in Kosovo.[4] On the surface, the issue at hand was straightforward: whether or not to intervene militarily. But the debate in Congress and within the administration showed that this was anything but a simple matter. Analogies were drawn with at least four different events from the past, each of which suggested a different definition of the problem and response. They were Vietnam, the Holocaust, Munich, and the outbreak of World War I. Debate over which of these analogies was correct slowed the American response and shaped the form it took.

In addition to selecting reference points for evaluating information, policy makers must make judgments about what is a piece of information (signal) and what is unimportant (noise). Discriminating between the two is no easy task. Moreover, having identified a piece of data as a signal does not tell the policy maker what to do; it only sets in motion the process of learning. Information received in the Philippines that Pearl Harbor was under attack did not tell policy makers there that they were the next target or what steps to take to defend themselves. Roberta Wohlstetter, in her classic account of the U.S. intelligence failure at Pearl Harbor, identifies fifty-six separate signals ranging in duration from one day to one month pointing to the Japanese attack. She also notes that prior to the attack there was a good deal of evidence to support all of the wrong interpretations. Wohlstetter suggests that the United States failed to anticipate the Japanese attack on Pearl Harbor, not for a lack of signals, but because there was too much noise.

Policy makers discriminate between signals and noise by making a series of assumptions about what motivates the behavior of others or what constitutes the underlying dynamics of a problem confronting them. Consider the intercepted Japanese directive to their U.S. embassy and consulates to burn their codes. In retrospect this is taken as a clear indication that hostilities were imminent. But during the first week of December, the United States ordered all of its consulates in the Far East to burn their codes, and no one took this to be the equivalent of a U.S. declaration of war against Japan.[5]

The assumptions policy makers bring to bear on foreign policy problems are influenced by their long-term experiences and immediate concerns. Long-term experience provides policy makers with a data base against which to evaluate an ongoing pattern of behavior. For Franklin Roosevelt and other U.S. policy makers, personal experiences and their reading of history led to a conclusion that the presence of the U.S. fleet at Pearl Harbor was a deterrent to a Japanese attack. They failed to appreciate that it also made a fine target. For their part, Japanese leaders drew upon their 1904 war-opening attack in the Russo–Japanese War as the model for how to deal with a more powerful enemy. Immediate concerns largely determine what we expect to see. Preoccupation with economic difficulties in country X will blind policy makers to evidence that they ordinarily would have recognized as pointing to a military coup. In the 1970s, U.S. policy makers were surprised by the Turkish invasion of Cyprus and the Portuguese coup, not because these events could not have been foreseen, but because so much attention was riveted on Vietnam.

Once they are in place, perceptual systems are not readily changed. They easily become obsolete and inaccurate. Holding onto one's views in the face of challenges is not necessarily irrational. No firm evidence exists that open-minded policy makers are better equipped to avoid surprises than are closed-minded ones. Some would even argue that a firm conceptual system is a necessary requirement for action, that in its absence one is condemned to indecision in the face of unfolding events. The principle involved here is cognitive consistency.[6] Individuals try to keep their beliefs and values consistent with one another by ignoring some information, actively seeking out other data, and reinterpreting still other information so that it supports the individuals' perception of reality. The result is that instead of being a continuous and rationally structured process, learning is sporadic and constrained. Policy makers do not move steadily from a simplistic understanding of an event to a more complex one as their experience and familiarity with it build. New information and new problems are fit into already well-established perceptual systems. Learning thus rarely produces dramatic changes in priorities or commitments, and changes in behavior tend to be incremental.

A well-documented case of this process at work is John Foster Dulles's perception of the Soviet Union.[7] Dulles was secretary of state for all but a few months of the Eisenhower administration and had a closed belief system. He saw the Soviet Union as a hostile state and interpreted any data that might indicate a lessening of hostility in such a way that it reinforced his original perceptions. Cooperative Soviet gestures were not a sign of goodwill but the product of Soviet failures and represented only a lull before they would engage in another round of hostilities.

Events Policy Makers Learn from

The sporadic and constrained nature of the learning process means that not all aspects of the past are equally likely to serve as the source of lessons. Two categories of events are turned to most often by policy makers in their search for lessons. The first is the dramatic and highly visible event. Policy makers turn to these events out of the conviction that because they are so dramatic and visible they must contain more information about international politics than do more commonplace happenings. The scars they leave in defeat and the praises sung in victory are so deeply entrenched in the collective memory of society that the individual does not have to experience them personally in order to see them as holding lessons for the present. Events of this magnitude are often referred to as generational events because an entire generation draws upon them for lessons. War is the ultimate dramatic event. A policy maker need not have been involved in the negotiations at Munich to invoke the analogy and point to the dangers of appeasement or in Korea to cite the military and political problems of fighting a limited war.

The corollary to paying a great deal of attention to highly dramatic events is to all but ignore the nonevent. The crisis that almost happened but did not is not learned from. Warnings about the weakness of the Shah of Iran were heard as early as 1961 when members of the Senate Foreign Relations Committee warned the newly installed Kennedy administration that no number of weapons could save him. Mass unrest and corruption, they argued, doomed him to defeat. Senator Hubert Humphrey declared: "This crowd they are dead. They just don't know it. . . . It is just a matter of time."[8] Policy makers will invoke the images of the Marines killed by terrorists in Lebanon in debating policy but will fail to cite the terrorist attacks that were prevented by the timely use of intelligence. Rather than crediting intelligence with having anticipated an attack, they will question whether it was ever to have taken place. The more often the warning is given and no attack occurs, the easier it is for policy makers to dismiss the next warning. The November 27 warning to Pearl Harbor that a Japanese attack was possible was not the first such warning received. An alarming dispatch had been received in October, and no attack had followed. Also, there had been several other warnings issued during the course of 1941 that the Japanese in Honolulu were burning their codes.

The second type of event typically searched for lessons is that which the policy maker experienced firsthand. Especially important are those experiences that took place early in the policy maker's career. The lessons drawn from events experienced firsthand tend to be overgeneralized to the neglect of lessons that might be drawn from the careful analysis of the experiences of others. U.S. thinking about the post–World War II role of the atomic bomb provides an example of the pull of personally experienced events on policy making.[9] The initial decisions were made by the men who had defeated Germany and Japan. In formulating ideas about the uses to which the bomb might be put, they drew heavily upon these experiences. From 1945 to 1950, the Soviet targets identified for destruction by the atomic bomb duplicated those emphasized in the U.S. World War II policy of targeting commercial and industrial centers. To these men the atomic bomb was not a qualitatively new weapon for which a new strategy had to be developed. It was only the latest and most powerful weapon developed to date. It would be left to politicians to put forward the first strategy tailored to the political and technological realities of the postwar era.

The influence of firsthand experience on analogy drawing was fully evident in foreign aid debates in the Truman administration that occurred in 1950.[10] So, too, is the danger of reading our own preferences back into history. With 20-20 hindsight, we would expect that the Marshall Plan that was created in 1947 would be the dominant point of reference since it is generally regarded as the most successful post–World War II foreign aid program. But it was not. Instead most participants cited other programs and activities with which they had more familiarity. Members of professional associations overwhelmingly referenced U.S. business experience abroad and nondevelopment U.S. foreign policy programs. Representatives from voluntary associations tended to refer to the efforts of the United Nations and the actions of missionary and volunteer groups. Those in the executive branch spoke most often about other U.S. foreign policy programs, while congresspeople drew analogies with the Fulbright Program and the Smith-Mundt (Educational Exchange) Act that Congress had recently authorized.

Firsthand experiences that occur early in a policy maker's career are especially important because perceptual systems are resistant to change. Individuals are most open to competing images of reality when they confront a situation for the first time. Once selected, a label or category establishes the basis for future comparisons. These early firsthand experiences are not necessarily related to foreign policy problems. They may be ways of thinking about problems that proved successful in the past, positions taken on issues that produced the desired outcome, or strategies used in winning political office.[11] Early firsthand experiences are also of special significance because of the conditions under which policy makers must try to learn from the past. Decisions must be made, and a policy maker's attention is constantly spread over a wide variety of situations demanding his or her attention. Henry Kissinger spoke to these problems in his memoirs when he stated that "policy makers live off the intellectual capital they have brought with them into office; they have no time to build more capital."[12]

Types of Calculations Made about Those Events

When an event is recognized as a possible source of lessons, policy makers frequently engage in three types of calculations. First, they pay attention to what happened and seldom to why. The iron curtain descended across Europe; Vietnam fell; the American embassy was attacked, and hostages were taken. Focusing on what happened rather than on why creates a type of tunnel vision that obscures from view the differences between the present situation and earlier ones. What can one conclude from the fact that for the 1968 invasion of Czechoslovakia, the 1979 invasion of Afghanistan, and the 1981 noninvasion of Poland the Soviet Union required three months' preparation time? Betts suggests not very much.[13] Policy makers could not assume that the Soviets would need three months in order to prepare for the next invasion. None of these were extremely urgent cases; they do not preclude more rapid mobilizations or a mobilization starting at a higher stage of readiness.

Second, in examining what happened, policy makers tend to dichotomize the outcome into successes and failures. They tend to forget that most policy initiatives are designed to achieve multiple objectives, that success and failure are rarely ever total, and that neither success nor failure is permanent. Problems are not so much solved as redefined and transformed into new challenges and opportunities.

When a policy is defined as a success, policy makers are especially prone to ignore three considerations in applying it as a lesson: (1) its costs, (2) the possibility that another option would have worked better or produced the same result at less cost, and (3) the role accident, luck, and chance play in affecting the outcome of events. In the 1960s, careful observers felt compelled to warn policy makers not to read into the 1965 invasion of the Dominican Republic a formula for successful invasions elsewhere in Latin America. They cautioned that focusing on the success of the invasion diverted attention from such key issues as general weaknesses of U.S. policy in the Caribbean, the unique aspects of the situation in the Dominican Republic, acts of omission by the United States that brought about the need for an invasion, and the costs the invasion brought in terms of a deepening involvement of the United States in the domestic politics of the Dominican Republic.[14]

When defined as a failure, a different set of biases tends to grip policy-maker thinking. There is (1) the presumption that an alternative course of action would have worked better and that policy makers should have known this and (2) an unwillingness to admit that success may have been unattainable or that surprise is inevitable. The congressional investigation into Pearl Harbor takes up thirty-nine volumes, and the success of the Japanese attack continues to bring forward a never-ending series of books asserting that U.S. policy makers knew of the attack and permitted it to happen.

Third, to the extent that policy makers do seek to discover explanations, they tend to treat the most visible features of the situation as having had the biggest impact on the outcome of events. Diplomatic and military histories are written in terms of personalities and actors' strategies. Rarely is organizational planning, careful staff preparation, or bureaucratic coordination placed at the center of analysis.

Lessons Learned

Three lessons are most often learned by policy makers from their studies of history. The first is to expect to see more of the same. The Shah was expected to continue in power in 1979 simply because he had ruled for so long. Iran without the Shah seemed inconceivable. The grain shortage of 1973 caught U.S. policy makers by surprise because for policy makers "the grain problem" was always one of too much grain. It did not occur to them that the combination of large-scale Soviet purchases of grain plus global drought would send the price of grain in the United States skyrocketing.

A second lesson learned is to expect continuity in the behavior of other actors. In part this occurs because policy makers are insensitive to the perceived costs of inaction as viewed by another state. The United States made this mistake at Pearl Harbor. U.S. estimates of Japanese behavior were based on the cost of attacking the United States. Insufficient attention was given to the costs that the Japanese would experience if they did nothing and allowed the status quo to continue into the future. For similar reasons the hostile acts or words of allies surprise policy makers more than the hostility of an enemy. Having labeled a state as an ally, policy makers tend to become insensitive to the continuing conflicts of interest between them and the possibility that the ally will act to resolve them.

Third, policy makers learn to avoid policies that failed and to repeat policies that brought success. This would be fine if two conditions did not work against the continued success of a policy. First, successful policies get overused. They are applied to problems and situations for which they were not intended. Second, a successful policy often changes the situation in ways that will frustrate its future use. In the 1960s military aid to the Shah may indeed have been responsible for averting the coup predicted by members of the Senate Foreign Relations Committee, but it also changed the situation so that by the late 1970s continued military aid became part of the Shah's problem instead of the answer.

These three lessons cast a long shadow over U.S. foreign policy making in the lead-up to the Iraq War. First, policy makers expected to see more of the same. There was an unstated expectation that the proliferation of weapons of mass destruction, especially in so far as rogue states was concerned, was an inevitable and dangerous feature of international relations. As Scott Sagan notes in speaking specifically about nuclear proliferation, the dominant view is that proliferation is a "strategic chain reaction."[15] Iraq under Saddam Hussein was the most recent addition to this chain. North Korea's public declaration that it was pursuing a nuclear capability as war neared gave added credence to the sense of historical inevitability. Second, it was assumed that Saddam Hussein was evil and could not be trusted to change his policies or at a minimum be contained as a security threat. Few doubted that he possessed weapons of mass destruction. Iraq had come close to possessing a nuclear capability at the time of the Persian Gulf War and used chemical weapons against Iran in the Iran–Iraq War. Evidence (now discredited) pointed to continuing weapons programs. Moreover, Saddam Hussein was engaged in an ongoing game of deception and obstruction with UN weapons inspectors. Why would he do this unless he was trying to hide something? After the fact, when no weapons of mass destruction were found, Kenneth Pollack suggests that a possibility existed that was not considered.[16] Saddam Hussein was acting out of a fear that if his bluff was exposed his enemies within Iraq would be emboldened and his hold on power seriously weakened. Finally, the George W. Bush administration was determined to avoid what it saw as the central mistake made by George H. W. Bush in the Persian Gulf War when, rather than continue fighting and remove Saddam Hussein from power, it sought to achieve this end through supporting domestic forces opposed to him.

Learning from the Past: Case Studies

Our attention now shifts to an examination of the cold war, Vietnam, and the Persian Gulf War. The primary concern in looking at the cold war is to illustrate the difficulty of drawing lessons from an event when there is so little agreement about its basic nature. Our focus is on three questions central to the process of learning from an event: When did it begin? Whose fault, if anyone's, was it? Why did it end? We cannot hope to learn from an event if we do not have a clear sense of its dynamics or of our own responsibility for how it unfolded. To err in the first instance will result in mistaking a symptom of a problem for the problem itself. To err in the second instance leads either to an arrogance of power as we overestimate our own importance or to a crippling sense of guilt as we blame ourselves for too much. The purpose of examining Vietnam is twofold. First, Vietnam is used to provide a look at the range of lessons used by policy makers in making decisions. The lessons of the past used by members of the Kennedy and Johnson administrations in arguing for and against various policy options provide the material for this part of the case study. The second reason for looking at Vietnam is to illustrate the range of lessons that American elites have drawn from U.S. involvement. We examine the Persian Gulf War in order to get a better understanding about the reasons for the failure of American efforts at deterrence and compellence. A debate is under way as to which of these two strategies is best suited for the post–cold war era. The Persian Gulf War may hold important insights because it provided the first post–cold war test of these two strategies.

THE COLD WAR

In 1989, academics as well as policy makers in both the Soviet Union and the United States proclaimed an end to the cold war. George Kennan, the father of the containment doctrine around which so much of U.S. cold war foreign policy was built, stated that "whatever reasons there may once have existed for regarding the Soviet Union primarily as a possible, if not probable, military opponent, the time for that sort of thing has clearly passed. . . . [It] should now be regarded essentially as another great power like other great powers."[17]

For all of the scholarship that has been directed at it, the cold war remains for many "the most enigmatic and elusive international conflict of modern time."[18] For our purposes we define it as a period of competition, hostility, and tension between the Western powers and communist bloc states. While frequently intense, it never escalated into direct and open warfare between the two bloc leaders—the Soviet Union and the United States. No single issue or geographic area dominated the conflict. At any one point in time, the U.S.–Soviet cold war interactions were characterized by some combination of political maneuvering, diplomatic wrangling, psychological warfare, ideological competition, economic coercion, arms races, and proxy wars.

Beginnings of the Cold War.   At least four different starting points have been given to the cold war. The conventional starting point is the immediate post–World War II period. World War II is also often employed as a starting point. Less frequently used are the 1917-to-1920 era and the interwar period. Our concern in this section is with evaluating the merits of these competing starting points. Is one position more compelling than the rest? Are they mutually exclusive? Can they be integrated into a composite explanation that is superior to any single explanation? Before taking up these issues, we briefly present the evidence typically cited supporting each of the four starting points.

1917 to 1920.   The earliest starting point for the cold war employed with any frequency is the period beginning with the November 1917 revolution and continuing through the ensuing civil war.[19] Table 5.1 presents a chronology of major dates in the history of the cold war. The March 1917 revolution caught all of the revolutionary parties unprepared. The czar was replaced by a provisional government that was backed by the Western Powers because of its pledge to continue Russia's participation in World War I. Within Russia this government walked a tightrope. It occupied an unstable middle ground between leftist revolutionary forces and right-wing reactionary groups. On November 7, 1917, its life came to an end when the Bolsheviks seized power. Lenin was unalterably opposed to Russia's continued participation in what he saw to be an imperialist war, and one day after taking control of the government, the Bolshevik party set in motion Russia's with-

TABLE 5.1   Chronology of the Cold War: 1917–1950

March 1917	Czar overthrown; provisional government established.
November 1917	Bolshevik Revolution.
March 1918	Treaty of Brest-Litovsk ends Russian participation in war.
April 1918	Japanese troops enter Russia followed by U.S., U.K., and France.
March 1919	COMINTERN established.
June 1919	Versailles Treaty signed.
December 1922	U.S.S.R. is officially established.
November 1933	U.S. recognizes Soviet Union.
September 1938	Munich Agreement.
August 1939	German–Russian Nonaggression Pact.
November 1939	Russia invades Finland.
June 1941	Germany invades Russia.
February 1945	Yalta Conference.
August 1945	Atomic bomb dropped on Hiroshima.
April 1946	Iranian crisis begins.
March 1947	Truman Doctrine announced.
June 1947	Marshall Plan for recovery of Europe outlined.
September 1947	COMINFORM created.
February 1948	Communists seize power in Czechoslovakia.
June 1948	Berlin crisis begins.
April 1949	NATO established.
August 1949	Russia explodes first atomic bomb.
June 1950	North Korea invades South Korea.

drawal by issuing a Declaration of Peace calling for an immediate peace without annexations or indemnities. A preliminary armistice was soon signed between Russia and Germany, and then on March 15, 1918, a final peace treaty was signed at Brest-Litovsk.

The Soviet exit from the war coupled with an almost simultaneous German offensive in the West spread panic through the allied leadership. On April 9, 1918, Japan sent troops into the Soviet Union. Great Britain, France, and the United States followed suit. Although a heavy dose of anti-Bolshevik sentiment influenced the U.S. decision to intervene, the objectives were pictured as quite limited. Militarily, it was to prevent allied war material from falling into German hands and to help the Czech Legion escape from the Soviet Union so that it could continue fighting on the Western Front. A political objective was to check the ongoing expansion of the Japanese presence in Siberia. By this rationale the Western presence in the Soviet Union should have ceased on November 11, 1918, with the ending of World War I, but it did not. American forces did not leave the Soviet Union until early 1920. From the end of World War I until their departure, Western troops took part in the Russian civil war lending support to the white (anticommunist) forces.

The Interwar Period.   U.S.–Soviet relations improved little during the interwar period.[20] Two points of tension were carryovers from their 1917-to-1920 encounters. The Soviets continued to feel slighted over the United States' withholding of diplomatic recognition, which did not come until 1933. For its part the United States remained suspicious of communist intentions. The Soviet Union was pursuing a two-track foreign policy. At the official level the Soviet Union sought normal relations with the West. On another level it was seeking to spread revolution and overthrow capitalism. The specific object of U.S. and Western concern was COMINTERN. Created in 1919, it was an international organization of communist parties headquartered in Moscow but theoretically not connected with the Soviet government. Its avowed purpose was to undermine capitalist society from within and to counter the actions of traditional Western European socialist democratic parties.

As World War II approached, new issues emerged that raised the level of distrust and suspicion existing between the Soviet Union and the United States and brought the two powers into ever closer and more continuous contact. One issue was the repeated rejection by the West of Soviet appeals at the League of Nations for a collective security system directed at Hitler. Matters came to a head with the Munich crisis of September 29–30, 1938. Without Soviet or Czech participation, the British and French sought to achieve "peace in our time" by acceding to Hitler's demand that the Sudetenland be incorporated into the Third Reich. In the Soviets' eyes this had the effect of both inviting a German attack on the Soviet Union and providing a gateway to carry it out.

The primary Soviet foreign policy goal since at least 1934 had been to keep the Soviet Union out of war. Stalin now acted with a renewed sense of urgency to accomplish this objective. His efforts culminated in the signing of the Molotov–Ribbentrop Pact on August 31, 1939. Stalin saw himself as having bought two things with the treaty: time to prepare for a possible war with Germany, and territory. Secret protocols to the pact gave the Soviet Union rights to eastern Poland and the Baltic region. The West saw duplicity in the treaty for at the same time that Stalin was negotiating with Hitler, he was also engaged in talks with the West about new security arrangements. Soviet motives and sincerity were further questioned with its November 1939 invasion of Finland.

World War II.   Hitler's surprise attack on the Soviet Union instantly transformed it from an aggressor state into a valuable Western ally. It did little, however, to bring a greater degree of trust to their relationship. Almost immediately, controversy developed over the delay in opening the second front. Promised by Roosevelt in 1942 and again in 1943, the Normandy landing did not take place until June 1944. Western leaders based their case for delay on a lack of invasion barges, the need for careful planning, and the time required to build up the necessary military forces. Soviet leaders saw it differently. They placed greater emphasis on Winston Churchill's declaration that there would be no invasion until Germany was weakened to the point where Western casualties would not be excessive.[21] The Soviets saw in Western delays an attempt to lock Germany and the Soviet Union into a series of battles that would leave them militarily exhausted and the Soviet Union vulnerable to future Western pressures.

From the Western point of view, Soviet unwillingness to commit itself to fighting Japan was a major irritation. The American military lobbied hard for a guarantee of Soviet participation in the war against Japan at the earliest possible date. Without such participation it was estimated that the war in the Pacific would continue eighteen to twenty-four months after the end of fighting in Europe. Soviet assurances were only given at Yalta in 1945 when Stalin pledged to commit Soviet troops no later than 90 days after the defeat of Germany. Of all the war-related controversies, it is the American decision to drop the atomic bomb that has emerged as one of the fundamental points of disagreement between the orthodox and the revisionist interpretations of the cold war. In the orthodox view, the use of the atomic bomb was based on military considerations. Without its use, not only would the war with Japan drag on, but its termination would require an invasion of the home islands at a high cost in American lives. The revisionist interpretation sees in the dropping of the atomic bomb not military necessity but political maneuvering. They see the Japanese military capability as being overstated by the orthodox interpretation. In the revisionist view, the atomic bomb was used to send a signal to the Soviet Union that the United States had "sufficient power to affect the developments in the border regions of the Soviet Union" and that the United States was prepared to take a "firm" stance in negotiations over the shape of the postwar world.[22]

The Post World War II Era.   Those who date the cold war as beginning in the post–World War II era place the greatest emphasis on events between 1946 and the beginning of the Korean War. It is in this period that the Soviet Union and the United States repeatedly collided over the political-geographic debris of World War II. At Yalta the United States and the Soviet Union had presumably reached an understanding on how the power vacuum in Eastern Europe was to be filled. Roosevelt felt that he had received Stalin's agreement to free elections in which all democratic parties could participate. The systematic exclusion of pro-Western parties from the electoral process in Poland and throughout Eastern Europe struck many in the West as a doublecross. To Stalin it was simple realpolitik. For its security the Soviet Union had to have a defensive corridor on its European border. The Soviet position was that U.S. troops occupied Italy and Japan and determined the nature of those governments. So, too, would Soviet troops determine the nature of the Eastern European governments.

The fate of Eastern Europe was only one of a host of issues that came together in rapid-fire succession to throw a cloud over postwar U.S.–Soviet relations. June 1945 saw a Soviet attempt to pressure Turkey into a revision of the Dardanelles Strait Agreement that would have given the Soviet Union partial administrative control over naval bases as well as the entry point from the Black Sea to the Mediterranean Sea. The year 1946 found the Soviet Union and the United States in conflict over Iran when Soviet troops refused to leave according to the schedule agreed upon at the Tehran Conference. Instead, the Soviet Union attempted to create Soviet-dominated republics out of Iran's northern provinces by first manipulating the Azerbaijanian population and then the Kurdish minority. Soviet pressure was also placed on Greece in 1946 in the form of an expansion and intensification of the ongoing civil war.

The year 1948 was pivotal in U.S.–Soviet cold war relations. First, the COMINFORM (Communist Information Bureau) was created. Like the COMINTERN before it, the COMINFORM was a vehicle for uniting communist parties under Soviet leadership. The COMINTERN had been disbanded during the war as a sign of good faith, and the creation of this new organization raised new doubts about the Soviet Union's true motives and fueled fears of communist subversion.

Second, there occurred the first of the post–war Berlin crises. The original intention of the allies was that Germany was not to be partitioned but only divided into occupation zones for administrative purposes. By 1948, however, the U.S. and British zones had been merged, and the Western powers were discussing the future of Germany without consulting the Soviets. On June 18, 1948, the Western allies instituted a currency reform in their zones. That evening the Soviet Union, informed the Western Powers that they no longer had any right of access to Berlin. The Soviets then cut off all surface traffic from Berlin to the Western zones. Three days later the United States and Britain launched a massive air supply operation to keep West Berlin afloat. Three hundred and twenty-four days later the blockade was lifted, with Germany and Berlin firmly divided into eastern and western zones.

Finally, 1948 saw the downfall of the pro-Soviet but noncommunist Benes government in Czechoslovakia. Alone among the Eastern European states, Czechoslovakia had a tradition of democracy. The first postwar election produced a coalition government. In February 1948, amid indications that the Czech communist party would not fare well in an upcoming election it engineered a coup. In its aftermath pro-Western political elements were purged, and Czechoslovakia came to resemble the other Soviet-dominated Eastern European satellite states.

The year 1949 brought little relief as tensions continued to mount. In April 1949 the United States and eleven of its Western European and Atlantic allies signed the treaty establishing the North Atlantic Treaty Organization (NATO). Through it, the United States pledged itself to the defense of Western Europe. In late 1949, U.S. security interests were dealt a double blow. The Soviet Union unexpectedly detonated an atomic bomb, which ended the American atomic monopoly years before U.S. policy makers had thought possible. Second, there was the "fall of China." It was inconceivable to most Americans that its ally, Jiang Jienshi (Chiang Kai-shek), could be defeated by the communist Mao Zedong. China now had to be added to the Soviet Union as a major communist power to be contained. All of these accumulated tensions spilled into the open in June 1950 when North Korea attacked South Korea. The cold war was now firmly established, and it had a global rather than just a European character to it.

When Did It Begin?   Having reviewed the historical record, the question remains, When did the cold war begin? The best answer may be, "It depends." It depends on what it is about the cold war that you are interested in or hold to be most important. If the overall pattern of U.S.–Soviet interaction is the primary concern, then the post–World War II era is the most appropriate place to date its origins. It is only at this point in time that overall U.S.–Soviet interactions take on the necessary degree of permanence, intensity, and tension to merit the label *cold war.* Prior to World War II, U.S.–Soviet interactions, while often adversarial in nature, were too intermittent and fragmented to produce the intensity or tension that later contacts did. Even during World War II when interactions did become permanent and intense, U.S.–Soviet tensions were always muted by the mutually recognized need to unite against Hitler. Stalin disbanded the COMINTERN and toned down the ideological rhetoric. Roosevelt earnestly sought to allay Soviet fears of Western duplicity and often distanced himself from Churchill's staunch anticommunist positions.

If, however, one sees in the historical record not one but many cold wars, then the post–World War II era is often a less satisfactory starting point.[23] Viewed as a conflict between rival ideologies, the 1917-to-1920 era is the most appropriate starting point. When viewed as a competition for global influence and prestige, the most appropriate starting point may not be until the late 1950s or early 1960s when Cuba, Africa, Asia, and Latin America became battlegrounds for U.S. and Soviet foreign policy. If one takes the cold war to be primarily an arms race between the superpowers, then the Korean War may be the date to select, for it is with its involvement in Korea that the United States reversed its policy of retrenchment and began to expand its armed forces.

Last, if the European balance of power is used as the focal point, we may have two different starting points. The Soviet Union clearly identified its national security interests with the distribution of power in Europe as early as the 1930s. Only after World War II did the United States act with an appreciation for the importance of Europe to its national security. In fact, it is this mutual recognition of the importance of Europe to their national security that first gave postwar U.S.–Soviet interactions the high degree of permanence, intensity, and tension that brought into existence the concept of a cold war.

Placing Responsibility.   Subject to even more disagreement than when the cold war began is who, if anyone, was responsible for it. According to the orthodox interpretation, responsibility for the cold war is placed on the Soviet Union.[24] The United States is pictured as basically reacting to and trying to check Soviet outward thrusts. Where advocates of the orthodox view see a constant pattern of Soviet expansion combined with an inflexible and Messianic ideology, the revisionists see an insecure and weak Soviet Union.[25] In their view, the United States is primarily responsible for the cold war. Its misreading of Soviet goals (which are held by revisionists to be fundamentally defensive in nature), exaggeration of Soviet military power, and obsession with communism combined to produce a series of policies that left the Soviet Union no choice but to act unilaterally in protecting its national interests.

As examples of unwarranted and overly aggressive U.S. policies, revisionists cite the dropping of the atomic bomb, the abrupt ending of lend-lease, British and U.S. actions in Germany, the handling of the Marshall Plan, the rhetoric of the Truman Doctrine, and the creation of NATO. They also cite the considerable evidence that Stalin was not determined from the outset to establish miniature Stalinist systems in Eastern Europe. The decision to do so was taken only as U.S.–Soviet relations deteriorated and the cold war intensified.

Other schools of thought on the origins of the cold war reject attempts to assign responsibility. Advocates of these interpretations see the United States and Soviet Union as victims of international politics and the nature of the state system. One version holds that a clash between the two states was all but inevitable given what had already transpired in Europe. Louis Halle, for example, asserts that the cold war is the fourth in a series of great wars that have been fought to maintain or restore the European balance of power. He lists the Napoleonic Wars, World War I, and World War II as its predecessors.[26] A second line of argument sees the United States and Soviet Union as having become locked into a conflict spiral. In such a situation the initial moves of each side are calculated to meet a specific end, but the struggle itself soon comes to dominate the players and impose a different logic and set of imperatives upon them. In essence, the conflict begins to feed upon itself, and players lose control over their own actions. Central to the dynamics of a conflict spiral are mutual fear and suspicion.[27] They combine to produce an inherent distrust of the opponent's motives and often distort the meaning of his actions. Breaking out of a conflict spiral is extremely difficult to accomplish. Economic or political exhaustion is one method; war is another. However, neither method is guaranteed to prevent the conflict spiral from starting up again.

Learning from the past requires making sense out of these alternative positions. One way of bringing a sense of order to these competing views is to disaggregate the cold war into various dimensions, as we did in discussing when it began, and raising the question of responsibility for each dimension. A second approach is to recognize that these interpretations are pitched at different levels of analysis. Interpretations that place the behavior of the United States and Soviet Union in the context of a conflict spiral or a struggle over the balance of power rest on a reading of the dynamics of the international systems. Systems-level analysis views foreign policy as an attempt by states to adapt to their geopolitical environment. The process of adaptation is often one that leaves few, if any, alternatives in the eyes of policy makers. The question of responsibility becomes secondary to the needs of adjustment and self-preservation.

Assessing cold war responsibility at this level involves asking types of questions that the orthodox and revisionist do not address. The concern is not with purpose. (Why did the Soviet Union refuse to leave Iran?) It is with identifying factors—including those that policy makers themselves may have been only dimly aware of—that provide the necessary and sufficient conditions for the emergence of a particular orientation toward the international system.[28]

The standard orthodox and revisionist interpretations operate on a strategic level of analysis. At this level, actions are evaluated by placing oneself in the position of the policy maker in an attempt to determine the rationale for his or her action. Typically, the state is viewed as a unified actor, and rationality is assumed. According to Charles Learche, the key to understanding strategic interactions is to identify the state's strategic concept, which he views to be a composite formulation of a state's sense of national purpose, a situational estimate, and its fundamental operating principles.[29] The question of responsibility then becomes one of identifying and judging the appropriateness of the strategic concepts employed by the United States and the Soviet Union.

Finally, cold war responsibility can be assessed at the decision-making level. Interpretations that stress Truman's or Stalin's personality, belief systems, or the impact of bureaucratic factors operate on this level. Responsibility is assigned here for specific actions on the assumption that strategic concepts lend themselves to more than one interpretation when applied to a specific situation. Defense of Greece and Turkey may have been dictated by U.S. strategic principles, but the rationale presented in the Truman Doctrine was not. It bore the imprint of specific personalities, belief systems, and bureaucratic interests.

The real challenge in addressing the question of responsibility is making judgments about how the forces associated with the three levels come together to produce a phenomenon as complex as the cold war. Under what conditions do forces at one level dominate those at another? Is the pattern consistent over time? What points of opportunity are open to policy makers who wish to limit conflict or simply direct events in a certain direction? When is the danger of war or a major escalation greatest?

Why Did the Cold War End?   That the cold war is over seems clear. What is not clear is why it ended. Both practitioners and scholars were caught off guard. Each group had come to treat it as a fact of life and had not anticipated the possibility that it might end. Consequently, neither their policies nor their theories were directed at bringing this about or predicting its occurrence.[30] The question of why it ended is important because the answer can be seen as validating the correctness of certain policy lines, thus promoting them as a way of settling future conflicts.

Initial efforts to explain the end of the cold war had a decidedly political coloring. Conservatives attributed it to the success of Reagan's foreign policy of "peace through strength." For them the end of the cold war was a vindication of George Kennan's containment strategy. Kennan had prophesied that should Soviet leaders be confronted by the constant application of counterpressure, not only would their expansionist efforts be thwarted but the Soviet political system would also be transformed. The Reagan administration's combination of military and ideological assertiveness signaled a marked reversal in U.S. foreign policy from the détente era of Nixon and

Carter. No longer was the United States interested in making the world safe for communism, according to this line of thought. The administration's disinterest in arms control and its rapid expansion in the size of the defense budget spoke to a new willingness to challenge the Soviet Union militarily. The avowed goal of the Reagan Doctrine was not only to contain the spread of communism but to unseat existing communist governments. Reagan's ideological rhetoric reinforced the point that there would be no compromises with Soviet leaders. The problem facing Soviet leaders in responding to a determined Reagan administration was that decades of neglect and mismanagement had reduced the Soviet economy to the point where it could not provide the basis for an effective counterchallenge.

Liberals saw the end of the cold war differently. They pointed to the importance of Western internationalist ideas. Of particular significance from their point of view were the influences of globalist values and antinuclearism. Both were important because of the lack of foreign policy sophistication on the part of Gorbachev and his key advisers. These ideas provided them with a means of putting their stamp on the foreign policy establishment and a way of advancing their domestic agenda. Globalism introduced these new Soviet leaders to such key concepts as interdependence and ecological sustainability. It also highlighted the role that international organizations such as the United Nations could play in ensuring Russian security. The principal Western proponent of antinuclearism was Ronald Reagan. This aspect of Reagan's thinking often is downplayed by conservatives, but to liberals it was crucial for the end of the cold war. From their perspective it was this part of Reagan's foreign policy agenda that Gorbachev was responding to and not his hardline military posture. Reagan's antinuclearism gave Gorbachev hope that arms control initiatives would not be dismissed out of hand and that they provided an avenue for redirecting Soviet expenditures so as to further economic reform. Beth Fischer suggests that this more conciliatory side of Reagan's foreign policy emerged some fifteen months prior to Gorbachev's coming to power. What remains unclear is why the shift away from its more confrontational policy took place.[31]

More recent efforts to explain the end of the cold war have drawn a much more complex picture. Attention has shifted away from simply identifying those aspects of American foreign policy or American society that challenged Soviet leaders or were found inviting by them to uncovering links between these forces and Soviet domestic politics.[32] One of the arguments made by many who take this approach is to caution against claiming too much credit on behalf of American foreign policy in ending the cold war. For example, Raymond Garthoff argues that "the American role in ending the Cold War was necessary but, naturally, not primary . . . in the final analysis, because the Cold War rested on Marxist-Leninist assumptions of inevitable world conflict, only a Soviet leader could have ended it."[33]

One of the consequences of treating Soviet politics as a key part to understanding why the cold war ended is that it directs attention to the process of learning that Soviet leaders may have engaged in after Brezhnev's death. Among the tentative findings put forward by researchers is that Gorbachev learned inductively through trial and error, and that one of the reasons that he was able to learn was that he was a relatively uncommitted thinker on national security problems and open to new ideas.[34] Also playing an important but even role in the process of learning that took place in both the East and West as the cold war ended were networks of transnational actors (scientists, policy analysts, political leaders) who were able to gain access to the Soviet political system.[35] They then helped put together a "winning coalition" that supported Gorbachev's new thinking in foreign policy.

VIETNAM

America's involvement in Vietnam spanned the terms of six presidents. The cost of the war and its level of destruction were enormous: 55,000 American dead; a maximum American troop presence of 541,000 men; a total cost of $150 billion; untold numbers of Vietnamese dead and wounded; seven million tons of bombs dropped; and 20 million craters left behind. Table 5.2 presents a chronology of major events in the history of the U.S. presence in Vietnam. Our purpose in examining Vietnam is not to establish responsibility but to highlight (1) the types and sources of lessons used by U.S. foreign policy makers in making decisions and (2) the lessons that have emerged from this involvement. This type of evaluation is necessary both to better understand Vietnam and to evaluate assertions that Angola, Nicaragua, or country X is another Vietnam. The need for it is evident in the ignorance of the public and U.S. policy makers about what happened there. A public opinion poll taken March 21–25, 1985, revealed that only three in five Americans knew that the United States supported South Vietnam. In a press conference on February 18, 1982, in response to a question about covert operations in Latin America, President Reagan stated:

> If I recall correctly, . . . North and South Vietnam had been, previous to colonization, two separate countries [and] provisions were made that these two countries could, by the vote of their people together, decide whether they wanted to be one country or not. . . . Ho Chi Minh refused to participate in such an election. . . . John F. Kennedy authorized the sending of a division of Marines. And that was the first move toward combat troops in Vietnam.[36]

Vietnam Chronology.   The first president to have to deal with Vietnam was Truman. Initially, his views on Indochina resembled those held during World War II by Roosevelt, who was sympathetic to Ho Chi Minh's efforts to establish independence for the region and unsympathetic to French attempts to reestablish their prewar position of colonial domination. In 1947 Truman resisted French requests for U.S. aid and urged France to end the war against Ho Chi Minh who, while one of the founders of the French communist party, had proven himself a valuable ally and nationalist in defeating Japan. Truman's views were soon to undergo a stark and rapid transformation. By 1952, the United States was providing France with $30 million in aid to defeat Ho Chi Minh, and in 1953, when his presidency ended, the United States was paying one-third of the French war cost. Ho Chi Minh was also redefined from a nationalist into a communist threat to U.S. security interests. Nothing

TABLE 5.2   Chronology of U.S. Involvement in Vietnam

September 1940	France gives Japan right of transit, control over local military facilities, and control over economic resources in return for right to keep nominal sovereignty.
March 1945	Gaullist French forces take over administration of Vietnam from pro-Vichy French troops.
September 1945	Ho Chi Minh declares Vietnam to be independent.
February 1950	U.S. recognizes French-backed Bao Dai government.
March 1954	French forces defeated at Dien Bien Phu.
April 1954	Geneva Peace Talks begin; end in July.
September 1954	SEATO created.
July 1956	No elections held in Vietnam.
October 1961	Taylor–Rostow mission sent to Vietnam; 15,000 advisers sent in as a result.
November 1963	Diem and Kennedy assassinated.
August 1964	Gulf of Tonkin incident.
February 1965	Pleiku barracks attacked; 8 U.S. dead and 60 injured; Operation Rolling Thunder launched in retaliation.
May 1965	Westmoreland requests 80,000 troops.
July 1965	Johnson announces an additional 125,000 troops to be sent to Vietnam.
January 1968	Tet Offensive.
March 1968	Bombing halted; Johnson steps out of presidential race.
April 1970	Cambodia invaded.
March 1972	Major North Vietnamese offensive launched.
April 1972	B-52 bombings of Hanoi and Haiphong.
May 1972	North Vietnamese harbors mined.
December 1972	Peace talks collapse and then resume after heavy bombing.
January 1973	Peace agreement signed.
March 1975	North Vietnamese offensive begins.
April 1975	South Vietnam surrenders.

had changed in Indochina to warrant this new evaluation of the situation. Dramatic events, however, were taking place elsewhere as cold war competition took root. In the process, decisions on Indochina came to be viewed in a larger context. France was reluctant to participate in a European Defense System, something the United States saw as vital if Europe was to contain communist expansionist pressures. In a virtual quid pro quo, the United States agreed to underwrite the French war effort in Indochina the same day France announced its intent to participate in plans for the defense of Europe.

The Eisenhower administration began by reaffirming Truman's financial commitment to France and then enlarged upon it. By the end of 1953, U.S. aid rose to $500 million and covered approximately one-half of the cost of the French war effort. For Eisenhower and Secretary of State John Foster

Dulles, expenditures of this magnitude were necessary to prevent a Chinese intervention that they both felt was otherwise likely to occur. Unfortunately for the French, U.S. aid was not enough to secure victory, and Eisenhower was unwilling to go beyond financing a proxy war.

The end came for the French at Dien Bien Phu. With its forces under siege there, France informed the United States that unless it intervened Indochina would fall to the communists. With no aid forthcoming, the process of withdrawal began. France's involvement in Indochina officially came to an end with the signing of the 1954 Geneva Peace Accords. According to this agreement, a "provisional demarcation line" would be established at the seventeenth parallel. Vietminh troops loyal to Ho Chi Minh would regroup north of it, and pro-French Vietnamese forces would regroup south of it. Elections were scheduled for 1956 to determine who would rule over the single country of Vietnam. The Geneva Accords provided the French with the necessary face-saving way out of Indochina. Ho Chi Minh's troops controlled three-quarters of Vietnam and were poised to extend their area of control. All parties to the agreement expected Ho Chi Minh to win the 1956 election easily.

The United States did not sign the Geneva Accords but pledged to "refrain from the threat or use of force to disturb" the settlement. However, only six weeks after its signing, the Southeast Asia Treaty Organization (SEATO) was established as part of an effort to halt the spread of communism in the wake of the French defeat. Signatory states to this collective security pact were Great Britain, France, New Zealand, Pakistan, the Philippines, Thailand, Australia, and the United States. A protocol extended coverage to Laos, Cambodia, and "the free people under the jurisdiction of Vietnam." The Vietminh saw the protocol as a violation of the Geneva Accords because it treated the seventeenth parallel as a political boundary and not as a civil war truce line. Political developments below the seventeenth parallel supported the Vietminh interpretation. In 1955, the United States backed Ngo Dinh Diem, who had declared himself president of the Republic of Vietnam. With U.S. support he argued that since South Vietnam had not signed the Geneva Accords, it did not have to abide by it and hold elections. The year 1956 came and went with no elections. By the time Eisenhower left office, U.S. military aid reached the point where one thousand U.S. military advisers were stationed in South Vietnam.

The landmark decision on Vietnam during the Kennedy administration came in October 1961 with the Taylor–Rostow Report. Receiving contradictory information and advice on how to proceed, Kennedy sent General Maxwell Taylor and Walt Rostow to Vietnam on a fact-finding mission. They reported that South Vietnam could only be saved by the introduction of eight thousand U.S. combat troops. Kennedy rejected this conclusion, but while skeptical of the argument, he did send an additional fifteen thousand military advisers. Kennedy's handling of the Taylor–Rostow Report is significant for two reasons. First, the decision was typical of those he made on Vietnam. He never gave the advocates of escalation all that they wanted, but neither did he ever say no. Some increase in the level of the American military commitment was always forthcoming. Second, in acting on the Taylor–Rostow Report, Kennedy helped shift the definition of the Vietnam conflict from a political problem to a military one. Until this point Vietnam was seen by the Kennedy administration as a guerrilla war in which control of the population was key. From now on, control of the battlefield was to become the priority item.

Under Johnson, U.S. involvement in the war steadily escalated. Pressures began building in January 1964 when the joint chiefs of staff (JCS) urged him to put aside U.S. self-imposed restraints so that the war might be won more quickly. They especially urged aerial bombing of North Vietnam. In August 1964 this bombing began in retaliation for an incident in the Gulf of Tonkin. The United States stated that two North Vietnamese PT boats fired on the *C. Turner Joy* and the *Maddox* in neutral waters. President Johnson also went to Congress for a resolution supporting his use of force against North Vietnam. The Gulf of Tonkin Resolution passed by a unanimous vote in the House and by an 88 to 2 vote in the Senate. It gave the president the authority to "take all necessary measures to repel any armed attack against the forces of the United States and to prevent further aggression." The incident itself is clouded in controversy. Later studies suggest that the incident was staged or that it never occurred. These views hold that Johnson was merely looking for an excuse to begin the bombing.[37] In the eyes of many, the Gulf of Tonkin Resolution became the functional equivalent of a declaration of war.

From that point forward, the war became increasingly Americanized. Operation Rolling Thunder, a sustained and massive bombing campaign, was launched against North Vietnam in retaliation for the February 1965 Vietcong attack on Pleiku. In June, the military sought 200,000 ground forces and projected a need for 600,000 troops by 1967. U.S. goals were also changing. A Pentagon Papers memorandum put forward the following priorities: 70 percent to avoid a humiliating defeat; 20 percent to keep South Vietnam from China; and 10 percent to permit the people of South Vietnam to enjoy a better, freer way of life.[38]

The Tet Offensive in January 1968 brought yet another challenge to the Johnson administration, and in many ways it was the final challenge. In March 1968 Johnson announced a halt in the bombings against North Vietnam and that he was not a candidate for reelection. The Tet Offensive was a countrywide conventional assault by communist forces on South Vietnam. It penetrated Saigon, all of the provincial capitals, and even the U.S. embassy compound. The U.S. response was massive and expanded bombings of North Vietnam. In the end the communist forces were defeated. As a final thrust to take control of South Vietnam, it had been premature, but it did demonstrate the bankruptcy of U.S. policy. Massive bombings and hundreds of thousands of U.S. combat troops had not brought the United States closer to victory.

Establishing détente was Nixon's primary concern, and this policy could be threatened by any weakness or vacillation in U.S. policy on Vietnam. American commitments to Vietnam had to be met if the Soviet Union and China were to respect the United States in the post-Vietnam era. The strategy selected for accomplishing this was Vietnamization. Gradually, the United States would reduce its combat presence such that by 1972 the South Vietnamese army would be able to hold its own when supported by U.S. air and naval power and economic aid.

The inherent weakness of Vietnamization was that the strategy could succeed only if the North Vietnamese did not attack in the transition period before the South Vietnamese army was ready. Nixon and Kissinger designed a two-pronged approach to lessen the likelihood that this would occur. Cambodia was invaded with the hope of cleaning out North Vietnamese sanctuaries, and the bombing of North Vietnam was increased. Nevertheless, the potential danger became a reality when in the spring of 1972 North Vietnam attacked across the demilitarized zone (DMZ). At this point Nixon was forced to re-Americanize the war in order to prevent the defeat of South Vietnam. Bombing of North Vietnam now reached unprecedented levels, and North Vietnamese ports were mined.

Being carried out against the backdrop of this fighting were the Paris Peace Talks. They had begun in earnest in 1969 but had made little progress. With this escalation of the war Nixon also offered a new peace plan, which included a promise to withdraw all U.S. forces after an Indochina-wide cease-fire and exchange of prisoners of war (POWs). Progress was now forthcoming. Hanoi was finding itself increasingly isolated from the Soviet Union and China, both of whom had become more interested in establishing a working relationship with the United States than in defeating it in Vietnam. It was now South Vietnam that began to object to the peace terms and stalled the negotiating process. In early December, the "final talks" broke off without an agreement. On December 18, 1972, the United States ordered the all-out bombing of Hanoi and Haiphong to demonstrate U.S. resolve to both North and South Vietnamese leaders. On December 30, talks resumed, and the bombing was ended. A peace treaty was signed on January 23, 1973.

President Ford was in office when South Vietnam fell in 1975. What had begun as a normal military engagement ended in a rout. On March 12, 1975, the North Vietnamese attacked across the DMZ. On March 25 Hue fell. Five days later Da Nang fell. The United States evacuated on April 29, and on April 30 South Vietnam surrendered unconditionally.

Lessons Used by Policy Makers.   In examining the lessons used by policy makers in their decision making on Vietnam, our focus is on the Kennedy and Johnson administrations because it is here that the major escalations in the type and level of the U.S. commitment took place. We can identify two broad types of lessons of the past held by U.S. policy makers. The first are political lessons, and the second are strategic and tactical ones.

The political lessons of the past differed for elected and appointed policy makers only in their details. The bottom line was the same: Personal survival in the upper circles of decision making in Washington required creating an image of toughness. The source of this lesson for elected officials was the "loss" of China. The Republicans had successfully leveled this charge against the Democrats. Kennedy applied the same strategy against Nixon in 1960, accusing the Eisenhower administration of losing Cuba. Politically, Kennedy saw Vietnam as his China. Johnson drew the same lessons as did Kennedy. As Johnson stated many times, he would not be the first president to lose a war. In a similar vein, David Halberstam suggests that "Johnson did not take the domino theory seriously; he was far more worried about . . . what this [the fall of Vietnam] would do to him in terms of domestic politics."[39]

The national security managers also drew upon the fall of China for lessons. To this they could add lessons from decision making in the Korean War. In each case the implications were the same. A reputation for toughness was the most highly prized virtue that one could possess.[40] The bureaucratic casualties in the decision-making process on China were those who, even though they were correct, had become identified with the soft side of a policy debate. Those who had been hawkish—but wrong—emerged relatively unscathed from McCarthyism. To a lesser extent, Korea produced a similar pattern. Dean Rusk, who had failed to predict the Chinese entry into Korea but was staunchly anticommunist, did not pay a price for being wrong. In 1961, he became Kennedy's secretary of state.

Standing out among the host of strategic and tactical lessons of the past drawn upon by policy makers on Vietnam was the Munich analogy and the danger of appeasement. Munich had become a symbol for a generation of policy makers.[41] Its impact was so great that even those with no personal contact with the European peace efforts in the late 1930s could draw upon it for insight. Johnson, for example, saw the central lesson of the twentieth century as being that the appetite for aggression is never satisfied. It was Rusk who drew most openly and repeatedly on the Munich analogy. While he recognized that differences existed between the aggressions of Ho Chi Minh and Hitler, the basic point remained the same. "Aggression by any other name was still aggression and . . . must be checked."[42]

Very different were the lessons of the French experience in Indochina. Ernest May states that it was on the mind of every participant in the debate on the Taylor–Rostow Report.[43] Yet it had a negligible impact on American thinking, falling far short of being a generational experience on the order of Munich. Only George Ball actively drew upon this analogy. He had firsthand experience with the French war effort, having served as a lawyer for France during the Geneva negotiations. To him the war was unwinnable, and he warned Kennedy that if he sent the 15,000 combat troops to Vietnam as recommended, the commitment would escalate to 300,000 men.

Ball became concerned with U.S. policy in Vietnam because he feared that it was diverting attention from Europe. This Europeanist orientation to world politics was not unique within the Kennedy–Johnson administrations. McGeorge Bundy was "totally a man of the Atlantic." He was also very much a product of the 1950s and the cold war, so that when he entered the debate on Vietnam, he was an advocate of the U.S. presence. Kennedy's first ambassador to Vietnam, Fritz Nolting, and his top aide, William Trueheart, were also Europeanists who were totally ignorant of Asia and Asian communism. The predominance of Europeanists illustrates the interaction of political and strategic and tactical lessons of the past. A president concerned with making sure Vietnam did not become his China had limited options in making appointments. A residue of doubt continued to hang over the credentials of most Asian experts. While they lacked knowledge about Asian affairs, a president could feel politically safe with Europeanists in key decision-making positions.

The lack of knowledge about Asia on the part of key policy makers comes through in the strategic and tactical lessons they drew from Asian events. In many respects Kennedy was more knowledgeable about Asia than most in his administration. He had taken a special interest in Indochina while in Congress and had read on guerrilla warfare. Yet for all of this his views were not particularly sophisticated. According to Halberstam, they rested more on intuitive feel than on knowledge.[44] The inadequacy of this intuitive feel is evident in Kennedy's favored set of lessons of the past: Magsaysay's struggle against the Huk guerrillas in the Philippines and the British experience in Malaysia. Both contests were of a far different order from what was being contemplated in Vietnam. For example, the Malaysian analogy was flawed in at least five respects according to the U.S. military.

1. Malaysian borders were far more controllable.

2. The racial characteristics of the Chinese insurgents in Malaysia made identification and segregation a relatively simple matter as compared with the situation in Vietnam.

3. The scarcity of food in Malaysia compared to the relative plenty in South Vietnam made the denial of food to the guerrillas a far less usable weapon.

4. More important, in Malaysia the British were in actual command of military operations.

5. Finally, it took the British twelve years to defeat an insurgency that was less strong than the one in South Vietnam.[45]

The professional military also proved unable to draw on Asia for insights into how to fight in Vietnam. Westmoreland was "a conventional man in an unconventional war." Vietcong challenges only brought a request for more and more men and more bombing. They did not produce innovative strategies or tactics. Robert McNamara was no different in this respect. Never challenging the assumptions of policy, he limited himself to translating ideas into workable processes. In the end, he was unable "to adapt his values and terms to Vietnam realities."[46] The approach of the chairman of the Joint Chiefs of Staff, General Maxwell Taylor, was not very different. While he spoke of the challenge of brush-fire wars, his cables from Vietnam and the Taylor–Rostow Report indicated that Taylor was not really talking in terms of fighting a guerrilla war. His concern was with the military problem in Vietnam, and he approached it in a very conventional manner. Additional troops were the answer; political reforms were not mentioned. Taylor's analogy was with Korea and not the Philippines or the French experience in Indochina. Looking at Korea, he drew favorable comparisons with battlefield conditions and terrain. Taylor overlooked the differing nature of the two wars. Korea had been a conventional war begun by a border crossing by uniformed troops who fought in large concentrations.[47] This was not Vietnam in 1964.

The lessons drawn by two other policy makers deserve mention. The first is Walt Rostow, who brought to Vietnam decision making a firm set of beliefs on how to win the war and of the necessity of winning it. In his eyes communist intervention had taken place in South Vietnam, breaking the first rule of peaceful coexistence. The boundaries of the two camps were immutable, and any effort to alter them had to be resisted. His solution was air power.

Rostow had selected bombing targets during World War II and was convinced that massive bombing would bring North Vietnam to its knees. He was challenged on this point by George Ball, who had been a member of the Strategic Survey Group that studied the impact of the allied bombing of Germany. It concluded that the bombing had been of limited value. Ball concurred in this conclusion and argued that bombing North Vietnam would be equally futile. The second person worth looking at is Lyndon Johnson, who drew heavily upon his experience in Texas politics in formulating his Vietnam strategy. He had opposed the idea of a coup against Diem. That simply was not the way things were done in Texas. "Otto Passman and I, we have our differences, . . . but I don't plan his overthrow."[48] Beyond that, the United States had given its word to Diem, and you don't go back on your word. Johnson also felt that displays of toughness were prerequisites for dealing with the Vietnamese. Here he drew upon analogies to his dealings with Mexicans. "If you don't watch they'll walk right into your yard and take it over . . . but if you say to 'em right at the start, 'Hold on just a minute,' they'll know they are dealing with someone who'll stand up. And after that you can get along just fine."[49]

Lessons Learned. Vietnam had a tremendous impact on public opinion and elite attitudes. It destroyed the postwar consensus on the ends and means of U.S. foreign policy and left in its place three competing belief systems: cold war internationalism, post–cold war internationalism, and neo-isolationism. That three competing belief systems have merged is an indication that the lessons of Vietnam are not self-evident or easily agreed upon. The identification of three belief systems understates the extent of disagreement on the lessons of Vietnam. In identifying the lessons of Vietnam, we rely on a survey conducted by Ole Holsti and James Rosenau.[50] Respondents were asked to assess the lessons of Vietnam, the sources of failure, and the consequences of that failure. They were also asked to identify their positions on Vietnam when the war first became an issue for them and toward the end of the U.S. involvement. The sample was divided into three parts. The first was made up of a random sampling of names from *Who's Who*. The second group was selected on a quota basis from key groups in society (foreign service officers, clergy, women, labor, media, academics, and politicians). The third group was made up of military personnel.

On the basis of attitudes held at the beginning and end of Vietnam, Holsti and Rosenau identify seven groups holding different notions about the sources, consequences, and lessons of Vietnam. These groups covered the entire range of opinion from consistent critics to consistent supporters. Fully 30 percent of the sample resides at the extremes, confirming the depth of the impact Vietnam had on American attitudes.

Looking first at the sources of failure, Holsti and Rosenau were able to identify twenty-one reasons why the United States lost in Vietnam, according to those they polled. The depth of the disagreement is great. Not only are the sources of failure ranked differently by the various groups, but no one explanation appears in all seven groups. Only three appear in six of these groups: the United States' lack of clear-cut goals, the presence of Soviet and Chinese aid, and North Vietnamese dedication.

A more coherent picture emerges when we look at the consequences of Vietnam cited by the seven groups. Supporters cited international system-related concerns as the most important consequences of Vietnam. Critics cited Vietnam's domestic impact as most significant. Only one consequence was cited by all seven groups but not with the same relative importance: The United States will limit its conception of its national interest.

The picture becomes cloudy again when turning to the lessons of Vietnam. Thirty-four lessons were cited. No one lesson appears in all seven groups. Only two appear in six groups: Executive-legislative cooperation is vital, and Russia is expansionist.

THE PERSIAN GULF WAR[51]

The Persian Gulf War can be divided into four periods. The first begins in early 1990 and ends with Iraq's August 2 invasion of Kuwait. The second encompasses the period between that invasion and the beginning of the bombing campaign in January 1991. The third stage involves the war itself, the five weeks of aerial bombardment and the hundred hours of ground warfare. The fourth and final stage involves the posthostility diplomacy between Iraq and the UN forces as well as Saddam Hussein's military action against the Kurds and Shiites. Each holds lessons for the future. We will examine the first two in detail because our concern is with the failure of U.S. deterrence and compellence strategies. Table 5.3 shows the chronology of the war.

TABLE 5.3   Persian Gulf War Chronology

August 2, 1990	Iraqi troops invade Kuwait.
August 6, 1990	UN Security Council imposes economic sanctions
August 7, 1990	President Bush begins Operation Desert Shield by ordering U.S. troops, aircraft, and warships to Saudi Arabia.
August 9, 1990	UN Security Council declares Iraqi annexation of Kuwait "null and void."
August 10, 1990	The United States begins a naval blockade of Iraq.
August 22, 1990	President Bush announces call-up of 40,000 military reservists.
November 29, 1990	UN Security Council passes Resolution 678 authorizing members to "use all necessary means" against Iraq unless it withdraws from Kuwait by January 15, 1992.
January 12, 1991	The Senate votes 52–47 to authorize Bush to use force to carry out UN Resolution 678; the House votes 250–183 supporting a presidential use of force.
January 15, 1991	At 7:00 P.M. EST, the air attack on Baghdad begins.
January 17, 1991	Iraq launches SCUD missiles at Israel.
February 22, 1991	Bush issues Saddam Hussein an ultimatum to leave Kuwait by noon February 23.
February 24, 1991	The ground war begins.
February 27, 1991	President Bush announces that offensive actions will end.

Period 1: February–August 1990.   On February 15, 1990, Voice of America (VOA) broadcast a story about how democracy was taking hold in countries that were once dictatorships. In the course of doing so, it identified Iraq as a state where the "secret police were still widely present." The Iraqi government complained to U.S. Ambassador April Glaspie that this constituted a "flagrant interference in the internal affairs of Iraq." Glaspie wrote a letter apologizing for the comment, stating that "it is absolutely not United States policy to question the legitimacy of the Government of Iraq nor to interfere in any way in the domestic concerns of the Iraqi people and government." Before the month was out, Saddam Hussein again complained about American foreign policy toward Iraq. At a February 24 meeting of the Arab Cooperation Council in Jordan, he warned other Arab states about "undisciplined and irresponsible behavior" on the part of the United States and that Israel might undertake "new stupidities . . . as a result of U.S. encouragement." Moderate Arab states felt threatened by Hussein's comments, which they read as veiled criticisms of their relationships with the United States.

There was little veiled in Hussein's other major pronouncement. He wanted the Gulf states to provide Iraq with $30 billion in aid for doing their bidding in the war against Iran. Should this money not be forthcoming, Hussein promised to "take steps to retaliate." Iraq's economy had been severely damaged by the 1980–1988 Iran–Iraq War. It had cost Iraq over $500 billion and left it with a staggering war debt. The key to Iraq's economic recovery lay in oil sales, but the price of oil had been dropping steadily from $20.50 per barrel in January 1990 to $13.00 per barrel in July. Each dollar drop cost Iraq an estimated $1 billion in annual revenues. Not surprisingly, Saddam Hussein blamed overproduction by Kuwait and other OPEC states for this situation.

In April, Saddam Hussein continued his verbal attacks on the United States and Israel, telling a group of Iraqi military officers that "this is the biggest conspiracy in modern history" and that "we have a duty to defend Iraq." He also implied that he would use chemical weapons against Israel, noting that "we will make the fire eat up half of Israel." In the following days Saddam Hussein sought to soften these remarks. He contacted the Saudis and arranged to meet with their ambassador to the United States, who was told that these remarks had been blown out of proportion and to pass this along to the Bush administration. Saddam Hussein went on to reassure the Saudi official that he had no designs over his neighbors but that he had to "whip them [the Iraqi people] into a sort of frenzy or emotional mobilization . . . so they will be ready for whatever may happen."

The State Department publicly termed Hussein's comments "inflammatory," and an official White House spokesperson labeled them "particularly deplorable and irresponsible." At this point the Bush administration began to contemplate economic sanctions against Iraq. Plans were drawn up to eliminate credits for wheat purchases by Iraq and the import of military and dual-use technologies. They were formally presented for consideration by an April 16 meeting of representatives from interested cabinet offices. There the plan ran into opposition and was dropped: Both the Commerce Department and the National Security Council objected. The White House also opposed the idea because at the time the Bush administration was trying to head off congressional pressures for economic sanctions against Iraq.

A congressional delegation visited Iraq shortly after Saddam Hussein's speech. Headed by Senator Bob Dole, it both threatened and reassured Iraq. Saddam Hussein was warned that a prerequisite for improvements in U.S.–Iraqi relations was a halt in Iraq's efforts to acquire chemical and biological weapons. In private conversations, however, members of the U.S. delegation apparently struck a more conciliatory note, indicating that they saw Saddam Hussein as a man of peace and that both the Bush administration and many in Congress opposed economic sanctions. In Washington, Bush received the Saudi ambassador and, while doubting Saddam Hussein's honesty and true intentions, agreed to obtain a statement from Israel that it had no intention of attacking Iraq. After this was done and communicated to Saddam Hussein, the Bush administration considered the matter closed.

Saddam Hussein, however, soon went back on the verbal offensive. At a May summit meeting of Arab states he charged that Kuwait and other quota-busting oil-producing states were "virtually waging an economic war against my country." He also promised that "one day the reckoning will come." In July Saddam Hussein unleashed a new round of attacks against OPEC states for their oil-pricing policies. On July 10, the OPEC oil ministers had agreed to raise the price of oil back to $18 per barrel, but Kuwait qualified its position by stating that it would review and possibly reverse this decision in the fall. For all practical purposes, this was an invitation to oil companies to wait and purchase Kuwaiti oil at a reduced price in the near future. Saddam Hussein responded by laying out the totality of his demands of Kuwait. He demanded $2.4 billion in compensation for oil that was dumped from disputed oil fields, $12 billion in compensation for the loss of revenues resulting from the depressed price of oil brought about by Kuwait's overproduction, Kuwaiti forgiveness of Iraq's $10 billion war debt from the Iran–Iraq War, and a lease on the strategic island of Bubiyan.

In a memorandum to the Arab League Saddam Hussein also charged Kuwait and the United Arab Emirates (UAE) with being part of a "Zionist plot aided by imperialists." At virtually the same time, Iraqi radio broadcast a speech by Saddam Hussein asserting that low oil prices were a "poisoned dagger" pointed at Iraq. In that speech he also threatened to take matters into his own hands if need be, stating that "if words fail to protect us, we will have no choice other than to go into action to reestablish the correct state of affairs and restore our rights."

Accompanying this hostile rhetoric were troop movements by key units in Iraq's Republican Guard toward the Kuwaiti border. While disturbed by this sudden military show of force, U.S. officials concluded that Iraq's purpose was to intimidate Kuwait and not to invade it. They reached this conclusion because of the absence of supply and support units necessary to sustain an invasion and because the number of troops observed was judged to be too small for an invasion of Kuwait. Still, Saddam Hussein's actions seemed to demand a countermove. Kuwait put its small army on alert, and Secretary of Defense Dick Cheney stated that the Bush administration would "take seriously any threat to U.S. interests or U.S. friends in the region." The United States also responded favorably to a request from the UAE for military assistance by providing it with two aerial tankers and quickly arranging for, and making public, a joint naval exercise. The UAE was not entirely pleased with the U.S. response. Wanting reassurance and the military aid, but not wanting to antagonize Saddam Hussein, it had hoped to keep matters secret.

Saddam Hussein's July outburst also set in motion a new round of diplomatic efforts in the region. Ambassador Glaspie also met with Saddam Hussein. Glaspie had been trying to arrange a meeting ever since his July 17 radio address. On July 25, she was summoned to meet with him on such short notice that she was unable to get instructions from the State Department. In her conversation with Saddam Hussein, Glaspie repeated the standard U.S. position. The United States "would not countenance violence or the threat of violence or in fact threat of intimidation." It would "defend our vital interests" and "defend the sovereignty and integrity" of our "friends in the Gulf." The United States wanted better relations with Iraq. And the United States had "no opinion on the Arab–Arab conflicts, like your border disagreement with Kuwait." After this meeting Glaspie cabled Washington that it should back off the public criticism of Saddam Hussein and that his interest in a peaceful settlement of the dispute was sincere.

The United States continued on this diplomatic course right up until the invasion. On July 31, John Kelly, Assistant Secretary of State for Near East and South Asian Affairs, in testimony before a House Foreign Affairs subcommittee, acknowledged that Iraq's military buildup along the Kuwaiti border was troubling and demanded a response. He argued, however, against economic sanctions and in favor of flexibility. When questioned as to how far the United States was prepared to go in defending the sovereignty of allied states, Kelly stated that "we have no defense treaty relationship with any Gulf country" and that "we do not have a treaty commitment which would oblige us to engage U.S. forces."

This same day, Pat Lang, the Defense Intelligence Agency's (DIA) national intelligence officer for the Middle East and South Asia, issued a warning that Iraq would soon go to war. Lang had been watching the Iraqi buildup since the middle of July. In a span of eleven days, he had seen eight divisions move a distance of 300 to 400 miles, placing some 100,000 soldiers on the Kuwaiti border. Neither the CIA nor DIA fully supported Lang's conclusion. The next day, August 1, additional satellite intelligence had come in, making it clear that an invasion was about to be launched. In his briefing to the Joint Chiefs of Staff and Secretary of Defense Cheney, General Norman Schwarzkopf, who headed the Central Command, stated that there was little or nothing that could be done. The United States only had 10,000 troops in the region and almost all of them were naval forces.

Period 2: August 1990–January 1991.   On August 2, Iraqi troops crossed into Kuwait and within a matter of hours took control of the entire country. On August 4, President Bush spoke out against the invasion, stating that "it would not stand." The next day the United Nations voted to impose economic sanctions against Iraq, and on August 24 it followed with a vote to authorize the use of force to impose those sanctions. Earlier the United Nations had voted to condemn the invasion and called for Iraq's immediate and unconditional withdrawal from Kuwait. In late September, Iraq's Revolutionary Command Council rejected the UN call for withdrawal and promised that any effort to bring this about would result in "the mother of all battles."

Military action was also forthcoming. On August 6, President Bush authorized the Pentagon to implement Operations Plan 90–1002. This was a top-secret contingency plan put together in the 1980s to deal with the prospect of a Middle East war against the Soviet Union or Iran. Because the possibility of an Iraqi attack had not been given high priority, 90–1002 had not been updated. Its central assumption that planners would have thirty days' notice prior to the start of fighting to begin deploying forces and moving supplies was not met. Schwarzkopf calculated that implementing 90–1002 would require seventeen weeks, 200,000 to 250,000 troops, and the cooperation of Saudi Arabia or some other Arab state where the United States could set up bases.

At the first postinvasion meeting of the National Security Council, Bush asserted that "we just can't accept what's happened in Kuwait just because it's too hard to do anything about it." General Powell argued that the United States ought to draw a firm line with Saudi Arabia because that was where real U.S. interests lay. UN Ambassador Thomas Pickering noted that this left Kuwait on the other side of the line. The danger of an Iraqi attack against Saudi Arabia struck many as particularly grave in the first days of the American deployment. It was only in late August that U.S. military commanders felt that the American military presence had grown to the point that Saddam Hussein would probably no longer consider attacking Saudi Arabia as a viable option.

U.S. diplomatic efforts were now directed at holding the anti-Iraq international coalition together and building support for military action designed to force Iraq out of Kuwait. Russian and French diplomatic initiatives in September and early October suggested a weakening of international resolve. Both put forward terms that were at variance with the UN demand for an Iraqi withdrawal. By early November, however, it was clear that these efforts had failed, and attention turned to laying the diplomatic groundwork for military action. In need of particular attention was Saudi Arabia. Its cooperation was seen as essential for the success of 90–1002. Intelligence information available to the Bush administration indicated that the Saudi leadership was anything but firm in its resolution to oppose Saddam Hussein. It appeared they were giving consideration to paying Saddam Hussein billions of dollars in oil revenues as a means of deflecting his attention away from their country.

With international support well on the way to being assured, President Bush announced on November 8 that the size of the U.S. military presence in the Persian Gulf would double. The purpose was to ensure that should they desire to do so, coalition forces could conduct a successful offensive operation. Bush then traveled to the Middle East to meet with Arab leaders to gain their backing for a military push against Iraq. On November 29, the Security Council voted 12 to 2, with one abstention (China), to set January 15, 1991, as the deadline for Iraq's peaceful exit from Kuwait. If this did not happen, it authorized member states cooperating with Iraq "to use all means necessary" to bring about Iraq's immediate and unconditional withdrawal.

A formidable force under U.S. command was being assembled very rapidly in the Persian Gulf. Over 400,000 U.S. forces would arrive in the Middle East. Coalition air forces would fly 109,876 sorties, drop 88,500 tons of bombs, and shoot down thirty-five Iraqi airplanes. The size of this force did not preclude a debate in the United States over the ultimate wisdom of going to war.[52] Three prominent former policy makers spoke out against war. Zbigniew Brzezinski, Carter's national security adviser, counseled against going to war in congressional testimony saying that "the threat posed by Iraq was far from catastrophic." Admiral William Crow, who was chairman of the Joint Chiefs of Staff under Reagan, stated that, although Iraq must leave Kuwait, "we should give sanctions a fair chance before discarding them." James Schlesinger, who served as secretary of defense and director of the Central Intelligence Agency, cautioned against using force given the unpredictable nature of the region and the possibility that the United States might have to involve itself deeply in Middle East affairs "in the aftermath of a shattering war." Speaking in favor of war, or at least accepting the need for it, was Henry Kissinger, former secretary of state and national security adviser, who feared that if Iraq's aggression went unchecked a domino effect would take place in which moderate governments would collapse amid escalating crises. Also supporting it was Jeane Kirkpatrick, who served as UN Ambassador under Reagan. She argued that Saddam Hussein must be punished in order to "deter future aggression from similar violence and make the world safer for all."

With U.S. war plans being finalized and the time of the attack set, Bush went to Congress to get its approval for the use of force. This move was debated within the administration, but by early January it became clear that Congress intended to take up the question whether or not the Bush administration asked. The debate was framed as a choice between two options: authorizing the president to use force or insisting that economic sanctions be given more time. Economic sanctions were imposed almost immediately. On August 2, the Bush administration froze all Iraqi and Kuwaiti assets; it also moved to prohibit trade and financial dealings with Iraq. Great Britain, France, Russia, and the United Nations all followed suit. In December, William Webster, the CIA's director, stated that Iraq had lost more than 90 percent of its imports and 97 percent of its exports, depriving Iraq of $1.5 billion in foreign exchange. He estimated that Iraq's foreign exchange reserves would be depleted by the spring and that it would not have the financial means to entice potential sanctions-busters to aid it. By the summer he expected only energy-related and some military industries to be fully functioning. Somewhat less optimistically, Webster also concluded that Iraqi ground and air forces could probably remain near their current levels of readiness for up to nine months.

After an often emotional debate, Congress voted on January 12, 1991, to support the president by a vote of 250 to 183 in the House and 52 to 47 in the Senate.

At the same time that Congress was debating the wisdom of going to war, the Bush administration was engaged in last-minute diplomatic negotiations with Iraq in Geneva. A January 8 meeting between Secretary of State Baker and Foreign Minister Tariq Aziz ended in deadlock. Aziz stated that the blunt language used by Bush in a letter given to him by Baker that demanded Iraq's withdrawal from Kuwait was "incompatible to the language that should be used in correspondence between heads of state." The following day, Saddam Hussein delivered a radio address in which he claimed that the Iraqi forces were ready for war and confident of victory. A last-minute visit by UN Secretary-General Javier Perez de Cuellar also failed. The United Nations–set deadline of January 15, 1991, arrived and passed. At about midnight, January 16, coalition aircraft took off from Saudi Arabia to begin the air campaign against Iraq.

Deterrence. The United States sought to deter two Iraqi actions in the time period chronicled above: an invasion of Kuwait and an invasion of Saudi Arabia. One lesson that we can try to learn from the Persian Gulf War will answer the question: Why did deterrence fail in the first case and succeed in the second? Was it because of inadequacies in deterrence theory or the inability to design and implement an appropriate strategy? The Persian Gulf War is an important test case. If deterrence could not be made to work outside of the context of deterring a Soviet nuclear attack on the United States or one of its key allies, then U.S. security policy would need to be anchored around a different strategic doctrine in the post–cold war era.

Deterrence theory builds upon a straightforward assumption about why states go to war. War is assumed to be the product of a rational decision calculus in which costs and benefits are weighed against each other. Only when the expected benefits of going to war exceed the expected costs of doing so will a state go to war. Once this decision has been made, other states face the prospect of (1) fighting a war to defend themselves, (2) appeasing the would-be aggressor—in essence giving it all or part of what it wants in the hopes of averting war, or (3) convincing the would-be aggressor to alter its plans and accept the status quo. Deterrence strategies are designed to accomplish this last outcome by rearranging the elements of this decision calculus in such a way that costs exceed benefits. To do so they must convincingly communicate both a willingness and an ability to raise the costs to the would-be aggressor should it go forward.

In regard to the first effort at deterrence, a strong case can be made that U.S. policy makers did not come close to implementing a coherent deterrence strategy. The United States neither possessed the capability to raise the costs to Iraq of an invasion of Kuwait (much less defeat any such effort) nor did it clearly communicate its position to Iraq.

From a military perspective the only counter to Saddam Hussein's attacking force was Kuwait's small army and air force. Bush administration officials gave little thought to augmenting this force. The only concrete move in this direction was the training exercise with the UAE and transfer of the two airborne refueling aircraft. Just days before the invasion, a high-ranking civilian defense department official proposed that, as a show of force, the United States move the maritime prepositioned ships from the Indian Ocean to the Persian Gulf. Each ship contained thirty days' worth of food, ammunition, and supplies for a Marine unit of sixteen thousand. General Powell objected to the idea and no ships were deployed. In making his case Powell noted that this move implied a commitment to send ground troops, that no one was proposing that the United States do this, and that Kuwait had not asked for such help.

The absence of a credible capability to defeat or punish Iraqi forces made signaling U.S. resolve a difficult task to accomplish. U.S. public pronouncements suggested an administration unsure of what it wanted to do and the image it wished to project. The statements by Ambassador Glaspie, Assistant Secretary of State Kelly, and other Bush administration officials did not point to a "line in the sand" beyond which Iraqi forces could not move with impunity. Instead, they contained expressions of concern mixed with declarations indicating limits to the extent of any potential U.S. involvement. When strong statements were made, they were quickly followed with retractions or modifiers. For example, at one point Secretary of Defense Cheney stated that U.S. defense commitments to Kuwait had not changed since the Iran–Iraq War when the United States had reflagged Kuwaiti tankers. That same day a Pentagon spokesperson stated that Cheney had been quoted "with some degree of liberty by the press." In commenting on the U.S.–UAE naval exercise, the Secretary of the Navy told Congress that U.S. forces had gone on alert status. Later, this statement was retracted.

It seemed that the Bush administration did not think it necessary to convey a credible threat because few believed that Saddam Hussein could seriously think of going to war so soon after the costly Iran–Iraq War of 1980–1988. This was the conclusion of a fall 1989 National Intelligence Estimate. It judged that Saddam Hussein wished to dominate the Gulf but that because of the costs suffered by Iraq in that war he was unlikely to use military force to do so. The conclusion that Iraq would not use force was also shared by most Arab leaders, and this reassuring message was regularly communicated to the Bush White House.

Iraqi aggression against Kuwait was not deterred because deterrence as it is supposed to be practiced was not attempted. The United States had sought to stop Saddam Hussein by engaging in a series of half-measures. An enemy making cost-benefit calculations about the consequences of an aggressive move was not likely to be deterred under these circumstances. An interesting question is raised by this conclusion: Could Saddam Hussein have been deterred if a deterrence strategy had been properly executed? The answer might be "no." If Saddam Hussein's primary motivation for invading Kuwait grew out of economic desperation, then it is possible that he would have pressed forward regardless of the military costs because of the perceived consequences of inaction—continued economic problems that could lead to his overthrow. Deterrence might also have failed due to the image of the United States held by Saddam Hussein. Janice Gross Stein observes that his

> judgment of American intentions was deeply rooted in the political and cultural context which reinforced the long-standing image of the United States as an imperialist power working through its wealthy agents in the Gulf against the interests of Arab states like Iraq.[53]

Because he saw the United States as engaged in a pattern of economic and covert warfare against him, Saddam Hussein may well have framed his choices as "open confrontation and long-term sabotage."

Having failed to deter the invasion of Kuwait, the United States turned its attention to deterring an invasion of Saudi Arabia. Implementing plan 90–1002, the United States moved quickly to place a credible deterrent force in his path. It also moved aggressively on the diplomatic front to garner support for Operation Desert Shield. The overall tactical requirements for a successful deterrence strategy were thus in place. But was the deterrence strategy a success? Just because Saddam Hussein did not invade Saudi Arabia does not prove that he was deterred. He may have had no intention of doing so. In fact, all agree that in the first weeks after the invasion of Kuwait before U.S. forces arrived in large numbers he could have successfully done so. Yet, he did not. General Powell believed that Saddam Hussein never intended to invade Saudi Arabia because of the larger geopolitical consequences of that move. These were consequences that existed quite apart from any display of U.S. force.

It is also possible to identify several shortcomings in the U.S. deterrent strategy that might have encouraged a calculating opponent to conclude that further aggression might still pay. First, the Bush administration was not completely clear why U.S. forces were being sent to the Persian Gulf. Defending Saudi Arabia was only one of several explanations put forward. Among the others were restoring the rulers of Kuwait, protecting American jobs, protecting the world order, dealing with Iraq's growing nuclear threat, and stopping a "mad dictator" who wanted to control "the economic well-being of every country in the world." Second, Saudi Arabia's resolve in the face of a possible Iraqi attack was in doubt at the very time the United States was searching for a military option. Should Saudi misgivings have been recognized by Iraq they could only have served to embolden it. These shortcomings may not have been crippling even if Saddam Hussein had been considering an invasion of Saudi Arabia. Studies show that secrecy does not have to be complete for strategic surprise to succeed (for example, Japan's attack on Pearl Harbor and Hitler's attack on the Soviet Union). The same may be true of deterrence. Credibility and capability gaps may arise but the overall policy may still succeed.

Compellence. Where deterrence seeks to prevent an unwanted action from taking place, compellence seeks to reverse an unwanted situation. It does so using the same underlying logic as deterrence and with the same set of strategic requirements. A credible compellent force must be created and a willingness to use it must be communicated to the enemy. Once again, the enemy is assumed to base its actions on cost-benefit calculations arrived at in a rational manner. With the shift from Desert Shield to Desert Storm, the United States moved from deterrence to compellence. The goal now became bringing about an Iraqi withdrawal from Kuwait. Compellence failed. Iraqi forces did not leave Kuwait on their own accord but were forced out through military combat. As was the case with the deterrence failure, the root causes may have rested either with the concept of compellence or how it was implemented.

Where American policy makers had not thought it necessary to commit deterrence forces to the Middle East prior to Iraq's invasion of Kuwait, none quarreled with the need for a large compellence force. General Powell outlined these requirements in the days prior to the November 8 decision to move from Desert Shield to Desert Storm. The size of his request surprised many of those who heard it, but no one tried to reduce it. President Bush commented: "If that's what you need, we'll do it." The United States also went to great lengths to communicate its commitment. Diplomatic efforts by other states to bring about something less than a full withdrawal from Kuwait were resisted; UN authorization for the use of force was obtained; a clear deadline was established; and Congress had come on board with its December vote.

Why then did compellence fail? One possibility is that, as in the case of the deterrence failure, Saddam Hussein was not basing his decisions on the type of cost-benefit calculation that displays of force and commitment could influence. A second possibility is that he was engaged in the very type of cost-benefit calculation expected by compellence theorists but that he came up with the "wrong" answer. Instead of calculating that he would be defeated, Saddam Hussein may have concluded that Iraq could win. Stein identifies a series of miscalculations that he could have made: (1) the UN coalition would not hold together; (2) the United States would not use massive force because of domestic opposition; (3) air power would not eliminate the need for a bloody ground war; (4) the United States would not tolerate large numbers of American casualties; (5) Israel would retaliate if attacked, splitting the Arab world; and (6) even in military defeat there would be a political victory. All were plausible and represented concerns voiced by U.S. policy makers.

Summary

The cold war, Vietnam, and the Persian Gulf War show that learning from the past is not easily done. Not only are the events tremendously complex, but the question of learning from them hides a host of less visible preliminary questions: What is it about the event you wish to learn? What phase of the event are you concerned with? Whose views are you concerned with? What set of values will you bring to your analysis? In looking at Vietnam or the cold war, we have the luxury of time and distance from the event itself. This is not always the case, and when it is not, the task of learning from the past becomes even more complex.

THE OCCUPATION AND RECONSTRUCTION OF IRAQ

Perhaps the most pressing foreign policy problem for which lessons from the past are needed today is the occupation and reconstruction of Iraq. As the formal turnover of power in June 2004 approached, the overriding themes in political commentaries were that of opportunities lost and naïve expectations. Because this is an ongoing event, we cannot engage in the type of post-mortem that we did in the three case studies covered in this chapter. We can, however, identify ways in which history might have been used better.

The post–World War II American occupations of Germany and Japan were put forward by the George W. Bush administration as the starting points for thinking about rebuilding Iraq. He observed, "America has made and kept this kind of commitment before . . . after defeating enemies, we did not leave behind occupying armies, we left constitutions and parliaments." A closer reading of the American experience in Germany and Japan would have given reason for caution both with regard to process and outcome. Douglas Porch maintains that for nearly a full decade many of those involved in these reconstruction programs considered their efforts to be nearly a complete failure.[54] Rather than encounter a welcoming population, they found resentment and resistance. Actions taken to bring about reform were often counterproductive. General Lucius Clay, who was in charge of the American occupation zone, called de-Nazification his biggest mistake. It was in his mind a "hopelessly ambiguous procedure" that linked together small and big Nazis and brought forward the hostility of the population at large because the implementation of this policy often appeared arbitrary and hypocritical. Yet, the United States moved quickly to de-Ba'athify Iraq by dismissing party members from government positions and decommissioning the army.

It can be argued that the reasons for the ultimate success of the occupation of Germany and Japan had little to do with American policy or the presumed natural inclination of people liberated from tyranny for democracy. Rather, it had to do with such factors as enlightened domestic leadership, economic miracles fueled by the Marshall plan in Europe and the Korean War in Asia, along with the prior experience of democracy and entrepreneurship within these two states. The key American contribution was creating domestic and regional security, laying the ground rules for democratic reform, and then getting out of the way.

Germany and Japan were not the only efforts at reconstruction (or more broadly, nation building) that might have been looked to for lessons. Minxin Pei identifies fourteen additional cases[55] including Cuba (1898–1902, 1903–1936, 1917–1922), the Dominican Republic (1916–1924, 1965–1966), South Vietnam, Cambodia, and Afghanistan. In only two of these cases, Panama (1989) and Grenada, was democracy in place after ten years. The cases embodied a wide variety of interim administrations in the nation-building period. In seven cases, the United States established governments that almost totally depended upon it for their survival. In none of these cases did democracy emerge. Pei concludes that the ideal form of transition involves a quick transfer of power to legitimately elected local leaders but cautions that his presupposes a functioning electoral system and moderate local leaders who have genuine support among the populace.

Two other historical precedents from which to learn lessons about the occupation and reconstruction of Iraq also are available for the taking.[56] One is the Philippines. It was suggested as a precedent by President George W. Bush in an October 2003 speech outside of the Philippine House of Representatives where he declared "America is proud of its part in the great story of the Filipino people . . . Together our soldiers liberated the Philippines from colonial rule." The historical record, however, suggests problems with the Philippines as a model for Iraq. After occupying the country as a result of the Spanish-American War of 1898, American forces fought a fourteen-year-long war against Filipino insurgents. Some 120,000 soldiers participated in this campaign; 4,000 were killed, as were more than 200,000 Filipinos. Decades later, after World War II, Philippine democracy succumbed to the excesses and abuses of Fernando Marcos who in 1973 declared himself president for life. He was overthrown in a 1986 coup. A second precedent is the Soviet experience in Afghanistan. The Soviet Union entered Afghanistan with superior firepower but soon succumbed to guerrilla warfare and terrorist attacks. By one Russian count, there were more than 1,800 terrorist attacks against non-military targets between 1985 to 1987. They came to modernize and transform an Islamic society and do it quickly. They hoped that local police and military forces would secure order and do the bulk of the fighting. They became the enemy of Islam.

Notes

1. Richard K. Betts, *Surprise Attack, Lessons for Defense Planning* (Washington, D.C.: Brookings, 1982), p. 8.

2. Richard Ned Lebow, *Between Peace and War: The Nature of International Crisis Behavior* (Baltimore, Md.: Johns Hopkins University Press, 1981), p. 199.

3. Roberta Wohlstetter, *Pearl Harbor: Warning and Decision* (Stanford, Calif.: Stanford University Press, 1962), p. 70.

4. Roland Paris, "Kosovo and the Metaphor War," *Political Science Quarterly* (117), 2002, 423–50.

5. Wohlstetter, p. 388.

6. On cognitive consistency and its application to world politics, see Robert Jervis, *Perception and Misperception in International Politics* (Princeton, N.J.: Princeton University Press, 1976); John D. Steinbruner, *The Cybernetic Theory of Decision: New Dimensions of Political Analysis* (Princeton, N.J.: Princeton University Press, 1974); and Lebow, *Between Peace and War.*

7. Ole Holsti, "The Belief System and National Images: A Case Study," *Journal of Conflict Resolution,* 6 (1972), 244–52.

8. *Washington Post,* December 23, 1984, p. 11.

9. These points are discussed in George Quester, *Nuclear Diplomacy, The First Twenty-Five Years* (New York: Dunellen, 1970); and Michael Mandelbaum, *The Nuclear Question: The United States and Nuclear Weapons, 1946–1976* (New York: Cambridge University Press, 1979).

10. Marijke Breuning, "The Role of Analogies and Abstract Reasoning in Decision Making," *International Studies Quarterly* (2003) 47: 229–45.

11. Jervis, *Perception and Misperception,* pp. 249–50.

12. Henry Kissinger, *The White House Years* (Boston: Little, Brown, 1979), p. 54.

13. Betts, *Surprise Attack,* p. 8.

14. Abraham Lowenthal, "The Dominican Intervention in Retrospect," *Public Policy,* 18 (1969), 133–48.

15. Scott Sagan, "Why Do States Build Nuclear Weapons?" *International Security,* 21 (1996–97), 58.

16. Kenneth Pollack, "Spies, Lies, and Weapons," *Atlantic Monthly,* 293 (January 2004), 78–92.

17. Kennan's comments were made in testimony before the Senate Foreign Relations Committee. They are reported in *Washington Post,* April 5, 1989.

18. Norman Graebner, "Cold War Origins and the Continuing Debate: A Review of the Literature," in Erik Hoffman and Frederick Fleron Jr. (eds.), *The Conduct of Soviet Foreign Policy,* expanded 2nd ed. (New York: Aldine, 1980), p. 217.

19. See, for example, D. F. Flemming, *The Cold War and Its Origins, 1917–1950* (Garden City, N.Y.: Doubleday, 1961).

20. On this period see Adam Ulam, *Expansion and Coexistence, Soviet Foreign Policy, 1917–1973* (New York: Praeger, 1974); and John Lewis Gaddis, *Russia, the Soviet Union, and the United States, an Interpretive History* (New York: Wiley & Sons, 1978).

21. John Spanier, *American Foreign Policy Since World War II,* 9th ed. (New York: Holt, Rinehart & Winston, 1983), p. 16.

22. Gar Alperowitz, *Atomic Diplomacy, Hiroshima, and Potsdam* (New York: Viking, 1965), p. 229.

23. On the existence of multiple cold wars, see John Lewis Gaddis, "Containment: Its Past and Future," *International Security,* 5 (1981), 74–101.

24. For an orthodox perspective see Herbert Feis, *Between War and Peace: The Potsdam Conference* (Princeton, N.J.: Princeton University Press, 1960).

25. For a revisionist perspective see William A. Williams, *The Tragedy of American Diplomacy,* rev. ed. (New York: World, 1962).

26. Louis Halle, *The Cold War as History* (New York: Harper & Row, 1967), p. 2.

27. On the role of perceptions, see Uri Bronfenbrenner, "The Mirror Image in Soviet–American Relations," *Journal of Social Issues,* 17 (1961), 45–56.

28. John P. Lovell, *Foreign Policy in Perspective* (New York: Holt, Rinehart & Winston, 1970), p. 134.

29. Charles Learche Jr., *The Cold War . . . and After* (Englewood Cliffs, N.J.: Prentice-Hall, 1965), Chap. 2.

30. See John Lewis Gaddis, "International Relations Theory and the End of the Cold War," *International Security,* 17 (1992/93), 5–58; Ted Hopf and John Lewis Gaddis, "Correspondence: Getting the End of the Cold War Wrong," *International Security,* 18 (1993), 202–15.

31. Beth Fischer, "Toeing the Hardline? The Reagan Administration and the Ending of the Cold War," *Political Science Quarterly,* 112 (1997), 477–96.

32. See Thomas Risse-Kappen, "Did 'Peace Through Strength' End the Cold War?" *International Security,* 16 (1991), 162–88; Robert English, "Power, Ideas, and New Evidence on the Cold War's End," *International Security,* 26 (2002), 70–92; and Stephen Brooks and William Wohlforth, "Power, Globalization, and the End of the Cold War," *International Security,* 25 (2000/2001), 5–53.

33. Raymond L. Garthoff, "Looking Back: The Cold War in Retrospect," *The Brookings Review,* 12 (Summer 1994), 10–13.

34. Janice Gross Stein, "Political Learning by Doing: Gorbachev as Uncommitted Thinker and Motivated Learner," *International Organization,* 48 (1994), 155–83.

35. Thomas Risse-Kappen, "Ideas Do Not Float Freely: Transnational Coalitions, Domestic Structures, and the End of the Cold War," *International Organization,* 48 (1994), 185–214.

36. Results of the public opinion poll are found in the *New York Times,* March 31, 1985, Sec. 6, p. 34. Reagan's comments can be found in the *Weekly Compilation of Presidential Documents,* 18 (February 18, 1982), 185.

37. John Stoessinger, *Why Nations Go to War,* 3rd ed. (New York: St. Martin's, 1982), p. 101.

38. *The Pentagon Papers* as published by the *New York Times* (New York: Quadrangle, 1971), p. 263.

39. David Halberstam, *The Best and the Brightest* (Greenwich, Conn.: Fawcett, 1972), p. 433.

40. On this point see Richard Barnett, *The Roots of War* (New York: Penguin, 1973), Chaps. 4 and 5.

41. Ernest May makes this point in his treatment of Vietnam in *"Lessons" of the Past: The Use and Misuse of History in American Foreign Policy* (New York: Oxford University Press, 1978).

42. Robert Gallucci, *Neither Peace nor Honor, the Politics of American Military Policy in Vietnam* (Baltimore, Md.: Johns Hopkins University Press, 1975), p. 33.

43. May, *"Lessons" of the Past,* p. 94.

44. Halberstam, *The Best and the Brightest,* p. 119.

45. May, *"Lessons" of the Past,* pp. 98–99.

46. Halberstam, *The Best and the Brightest,* p. 304.

47. Ibid., p. 212.

48. Ibid., p. 356.

49. Ibid., p. 643.

50. Ole Holsti and James N. Rosenau, "Vietnam, Consensus, and the Belief Systems of American Leaders," *World Politics,* 32 (1979), 1–56.

51. Material for this section is drawn from Michael Mazarr, Don M. Snider, and James A. Blackwell Jr., *Desert Storm: The Gulf War and What We Learned* (Boulder, Colo.: Westview, 1993); Bob Woodward, *The Commanders* (New York: Simon & Schuster, 1991); and Janice Gross Stein, "Deterrence and Compellence in the Gulf, 1990–91: A Failed or Impossible Task?" *International Security,* 17 (1992), 147–79.

52. The following perspectives are presented in Mazarr, Snider, and Blackwell, *Desert Storm,* 72–73.

53. Stein, "Deterrence and Compellence in the Gulf, 1990–91," 167.

54. Douglas Porch, "Occupational Hazards," *The National Interest* (2003), 35–46.

55. Minxin Pei, "From Victory to Success: Afterwar Policy in Iraq," *Foreign Policy,* 137 (July 2003), 1–55.

56. John Judis, "Imperial Amnesia," *Foreign Policy,* 143 (July 2004), 50–59.

— 6 —

THE DOMESTIC CONTEXT
OF AMERICAN FOREIGN POLICY

The end of the cold war did more than present American foreign policy with a new set of challenges and opportunities. It also has helped change the way in which foreign policy is made. Echoing what is now the conventional wisdom, one commentator observes:

> There is every indication of a new dynamic at work, one that redefines the relative roles of the public and leadership in the formulation of foreign policy, with the public assuming a larger role than some leaders may be comfortable with.[1]

The interplay of leaders and the public is of pivotal importance because a successful foreign policy must combine a well-crafted response to the challenges and opportunities of the international system with public support. Achieving public support is not always easily realized, and many questions surround how the public voice should be injected into the policy process. Should it come through the active participation of the public in making foreign policy decisions? If so, how should the public voice be expressed? Should it come early in the formulation of policy alternatives or only exist as a type of yes–no statement of support after policy makers have applied their expertise to the problem? Or should the public be largely passive, allowing policy makers a great deal of freedom of action in formulating foreign policy initiatives? James Billington argues the case for an active and involved public. "International affairs cannot be a spectator sport any more than policymaking can be the preserve of a small group of elites. Many must be involved; many more persuaded."[2] Walter Lippmann presents the opposite position.

125

The people have imposed a veto upon the judgement of the informed and responsible officials. They have compelled the governments, which usually knew what would have been wiser, was necessary, or was more expedient, to be too late with too little, or too long with too much, too pacifist in peace and too bellicose in war, too neutralist or too appeasing in negotiation or too intransigent. Mass opinion . . . has shown itself to be a dangerous master of decisions when the stakes are life and death.[3]

In this chapter we examine the major avenues available to the public in exercising its voice on foreign policy matters: public opinion, elections, interest group activity, and political protest. We also discuss how policy makers view the public voice in making foreign policy decisions and the role of the media.

Before examining these avenues of influence, preliminary questions must be asked: Who is the public? How does one go about making distinctions among a population as diverse as that in the United States? The organizing principle found to be most helpful is the individual's level of awareness on foreign policy matters. Approached from this perspective, the American public is composed of four groups that have remained relatively consistent in size over time. Writing in 1950, Gabriel Almond broke the American public into three categories: a large mass public made up of 75 to 90 percent of the adult population which is largely disinterested in and unattentive to foreign affairs; a smaller, attentive public made up of 10 percent of the adult population which is informed and interested and listens to the ideas and policies put forward by the policy and opinion elite; and another group made up of 1 to 2 percent of the adult population which also includes the last group made up of the official policy leadership: legislators, bureaucrats, and office holders in the executive branch.[4]

In 1978, Barry Hughes outlined a quite similar profile of the American public.[5] First, he found a large group comprising 30 percent of the public that was unaware of all but the most significant international events. Members of this group had at best vague and weak opinions. Second, there existed a large group comprising 45 percent of the public that was aware of many major international events but was not deeply informed about them. Hughes characterized the remaining 25 percent as being generally knowledgeable about foreign issues and holding relatively firm convictions. He labeled this group the opinion holders. Within it he identified a smaller group of activists (1 to 2 percent) who served as opinion mobilizers for the other segments of the public.

Recent evidence suggests that this picture of the American public as being largely ill-informed and inattentive to foreign policy issues is somewhat out of focus. According to Catherine M. Kelleher, "almost every general foreign policy survey . . . [now] shows that the American public is increasingly well-informed about global issues, devotes attention to evolving international events, and has opinions on most major foreign and defense policy questions."[6] This is not to say that the public necessarily favors the "correct" policy or the one best suited to protect American interests. But evidence does point to an American public that knows which policies it favors and which it opposes and that is consistent in its preferences.

The Media and American Foreign Policy

Not unexpectedly, it is the mass media—especially television—that many commentators point to as a major reason for this change. It is only recently that television has emerged from the shadows of the print media to become a major force in the foreign policy process.[7]

Consider how differently the October 1962 Cuban missile crisis might have been played out had it occurred in the 1990s.[8] Robert McNamara, President Kennedy's secretary of defense, observed, "I don't think that I turned on a television set during the whole two weeks of that crisis." During the 1990 Persian Gulf War, CNN was monitored regularly by government officials. Bush's Secretary of Defense Dick Cheney followed CNN in the period leading up to the air war for the first sign of leaks. CIA Director William Webster told National Security Adviser Brent Scowcroft to turn on CNN to find out where Iraqi missiles were landing. A similarly stark contrast exists among the viewing habits of the American people. In 1962, only 29 percent of Americans considered television news to be the most credible source of information, and the network evening news broadcasts on the major networks were only fifteen minutes long and relied heavily on sixteen-millimeter black-and-white footage of international events that were at least a day old because of the need to develop, edit, and transport the film to the United States. By 1980, 51 percent of Americans found television news to be their most credible news source, and that same year CNN came on the air with its twenty-four-hour news format.

During the Cuban missile crisis the Kennedy administration knew about the missiles in Cuba for six days before the information was broadcast to the American people. By contrast, President Bush was expected to respond almost instantly to Iraq's invasion of Kuwait and to pictures of starving people in Somalia. Today, it is not unreasonable to suspect that American television satellites might have discovered the presence of Russian missiles in Cuba at about the same time; that they would have run this story on *Nightline* or some other news program in which the pictures of Russian missiles were displayed along with recordings of Kennedy's September statement that there were no missiles in Cuba. Republican congressional leaders would have been invited to comment—and some would have demanded military action. Administration spokespeople would be inundated with questions about what they planned to do about the missiles and asked to explain how such a policy failure could have come about. Using military force was the option first embraced by the Kennedy administration, but it was abandoned as the week progressed in favor of the blockade. McNamara is uncertain that in such an altered decision-making environment the same decisions would have been reached.

To cope with the ability of the media to place administration foreign policy decisions under a telescope, it has become necessary for presidents to develop a television policy to accompany their foreign policy. The Bush administration succeeded in doing so during the Gulf War but failed with its Haitian, Bosnian, and Somalian policies, failures shared by the Clinton administration. In the former, the Bush administration was able to frame the policy issue in its own terms and control the media's coverage of it.[9] In the Gulf War, a "pool system" was put in place that served to limit the scope and depth of media reporting (such as denying permission to go to a bombed Iraqi nuclear facility for security reasons). This allowed the administration to place its "spin" on unfolding events. The Pentagon also initiated a Hometown News Project that flew over nine-hundred members of the press to Saudi Arabia to write stories about local servicepeople stationed in the Gulf. Not surprisingly, these human interest stories tended to be positive and served administration interests well.

Uncertain over how to proceed in Haiti, Bosnia, and Somalia, the Bush and Clinton administrations found the media far more troublesome.[10] Efforts to orchestrate coverage of Somalia failed. One Yugoslav commentator noted about coverage of the Balkans conflict, "confronted by the confusing new complexities of the post–cold war world, the world media had no clear guidance from their governments on how to view events." He continued, "in the absence of defined national interest, the U.S. media reported from the human side." The inability of U.S. administrations to respond to these images led to a chorus of congressional demands to "do something" and reinforced the view that American foreign policy had lost its sense of vision and competence. A similar failure to frame the issue on its own terms was evident on Haiti where the media gave extensive coverage to a hunger strike by Randall Robinson, executive director of TransAfrica, who was protesting Clinton administration policy.

Many in the media, responding to administration complaints that they are not fairly portraying American foreign policy or that they are hampering its conduct, make two points. First, very often administrations have developed television policies but not foreign policies. They are only showing the American public what is happening. If that does not correspond to declaratory statements of American foreign policy, it is not the media's fault. Second, the clearest way to limit the influence of the media is to enunciate a clear policy. The media's foreign policy influence is directly tied to the absence of a clear policy and the absence of contextual information to evaluate what they are seeing or reading about. Drawing upon his experience as a historian and CNN commentator, Michael Beschloss offers sixteen lessons to future presidents as they make foreign policy in the television age. They are found in Table 6.1.

The influence of the media extends beyond that of serving as a catalyst and accelerator of the decision-making process in Washington. It also affects the diplomatic dialogue between states.[11] In 1962, it took six to eight hours for classified communications to go from Moscow to Washington. This time gap was a major concern as both sides sought to end the crisis. McNamara states that it was because of Khrushchev's interest in closing this gap that his message of October 28 was sent in the clear over Radio Moscow.

The pace and restricted nature of international communications also gave added weight to the intelligence reports and views put forward by government sources such as the KGB and defense ministry. Bush administration officials note that they tried to use television to communicate directly with Saddam Hussein and provide him with "the bad news" they felt his aides tried

TABLE 6.1   Media Lessons for Modern-Day Presidents

1. Television offers presidents a superior weapon for framing issues and selling policy in crisis.

2. Television also amplifies public opposition; most presidents forget it, but this can improve and strengthen policy.

3. Television can encourage presidents to favor crisis management over long-term planning.

4. Television can drastically reduce the time, secrecy, and calm available to a president for deliberating with advisers on an urgent foreign policy problem.

5. Presidents cannot presume that they can maintain a monopoly on information for long.

6. Television allows presidents to communicate with adversary leaders and populations.

7. Television can seriously affect relations with allies.

8. LBJ's notion that Vietnam was lost on television is questionable.

9. Nonetheless, experience suggests that it is in a president's interest to design U.S. military ventures to be as brief and telegenic as possible.

10. Presidents shouldn't be obsessed in public over hostages.

11. Unexpected events shown on television can have inordinate influence on the public's perception of a foreign crisis.

12. When appearing on television during a crisis, a president and his high officials must be absolutely honest with the public.

13. Censorship can risk a damaging backlash.

14. During the use of force, there is no such thing as too much military success.

15. Television can help create an unexpected agenda, especially during the run-up or endgame of a war.

16. Presidents who fail to craft an implicit or explicit television strategy while dealing with a foreign crisis do so at their own peril.

Source: Hearings, Committee on Foreign Affairs, House of Representatives, 103rd Congress, April 26, 1994. (Washington, D.C.: U.S. Government Printing Office, 1994), pp. 52–53.

to hide from him. It could even be argued that under the glare of today's media coverage Khrushchev might not have tried to put Soviet missiles in Cuba, or that he might have proceeded differently. Only in places that the U.S. media "does not care about" might Khrushchev's strategy work today.

The media has had a similar impact on the relationship between diplomats and battlefield commanders and their respective superiors in Washington. During the Cuban missile crisis a great deal of concern was expressed that military action might be initiated in Cuba against the wishes of Khrushchev and that once begun their effect would be difficult to assess. The modern media and its associated technologies provides a direct link between decision makers in Washington and events abroad. The American media offered policy makers and citizens live broadcasts of incoming SCUD missiles and the Patriot antimissile defense system in operation. CNN provided live accounts of the effect of American bombing of Baghdad. It was not reports from the American embassy in Moscow that persuaded Bush that Yeltsin would survive the 1991 coup attempt but television images of him sitting atop a tank addressing his supporters.

That the American media does not care equally about all areas of the world or types of international relations problems is seen as a major source of bias in its impact on American foreign policy. Coverage decisions are based on three factors: "sizzle," parochial self-interest, and cost. Sizzle refers to a story's ability to stir emotions. It directs the media's attention to short-run, highly visual events and away from long-term stories that cannot be captured readily on film. Coups, civil war, demonstrations, and earthquakes are more visual and hence more likely to hold the audience's attention than are stories about grain production, trade in semiconductors, international debt, or rural development projects. But even graphic pictures are not enough to guarantee coverage. Footage of widespread famine in Ethiopia was first rejected by American television networks because it was not visual enough. When finally run, it was the last item on the national news broadcast for the evening.

Parochial self-interest deals with the perceived American stake in an issue. Typically, this is seen as involving areas where the United States has historically had close economic or cultural ties (Latin America, Israel, Western Europe) or where American troops are stationed (Korea, Vietnam). In other instances, parochial self-interest is largely defined by the White House. Presidential travel, presidential policy statements, and presidential agreements serve to drive the media's definition of what is important.

Cost considerations have always played a prominent role in decisions about international news coverage. One of the first challenges facing Ted Turner in setting up CNN was making it cost-effective. To hold down costs, CNN developed exchange agreements with other states that would be conducted over satellites. For the same reason it decided to go with a newswire format that emphasized live programming and to go live with breaking stories wherever possible. The initial costs were estimated at about $15 to $22 million per year. At this time, ABC, CBS, and NBC were spending $110 to $150 million per year on news. By 1991, CBS had closed bureaus in Hong Kong, Rome, and Frankfurt, leaving it with nine. NBC had ten and CBS seven. The consequence was felt almost immediately. In 1992, they covered less international news than in any of the previous three years, and the number of long pieces they presented was also down from earlier years.

THE MEDIA, PUBLIC OPINION, AND WAR

One of the most hotly debated aspects of television's coverage of foreign policy is the role it plays in shaping public opinion. Is it a window that policy makers can use to judge the temper of public opinion on a policy issue, a device that policy makers can use to manipulate public attitudes, an instrument that the politically active can use to pressure policy makers, or a little bit of each? The answer is important because media coverage can increase or restrict presidential powers vis-à-vis Congress.

Two points of reference for thinking about the relationship between the media, policy makers, and citizens have been suggested. The first involves "indexing." The media takes it cues about what to report from the political debate in Washington. If there is no debate; then there is no debate in the media. Somalia provides an example. Most commentators cite it as a text-book case of the media driving foreign policy decisions.[12] First, images of starving infants pushed the Bush administration to take action, and then im-ages of a dead American soldier being dragged through the streets com-pelled the Clinton administration to leave. Jonathan Mermin paints a more complex picture.[13] He argues that for the most part the media only "discov-ered" Somalia after it had already become a major concern for key policy makers in Washington.

The second is an "opinion cascade."[14] According to it, journalists look to the White House first for cues on how to define a problem. This is impor-tant because first impressions are often difficult to challenge. With this frame of reference in hand, journalists then go to other lesser news sources such as members of Congress, ex-government officials, and experts for commentary and input. At the next stage, these ideas frame how the media present the topic to the public. Dissenting opinion reaches the public under two condi-tions. First, when opponents to the administration use its frame of reference to challenge a policy. Most commonly this takes the form of arguing the pol-icy is good but implementation is bad. Second, when the political landscape is unsettled and no clear frame of reference exists for defining the problem. Under these conditions, the media looks just as much to the public as to elites in trying to frame a topic.

The Persian Gulf War.   American public opinion about the wisdom of using military force against Iraq underwent several abrupt shifts during the period between the August 1990 Iraqi invasion of Kuwait and the conclusion of hostilities in July 1991. Initially, the American public was sharply divided on the issue, with support for the war hovering around the 50 percent mark until President Bush's January 16, 1991, speech announcing the beginning of the bombing campaign. Support then shot up to 72 percent. Support surged again in February, this time to a high of 80 percent, when Bush an-nounced the beginning of the ground war, and it remained high for the remainder of the conflict. One explanation for this pattern is the "rally-around-the-flag" argument, which pictures the public as being very respon-sive to cues from policy makers and as predisposed to support the president in times of international crisis. Looked at from this perspective, the media becomes little more than a transmission belt for the exchange of one-sided supportive messages.

While not denying the impact of the rally-around-the-flag effect in the first surge in public support for the war, Barbara Allen and her colleagues assert that a much more complex picture emerges if the entire Persian Gulf crisis is examined.[15] They center their analysis on a "spiral of silence" hypoth-esis. According to it, when individuals hold opinions that they do not hear voiced by others they exercise self-censorship as a way of protecting them-selves from criticism. The opposite reaction takes place among those who re-ceive positive reinforcement for their views. They become even more vocal and confident in their beliefs, leading the dissenters to exercise even more self-censorship. The media plays a key role in this process by the way in which it frames issues through the use of symbols and causes individuals to access and use particular attitudes in evaluating an issue.

In the case of the Gulf War, in which the media in its selection of stories portrayed a growing American consensus in favor of military action, actual polling data pointed to the existence of an American public that was closely divided on the question at the start of the conflict. The networks all but ignored antiwar stories. Of 2,855 minutes of network news coverage of the war between August 8 and January 3, only twenty-nine minutes showed popular opposition to the American military buildup. Once military activities designed to liberate Kuwait began, network stories on opinion in the United States were framed in terms of patriotism, militarism, and nationalism. Film clips of war protesters were paired with scenes of Americans praying in churches. The views of congresspeople opposing the war were defined as "atypical" and the media declared that "of course, the political leaders are falling in behind the President."

The Iraq War.   One of the most fascinating questions raised by the Iraq War is why was the public so accommodating to presidential leadership to go to war when prior to the decision 65 percent agreed with the statement that the United States "should only invade Iraq with UN approval and the support of its allies.[16] Of those polled, 13 percent opposed the war altogether. Polling evidence suggests that misperceptions played a key role. In particular, many Americans were wrong about three "facts" according to polling done after the war, from June–September 2003. First, 45 to 52 percent of Americans questioned believed that evidence existed of a link between Iraq and al-Qaeda. Second, some 23 percent believed that weapons of mass destruction had been found. Third, about 25 percent of those questioned believed that the majority of people around the world supported the U.S. decision to go to war. Further analysis of the polling data showed the impact of these post–war misperceptions and support for the war. Only 23 percent of those polled who correctly answered these questions supported the war. In contrast, 86 percent of those who were wrong on all three counts supported it. Those who held that the majority of people in the world supported the war were 3.3 times more likely to support the war than those who correctly stated the majority of the world's people opposed the war.

When questioned as to where they received most of their news from, 19 percent said the print media and 80 percent said TV or radio. Fox was the news source of choice for those who had the most misperceptions (80 percent of its viewers held at least one of the three misperceptions), while NPR viewers held the least misperceptions (23 percent of its viewers held at least one of the three). So powerful is the impact of the source of news for holding misperceptions about the Iraq War that it is a more powerful predictor than level of education, party identification, and support for the President. Just as striking is the fact the no relationship existed between the degree to which people paid attention to the news and their holding misperceptions. In fact, the more one reported paying attention to Fox news slightly increased the chance of holding a misperception.

Public Opinion

Public opinion provides a first avenue open to the public for expressing its views on foreign policy. And while every president claims that they do not care what polls say the public thinks, every president since Richard Nixon has employed pollsters to do just that.[17] Nixon asked questions about Vietnam and admitting China to the United Nations. Ronald Reagan spent $4.1 million over eight years and tracked views on Iran–Contra and the bombing of the Marine barracks in Lebanon. During George W. Bush's administration, no issue has been followed more closely than the public's perceptions of the Iraq War.

As we have already noted, prior to the war the public was permissive in its outlook. Support for war ranged between 52 to 59 percent from August 2002 through early March 2003, while the number opposed fluctuated more widely between 35 to 43 percent. Looking beneath these overall figures shows that the country was divided on the war along a number of different lines. Six of ten young Americans (eighteen to twenty-nine) supported the war while less than five in ten older Americans (sixty-five and older) did so. Black Americans (56 percent) opposed the war, but Hispanic-Americans (60 percent) supported it. Women supported the war but only barely (51 percent).

Once the war began, the widely anticipated "rally around the flag" effect surfaced. The last Gallup poll before the war showed 64 percent in favor of it. Once war began on March 19, support for it jumped to 72 percent, and President George W. Bush's favorable rating jumped to 13 points. While significant, this was less than the 39-point jump in his ratings following the 9/11 attacks from 51 to 90 percent, or the 24-point jump to an 83 percent approval rating enjoyed by his father at the outset of the Persian Gulf War.

Interpreting a public opinion poll is not always easy. The public's response can easily be swayed by the wording of a question. For example, in 1964, 53 percent of those polled responded positively to a question asking if the United States should give aid to other countries if they needed help. Two years later a question asking if the United States should give aid to a country that failed to support it on a major foreign policy issue such as Vietnam produced a 75 percent anti-foreign aid response. A similar sensitivity to wording surfaced almost 30 years later. When asked if the United States should take all action necessary including military force to make sure Iraq withdrew from Kuwait, 65 percent said yes. When asked if the United States should initiate a war to force Iraq out of Kuwait only 28 percent said yes.

We can find a similar sensitivity to wording in the public's evaluation of the U.S. peacekeeping effort in Somalia. A CBS/New York Times poll asked the public, "Do you think the United States is doing [did] the right thing in sending U.S. troops to Somalia to try and make sure shipments of food get through to the people there or should U.S. troops have stayed out?" They also asked, "Given the [possible] loss of American lives and the other costs involved, do you think sending U.S. troops to make sure food gets through to the people of Somalia is worth the cost or not?" The first wording always produced more positive answers.[18]

TRENDS AND CONTENT

Given these types of problems, analysts conclude that when taken out of context, answers to foreign policy questions seldom provide an accurate reading of public opinion. Far more valuable is trend analysis where responses to questions are traced over time for their content and stability. Approached this way, public opinion polls have captured several clearly identifiable changes in the structure of American public opinion about foreign affairs issues. The pivotal event for the first change was World War II. Public opinion polls prior to World War II suggested a strongly isolationist outlook. In 1939, 70 percent of opinion holders said that the American entry into World War I was a mistake, and 94 percent of those with opinions felt that the United States should "do everything possible to stay out of foreign wars" rather than try to prevent one. The outbreak of fighting in Europe had little impact on U.S. attitudes. Public support for war against Germany only rose from 13 percent to 32 percent between late 1939 and late 1941.[19] Following the attack on Pearl Harbor, this situation changed dramatically. Internationalist sentiment came to dominate public perceptions about the proper U.S. role in the world. Between 1949 and 1969, 60 to 80 percent of the American public consistently favored an active U.S. participation in world affairs.[20]

Prior to Vietnam virtually all internationalists were in fundamental agreement on the nature of the international system and the makeup of U.S. foreign policy. Ole Holsti and James Rosenau suggest that eight axioms, or universally recognized truths, made up the foundation of this consensus. They included the beliefs that the United States had both the responsibility and the capability to create a just and stable world order, that peace and security are indivisible, that the Soviet Union was the primary threat to world order, and that containment was the most effective way of meeting the Soviet challenge.[21] Foreign policy based on these axioms could expect to receive the support of the American people. When disagreements arose, they tended to be over the process of making foreign policy rather than over its substance.

Vietnam was the next pivotal event shaping the direction of public attitudes. Lloyd Free and William Watts have traced the shifting fortunes of internationalism from the time of the U.S. involvement in Vietnam.[22] Beginning with 1964 data, they have classified responses to public opinion polls along an internationalist–isolationist continuum. What emerges from their study is a steady and precipitous erosion of internationalist sentiment from 1964 to 1974 and its reemergence as the majority perspective in 1980. In 1964, 65 percent of the public was defined as internationalist. This fell to 59 percent in 1968, 56 percent in 1972, and 41 percent in 1974. That year also saw a dramatic increase in the number of isolationist responses from 9 percent in 1972 to 21 percent. While isolationist sentiment would build to a high of 23 percent in 1976, 1974 was the low point for internationalism. Those supporting an active U.S. role rose in number to 61 percent in 1980. By that time isolationist sentiment had fallen back to 13 percent. No single, pivotal event seems to be associated with this rebirth of internationalism, although the 1972 to 1973 oil crisis is closely linked with it in terms of time. Instead, the American public gradually came to see the international system as threatening and out of control and had a renewed willingness to use U.S. power and influence to protect U.S. national interests.

Pronounced changes have occurred in Americans' self-image and the types of foreign policy problems they worry most about. A poll conducted by the Chicago Council on Foreign Relations in late 1998 found that the American public appears to have grown more self-confident as the cold war receded.[23] Fifty percent feel that the United States now plays a more important and more powerful role in the world than it did ten years ago. Seventy-nine percent of the public anticipates that the United States will play an even greater role in ten years. Sixty-three percent of the public now view economic strength as the key determining factor to overall power and influence in the world. The four most highly ranked U.S. foreign policy goals were (1) preventing the spread of nuclear weapons, (2) stopping the flow of illegal drugs into the United States, (3) protecting the jobs of American workers, and (4) combating international terrorism. From the public's vantage point, the four most important countries to the United States are, in order, Japan, Russia, Saudi Arabia, and China. The public's attitudes toward Russia have undergone considerable change with the sense of goodwill that appeared in the immediate post–cold war era now replaced by a sense that Russia should solve its own problems.

On a deeper level, however, neither the Cold War nor the war on terrorism appears to have changed the underlying structure of American attitudes on foreign policy. A 1992 study conducted by Ole Holsti found that it continued to be possible to place American opinion leaders into one of four categories that were developed by Eugene Wittkopf in the mid-1980s.[24] They are hard-liners, accommodationists, internationalists, and isolationists. Holsti's study found little support among opinion leaders for a return to across-the-board isolationism as the cornerstone of American foreign policy. Only 9 percent of respondents were classified in this manner. Fifty-three percent were accommodationists, 33 percent internationalists, and 9 percent hard-liners. Even more important than the distribution of opinion leaders across categories is that knowing where individuals fit continues to allow one to predict with great confidence their positions on issues involving the use of force, strengthening the United Nations, and the nature of future security threats facing the United States. One important policy area that does not fit into the framework (that is, one could not make accurate predictions about a respondent's policy position) is trade and protectionism.

Similarly, public opinion data suggest that the 9/11 terrorist attacks did not fundamentally alter the basic internationalist beliefs of Americans.[25] A poll conducted in November 2001 showed that 81 percent of Americans felt it was important for the United States to take an active role in the world. This was the highest level ever recorded since the question was first asked in 1947. Both before and after 9/11, a strong majority of Americans voiced support for sharing the burdens of international activism with others. Also consistent with the pre–9/11 post–cold war public opinion polls is the continued emphasis placed by Americans on domestic matters. A May 2002 Gallup poll found that 53 percent of Americans think the government is spending the right amount to fight the war on terrorism. The 2002 Chicago Council on Foreign Relations poll found that 65 percent of Americans wanted to spend more money on homeland security and 44 percent wanted to spend more on defense. This compares with 77 percent (the highest response) who want to spend more on health care, 75 percent who want increased aid to education, and 70 percent who want more money to combat crime and violence. The single greatest area of support for increased spending in foreign affairs was for added funds for intelligence gathering. It grew 39 percent from 27 percent to 66 percent.

PUBLIC OPINION AND THE USE OF FORCE

The conventional wisdom inherited from the Vietnam era was that the public was unwilling to support the use of force if it resulted in casualties. The policy implication of this reading of the public led policy makers to either avoid the use of force altogether or use it under highly controlled settings. The accumulated evidence on the use of force from the 1960s through the 1990s now points in a different direction. The public is not totally gun shy. It will support the use of military force even when casualties occur depending upon (1) the policy purpose behind its use, (2) the success or failure of the undertaking, and (3) the degree of leadership consensus. In a related vein, other studies suggest that the public is sensitive to the domestic costs of foreign policy activism. The more serious the domestic problems relative to the external challenge the more powerful will be the public's isolationist impulse. Thus, the weaker the economy the less support a president is likely to find for an activist foreign policy.[26]

Of particular interest on the first point is a study undertaken by Bruce Jentleson[27] who argues that the American public is most likely to use military force when the purpose is to restrain the foreign policy actions of a hostile state and least likely to do so when the purpose is to bring about internal political change. A summary of his findings is presented in Table 6.2. This shows that all five uses of force that involved attempts to curb the foreign policy activities of another state ranked higher than any effort to use military force to bring about internal political change. Public support for the war against Iraq bears out Jentleson's argument. Support was highest for Operation Desert Shield and Operation Desert Storm, which were designed primarily to curb Iraqi foreign policy adventurism by defending Saudi Arabia and liberating Kuwait. The American public was distinctly less interested in using American military power to protect the Kurds or Shiites in southern Iraq after President Bush announced the cease-fire. A similar pattern of public support emerged in 1999 for NATO's bombing in Kosovo to stop Serb aggression.

The impact of race and gender has been an important area of inquiry in the study of public opinion and the use of force. Distinct racial differences appear to exist. When the Iraq War started, only 29 percent of blacks polled

TABLE 6.2   Policy Objectives and Public Support

Case	Principal Policy Objective	Public Support Score (re-ranking)*
Libya: antiterrorism	FPR	1
Persian Gulf reflagging	FPR	2
Lebanon	Mixed	3
Afghanistan	Mixed	4
Nicaragua: military exercises	FPR	5
Panama (preinvasion)	IPC	6
El Salvador	IPC	7
Libya: get Qaddafi	IPC	8
Nicaragua: overthrow Sandinistas	IPC	9

*Re-ranking excludes halo-effect cases
FPR = foreign policy restraint
IPC = internal political change
Source: Bruce W. Jentleson, "The Pretty Prudent Public," International Studies Quarterly, 36 (1990), 64.

supported it. This is significantly down from the 59 percent who supported the Persian Gulf War, but in each case it is below the level of support offered by white. A Chicago Council of Foreign Relations poll in the mid-1990s found that the only hypothetical conflict situation in which nonwhites were more willing than white to use military force was in a South African civil war.[28] Research on gender also shows differences. On average, regardless of the purpose, women are less supportive of the use of military force. They are also more sensitive to humanitarian concerns and the loss of life. Having said this, women are not pacifists. Richard Eichenberg notes "any differences occur at the margins, in response to specific circumstances."[29] At the same time, they conclude that the magnitude of these differences on some issues "have the potential to be a significant factor in political decisions to employ military force and in the political response to the use of force." Table 6.3 presents a snapshot view of how men and women responded differently to the use of force between 1990 and 2003.

IMPACT

The question of how much influence opinion has on American foreign policy can be answered two ways. One can look (1) to the type of impact it has and (2) to the conditions necessary for it to be heard. Public opinion can have three types of impact on the policy process and the nature of American foreign policy. It can serve as a constraint on policy innovation, a source of policy innovation, and a resource to be drawn upon by policy makers in implementing policy. Public opinion acts as a constraint by defining the limits to what is politically feasible. As we have just seen, many regard the existence of unstable moods as a powerful constraint on U.S. foreign policy. A case can

TABLE 6.3   Gender-Based Differences on Use of Military Force

Policy Issue	Female % in favor	Male % in favor
Conflict		
War against terror	70.5	80.0
Persian Gulf War	49.8	66.8
Somalia	52.6	61.4
Kosovo/Serbia	47.0	54.4
Type of Military Action		
Air/missile strikes/bombing	54.1	66.6
Send troops abroad	48.1	60.0
Policy Objective		
Foreign policy restraint	54.9	68.1
Humanitarian intervention	63.4	68.1
Internal political change	43.8	53.2
Peacekeeping	43.4	49.6
Mention of Casualties		
War on terror/no casualties mentioned	73.8	82.4
War on terror/casualties mentioned	58.0	71.5
Haiti/no casualties mentioned	31.3	42.5
Haiti/casualties mentioned	26.0	37.7

Source: Richard Eichenberg, "Gender Differences in Public Attitudes toward the Use of Force by the United States, 1990–2003," *International Security,* 28 (2003), Tables 2, 3, 4, 5.

also be made that the existence of too firm an outlook or too rigid a division of opinion is just as much a constraint. The deeply entrenched isolationist outlook of the American public during the 1930s made it extremely difficult for Roosevelt to prepare the United States for World War II. A firm but divided opinion is cited by one major study as responsible for the prolonged U.S. presence in Vietnam.[30] Faced by a damned-if-they-do-and-damned-if-they-don't dilemma, successive administrations are seen as having followed a strategy of perseverance until a public consensus developed for either a strategy of victory or withdrawal. Richard Sobel reaches a similar conclusion about the influence of public opinion in his study of U.S. interventions after Vietnam.[31] By matching public opinion poll data with the comments made by policy makers about the decisions they participated in either through memoirs or public statements, he finds that public opinion constrains policy makers but does not determine U.S. intervention policy.

Observers generally agree that public opinion rarely serves as a stimulus to policy innovation. Policy makers fear losing public support much more than they feel compelled to act because "the public demands it." One commentator argues that "no major foreign policy decision in the U.S. has been made in response to a spontaneous public demand."[32] While this may be the case, public opinion today does appear to be capable of placing new items on the political agenda. The nuclear freeze movement demonstrates both the potential and the limitations of public opinion as a source of policy innovation. Springing spontaneously from the American public in winter 1982, the nuclear freeze movement did not produce a major breakthrough in arms control policy. It did, however, give renewed life to the arms control process that had stalled in the Reagan administration's first term. As an aide to Senator Edward Kennedy noted, Kennedy's legislative leadership on nuclear freeze matters was not a case of his mobilizing public opinion in opposition to Reagan's policies but one of Kennedy's trying to "catch up with the country."[33]

Four factors have been identified as playing a key role in determining how much influence public opinion will have on American foreign policy.[34] First, at least 50 percent of the American public must share the opinion. According to Thomas W. Graham, when 79 percent of the American public is of one mind the influence of public opinion will be nearly automatic. At 60 percent it should be enough to overcome strong bureaucratic opposition. Second, public opinion's influence is greatest if exercised at the agenda-building stage and ratification stages of the policy process. It will be indirect at best in the negotiation and implementation stages. Third, political elites must be open to public opinion. One study found that great variation existed among presidents in terms of their beliefs that listening to public opinion was either desirable or a practical necessity in making decisions. Interestingly, regardless of outlook presidents tended to respond to how they anticipated the public would respond rather than the public's actual views on a problem.[35] The final limiting factor is the ability (or, more commonly, inability) of political leaders to structure their policy positions in ways that allow them to turn existing public attitudes into a political resource.

Elections

Almost invariably, the winning candidate in an election cites the results as a mandate for his or her policy program. Yet is this really the case? Do elections serve as a mechanism for translating the public voice into policy? The evidence suggests that claims of popular mandates are overstated and are based on a flawed reading of election returns. A look back at the Lyndon Johnson–Barry Goldwater election of 1964 and the 1968 Democratic New Hampshire primary shows just how deceptive electoral outcomes can be. In each case Vietnam was the major issue. In 1964 Johnson won a landslide victory over Goldwater, who had campaigned on a platform of winning the war against communism in Vietnam "by any means necessary." The results were commonly interpreted as a mandate for restraint in the war effort. National surveys, however, revealed a far more complex picture: 82 percent of those who wanted to maintain the U.S. presence in Vietnam supported Johnson over Goldwater, as did 63 percent of those who favored withdrawal and 52 percent of those who favored a stronger stand such as invading North Vietnam.[36] In 1968 Eugene McCarthy "upset" Johnson in the New Hampshire primary even though Johnson received more votes than he did (49 to 41 percent). McCarthy's strong performance was widely interpreted as a repudiation of Johnson's handling of the war and an endorsement of McCarthy's dovish position. Analysis reveals that in terms of overall numbers, McCarthy received more votes from dissatisfied hawks than from doves. Quite simply, it often becomes difficult to tell whether people voted for candidates out of support for their policy stance or in spite of it.[37]

For elections to confer a mandate upon the winner, three demands are made of the voter: (1) they must be knowledgeable, (2) they must cast their ballots on the basis of issue preferences, and (3) they must be able to distinguish between parties or candidates.

VOTER KNOWLEDGE AND ISSUE VOTING

Evidence on the first point is not encouraging. The large majority of citizens lack both a knowledge of foreign affairs and an interest in them. The lack of widespread public understanding about foreign affairs issues never ceases to amaze commentators. In 1996, Republican presidential candidate Robert Dole sought to make President Clinton's refusal to build an antimissile system an issue in the campaign. It failed to catch on because many voters refused to believe the United States did not already have one. A participant in a focus group, when told no missile shield existed, stated: "I don't believe you, you couldn't pay me enough to believe you . . . you see it in the movies." Other examples are equally telling:

1964: 38 percent know that Russia was not a member of NATO.

1964: 58 percent know that the United States was a member of NATO.

1966: Over 80 percent fail to properly identify the Vietcong.

1972: 63 percent could identify China as communist.

1979: 23 percent knew which countries were involved in the SALT talks.

1983: 8 percent knew that the United States supported the government in El Salvador and the insurgents in Nicaragua.

1987: Following the Reagan–Gorbachev summit in Washington, only 50 percent of the public correctly answered one or more of five questions regarding the basic provisions of the INF treaty.

1993: 43 percent could not identify which continent Somalia was on.[38]

2003: 68 percent believed Iraq played an important role in the terrorist attacks of 9/11.

Do candidates win because of their policy preferences or in spite of them? Much evidence supports the view that voters do not respond to issues when casting their ballots. Instead, they are heavily influenced by party affiliation, candidate image, incumbency, or some other nonissue factor. Historically, foreign policy has not been a good issue on which to conduct a campaign. Economic issues have exerted a greater influence on people vote. For example, in 1992 by a margin of 57 to 36 percent, Americans felt that George H. W. Bush would do a better job of handling foreign policy than Bill Clinton but did not return him to office. Foreign policy issues have their biggest electoral impact when a stringent set of conditions are present. First, candidates must take different positions on issues (a point we return to in the next section). Second, the issue must be important to the voter. Third, the voter was knowledgeable about the issue. Moreover, the number of Americans for whom a single issue, domestic or foreign policy, is likely to be of intense concern to Americans is very small other than something like terrorism. In the absence of these conditions, party identification, candidate image, incumbency, or some other nonissue factor play the most important roles. The influence of party on candidate evaluation is fully evident in how the public viewed the Bush administration's pre-war claims about Iraq's possession of weapons of mass destruction. Of those polled, 75 percent of Democrats said that Bush had lied or exaggerated on the subject. An equally large number of Republicans said he had not. Among swing voters (those defined as independents who expected to vote in the 2004 election), 52 percent felt that Bush had misled the public.

Charles Whalen, a six-term Republican from Ohio who retired in 1980, sees the sporadic interest and low information level of constituents on foreign policy matters as a point of vulnerability to incumbents.[39] Challengers attempt to create an image of having policy differences with the incumbent and to cast the incumbent in a negative light. They find a powerful weapon in foreign affairs voting records. These issues are often complex and when taken out of context can place the incumbent on the defensive and greatly increase the cost and uncertainty of a reelection campaign.

Examples of what concerns Whalen are easy to find. Representatives Morris Udall and Paul Findley voted with the administration against the Young Amendment to the FY1980 Foreign Aid Appropriations Bill, which would have barred any indirect aid from going to a specified list of communist states. The United States had no intention of sending any aid to these states but objected to the wording "indirect" aid because it would have violated the charters of the international organizations distributing the aid. Both faced electoral campaign charges of being in favor of giving aid to communist states. In 2000, the Cuban-American National Foundation, a powerful anti-Castro lobbying force, targeted congresspeople George Nethercutt, Jr., and Blanche Lincoln who supported lifting U.S. economic sanctions against Cuba. Advertisements asserted that by voting to lift these sanctions voters would be strengthening Castro and allowing him to continue to engage in forced child labor and child prostitution, sponsoring international terrorism, and imprisoning political prisoners.

PARTY AND CANDIDATE DIFFERENCES

The third prerequisite for elections to serve as a mandate is that voters must be able to distinguish between party and candidate positions. Compared to their European counterparts, American political parties do not offer voters a clear and consistent choice. They are neither ideologically distinct nor internally cohesive. Election campaigns generally find the two major parties on the same side of an issue. Both are for peace, opposed to corruption, and for a stronger defense. In 1980 both Carter and Reagan favored increasing U.S. military capabilities. In 1964 neither Johnson nor Goldwater advocated getting out of Vietnam, while in 1968 both Humphrey and Nixon did. The 1992 election found Clinton and George Bush in general agreement on cutbacks in defense spending, NAFTA, and the conduct of the Persian Gulf War. In the 2000 George W. Bush–Al Gore campaign, both candidates endorsed higher military spending, expressed concern about committing U.S. forces abroad, and were willing to proceed with work on a ballistic missile defense system. William Schneider argues that candidates stress issues that find most people on the same side of the argument out of the need to form and hold together broad electoral coalitions. Issues where candidates may truly advocate competing policy positions are best suited to primary campaigns where the candidate is trying to stand out apart from other competitors. General elections thus turn out to be less a debate on the issues and more a contest in who the public feels is best capable of achieving the same goals.[40] In this respect, a strong foreign policy record does provide incumbents with an electoral edge because it can be used to demonstrate their leadership abilities.

IMPACT

What then is the impact of elections on U.S. foreign policy? Elections do serve to change leaders and thereby alter policies. They do not, however, appear capable of providing policy makers with a foreign affairs mandate. The preconditions for such a role go largely, although not entirely, unmet. Thus, while policies may change as the result of an election, the correspondence between this change and public attitudes is often tenuous. Many observers see one significant impact of elections on foreign policy that exists quite apart from its ability or inability to confer a mandate. "Foreign governments have long understood the difficulty of doing business with the U.S. in election years."[41] Foreign policy initiatives come to a halt as all sides await the outcome of the election, and U.S. foreign policy takes on a nationalistic and militant character. For example, in May 1988 the Senate by a vote of 83 to 6 voted to give the military a major new role in the war on drugs. In doing so the Senate was described as lining up in the election-year crusade against illegal drugs and critics were quoted as condemning the measure as election-year "posturing."[42] A recent example of posturing is the 97 to 3 vote by the Senate in 1999 committing the United States to build a national ballistic missile defense system. The bill did not authorize the spending of any funds or set a target date and did not reflect the true—and much closer—division of opinion on this program in the Senate. Candidates attempting to read the climate of opinion sense a general lack of interest in foreign policy initiatives. It is politically safer to restrict oneself to pledges of maintaining U.S. prestige and military strength than to advocate specific courses of action. Foreign policy initiatives always run the risk of failure and even in success can bring with them charges of having paid too high a price or of having let allies off too easily.

William Quandt believes that the influence of American elections on foreign policy extends well beyond the presidential election year.[43] He sees an electoral cycle existing that influences noncrisis foreign policy decisions during a president's entire term in office. The first year in office generally is characterized by policy experimentation, false starts, and overly zealous goals. This is due to the continued influence of overly simplistic campaign rhetoric that comes about because presidents are forced to take positions on issues before they have mastered the intricacies of managing the presidency. Instinctively, they return to the themes that served them so well during the campaign. During the second year in office pragmatism becomes more evident. This is because of both the increased knowledge and skill of the administration and the realization that a foreign policy mishap may lead to the loss of House and Senate seats in the mid-term election. Quandt suggests that in the third year foreign policy issues will largely be evaluated in terms of their impact on the reelection campaign. Potential successes will be pursued vigorously even if the price tag is high, while the administration will try to disengage itself from potential losses. As noted above, the final year brings stalemate to the foreign policy process. The most propitious time for foreign policy undertakings is the first year and one-half of a second term. Here one finds an experienced president who knows what he wants to do in foreign affairs operating under the halo effect of a reelection victory. By late in the second year of a president's second term, electoral considerations begin to overwhelm foreign policy as jockeying begins in both parties for their respective presidential nominations. At some point, the president will come to be regarded at home and abroad as a "lame duck," which limits his or her ability to conduct foreign policy.

The 2004 election year largely confirmed to these expectations. Bilateral free trade agreements signed by the Bush administration were not submitted to the Senate in order to avoid a public debate on trade policy. The nomination of a new head of the CIA was postponed until after the election. According to press accounts, the Bush administration placed great pressure on Pakistan in spring 2004 to capture or kill Osama bin Laden or one of his key aides before November.

Interest Groups

The third avenue open to the public for expressing its outlook on foreign policy issues is interest group activity. Here the public communicates to policy makers through an intermediary rather than directly, as with public opinion and elections. To its advocates the interest group approach holds several advantages over the real or perceived limitations of the more direct mechanisms for expressing opinions about foreign policy. First, the informational demands on individuals are lessened. They need not stay up-to-date in their knowledge of foreign policy matters because they can rely on group leaders to look after their interests. Second, interest groups provide a more continuous and concrete form of input than do periodic elections and occasional public opinion polls. Third, this input brings with it more political clout than does the individual expression of an opinion or the anonymous act of voting.

Critics of the interest group approach raise two major, but quite different, objections to the utility of pressure group lobbying as a means of influencing policy. The first objection is that interest groups have little influence over foreign policy decision making. Two reasons are commonly given. Ineffective interest group activity is held to stem from the division of opinion within interest groups, the existence of competing interest groups within a policy area, and the very nature of lobbying. The first problem typically has plagued large business groups such as the Chamber of Commerce. Divisions within their ranks over the merits of protectionist legislation and restrictions on trade with communist states make it difficult for these groups to adopt a single policy position. The second problem is that interest groups and lobbyists typically are found on both sides of an issue. It was not the case that all interest groups opposed the SALT II treaty. Protreaty groups (the Federation of American Scientists and the Council for a Livable World) competed with those opposed to it (the Committee for the Present Danger and the Coalition for a Democratic Majority).

The second major objection to interest group activity is the reverse of the first. Interest group activity is too successful—but only for some. The resources needed for success (money, organizational infrastructure, leadership, access) are unevenly distributed. Instead of competition among groups to determine policy outcomes, there exists the permanent domination of a select group of interests against all the rest. "Iron triangles" are created in which interest groups, congressional committees, and bureaucrats are linked together, short-circuiting the open access of the policy process to domestic influences.

The most powerful statement of this point of view is expressed in the idea of a military industrial complex.[44] At the core of this argument is the assertion that there exists within U.S. policy-making circles a dominant force consisting of professional soldiers, industrialists, and government officials. Acting in unison, they determine policy on defense-related matters. The resulting policies are based on an ideology of international conflict that requires high levels of military spending, a large defense establishment, and a belligerent, interventionist foreign policy.

The idea of a military industrial complex is relatively recent. The term was coined by C. Wright Mills in 1956 and given high visibility by President Eisenhower in his farewell address when he warned against its unwarranted influence and the dangers of misplaced power.[45] In the 1960s, it became a major theme in writings of those who opposed the U.S. involvement in Vietnam. Concerns about its influence waned in the 1970s with the shift in emphasis from confrontation and containment to détente.

The Iraq War with its heavy reliance on private-sector contractors to provide key services brought forward new allegations about the existence of military-industrial complex. At the center of the storm was Halliburton. One of the world's largest companies providing products and services to the oil industry, it employs over 100,000 people and operates in over 120 countries. In the early 1990s, it gained notoriety for supplying Libya and Iraq with oil drilling equipment that could be used to detonate nuclear weapons. In 1995, it paid a $1.2 million fine for violating the U.S. export ban to Libya. That same year Dick Cheney became Halliburton's CEO. He would speak out against export bans to rogue states such as Iran and Libya as being motivated by political pressure groups. During the Iraq War, Halliburton was one of the major beneficiaries of the government's awarding of no-bid contracts for services and saw its net profit fro the second quarter of 2003 reach $26 million when it showed a second quarter loss of $498 million in 2002. The company has come under investigation by the Defense Department for overcharging for some of the services provided under the terms of the $1.7 billion worth of contracts it holds as part of Operation Iraqi Freedom.

Efforts to establish the validity of assertions about the influence of the military industrial complex on U.S. foreign policy have produced mixed results. General agreement exists on the presence of a military-industrial complex, but there is disagreement on how to interpret its influence. One observer suggests that the competing judgments can be reconciled if we make a distinction between the major political decisions, which set into motion high rates of defense spending, and the legislative and administrative decisions, which translate them into concrete programs. The influence of the military industrial complex is greatest in the second area and far less in the first where it faces strong competition from ideological, economic, and other nonmilitary influences.

TYPES OF GROUPS

A wide variety of groups actively try to influence U.S. foreign policy. Consider its China policy. In the early 1980s, when there was a general consensus on what that policy should be, interest group activity was relatively contained. When that consensus broke down in 1989 to 1990, a surge of interest group activity tried to exploit policy disagreements over the relative importance of political, religious freedom, trade, nonproliferation, Taiwan, and Tibet in American foreign policy.[46] A representative list of interest groups active in this policy area would include such diverse groups as the AFL-CIO, Amnesty International, the Christian Coalition of America, the Committee of 100 for Tibet, the Emergency Committee for American Trade, the Family Research Council, the National Endowment for Democracy, the Asia Society, and the U.S.-China business council.

Ethnic Groups.   Three aspects of the policy-making process are particularly favorable to ethnic lobbying: framing issues, providing information and analysis to support policy options and engaging in oversight of how policies are implemented. The most successful ethnic lobbies have relied on three ingredients to give them political clout: the threat of switching allegiances at election time either from one party to another or to another candidate in the same party, a strong and effective lobbying apparatus, and the ability to build their case around traditional American symbols and ideals.[47]

Currently, the Jewish-American lobby possesses the most formidable combination of these elements. The centerpiece of the Jewish lobbying effort for Israel is the highly organized, efficient, and well-financed American–Israel Public Affairs Committee (AIPAC), which serves as an umbrella organization for pro-Israeli groups. It "promptly and unfailingly provides all members [of Congress] with data and documentation, supplemented, as circumstances dictate, with telephone calls and personal visits on those issues touching upon Israeli national interests."[48] The successes of the Jewish lobby have been many. Beginning with the Truman administration's recognition of Israel in 1947 and later on matters of foreign aid and arms sales, successive administrations have privately acknowledged or publicly confronted its power.

In the 1980s AIPAC became an active force in American electoral politics. During the 1986 election campaign it was estimated that eighty pro-Israeli PACs donated nearly $7 million to candidates. A 1986 memo that was obtained by the *Washington Post* from AIPAC to other pro-Israeli lobbies urged them to make donations to five specific Senate candidates that it wished to see reelected. In 1984 Senator Rudy Boschwitz, who chaired the Senate Foreign Relations Subcommittee on the Middle East, received more than one-third of the $4.25 million that pro-Israeli PACs gave to congressional candidates. Incumbents have also felt the wrath of AIPAC. Opponents of Representative Paul Finley, Senator Charles Percy, and Senator Jesse Helms all received hearty backing from pro-Israeli forces. (In Finley's case, 90 percent of his opponent's funds came from Jewish sources.) Finley and Percy were defeated and Helms became a strong supporter of Israel following his hard-fought reelection victory.

In August 2002, the perils of ethnic lobbying also surfaced. Israeli Prime Minister Ariel Sharon was scheduled to appear the next month in Florida as the guest of the Greater Miami Jewish Federation. Democrats argued his presence just before the primary was also designed to help Republican Governor Jeb Bush's reelection bid. Stung by this attack, Sharon cancelled the trip citing domestic matters in Israel that needed attending.

No Arab-American lobbying force equal to AIPAC has yet emerged.[49] In 1972 a central organization, the National Association of Arab Americans (NAAA), was founded, and in the mid-1980s it had field coordinators in every congressional district and a membership of some 100,000 Arab-American families. In 1984, it founded a political action committee and provided $20,000 in campaign funding to twenty-two Democratic and twenty-four Republican candidates. This compares to the $2.8 million in funding provided by some seventy-six pro-Israeli political action committees. A major obstacle in the way of creating an effective Arab lobbying force is the ethnic diversity of Arab Americans. Until 1948 most Arabs coming to the United States were Christians from Syria and Lebanon. Since 1978 most have been Muslims. The result is that no single political agenda exists for Arab Americans. A consensus exists only on the broad issues of pursuing a comprehensive peace plan in the Middle East and establishing better U.S. relations with the Arab world. Of special concern in this regard are U.S. foreign aid and arms sales policies.

By the mid-1980s, African Americans had made great strides toward meeting two of the three prerequisites we listed. First, as the Reverend Jesse Jackson's 1984 bid for the presidency made clear, blacks make up an important constituency within the Democratic party. Second, an organizational base, TransAfrica, now exists. Founded in 1977, TransAfrica now has over 10,000 members and an annual budget of over $1.4 million. The major focus of black lobbying in the mid-1980s was reorienting U.S. policy toward South Africa. With this issue behind it, African Americans have had a more difficult time mobilizing on foreign policy issues.[50] On genocide in Rwanda, the African-American community evidenced an overall lack of interest. This has been explained by the absence of a clear-cut black-white dimension to the problem. The crisis in Haiti during the Clinton administration more closely resembled this type of situation and, in fact, one of the reasons Clinton felt forced to act was lobbying by African Americans led by Randall Robinson, who threatened to go on a hunger strike if action were not taken to return Jean-Bertrand Aristide to power.

Ethnic diversity is a problem for Hispanic-American lobbying on foreign policy.[51] Mexican immigration has been motivated largely by economic considerations, is concentrated in the Southwest, and is largely Democratic. (In 1980, Carter got 72 percent of this vote.) Cuban immigration is concentrated on the East Coast, has been motivated largely by political concerns, and is politically conservative and Republican. (Reagan got 59 percent of Florida's Hispanic vote.) To this, one must also add Puerto Ricans, who are concentrated largely in the Midwest and Northeast and who vote Democratic.

Two additional fissures exist within the Hispanic community that makes the establishment of an effective lobbying force difficult. It pits American-born Hispanics against immigrants.[52] The only real area of overlapping concerns is immigration policy. When questioned as to their policy priorities American-born Hispanics give greatest weight to domestic issues such as education, crime, economic growth, and the environment. Only American-born Cuban-Americans consistently site foreign policy problems. Immigrants, on the other hand, are home-oriented. This is particularly notable in two respects. First, they send considerable amounts of money home each year. In 1999, more than $5.6 billion was sent back to Mexico, $1.4 billion to El Salvador, and $1.5 billion to the Dominican Republic. Second, candidates from Latin America now routinely come to the United States in search of votes and campaign funding from immigrant communities. The second fissure is generational. It came through clearly in the differing reactions to Bush's June 2004 imposition of tight restrictions on travel to Cuba and on the practice of sending money to relatives still there. The ban was supported by the 250,000 remaining "historic exiles" who fled Cuba right after Castro seized power and opposed by those who fled more recently.

The most successful Hispanic lobby is the Cuban-American National Foundation.[53] It vehemently opposes any change in American policy toward Cuba and has been charged with intimidating and harassing those members of the Cuban-American community in Florida who wish to open a dialogue with Castro. Former Reagan administration UN Ambassador Jeane Kirkpatrick and Florida Senators Bob Graham and Connie Mack have served on commissions that the foundation has established. Its Free Cuba political action committee (PAC) made $114,000 in campaign contributions in the 1989–1990 elections. In mid-1992 it had contributed to twenty-six congressional candidates and "maxed out" on its contribution to Representative Robert Torricelli, who represented a large Cuban-American community in New Jersey and authored the 1992 Cuban Democracy Act. Passed by Congress in an election year and endorsed by both Bush and Clinton in an effort to gain the support of the Cuban-American community, this piece of legislation has been derided by its critics as an "economic declaration of war" against Castro and a violation of international free trade agreements. The act prohibits foreign affiliates of U.S. firms from doing business in Cuba.

While ethnic groups have long been active in trying to influence U.S. foreign policy toward their homelands, the end of the cold war and the accompanying decline in influence of traditional foreign policy elites have ushered in a new era of activism and heightened influence. The 1996 senatorial race in South Dakota saw a battle in which the Democratic candidate raised over $150,000 from Pakistani-American groups while the Republican candidate (who authored legislation cutting U.S. foreign aid to Pakistan) raised approximately the same amount from Indian-American sources. The influence of these groups is now also found in the halls of Congress. Founded in 1993, the Congressional India Caucus now has some 115 members. Twice in 1999 India's supporters blocked legislation that would have cut off aid to India. Also emerging are signs of joint ethnic group lobbying efforts. In 2003, India and Israel jointly lobbied Congress on the terms of a $3 billion foreign aid package for Pakistan. They successfully got language inserted that pressured Pakistan to stop Islamic militants from crossing into India. Earlier they worked together to get Bush administration approval of an Israeli arms sale to India. In 2000, the United States had blocked a similar sale to China. U.S. approval is needed because the weapons in question contain American-built parts.

Foreign Lobbying.   Foreign lobbying has become big business in Washington. In 1990, with his capital under attack by rebel forces and the United States lukewarm in its support for him, Liberian President Samuel Doe paid a Washington lobbyist $800,000 to improve his image. One of the main objectives of Nelson Mandela's 1990 trip to the United States was to lobby Congress and mobilize public support for continued economic sanctions against South Africa. In 1993 Libya hired Abraham Stofaer to represent its interests in Washington. Stofaer had served in the State Department between 1985 and 1990 and was one of those who put together the 1986 economic sanctions directed at Libya for its role in the terrorist attack on Pan Am Flight 103, which exploded over Lockerbie, Scotland, killing 270 people. In 1988 alone, 152 Japanese firms and government agencies contracted with 113 Washington lobbying firms. And they were not alone. Canada had 61 organizations working on its behalf; Great Britain had 44. All told, there are now some 8,000 foreign agents registered with the Justice Department.[54] A virtual *Who's Who* of Washington "in-and-outers" and ex-legislators can be found in the employment of foreign concerns. For example, Bob Livingstone (R-LA), former Chair of the House Appropriations Committee, built the tenth-largest lobbying firm in Washington in four years. In 2003, he beat back an effort by Republicans to strip Turkey of $1 billion worth of foreign aid. They were angered by its failure to participate more fully in the Iraq War. He provided Turkey with advice on how to approach members of Congress, personally contacted his former colleagues, and arranged for embassy officials to stand just off the House floor as the vote was being taken.

Taiwan has been particularly active in cultivating ties with U.S. officials. In 1996, defeated Republican presidential candidate Robert Dole registered as an agent for Taiwan with a $30,000-a-month retainer. In 2002 evidence surfaced of a secret $100 million fund to buy influence with foreign governments and individuals. Between 1995 and 2000, it provided Washington-based lobbying firms with $9.8 million in contracts. One service provided was to help draft a letter from then Majority Leader Trent Lott to President Bill Clinton suggesting that congressional approval of normal trade relations with China might depend on the administration's prompt approval of Taiwan's request for additional weapons. It also funded $30,000 of research by John Bolton who became undersecretary of state for arms control and international security in the George W. Bush administration and provided James Kelly, Bush's assistant secretary of state for East Asia and Pacific Affairs, with $100,000 for two years at Harvard.

Both foreign governments and foreign firms engage in lobbying. The most common concerns of foreign governments are foreign aid legislation and arms sales. The typical plan of attack involves two steps. First, one must secure the support of the executive branch. The second step is to lobby Congress. The goal here is to prevent resolutions of disapproval or amendments that would block the transfer of aid or weapons. The effort involved is often considerable. Charles Goodell, a former Republican senator and representative from New York, reported having a total of 253 meetings, lunches, and phone calls in his successful lobbying effort to get approval for a Moroccan arms sales package.

The primary concern of foreign firms is their ability to conduct business in the United States. Accordingly, their lobbying activities are directed at all levels of the American political system. Of particular concern at state and local levels are taxation, zoning, and labor laws. SONY threatened not to go ahead with plans to build new plants in California and Florida unless those states repealed that portion of the state tax code that would have taxed their earnings based on worldwide sales rather than just on what was produced within the state. Both states succumbed to the foreign lobbying campaign. The most intense and successful foreign lobbying campaign to date is that conducted by Toshiba in 1987–1988. In July 1987, the Senate, angered at the news that Toshiba had illegally sold sensitive technology to the Soviet Union, voted to ban it from the U.S. market, a move that would cost Toshiba $10 billion per year. By May 1988, that legislation had been amended so that Toshiba only lost its U.S. government contracts (which were valued at $100 million annually) for a period of three years. In the intervening months, Toshiba unleashed what Senator Jake Garn labeled the most intense lobbying campaign he had seen in his fourteen years in Washington. The total cost has been placed at over $9 million dollars. One Washington, D.C., law firm alone was paid $4.3 million for its services. The message sent out by the lobbyists was that punishing Toshiba would cost 100,000 American jobs. A last point on this case is worth noting: Because Toshiba America is considered a U.S. corporation, its lobbyists were not required to register as foreign agents.

Ideological-Public Interest Groups.   A wide variety of groups fall under this category. At one extreme we find highly institutionalized and well-funded organizations that we do not normally think of as interest groups. These are "think tanks" that have as part of their mission the propagation and advancement of ideas on how to address public policy problems. The Brookings Institution was long the most prominent foreign policy think tank advancing a liberal-democratic foreign policy agenda. Over the years it has become more moderate and centrist in its orientation. Two of the most visible think tanks now occupy positions at the conservative end of the political spectrum: the Heritage Foundation and the Cato Institute. The former sees its mission as advancing policies based on free enterprise, limited government, and traditional American ideals and calls for a foreign policy that is based on a strong military defense, limited involvement in humanitarian undertakings, and advancing free market principles in international trade. The latter is a libertarian organization that has advanced an isolationist foreign policy agenda for the United States.

Think tanks make their mark in Washington in many ways. Their members serve as a source of expertise for administrations and congressional committees to draw upon either as outside experts or employees. Less visibly but perhaps most significantly, they serve as a focal point for bringing like-minded individuals together to address common concerns. For example, think tanks were prominent members of the "blue team," a loose alliance of members of Congress, staffers, conservative journalists, and lobbyists for Taiwan who have worked to present China as a threat to the United States. They succeeded in restricting the scope of U.S.–Chinese military contacts, getting the State Department to address human rights concerns, and forcing the Pentagon to do a study of the China–Taiwan military balance.

Also included in this category are more traditional interests groups, the most prominent of which today may be the "religious right."[55] Primarily identifying with the Republican Party, members of the religious right were staunch supporters of Ronald Reagan and found foreign policy a powerful venue onto which to project their values. Pat Robertson's Christian Broadcasting Network gave $3–7 billion to U.S.-backed anticommunist forces in Central America. In 2003, Robertson defended about-to-be-deposed Liberian leader Charles Taylor against charges that he was a war criminal and urged the Bush administration to stop "undermining a Christian, Baptist president to bring in Muslim rebels to take over the country." Jerry Falwell emerged as a strong defender of apartheid in South Africa. More generally, the religious right has supported Israel to the point of creating visions of a new crusade in Palestinian minds. The United Nations and International Monetary Fund have also become lobbying targets for their funding of family planning and population control programs. Finally, an important mobilizing issue for the religious right has been the persecution of Christians, particularly in Russia, China, and the Sudan.

The religious right does not hold a monopoly on interest group activity by religious organizations. The prelude to the Iraq War found groups active on both sides. For example where fundamentalist groups tended to support the war the Catholic Church, the Religious Society of Friends (Quakers), the

United Church of Christ, the World Council of Churches, the Muslim Peace Fellowship, and the Shalom Center all spoke out against it. The story of religious groups lobbying on foreign policy issues is not a new one. Leo Ribuffo notes that it is an old and complex story. He concludes that religious ideals have at most an indirect impact on policy makers and that no major diplomatic decision has turned on religious issues alone.[56]

IMPACT

Establishing the influence of an interest group on a specific policy is difficult. More is required than revealing the presence of group activity. A concrete link must be established between the group's actions and the actions taken by those who were influenced. "Koreagate," the influence-peddling activities of South Korean businessman Tongsun Park, made headlines and led to House and Senate investigations in 1978. Significant breaches in law and ethics were uncovered, but no policy change or votes were found tied to his efforts.

Success is also not an all-or-nothing condition, and this further complicates the problem of establishing influence. Consider the Jewish lobby and its efforts on behalf of the Jackson–Vanik Amendment. At the time, passage of this amendment was viewed as a major success and a show of strength. It is now seen by many as a hollow victory that brought with it ruinous costs. The Jackson–Vanik Amendment made freedom to emigrate from the Soviet Union a prerequisite for the granting of MFN status to Soviet goods. It did not have its intended impact. The amendment strained détente and embroiled the emigration issue in the larger context of rising U.S.–Soviet competition. Human rights remained largely an illusion within the Soviet Union, and emigration quickly became more difficult. From its high of thirty-five thousand in 1973, emigration fell to a low of thirteen thousand in 1975. It would then climb up again with the signing of SALT II, only to fall once more with the Soviet invasion of Afghanistan.

Political Protest

Images of protesters clashing with police in Seattle in December 1999 at a meeting of the World Trade Organization and in Quebec in 2001 over a meeting to establish a free trade zone for the Americas brought back vivid memories of political protests against the war in Vietnam, which were prominent scenes on the American political landscape in the late 1960s and early 1970s. These images also serve as an important reminder that the public voice is not only expressed through officially sanctioned avenues. It can, on occasion, come through in highly unorganized and violent forms.

Not unexpectedly, public pronouncements by President George W. Bush and other administration officials were not any more supportive of the antiglobalization goals of the political protests than were the Johnson and Nixon administrations of the anti-Vietnam goals of the protesters they faced. Still, we would be wrong to dismiss political protest as an ineffective means for expressing the public voice. First, political protests, when they take on the scale of the peace movement and the antiglobalization movement, do alter the political agenda. In the case of the antiglobalization protests they have ensured that environmental, labor, and democracy issues cannot be ignored. Second, they serve to energize long-established political forces such as labor or bring new voices into the political arena.

This last point may be particularly important today. James Lindsay observes that an "apathetic internationalism" is reshaping American politics. First, it encourages policy makers to ignore foreign policy problems. More significantly, it empowers squeaky wheels and favors those who make the loudest noise about foreign policy problems. More often than not this condition favors those organized interests who can mobilize their supporters most effectively to pressure policy makers. But when thousands of protesters repeatedly take to the streets, a new element is added to the equation.[57]

The Iraq War brought forward political protest in both conventional and new forms. Before the war began, hundreds of thousands marched in protest across the United States, and in October 2003, tens of thousands of protesters marched in Washington calling for an end to the occupation. There also occurred a virtual protest march on Washington in which antiwar forces flooded congressional offices with emails announcing their opposition to the war. A similar tactic was used in July 2003 to pressure Congress into investigating the prewar intelligence claims made by the George W. Bush administration as more than 400,000 people from every state contacted members of Congress.

Policy-Maker Response

Policy makers do not tend to share the view that the public voice on foreign policy is an important influence on policy—or that it should be. The prevailing view among policy makers holds that foreign policy is too important to be left to the uninformed and unstable flow of public perceptions of world affairs. It should be made by that small group of public officials who are informed about international problems. Public attitudes are something to be formed and shaped by the policy makers rather than followed by them. On one level of activity, this perspective takes the form of a preoccupation with educating the public. On another level it takes the form of a manipulative attitude toward public perceptions.[58] In either case the objective is to secure the widest possible area of freedom for the policy maker to practice his or her craft.

The tendency of policy makers to discount the positive contribution of the public voice to foreign policy making also shows up in where they look to uncover the public voice. Our discussion has stressed public opinion polls, election results, and interest group activity. State Department officials emphasize public attitudes as interpreted by personal contacts, other institutions, and the working press. Especially important for the State Department is the view Congress has of public opinion. As one State Department official observed, "If a given viewpoint different from our own does not have congressional expression, forget it."[59] The inevitable result of this perspective is to narrow greatly the range of public attitudes taken into account in making policy.

Steven Kull and I. M. Destler bring still another perspective to bear on the problem of policy makers responding to the public voice.[60] They assert that the fundamental problem is that policy makers misread the public. In their view, this is particularly true in such areas as support for the United Nations, peacekeeping operations, and foreign aid. They see the public as tired of global involvement and wanting to disengage, a set of attitudes that they feel leaves them little leeway to conduct a robust and internationalist foreign policy. Kull and Destler assert that there is little trend-line data to support this view of limited foreign policy options.

Why then the misreading of the public? In large part, the answer is that policy makers seek out little information about how the public views foreign policy. A congressional staffer could not remember the last time he was asked to do a foreign policy poll. A member of the executive branch said that most information on this score was anecdotal. Kull and Destler explain this situation largely in terms of convenience, inertia, and political incentives. It is convenient for policy makers to think about the public as setting boundaries on what they can do while giving them great latitude within those boundaries. Once established, these boundaries are perpetuated by inertia and become part of the mythology of the political landscape. Finally, the electoral market neither regularly punishes policy makers who misread the public on foreign policy nor rewards them for doing so correctly. There is thus no incentive to explore the margins of these mythical boundaries to determine how accurate they are.

AN EXAMPLE: THE PUBLIC USE OF INTELLIGENCE AND THE IRAQ WAR

Intelligence analysis by governments is conducted in secret. Yet intelligence does not always remain secret. This is because not only does intelligence help policy makers understand situations and frame options, but it also is a valuable political resource for helping sell government policies to the American public at large. Republican and Democratic presidents have used intelligence publicly to bolster the case for their policies. One of the most sustained efforts was by the Reagan administration in promoting the case for anticommunist involvement in Central America. In the case of the lead-up to the Iraq War, the George W. Bush administration engaged in a campaign of orchestrated public intelligence that was part of the administration's broader campaign to build support for the war.

The campaign began in August 2002 with two comments made by Vice President Dick Cheney. The first came on August 7. Responding to a question at the Commonwealth Club in San Francisco, Cheney said "it is the judgment of many of us that in the not too-distant future he [Saddam Hussein] will acquire nuclear weapons." In a speech to the National Convention of the Veterans of Foreign Wars on August 26, he referenced intelligence in highlighting the threat posed by Saddam Hussein. Cheney stated "there is no doubt that Saddam Hussein has weapons of mass destruction." He continued, "we now know that Saddam has resumed his efforts to acquire nuclear weapons. Among other sources we've gotten this from firsthand testimony from defectors, including Saddam's own son-in law, who was subsequently murdered at Saddam's direction."

Also in August 2002, under the direction of Chief of Staff Andrew Cord, the Bush administration set up a White House Iraq Group (WHIG) to ensure that the various parts of the White House were working in harmony on Iraq. Under its direction, a strategic communications task force operated to work on speeches and white papers dealing with Iraq. The first white paper produced, "A Grave and Gathering Danger: Saddam Hussein's Quest for Nuclear Weapons," contained the claim that Iraq "sought uranium oxide, an essential ingredient in the enrichment process from Africa." It claimed that a satellite photograph shows "many signs of the reconstruction and acceleration of the Iraqi nuclear program." And it stated that "since the beginning of the nineties, Saddam Hussein has launched a crash program to divert nuclear fuel for . . . nuclear weapons."

President Bush and British Prime Minister Tony Blair met at Camp David on September 7, and each made public pronouncements regarding the seriousness of the threat. Blair cited a report from the International Atomic Energy Agency showing "what's been going on at the former weapons sites" and Bush said an IAEA report placed Iraq "six months away from developing a [nuclear] weapon. I don't know what more evidence we need." The following day, the *New York Times* quoted anonymous administration officials on Iraq's possession of aluminum tubes whose specifications made them ideally suited as component parts of a centrifuge. That morning, Rice, Cheney, Rumsfeld, and Secretary of State Colin Powell made appearances on TV talk shows. Rice stated on CNNs *Late Edition* that "we do know that there have been shipments going . . . into Iraq, for instance of aluminum tubes that really are only suited to . . . nuclear weapons programs, centrifuge programs." She noted that "there will always be some uncertainty about how quickly he can acquire nuclear weapons . . . but we don't want the smoking gun to be a mushroom cloud." Cheney on NBC's *Meet the Press,* in speaking of the Iraqi nuclear program, said "increasingly we believe the United States will become the target." Rumsfeld on CBS's *Face the Nation* asked viewers to imagine a September 11th with weapons of mass destruction.

Next to speak for the administration was President Bush. At the United Nations on September 12, he repeated the charge that Iraq "has made several attempts to buy high-strength aluminum tubes used to enrich uranium for a nuclear weapon. Should Iraq acquire fissile material, it would be able to build a nuclear weapon within a year." Seized shipments were cited as proof. To buttress its case, the same day that Bush addressed the UN the administration released a background paper, "A Decade of Deception and Defiance: Saddam Hussein's Defiance of the United Nations." On September 26, President Bush continued this theme of certainty stating "the Iraq regime possesses biological and chemical weapons. The Iraq regime is building the facilities necessary to make more biological and chemical weapons."

On October 2, between President Bush's address to the United Nations and his speech in Cincinnati on October 7 in which he stated "the evidence indicates Iraq is reconstituting its nuclear weapons program" and that "satellite photographs reveal that Iraq is rebuilding facilities at sites that have been part of its nuclear program in the past," the administration released a white paper based on the classified National Intelligence Estimate it had just produced. Entitled, Iraq's Weapons of Mass Destruction Program," its lead "key judgment" was that "if left unchecked it [Iraq] probably will have a nuclear weapon during this decade." The white paper repeated the conclusion expressed by Bush on September 26 that Baghdad "has chemical and biological weapons" and that it "has begun renewed production of chemical warfare agents." The white paper also contained maps and aerial photographs and made the case that new construction facilities were related to Iraq's nuclear program.

In Bush's October 7 speech, the president stated "we have discovered through intelligence that Iraq has a growing fleet" of unmanned aircraft and worried they might be targeted on the United States. He also asserted that in 1998 "information from a high-ranking Iraqi nuclear engineer who had defected revealed that despite his public promises, Saddam Hussein had ordered his nuclear program to continue." This could, Bush continued, provide weapons of mass destruction to terrorist groups or allow Iraq to attack the United States.

The next major salvo involving the orchestrated use of public intelligence came in President Bush's January 28, 2003 State of the Union Address. In it he stated, "the British government has learned that Saddam Hussein recently sought significant quantities of uranium from Africa."

Public intelligence was at the heart of Secretary of State Powell's February 5, 2003 address to the UN Security Council. A few days before the speech, he cautioned observers that he would not present a "smoking gun." In making his case, however, he affirmed that "every statement I make today is backed up by sources, solid sources. . . . These are not assertions. What we are giving you are facts and conclusions based on solid intelligence." Powell was accompanied by DCI George Tenet in a move intended to symbolize the certainty of the information that he presented in his ninety-minute multimedia presentation that included photographs, intercepted phone conversations, and charts linking Iraq to al-Qaeda. Powell stated "we know from sources that a missile brigade outside Baghdad was dispersing rocket launchers and warheads containing biological agents to various locations. Powell also asserted the United States has "satellite photos that indicate banned materials have recently been moved from a number of Iraqi weapons of mass destruction facilities." He also affirmed that "we have firsthand descriptions of biological weapons factories on wheels and rails." President Bush would later cite the capture of two of these facilities as proof that Iraq had weapons of mass destruction.

President Bush would publicly reference intelligence at least twice more before the war began. In his February 8, 2003 radio address to the nation, he stated, "we have sources that tell us that Saddam Hussein recently authorized Iraqi field commanders to use chemical weapons." Then in delivering his final ultimatum to Iraq on March 17, the president told the nation "intelligence gathered by this and other governments leaves no doubt that the Iraq regime continues to possess and conceal some of the most lethal weapons ever devised."

Virtually all of the intelligence made public during this campaign was either challenged in secret by elements of the intelligence community at the time, taken out of context so that their importance was overstated, or later proven to be inaccurate. This is not surprising since by its very nature public intelligence is incomplete intelligence. Its purpose is not to tell the whole story but to highlight a certain aspect of a policy problem and prompt action.

Summary and Future Issues

What can we say of the future? First, we can expect the impact of public attitudes to vary from issue area to issue area. The public's influence is the greatest today on issues where economic and security concerns are present and when the decision time is long. As these conditions are removed, the public's influence progressively lessens.[61] Bold and self-contained foreign policy initiatives that allow the president to control the flow of information, such as the Reykjavik Summit, the invasion of Grenada, air attacks on Libya, and the invasion of Panama, have been viewed quite favorably by the public regardless of the actual merits of the policy initiative or its concrete accomplishments. In contrast, the longer the issue remains in the public's eye and the less able the president is to control the information flow, as was the case with the Iranian hostage crisis and the Iran–Contra scandal, the more critical the *public's* assessment of the *president's* performance becomes.

Second, there is a need to bridge the gap between elites and the American public. Not only do policy makers misread the public on foreign policy but there is a pronounced gap in how to look at foreign policy problems. We have a reasonable public that is basically centrist in outlook and an elite that is highly partisan, opportunistic, and in search of ideological advantage. In recent years, the Comprehensive Test Ban Treaty, Fast Track trade negotiating authority, and funding for the United Nations have all fallen victim to this polarization of the foreign policy process.

Third, even more fundamentally, policy makers may need to rethink the way in which they engage the public. Daniel Yankelovich and John Immerwahr note that while foreign policy leaders have generally been reluctant to engage the public in complex foreign policy issues they have never doubted their ability to do so.[62] One indication that this standard wisdom is no longer relevant (if it ever was) is the George W. Bush administration's inability to block the creation of an independent commission to look into the quality of intelligence prior to 9/11 and its later failure to bring the commission's life to an early end. Further evidence on this point comes from a study of presidential popularity and foreign policy behavior. Particularly interesting is the finding that presidential drama (i.e., speeches, forceful actions) if properly carried out can produce a short-term increase in public support for a president, but there are no guarantees attached.[63] Travel, for example, may hurt a president's standing. Sending troops to a region that the public does not consider important will also hurt it.

Notes

1. Daniel Sharp, "Preamble," in Daniel Yankelovich and I. M. Destler (eds.), *Beyond the Beltway: Engaging the Public in U.S. Foreign Policy* (New York: Norton, 1994), p. 13.
2. James Billington, "Realism and Vision in Foreign Policy," *Foreign Affairs*, 65 (1987), 630.
3. Walter Lippmann, quoted in Amos Jordan and William J. Taylor Jr., *American National Security Policy and Process* (Baltimore, Md.: Johns Hopkins University Press, 1981), p. 43.
4. Gabriel Almond, *The American People and Foreign Policy* (New York: Praeger, 1961).
5. Barry Hughes, *The Domestic Context of American Foreign Policy* (San Francisco: Freeman, 1978), pp. 23–24.
6. Catherine M. Kelleher, "U.S. Public Opinion on the Use of Force," *The Brookings Review*, 12 (Spring 1994), 26–29.
7. Lewis A. Friedland, *Covering the World: International Television News* (New York: Twentieth Century Fund, 1992).
8. See prepared statement by Michael R. Beschloss, "Impact of Television on U.S. Foreign Policy," *Hearing before the Committee on Foreign Affairs, House of Representatives*, 103rd Congress, 2nd session, April 26, 1994.
9. Trevor Thrall, "The Gulf in Reporting the Gulf War," *Breakthroughs*, 2 (1992), 9–13.
10. Jacqueline Sharkey, "When Pictures Drive Foreign Policy," *American Journalism Review*, 15 (December 1993), 14–19.
11. Timothy J. McNulty, "Television's Impact on Executive Decisionmaking and Diplomacy," *Fletcher Forum*, 17 (Winter 1993), 67–83.
12. Frank J. Stech, "Winning CNN Wars," *Parameters*, 24 (1994), 37–56.
13. Jonathan Mermin, "Television News and American Intervention in Somalia: The Myth of a Media Driven Foreign Policy," *Political Science Quarterly*, 112 (1997), 385–403.
14. Robert Entman, *Projections of Power* (Chicago: University of Chicago Press, 2004).
15. Barbara Allen, Paula O'Loughlin, Amy Jasperson, and John L. Sullivan, "The Media and the Gulf War: Framing, Priming, and the Spiral of Silence," *Polity*, 37 (1994), 255–284.
16. Steven Kull, Clay Ramsey, and Evan Lewis, "Misperception, the Media, and the Iraq War," *Political Science Quarterly*, 118 (2003–2004), 569–98.
17. Kathryn Tempas, "Words vs. Deeds," *The Brookings Review* (Summer 2003), 33–35.
18. On foreign aid see Robert S. Erickson, Norman Luttbeg, and Kent Tedin, *American Public Opinion*, 2nd ed. (New York: John Wiley, 1980), p. 43. On the Persian Gulf War see John Mueller, "The Polls-A Review." *Public Opinion Quarterly* 57 (1993), 86–87.
19. Robert S. Erickson, Norman R. Luttbeg, and Kent L. Tedin, *American Public Opinion: Its Origins, Content, and Impact*, 2nd ed. (New York: Wiley & Sons, 1980), p. 44.
20. Hughes, *The Domestic Context of American Foreign Policy*, p. 31.
21. Ole R. Holsti and James N. Rosenau, *American Leadership in World Affairs, Vietnam and the Breakdown of Consensus* (Winchester, Mass.: Allen & Unwin, 1984), pp. 218–20.
22. Lloyd Free and William Watts, "Internationalism Comes of Age . . . Again," *Public Opinion*, 3 (1980), 46–50.
23. John Rielly, "Americans and the World: A Survey at Century's End," *Foreign Policy*, 114 (1999), 97–113.
24. Ole R. Holsti, "Public Opinion and Foreign Policy: Attitude Structures of Opinion Leaders After the Cold War," in Eugene R. Wittkopf (ed.), *Domestic Sources of American Foreign Policy: Insights and Evidence*, 2nd ed. (New York: St. Martin's, 1994), 36–56.
25. Shoon Kathleen Murray and Christopher Spinosa, "The Post 9/11 Shift in Public Opinion," in Eugene Wittkopf and James McCormick (eds.), *The Domestic Sources of American Foreign Policy*, fourth edition (Lanham, MD: Rowman and Littlefield, 2004), 97–116).
26. Miroslav Nincic, "Domestic Costs, the U.S. Public, and the Isolationist Calculus," *International Studies Quarterly*, 41 (1997), 593–610.
27. Bruce W. Jentleson, "The Pretty Prudent Public: Post-Vietnam American Opinion on the Use of Military Force," *International Studies Quarterly*, 36 (1990), 49–74.
28. John Rielly, "The Public Mood at Mid-Decade," *Foreign Policy*, 98 (1995), 76–95.

29. Richard Eichenberg, "Gender Differences in Public Attitudes toward the Use of Force by the United States, 1990–2003," *International Security,* 28 (2003), 110–41.

30. Leslie Gelb and Richard K. Betts, *The Irony of Vietnam: The System Worked* (Washington, D.C.: Brookings, 1979).

31. Richard Sobel, *The Impact of Public Opinion on U.S. Foreign Policy Since Vietnam* (New York: Oxford University Press, 2001).

32. Richard J. Barnett, *The Roots of War* (New York: Penguin, 1977), p. 243.

33. Quoted in William Schneider, "Conservatism, Not Interventionism: Trends in Foreign Policy Opinion, 1974–1982," in Kenneth A. Oye, Robert J. Lieber, and Donald Rothchild (eds.), *Eagle Defiant: United States Foreign Policy in the 1980s* (Boston: Little, Brown, 1983), p. 138.

34. Thomas W. Graham, "Public Opinion and U.S. Foreign Policy Decision Making," in David A. Deese (ed.), *The New Politics of American Foreign Policy* (New York: St. Martin's, 1994), pp. 190–215.

35. Douglas Foyle, *Counting the Public In* (New York: Columbia University Press, 1999, p. 267).

36. Gerald M. Pomper, *Elections in America: Control and Influence in Democratic Politics* (New York: Dodd, Mead, 1968), p. 251.

37. Erickson, Luttbeg, and Tedin, *American Public Opinion,* p. 216.

38. The figures for 1983 are reported in the *New York Times,* July 1, 1983, p. 1. The remaining figures are discussed in ibid., p. 19; and Hughes, *Domestic Context of American Foreign Policy,* p. 91. The 1987 figure is from William Galston and Christopher Makins, "Campaign '88 and Foreign Policy," *Foreign Policy,* 71 (1988), 9. The 1993 data is from *Time* (October 4,1993). The 2003 data if from Kull, FN 16.

39. Charles Whalen, *The House and Foreign Policy* (Chapel Hill: University of North Carolina Press, 1982).

40. Schneider, "Conservatism, Not Interventionism."

41. Laurence Radway, "The Curse of Free Elections," *Foreign Policy,* 40 (1980), 61–73.

42. *Washington Post,* May 13, 1988, p. 4.

43. William B. Quandt, "The Electoral Cycle and the Conduct of American Foreign Policy," *Political Science Quarterly,* 101 (1986), 825–37.

44. See Steven Rosen (ed.), *Testing the Theory of the Military Industrial Complex* (Lexington, Ky.: Heath, 1973).

45. C. W. Mills, *The Power Elite* (New York: Oxford University Press, 1956).

46. Kerry Dumbaught, "Interest Groups," in Ramon Myers et al. (eds.), *Making China Policy* (Lanham, MD: Rowman & Littlefield, 2001), 149–72.

47. Martin Weil, "Can the Blacks Do for Africa What the Jews Did for Israel?" *Foreign Policy,* 15 (1974), 109–29.

48. Charles McMathias Jr., "Ethnic Groups and Foreign Affairs," *Foreign Affairs,* 59 (1981), 975–99.

49. David J. Sadd and G. Neal Lendenmann, "Arab American Grievances," *Foreign Policy,* 60 (1985), 17–29.

50. Fran Scott and Abdulah Osman, "Identity, African-Americans and U.S. Foreign Policy," in Thomas Ambrosio (ed.), *Ethnic Identity Groups and U.S. Foreign Policy* (Westport, CT: Praeger, 2002), 71–92.

51. Bill Richardson, "Hispanic American Concerns," *Foreign Policy,* 60 (1985), 30–39.

52. Michael Jones-Correa, "Latinos and Latin America," in Ambrosio (ed.), *Ethnic Identity Groups and U.S. Foreign Policy,* 115–30.

53. See Shawn Miller, "Trade Winds Stir Miami Storm," *Insight,* June 7, 1993; and Carla Anne Robins, "Dateline Washington: Cuban-American Clout," *Foreign Policy,* 88 (1992), 165–82.

54. Congressional Quarterly, *The Washington Lobby,* 4th ed. (Washington, D.C.: Congressional Quarterly, 1982), pp. 155–62; and *Washington Post,* June 19, 1988.

55. William Martin, "The Christian Right and American Foreign Policy," *Foreign Policy,* 114 (1999), 66–80.

56. Leo Ribuffo, "Religion and American Foreign Policy," *The National Interest,* 52 (1998), 36–51.

57. James Lindsay, "The Apathy: How an Uninterested Public Is Reshaping Foreign Policy," *Foreign Affairs,* 79 (2000), 2–8.

58. Bernard Cohen, *The Public's Impact on Foreign Policy* (Boston: Little, Brown, 1973).

59. Ibid., p. 117.

60. Steven Kull and I. M. Destler, *Misreading the Public: The Myth of the New Isolationism* (Washington, D.C.: Brookings, 1999).

61. On the matter of issue areas, see Hughes, *The Domestic Context of American Foreign Policy,* Chap. 7.

62. Daniel Yankelovich and John Immerwahr, "The Rules of Public Engagement," in Daniel Yankelovich and I. M. Destler (eds.), *Beyond the Beltway: Engaging the Public in U.S. Foreign Policy* (New York: Norton, 1994), 43–78. The quote is on p. 45.

63. Robin F. Marra, Charles W. Ostrom Jr., and Dennis M. Simon, "Foreign Policy and Presidential Popularity," *Journal of Conflict Resolution,* 34 (1990), 568–623.

7

THE CONSTITUTION
AND FOREIGN AFFAIRS

On February 16, 1990, President George H. W. Bush signed into law a bill that provided operating funds for the State Department. In doing so he stated that "many provisions of this act could be read to violate fundamental constitutional principles by using legislation to direct . . . the conduct of negotiations with foreign nations" and that therefore he did not consider himself bound by all of its provisions.[1] Among the points he objected to were:

- The denial of funding to the U.S. delegation to the Conference on European Security and Cooperation unless a congressional representative is included in the delegation.
- The denial of funds to carry out the current Middle East peace process with the PLO if the president knows and advises Congress that the PLO has directly participated in the planning or execution of terrorist acts.
- The denial of permission to the Soviet Union to occupy a consulate facility in New York until the United States is certified to occupy an interim facility in Kiev.

Bush was not the first president to do battle with Congress over the proper division of authority in the conduct of U.S. foreign policy. In this chapter we examine the constitutional basis for presidential and congressional interaction in making U.S. foreign policy. Four powers are discussed: treaty making, appointments, war, and commerce. In the following chapters we examine how each of these two institutions has built on these powers to exercise its foreign policy powers.

Treaty-Making Powers

SENATORIAL ADVICE AND CONSENT.

The Constitution states that the president, by and with the advice and consent of the Senate, has the power to make treaties. The president's role in the treaty-making process has not been a source of serious controversy. He nominates the negotiators, issues instructions to them, submits the treaty to the Senate for its advice and consent, and if its consent is given, he makes a decision on whether or not to ratify the treaty and make it law. Far more controversial have been the nature of senatorial advice and consent, the topics to be covered by treaties, and the role of the House of Representatives in the treaty-making process.

Virtually from the start senatorial advice and consent have been given at the same time. The Constitution does not require that it be done this way. Louis Henkin argues that the Senate was originally intended to be a kind of advisory council, making recommendations to the president throughout the treaty-making process and on all aspects of the negotiations.[2] He also notes that neither the president nor the Senate ever accepted this model. In the place of formal Senate input into the negotiating process, presidents have developed a number of informal means for obtaining senatorial advice. A frequently used method is to include key members of the Senate in the delegation to the negotiations as observers. The impetus for this move can be found in Woodrow Wilson's experience with the League of Nations Treaty. Wilson went to Versailles to negotiate the treaty personally and did not include any senators or important Republicans in the American Peace Commission. On July 10, 1919, Wilson presented the 264-page Treaty of Paris to the Senate. Wilson indicated that he would accept no reservations to the treaty. This was not to be the case. The Senate split into four groups, only one of which supported the treaty without reservation. After a series of preliminary votes, all of which went against Wilson, in March 1920 a final vote was taken and the treaty was rejected 49 to 35.

On the basis of quantitative measures, the use of informal means of consultation has proven to be quite successful. Over fifteen hundred treaties have been ratified by the Senate and only twenty-one rejected. Fifteen of those occurred between 1789 to 1920.[3] A list of rejected treaties is presented in Table 7.1. These figures do not tell the full story. Omitted in this counting are treaties negotiated by presidents but never voted on by the Senate or those the Senate consented to only after prolonged delays. President Carter's withdrawal of the SALT II Treaty is only one example of major Senate "nonrejections." President Truman negotiated a treaty establishing an International Trade Organization that was to be part of the Bretton Woods system along with the World Bank and the International Monetary Fund. Because of certain Senate opposition, Truman never submitted the treaty for advice and consent, and the interim General Agreement on Tariffs and Trade (GATT) became the formal international vehicle for lowering tariffs. In 1988 the Senate gave its consent by a vote of 83 to 11 to a Convention on the Prevention and Punishment of Genocide that was signed by the United States in 1948

TABLE 7.1   Rejected Treaties

Bilateral		Multilateral	
Suspension of Slave Trade/Columbia	1825	Treaty of Versailles	1920
Property Rights/Switzerland	1836	World Court	1935
Annexation/Texas	1844	Law of Sea Convention	1960
Commercial Reciprocity/Germany	1844	Montreal Aviation Protocol	1983
Transit and Commercial Rights/Mexico	1860	Comprehensive Test Ban	1999
Cuban Claims Commission/Spain	1860		
Arbitration of Claims/United Kingdom	1869		
Commercial Reciprocity/Hawaii	1870		
Annexation/Dominican Republic	1870		
Interoceanic Canal/Nicaragua	1885		
Fishing Rights/United Kingdom	1888		
Extradition/United Kingdom	1889		
Arbitration/United Kingdom	1897		
Commercial Rights/Turkey	1927		
St. Lawrence Seaway/Canada	1934		

Source: David M. O'Brien, "Presidential and Congressional Relations in Foreign Affairs," in Colton Campbell et al. (eds.), Congress and the Politics of Foreign Policy (Upper Saddle River, NJ: Prentice Hall, 2003), 74.

and first submitted to the Senate by Truman in 1949. Potentially joining this list is the Law of the Sea Convention. Negotiated in 1982 the United States did not ratify the treaty because of concerns over the provisions governing deep seabed mining and questions of autonomy. Still, it abided by all of its provisions except those in the above areas. In April 2004, the George W. Bush administration determined that these concerns had now been addressed in a legally binding manner through 1994 amendments and asked the Senate to give its advice and consent. In making its case, the administration also argued that the convention supported the war on terrorism by providing for navigational freedom and overflight rights.

An overall tally such as the one presented above also makes no mention of senatorial attempts to change the treaties. Between 1789 and 1963, the Senate made changes in 69 percent of the treaties that came before it. In the heated debate over the Panama Canal Treaties, 145 amendments, 76 reservations, 18 understandings, and 3 declarations were proposed. Senatorial changes are often designed to improve a treaty. But this need not be the case. In the debate over the SALT II Treaty, "killer amendments" were introduced in order to ensure its nonacceptance by the Soviet Union. Changes have also created serious problems for the president in his dealings with other states. Senatorial changes in a Treaty of Friendship and Cooperation with Spain brought forward changes of interference in Spanish domestic affairs and almost resulted in Spain's refusal to ratify the treaty.[4]

President Clinton's term in office ended with a major executive-legislative battle over the Comprehensive Test Ban Treaty (CTBT).[5] The treaty was signed by Clinton on September 24, 1996, and submitted to the Senate for ratification in September 1997. There it sat until 1999 as a political hostage because Senate Foreign Relations Committee chairperson Jesse Helms (R-N.C.) wanted two other treaties, a 1996 treaty with Russia that would permit the deployment of a limited antiballistic missile defense system and the 1997 Kyoto Protocol on global climate control, submitted for ratification first. Helms opposed both treaties. In spring and summer 1999 Democrats made a major political push to force the CTBT out of committee. Fearful that the Democrats would make the Republican-controlled Senate's refusal to act on the CTBT a campaign issue in the upcoming presidential election, Majority Leader Trent Lott (R-Miss.) marshaled his forces so that the CTBT could be released and then defeated on the Senate floor. Debate began on October 8 and by agreement would be limited to fourteen hours followed by an immediate vote. It quickly became apparent to Clinton that he lacked the votes to obtain ratification, and on October 11 he sent a letter to the Senate urging a postponement. The following day, sixty-two Senators circulated a letter asking that the vote be delayed until the next Congress. Both of these efforts failed, and on October 13 by a vote of 51 to 48 the Senate rejected the CTBT. The vote fell largely along party lines with only four Republicans joining forty-four Democrats in support of the treaty.

This was not the only treaty that found the Clinton administration and Congress on opposite sides. On December 31, 2000, just weeks before leaving office, Clinton signed a treaty creating the first permanent international criminal court (ICC) designed to try individuals accused of crimes against humanity and war crimes. Jesse Helms quickly observed that "the decision will not stand." In fact, Clinton indicated that he would not submit the treaty to the Senate for ratification nor recommend that President-elect George W. Bush do so. The United States was one of the original proponents of an ICC but moved into an opposition mode over concerns about procedures and jurisdiction. The military was particularly concerned that U.S. soldiers participating in humanitarian peacekeeping efforts would fall under the jurisdiction of the court. In May 2002 the George W. Bush administration announced its decision not to participate in the ICC. Four reasons were given: 1) it undermines the role of the UN Security Council in maintaining peace and security; 2) the document has an absence of checks and balances; 3) it threatens U.S. sovereignty; and 4) it lends itself to politically motivated decisions.

Presidents and the Senate have already clashed several times in the post–cold war period over the content and advisability of treaties. On the whole, the lines of conflict have been quite predictable and point to the continued weight of traditional congressional concerns for protecting its prerogatives. One frequently expressed concern has been the possibility that a treaty might infringe on U.S. sovereignty. Opponents of the GATT treaty pointed to a 1991 GATT ruling that the U.S. ban on tuna from Mexico and other states whose fishing fleets killed large numbers of dolphins was illegal. They used this as evidence that by signing the treaty U.S. environmental laws would be weakened. Similar fears were expressed regarding the possibility that GATT might consistently rule against the United States on economic matters. The Clinton administration argued that no loss of sovereignty was at stake in the treaty, but it took a last-minute deal struck between Clinton and Senate Minority Leader Robert Dole allowing the United States to leave GATT should this happen to secure its passage. Finally, conservative groups have long objected to provisions of the UN Children's Rights Treaty because they argue it would weaken the role of parents. The United States remains one of the few countries not to have ratified this 1989 convention.

A second familiar problem confronting presidents in the post–cold war period has been that of securing a political majority in the Senate to support the treaty. The GATT treaty ratified by a wide bipartisan margin in a special post-1994 session of Congress is a case in point. The Clinton administration hoped to have the Senate give its consent to the treaty prior to the November elections but was unable to do so because of Republican opposition. With many key Democratic leaders opposing the treaty, Clinton needed Republican votes to gain approval. A particularly troublesome point was the need to get at least 60 votes in the Senate to waive a requirement written into recent budgetary legislation that any revenues lost by a tariff agreement be offset with equal spending reductions. Part of the price that Clinton was forced to pay to get Republican support for the GATT treaty was dropping his request for "fast track" authority to negotiate trade agreements. Under the terms of a "fast track" agreement, Congress is presented with a "take-it-or-leave-it" vote. No amendments are permitted.

Finally, we find the president and Congress in continued conflict over who has the power to interpret treaty language. A significant presidential-congressional clash over the language of a treaty came in 1988. The centerpiece of the dispute was whether a president could reinterpret the language of a treaty (in this particular case the INF Treaty) without congressional approval. President Reagan had done so with the 1972 ABM Treaty, and on the basis of this new interpretation his administration asserted that it could legally test elements of his SDI shield. Here, the focus of concern was unclear language over how laser weapons and other futuristic technologies were to be dealt with. The Senate position prevailed and language was written into the INF Treaty banning any reinterpretation of it without Senate approval.[6] At the same time, the Senate beat back efforts by Senators Jesse Helms and Larry Pressler to "kill" the treaty by attaching amendments to it that the Soviet Union would find totally unacceptable. Helms wanted a ban on noncruise missiles included in the treaty and Pressler wanted its implementation tied to the achievement of parity in conventional military forces.

The Clinton administration also found itself at odds with the Senate over the ABM Treaty. It approached Russia about modifying the language of the treaty in order to permit the deployment of mobile defensive systems against intermediate missiles. The Clinton administration said its proposal was only intended to clear up ambiguities in the treaty. Senate leaders responded that the administration should not try to put any change into effect without Senate approval. The Clinton administration ultimately conceded this point in 1997. It recognized the Senate's right to review the revised treaty language as part of a deal that allowed the global treaty on banning the production and use of chemical weapons to come up for a vote. Action on the treaty had been held up for four years, largely due to the opposition of Senate Foreign Relations Committee chairperson Jesse Helms. In return for permitting a vote, Helms was promised that the administration would move forward on a foreign affairs bureaucratic reorganization that he favored. The Clinton administration also sent letters to Senate Majority Leader Trent Lott promising to withdraw from the treaty if others exploited its provisions and promising to submit for Senate ratification two existing treaties that it had previously maintained did not require Senate action. President George W. Bush formally withdrew the United States from the ABM Treaty in June 2002. Thirty-one members of Congress unsuccessfully brought legal action against the administration asserting that the president lacked the constitutional power to do so.

It is important to note that not all treaty votes are controversial. During the Clinton administration, NATO enlargement and the START II Treaty received overwhelming support in the Senate in spite of the presence of serious disagreements within the academic and policy communities about their merits.

EXECUTIVE AGREEMENTS

The Constitution specifies that the Senate should give its advice and consent to treaties, but it does not define what a treaty is or what international agreements are to be made in this form. From the outset presidents have claimed the constitutional authority to engage in international agreements by means other than treaties. This alternative is known as the *executive agreement,* and over time it had become the favored presidential method for entering into understandings with other states.

Unlike a treaty, an executive agreement does not require the consent of the Senate before coming into force. The Supreme Court has ruled that it carries the same legal force as a treaty. The principal limit on its use is political, not legal. This came through quite clearly in the dispute between Bush and Congress over how best to protect Chinese students in the United States following the Tiananmen Square massacre. Bush promised to issue an executive order while Congress passed legislation. Each viewed the other's action as misguided. Congress felt the president's action did not make enough of a symbolic statement, and Bush argued that the congressional action was unnecessary and complicated his foreign policy dealings with China. Bush vetoed the legislation and, while the House voted to override it, the Senate sustained Bush's position.

The number of executive agreements compared to treaties has increased steadily over time. Between 1789 and 1839, the United States entered into 60 treaties and 27 executive agreements. A century later, between 1889 and 1939, those numbers had grown to 524 treaties and 917 executive agreements. Since the Nixon administration, presidents have favored executive agreements over treaties by ratios ranging from 25.6:1 under Gerald

Ford to 9.9:1 under Clinton. In his first two years in office, George W. Bush's administration entered into 21 treaties and 262 executive agreements for a ratio of 12.5:1.[7]

Additional insight can be gained by looking at how heavily the president has relied on executive agreements in different policy areas. One study showed that between 1946–1972 371 diplomatic agreements were entered into by the United States. Only 26.7 percent were done as executive agreements. At the same time only 12.4 percent of over 1,146 military agreements and 4.6% of 2,229 economic agreements were done as executive agreements.[8] Of the forty-two treaties signed in this time period, thirty-two dealt with major defense obligations such as security agreements with Japan, arms control accords, and the 1963 Nuclear Test Ban. Another nine treaties dealt with administrative aspects of major military pacts such as NATO. However, throughout this period every president relied more heavily on executive agreements than treaties for making major military commitments. Numbered among the ninety-nine agreements are establishing military bases in the Philippines (1947), a military security agreement with South Korea (1949), a U.S. military mission in El Salvador (1957), security pledges to Turkey, Iran, and Pakistan (1959), and the military use of Bahrain (1971).

On a number of occasions, the Senate has attempted to curb the president's use of executive agreements. Three efforts have been particularly noteworthy. The first was the Bricker Amendment. It would have required that executive agreements receive the same two-thirds vote of approval from the Senate that treaties must get. In 1954 it failed by one vote to get the necessary two-thirds majority in the Senate needed to set into motion the amendment ratification process at the state level.

The second effort by Congress to reclaim a role in making international agreements was the 1969 National Commitments Resolution declaring that it was now the sense of the Senate that no future national commitments be made without affirmative action by Congress. It defined a national commitment as the use of the armed forces of the United States on foreign territory, the promise to use them, or the granting of financial aid. In making this statement, Congress was trying to undo what had become standard practice for two decades: recognizing in advance the president's authority to use force to protect American interests. The vehicle used for this purpose was the area resolution. The first area resolution came in 1955 and recognized U.S. interests in protecting Taiwan from China. Later resolutions dealt with the Middle East (1957), Latin America (1962), Berlin (1964), and Southeast Asia (1964). Known as the Gulf of Tonkin Resolution, this last resolution was cited by presidents Johnson and Nixon whenever they were challenged on the legality of U.S. involvement in Vietnam.

The most recent effort by Congress to reassert itself was the 1972 Case–Zablocki Act, which required that Congress be informed of all executive agreements. The goal was to give Congress the opportunity to take action blocking these agreements if it saw fit. According to Senator Clifford Case, this act was needed because there were at least 4,000 executive agreements in effect in the early 1970s that Congress knew nothing about.[9] The Case–Zablocki Act did not end the practice of secret executive agreements. In part the problem is definitional. In 1975, Representative Les Aspin estimated that 400 to 600 agreements had not yet been reported to Congress because the White House claimed that they were either understandings, oral promises, or statements of political intent.[10] Included among these were a 1973 secret message that Nixon had sent to North Vietnam promising them reconstruction aid in return for a peace agreement, Kissinger's 1975 understanding with Israel and Egypt that U.S. personnel would be stationed in the Sinai as part of the disengagement process, and the 1975 Helsinki Accords, which were referred to as a statement of political intent.

Documents uncovered in the National Archives after the Persian Gulf War revealed a lengthy history of secret presidential agreements with Saudi Arabia.[11] In 1947, President Truman entered into an agreement with King Ibn Saud that stated that "one of the basic policies of [the] United States in [the] Near East is unqualifiedly to support [the] territorial integrity and political independence of Saudi Arabia." The document continued, "If Saudi Arabia should therefore be attacked by another power or be under threat of attack, the United States through medium of [the] United Nations would take energetic measures to ward off such aggression." In 1963, President Kennedy also entered into a secret agreement with Saudi Arabia. On the heels of an Egyptian-inspired coup and the assassination of a member of the Saudi royal family, Kennedy sent a U.S. fighter squadron to train in Saudi Arabia as a public show of support for that government. What was not made public was that Kennedy had authorized these units to use force against Egypt if provoked.

THE ROLE OF THE HOUSE
AND THE PANAMA CANAL TREATIES

The third and most recent area of controversy involving treaty-making powers involves the role of the House of Representatives. The Constitution gives the House no formal role in the treaty-making process, and traditionally it has played the part of a spectator. This has begun to change as the House has seized upon its budgetary powers as the vehicle for making its will known to both the Senate and the president. Treaties are not always self-executing. They typically require enabling legislation and the expenditure of funds before their provisions take effect. In exercising its budgetary and legislative powers, the House possesses the ability to undo what the Senate and president have agreed upon. According to one observer, the House came quite close to destroying the Panama Canal Treaties by inserting into the implementing legislation language that disagreed with and contradicted parts of the treaty just approved by the Senate.[12] The need for House approval of implementing legislation is not unique to the Panama Canal Treaties. The House also voted on implementing legislation for the 1994 GATT treaty. It did so by a bipartisan vote of 288 to 146 in favor of the necessary legislation. The GATT treaty then went to the Senate where the final ratification vote took place.

On September 16, 1977, President Carter submitted one document containing two treaties defining the future status of the Panama Canal to the

Senate for its consideration.[13] The Panama Canal Treaty abolished the Panama Canal Zone by terminating the 1903 treaty that established it. The United States would retain the right to manage and operate it until December 31, 1999, through a newly created Panama Canal Commission. At that time, Panama would get complete control. Until then, the United States would have military base rights and the primary responsibility for defending the canal, and a Neutrality Treaty established the permanent neutrality of the canal and guaranteed that it would always remain open. Furthermore, U.S. and Panamanian warships were to be allowed to pass through the canal "expeditiously." On March 16, 1978, by a vote of 68 to 32, the Senate gave its consent to the Neutrality Treaty. On April 18, it consented to the Panama Canal Treaty by a similar vote. The Senate debate on the merits of the two treaties consumed more time than had any treaty debate since that on the Treaty of Versailles: 192 changes were offered during the course of the debate, and 88 were voted on.

The controversy did not end here. It merely shifted to the House where the required implementing legislation now had to be passed. The administration bill was assigned to four committees. Primary jurisdiction was held by the Merchant Marine and Fisheries Committee whose chair, Representative John Murphy, opposed the treaty. He proposed his own version of the implementing legislation. Instead of creating a government corporation to run the canal, which would pay its expenses out of tolls as the Carter administration proposed, Murphy's bill would create a government agency whose budget would be voted on annually by Congress. The administration's bill would also have transferred property to Panama automatically; Murphy's bill required a vote on each transfer. A third bill would have required Panama to pay the cost of implementing the treaties and to reimburse the United States for the net cost of building the canal.

Eventually, the Carter administration abandoned its own bill in favor of the Murphy bill. After a series of extremely close votes, the House accepted the Murphy bill by a vote of 224 to 202. The result angered Panama. President Aristides Royo cited almost 30 articles of the House bill that violated provisions of the treaty. The Senate passed implementing legislation more in line with the administration's original proposal, and because the two bills disagreed, the matter was sent to a conference committee. By a vote of 308 to 90, the House instructed its conferees to insist on the House language regarding the transfer of property and the status of the Panama Canal Commission. The House rejected the first conference report by a vote of 192 to 203 and finally gave its acceptance by a vote of 232 to 188 only four days before the treaty was scheduled to take effect and 60 percent of the Panama Canal Zone was to be transferred to Panama.

Appointment Powers

As originally envisioned, the power to approve or reject presidential appointments was closely related to the power to give advice and consent to treaties. By exercising a voice in who negotiated the treaty, the Senate would be able to influence its content. In practice this linkage was never fully put into place, and it had long since unraveled. The Senate has failed to actively or systematically exercise its confirmation powers. Frequently, it has not hesitated to approve ambassadors appointed solely for political purposes and without any other apparent qualifications for the post. In 1956 a contribution of $22,000 to the Eisenhower campaign "bought" the ambassadorship to Sri Lanka. During the Nixon administration the ambassadors to Switzerland, Austria, and France all made contributions in excess of $100,000 to the Republican party. At the end of President Bush's term in office, 20 percent of the ambassador corps was made up of political or noncareer appointments. About 30 percent of Clinton's ambassadorial appointments could be classified as political in nature. In his first term, major campaign contributors were rewarded with ambassadorships to Luxembourg, Switzerland, Singapore, and Sweden. Early in his second term, campaign contributors were nominated for posts in Chile, the Bahamas, Barbados, and the Dominican Republic. The pattern of using ambassadorships as rewards for political support continued under George. W. Bush. Many went to "Pioneers," individuals who raised a minimum of $100,000 for his presidential race. Among those receiving appointments were Stephen Brauer as ambassador to Belgium (he contributed $190,000), W. L. Brown Jr., as ambassador to Austria (($169,000), Clifford Soebel as ambassador to the Netherlands ($331,000), and Richard Egan as ambassador to Ireland ($106,000).

Among the most controversial nominees for State Department positions was his selection of Reagan-era Central America policy veterans for ambassador to the United Nations, assistant secretary of state for Western Hemisphere affairs, deputy assistant secretary of state for inter-American affairs, and ambassador to the Organization of American States. While some of these nominations sailed through with little debate, others brought forward strong opposition. The nomination of Otto Reich to be assistant secretary of state was rejected twice by the Senate Foreign Relations Committee in 2001 without ever holding a hearing. Democrats asserted that he was too divisive while Republicans claimed that he was being punished for his intense opposition to Fidel Castro.

As this case indicates, typically when the Senate has raised its voice in opposition, concern has been directed more at making a policy statement than questioning the qualifications of the nominee. Three nominees to head the CIA, Theodore Sorensen (by Carter), Robert Gates (by Reagan), and Anthony Lake (by Clinton) were "defeated." While she was easily confirmed as Secretary of State in January 2005, Democrats used Condoleezza Rice's nomination for that post to air objections to the George W. Bush administration's Iraq policies rather than challenge her credentials.

The resolution of these cases again points to the need for caution in making judgments about the Senate's use of its constitutional powers. Halperin, Sorensen, and Gates all withdrew their names from consideration before a vote was taken. Gates would later be nominated again by Bush and win confirmation as head of the CIA. Pastor's nomination was withdrawn after it had been approved by the Senate Foreign Relations Committee. This approval came prior to the 1994 election but was vigorously opposed by Senator

Jesse Helms, who became chairperson of that committee after the Republicans won control of the Senate. Helms blamed Pastor, a Latin American expert who served on Carter's National Security Council, for the Panama Canal Treaties. Political memories often can be quite long. In 2005 President George W. Bush nominated John Negroponte to be the first national intelligence director. Opposition to his nomination came from human rights activists who served as ambassador to Honduras under Reagan at a time when dozens of Hondurans disappeared at the hands of the military.

Presidents have also turned the confirmation powers into something less than what was originally intended by using personal representatives as negotiators. Franklin Roosevelt relied heavily on Harry Hopkins in making international agreements, leaving Secretary of State Cordell Hull to administer over "diplomatic trivia." Carter used Hamilton Jordan to conduct secret negotiations during the Iranian hostage crisis, and in the Reagan administration National Security Council (NSC) staffers and private citizens were relied on to carry out the Iran–Contra initiative. A similar problem confronts the Senate if it wishes to influence the type of advice that the president gets. Presidents are free to listen to whom they please. Under Woodrow Wilson, Colonel House, a friend and confidant, was more influential than secretaries of state William Jennings Bryan and William Lansing. Today it is widely recognized that the national security adviser often has more influence on presidential thinking than does the secretary of state. Yet the former's appointment is not subject to Senate approval.

Two early personnel moves by George W. Bush highlight the Senate's continued problems in using its appointments power to control the president. First, Karl Rove, a senior political adviser in the White House who was not subject to confirmation, emerged as an important force in such foreign policy decisions as ending the bombing on Vieques and proposing amnesty for illegal Mexican immigrants in the United States. Both were widely interpreted as politically inspired moves. Second, he appointed Elliot Abrams to a senior position in the NSC responsible for promoting democracy and human rights. Again, Senate confirmation was not necessary. Abrams, along with Reich, was identified by the Iran–Contra investigations as having engaged in illegal activities. In 1991 Abrams pleaded guilty to two counts of misleading Congress about funding for the Contras. He was pardoned by President George Bush in 1992.

War Powers

The war powers of the Constitution are split into three basic parts. Congress is given the power to declare war and the power to raise and maintain an army and navy, while the president is designated as commander in chief of the armed forces. In the abstract these powers fit together very nicely, but in practice a far different picture prevails. A problem immediately arises over defining when a state of war exists. Is it any instance where U.S. troops are placed into combat, or must a war be declared into existence? In its Prize Cases decision of 1862, the Supreme Court ruled that the existence of a war was found in the prevailing conditions and not in a formal congressional declaration. U.S. practice has borne this out. Congress has declared only 5 of the over 125 "wars" that the United States has fought: the War of 1812, the Spanish-American War, the Mexican War, World War I, and World War II.

In addition, no state today can wait until a war has broken out or has been declared to begin mobilizing its armed forces. Successful military action requires forces in being. The dilemma facing Congress is that once it has created a standing military establishment capable of going into combat without further mobilization, it has lost control over the president. The Cuban missile crisis and the Bay of Pigs invasion were played out without a declaration of war. Carter presented Congress with a *fait accompli* with the Iranian hostage rescue effort; Reagan acted unilaterally in invading Grenada and bombing Libya; George H. W. Bush did the same in invading Panama and sending troops to Somalia.

President Clinton did not seek congressional authorization for his use of troops to return President Jean-Bertrand Aristide to power in Haiti. In fact, the Clinton administration asserted that the War Powers Resolution should be interpreted as recognizing and presupposing "the existence of a unilateral Presidential authority to deploy armed force." Neither the Clinton administration nor anyone in Congress mentioned the War Powers Resolution in February 1998, when President Clinton was contemplating air strikes against Iraq for its refusal to permit UN inspectors to search weapons sites. President George W. Bush began the war against terrorism in Afghanistan without a declaration of war or any reference to the War Powers Resolution. The single major congressional action was the September 12 Senate Joint Resolution #22 that "supports the determination of the President, in close consultation with Congress, to bring justice and punish the perpetrators of these attacks as well as their sponsors. . . ."

Presidents have defended such uses of force, citing their commander-in-chief powers. The exact meaning of these powers is unclear. Alexander Hamilton saw it as a symbolic grant of power with the actual power to decide military strategy and tactics being held by professional soldiers. Yet many presidents have taken this grant of power quite literally. Franklin Roosevelt actively participated in formulating military strategy and tactics during World War II, and Lyndon Johnson actively participated in selecting bombing targets during Vietnam.

WAR POWERS RESOLUTION

The most visible means available to Congress in trying to limit the president's use of force is the 1973 War Powers Resolution that was passed over President Nixon's veto.[14] It requires the president to do the following:

1. "In every possible instance" consult with Congress before committing U.S. troops in "hostilities or into situations where imminent involvement in hostilities" is likely.

2. Inform Congress within forty-eight hours after the introduction of troops if there has been no declaration of war.

3. Remove U.S. troops within sixty days (or ninety days in special circumstances) if Congress does not either declare war or adopt a concurrent resolution approving the action.

Congress also can terminate the U.S. military involvement before the sixty-day limit by passing a concurrent resolution. Such a resolution does not require the president's signature and, therefore, cannot be vetoed. From the outset, the War Powers Resolution has been controversial. Senator Jacob Javits saw in it the basis for a new foreign policy compact between the president and Congress. Senator Thomas Eagleton, an original supporter of the legislation with Javits, voted against it because he claimed that it gave the president powers he never had: the power to commit U.S. troops abroad without prior congressional approval.

Presidents have argued that the act was unconstitutional. The particular object of presidential hostility is the provision granting Congress the right to terminate hostilities through the use of a legislative veto. The legislative veto is a device that Congress has relied on to reinsert its voice into foreign affairs decision making. It allows the Congress to approve or disapprove executive branch actions after the fact in a form short of legislation. In addition to the War Powers Resolution, Congress has inserted legislative vetoes into a wide range of foreign policy legislation, including arms sales, the export of nuclear fuel and facilities, presidential decisions not to grant relief to industries injured by imports, the continuation of most favored nation status of communist states, the stationing of U.S. personnel in the Sinai, presidential declarations of emergency, and national defense contracts in excess of $25 million.[15]

Presidents have maintained that only congressional action that has been approved by the president or is passed by Congress over his veto is legally binding. On January 23, 1983, in a landmark case, the Supreme Court agreed with the presidential interpretation in making its ruling in *U.S. v. Chadha*. The case centered on the exercise of a legislative veto by the House of Representatives of the Attorney General's decision to allow Chadha, an East Indian student holding a British passport, to stay in the United States. The Supreme Court reaffirmed this position thirteen days later in a second case and explicitly linked its ruling to the legislative veto provisions of the War Powers Resolution. It should be noted that a foreign affairs legislative veto has never been exercised. The closest it came to being used was with the transfer of nuclear material to India in 1980 and the sale of an AWACS (Airborne Warning and Control Systems aircraft) and F-15 enhancement package to Saudi Arabia in 1981.

Another sore point with presidents is the 60-day time limit imposed by the act. From the very outset presidents have challenged the time limit on constitutional and practical grounds while at the same time they have acted in accordance with its reporting provisions. Of interest is the language used by presidents in making their reports.[16] In some cases (the transportation of refugees from Da Nang in April 1975, the evacuation of U.S. nationals from Cambodia and Vietnam in April 1975, and the evacuation of U.S. nationals from Lebanon in 1976), the president reported his action in a perfunctory manner. In reporting the *Mayaguez* rescue operation in 1975, President Ford stated that he was "taking note" of the War Powers Resolution but asserted that he acted on the basis of his commander-in-chief powers. In this case, it is also unclear whether the advance consulting provisions were met. Senator Hugh Scott, deputy minority leader and a member of the Senate Foreign Relations Committee, stated: "We were informed. We were alerted. We were advised. We were notified. . . . I don't know whether that's consultation or not."

Presidents have also sought to characterize their decision to use force as lying beyond the jurisdiction of the War Powers Resolution. Carter did not engage in advance consultations with Congress in carrying out the hostage rescue effort. He claimed it was a humanitarian action. Reagan used the same logic in bypassing Congress on the invasion of Grenada. He would later argue that since the marines were invited in by the Lebanese government they were not being sent into a combat situation and the War Powers Resolution did not apply. About to use military force against Haiti without congressional authorization, Clinton proclaimed he was prepared to "carry out the will of the United Nations." George H. W. Bush followed Carter and Reagan's logic arguing that since Somalia was a humanitarian operation no congressional approval was needed. He went to Congress for approval of military action against Iraq in the Persian Gulf War with great reluctance with Secretary of Defense Dick Cheney asserting that no additional authorization from Congress was necessary since the UN had sanctioned the use of "all necessary means" to force Iraq to withdraw from Kuwait. Even after Congress passed supporting resolutions in January 1991, George H. W. Bush continued to stress that "I don't think I need it. . . . I feel that I have the authority to fully implement the United Nations resolution."

In preparing for the Iraq War, the George W. Bush administration put forward two arguments for why the War Powers Resolution did not apply.[17] First, they argued that the 1991 resolution passed before the Persian Gulf War provided continuing military authority to the president. Second, they maintained that the use of force was authorized by the 1998 Iraq Liberation Act that called upon the president to provide for the overthrow of Saddam Hussein. In fact, the act specifically stated that none of its provisions "shall be construed to authorize or otherwise speak to the use of United States Armed Forces . . . in carrying out this Act."

CIVIL LIBERTIES

The most common point of reference for thinking about presidential war powers is with regard to Congress. But this is not always the case. Periodically the issue has been the power of the president versus the rights of the public. In the 1952 case of *Youngstown Sheet and Tube Co. v. Sawyer,* the Supreme Court ruled 6 to 3 against the constitutionality of Truman's order to nationalize the country's steel mills, an action he had taken because of the ongoing Korean War and the disruption a strike would cause for the war effort. A second famous case involved publication of the Pentagon Papers by the New York Times in 1971. The Pentagon Papers were a secret Defense Department study of U.S. involvement in Vietnam. Citing national security threats, the Nixon administration tried to stop their publication after the first three installments appeared. The Supreme Court ruled by a 6 to 3 vote to reject the Nixon administration's argument and permit the newspapers to continue to publish them.

The war against terrorism has brought forward renewed concerns about the protection of civil liberties on several fronts. One issue has been the rights of some 660 detainees in Guantanamo Bay, Cuba, where they have been held without trial and interrogated. Most were captured in military or intelligence operations in Afghanistan and Pakistan against al-Qaeda. The Bush administration claimed that they did not have access to U.S. courts and could be held as long as the president felt appropriate because they were un-lawful enemy combatants captured on the battlefield and because Guantanamo Bay was not part of the United States. In a series of decisions announced in June 2004, the Supreme Court rejected the administration's claim to such sweeping powers. Their decisions did not, however, clearly establish the outermost reaches of presidential authority here. A second issue grew out of revelations of abuse at of Iraqi prisoners by American guards at the Abu Ghraib prison. Of concern here was an assertion by George W. Bush he "had the authority under the Constitution" to deny the Geneva Prisoner of War Conventions to combatants captures in Afghanistan even though he would not invoke that power.

Commerce Powers

Two trade issues have dominated congressional-presidential relations in the last several decades. The first has been largely put to rest. It involved extending "permanent normal trade relations," long referred to as most favored nation (MFN) status, to communist states. The early focus was on the Soviet Union. Increased trade with the United States was to be one of the main carrots held out by the Nixon administration to the Soviet Union as part of its détente policy. It was to be an inducement for signing arms control agreements and refraining from opportunistic behavior in the third world. Quickly, however, Congress inserted language into trade legislation through the Jackson–Vanik Amendment, which linked improved trade terms with changes in Soviet domestic human rights behavior, most notably its treatment of Soviet Jews. Most recently the focus has been on China. For twenty years Congress held yearly votes on the terms by which Chinese goods would enter and compete in the U.S. market. In September 2000 the Clinton administration scored a major victory when by a vote of 83 to 15 the Senate voted to permanently award China normal trade relations, opening the way for China to join the World Trade Organization (WTO). Supporters cited the economic benefits of increased trade with China, while opponents cited China's poor human rights record, unfair trading practices, and involvement in provocative arms sales.

The second point of conflict is very much alive. It involves granting the president "fast track" authority to negotiate international trade agreements. As we will note later, fast track authority severely limits the ability of Congress to modify trade agreements when they are presented for its approval. President Clinton was forced to allow this authority to lapse as part of the political price for getting the Senate to ratify the GATT treaty establishing the WTO.

In December 2001, the House of Representatives passed a bill restoring Fast Track authority (now renamed Trade Promotional authority) to President George W. Bush by a vote of 215 to 214. The Senate, which historically has been solidly pro-free trade, supported the measure with little opposition. In the House vote, only twenty-one Democrats supported the measure. Many of those opposed represented "high-tech" communities whose firms depend on selling to export markets and traditional free traders. Opponents are concerned that trade offs between environmental protection, intellectual property rights, and labor standards may be made at the Doha Round of WTO talks, set to run from 2002 to 2005, in the name of furthering free trade.

The president and Congress have clashed over these and other trade matters because the Constitution gives Congress the power to regulate commerce with foreign nations. In theory this power belongs exclusively to Congress. No parallel statement exists laying out presidential powers. In practice, power sharing between the two branches has been necessary. Congress may have the power to regulate foreign commerce, but only the president has the power to negotiate treaties, and it is the president whom the Supreme Court has designated as the "sole organ of the government in the field of foreign affairs." Power sharing in international economics has not produced the same level of conflict between the two branches as it has in other areas. Instead, it has produced a series of innovations that have brought a high degree of continuity and consistency to U.S. policy. The first innovative power-sharing arrangement is found in the 1934 Trade Agreements Act by which Congress delegated to the president the authority to "implement into domestic law the results of trade agreements as they relate to tariffs." This procedure greatly enhanced the president's power position in multilateral trade negotiations by removing the threat of congressional obstructionism in the formal approval and implementation of the negotiated agreement. Congress periodically renewed this grant of authority for a succession of presidents, changing only the time frame involved and the value of the reduction permitted and inserting legislative veto provisions. This procedure worked well until the Kennedy Round negotiations (1964 to 1967), when for the first time nontariff barriers to trade became the major points of contention. Changes in U.S. law and the congressional delegation of authority were now widely seen as necessary before the United States could effectively engage in another round of international trade negotiations.

The Trade Reform Act of 1974 introduced the second major innovative power-sharing arrangement. It created a "fast track" reporting procedure. The president would be able to send a draft bill containing the necessary implementing legislation to Congress, which would be required to vote yes or no within 90 days and which was prohibited from adding any amendments. The 1974 Trade Reform Act also created an elaborate set of advisory committees and targets to guide the negotiating process. These procedures were used with great success in the Tokyo Round negotiations (1973 to 1979). The president's representatives negotiated, and Congress quickly approved, an incredibly complex series of agreements with very little acrimony at a time when the two branches could agree upon little else.[18]

I. M. Destler suggests that these types of legislative innovations have allowed Congress to insulate itself from domestic pressures for protectionist trade legislation. The result is that congressional representatives can "advocate, even threaten, trade restrictions, while nicely relieving them of the need to deliver on their threats." Such protection for Congress was necessary because congressional tariffs invariably meant high tariffs, and after the experience of the 1930s and the Smoot–Hawley Tariff, all agreed that this had to be avoided. The concern expressed today is that Congress has today once again made itself vulnerable to these pressures because of its reluctance to grant fast-track authority and support free-trade agreements that the public perceives as costing Americans jobs.

Federalism and the States

The past several decades have seen an explosion in the foreign policy activity of states and local governments. They have surfaced as visible and active lobbyists on important foreign policy issues. State government associations spoke out vehemently against what they saw as a GATT treaty that discriminated against states.[19] They objected to provisions that in their view would reduce state and local taxes paid by foreign companies and transfer authority to determine state and local tax policies away from U.S. courts to international trade panels. States were also active in their opposition to certain facets of U.S. refugee policy. In 1994, Florida sued the federal government to recover millions of dollars state and local governments spent providing social services and law enforcement for illegal immigrants. California, Illinois, and Texas had voiced similar complaints. Later that year, Florida Governor Lawton Chiles followed this up by "declaring a state of emergency" and calling on the Clinton administration to change its policy of allowing Cuban boat people to enter the United States.

Even more significant from a constitutional perspective is the emergence of state and local foreign policies. The range of these foreign policy initiatives is great.[20] At the local level, eighty-six communities formed linkages with Nicaragua and provided its people with humanitarian assistance. Twenty-nine communities provided sanctuary for Guatemalan and Salvadoran refugees. The U.S. Conference of Mayors demanded cuts in military spending and 120 localities refused to cooperate with the Federal Emergency Management Agency's nuclear war exercises. Over 900 communities passed resolutions supporting a freeze in the arms race during the later part of the Cold War. More recently, over 150 local governments and three states passed resolutions condemning all or parts of the USA Patriot Act. Its provisions permit the government to seize business, library, and computer records without disclosing that it has done so.

States have become particularly prominent actors in international economic transactions.[21] Raw economic figures point to their potential for global influence. Ten states would rank among the world's top twenty-five economies. All fifty states would rank in the top seventy-five. This economic strength has become the foundation for an overseas economic presence. In

1970, only four states had offices abroad, but in 1990, forty-three states were operating 163 offices around the world. All fifty states now offer export assistance programs and many provide investment incentive packages in order to attract foreign investors. Increasingly states and localities have flexed their economic power in an effort to influence events abroad. In 1998, cities in California, Colorado, Wisconsin, Michigan, North Carolina, Rhode Island, New York, Florida, and Massachusetts had imposed investment or purchasing sanctions (or had them pending) against Burma, Nigeria, Cuba, Indonesia, and Tibet. Also in 1998, a committee representing about 800 municipal and state financial officers decided to go ahead with sanctions against Switzerland's three largest banks in an effort to force a settlement of claims from Holocaust survivors. In doing so, it rejected a warning from the State Department that their actions would worsen U.S.–Swiss relations and damage the reputation of the United States in international financial markets.

The U.S. Constitution established a federal system of government in which some powers were given exclusively to the national government, some to the states, and others were shared among them. Among those granted exclusively to the national government are the powers "to conduct foreign relations" and "to regulate commerce with foreign nations and among states." As states and localities become more active in these areas and pursue policies at variance with those advocated by the federal government, the potential for conflict grows. For example, in 1989 Texas shipped hormone-fed beef to Great Britain over the objections of the federal government, and the Department of Agriculture at first refused to certify that the meat was drug-free. In 1991, only days after President Bush lifted U.S. economic sanctions against South Africa, New York City moved to tighten its restrictions on trade with that country.

In 2000, the Supreme Court struck a blow against state activism in foreign policy matters when it ruled that a Massachusetts law banning companies from doing business in Burma from holding state contracts was unconstitutional. Justice David Souter wrote that the Massachusetts law "undermines the president's capacity in his instance for effective diplomacy." The Supreme Court found that the law had been preempted when, three months before it was passed in 1996, Congress enacted sanctions against Burma. Although tightly written, this ruling invalidated as many as twenty-two laws passed by other state and local jurisdictions. A listing of these laws is found in Table 7.2. Massachusetts had argued that state purchasing decisions and investment decisions did not properly fall under the heading of international commerce.

The question of where states and localities fit into the overall scheme of American foreign policy is sure to remain unanswered for the foreseeable future. Beyond the legal issues involved, the debate promises to center on three concerns.[22] First, can the United States have an effective foreign policy if it speaks with more than one voice? Second, since foreign policy decisions affect everyone, should they be made by state and local groups? Third, do states and local governments have the expertise to engage in foreign policy making? The traditional answer to all three questions is no. Defenders of state foreign policy making argue that the United States has never spoken with

TABLE 7.2   State and Local Sanctions Legislation in Place, 2000

States	Massachusetts
• Massachusetts	• Amherst
• California (2)	• Brookline
• Vermont	• Cambridge (3)
• Washington	• Newton
Localities	• Quincy
California	• Somerville
• Alameda County (2)	*Michigan*
• Berkeley (3)	• Ann Arbor
• Los Angeles	*New York*
• Oakland (2)	• New York City
• Palo Alto	*North Carolina*
• San Francisco	• Carrboro
• Santa Cruz	• Chapel Hill
• Santa Monica	*Ohio*
• West Hollywood	• North Olmstead
Colorado	*Oregon*
• Boulder	• Portland
Florida	*Pennsylvania*
• Dade County	• Philadelphia
Maryland	*Wisconsin*
• Takoma Park	• Madison

Source: adapted from Terrence Guy, "Local Government and Global Politics," *Political Science Quarterly* 115 (2000), p. 357.

one voice in foreign policy; that there is a great deal of local- and state-level expertise on environmental, economic, and human rights issues; and that municipal and state foreign policies that affect voters' lives are more readily controlled by voters than is decision making in Washington.

Summary and Future Issues

In this chapter we have reviewed the constitutional distribution of powers in foreign affairs as they exist in the areas of treaty making, appointments, war making, and commerce. This distribution of powers is not exhaustive. Gaps exist. No mention is made of the power to terminate a treaty, declare neutrality, make peace, or break diplomatic relations. The constitutional distribution of powers establishes only a starting point for foreign policy decision making. In the words of Edward Corwin, it is an "invitation to the president and Congress to struggle over the privilege of directing U.S. foreign policy."[23]

We can see that most of the time the struggle between the two branches takes the form of imposing (and resisting) specific restrictions on the exercise of presidential power. The perennial focus of attention is the War Powers Resolution. Recently Louis Fisher and David Gray Adler have argued that after twenty-five years of experience, it would be better for both branches—and for constitutional government—to repeal the War Powers Resolution and rely upon traditional political pressures and the regular system of checks and balances, including impeachment. Over the long term, outright repeal would be less risky than continuing along the present path.[24]

More frequently heard than calls for its repeal are proposals for the revision of the War Powers Resolution. Congressional leaders in both parties have proposed that the section requiring that the president notify Congress be repealed and replaced by provisions allowing for (1) the expedited consideration of legislation to terminate any troop deployments that Congress objects to and (2) the establishment of a permanent congressional consulting group that the administration would be in touch with before and during military operations. Failing this, observers such as Destler believe that we will see congressional-presidential dealings in this area beginning to move on two separate tracks.[25] On big issues such as the war powers question, the president may gain additional leeway. On more routine issues such as arms sales and economic policy, the president will lose flexibility. In these areas Congress will develop more cumbersome means of regulating executive branch behavior.

After watching U.S. forces serve in international peacekeeping efforts in Somalia and Haiti, and fearing that the same thing might happen in places like Bosnia, Senate Majority Leader Robert Dole started off the 104th Congress by introducing a "peace powers act" that would place restraints on a president's ability to send U.S. troops and spend U.S. dollars policing post–cold war trouble spots. Dole's resolution would repeal that part of the War Powers Resolution that required a president to withdraw troops from hostile situations in 60 days unless Congress gave its approval. The notification and reporting requirements would be retained. With regard to peacekeeping operations, Dole's resolution would prevent the president from moving to initiate, expand, or extend peacekeeping operations without detailing in advance how they would be paid for. A second Republican bid to repeal the War Powers Resolution was turned back in the House in 1995 by a vote of 217 to 201. A letter from Clinton supporting the repeal was held back when it became clear that the move would fail.

The emergence of divided government in the post-cold war era has also produced calls for a more fundamental reexamination of the balance of power between the two branches. Most often cited as proof positive of the need for these changes are the inability to pass foreign policy legislation in a timely fashion and the transformation of "advise and consent" into "harass and maim." Reforms have also been sought at a much more fundamental level. William Fulbright, former chairman of the Senate Foreign Relations Committee, was among the first to speak out for such a reform, questioning whether "our constitutional machinery, admirably suited for the needs of a remote 18th century agrarian republic" was "adequate to the formulations and conduct of foreign policy of a 20th century nation."[26]

The most recent development holding the potential for altering the constitutional distribution of powers in foreign policy comes from outside the United States in the form of the growing support for the principle of universal jurisdiction, which holds that national standards of justice are subservient to internationally agreed-upon standards. We see this issue raised in three different areas. The first is in the establishment of an International Court of Justice. Second, there is the question of prisoner rights and the relative standing of international agreements such as the Geneva Convention and U.S. policy. The third area involves the relationship of U.S. trade laws to the rulings of the World Trade Organization (WTO). Several times in recent years, the WTO has ruled American trade practices and tax laws to be in violation of international agreements. If they are not changed, the United States is vulnerable to retaliatory action and heavy fines from the injured countries.

Henry Kissinger, himself the subject of calls for trial by a the ICC for his involvement in the U.S. covert action against Chilean President Salvadore Allende, warns that an overly eager embrace of the principle of universal jurisdiction runs the risk of "substituting the tyranny of judges for that of governments."[27] Expressing a classic balance-of-power outlook on international affairs, he asserts that there is no evidence that if politics is replaced by law, peace will be realized.

Notes

1. Quoted in the *Washington Post,* February 17, 1990, p. 23.
2. Louis Henkin, *Foreign Affairs and the Constitution* (Mineola, N.Y.: Foundation Press, 1972), p. 131.
3. David M. O'Brien, "Presidential and Congressional Relations in Foreign Affairs," in Colton Campbell et al. (eds.), *Congress and the Politics of Foreign Policy* (Upper Saddle River, NJ: Prentice Hall, 2003), p. 73.
4. Theodor Meron, "The Treaty Power: The International Legal Effect of Changes in Obligations Initiated by the Congress," in Thomas M. Franck (ed.), *The Tethered Presidency* (New York: New York University Press, 1981), pp. 103–40.
5. Stephen Schwartz, "Outmaneuvered, Outgunned and Out of View: The Test Ban Debacle," *The Bulletin of the Atomic Scientists,* 56 (January 2000), 24–31.
6. For a discussion of the Reagan administration's tendency to unilaterally reinterpret laws, see David Scheffer, "Nouveau Law and Foreign Policy," *Foreign Policy,* 76 (1989), 44–65.
7. James Pfiffner, *The Modern Presidency* (Boston: Bedford/St. Martins, 2004), p, 187.
8. Loch Johnson and James M. McCormick, "Foreign Policy by Executive Fiat," *Foreign Policy,* 28 (1977), 117–38.
9. James A Nathan and Richard K. Oliver, *Foreign Policy Making and the American Political System* (Boston: Little, Brown, 1983), p. 115.
10. Charles W. Kegley Jr., and Eugene R. Wittkopf, *American Foreign Policy: Pattern and Process,* 2nd ed. (New York: St. Martin's, 1982), p. 418.
11. *Washington Post,* February 9, 1992.
12. William L. Furlong, "Negotiations and Ratification of the Panama Canal Treaty," in John Spanier and Joseph Nogee (eds.), *Congress, the Presidency, and American Foreign Policy* (Elmsford, N.Y.: Pergamon, 1981), pp. 77–107.
13. The material in this section is drawn from the accounts by Furlong; and Cecil Crabb, Jr., and Pat M. Holt, *Invitation to Struggle: Congress, the President, and Foreign Policy,* 2nd ed. (Washington D.C.: Congressional Quarterly, 1984).

14. Robert F. Turner, *The War Powers Resolution: Its Implementation in Theory and Practice* (Philadelphia: Foreign Policy Research Institute, 1983), presents a thorough and critical review of the cases to which the War Powers Resolution has been and could have been applied.

15. Congressional Research Service, *Foreign Policy Effects of the Supreme Court's Legislative Veto Decision* (Washington, D.C.: Congressional Research Service, February 23, 1984).

16. House Committee on Foreign Affairs, *The War Powers Resolution: Relevant Documents, Correspondence, and Reports* (Washington, D.C.: U.S. Government Printing Office, 1983); Reagan's actions are examined in Charles Madden, "Foreign Policy Report," *National Journal,* May 19, 1984, pp. 989–93.

17. On the Iraq War see, Louis Fisher, "Deciding on War Against Iraq," *Political Science Quarterly,* 118 (2003), 389–410; and "Presidential Wars," in Eugene Wittkopf and James McCormick (eds.), *The Domestic Sources of American Foreign Policy,* 4th ed. (Lanham, MD: Rowman & Littlefield, 2004), pp. 155–70.

18. I. M. Destler and Thomas R. Graham, "United States Congress and the Tokyo Round: Lessons of a Success Story," *The World Economy,* 3 (1980), 53–70.

19. Dan R. Bucks, "Trade Trouble Ahead," *State Government News,* May 1994, pp. 6–9.

20. Michael H. Shuman, "Dateline Main Street: Courts v. Local Foreign Policies," *Foreign Policy,* 86 (1992), 158–77.

21. Earl H. Fry, "States in the International Economy: An American Overview," in Douglas M. Brown and Earl H. Fry (eds.), *States and Provinces in the International Political Economy* (Berkeley, Calif.: Institute of Governmental Studies Press, 1993), 45–64.

22. Shuman, "Dateline Mainstreet."

23. Edward S. Corwin, *The President: Office and Powers* (New York: New York University Press, 1957), p. 171.

24. Louis Fisher and David Gray Adler, "The War Powers Resolution: Time to Say Goodbye," *Political Science Quarterly,* 113 (1998), 1–18.

25. I. M. Destler, "Dateline Washington: Life after the Veto," *Foreign Policy,* 52 (1983), pp. 181–86.

26. William J. Fulbright, "American Foreign Policy in the 20th Century Under an 18th Century Constitution," *Cornell Law Quarterly,* 47 (1961), 1–13. A similar argument is made by John G. Tower, "Congress Versus the President," *Foreign Affairs,* 60 (1981/82), 229–46.

27. Henry Kissinger, "The Pitfalls of Universal Jurisdiction," *Foreign Affairs,* 80 (2001), 86–96.

8

THE PRESIDENCY

In the public's eye, it is the president who makes American foreign policy. As the following excerpts illustrate, memoir and journalist accounts of key moments in American foreign policy reinforce this image. In speaking to an interviewer of his administration's debate on how to proceed after 9/11, President George W. Bush said this of his key advisors:

> I've grown comfortable with them as human beings and as people that were capable of handling their responsibilities. And therefore I—when they give me advice, I trust their judgment. Now sometimes that advice isn't always the same, in which case my job—look the job is to grind through these problems and grind through scenarios, and hopefully reach a consensus of six or seven smart people, which makes my job easier.[1]

President Nixon gave this account of how he decided it was necessary to send troops into Cambodia during the Vietnam War.

> My immediate reaction was to do everything possible to help Lon Nol, but [Secretary of State] Rogers, and [Secretary of Defense] Laird strongly recommended that we hold back. . . . By the end of April . . . it was clear that Lon Nol needed help to survive. . . . Support for Lon Nol was discussed at an NSC meeting on April 22. I woke up early that morning and dictated a memorandum to [National Security Adviser] Kissinger: Assuming that I feel the way today at our meeting as I feel this morning . . . I think we need a bold move in Cambodia to show that we stand with Lon Nol. . . . On Monday morning I met with Rogers, Laird, and Kissinger. It was a tense meeting, because even though Rogers and Laird had by now given up hope of dissuading me from taking some action in Cambodia, they still thought they could convince me not to involve American troops. . . . That night I sat alone going over

the decision one last time. . . . I took a pad and began to make a list of the pluses and minuses of both operations.[2]

Carter gives this account of how he came to his decision to hold the Camp David summit conference between Israeli prime minister Begin and Egyptian president Sadat. He begins the account with a diary entry from February 3, 1978.

> We had quite an argument at breakfast with me on one side and Fritz [Vice President Mondale], Cy [Secretary of State Vance], Zbig [National Security Adviser Brzezinski], and Ham [presidential aide Jordan] on the other. I think we ought to move much more aggressively on the Middle East question than any of them seem to. . . . Late in June, I called in a small group of Democratic "wisemen"—senior leaders who were experienced in political affairs. Their advice was to "stay as aloof as possible from direct involvement in the Middle East negotiations; this is a losing proposition." At the time, I could not think of any reason to disagree with them, but there was just no way I could abandon such an important commitment. . . . At our regular Friday morning foreign-affairs breakfast we spent much of our time talking about the Middle East. . . . I discussed the situation with Rosalynn, who was thoroughly familiar with the issues involved in the Middle East dispute and understood what was at stake. . . . There was only one thing to do. . . . I would try to bring Sadat and Begin together for an extensive negotiating session with me. . . . I asked Mondale, Vance [Secretary of Defense], Brown, Brzezinski, and Jordan to come to Camp David for a special meeting on the Middle East. There I described what I had in mind. None of us thought we had much chance of success but we could not think of a better alternative.[3]

Not all presidents are as deeply involved in making foreign policy decisions. In his videotaped testimony for the trial of one of his former national security advisers, John Poindexter, President Reagan made many comments that were at variance with the documentary evidence amassed by the Tower Commission and the testimony of other participants. The following is his response to a question regarding his recollection of a 1986 briefing by Poindexter on sending HAWK missile spare parts to Iran.

> The only thing that I am aware of, and I cannot remember any meeting on this or not, was I do have a memory of learning or hearing that the Israelis, prior to these other things, had sent some of their HAWK missiles to Iran evidently in that sale. . . . And the thing that makes me remember this is that, apparently, the understanding was that this was going to be in return for some, perhaps, hostages of their own or the people that were held. That if these individuals had not been released by the time the plane of delivery had reached a certain point, the plane would turn around and come back without continuing the delivery.[4]

Hugh Heclo suggests that "far from being in charge of, or running the government, the president must struggle even to comprehend what is going on."[5] Information does not come to the president automatically. Nor can presidents count on speed and secrecy in making and carrying out decisions. Theirs is often the power to persuade rather than the power to command.[6] In this chapter we examine the interplay of personality and organization in presidential foreign policy leadership.

Presidential Personality

Textbooks and newspaper accounts of U.S. foreign policy are dominated by references to policies that bear a president's name: the Monroe Doctrine, the Truman Doctrine, the Nixon Doctrine, the Carter Doctrine, the Reagan Doctrine. Personalizing the presidency this way suggests that the identity of the president matters greatly and that if a different person had been president, U.S. foreign policy would look different. Certainly this is the case in terms of how presidents approach certain aspects of their job. Consider the differences between the trips to Africa made by Bill Clinton in 1998 and by George W. Bush in 2003. Clinton spent eleven days in Africa and visited six countries. Bush saw five countries in five days. Clinton spent two days on safari. Bush spent one hour on safari. Clinton traveled with an entourage of forty. Bush brought few guests. Where Clinton routinely commented that it was wrong for the United States to have taken slaves from Africa, Bush spoke out aggressively against the failure of African leaders to do enough about AIDS. Clinton toured Nelson Mandela's prison and visited Soweto, while Bush went to Pretoria where the white-only government ruled. Yet does it matter? Africa largely was neglected by both administrations and continues to operate at the periphery of world politics. Presidents seem attracted to it for reasons that have little to do with Africa per se. Clinton's trip occurred against the backdrop of the Monica Lewinsky scandal and was a means of getting out of Washington. Bush was drawn to Africa because of the link between failed states and terrorism, and because his administration was about to reluctantly commit U.S. troops to Liberia. Stated more generally, a persuasive case can be made that situational factors, role variables, and the common socioeconomic backgrounds of policy makers place severe constraints on the impact of personality on policy. In this section we first look at a leading effort to capture presidential personality and then examine under what conditions we should expect presidential personality to make a difference.

The most famous effort to classify presidential personality and explore its implications for policy is by James David Barber, who defines personality in terms of three elements.[7] The first is worldview, which Barber defines as an individual's politically relevant beliefs. The second element is style, which refers to an individual's habitual ways of responding to political opportunities and challenges through "rhetoric, personal relations, and homework." They are both heavily influenced by the third and most important component of personality: character, which develops in childhood. Character is the way the individual orients himself or herself toward life and involves two dimensions. The first is the amount of energy put into the presidency. Presidents are classified as either passive or active. The second dimension is whether the president derives personal satisfaction from the job. A president who does is classified as positive, and one who gets no personal satisfaction from being president is classified as negative. Together these two dimensions produce four presidential personalities.

Active-positives such as Truman, Carter, Kennedy, Clinton and George H. W. Bush put a great deal of energy into being president and derive great satisfaction from doing so. They are achievement oriented, value productivity, and enjoy meeting new challenges. Active-negatives such as Johnson and Nixon are compulsive individuals who are driven to acquire power as a means of compensating for low self-esteem. Active-negatives adopt a domineering posture toward those around them and have difficulty managing their aggressive feelings. Passive-positives are directed individuals who seek affection as a reward for being agreeable. Passive-positive presidents such as Reagan and George W. Bush do not make full use of the powers of the presidency but feel satisfied with the job as they define it. Passive-negatives such as Eisenhower get little satisfaction from the job and use few of the powers available to them. They are only in politics because others have sought them out, and they feel a responsibility to meet these expectations. Their actions are plagued by low self-esteem and feelings of uselessness. They do not enjoy the game of politics. Rather than bargain and compromise, they seek to avoid confrontation by emphasizing vague principles and procedural arrangements.

Barber argues that his typology can be used to predict presidential performance. In Barber's original presentation he argued for the active-positive character as the one best suited for the modern presidency. A preferable approach is to recognize that each type of presidential character has different implications for U.S. foreign policy. Barber favored the active-positive personality for its flexibility and emphasis on the rational mastery of problems. Carter's handling of the Panama Canal Treaties illustrates the ability of active-positives to productively engage in coalition-building efforts and to accept the compromises necessary to get a policy measure passed. Carter's presidency also illustrates the problem with active-positive presidents. They may overreach themselves by pursuing too many goals at once and be insensitive to the fact that the irrationalities of politics can frustrate even the best laid plans. Carter was roundly criticized for being too flexible in the search for results and for trying to do too many things at the outset of his administration: negotiate a SALT II Treaty, negotiate a Panama Canal Treaty, and reorder U.S. foreign policy priorities by emphasizing human rights and economic problems over the Soviet threat. Bill Clinton is a second example. Clinton is a perfect fit for classification as an active-positive president. He is a supremely political animal who enjoys the game of politics; when defeated he bounces back; and he displays a fundamental pragmatism in approaching policy problems.[8]

The great danger of active-negatives is that they will rigidly adhere to a disastrous foreign policy. Woodrow Wilson did so in the League of Nations controversy; John Adams, with the Alien and Sedition Act; Lyndon Johnson, with Vietnam; and Richard Nixon, with his actions in the Watergate scandal and the impeachment proceedings.

George W. Bush fits comfortably into the passive-positive category. Delegation of authority to others, focusing on a few select themes, and preference for binary black-white thinking that allows him to make decisions without getting into the deeper questions involved in an issue are widely acknowledged to be key characteristics of how he approaches problems. Bob Woodward, who chronicled the Bush administration's decisions to go to war in Afghanistan and Iraq, said his decision-making style "bordered on the hurried. He wanted actions, solutions. Once on course, he directed his energy at forging on, rarely looking back, scoffing at—even ridiculing—doubt and anything less than 100 percent commitment."[9] Richard Clarke who worked for both Bush and Clinton on terrorism matters says of Bush, he "asked us soon after September 11 for cards or charts of senior al-Qaeda managers as though dealing with them would be like a Harvard Business School exercise in a hostile takeover.[10] He announced his intention to measure progress in the war on terrorism by crossing through the pictures of those caught or killed."

His administration also provides illustrations of two of the major dangers presented by passive presidents. First, there is policy drift. While the administration moved quickly and assertively to deal with the threat of terrorism after 9/11, it was slow to recognize that the issue was a major problem. Clarke maintains that is was only on September 4, 2001 that the meeting on al-Qaeda he had urgently called for on January 25 was held. He describes the meeting as a nonevent that ended without a decision having been made. The second potential danger is the absence of accountability. This comes through in the administration's inability to present a timeline indicating what Bush knew regarding the permissibility of using extreme measures to obtain information from prisoners held at Guantanamo Bay or the Abu Ghraib prison, and when he knew it. At the same time, Secretary of State Colin Powell maintained that the president was kept fully informed about detainee issues raised by the Red Cross. He indicated they were discussed in national security council meetings and elsewhere in the president's presence.

Placing a president in one of Barber's categories involves a great deal of subjective judgment. Consider the case of Eisenhower. Fred Greenstein suggests that Eisenhower was not a passive-negative president as he is defined by Barber.[11] Based on previously unavailable materials, Greenstein concludes that Eisenhower deliberately cultivated the image of not being involved in policy making in order to deflect political pressures away from him. Eisenhower's "hidden hand leadership" employed a behind-the-scenes activism combined with a low profile in public.

Categorizing presidents in terms of shared qualities is useful because it allows us to move beyond making a series of singular observations. We must remember, however, that placing presidents in categories is only the beginning step in an analysis of their presidency and not the end. Attributes alone do not tell us what to expect from a president in terms of either policy or leadership style. Few would have predicted that Ronald Reagan, the arch anticommunist, would end his administration as an advocate of arms control or bring about a major improvement in U.S.–Soviet relations.[12]

When Does the Individual Matter?

In a study of twentieth-century U.S. foreign policy, John Stoessinger was struck by how few individuals made crucial decisions shaping its direction.[13] He found that "movers" (exceptional individuals who for better or worse not only find turning points in history but help create them) have been far outnumbered by "players" (individuals caught up in the flow of events who respond in a standard and predictable fashion). One explanation for this imbalance is that there may exist relatively few situations where the personal characteristics of the policy maker are important for explaining policy.

A useful distinction can be made between action indispensability and actor indispensability.[14] Action indispensability refers to situations in which a specific action is critical to the success or failure of a policy. The identity of the actor is not necessarily a critical factor in explaining the action. It is possible that any individual (player) in that situation would have acted in the same manner. Actor indispensability refers to those situations where the personal characteristics of the involved are critical to explaining the action taken. In Stoessinger's terms the individual involved is a mover. This is someone who increases the odds of success or failure by bringing his or her unique qualities to bear on a problem.

A crucial element of action indispensability is the degree to which the situation permits restructuring. Some situations are so intractable or unstable that it is unreasonable to expect the actions of an individual policy maker to have much of an impact. The most favorable condition for individual actions to have an impact is when a "precarious equilibrium" exists and events are primed to move in any number of directions. This is seldom the case. Many of the foreign policy problems that a president confronts are either highly intractable situations or very unstable ones. Presidents do not ignore these policy problems. Peace initiatives in the Middle East have become a common feature of U.S. foreign policy. Economic summit conferences bringing together the leaders of the advanced industrial states now occur at regular intervals. It is just that either the instability of the situation overtakes policy initiatives, or its persistent features dilute the policy initiative, perpetuating the status quo.

In concrete terms we can suggest that the president's personality will have its greatest impact on policy under these conditions. First is when the issue is new on the agenda. Carter's involvement in human rights policy and Reagan's championing of the strategic defense initiative are cases in point. Second is when the issue is addressed early in the administration. Carter's decision not to simply wrap up the SALT II package left him by Ford but to negotiate his own treaty illustrates this point. Clinton's handling of Somalia is another example. Third are those ongoing issues where the president is deeply involved. Vietnam was such an issue for Johnson and Nixon. Release of the American hostages in Lebanon was such an issue for Reagan. Finally, we can expect presidential personality to matter when the issue is in a state of precarious equilibrium. Recent issues that could be classified this way include arms control, the Middle East peace process, Bosnia, and the democratization movement in Russia. All three of these conditions are met by the events of 9/11. The issue was new on the agenda. While the Clinton administration had given terrorism more attention than did the incoming Bush administration, no firm plan of action was in place. The attack occurred early in the administration. And certainly from the point of view of key individuals within the administration, the terrorist attacks presented the United States with a unique opportunity to remake the political map of the Persian Gulf.

Presidential Bureaucracy

Presidents have discovered that the strength of their personality alone is not enough to get others to follow. Leadership also requires an organizational foundation, and experience has taught them that the executive branch bureaucracy is not that organization. The bureaucrat's time frame is different from that of the president. Presidents have only four years (eight if they are lucky) to implement their agenda. Bureaucrats know that they will be there long after the current administration leaves office and the next one, claiming a new mandate, arrives. The result is that presidents have been forced to look elsewhere to create an organization that will allow them to lead. The central foreign policy structure that presidents have grown to rely on is the National Security Council (NSC). Before reviewing its history, it is important to recognize that a prerequisite for effectively using the presidential bureaucracy to exercise foreign policy leadership is presidential control over it. How this is done is up to the president and varies from president to president.

Four basic options exist.[15] None is by definition superior to another. All have contributed to foreign policy successes and failures. The first is a competitive model in which a great deal of emphasis is placed on the free and open expression of ideas. Jurisdictions and grants of authority overlap as individuals and departments compete for the president's attention in putting forward ideas and programs. Franklin Roosevelt is the only president who successfully employed such a model. Lyndon Johnson is seen as having tried and failed to emulate him. A second leadership style involves setting up a formalistic system in which the president establishes orderly routines and procedures for organizing the administration's policy deliberations. The system is hierarchically structured with the president deeply involved as the final arbitrator in defining strategy and policy choices. Truman, Eisenhower, Nixon, Ford, and Reagan set up formalistic systems. The third management style centers on the creation of a collegial system in which presidents try to bring together a group of advisers to operate as a problem-solving team. Kennedy, Carter, George H. W. Bush, and Clinton set up this type of system.

The fourth management style has been introduced by George W. Bush. In spirit, it harkens back to a Nixon-style attempt to govern by stressing loyalty, tightly controlling the flow of information, and surrounding himself with an "iron triangle" of aides. In his first term this consisted of, national security advisor Condoleezza Rice, chief of staff Andrew Card, Jr., and Vice President Dick Cheney. There are also noticeable managerial differences. Whereas the

Nixon national security council system stressed hierarchy and centralized control, Bush is widely described as the first president to bring a CEO (chief executive officer) perspective to the presidency. Central to this model of presidential leadership is setting the overall tone of the administration and policy agenda so as to establish the general direction of policy, and flattening the power structure so that responsibility for carrying through on policy can be effectively delegated to key individuals.

The National Security Council

The history of the National Security Council (NSC) system can be broken down into four phases, each of which introduced distortions into the operation of the system that ultimately hindered the pursuit of foreign policy goals and its ultimate purpose. According to the 1947 National Security Act, this was to advise the president "with respect to the integration of domestic, foreign, and military policies relating to national security."[16] The first phase of the NSC's history runs from 1947 to 1960. During this period the NSC became overly institutionalized. Truman was the first president to have the NSC, and he was cautious in using it. He particularly wanted to avoid setting any precedents that would give it the power to supervise executive branch agencies or establish a norm of group responsibility for foreign policy decisions as some had hoped when the establishment of the NSC was being debated. For Truman foreign policy was the responsibility of the president alone. The NSC was to be an advisory body and nothing more. To emphasize this point, Truman did not attend early meetings of the NSC. The outbreak of the Korean War changed Truman's approach to the NSC. He started to use it more systematically and began attending its regularly scheduled meetings. Organizational changes also took place. All national security issues were now to be brought to his attention through the NSC system, the NSC staff was reorganized, and the emphasis on outside consultants was replaced by a senior staff served by staff assistants.

Institutionalization continued under Eisenhower, who transformed the NSC system into a two-part unit that would be actively involved in making policy. A Planning Board was created to develop policy recommendations for the president, and an Operations Coordinating Board was established to oversee the implementation of national security decisions. Eisenhower also established the post of Assistant for National Security Affairs (commonly known as the president's National Security Adviser) to more forcefully coordinate the national security decision-making process. Conventional accounts conclude that the NSC system never really functioned as envisioned. Instead of producing high-quality policy recommendations, the concern for touching all the bureaucratic bases produced decisions made on the basis of the lowest common denominator. Rather than increasing presidential options, it limited them. Policy implementation continued to be governed by departmental objectives and definitions of the problem rather than by presidential goals and perspectives.[17]

The second phase of the NSC's history, in which it became overly personalized, began with the Kennedy administration and lasted until 1980. Under Kennedy the formal and hierarchically structured system that Eisenhower had created declined in importance. Kennedy adopted an activist approach to national security management grounded on informal operating procedures. Stress was placed on multiple lines of communication, direct presidential contacts with second- and third-level officials, and securing outside expert advice. Ad hoc interagency task forces replaced the formal NSC system as the primary decision-making unit for dealing with such international problems as the Cuban missile crisis, Berlin, and Laos. Within the NSC system, emphasis switched from the council itself to the NSC staff. The staff came to be viewed less as a body of professionals who would stay on from administration to administration and more as a group that closely identified with the current administration and was loyal to it. The NSC staff became the vehicle by which Kennedy could serve as his own Secretary of State.

In the revamped management system, the national security adviser played a key role. This person was responsible for ensuring that the staff operated from a presidential perspective. McGeorge Bundy held this post under Kennedy and in the first part of the Johnson administration. He was replaced by Walt Rostow in 1966. The change in advisers brought with it a change in operating style. Bundy saw his role as a facilitator whose job it was to encourage the airing of ideas and policy alternatives. Rostow was more of an ideologue concerned with policy advocacy over process management.

Like Kennedy, Johnson took an activist stance and favored small, informal policy-making settings over the formal NSC system. Major Vietnam decisions were made at the Tuesday lunch group that brought together Johnson and his key foreign policy advisers. The Tuesday lunch group was a "procedural abomination" lacking a formal agenda and clearly stated conclusions, wearing on participants, and confusing to those at the working levels.[18] The NSC coordinating system was overwhelmed by the pressures of Vietnam, was often bypassed due to the tendency to make key policy decisions in the White House.

Nixon began his presidency with a pledge to place the NSC system back at the center of the foreign policy decision-making process.[19] This was achieved by first selecting Henry Kissinger as his national security adviser and William Rogers as his secretary of state. The combination of a strong, opinionated, and activist national security adviser and a secretary of state with little foreign policy experience guaranteed that foreign policy would be made in the White House. Second, Nixon created an elaborate NSC committee and staff system. Separate bodies were created to deal with SALT-related verification issues, Vietnam, intelligence programs, covert action, crisis management, and defense programs. There also existed an Under Secretaries Committee and interdepartmental groups.

Positioned at the center of this elaborate system, Kissinger was able to direct the flow of paper in the direction he wanted, bringing the NSC system into play on certain issues and cutting it out of others. By the end of the Nixon administration, the NSC was largely on the outside looking in. It met only three times in 1973, compared with thirty-seven times in 1969. Such important decisions as the invasion of Cambodia, Kissinger's trip to China, the Paris Peace Negotiations, bombing in Vietnam, and putting U.S. troops on worldwide alert in the Yom Kippur War were made outside the NSC system.

Carter dismantled the elaborate Nixon–Ford–Kissinger committee system in favor of two committees. The Policy Review Committee was charged with handling long-term projects. A Special Coordinating Committee (SCC) was created to deal with short-term problems, crisis situations, and covert action. Originally, these two committees were to be equally important, but over time the SCC dominated. This was especially true with the advent of the Iranian hostage crisis and the Soviet invasion of Afghanistan. Collegiality was evident in the prominent policy-making roles played by the Friday foreign policy breakfasts (attended by Carter and his key foreign policy advisers) and the Thursday lunch meetings (at which these advisers met to prepare for the Friday meeting).

Carter's activism often overloaded the foreign policy agenda and created a number of problems for his NSC system. Many of them centered on the workings of the Friday foreign policy breakfasts, which became substitutes for full NSC meetings. The problem was that decisions arrived at here were not always fully integrated into the NSC system, nor did they necessarily produce clearly articulated positions.[20]

During the Reagan administration, the NSC entered a third phase. Pledging to depersonalize the system, Reagan pushed too far in the opposite direction, causing it to go into decline. The national security adviser became a nonperson with little foreign policy influence or stature. And, as a direct consequence, the NSC staff ceased to function as either a policy-making or policy-coordinating body. With no force able to coordinate foreign policy, an unprecedented degree of bureaucratic infighting and fragmentation came to characterize (and paralyze) Reagan's foreign policy. Only with the arrival of General Powell as national security adviser and the passage from the cabinet of such powerful and highly opinionated figures as Secretary of Defense Caspar Weinberger and Director of Central Intelligence William Casey did a coherent foreign policy agenda appear.[21] While this was happening the NSC staff moved in two different directions. On the one hand it became preoccupied with bureaucratic trivia. (There were twenty-five committees, fifty-five mid-level committees, and some one hundred task forces and working groups.) On the other hand it became involved in the actual conduct of foreign policy in the Iran–Contra initiative.

Beginning with the George Bush administration, decision making in the NSC became transformed again. It is now more collegial in nature. George H. W. Bush, Bill Clinton, and George W. Bush all selected low-key national security advisers who were expected to stay out of the public limelight. The move to collegiality was applauded by most as a necessary step to overcome many of the past excesses of the NSC system. In each case, however, the final result has been less than hoped for as the necessary foundation for a collegial decision-making system was not put in place. The primary problem encountered in George H. W. Bush's administration, which followed Reagan's, was too much homogeneity in outlook. All of the participants, including the president, were confident that they understood the world and were slow to adapt to the end of the Cold War. Clinton failed to make his collegial system work because he was unable to provide a constant vision to guide his team or to construct an effective division of labor among its members.

George W. Bush, in contrast to Clinton, has been a disciplined delegater of authority, but this, too, has had its costs. Bush brought together an experienced national security team, many of whom had served in his father's administration and that of Ronald Reagan. While loyalty and teamwork were prime values Bush focused on in making his selections he did not bring together people who were all of one mind. Colin Powell became secretary of state and brought a conservative-realist perspective to the office that stressed caution in using force and the pursuit of limited objectives. Key posts in the Pentagon and the vice president's office (and to a lesser extent at the State Department) were staffed by neoconservatives whose outlook on world affairs was firmly anchored in the belief that the United States was the world's only superpower and that it had a special role to play in transforming the world. They also held that unilateral exercise of American military power was an appropriate means of achieving this goal. Condoleezza Rice, who was selected to be national security advisor, in his first administration was not overly identified with either faction. Under George W. Bush these individuals and their aides came together in a three-tiered NSC system.[22] Those meetings where Bush is present are officially designated as NSC meetings. Those at which Cheney or Rice presided were designated as a Principals Committee meeting. At the lowest level are Deputies Committee meetings that focus on implementing decisions. It is chaired by the deputy national security advisor. Sitting atop this system is an informal committee, the "War Cabinet." This group consists of some twelve key Bush advisors on the war against terrorism and is the group who made major decisions regarding the wars in Afghanistan and Iraq.

The philosophical and personal tensions between these two factions have not been effectively constrained by this NSC system, although they did not surface with great intensity until after 9/11. One commentator describes the NSC as having become transformed from a collegial system into one of "unrestrained ideological entrepreneurship" in which collegial scrutiny of policy proposals is replaced by pockets of officials with strongly held views competing to sell their policy preferences to the president. Several factors are seen as contributing to this transformation.[23] One is the dominant role played by Cheney who holds strong opinions and supervises a mini-NSC staff of his own. A second was the inability of Rice to hold these competing forces in line. In particular, Donald Rumsfeld and the Defense Department are seen as having captured Iraq policy. More and more Rice stressed her role as advisor to the president over that of manager with the result that decisions such as those on Iran and North Korea were often made and then reversed. Finally, there is Bush's leadership style. BobWoodward recounts the meeting in which the CIA made its best case of Iraq possessing weapons of mass destruction. After hearing the case Bush remarked, "Nice try. I don't think this is quite—it is not something Joe Public would understand . . . Is this the best we've got." Director of Central Intelligence George Tenet replied, "It's a slam dunk case!"[24] While Bush noted the case needed more work, there is no record of penetrating questions being asked or the issue being brought up for renewed debate. It simply went forward.

Other Voices

THE VICE PRESIDENT

Political folklore assigns the vice president little more than a ceremonial position in the policy making process barring the death of a president. There is often great truth in these images. Harry Truman spoke with Franklin Roosevelt only eight times and knew nothing of the development of the atomic bombs or discussions that Roosevelt had with Winston Churchill and Joseph Stalin on the shape of the post–World War II international system. Of late, however, much as changed. The last three vice presidents have played important foreign policy roles.[25] George H. W. Bush's vice president, Dan Quayle, became the administration's most active voices on Latin American affairs and his decidedly pro-Israeli position was important in maintaining the Persian Gulf War alliance against Iraq. Quayle also stressed to the president the importance of obtaining congressional support for the Persian Gulf War. Al Gore, Clinton's vice president, established himself as a key administration expert on Russia and some of the key newly emerging states such as Kazakhstan and Ukraine.

The foreign policy roles played by Quayle and Gore, however, pale in comparison to that of Dick Cheney, George W. Bush's vice president. Cheney brought considerable foreign policy experience to that position. He had served as Secretary of Defense under George H. W. Bush and served on the House Select Committee on Intelligence. Building upon this background and Bush's trust in him, Cheney quickly became a powerful foreign policy voice within the administration. Prior to 9/11 terrorist attacks, he was charged with leading the administration's planning for homeland security and after those attacks he became a powerful voice for bringing that war to Iraq, often engaging in spirited exchanges with Secretary of State Colin Powell, who opposed such a move. This position was advanced in NSC meetings and in private meetings with the president. Both before and after the war, Cheney vehemently asserted in public that Iraq possessed weapons of mass destruction and that a link existed between Iraq and al-Qaeda. His behind-the-scenes efforts to root out intelligence supporting this position are among the most controversial aspects of the administration's handling of prewar intelligence. Defenders assert it was necessary to overcome the lethargy of the CIA in pursuing intelligence on Iraq, while critics charge that his actions politicized intelligence.

THE WHITE HOUSE CHIEF OF STAFF

By convention, a division of labor has evolved in White House decision-making circles between the Chief of Staff (COS) and the national security advisor. Each acts as a principal source of advice for the president, the COS for domestic policy and the national security advisor for foreign policy. In addition, the COS acts as a gatekeeper regulating those who have access to the president. This latter power is seen as making the COS more of a political (and powerful) figure than the national security advisor in an administration.[26] Without much fanfare, however, this division of labor is disappearing, and more and more the COS has come to have an important voice in foreign policy matters. This trend began with Alexander Haig, who was COS under Nixon, and Hamilton Jordan, who held the post under Carter. Their efforts have not always been judged a success. For example, while Howard Baker, Jr., who was COS under Reagan, is credited with persuading him to hold frequent summits with Soviet leaders, Thomas McLarty's actions as Clinton's first COS are seen as having threatened congressional approval of the NAFTA. President George W. Bush chose Andrew Card to be his COS. Card's portfolio extended into foreign policy almost immediately. He was widely associated with an early Bush immigration initiative that was seen as designed to garner Hispanic votes for the Republican Party. After 9/11, he was one of those placed in charge of the Homeland Security Council. As the Bush administration moved toward war with Iraq, Card established the White House Iraq Group to make sure that the various parts of the White House were working in harmony on Iraq.

Several reasons stand out for why the COS is now a potentially important foreign policy voice. Foremost among them is the blurring of the boundary between foreign and domestic policy. Today many traditional foreign policy problems have characteristics of both and can be characterized as intermestic issues. One consequence of this is to make the COS's domestic political expertise relevant for how many foreign policy issues are decided. As Hamilton Jordan recalls that he sought to play the role of an early warning system and alert officials to potential domestic political problems embedded in foreign policy decisions. In speaking of the timing of the Iraq War, Andrew Card observed that from a marketing perspective it was not wise to introduce a new product in August. A second consequence of the intermestic nature of foreign policy problems is that presidents have increasingly turned to advisory groups to help manage and coordinate policy decisions in these areas. The COS's role as power broker and gatekeeper has become crucial for ensuring that the president stays atop the policy process. Leon Panetta, Clinton's second COS, insisted that all decision papers, including those from the NSC went to the president only after his review. If he felt there were not enough options given to Clinton the paper was returned.

Presidential Decision Making

We began this chapter by introducing several episodes of presidential decision making. Each focused on presidential involvement in a specific problem. We conclude by examining an ongoing foreign policy making situation that every president must deal with: decision making early in an administration where the influence of presidential transitions is strong.[27] Much of the controversy surrounding some of President George W. Bush's early foreign policy decisions, such as withdrawing from the Kyoto Protocol and proceeding with the national ballistic missile defense system, can be best understood in terms of the dynamics of presidential transitions and foreign policy.

PRESIDENTIAL TRANSITIONS

The first months of a new presidency are a unique time in American politics. It is a "honeymoon" period when relations between the president and Congress, and the president and the media are at least cordial if not deferential. Significantly, it is also a period in which foreign policy challenges and opportunities may arise that demand a presidential response. The extent to which a successful foreign policy response is crafted is heavily dependent upon the advanced planning and learning that takes place during the transition period from one administration to another. This challenge is particularly daunting with presidential transition from one party to another.

Reviewing recent transitions of this type suggests that the qualities of hubris, haste, and newness that are associated with new administrations tend to produce a three-part transition syndrome in the area of foreign policy. First, key policy positions are adopted during the transition period on the basis of broad strategic principles or campaign themes before the realities of governing have a chance to replace the euphoria of victory. Second, desiring to separate itself from its predecessor, the incoming administration commits itself to deal with policies before it has established procedures for policy guidance, coordination, or implementation. Third, the primary point of reference is internal: the personal preferences and strategic perspectives of those who have joined the new administration.

Reagan and AWACS.   The first major foreign policy crisis for the new Reagan administration was a self-inflicted blow that had its roots in the transition process. At issue was a $8.5 million arms sale to Saudi Arabia that involved tanker planes, fuel tanks and sophisticated air-to-air missiles for sixty F-15 fighters whose transfer Congress had already approved, and AWACS reconnaissance aircraft.

One of Reagan's complaints about Carter's foreign policy had been its moralizing. That administration's arms sales policy very much fit this profile. By Carter's presidential directive, arms sales were not to be a normal part of American foreign policy and dollar limits were set. During the campaign, Reagan had opposed placing constraints on arms sales, and once elected he directed the State Department to come up with a different policy. In May 1981, the Reagan administration rescinded Carter's Presidential Directive 13 and put its own guidelines in place. In its haste to act and (over) confident of the merits of its proposed change in policy, the Reagan administration did not wait for its own internal review of U.S. arms sales policy to be completed or its findings approved before making specific arms sales decisions. It approved several that the Carter administration had not acted upon. One of these was the proposed Saudi arms sale.

Reagan was surprised by the opposition his announcement met with. Under pressure from pro-Israeli lobbyists who argued that the proposed arms sale would provide Saudi Arabia with an offensive capability that threatened Israeli security, Reagan first scaled back the package and then announced on March 2 that he would put the proposed sale on hold while his advisers took a closer look at it. In April, before this review was completed, the Reagan administration announced that not only would it supply Saudi Arabia with the requested upgrades, but that it would also provide it with five AWACS, seven tankers, and twenty-two ground radar stations. Once again, Reagan was caught off guard by the opposition to his proposal with even its supporters stating that "the administration failed from the outset to recognize its repercussions." So intense was the opposition that Reagan did not formally notify Congress of the arms sale until October. Haste and newness also took their toll on the administration's lobbying effort. Senator John Glenn, who voted against the arms sale, stated that "I know of no one on either side who does not think this has been grossly mishandled." The sale was approved by Congress by a vote of 52 to 48, largely on the basis of the argument that to defeat Reagan on his first major foreign policy initiative would cripple American foreign policy for the remainder of his term.

In trying to explain the Reagan administration's position, its defenders emphasized broad strategic considerations that centered on the dynamics of the Middle East balance of power. The emphasis on strategic principles as a guide to action came at the expense of an attention to the political realities of the proposed arms sale. J. Brian Atwood, who lobbied Congress on behalf of the State Department during the Carter administration, observed that Reagan may not have realized the political costs of letting the opposition get so organized. Moreover, "a lot of those senators who reversed themselves under great pressure have been embarrassed by this whole thing and they're going to suffer the political consequences of it." He predicted that in the future they would be less willing to take risks for Reagan. At least insofar as Middle East arms sales were concerned, Atwood's prediction was accurate. Between 1983 and 1985 three arms sale packages to Lebanon had to be withdrawn due to congressional opposition, and a 1985 arms sale to Saudi Arabia was voted down in the House and survived an override attempt in the Senate by only a single vote.

Clinton and Gays in the Military.   At a 1991 campaign stop at Harvard University's John F. Kennedy School of Government, presidential candidate Bill Clinton indicated that if elected he would lift the ban on homosexuals in the military. Clinton's statement was made in response to a student's question, and according to Clinton, was offered without prior consultation with campaign aides or consideration of the broader issues involved. Nevertheless, that promise soon became a staple on the campaign trail. The potentially explosive nature of Clinton's campaign promise generated remarkably little negative publicity during the postconvention phase of the campaign. All of that changed shortly after the election. During the transition, members of the Joint Chiefs of Staff (JCS) worked through retired Admiral William J. Crowe, who publicly supported Clinton during the campaign but opposed lifting the ban, and Representative Dave McCurdy to try to convince Clinton not to act on his campaign promise. Reportedly, they urged Clinton to appoint a presidential commission to examine the issue over a one- or two-year period.

The tone of these discussions was not conducive to compromise. Clinton's transition team placed John Holum, a Washington lawyer, in charge of preparing a plan for lifting the ban. Holum's position was that he "wasn't there to ask whether it should be done . . . [but] how it could be done to minimize the impact on combat effectiveness." (Holum's report was finished in early January and sent to Little Rock for Clinton to read. It contained warnings by two of Secretary of Defense Les Aspin's advisers of the danger that lay ahead. They urged the new administration to develop a strategy for heading off the impending conflict with Congress. "Early legislative action on this issue will be detrimental . . . to the president's long-term relations with Congress, his relationship with the military as commander-in-chief and may hinder the intended policy of change."

The Clinton administration's effort to act quickly only served to reinforce congressional fear about the consequences of this move. The new administration compounded its problems by meeting with gay rights groups and reassuring them of Clinton's continued support, a move that only made compromise with Congress more difficult. Aspin's aides called for a personal meeting between Clinton, Senator Sam Nunn, Majority Leader George Mitchell, and Senator Ted Kennedy to plot out a strategy. This advice was not followed and no such meeting ever took place. In fact, Clinton did not meet face-to-face with the JCS until January 18, a delay that angered the chiefs and their supporters in Congress who felt that they should have been consulted from the outset about a major change in military policy. Aspin himself urged Clinton to approach this meeting not as a negotiation but "as the first step in the consultation that you have promised."

In the end, Clinton compromised and set July 15 as the date for a formal executive order lifting the ban on gays in the military. His action allowed Majority Leader Mitchell to postpone any votes on the subject with the argument that the administration's position was not yet in place. The six-month breather also allowed for congressional hearings and for continued negotiations between Aspin and the JCS. These tense meetings produced an agreement under which recruits will not be asked about their sexual orientation but they will be dismissed for homosexual conduct.

Summary and Future Issues

Our look to the future needs to be directed at two different levels of concern. The first involves the need for continued refinement in the structure and operation of the executive branch. In the future as in the past, presidents will turn to the NSC and other organizations to establish leadership in foreign policy. No one organizational structure will be the "right" one for a president to select. As the Tower Commission stressed, "There is no magic formula which can be applied to the NSC structure and process. . . . It must adapt to each individual president's style and management philosophy." It goes on to note that this does not mean that guidelines cannot be put forward. In the eyes of some, such guidelines are desperately needed. In criticizing past presidential choices, Destler argues that the evolution and pattern of White House staffing has served the illusion of presidential power rather than its reality. Along with Ivo Daalder, he argues that what is needed are reforms that allow the NSC to do those few critical tasks for which it is uniquely suited: (1) managing the president's daily foreign policy activity, (2) coordinating the process by which key decisions are made, (3) driving the policy-making process to make real choices in a timely fashion, and (4) monitoring the implementation of decisions.[28]

At a more fundamental level, we also need to look at the role of the presidency in making foreign policy. In the 1960s it was commonplace to talk about the imperial presidency, as neither Congress nor the public seemed capable of challenging the president in foreign policy. The situation has changed. In the words of one commentator, the presidency has become a bullied pulpit.[29] "A cutthroat legal culture, an obstructionist Congress, relentless media criticism, and endless polls . . . [and] a staff filled with temporary appointees" has robbed presidents of their ability to lead. All too often all that is left for them is resort to moral rhetoric and exhortations to do the right thing, whether it is for Congress to ratify a treaty and support free trade, or for other states to end the violence in the Middle East or Balkans. They do so because they have little hope of engineering a timely policy response. Dual dangers lie in this strategy. If not listened to, the president risks losing prestige, and the appearance of weakness may make it even more difficult to exert leadership in the future. On the other hand, if by engaging in moral rhetoric other political institutions are moved to action, the president runs the risk of having oversold a policy that can never produce the promised results.

Notes

1. Kathyrn Tenpas and Stephen Hess, "Organizing the Bush Presidency," in Gary Gregg II and Mark Rozell (eds.), *Considering the Bush Presidency* (New York: Oxford, 2004), p. 43.

2. Richard M. Nixon, *RN: The Memoirs of Richard Nixon* (New York: Grosset & Dunlap, 1978), pp. 447–50.

3. Jimmy Carter, *Keeping Faith: Memoirs of a President* (New York: Bantam, 1982), pp. 305–16.

4. Excerpts from Reagan's videotaped testimony can be found in the *Washington Post,* February 23, 1990, pp. 10–11.

5. Hugh Heclo, "Introduction: The Presidential Illusion," in Hugh Heclo and Lester M. Salamon (eds.), *The Illusion of Presidential Government* (Boulder, Colo.: Westview, 1981), p. 1.

6. Richard Neustadt, *Presidential Power: The Politics of Leadership* (New York: Wiley & Sons, 1960).

7. James David Barber, *The Presidential Character: Predicting Performance in the White House,* 3rd ed. (Englewood Cliffs, N.J.: Prentice-Hall, 1985). Also see Alexander George, "Assessing Presidential Character," *World Politics,* 26 (1974), 234–82. For other formulations of presidential personality, see Lloyd S. Etheridge, "Personality Effects on American Foreign Policy, 1898–1968: A Test of Interpersonal Generalization Theory," *American Political Science Review,* 72 (1978), 434–51; and John Stoessinger, *Crusaders and Pragmatists: Movers of Modern American Foreign Policy* (New York: Norton, 1979).

8. Fred I. Greenstein, "The Presidential Leadership Style of Bill Clinton: An Early Appraisal," *Political Science Quarterly,* 108 (1993/94), pp. 589–601.

9. Bob Woodward, *Bush at War* (New York: Simon & Schuster, 2002), p. 256.

10. Richard Clarke, *Against All Enemies* (New York: Free Press, 2004), p. 287

11. Fred I. Greenstein, *The Hidden Hand Presidency: Eisenhower as Leader* (New York: Basic, 1982).

12. John Lewis Gaddis, "The Unexpected Ronald Reagan," in John Lewis Gaddis (ed.), *The United States and the End of the Cold War: Implications, Reconsiderations, Provocations* (New York: Oxford University Press, 1992), pp. 119–32.

13. Stoessinger, *Crusaders and Pragmatists.*

14. Fred I. Greenstein, *Personality and Politics* (Chicago: Markham, 1969).

15. Donald M. Snow and Eugene Brown, *Puzzle Palaces and Foggy Bottom: U.S. Foreign and Defense Policy-Making in the 1990s* (New York: St. Martin's, 1994), pp. 44–70.

16. Zbigniew Brzezinski, "The NSC's Midlife Crisis," *Foreign Policy,* 69 (1987/88), pp. 80–99.

17. For a reinterpretation of the Eisenhower NSC experience, see Fred Greenstein and Richard Immerman, "Effective National Security Advising: Recovering the Eisenhower Legacy," *Political Science Quarterly,* 115 (2000), 335–45.

18. William P. Bundy, "The National Security Process: Plus Change. . . ," *International Security,* 7 (1982/83), pp. 94–109.

19. On the Nixon NSC system, see John P. Leacacos, "Kissinger's Apparat," *Foreign Policy,* 5 (1971), pp. 2–27.

20. Robert E. Hunter, *Presidential Control of Foreign Policy: Management or Mishap,* Washington Paper #91 (New York: Praeger, 1982), pp. 35–36.

21. Terry Diehl, "Reagan's Mixed Legacy," *Foreign Policy,* 75 (1989), 34–55.

22. John Prados, "The Pros From Dover," *Bulletin of the Atomic Scientists,* 60 (2004), 44–51.

23. Colin Campbell, "Unrestrained Ideological Entrepreneurship in the Bush II Advisory System," in Colin Campbell and Bert Rockman (eds.), *The George W. Bush Presidency* (Washington, D.C.: Congressional Quarterly Press, 2004), 73–104.

24. Bob Woodward, *Plan of Attack* (New York: Simon & Schuster, 2004), p. 249.

25. Paul Kengor, "Cheney and Vice Presidential Power," in *Considering the Bush Presidency* (New York: Oxford University Press, 2004), 160–176; and "The Vice President, Secretary of State, and Foreign Policy," *Political Science Quarterly,* 115 (2000), 175–99.

26. David Cohen, Chris Dolan, and Jerel Rosati, "A Place at the Table," *Congress and the Presidency,* 29 (2002), 119–49.

27. Material in this section is drawn from Glenn Hastedt and Anthony Eksterowicz, "Perils of Presidential Transitions," *Seton Hall Journal of Diplomacy and International Relations,* 2 (2001), 67–85.

28. I. M. Destler, "National Security II: The Rise of the Assistant," in Heclo and Salamon (eds.), *The Illusion of Presidential Government,* p. 278; Ivo Daalder and I. M. Destler, "A New NSC for a New Administration," *Brookings Institution Policy Brief #68* (Washington, D.C.: Brookings, November 2000).

29. Sebastian Mallaby, "The Bullied Pulpit: A Weak Chief Executive Makes Worse Foreign Policy," *Foreign Policy,* 79 (2000), 2–8.

— 9 —

CONGRESS AND FOREIGN POLICY

Whether it is reconstruction funds for Iraq, trade legislation, or a new weapons system, to a president Congress often appears to be an obstacle course through which his foreign policy proposals must first pass. It is an obstacle course made up of two parts: the constitutional distribution of powers between the Congress and the president that we examined in Chapter 7 and Congress's internal structure and operating procedures. These internal obstacles are every bit as formidable as those obstacles rooted in the constitutional separation of powers, and they are our focus in this chapter.

Before proceeding, two points need to be stressed. First, just as the structure of the presidency has changed, so too has that of Congress. This is important because it means that the obstacles we will discuss in this chapter have been grafted onto one another over time and that as Congress continues to evolve, new ones may be added to this list and old ones shed. Second, not everyone regards congressional participation in foreign policy making as an evil to be avoided. Congressional participation raises the public's awareness about issues, provides additional information to policy makers, and, in the long run, may improve the quality of U.S. foreign policy.[1] Former Director of Central Intelligence Stansfield Turner makes the same point regarding congressional oversight of the CIA. "It forces the DCI and his subordinates to exercise greater judiciousness in making decisions . . . it helps keep them [CIA people] in touch with national views."[2]

Congressional Structure and Foreign Policy

BLUNT FOREIGN POLICY TOOLS

Foremost among the tools Congress relies upon to influence policy are its general legislative, budgetary, and oversight powers. While they are formidable powers, Congress often finds itself frustrated in its efforts to fine-tune U.S. foreign policy or give it a new sense of direction due to their bluntness and essentially negative character.

Four basic forms of congressional action exist. Included are the simple resolution, which is a statement made by one house; the concurrent resolution, a statement passed by both houses; and the joint resolution, a statement made by both houses that is signed by the president. None of these carry the force of law; they are simply statements of opinion by Congress. Last, there is the legislative bill, which is passed by both houses and is signed by the president (or passed over the president's veto) and becomes law. In an early postwar study of Congress, James Robinson found that while presidential policy proposals were primarily phrased as bills, congressionally initiated actions tended to be expressed as simple resolutions.[3]

The situation today is much the same with one major exception. Congress still relies heavily on resolutions to express its will. The very consideration of a resolution can spark political controversy because of its potential for complicating relations with other states. In 2000, a scheduled House vote on a nonbinding resolution labeling Turkey's treatment of Armenians between 1915 to 1923 as genocide became the focal point of intense politicking between the White House and Congress. Passed by the House International Relations Committee by a vote of 24 to 11, the measure was cosponsored by 141 representatives and had bipartisan support. The measure was proposed by Congressman James Rogan (R-Calif.), who was locked in a tight reelection race and whose district has the largest concentration of Armenian Americans in the United States. Turkey protested the action to the Clinton administration and threatened to deny the United States use of its air bases for staging flights over northern Iraq. To press their case Turkey made full use of its lobbyists. Under pressure from the White House, House Speaker J. Dennis Hassert cancelled the vote, thereby avoiding the diplomatic confrontation between the United States and Turkey.

In 2002, the George W. Bush administration was unable to prevent the House (352 to 21) and Senate (92 to 2) from voting favorably on slightly differing resolutions that endorsed Israel's military campaign to dismantle the "terrorist infrastructure" in the occupied territories. Both resolutions characterized its actions as self-defense and part of the global war on terrorism. The Bush administration argued that these resolutions complicated its efforts at mediating a Middle East peace agreement.

One trend that has become more pronounced over time is the amount of legislation that bears on U.S. foreign policy and Congress's use of its legislative powers to limit or amend presidentially initiated foreign policy legislation. President George W. Bush discovered this reality early in his administration when both the House and Senate passed legislation preventing Mexican trucks from entering more than twenty miles into the United States. Free access to the United States had been a key part of the NAFTA agreement but was strongly opposed by a coalition of labor and consumer safety groups. The White House described the votes as "isolationist" and "anti-Hispanic" and promised to continue pressing forward on the issue. He rediscovered this reality again in 2002 and 2003. In 2002, the Senate granted the president trade promotion authority only after coupling it with a multibillion-dollar expansion of funding for American workers hurt by foreign competition. In 2003, the Senate approved an $87.5 billion spending bill for military and reconstruction operations in Iraq. Passage of the bill followed vigorous debate over whether Iraq should have to pay for some of the projects in the bill out of its own funds. The Senate supported that position but it was removed by a House–Senate conference. Money was reduced for several rebuilding projects while other projects were dropped entirely from the bill.

The sheer volume of foreign policy legislation has become staggering. The 1960 edition of *Legislation on Foreign Relations* ran 519 pages. The 1975 edition had 1,856 pages, and the 1985 edition was divided into two volumes with a total of 2,698 pages. The 1979 decision to normalize relations with the People's Republic of China required the United States to recast its relations with Taiwan from government-to-government relations to government-to-people relations. Thirty-four pages of statutes were affected by this simple change in language.[4]

Congress also has sought to make its voice heard by attaching amendments or "barnacles" to foreign policy legislation sought by the president.[5] One type of barnacle is to earmark or designate funds contained within a piece of legislation for a specific country. In passing the fiscal year 1990 foreign aid bill, Congress earmarked $4 billion in aid for traditional U.S. ally Israel. All totaled, $2.8 billion out of $3.2 billion from the Economic Support Fund was earmarked for specific countries.

Most barnacles contain escape clauses that allow the president to get around them. Some of the most prominent barnacles lie in the areas of human rights (the State Department's 1989 Human Rights Report ran 1,641 pages) and drug trafficking. A 1986 law requires that the State Department annually certify that recipients of U.S. foreign aid are "fully cooperating" in eradication efforts and the worldwide fight against drugs. Congress then votes to support or reject the State Department's judgment. If a country fails to win certification it loses American military and economic aid and trade preferences. In 1988, "national interests" were cited in the certification of Panama and Mexico. Five states, Afghanistan, Laos, Paraguay, Syria, and Iran, were decertified. The Senate voted 63–27 to decertify Mexico, but the House refused to do so and Mexico was able to continue receiving U.S. aid. Because of the constant controversy surrounding the certification process a move was made to suspend it for two years as part of the 1998 foreign aid spending bill. The move was rejected by the Senate with many Senators fearing that a yes vote would portray them as soft on drugs. An escape hatch also exists in the Burmese Freedom and Peace Act of 2003. It called for the ban of all imports from Burma for one year but allowed the president to lift the ban at any time if he concluded that Burma was making "substantial and measurable progress" in ending human rights violations and creating a democratic government or that it was in the U.S. national interest to do so.

Congress's budget powers are equally blunt and difficult to use. In part this is because doing so involves three different sets of decisions. Congress must decide upon an overall authorization level for the budget under consideration, authorize the expenditure of funds for the programs contained in the budget, and then allocate funds for those programs. These decisions are made in different settings, at different times, and by individuals and committees that are responding to different sets of outside pressures. The decision on the overall budget ceiling is made by Congress as a whole and takes the form of a budget resolution. Authorization decisions are made separately by the committees with legislative jurisdiction over the policy area. Appropriation decisions are made by the House and Senate Appropriations Committee and their subcommittees.

An additional problem with using the budget as an instrument to shape the direction of U.S. foreign policy is that programs cost money but "policies" may not. What policies are able to do is raise expectations, place U.S. prestige on the line, or commit the United States to a course of action in the eyes of other states. When this occurs, Congress tends to find that it has little choice but to support—fund—the policy initiative, at least on a cosmetic basis. Senator John Kerry (D-Mass) spoke to this same point in expressing his opposition to the congressional resolution supporting the Persian Gulf War. He noted:

> I hear it from one person after another—"I do not want the President to look bad. . . . The President got us in this position. I am uncomfortable—but I cannot go against him. . . . Are we supposed to go to war because one man—the President—makes a series of unilateral decisions that put us in a box. . . . Are we supposed to go to war because once the President has announced publicly, to reverse or question him is somehow detrimental to the Nation. . . ."[6]

Problems also confront Congress in attempting to cut off funding for overseas military action. During the Reagan administration votes on cutting off aid to the Contras continually reappeared, and none was decisive. This continued hesitancy to use its budgetary powers is not new. Efforts to cut off funding for Vietnam routinely failed, and the vote that actually ended U.S. involvement in Vietnam came on a procedural vote to table the legislation before Congress. A notable exception to this pattern is the Clark Amendment to the 1976 appropriations bill, which forbade the use of funds for "any activities involving Angola directly or indirectly." This measure was passed at a time when the Nixon administration was already involved in the Angolan civil war and was engaged in planning for additional undertakings.[7]

Finally, there is a problem with presidential implementation of congressional budgetary decisions. In 1971, Congress appropriated $700 million for a manned bomber. The funds went unspent by the Nixon administration because it opposed the project. During Vietnam the Pentagon transferred several million dollars appropriated as military aid for Taiwan for the war effort. It then went back to Congress and asked for supplemental appropriations to cover these funds. Unless it was willing to offend Taiwan, Congress had little choice but to grant the request. The reconstruction of Iraq provides another example of the limited ability of Congress' budgetary powers to influence the implementation of American foreign policy. In 2003, the Bush administration called for a quick infusion of money into Iraq to speed its recovery and transformation in the aftermath of the war. Yet, much to the dismay of many in Congress, in June 2004, just days before power was transferred to a new Iraqi government, only 2 percent of that money had been spent. None of the $500 million for health care, $400 million for roads and bridges, or the $4.2 billion for water and sanitation improvements had been spent. The largest area of expenditure was for security and law enforcement where $194 million of the appropriated $3.2 billion had been dispersed.

Oversight refers to the actions of Congress regarding the bureaucratic implementation of policy. Congress was long accused of shunning its oversight responsibilities in favor of looking after state and district interests and passing legislation. The mood changed markedly in the late 1970s and early 1980s as a new interest in oversight gripped Congress. At the same time the nature of oversight also began to change; the traditional investigatory approach to oversight was replaced by a desire to be informed in advance of how policy was going to be implemented.[8]

Questions about Congress' fundamental right to engage in oversight of foreign policy were at the center of the debate over creating the Department of Homeland Security.[9] On September 20, 2001, nine days after the terrorist attacks of September 11, George W. Bush addressed a joint session of Congress. As part of his administration's response to these attacks, he announced the creation of an Office of Homeland Security (OHS) that would be located in the White House Office. Its director would have cabinet rank and report directly to him. OHS was charged with leading, overseeing, and coordinating the development of a "comprehensive national strategy" to safeguard the United States against terrorist attacks and to respond to any such attacks if they happen. Tom Ridge was named Assistant to the President for Homeland Security. Moving forward using an executive order instead of a piece of legislation passed by Congress to create OHS carried with it several important political and administrative implications. First, it meant that Ridge's appointment was not subject to Senate approval and that Congress could not easily compel him to testify. Presidents routinely invoke the power of "executive privilege" to block such requests. Second, funding for the OHS would come from discretionary funds appropriated by Congress to the president and the White House Office. This removed OHS from the normal pattern of budgetary oversight exercised by Congress over agency budgets where funds are authorized and appropriated annually by congressional committees. In this case, Bush used $25.5 million from the Emergency Response Fund set up by Congress in response to the September 11 terrorist attacks to finance the initial business of OHS. Third, since OHS was not created via a law, its organizational structure, as well as goals and missions, could be changed at the will of the president simply by issuing another executive order.

OHS got off to a rocky start, and there soon arose a chorus of doubt over the adequacy of Ridge's authority. Members of Congress led by Rep. William "Mac" Thornberry (R-Texas) and Sen. Joseph Lieberman (D-Conn.) led calls for creating a Department of Homeland Security (DHS). Not only did the administration reject this alternative, but refused to allow Ridge to testify on the grounds of executive privilege under which a president can prevent an advisor from testifying. Many Republicans and Democrats in Congress argued the real issue was that Congress had the right to oversee the bureaucracy and Ridge had been put in charge of running a large organization. The standoff between the two branches ended in June 2002 when George W. Bush abruptly altered course and announced he now supported a DHS. The strength of the congressional forces for a DHS and revelations of failures to share intelligence between the CIA and FBI led him to this move in an attempt to regain the political initiative in the area of homeland security.

Congress has been especially vigorous in using "reporting requirements" as a tool of oversight. Few policy areas have escaped the reach of congressional reporting requirements initiatives. In addition to the example of drug certification that was just discussed, Congress has required the executive branch to certify such practices as the human rights records of states, their stance on the nonproliferation or nuclear weapons, and their willingness to comply with trade agreements.

Ruth Collier has identified three major types of reporting requirements that Congress has used.[10] Periodic reports are produced in a policy area on a regular basis. For example, each year the State Department is required to submit a country report on human rights practices. A second type is the notification that a particular type of foreign policy action has been taken or will be taken. From Congress's point of view, the absence of presidential notifications of covert action was a major issue in the Iran–Contra affair. Most of these reports, however, are far less politically charged and involve changes in the distribution of foreign aid funds, arms sales, and arms control initiatives. In the mid-1980s an average of over 700 notifications were sent to Congress. The third type of reporting requirement is a one-time report where Congress is seeking a particular piece of information from the executive branch. In the 1986 Anti-Apartheid Act, Congress identified ten issues on which it wanted the president to furnish it with information.

DECENTRALIZATION

Traditionally, the work of Congress was done in committees. It was here that the political deals were made and the technical details of legislation were worked out. Congress as a whole was expected to quietly and expeditiously give its consent to committee decisions, and more often than not, it did. Beginning in the early 1970s, all this began to change, and the focus of decision making shifted from the full committee to the subcommittee. The result has been an even greater decentralization of Congress, which is visible in a number of ways. First, there is the increased attention that the executive branch must give to the foreign policy views of all members of Congress. As one State Department official put it, "It used to be that all one had to do was contact the chairman and a few ranking members of a committee, now all 435 members plus 100 senators have to be contacted."[11] The Defense Department has experienced a similar change in its dealings with Congress. In 1964 Defense

Department representatives spent 1,575 witness hours before Congress. In 1976 that number increased to 7,746.[12]

As a result, we have to look in many places to find foreign policy legislation, and these pieces are not easily assembled into a coherent whole. In 2000, legislation allowing the sale of food to Cuba was part of an agricultural spending bill. In 1998 Congress sought to limit President Clinton's ability to move forward on the Kyoto Protocol by attaching an amendment to the appropriations bill for the Environmental Protection Agency that prohibited it from spending money on planning efforts related to the treaty.

Second, there is the growing tendency for prospective pieces of legislation to be referred to more than one committee. Multiple referrals are necessary because of the lack of fit between the jurisdictions of congressional committees and policy areas. Thomas Brewer found a dozen Senate committees involved in foreign economic policy and nearly fifty subcommittees involved in foreign policy toward the third world.[13] Another study found that the House Armed Services Committee had jurisdiction over thirteen agencies and departments and twelve legislative areas while its Senate counterpart had jurisdiction over ten agencies and eleven legislative areas. Former Congressperson Lee Hamilton asserts that the greatest concentration of foreign policy power is now in the appropriations committees where domestic concerns hold greater weight than do foreign policy ones.[14]

Third, the impact of decentralization can be seen in the increased power that accrues to subcommittee chairs. Hamilton notes that it is now common for foreign policy bills to come directly to the floor without consideration by the full foreign policy committees. Under these conditions, foreign policy issues tend to be looked upon as isolated issues and not part of a broader strategic plan of action. Power then goes to subcommittee chairs. Late in the Clinton administration, Senator Judd Gregg (R-N.H.), who was chair of the Appropriations subcommittee with jurisdiction over the State Department's budget, held up funding that had been approved the previous year because of what he termed its "capitulation" to rebel forces in Sierra Leone. Only after being presented with a multilateral plan that took a hard line against these forces was he prepared to release these funds. His actions forced Secretary of State Madeline Albright to meet with Senate Appropriations Committee chair Ted Stevens (R-Alaska), who promised to try to work out a compromise that would release at least part of these funds before Congress recessed. Gregg's actions had repercussions beyond his area of jurisdiction as well. Officials noted that they complicated efforts to reduce U.S. dues to the United Nations.

POLICY ENTREPRENEURSHIP

A change in attitude has accompanied the trend toward increasing decentralization. Policy individualism has replaced party loyalty as the motivation behind much congressional action. As a result the long-standing congressional norms of deference and apprenticeship have been replaced by expectations of power sharing and policy input. *Entrepreneurship* is the label frequently attached to this new outlook. David Price defines a policy entrepreneur as someone who is committed to a continuing search for policy gaps and opportunities.[15] The entrepreneur is different from the traditional foreign policy "gadfly" who raises issues in order to influence the terms of the policy debate and is concerned with long-term policy gains.[16]

Gadflies are found across the political spectrum. Prominent conservatives have included Jesse Helms, while George McGovern was a noteworthy liberal. Among the most outspoken gadflies today are John McCain and Chuck Hegal. The policy entrepreneur is largely motivated by short-term considerations. The primary one is reelection and the belief that the likelihood of being reelected is enhanced if one can claim credit for authoring or amending important bills or publicly exposing a major problem or scandal. As I. M. Destler notes, the problem with credit taking, position taking, and self-advertising is that all three are concerned with the public's image of a piece of legislation and not with how it actually turns out.[17]

Foreign policy has always been a major area of entrepreneurial activity. The Senate Foreign Relations Committee long has been a focal point of media attention and a breeding ground for presidential candidates who used its visibility to their political advantage. International economic issues have also attracted the attention to congresspeople. "Japan bashing" in the form of harshly worded congressional resolutions has become a common staple of U.S. international economic policy. In 1995, many in Congress moved aggressively to promote retaliatory trade legislation against those who trade with Cuba and Iran. Senator Jesse Helms and Representative Dan Burton sought to bar sugar imports to the United States from anyone purchasing or renting property in Cuba that was confiscated after Castro seized power in 1959. Canada saw itself as the target of this legislation and sent a sharply worded protest to the United States stating that Helms–Burton violated NAFTA and World Trade Organization obligations entered into by the United States. At the same time that this legislation was being debated, the Clinton administration and Congress were engaged in a race to see who could propose the toughest actions against Iran. The administration barred Texas-based Conoco Oil Company from developing oil and gas fields with Iran, but Republicans in Congress wanted to go even further. Senator Alfonse D'Amato and Representative Peter King introduced a bill that according to D'Amato would force a foreign corporation or individual to "choose between trade with the United States or trade with Iran."

Individual activity, whether done as a policy entrepreneur or as a gadfly, has left a distinct mark on the conduct of American foreign policy by forcing foreign dignitaries to expand their negotiating agendas. Seeking to gain congressional support for the Clinton administration's plan to pay off a portion of its UN debt, Secretary General Kofi Annan met with Senate Foreign Relations Committee chairperson Jesse Helms. Annan agreed to the meeting only after President Clinton told him it was essential to gain Helms's support if he hoped to see the United States pay its back dues.

STAFF AIDES

Information has always been a problem for Congress when it comes to making foreign policy. Thomas Brewer identified more than 100 House roll call votes on foreign policy issues in just one year.[18] Few members can hope to acquire the background and expertise to understand and stay on top of such a wide range of issues as Defense Department appropriations, export controls, world hunger, and recognizing the Transkei territory in South Africa. The emergence of a large and well-informed number of staff aides has given the problem a new focus.[19] The problem is no longer one of acquiring needed information from the executive branch or party leaders. It is now also one of using information in a controlled and coherent fashion. Concerns have been expressed over whether (1) the staffer is serving Congress or just leading willing congresspeople from issue to issue as they build their own reputations, and (2) an activist staff might not be overloading Congress with new issues, thereby robbing it of the time needed for debate and deliberation.

The tremendous increase in staff size is visible throughout Congress. In 1947, there existed roughly five hundred committee and two thousand personal staffers. In 1979, these numbers had jumped to three thousand committee staff aides and over ten thousand personal staff aides. Congress as a whole has also increased its information-gathering and processing capabilities by establishing or increasing the size of the Congressional Research Service (established in 1914), the Congressional Accounting Office (1921), the Office of Technology Assessment (1972), and the Congressional Budget Office (1974). In 1976, the Office of Technology Assessment supervised a study for the Senate Foreign Relations Committee that estimated the number of American casualties in a nuclear war. Its findings challenged Defense Department assumptions and methodology. It has also studied questions relating to nuclear terrorism and energy policy.

In addition to being able to draw upon vast amounts of information from their staffs and congressional research services, congresspeople and senators can also draw upon the products of private nonprofit research institutes and think tanks such as the Brookings Institute, the Cato Institute, and the Heritage Foundation.[20] Until the 1970s, think tanks were relatively few in number. Today they are prominent fixtures on the Washington, D.C., political landscape, providing a base of operations for policy-oriented academics, defeated and would-be elected officials, and foreign policy experts who hope to enter or reenter government service in a future administration. Think tanks provide policy makers with a wide array of products, ranging from scholarly papers and conferences to serving as informal "talent banks" that can be drawn upon in debating policy choices.

The Influence of Party and Region

From what we have seen so far, it is clear that Congress has great difficulty speaking with one voice on foreign policy matters. We can bring this difficulty into even greater focus by examining the influence of party and region on foreign policy decisions. Current evidence suggests that the ability of party identification to unite individuals around a policy choice is not as great as we might expect, while the pull of regionalism is greater than commonly believed.

We need to look no further than the problems the Republican Party in Congress was having in formulating a unified foreign policy position in the late 1990s to see splits beneath the surface of party unity on foreign policy matters.[21] Where senior Republican leaders embrace an internationalist outlook rooted in cold war foreign policy triumphs, those elected for the first time in the 1990s and later have a different worldview. It is one that places budget deficits and eroding values at center stage. Junior Republicans have opposed supporting loan guarantees to Mexico, favor privitization of foreign aid, oppose expensive new weapons systems, and show little interest in bipartisan resolutions supporting the President in Bosnia or elsewhere. Past accomplishments mean little to them. This internal split in the Republican Party surfaced again in 2004, pitting defense hawks against deficit hawks as a result of the sharp increase in defense spending under George W. Bush. In the Senate, the Budget Committee cut $7 billion from Bush's defense request. The House Budget Committee was leaning in the same direction. To counter these moves, the Chair of the Armed Services Committee and thirty-three other House Republicans sent a letter to the Chair of the Budget Committee warning that they would not support a resolution cutting Bush's request. The Democratic Party is not immune from the problems growing out of internal disunity. Led by organized labor, a protectionist wing of the Democratic Party has gained in influence at the expense of the more liberal free traders. The combined result of these divisions was the inability of President Clinton and House Speaker Newt Gingrich working together to deliver enough votes to gain passage of legislation that would have granted Clinton fast track authority in trade negotiations.

It is commonly accepted by students of world politics that the globalization of the world's economy creates winners and losers. This is equally true for regions of a country as it is for countries as a whole. Peter Trubowitz asserts that today as in the 1890s and 1930s the changing nature of the global economy and the uneven impact it has on different areas of the United States has produced regional conflict over how to define the American national interest.[22] He sees U.S. foreign policy as being driven by a coalition of the South and the West, regions that benefit from a foreign policy designed to promote free trade and assure international stability. Opposed to it is the Northeast, which while once benefiting from such policies now sees itself as economically disadvantaged by them and favors protectionism and cuts in defense spending. This regional alignment of forces, rather than a Republican-Democratic divide, is what steered the Reagan buildup through Congress.

We can also see the impact of geography in more traditional terms of "pork barrel" politics. Senator Mitch McConnell (R-Ky.) was a leading opponent of foreign aid until he became chair of the Senate Appropriations foreign operations subcommittee. Under his leadership, funds flowed to Kentucky contractors, Kentucky universities, and the Mitch McConnell Conservation Fund. There was also a dramatic increase in foreign aid funds for Armenia. Though few Armenians reside in Kentucky, since the late 1990s, Armenian Americans have contributed generously to the Republican Party in Kentucky and the Republican National Committee, which he headed. Base closings and weapon system terminations are guaranteed to produce strong geographic responses. George W. Bush has tried to do both, cutting military bases and mothballing one-third of the B-1 bomber force. Senators and representatives of both parties from Florida, Georgia, and Idaho whose B-1 bases would be closed noted with displeasure that the two B-1 bases that would be left operational were in Texas and South Dakota, home states of the president and Speaker of the House. Senator John Warner (R-Va.), the ranking Republican member of the Senate Armed Services Committee and one who supports base closings as a cost-saving device, spoke out angrily against the notion that bases such as those in the Norfolk area should be closed because they were in heavily populated areas.

FOREIGN POLICY IMPACT

All of the above factors combine to place a heavy burden on congressional participation in foreign policy making. First, congressional participation is sluggish. In large measure this is by design. James Sundquist asserts that "from the beginning, the Congress has shown that its most deep-seated fear is not obstructionism but quick majoritarian decisions."[23] Second, Congress's participation is parochial and unpredictable at both the institutional and individual levels. In 1978, for example, Carter won five major foreign policy victories: the Panama Canal Treaties, an arms sales package to the Middle East, energy legislation, lifting the Turkish arms embargo, and a foreign assistance bill. Only eleven senators voted yes on all five; only one voted no to all of them.[24] Parochialism is present regardless of which party is in control of Congress. Senator Henry "Scoop" Jackson, a conservative Democrat from Washington and long-time fixture on the Armed Services Committee, was known as the "Senator from Boeing" for his ability to steer contracts to Boeing aircraft, which was headquartered in Washington. In 1995, the Republican-controlled Senate Armed Services Committee added $5 billion in funds for weapons spending on to Clinton's request. Eighty-one percent of these funds were to go to states represented by committee members. A similar pattern took place in the area of military construction, where $345 million was added. Of the forty-four projects added, thirty-two were in states represented on the committee. Parochialism extends beyond the committee system. The B-1 bomber, for example, had 400 subcontracts in over 400 of the 435 districts of the House.

When Congress acts, it acts with blunt instruments that often seem to produce overkill or make the problem worse. A compelling example occurred in May 1994 when on back-to-back votes of 50 to 49 the Senate first instructed Clinton to obtain allied support for lifting a multilateral weapons embargo against Bosnia and then voted to force him to do so unilaterally and immediately. Senator John Glenn summarized the votes this way: "We give clear guidance except when we change our minds."

The picture is not entirely negative. Robert Pastor argues that Congress actually possesses some comparative advantages over the White House in setting the direction of American foreign policy.[25] An assertive Congress helps the United States "adapt its means and its goals to changes within and outside itself" and provides skillful negotiators with a powerful bargaining lever in dealings with other countries. Congress is also able to provide a corrective for narrow presidential definitions of foreign policy problems. Pastor contends that this often has been the case with regard to Latin America. Under Carter, Congress insisted that long-standing American security concerns not be abandoned in the signing of the Panama Canal Treaty, and under Reagan it exerted pressure to make sure that human rights concerns were not ignored.

A more complicated and nuanced picture of Congress's impact on foreign policy emerges when we direct our attention to specific policy areas. Stephen Cohen identifies eight principles that are central to understanding congressional activity in international economic policy.[26] By collapsing some of his arguments, we can summarize his main findings as follows:

1. Congress is not equally concerned with all aspects of international economic policy. Simply put, some things matter more than others. Most important is international trade, followed by foreign assistance. International monetary, investment, and energy policy are far less important.

2. Extremely important for understanding congressional influence is the relationship between key congressional and administration officials. Good working relations can do a lot to defuse congressional anger and give the White House room to maneuver.

3. Congress is willing to take the lead; it is not simply a reactive body. But Congress deals with international economic issues at a slow, deliberate speed. Quick decisive actions are rare.

4. Congress has a two-tiered trade philosophy. On the one hand, it believes that free trade is important. On the other it believes that exceptions must be made due to economic or political considerations. Over time it has developed a finely tuned set of expectations regarding how the White House is supposed to manage these two sets of concerns in its dealings with other countries.

5. The dominant factors explaining a congressperson's position on international economic policy is geography (for trade policy) and committee assignments, not party affiliation or political philosophy.

Congress and the President: The Changing Relationship

The relationship between Congress and the president is not static. Viewed over time, congressional–presidential relations have moved from a long period of presidential dominance to one where Congress has emerged as an important player fully capable of frustrating presidential initiatives. This change can be measured many different ways. For example, one can chart the number of times presidents and Congress have opposed each other on foreign policy legislation. Before 1973, of the forty-five major pieces of foreign policy legislation considered by Congress, twenty-one (47 percent) failed. Since then thirty-eight of sixty-four major pieces of legislation (77 percent) have failed. Presidents have also found themselves opposing foreign policy legislation more frequently. Prior to 1973, they opposed 22 percent of the bills being considered. After 1973, this number has risen to 53 percent.[27]

If we look beyond these numbers, we see that the relationship between Congress and the president cannot simply be categorized as one of deference, dominance, or defiance. James Scott and Ralph Carter suggest that changes in congressional–presidential relations in foreign policy can be thought about in terms of differing levels of activity and assertiveness.[28] Combining them produces four patterns. A competitive Congress is both active and assertive in foreign policy and thus quite willing to challenge a president's lead. A disengaged Congress is neither active nor assertive and tends to readily follow a president's foreign policy preferences. A supportive Congress is one that is active but not aggressive. It cooperates with the president on a broad range of foreign policy initiatives without challenging him. Finally, a strategic Congress is not particularly active but is willing and capable of challenging a president on specific issues that conflict with its foreign policy agenda.

From the end of World War II until about 1958, a supportive Congress existed. Relations between the two branches were largely harmonious. Bipartisanship was the order of the day. The president was the acknowledged architect of American foreign policy and Congress' role was to reaffirm his policy initiatives and provide him with the means necessary to act. Often its participation took on a plebiscitary character with the passage of area resolutions such as those on the Middle East, Taiwan, and Latin America. Periods of dissent did occur, such as after the "loss of China" and during the McCarthy hearings, but overall the cold war consensus held. The next decade, 1958 to 1968, saw the emergence of a strategic Congress. The cold war principles around which the earlier bipartisan consensus was built had by now begun to fray. Congress was not in an open revolt against the president. Proclamations of support were still present, most notably the Gulf of Tonkin Resolution, and failures such as the Bay of Pigs did not bring forward partisan attacks. But pockets of resistance had now formed, and Congress did move to challenge the president selectively. Two key points of confrontation were the Vietnam War and the existence of a missile gap. From 1968 into the mid-1980s, Congress was both active and assertive. This competitive Congress not only sought to limit the president's ability to conduct foreign policy by passing such measures as the War Powers Resolution and the Case–Zablocki Act, it resisted many of his most important foreign policy initiatives. The Jackson–Vanik Amendment undermined Nixon's détente policy, Carter was challenged on the Panama Canal Treaties, and Ford was rebuffed on an arms sales agreement to Turkey. The period from the mid-1980s until September 11, 2001 marked a return to a strategic Congress. Once again, Congress selectively engaged the president on foreign policy issues. In some cases, such as the annual vote on Most Favored Nations Status for China, the interactions became almost ritualistic. On other occasions, such as the Comprehensive Test Ban Treaty, ratifying NAFTA, and granting fast-track trade authority, the conflicts were highly partisan and spirited.

The terrorist attacks of 9/11 led to the emergence of a disengaged Congress, one that was willing to cede the authority to make crucial foreign policy decisions to the president. Nowhere is this more evident than in George W. Bush's ability to obtain a use-of-force resolution from Congress against Iraq by votes of 77 to 23 in the Senate and 296 to 133 in the House. Congress was not totally compliant, but it did not directly challenge the president. Objections to the Bush administration's proposed language that authorizing the president "to use all means that he determined to be appropriate" was addressed in behind-the-scenes meetings. In its place was language acceptable to the administration that authorized Bush to "defend the security of the United States against the continuing threat posed by Iraq and to enforce all relevant UN resolutions." Also inserted was reporting language consistent with that used in the War Powers Resolution, language that the administration accepted without at the same time accepting the constitutionality of the War Powers Resolution. Key parts of the resolution are found in Box 9.1. Leading Democrats put very different readings on the importance of the resolution. Senate Majority Leader Tom Daschle, who supported the resolution, expressed the prevailing sentiment in Congress saying "the bottom line is . . . we want to move on." Robert Byrd who opposed the resolution said, "How have we gotten to this low point in the history of Congress? Are we too feeble to resist the demand of a president who is determined to bend the collective will of Congress to his will?"[29] This disengaged Congress has already shown signs of moving back toward a strategic Congress. Presidential authority to engage in fast-track trade negotiations was approved by the thinnest of margins. And, most significantly, Congress held hearings into the state of intelligence prior to 9/11 and issued a highly critical report.

Box 9.1

Excerpt: **HOUSE RESOLUTION AUTHORIZING THE USE OF FORCE AGAINST IRAQ,** *OCTOBER 2, 2002*

SECTION 1:

This joint resolution may be cited as the "Authorization for the Use of Military Force Against Iraq."

SECTION 2.

SUPPORT FOR UNITED STATES DIPLOMATIC EFFORTS.

The Congress of the United States supports the efforts by the president to:

(a) strictly enforce through the United Nations Security Council all relevant Security Council resolutions applicable to Iraq and encourages him in those efforts; and

(b) obtain prompt and decisive action by the Security Council to ensure that Iraq abandons its strategy of delay, evasion and noncompliance and promptly and strictly complies with all relevant Security Council resolutions.

SECTION 3:

AUTHORIZATION FOR USE OF UNITED STATES ARMED FORCES.

(a) AUTHORIZATION. The president is authorized to use the Armed Forces of the United States as he determines to be necessary and appropriate in order to

(1) defend the national security of the United States against the continuing threat posed by Iraq; and

(2) enforce all relevant United Nations Security Council Resolutions regarding Iraq.

Box 9.1 *(Continued)*

(b) PRESIDENTIAL determination.

In connection with the exercise of the authority granted in subsection (a) to use force the president shall, prior to such exercise or as soon there after as may be feasible, but no later than 48 hours after exercising such authority, make available to the Speaker of the House of Representatives and the president pro tempore of the Senate his determination that

(1) reliance by the United States on further diplomatic or other peaceful means alone either (A) will not adequately protect the national security of the United States against the continuing threat posed by Iraq or (B) is not likely to lead to enforcement of all relevant United Nations Security Council resolutions regarding Iraq, and

(2) acting pursuant to this resolution is consistent with the United States and other countries continuing to take the necessary actions against international terrorists and terrorist organizations, including those nations, organizations or persons who planned, authorized, committed or aided the terrorists attacks that occurred on Sept. 11, 2001.

(c) WAR powers resolution requirements.

(1) Specific statutory authorization. Consistent with section 8(a)(1) of the War Powers Resolution, the Congress declares that this section is intended to constitute specific statutory authorization within the meaning of section 5 (b) of the War Powers Resolution.

(2) Applicability of other requirements. Nothing in this resolution supersedes any requirement of the War Powers Resolution.

SECTION 4:

REPORTS TO CONGRESS.

(a) The president shall, at least once every 60 days, submit to the Congress a report on matters relevant to this joint resolution, including actions taken pursuant to the exercise of authority granted in section 2 and the status of planning for efforts that are expected to be required after such actions are completed, including those actions described in section 7 of Public Law 105-338 (the Iraq Liberation Act of 1998).

(b) To the extent that the submission of any report described in subsection (a) coincides with the submission of any other report on matters relevant to this joint resolution otherwise required to be submitted to Congress pursuant to the reporting requirements of Public Law 93-148 (the War Powers Resolution), all such reports may be submitted as a single consolidated report to the Congress.

(c) To the extent that the information required by section 3 of Public Law 102-1 is included in the report required by this section, such report shall be considered as meeting the requirements of section 3 of Public Law 102-1.

Summary and Future Issues

The fundamental problem facing Congress in exercising its foreign policy voice in the future will be the one that we have outlined in this chapter: to establish its right to participate in making decisions and to manage the contradictory pressures for efficiency and participation. The optimal mix has yet to be found, and as we have seen, the nature of the relationship between Congress and the president has varied greatly. Congress cannot be ignored. The Constitution mandates its participation in foreign policy making. Its participation is also politically necessary. Robert Zoellick, writing before he became George W. Bush's special trade representative, asserted that "without congressional support, the Executive cannot sustain long-term public support."[30] The question is how to do so.

One approach is to focus on correcting those facets of Congress that contribute to its inefficiency in foreign policy making. As an example, one could focus on improving its ability to conduct oversight. This point was stressed repeatedly in the debate over creating a Department of Homeland Security. The Bush administration initially argued against a department citing oversight problems. According to its count, thirteen full committees in each House and eighty-eight committees and subcommittees in total shared responsibility for homeland security. After voting a Department of Homeland Security into existence, the House and Senate took different routes toward creating oversight structures. The House created a Select Homeland Security Committee, many of whose members were powerful committee chairs already giving them a prime vantage point from which to protect their turf. The Senate made no changes in its committee structure beyond the creation of an Appropriations Committee for Homeland Security. While Congress failed here to make major oversight changes, it has improved its oversight of trade policy by creating a Congressional Oversight Group composed of the chairs and ranking members of the Senate Committee on Finance, the House Ways and Means Committee, and three other members to facilitate information sharing and consultation with the Office of the U.S. Trade Representative. An even more ambitious suggestion is to create a joint committee on national security that would oversee the workings of the National Security Council.

Although our focus in this chapter is on Congress, some have argued that improving congressional participation in foreign policy actually requires a change in the operating style of presidents. They continue to operate on the basis of what James MacGregor Burns refers to as a presidential style of leadership.[31] According to this model, leadership requires that presidents guard and protect their power, especially from congressional encroachments. The cold war served as a catalyst and source of support for this style of presidential leadership. The problem is that presidents have not changed their leadership style. Rather they have engaged in foreign policy "ad hocism" in which periodic understandings with Congress on how to conduct foreign policy are interspersed with presidential attempts to reassert primacy.

Some commentators argue that what is needed is a collaborative model of leadership based upon Madison's notion of separate institutions sharing power. Thus each branch, while mindful of its own powers, would construct mechanisms or tools to aid interbranch collaboration.[32] Possible building blocks on which this leadership might be based are already in place or have been tried on an experimental basis. In the area of arms control the Carter administration established the practice of appointing congressional advisers to the SALT II Geneva negotiations. These advisers were involved in both formal and informal treaty discussions and reviewed the draft of the SALT II agreement.[33] The congressional advisory group continued under the Reagan administration despite its very different approach to arms control.

Notes

1. Douglas Bennett Jr., "Congress in Foreign Policy: Who Needs It," *Foreign Affairs,* 57 (1978), 40–50.

2. Stansfield Turner, *Secrecy and Democracy* (Boston: Houghton Mifflin, 1985), pp. 150–51.

3. James A. Robinson, *Congress and Foreign Policy Making: A Study in Legislative Influence and Initiative* (Homewood, Ill.: Dorsey, 1962), p. 110.

4. Lee R. Marks, "Legislating and the Conduct of Diplomacy: The Constitution's Inconsistent Functions," in Thomas M. Franck (ed.), *The Tethered Presidency: Congressional Restraints on Executive Power* (New York: New York University Press, 1981), p. 201.

5. I. M. Destler, "Dateline Washington: Congress as Boss," *Foreign Policy,* 42 (1981), 161–80.

6. *The Congressional Record,* January 11, 1991, pp. S250–51.

7. This point and others about the budgetary powers of Congress are discussed by Charles W. Kegley Jr., and Eugene R. Wittkopf, *American Foreign Policy: Pattern and Process,* 2nd ed. (New York: St. Martin's, 1982), pp. 417–29.

8. Abner J. Mikva and Patti B. Solis, *The American Congress: The First Branch* (New York: Watts, 1983), pp. 302–7.

9. Glenn Hastedt, "The Department of Homeland Security: Politics of Creation," in Ralph Carter (ed.), *Contemporary Cases in U.S. Foreign Policy* (Washington DC., CQ Press, 2004), pp. 149–80.

10. Ruth Collier, "Foreign Policy by Reporting Requirement," *Washington Quarterly,* 11 (1988), 74–84.

11. Roger H. Davidson, "Subcommittee Government: New Channels for Policy Making," in Thomas E. Mann and Norman J. Ornstein (eds.), *The New Congress* (Washington D.C.: American Enterprise Institute, 1981), p. 130.

12. Amos A. Jordon and William J. Taylor Jr., *American National Security: Policy and Process* (Baltimore, Md.: Johns Hopkins University Press, 1981), p. 121.

13. Thomas L. Brewer, *American Foreign Policy: A Contemporary Introduction,* 2nd ed. (Englewood Cliffs, N.J.: Prentice-Hall, 1986), p. 119.

14. Lee Hamilton, *A Creative Tension* (Washington, D.C.: Woodrow Wilson Center Press, 2002).

15. David Price, *Who Makes the Laws?* (Cambridge, Mass: Schenkman, 1972), p. 330.

16. Joshua Muravchik, *The Senate and National Security: A New Mood,* Washington Paper #80 (Beverly Hills: Sage, 1980), pp. 57–60.

17. I. M. Destler, "Executive–Congressional Conflict in Foreign Policy: Explaining It: Coping With It," in Dodd and Oppenheimer (eds.), *Congress Reconsidered,* p. 301.

18. Brewer, *American Foreign Policy,* p. 119.

19. For a discussion of congressional staffs, see Michael J. Malbin, "Delegation, Deliberation, and the New Role of Congressional Staff," in Mann and Ornstein (eds.), *The New Congress,* pp. 134–77; and Muravchik, *The Senate and National Security.*

20. James A. Smith, *The Idea Brokers: Think Tanks and the Rise of the New Policy Elite* (New York: Free Press, 1991, and David Newsom, *The Public and Foreign Policy* (Bloomington: Indiana University Press, 1996).

21. James Kitfield, "The Folk Who Live on the Hill," *The National Interest,* 58 (1999/2000), 48–55.

22. Peter Trubowitz, *Defining the National Interest* (Chicago: University of Chicago Press, 1998).

23. Sundquist, *Decline and Resurgence of Congress,* p. 156.

24. Destler, "Executive–Congressional Conflict in Foreign Policy," pp. 296–316.

25. Robert Pastor, "Congress and U.S. Foreign Policy: Comparative Advantage or Disadvantage?" *Washington Quarterly,* 14 (1991), 101–14. Pastor writes in rebuttal to the argument put forward by Aaron L. Friedberg, "Is the United States Capable of Acting Strategically?" *Washington Quarterly,* 14 (1990), 5–23.

26. Stephen D. Cohen, *The Making of United States International Economic Policy,* 3rd ed. (New York: Praeger, 1994).

27. Jeffrey Peake, "Coalition Building and Overcoming Legislative Gridlock in Foreign Policy, 1947–98," *Presidential Studies Quarterly,* 32 (2002), 67–73.

28. James Scott and Ralph Carter, "Acting on the Hill," *Congress & the Presidency,* 29 (2002), 151–69.

29. James Lindsay, "Deference and Defiance," *Presidential Studies Quarterly,* 33 (2003), 543.

30. Robert Zoellick, "Congress and the Making of U.S. Foreign Policy," *Survival,* 41 (1999–2000), 23.

31. James MacGregor Burns, *Presidential Government: The Crucible of Leadership* (Boston: Houghton Mifflin, 1973).

32. For essays on this theme see Thomas Mann (ed.), *A Question of Balance: The President, the Congress, and Foreign Policy;* also see Barry Blechman, "The Congressional Role in U.S. Military Policy," *Political Science Quarterly,* 106 (Spring 1991), 17–32.

33. Stephen Flanagan, "The Domestic Politics of SALT II," in John Spanier and John Nogee (eds.), *Congress and the Presidency* (New York: Pergamon Press, 1981), pp. 44–76.

— 10 —

THE FOREIGN AFFAIRS BUREAUCRACY

According to Henry Kissinger, "The purpose of bureaucracy is to devise a standard operating procedure that can cope effectively with most problems."[1] In doing so it frees high-level policy makers to concentrate on the unexpected and exceptional and to pursue policy innovations. When it fails to identify options or when those options prove to be irrelevant, bureaucracy becomes a hindrance, forcing policy makers to redirect their efforts away from problem solving to forging a bureaucratic consensus. The critical problem identified by Kissinger is integrating the roles of the professional expert and the political generalist. But this is not the only challenge that must be addressed if the bureaucracy is to become part of the answer to having a successful foreign policy rather than part of the problem that prevents this from happening. Two other endemic problems exist.[2] The first is policy coordination. This involves the successful management of the day-to-day formulation and execution of specific policies by specific bureaucratic units. Without it, contradictory policies are put forward and the implementation of decisions is cumbersome. The second challenge is programmatic coherence. The bureaucratic focus here is on constructing sound and reasoned long-term plans of action to further U.S. strategic interests. Without it, policy often "hangs on a thread" as goals are articulated but few funds are assigned to the task and no one claims ownership. Under those circumstances, policy flounders, and challenges and opportunities go unrecognized because of neglect or bureaucratic rivalry.

From one perspective, these three challenges represent managerial problems that can be solved by more clearly identifying organizational responsibilities, establishing clear lines of communication, and carefully selecting personnel. Viewed from another perspective, these tensions reflect the fundamentally dual nature of all organizations and defy permanent solutions. Organizations can be divided into formal and informal subsystems.[3] The formal system is built around the legal lines of authority, rules, and regulations that make up the organization. It is embodied in organizational charts that reveal the tasks that the organization is charged with and lines of accountability. It is a goal-oriented system whose logic and coherence are derived from the tasks assigned to it by forces outside the organization. In the case of public bureaucracies, Congress, the president, and interest groups all participate in defining official organizational goals. The informal system springs up spontaneously around the formal system and consists of the unwritten rules of conduct and fundamental assumptions that guide the day-to-day behavior of those employed in the organization. The two systems frequently collide: Where the formal system is concerned with goal achievement, the informal system is concerned with the survival of organizational members. But no formal system can survive for long without an effectively operating system of unwritten rules and redundancy that allow it to cope with contingencies and problems that were not anticipated when the organization was set up. At the same time it also confronts policy makers with a challenge. As a spontaneous structure the informal system defies total control, and attempts to manipulate it will fail.

Our concern in this chapter is with the foreign affairs bureaucracy. The management dilemmas and the basic organizational realities sketched above are very much present here. We begin by examining the three organizations that dominate the foreign affairs bureaucracy: the State Department, the Defense Department, and the Central Intelligence Agency (CIA). We then take a brief look at bureaucracies that have traditionally been classified as domestic but now also have a foreign policy role: the Treasury, Commerce, and Agriculture Departments. Finally, we will look at the Department of Homeland Security, the newest bureaucratic unit with a foreign policy role.

The State Department

STRUCTURE AND GROWTH

According to historical tradition and government documents the president looks first to the State Department in making foreign policy. The State Department must serve as a transmission belt for information between the United States and foreign governments and as a resource for senior policy makers to draw upon as needed. Both of these tasks have become increasingly difficult to accomplish with the ever expanding agenda of American foreign policy. Annually, the State Department represents the United States in over fifty major international organizations and at over eight hundred international conferences. The volume of information that it must process has grown at a staggering rate. In the late 1960s and early 1970s, an average of over four thousand messages were processed each day. Over one-half were classified. By the mid-1980s, approximately ten thousand messages, reports, and instructions were sent and received by the State Department each day.

Dean Rusk, Secretary of State under John Kennedy and Lyndon Johnson, estimated that he saw only six of every one thousand cables sent to the State Department each day and that the president saw only one or two. Rusk also estimated that he read only twenty to thirty of the thirteen hundred cables sent out each day.[4] By the end of the twentieth century, the State Department was electronically processing over fourteen thousand official records and ninety thousand data messages each day along with over twenty million email messages per year.

Management challenges also lie in the number of non–State Department personnel that can be found in American embassies. In 1994, only 38 percent of U.S. government personnel in embassies worked for the State Department; 36 percent worked for the Defense Department, 5 percent for the Justice Department, 3 percent for the Transportation Department, and 18 percent for the Treasury, Commerce, and Agriculture Departments. The concept of a country team has been developed to bring coherence to the welter of agencies and programs now found represented at an embassy.

As chief of mission, the ambassador heads the country team. In practice, ambassadors have found it quite difficult to exercise enough authority to transform a set of independent and often competing policies into a coordinated and coherent program. They have been frustrated by the scope and complexity of the programs being carried out, the access of non–State Department personnel to independent reporting channels, and the need of these individuals to meet the performance and promotion standards set by their own bureaucracies. Also complicating the problem is the background of the ambasssador. Frequently, the ambassador is not a career diplomat. Under Carter 75 percent of all ambassadors were career diplomats. This was up from 40 percent in 1955 and 68 percent in 1962, but under Reagan it fell back to 60 percent.[5] Approximately 30 percent of President Clinton's appointments were noncareer diplomats.

The State Department's basic structure remained largely unchanged for the duration of the cold war. Beneath the secretary of state were a small number of deputy secretaries of state with responsibility for political, economic, international security, and management affairs. The remainder of the State Department was organized around geographical areas and functional tasks. While the number and identity of the regional areas remained steady, the functional bureaus showed considerable change over time. An inspection of organizational charts dating back to 1960 would show the continued presence of bureaus responsible for intelligence and research, international organizations, economic and business affairs, and political-military affairs. It would also reveal the disappearance of the education and culture bureau and the addition of the refugee bureau and a bureau responsible for human rights and humanitarian affairs. Bureaus were also transformed as the international agenda changed. For example, the International Scientific and Technical Bureau to the Oceans became the International Environment and Science Bureau.

In part, organizational stability was realized by setting up semiautonomous organizations to deal with three of the more pressing problem areas of cold war diplomacy: foreign aid, arms control, and dispersal of information.

Their emergence reflects a trend begun in World War II when rather than incorporate new foreign policy tasks into the State Department system, separate organizations operating under White House control were established. The Agency for International Development was established in 1961 and is responsible for administering the U.S. foreign economic aid program. The Arms Control and Disarmament Agency (ACDA) was also established in 1961 and is responsible for conducting studies on arms control and disarmament policies, managing U.S. arms control and disarmament negotiations, overseeing U.S. participation in arms control agreements, and advising the president, NSC, and secretary of state on arms control and disarmament matters. The United States Information Agency (USIA) was established in 1953 and is charged with promoting a better understanding of the United States in other countries. The "Voice of America" is one of its best-known undertakings.

Today, the State Department is undergoing two profound changes. One change involves the State Department's "shrinking presence" overseas. Between 1993 and 1996, the State Department cut more than two thousand employees and closed five embassies, twenty-three AID missions, and twenty-six consulates, consulate generals, and State Department branch offices. This reduction is a by-product of a reduction in the international affairs budget from $37.5 billion in 1984 to $18.6 billion in 1996.

The second change involves the formal integration of USIA and ACDA into the State Department and an end to their status as semiautonomous agencies. AID is to retain its independent status, but its director will report to the Secretary of State rather than to the president. This reorganization is the by-product of reform initiatives within the executive branch and the insistence of Senate Foreign Relations Committee chair Jesse Helms that streamlining the foreign affairs bureaucracy was the price to be paid for his willingness to allow the Chemical Weapons Convention to come up for a vote.

THE STATE DEPARTMENT'S VALUE SYSTEM

The Secretary of State.   Capturing the essence of the State Department's value system is best done by looking at how secretaries of state have defined their role and how the Foreign Service Officer (FSO) corps approaches its job. The job of secretary of state is not an easy one. Cecil Crabb suggests that "almost without exception, every post war Secretary of State has left under a cloud of criticism." Lack of leadership (James Byrnes, Dean Rusk), aloofness and arrogance (Dean Acheson), and overly zealous attempts to dominate foreign policy making (John Foster Dulles, Henry Kissinger, Alexander Haig) are among the charges that have been leveled.

Secretaries of state have also found themselves excluded from key decisions. Cyrus Vance resigned from the Carter administration partly in protest over his exclusion from decision making on the Iranian hostage rescue effort. Edmund Muskie, his successor, suffered the embarrassment of not being informed about PD-59, the presidential directive that shifted U.S. strategic thought away from a strictly second-strike posture to one emphasizing nuclear flexibility and limited strategic options. George Shultz claimed that he was only marginally informed of the NSC plan to sell U.S. weapons to Iran and secure the release of U.S. hostages in Lebanon.

In order to effectively participate in foreign policy making, secretaries of state, just as their counterparts at Defense and the CIA do, need a power base to work from. In practice, this has required that they must either become advocates of the State Department perspective or serve as the loyal ally of the president.[6] Haig adopted the first role orientation. Rusk, Dulles, and Shultz adopted the second. Vance and Christopher tried to combine elements of both. Each has its dangers and limitations. Adopting the first perspective makes one suspect in the White House, while the second makes one suspect within the State Department and runs the risk of letting it drift for lack of effective oversight. The greatest danger comes with the failure to establish any power base at all. Madeline Albright assumed that office with great fanfare, but by the end of the Clinton administration she was described as an insecure and indifferent leader who was the least influential secretary of state since William Rogers in the Nixon administration. Within the White House, national security advisor Sandy Berger was closer to Clinton and dominated decision making on key issues such as Bosnia, and she isolated herself from the State Department by surrounding herself with a small and closed circle of advisors.

Colin Powell served as Secretary of State under George W. Bush in his first administration. His primary role orientation was as a spokesperson for the State Department perspective. In the war on terrorism, the build-up to the war with Iraq, confrontations with North Korea, and U.S. policy toward the Israeli–Palestinian conflict, Powell repeatedly called for giving diplomacy a chance and was reluctant to advocate the use of force. A March 2003 study by the Foreign Affairs Council credited Powell with "historic" accomplishments in getting resources for the State Department and changing its culture.[7] The net result, however, was not a dominant voice in foreign policy making. Powell's position repeatedly lost out to more hawkish ones advanced by Secretary of Defense Donald Rumsfeld and Vice President Dick Cheney. So often did this happen that both before and after 9/11, Powell was on occasion described in the press as "missing in action."

Powell's case highlights challenges faced by secretaries of state who try to make the State Department their power base in still another way. Powell traveled less as Secretary of State than anyone who held this position since Kissinger who was abroad for 313 days in his 39 months as Secretary of State.[8] Kissinger's average trip lasted 8.7 days compared to 3.3 days for Powell. To bring the comparison up to date, his three immediate predecessors (Albright, Warren Christopher, and James Baker III) averaged 45 percent more time abroad than he has. In choosing to remain and work out of Washington, Powell is heeding the advice of George Kennan, the architect of the containment doctrine, who believes that secretaries of state have "seriously misused and distorted their position" by engaging in so much travel. It is far preferable from his point of view to rely on lower-level officials and ambassadors to become the voice of the United States abroad. (Powell does make heavy use of the phone, placing more than fifteen hundred calls to foreign leaders in the two years after 9/11). Yet, his giving primary attention to the state of affairs in Washington and reliance on diplomatic professionals to practice their craft has not met with universal approval from them. Some feel that his lack of travel has contributed to the general decline in America's image abroad. Former UN ambassador Richard Holbrooke asserts "in the modern age, like it or not, secretaries have to travel."

Condoleezza Rice, who served as national security advisor in the first George W. Bush administration, assumed the post of Secretary of State in his second administration. Her presence was expected to tighten the White House's control over the State Department. She also sought to distance herself from Powell's administrative style by immediately embarking on a series of high profile overseas trips.

Foreign Service Officers. At the heart of the State Department system is its FSO corps. The foreign service was created in 1924 by the Rogers Act. Foreign service officers were intended to be generalists, "trained to perform almost any task at any post in the world."[9] The principal organizational device for producing such individuals is to rotate them frequently among functional tasks and geographic areas. The civil service, which existed apart from the FSO corps, was relied on to perform the State Department's "lesser" technical and administrative tasks. In 1954, a reorganization proposal developed by Harry Wriston led to the merger of these two personnel systems. Provisions were also made for widespread lateral entry into the restructured FSO system. "Wristonization" was not a complete success. Integrating the two career tracks did not bridge the differences in outlook that had arisen between them. Some had hoped that lateral entry would "Americanize" the foreign service by bringing into the FSO individuals with pasts different from the eastern, Ivy League, and upper-class backgrounds associated with it. Wristonization also created new problems. It created resentment in the ranks of the FSOs who felt that the corps was being diluted by the addition of outsiders, which caused an overcrowding at the top of the FSO career pyramid because while the number of FSOs had increased, there was no increase in the number of highly desirable positions. Further reform of the FSO system took place in 1980 with the passage of the Foreign Service Officer Act. It too trimmed the number of positions available for senior FSOs. From 1986 to 1990 between 350 and 450 upper-grade FSOs were forced to retire. The American Foreign Service Association contends that the negative impact of the 1980 reforms goes deeper than number cuts and extends to the quality of U.S. foreign policy:

> No one wants to serve as the political or economic counselor at overseas embassies because these are not management jobs. No one is going to be willing to spend two or three years learning Chinese or Japanese, because it's likely to be regarded as dead time when you come before a promotion board. The word in the corridors now is get a job managing something and forget everything else, or you're dead.[10]

FSO misgivings about their place in the making of American foreign policy have grown over time. Under Reagan and George H. W. Bush the concern was "political creep." By this, FSOs meant the tendency for political appointees to be placed at the assistant secretary and deputy secretary positions. In the 1950s, few political appointees could be found at these levels. In 1973 only 11 of 63 deputy assistant secretaries of state were political appointees. In 1984 almost one-half (59 of 136) were political appointees. Beyond the loss of job opportunities, FSOs complained that the presence of this "new blood" made it difficult to have frank discussions of thorny issues.[11] Under Clinton, the problem was the potential outright elimination of these positions as part of the effort to hold down costs. The administration's initial reorganization plan called for cutting as many as 40 deputy assistant secretary positions. Many FSOs have responded to these challenges by becoming politically active. Perhaps no one has symbolized this shift in outlook as much as John Brady Kiesling, Ann Wright, and John Brown, who resigned from the foreign service in protest over what they saw as the misguided policies of the George W. Bush administration and the movement to war with Iraq.

The representativeness of the FSO corps continues to be a major problem. Minorities and women are particularly underrepresented. In late 1993, 56 percent of the FSO corps was white male, 24 percent white female, 7 percent minority male, and 4 percent minority female. The distribution is even more skewed if attention is paid only to the senior ranks of the FSO Corps, from which ambassadors and policy makers are selected. At this same time, 84 percent were white male, 9 percent white female, 5 percent minority male, and 1 percent minority female.[12] Over one eleven-year period, 586 appointments were made to the post of deputy chief of mission. Women received only nine of them. At the same time, women were appointed to consular positions (which deal largely with passport and visa matters) as opposed to political posts (where one is likely to be involved in policy making) so much more frequently than men that the odds of its happening were one to one million. These revelations came about as part of a lawsuit filed against the State Department in 1976. In 1989 the State Department finally admitted that discrimination did exist and began taking steps to address the problem. In March 2000, the State Department settled the largest employment discrimination case ever by agreeing to pay $508 million to approximately 1,100 women who were denied employment or promotion by the U.S. Information Agency (USIA) and the Voice of America between 1974 and 1984.

The president of the American Foreign Service Association (FSO) wrote in 1994: "Many male officers have complained of their perceived inability to compete fairly against women and minority officers for attractive positions."[13] Black FSOs, who brought their own still-pending discrimination suit in the mid-1980s, continue to assert that they are being "ghettoized" by being posted primarily to Africa and Latin America instead of the more prestigious areas such as Europe, the Middle East, and Asia. In 1996, the State Department agreed to pay $3.8 million to compensate black FSOs and to grant retroactive promotions to 17 individuals.

The State Department is not alone in facing charges of discrimination. In 1993, "Jane Doe Thompson," a CIA professional with over twenty years experience in the clandestine service and who had once served as station chief, sued the CIA because of sex discrimination. In a separate legal action, over one hundred female officers in the clandestine division, almost one-third of all female case officers, joined in a class action lawsuit alleging discrimination. The CIA settled both matters out of court. In the class action suit, it agreed to pay $990,000 in back salaries and to make twenty-five retroactive promotions. For its part, the military came under heavy criticism for its handling of the Tailhook investigation. It has also struggled to find answers to such broader issues as gays in the military and the role of women in combat.

The heart of the FSO corps is its value system. The subject of repeated studies, the FSO value system consists of a clearly identifiable world outlook and set of guidelines for survival within the State Department bureaucracy.[14] Agreement also exists in the belief that these qualities are not conducive to the formulation and administration of U.S. foreign policy and that they are one reason for the State Department's declining influence on foreign affairs. Central to the belief system of the FSO is the dual conviction that the only career experience relevant to the work of the State Department is that gained in the foreign service and that the core of this work lies in the areas of political reporting, negotiating, and representing U.S. interests abroad. The FSO is empirical, intuitive, and cautious. John Harr concludes that the "systematic and methodological approach associated with planning is largely alien to the FSO."[15] Risk taking in the preparation of analysis or processing of information is avoided. As many as twenty-seven signatures have been required before instructions were sent regarding the Food for Peace program. As I. M. Destler put it, the "desk officer 'inherits' a policy toward country X, he regards it as his function to keep that policy intact."[16]

From the perspective of the FSO, the key to survival (and promotion) within the State Department is winning the respect of one's colleagues. On the one hand, this is a logical position to take because promotion in the foreign service is by peer review. On the other hand, an excessive concern for how one is viewed by one's peers stifles thinking and produces conformity in thought and action. Chris Argyris identified four norms operating within the FSO corps that inhibit open confrontation on difficult issues and penalize risk takers.[17] They are the following:

1. Withdrawal from interpersonal difficulties and conflict
2. Minimum interpersonal openness, leveling, and trust
3. Mistrust of others' aggressiveness and fighting
4. Withdrawal from aggressiveness and fighting

FOREIGN POLICY IMPACT

Once the centerpiece of the foreign affairs bureaucracy, the State Department has seen its power and influence steadily erode. It has gone from being the leading force behind such policies as the Marshall Plan, NATO, and containment to largely playing the role of the critic who finds fault with the proposals of others. It has become defensive and protective in interdepartment dealings, unable to centralize and coordinate the activities of the foreign affairs bureaucracy. Two complaints frequently are voiced about the State Department's performance. First, its recommendations are too predictable. Regardless of the problem, the State Department can be counted on to advocate minimizing risks, avoiding quick action, and adopting a long-term perspective on the problem. Second, its recommendations are insensitive to the presidential perspective on foreign policy matters. It fails to frame proposals in ways that will produce political support or at least minimize the political costs to the president. The combined result is that State Department recommendations are easily dismissed. In the eyes of many, it has become more of a spokesperson for foreign viewpoints within the U.S. government than an advocate of U.S. national interests. This situation is not condemned by all. To some it is the role the State Department should play (and a role it plays well), and they believe it should stop trying to perform functions it is no longer suited for.[18]

Nowhere is the State Department's decline as evident as in the area of international economic policy. It has been surpassed in influence by the Office of the U.S. Trade Representative. Created in 1963 out of congressional frustration with the State Department's perceived reluctance to defend American economic interests in dealings with other states, the Office of the U.S. Trade Representative is located in the White House and reports directly to the president. The special trade representative is charged with responsibility for overseeing U.S. activity in multilateral trade negotiations, negotiating trade issues with other states, and negotiating trade issues within the United Nations system of organizations. Thus it was Robert Zoellick, rather than Colin Powell, who accompanied George W. Bush to Quebec to meet with Latin American leaders in hopes of laying the foundation for Free Trade of the Americas. It was Zoellick who announced that the United States and the European Union had reached an agreement resolving a long-standing dispute over trade in bananas. It was Zoellick who accompanied Bush to the G-8 Economic Summit in Genoa, and it was Zoellick who supervised U.S. negotiations at the Qatar Round of WTO talks.

The State Department's inability to exercise leadership in foreign policy repeatedly has produced calls for reform. Former Secretary of State Lawrence Eagleburger asserts that the proliferation of assistant secretaries has balkanized the administrative apparatus making it difficult for the State Department to speak with one voice.[19] Calling it a "crippled institution," longtime critic former Speaker of the House of Representatives Newt Gingrich has called for a "top-to-bottom" transformation of the State Department that will place it more effectively under the control of the president and bring it more in line with American values.[20] This is not the first time the State Department has come under fire. In the 1950s, it was a prime target of the McCarthy investigations into un-American activities. In 1953 alone, some 70 to 80 percent of the highest-ranking Foreign Service Officers were dismissed, resigned, or were reassigned to politically safe positions.[21]

The Defense Department

STRUCTURE AND GROWTH

For most of its history, the military security of the United States was provided by forces under the command of the War Department and the Department of the Navy. No political or military authority other than the president existed above these two departments to coordinate and direct their affairs. During World War II the ineffectiveness of this system became apparent and led U.S. policy makers to take a series of ad hoc steps to bring greater coherence to the U.S. war effort. In 1947 the National Security Act formalized many of these arrangements by establishing a Department of the Air Force and giving legal standing to the Joint Chiefs of Staff (JCS). It also created a National Military Establishment and the position of Secretary of Defense. Further changes were made in 1949 when the National Military Establishment was redesignated as the Defense Department. As part of the reorganization, the Army, Navy, and Air Force departments were made military departments within the Department of Defense and were dropped from the cabinet and the NSC. In addition, a chairperson was added to the JCS, and the office of Secretary of Defense was created. The objective of these reforms was to place the military services more fully under civilian control and to provide for greater coordination of their activities. These same motivations guided Defense Department reorganizations in 1953 and 1958. Since 1958 only minor changes have been made in the formal structure of the military establishment.

The dominant reform issue of the early 1980s within the defense establishment was improving the operational efficiency of the armed forces. The failed 1979 hostage rescue effort, the 1983 terrorist attack on the Marines in Beirut, and problems encountered in the 1983 invasion of Grenada were cited by many military reformers as proof that reforms were needed beginning at the very top.[22]

Congress shared the concerns of defense reformers. Over the objections of the executive branch and many in the military, in 1986 it passed two pieces of legislation designed to remedy perceived shortcomings in the performance of the U.S. military. The Goldwater–Nichols Act strengthened the position of the JCS relative to that of the individual services. It also gave added weight to those parts of the Pentagon that had an interservice perspective. The second piece of legislation, the Cohen–Nunn Act, established a unified command for special operations and created an Assistant Secretary of Defense for special operations and low-intensity conflict.

Today two fundamental and underlying issues dominate the military reform agenda. The first is the decreasing size of the military. While reductions in the number of active-duty military personnel have taken place in all four services, the impact has been especially pronounced in the Army. In 1990, at the end of the cold war, the Army had 732, 403 active-duty soldiers. In 2002, this number was down to 486,542, which was as high as it had been since 1997. The military had sought to soften the blow of these decreased numbers on its operational preparedness through two actions. One was to outsource many tasks to private contractors. They ranged from the mundane (feeding personnel and cutting lawns) to the complex (maintaining tactical systems and drone aircraft), to the highly sensitive (interrogating prisoners). During the Persian Gulf War some military units operated at one contractor for every twenty-five to fifty military personnel. In the Balkans, the ratio was one contractor per ten combatants, and this carried over to the start of the Iraq War.[23] Relying on contractors has raised questions about cost-effectiveness and lines of accountability. The second compensatory action was by relying more heavily on National Guard and reserve forces. Almost 400,000 of the nearly 870,000 members of the reserves have been activated since 9/11. This represents the greatest proportional use of the National Guard and reserves since WW II. As a result the "weekend warrior" image of the National Guard has been severely shaken. Concerns have been expressed for retention and enlistment rates as tours of duty grow longer and allegations surface over differential treatment for active-duty military personnel and reservists.

Also contributing to problems in this area are the costs of major weapons systems. The weapons procurement budget dipped in the early 1990s but has grown steadily since then. By 2008, it is expected to exceed $100 billion. The reasons are easy to find. As originally planned, the Air Force was going to obtain 132 B-2 stealth bombers at a cost of $500 million each. In 1991, that figure was reduced to 75 planes with a per-plane cost of over $2 billion. In 2003, the Navy announced the purchase of 6 nuclear-powered attack submarines for $8.7 billion. It is part of a 30 submarine purchase program that will cost $81 billion, a 24 percent price jump since the price was calculated in 2001. Increased costs are also a problem with less glamorous weapons systems. The Iraq War produced a huge increase in equipment replacement costs. In FY2002, the replacement costs of helicopter blades was $50 million, in FY2003 it rose 300% to $200 million. The cost of replacement tank tracks rose from $78 million to $230 million.

Transforming the structure of the Defense Department is the second major reform issue. The impetus for reform in this area is the passing of the cold war with its predictable set of threats and, especially after 9/11, the emergence of a very different and shifting threat environment. In 2001, the Bush administration's Quadrennial Defense Review moved away from a two-war concept, in which the United States would have to possess the capability of fighting and winning two major wars at the same time, to one which emphasized the need to defeat two aggressors at the same time but removed the requirement of being able to occupy both countries. The 2001 Review also called for the ability to engage in peacekeeping operations while this was happening. More fundamentally according to Secretary of Defense Donald Rumsfeld, the U.S. was moving from a threat based to a capabilities based defense strategy.[24] A draft document called the "Terms of Reference" that lays the foundation for the next Quadrennial Defense Review calls for a more fundamental change placing less emphasis on conventional warfare and a greater emphasis on dealing with insurgencies, terrorism and failed states. The Pentagon is already moving in this direction as evidenced by revelations that Rumsfeld secretly created a Special Support Branch to engage in clandestine activity abroad.

THE DEFENSE DEPARTMENT'S VALUE SYSTEM

Secretary of Defense. Secretaries of defense generally have adopted one of two roles.[25] The first is that of the generalist. According to James Roherty, the generalist recognizes and defers to military expertise. He is concerned with coordinating and integrating the judgments he receives from the military professionals. He sees himself as being the Defense Department's representative in the policy process. In contrast, the functionalist is concerned with consolidating management and policy control in the office of the secretary of defense. The functionalist rejects the notion that there exists a unique area of military expertise, and he sees himself as first among equals in defense policy decision making. Above all else, the functionalist seeks to efficiently manage the system in accordance with presidential policy objectives.

Among the early secretaries of defense, James Forrestal adopted the generalist perspective while Robert McNamara was a functionalist. McNamara's tenure was significant for his efforts to expand the range of issues that the secretary of defense had control over and the methodology used in making decisions. Until McNamara, even functionalist-oriented secretaries of defense largely restricted themselves to managing the budgetary process and mediating between interservice rivalries. McNamara sought and acquired a voice in designing defense policy. In doing so he brought Planning, Programming, and Budgetary Systems (PPBS) analysis to the Defense Department. As was commonplace in other government bureaucracies, the Defense Department's budget was organized by department (Army, Navy, Air Force) and broken down into such traditional categories as personnel, maintenance, and construction. Under PPBS "all military forces and systems were grouped into output-oriented programs according to their principal missions [conventional defense of Europe, nuclear deterrence], even though missions cut across traditional service boundaries categories."[26] Cost-benefit calculations were then made on whether or not to acquire a new system. Based on this type of decision calculus, the B-70 manned bomber, the Skybolt missile, and nuclear naval vessels were rejected while the Poseidon submarine, F-111 fighter, and the Minuteman III missile were accepted.

Donald Rumsfeld, George W. Bush's secretary of defense, established himself from the very outset of the administration as a functionalist who intended to alter the fundamental direction of American military policy and organization. Rumsfeld's tenure in office has been marked by widely varying degrees of success in his efforts at transformation. Prior to the terrorist attacks of 9/11, his outspoken criticism of the military, intrusive management style, and abrasiveness alienated so many that he was widely rumored to be in danger of being forced from office. Victory against the Taliban in Afghanistan and the success of his military strategy of a rapid military advance with minimum forces against Baghdad appeared to vindicate his arguments and greatly elevated his standing in the White House and Congress. Subsequent problems with the occupation and reconstruction of Iraq led to renewed questioning of his ideas and management style. This was particularly true with questions about the chain of command in the interrogation abuses at the Abu Ghraib prison and the inadequate number and overall lack of preparation of U.S. occupation forces.

Professional Military. To understand the system of values operating inside the Defense Department, we must also look at the outlook that the professional military has on policy making. Two different general sets of perspectives exist.[27] The traditional view sees the professional soldier as being above partisan politics. A clear line separates military and political affairs, and professional soldiers are expected to restrict themselves to speaking out only on those subjects falling within their sphere of expertise. In the fusionist perspective the professional soldier must acquire and use political skills if he or she is to exercise an effective voice on military matters. Moreover, the line separating military decisions from political ones is blurred. No pure area of military expertise exists wherein the professional soldier can expect to find his or her opinion accepted without challenge by civilian policy makers. To the fusionist, military involvement in traditional nonmilitary areas is all but guaranteed by the increasing use of the military as an instrument of foreign policy and by problems of resource scarcity.

Differences in outlook also exist among the military services. They each have different "personalities."[28] The Navy, it is said, worships at the altar of tradition, the Air Force at the altar of technology, and the Army at that of country and duty. They also have different views of their own identities. The Navy sees itself above all else as an institution whose stature and independence must be protected. The Air Force sees itself as the embodiment of the idea that air power is the key guarantor of national security in the modern age. The Army views itself as artisans of warfare, whose members are divided into mutually supportive guilds—infantry, artillery, and armor (cavalry). These traits combined with still other differences give each service a distinct outlook on questions of war and peace and the use of force as an instrument of U.S. foreign policy.

One of the most talked about issues today in civil-military relations is the growing dominance of the fusionist perspective along with emerging points of conflict between professional military officers and their civilian counterparts.[29] The split is not total. A study by the Triangle Institute of Security Studies (TISS) found the two groups shared a broad consensus on a number of issues regarding foreign policy goals and the efficacy of the military as an instrument of foreign policy. Supporting the growing fusionist definition, a majority of the officers surveyed believed it was proper for them to engage in public discussions of military policy. The TISS study also found that beneath this area of agreement each side possessed negative and stereotypical attitudes about the other. Officers believe that the military has dealt successfully with many of the social problems that plague civilian society, such as drug use and racial conflict. Civilian leaders do not share their view that the military is a model for cultural reformation. The data on this score do not support the military officer's self-image. In 2001, it was reported that the number of soldiers leaving the military after declaring themselves gay jumped

28 percent to 1,106. This followed the much-publicized beating death of a gay soldier at Fort Campbell in July 1999. Also in 1999, a survey reported that 75 percent of the military's minorities complained that they had experienced racially offensive behavior, and less than half felt that complaints of discrimination were thoroughly investigated.

A second point of intense study is the attitude of military professionals to the much-talked-about "revolution in military affairs" (RMA) that places information technologies at the center of the military process, both in its planning stages and on the battlefield.[30] Implicit in the embrace of RMA is a deemphasis on traditional military values, weapons systems, and structures. Studies conducted in 1999 and 2001 found that officers held widely different views about the value of the RMA that were not related to combat experience but were related to age, with senior officers being more supportive than junior ones. On an abstract level, less than one-half those surveyed felt the United States could remain competitive without radical change, but most were uncertain as to what needed to be done. Nearly half questioned believed their service was on the way toward making radical changes. Each service appeared to have a different read on RMA. Air Force and Navy officers tended to be more receptive to new ways of conducting warfare than Army and Marine Corps officers. These latter two groups of offices were most skeptical about claims that RMA would reduce the duration of conflicts or lower casualties. Not surprisingly Army officers were most convinced of the continued value of armored and mechanized formations and Navy officers were most enthusiastic about the future role of aircraft carrier battle groups. Consensus across services returned when asked about the merits of reducing current readiness to invest in new approaches. More negative responses were given to this question than any other with nearly three-quarters saying they leaned toward strong disagreement with the statement.

FOREIGN POLICY IMPACT

The professional military's foreign policy impact is a subject often discussed with great emotion. Some believe that military professionals are more aggressive than their civilian counterparts. Richard Betts rejects this argument.[31] Where the military professional and the civilian policy maker part company is over how and when to use force, not over whether to use it. The military prefers to use force quickly, massively, and decisively, and it is skeptical of making bluffs that involve the threatened use of force. Diplomats, on the other hand, prefer to avoid using force as long as possible because they see its use as an indication of a failure in policy, but they are positively predisposed to making military threats. Betts also found divisions within the military on advocating the use of force. Since World War II the most bellicose recommendations have come from the Chiefs of Naval Operations and field commanders. The Army Chiefs of Staff have been the most cautious in advocating the use of force.

Betts argues that military influence can operate on four levels in the decision making on military intervention and escalation.[32] The highest level of influence is when the military participates directly in the policy process and makes a negative recommendation against the use of force. Clinton did just this in ordering NATO bombing against Serbia in 1999. The next highest level is when the military participates indirectly in the policy process and opposes the use of force. In these cases the military does not make explicit recommendations against the use of force but presents alternatives or gives only conditional endorsement to the plan. One step below this is when the military participates indirectly in the policy process and favors the use of force. At this level the military's advice is not necessarily accepted, but it still influences the decision to use force through its presentation of data and policy alternatives. At the lowest level of influence, the military's participation is direct, and it supports the use of force. Betts finds that in these cases the military's recommendations are either superfluous (a civilian consensus already exists on the use of force) or rejected. For example, in the Cuban missile crisis, Kennedy rejected a nearly unanimous military recommendation for an armed attack.

Betts concludes that the military's real policy influence comes not through its direct participation in the policy process but through its indirect influence: its ability to get the context of a decision through the presentation of information, capabilities, and tactics. Bob Woodward, author of *The Commanders,* similarly reflects on how variable the influence of the military is on decisions regarding the use of force.[33] The Pentagon, he notes, "is not always the center of military decision making." It was in the months before the Bush administration's invasion of Panama when the attention of the White House was on other matters. In the case of the Persian Gulf War the White House paid attention to little else. "When the President and his advisors are engaged, they run the show." The same can be said for the Iraq War. Planning was not taken out of the hands of the military, but their input into the construction of a war plan was highly structured by Rumsfeld. The Iraq War also highlights the danger of overgeneralizing about the influence of the military. Doubts within the military were not given much weight and were publicly chastised as was Army Chief of Staff Gen. Eric Shinseki who publicly stated early in 2003 that the Bush administration was underestimating the number of forces needed to win the war and occupy postwar Iraq.

The CIA and the Intelligence Community

STRUCTURE AND GROWTH

Created in 1947, the Central Intelligence Agency (CIA) is not the first effort to centralize intelligence within the government. In 1939, Roosevelt established an Interdepartmental Intelligence Committee to coordinate the activities of the FBI, the Office of Naval Intelligence, and the Military Intelligence Division of the War Department.[34] This arrangement proved unsatisfactory, and after experimenting with another organizational arrangement, Roosevelt assigned the task to the Office of Strategic Services (OSS). The OSS was to "collect and analyze strategic information" as directed by the JCS and to "plan and operate such special services" as instructed by it. The OSS, in turn, became a victim of postwar demobilization.

The breakup of the OSS did not end the ongoing dispute over whether a central or federal intelligence system was best suited for the postwar era. In the end the federal principle prevailed when, in 1946, Truman established a National Intelligence Authority (NIA) and a Central Intelligence Group (CIG). The NIA was to plan, develop, and coordinate intelligence. The CIG operated under the direction of the NIA and was headed by a director of Central Intelligence (DCI). Its job was to coordinate, plan, and disseminate intelligence and to carry out covert action. One of the considerable handicaps that the DCI labored under was that all of the people working under him in the CIG were still formally part of other intelligence organizations and, in a sense, were only on loan to him. Both the NIA and CIG were dissolved by the 1947 National Security Act when they were replaced by the NSC and CIA, respectively.

Three points need to be stressed before outlining the makeup of the intelligence community. First, the concept of a community implies similarity and likeness, and it suggests the existence of a group of actors who share common goals and possess a common outlook on events. In these terms the U.S. intelligence community is a community only in the loosest sense. More accurately, it is a federation of units existing with varying degrees of institutional autonomy in their contribution to the intelligence function. Second, the concept of an intelligence community is not inherent in the definition of intelligence or in the common practice among states. The National Security Act of 1947, which created the CIA and assigned it the task of coordinating the activities of other departments, did not use the term *community* or identify those departments whose activities were to be coordinated. Third, the intelligence community is not a static entity. Its composition, as well as the relative importance of its members, has changed over time as new technologies have been developed, the international setting has changed, and bureaucratic wars have been won and lost.

The status of charter member is best conferred upon the CIA; the State Department's intelligence unit, the Bureau of Intelligence and Research (INR); and the intelligence units of the armed forces. All of these were given institutional representation on the NSC at the time of its creation. Three institutions that have a long-standing but lesser presence in the intelligence community are the FBI, the Treasury Department, and the Atomic Energy Commission (AEC) that is now found in the Energy Department. The newest addition to the intelligence community is the Department of Homeland Security. It does not possess an independent intelligence-gathering ability. Its primary intelligence missions are to monitor, assess, and coordinate indications and warnings related to terrorist threats against the United States and to gather and integrate terrorist-related information from its component agencies. Table 10.1 presents a listing of the current members of the intelligence community and their key tasks.

Historically, the most significant additions to the intelligence community have been military-related intelligence agencies. The first addition came

TABLE 10.1   Members of the Intelligence Community

Air Force Intelligence

Army Intelligence

Central Intelligence Agency

Defense Intelligence Agency

Department of Homeland Security

Energy Department

Federal Bureau of Investigation

Marine Corps Intelligence

National Geospatial-Intelligence Agency

National Reconnaissance Office

National Security Agency

Navy Intelligence

State Department

Treasury Intelligence

United States Coast Guard

Source: www.intelligence.gov/ic_brochure

in 1952 when Truman issued a presidential directive transforming the recently created Armed Forces Security Agency into the National Security Agency (NSA).[35] This operates as a semiautonomous agency of the Defense Department and is charged with (1) maintaining the security of U.S. message traffic and (2) interpreting traffic, analyzing, and cryptanalyzing the messages of all other states. In 1961 the Defense Intelligence Agency (DIA) joined the intelligence community as its newest major member. The Defense Intelligence Agency emerged as part of the centralization process then occurring within the Defense Department. The major objectives behind its creation were to unify the overall intelligence efforts of the Defense Department and to more effectively collect, produce, and disseminate military intelligence. Over the years, DIA emerged as the principal challenger to the CIA in the preparation of intelligence estimates. Under George W. Bush, the challenge to the CIA came from a newly created Office of Special Plans (OSP). Its mission was to provide an independent review of raw intelligence and dispute the mainstream interpretations given to it by the intelligence community. Both the CIA's and OSP's intelligence analysis prior to the Iraq War came in for criticism but for different reasons. The CIA was criticized for missing warnings of the 9/11 attack and its failure to express its doubts over the quality of intelligence behind the decision to go to war. OSP was criticized for "cherry-picking" intelligence that suited the pro-war case being advanced by Rumsfeld and Cheney and "stovepiping" it forward out of normal channels into the intelligence estimating process.

Organizationally, the CIA is divided into five operational components. Each is headed by a deputy director who reports to the DCI.[36] The Directorate of Administration is responsible for recruitment, training, support activities, communications, and the physical security of CIA buildings. The Directorate of Science and Technology (DS&T) is the newest major directorate. It was established in the early 1960s out of the conviction that technology had begun to change the nature of the intelligence function and that the CIA had to stay on top of this trend. The results of these efforts have been considerable. The U-2 and SR-71 spy planes and satellite reconnaisance systems all owe much to the efforts of this directorate.

The third operating unit of the CIA is the Directorate of Intelligence (DI). The DI is the primary producer of government intelligence documents which range in frequency from daily briefs (at varying levels of secrecy) to weekly, quarterly, and yearly summaries, to occasional special reports. The best known of these reports are the National Intelligence Estimates (NIEs). Until 1973 they were produced by the Office of National Estimates, which was part of the DI. At that time the office was replaced by a National Intelligence Officer system that currently operates out of the DCI's office. The change was made in order to increase the responsiveness of the intelligence community to policy maker needs and to improve the overall quality of the product. The purpose of an NIE remains the same: to present the intelligence community's best judgment on a given topic. Using 1982 as an example, sixty-seven NIEs were produced; the DCI requested twenty-one of them, and approximately that same number were done on a routine basis; 58 percent of them were drafted in DI while another 24 percent were drafted by the National Intelligence Center, which supervises the work of the National Intelligence Officers. The Soviet Union was typically the most frequent subject of an NIE. Europe, the Near East, and Latin America were also frequent subjects. The time required to put together an NIE varies widely. In 1982 thirty-one of the sixty-seven NIEs were "time urgent" and produced under a tight deadline.

The fourth directorate is the Directorate for Operations (DO). It has been the most controversial component within the CIA. The major problem identified today is the failure to shift resources away from the cold war communist threats to the newly emerging threats of terrorism and rogue states. In particular, its leadership has been chastised for failing to place agents within Saddam Hussein's Iraq or in Taliban controlled Afghanistan. Earlier complaints focused on its unlawful foreign activities and produced calls for its splitting off from the CIA or outright abolition. Like the DI, it was created in 1952. The Directorate for Operations has three basic missions: the clandestine collection of information, counterintelligence, and covert action. Within DO there exists a staff for each mission. The Foreign Intelligence Service monitors, assesses, and directs the clandestine collection of information; the counterintelligence staff is concerned with protecting the CIA from foreign penetrations; and the covert action staff plans and carries out covert action. The actual operations of DO are grouped on regional lines and subdivided into stations. Each station is headed by a station chief and is generally housed in the U.S. embassy. Their size varies from that of only a few individuals to several hundred. The last directorate, for planning and coordination, was set up in 1990. It is to focus on identifying the changing requirements for intelligence in today's world.

Periodically throughout its history, the CIA has found itself to be an institution under siege. As we will detail in Chapter 14, this has usually been because of failings in the area of covert action. Since the 1990s, however, it is the CIA's intelligence failures that have led to demands for reform, restructuring, and transferring its duties to other agencies. Well before 9/11 calls for action came from all quarters. In the Senate, Daniel Patrick Moynihan, who once chaired the Senate Select Committee on Intelligence, was so outraged over the CIA's failure to anticipate the fall of communism in the Soviet Union that he called for its abolition. Post–cold war Directors of Central Intelligence Robert Gates and R. James Woolsey commented publicly on the need for the CIA to undertake institutional changes and reexamine its intelligence priorities.[37] In November 1991, President George H. W. Bush issued National Security Directive 29 calling for a "top to bottom examination of the mission, role, and priorities of the intelligence community." President Bill Clinton issued a classified executive order that for the first time established formal priorities for intelligence agencies. At the top of the list were renegade states such as Iraq, Iran, and North Korea. Also receiving high priority were weapons proliferation and transnational forces such as Muslim Fundamentalism.

Demands for reform were a common theme in the investigations conducted by the House and Senate intelligence committees, and the special commission set up to investigate 9/11. Included in the commission's recommendations were the creation of a new national terrorism center and the establishment of a cabinet-level post of Director of National Intelligence to oversee the CIA, FBI, and other intelligence agencies. Support was strong in Congress for such reforms but they were opposed within the Executive Branch. The CIA called them unnecessary and the Defense Department feared the budgetary and control implications of a new national director of intelligence. An estimated 80 to 90 percent of the intelligence budget is allocated to Pentagon intelligence units. Under pressure to act and in the middle of a close election campaign a reluctant President George W. Bush endorsed the concept of a White House-based national intelligence director in August. The position was officially created in December 2004 with the signing into law of the Intelligence Reform and Terrorism Prevention Act. John Negroponte, a career diplomat who was serving as ambassador to Iraq, was named by the president to be the first national intelligence chief. He is the president's chief advisor on intelligence matters but did not obtain the budgetary power sought by many reformers.

THE INTELLIGENCE COMMUNITY'S VALUE SYSTEM

Criticism of the CIA was not directed only at its structure. Also coming in for censure was the manner in which both its top leadership and professionals approached their job. The Senate intelligence committee's report placed a major portion of the blame for the intelligence failures on Iraq and before 9/11 on "a broken corporate culture and poor management." It is to this side of the CIA that we now turn.

Director of Central Intelligence.   The DCI simultaneously is head of the intelligence community and the CIA. Because of this dual position, DCIs have many role orientations available to choose from. Few have sought, and none have achieved, real managerial control over the intelligence community. The most recent to try was Stansfield Turner, Carter's DCI, who ran into stiff and successful resistance from Secretary of Defense Brown. The DCIs have not given priority to their role as head of the intelligence community because significant weaknesses lie beneath their formal position. Of all the members of the intelligence community, only the CIA exists as a separate organizational entity; all the others are parts of larger departments, most often the Defense Department. Consequently, the other members of the intelligence community look with only one eye to what the DCI demands while keeping the other eye firmly fixed on departmental positions and priorities. As a result, the DCI's budgetary authority over the other members of the intelligence community remains largely unrealized, and his ability to direct their collection efforts is imperfect.

When defining their role as head of the CIA, three outlooks have been dominant: managerial, covert action, and estimating. Only John McCone (1961 to 1965) gave primacy to the intelligence estimating role, and he was largely an outsider to the intelligence process before his appointment. Allen Dulles (1953 to 1965) and Richard Helms (1966 to 1973), both stressed the covert action side of the agency's mission. Since the replacement of Helms by James Schlesinger, DCIs have tended to adopt a managerial orientation. Although their particular operating styles have varied, a common theme to these managerial efforts was to increase White House control over the CIA.

Controversy has surrounded the managerial orientations of recent DCIs. A criticism directed at both Robert Gates and R. James Woolsey was that they were ill-suited to managing the CIA's transition to the post–cold war world: Gates because he was too much of a cold warrior and Woolsey because he was an outsider to the intelligence community with no internal base of support to build on. Gates, a protégé of Casey, encountered unprecedented public opposition from active and retired intelligence professionals when nominated for the post by George H. W. Bush.[38] At the heart of their critique was the charge that as Director of Intelligence under Casey, Gates had politicized the intelligence process. By this they meant that he had tightened managerial control over the intelligence product to the point that its conclusions were being driven by the policy concerns and values of senior management. If Gates embodied the dangers inherent in an overly intrusive managerial style, Woolsey came to symbolize the problems that arise when an outsider DCI tries to manage change without the support of the White House. Clinton frequently did not attend the CIA's daily White House briefing, and Woolsey's access to the president reportedly was blocked by National Security Adviser Anthony Lake. John Deutch, still another outsider to intelligence, replaced Woolsey in 1995. By his own admission, he was uncomfortable with the CIA's culture and was frustrated by his inability to bring about meaningful reform. He resigned fifteen months later. Deutch was replaced by George Tenet, who earlier in his career had served as staff director for the Senate Intelligence

Committee. Tenet was described as the "ultimate staff guy," and his appointment was seen as proof of "the rewards of being a loyal and obedient servant of one's boss."[39] Tenet retained his position as DCI under George W. Bush and true to his past, he quickly became regarded as a team player. In doing so, he reestablished the CIA's access to the White House, meeting with Bush several times a week in contrast to Woolsey, who described his relationship with Clinton as "nonexistent." Tenet has adopted a managerial outlook that stresses providing information and not policy input. Under Tenet, the CIA's foreign policy role has expanded in unexpected ways as he and the CIA played major roles as mediators in attempting to broker an Arab–Israeli peace agreement.

Tenet resigned in June 2004. He had become a central figure in the debate over whether the CIA as an organization or he personally had overstated the case for war with Iraq. He was replaced by J. Peter Goss, a retired CIA official and member of Congress who chaired the House Intelligence Committee. Goss left no doubt that his primary orientation was to serve the president and moved quickly to exert control over the CIA by bringing about the resignation of several high ranking officials. At the same time the creation of a new position to oversee all intelligence expenditures placed limits on his ability to exert control beyond the agency's boundaries. The reach of his managerial powers was further called into question by revelations that the Defense Department had set up a clandestine intelligence unit of its own.

Intelligence Professionals.   In order to understand how the intelligence professional thinks about intelligence, we first need to note how the consumers of intelligence think about it because it is their demands and inquiries that the intelligence professional responds to.[40] First is the conviction that analysts should furnish information and nothing more. Analysts are not expected to explore alternatives or come to conclusions—this is the responsibility of the consumer. The underlying assumption is that the facts contain self-evident implications and that if all the facts are known, then any question can be answered. Second is the assumption that experience rather than the application of analytical techniques to a problem provides the most insight into the meaning of raw data. Third is an emphasis on current events. The perceived need is for up-to-the-minute information to solve an ongoing problem. Long-range planning is too academic an exercise and too far removed from the policy maker's most immediate concerns to be highly valued. A final shared attitude toward intelligence is the tendency to treat it as a free good. Intelligence is seen as something "on tap" and always on call.

The views on intelligence existing within the intelligence community are far from uniform. Differences exist both between and within organizations.[41] With this qualification in mind, it is possible to identify four tendencies in the approach to intelligence adopted by members of the intelligence community.[42] One tendency is to be current events-oriented, to be a "butcher," cutting up the latest information and presenting the choicest pieces to the consumer. This perspective appears to be adopted only grudgingly by analysts out of a desire to participate in the policy process. Analysts see their most important role as that of giving warning, but to stick to this role orientation in the face of policy maker disinterest condemns them to working on the fringe of the policy process. A second tendency is for analysts to adopt a "jigsaw theory" of intelligence. The analyst here acts like a "baker"; everything and anything is sought after, classified, and stored on the assumption that at some point in time it may be the missing ingredient to solving a riddle. Like the butcher, the baker's role orientation is consistent with the policy maker's notion of intelligence as a free good and the assumption that the ambiguity of data can be overcome by collecting more data.

A third tendency is for the production of "intelligence to please" or "backstopping." Often when consumers of intelligence stress current data, they combine it with known policy preferences. The analyst is then placed in a very difficult position. Efforts at providing anything but supportive evidence will be ignored. Decisions on troop strength in Vietnam and target selection for bombing and rescue raids reveal the extent to which pressures to produce "intelligence to please" can be felt and the detrimental effect this can have on the intelligence function. The final role orientation is that of the "intelligent maker" who acts as an organizational broker forging a consensus on the issue at hand. Because a consensus is needed for action, this role orientation is valuable, but a danger exists in that the consensus does not have to be based on an accurate reading of events. Facts bargained into existence provide an equally suitable basis for a consensus.

FOREIGN POLICY IMPACT

The purpose of intelligence is to provide policy makers with enough warning to allow them to act in the face of a challenge to national security. This is not easily done. Surprise is a fundamental reality of international politics, and no foreign policy or defense establishment can expect to escape completely from its negative consequences. Yet intelligence is not easily integrated into the policy process.[43] The conventional wisdom holds that policy and analysis must be kept separate, or policy will corrupt analysis. The alternative view holds that analysis cannot be kept value free or separate from policy making. The position holds that analysts must articulate and evaluate policy options as well as force policy makers to confront alternatives.

The relationship between the CIA and the president is the key determinant of its impact on the policy process. This relationship is marked by a series of tensions that often serve to make the impact of intelligence on policy less than what it could be under optimum circumstances. The first tension is between the logic of intelligence and the logic of policy-making.[44] The logic of intelligence is to reduce policy options by clarifying issues, assumptions, and consequences. The logic of policy-making is to keep options open for as long as possible. One way to do this is to keep secrets from intelligence agencies. The second tension is between the type of information the president wants to receive and the type of information that the intelligence community is predisposed to collect and disseminate. Commenting on his experience at INR, Thomas Hughes states that policy makers were most eager to get information that would help them convince Congress or the public about the merits of a policy. They were most frustrated with information that was politically impossible to use and generally skeptical about the incremental value of added information for policy-making purposes.[45] Third, intelligence produced by the intelligence community is not the only source of information available to policy makers. Interest groups, lobbyists, the media, and personal acquaintances all compete with it, and presidents are free to choose which intelligence they wish to listen to. No one can make a policy maker accept or act on a piece of intelligence.

The Domestic Bureaucracies

The most recent additions to the foreign affairs bureaucracy are organizations that have been classified traditionally as domestic in their concerns and areas of operation. Raymond Hopkins argues that the foreign policy involvement of these agencies parallels a process that happened earlier with the Defense Department. After World War II the Defense Department was instrumental in shaping global arms development programs and international security arrangements.[46] A similar process is at work in the areas of food, energy, and raw material production. The responsibility for the international management of these commodities has fallen on the U.S. government and, more specifically, non–State Department agencies. Hopkins cautions that there is nothing irreversible in this trend to greater involvement in international affairs. There is no reason why in the future the domestic bureaucracies might not once again have only a minor foreign policy role.

Integrating these newcomers into the foreign affairs bureaucracy has not been an easy task. At the core of the problem is finding an agreed-upon balance between foreign policy and domestic concerns. In the early postwar period, the foreign policy goal of containing communism dominated over private economic goals, but more recently, domestic goals have become dominant and are often pursued at the cost of broad foreign policy objectives.

TREASURY, COMMERCE, AND AGRICULTURE

Foremost among the domestic bureaucracies are the Treasury, Commerce, and Agriculture departments. By the mid-1970s the State Department had become more of a participant than a leader in the field of international economic policy. Its chief bureaucratic challenger is the Treasury Department, and the two approach international economic policy from quite different perspectives. Like the other domestic bureaucracies, the Treasury Department takes an "America first" perspective and places the needs of its clients at the center of its concerns. One author describes it as having an "undifferentiating adversary attitude" toward world affairs.[47] This is in contrast to the State Department's tendency to adopt a long-range perspective on international economic problems and one sensitive to the position of other states. A type of standoff currently exists between the State Department and Treasury Department for influence in the policy process. Each exercises a virtual veto over intragovernmental agreements on international economic policy. When disagreements arise, the issue gets kicked up the bureaucratic ladder for a decision by higher authorities. However, it now takes a strong secretary of state to neutralize the influence of the Treasury Department and its domestic allies.[48]

The Commerce Department has also emerged as a major foreign affairs bureaucracy, but its influence is not on the level of the Treasury Department's. It still functions as somewhat of a junior partner and is more involved in operating issues than in policy ones. Until 1969 the Commerce Department's primary foreign policy involvement stemmed from its job of overseeing U.S. export control policy. These controls were largely aimed at restricting the direct or indirect sale of strategic goods to communist states. In 1969 its mandate was expanded to include encouraging "peaceful trade with the East" while at the same time "vigilantly protecting" U.S. national security interests. Since 1980 the Commerce Department has become the primary implementor of nonagricultural trade policy and the chief administrator of U.S. export and import programs. As part of this task, it supervises the enforcement of antidumping regulations and the distribution of assistance to those industries injured because of lower-priced imports. Through its Foreign Commercial Service, the Commerce Department has representatives stationed in 66 countries and has become active in export promotion activities. The Commerce Department is not without its own challengers for influence on trade policy. The Office of the U.S. Trade Representative has also benefited at the expense of the State Department and enjoys a great deal of congressional support for its activities.

The Agriculture Department also remains a junior partner in the foreign affairs bureaucracy. It is active in administering U.S. food export programs throughout the world and has representatives in approximately 40 embassies. Its best-known foreign policy role is as the administrator of P.L. 480, the Food for Peace program, which provides for the free export of government-owned agricultural commodities for humanitarian and developmental purposes. In 2003, the Agriculture Department became embroiled in controversy for providing export help to American tobacco companies. The Foreign Agriculture Service provided market information to firms about where the demand for American cigarettes was high and where control laws were weak.

HOMELAND SECURITY

The Department of Homeland Security was established on November 25, 2002 as a response to the terrorist attacks of 9/11. Its creation combined 22 different agencies from 8 different departments with a projected budget of $37.45 million and 170,000 employees into one. It absorbed all of the Federal Emergency Management Agency, the Coast Guard, Secret Service, the Immigration and Naturalization Service, and the Customs Service along with the new Transportation and Security Administration. The FBI and CIA would not be affected by the creation of the Department of Homeland Security, but the new department was to have an "intelligence and threat analysis" unit that would serve as a customer of FBI and CIA intelligence for purposes of assessing threats, taking preventive action, and issuing public warnings.

Conceptually the Department of Homeland Security is built on four pillars. The first is border and transportation security. Its mission is to prevent terrorists and materials they might use from entering the United States. The second pillar is emergency preparedness and response. It will be the lead force in coordinating efforts by the private sector, and federal, state, and local agencies in responding to and preparing for terrorist attacks. The third pillar is responsibility for chemical, biological, radiological and nuclear counterterrorism measures. The focus is on preventing the importation of these materials as well as detecting, preventing, protecting against, and responding to terrorist attacks using them. The fourth and final pillar centers on information analysis and infrastructure protection. Its purpose is to assess terrorist threats and to determine the vulnerability of key resources and critical infrastructure to possible terrorist attacks and then develop countermeasures.

Newness does not exempt the Department of Homeland Security from the challenges of policy coordination and programmatic coherence that we noted in the beginning of the chapter. The policy coordination problem is simply stated. While billed as the largest reorganization since the creation of the Defense Department, by the Bush administration's own calculations creating the Department of Homeland Security it still left at least seventy-eight units involved in homeland security outside of the new department. Foremost among them were the Defense Department, FBI, CIA, and Center for Disease Control. Programmatic coherence problems stem in part from the fact that homeland security is not a self defining term. For example, President George W. Bush's *National Strategy for Homeland Security* released in July 2002 targeted six critical mission areas while the organizational structure of Department of Homeland Security identifies four pillars of activity. This lack of definitional clarity finds expression in the department's budgets that have come under repeated attack for providing insufficient funds for "first responders." Programmatic incoherence also results from the unwillingness of affected agencies, most notably the CIA, FBI, and Defense, to voluntarily cede power to it.

Summary and Future Issues

Viewed solely in terms of lines on an organizational chart, the foreign affairs bureaucracy offers presidents a powerful set of organizations to use in pursuit of their foreign policy agendas. Looked at from the perspective of values and roles, a more challenging picture emerges. The bureaucracy cannot be used as freely as would be liked. Not only must coordination be achieved between and within organizations, but the way in which bureaucrats approach their jobs must also be addressed. The problem of forging a consensus is a real and enduring one because different bureaucratic units see different sides of an issue.

In looking to the future, we see that the greatest challenge in each of the bureaucratic areas we highlighted will be creating what Paul Bracken refers to as "the military after next."[49] Bracken observes that it will not be very hard to anticipate the shape of the next U.S. military. It will be a product of trends and pressures either already in place or that are very visible. Much of this military is already in place. Where creative thinking needs to take place is in looking beyond the next decade to the military after it, that we must soon begin to create and that will be in place thirty years from now. Bracken argues that the next military, the one whose structure, roles, and missions we are presently debating, will be all but blind to fundamental changes in the international system as it struggles to find solutions for the immediate problems confronting it. He asserts that in thinking about the "military after next" we must reexamine such fundamental concepts as hierarchy, span of control, and response time. Even more fundamentally, Bracken states that we must rethink the competitive environment in which the United States operates, find new ways to distinguish among military competitors, and devise strategies to deal with each. Extending Bracken's arguments, the need also exists to begin thinking about the "CIA after next," the "State Department after next," and the "Treasury Department after next." The demands for reforming the CIA highlight one of the difficulties of thinking about future reforms. Historically, the CIA problem was controlling overly zealous individuals and organizations. The problem identified by the various 9/11 investigations is how to get individuals and organizations to be more aggressive in pursuing intelligence and analyzing it.[50]

Cost will emerge as an important constraint in the ability to re-create the foreign affairs bureaucracy. Richard Gardner observes that "a dangerous game is being played in Washington."[51] He refers to it as the "one percent solution." This is the notion that a successful foreign policy can be constructed on the basis of about 1 percent of the federal budget. Calculated on a per capita basis, every American currently contributes $29 per year to development and humanitarian aid. Gardner concludes that doing our fair share in sustainable development funding would require about $10 billion more per year by FY2005. That would raise American aid levels back up to the level they were at twenty years ago.

We conclude by noting one of the classic defenses of the State Department's performance. When asked by President Kennedy what was wrong with the State Department, career diplomat Charles Bohlen replied, "You are."[52] George Ball, also a career diplomat, seconds this observation by suggesting that the State Department is being used by presidents as a scapegoat for foreign policy failures. Presidents claim all of the successes but none of the failures.[53] Diplomats are not alone in this view that much of what is wrong with the foreign affairs bureaucracy is the doing of elected officials. The professional military view was that escalation in Vietnam would fail. They also believed that when the war ended and the civilians who championed escalation were no longer in office, the professional military would be left to shoulder the blame for what went wrong.[54]

Notes

1. Henry Kissinger, "Conditions of World Order," *Daedalus,* 95 (1966), 503–29.
2. Amy Zegart, "The Organization and Architecture of Nonproliferation," in Janne Nolan et al. (eds.), *Ultimate Security* (New York: Century Foundation Press, 2003), 17–44.
3. Victor A. Thompson, *Modern Organization* (New York: Knopf, 1961).

4. On the volume of State Department message traffic, see Werner Feld, *American Foreign Policy: Aspirations and Reality* (New York: Wiley & Sons, 1984), p. 61; and Gene Rainey, *Patterns of American Foreign Policy* (Boston: Allyn & Bacon, 1975), p. 175.

5. Henry T. Nash, *American Foreign Policy: A Search for Security,* 3rd ed. (Homewood, Ill.: Dorsey, 1985), pp. 134–35.

6. Leslie H. Gelb, "Why Not the State Department," in Charles W. Kegley Jr., and Eugene R. Wittkopf (eds.), *Perspectives on American Foreign Policy: Selected Readings* (New York: St. Martin's, 1983), p. 286.

7. Glenn Kessler, "State-Defense Policy Rivalry Intensifying," *The Washington Post,* April 22, 2002, A1.

8. Glenn Kessler, "Powell Flies in the Face of Tradition," *The Washington Post,* July 14, 2004, A1.

9. Donald P. Warwick, *A Theory of Public Bureaucracy: Politics, Personality and Organization in the State Department* (Cambridge, Mass.: Harvard University Press, 1975), pp. 29–30.

10. *Washington Post,* March 28, 1986, p. 13.

11. David Corn, "At the Foggy Bottom of the Barrel, Political Hacks," *Washington Post,* January 10, 1993, p. C3.

12. John M. Goshko, "Foreign Service's Painful Passage to Looking More Like America," *Washington Post,* April 21, 1994, p. 29.

13. Ibid.

14. In addition to other studies cited in this chapter, see Andrew Scott, "The Department of State: Formal Organization and Informal Culture," *International Studies Quarterly,* 13 (1969), 1–18; and his "Environmental Change and Organizational Adaptation: The Problem of the State Department," *International Studies Quarterly,* 14 (1970), 85–94.

15. John Harr, *The Professional Diplomat* (Princeton, N.J.: Princeton University Press, 1969), pp. 197–98.

16. I. M. Destler, *Presidents, Bureaucrats, and Foreign Policy: The Politics of Organizational Reform* (Princeton, N.J.: Princeton University Press, 1972), p. 158.

17. Cited in Harr, *The Professional Diplomat,* p. 230.

18. Robert Pringle, "Creeping Irrelevance at Foggy Bottom," *Foreign Policy,* 29 (1977/78), 128–39; and Warwick, *A Theory of Public Bureaucracy,* p. 72.

19. Lawrence Eagleburger and Robert L. Barry, "Dollars and Sense Diplomacy," *Foreign Affairs,* 75 (1996), 2–8.

20. Newt Gingrich, "Rogue State Department," *Foreign Policy,* 137 (2003), 42–48.

21. Nash, *American Foreign Policy,* p. 141.

22. For a discussion on the pros and cons of reorganizing the JCS system, see William J. Lynn and Barry R. Posen, "The Case for JCS Reform," *International Security,* 10 (1985/86), 69–97; MacKubin Thomas Owen, "The Hollow Promise of JCS Reform," *International Security,* 10 (1985/86), 98–111; and Edward Luttwak, *The Pentagon and the Art of War* (New York: Touchstone, 1985).

23. Renae Merle, "More Civilians Accompanying U.S. Military," *The Washington Post,* January 22, 2003, A10.

24. Donald Rumsfeld, "Transforming the Military," *Foreign Affairs* 81 (2002), 20–32.

25. James Roherty, "The Office of the Secretary of Defense," in John E. Endicott and Roy W. Stafford (eds.), *American Defense Policy.* 4th ed. (Baltimore, Md.: Johns Hopkins University Press, 1977). pp. 286–96.

26. Amos A. Jordon and William J. Taylor Jr., *American National Security: Policy and Process* (Baltimore, Md.: Johns Hopkins University Press, 1981), p. 185.

27. John H. Garrison, "The Political Dimension of Military Professionalism," in Endicott and Stafford (eds.), *American Defense Policy,* pp. 578–87.

28. Carl Builder, *The Masks of War* (Baltimore, Md.: Johns Hopkins University Press, 1989).

29. On this theme see Don Snider, "America's Postmodern Military," *World Policy Journal,* 17 (2000), 47–53; Thomas Ricks, "The Widening Gap Between the Military and Society," *Atlantic Monthly* (July 1997), 67–78; Ole Holsti, "A Widening Gap Between the U.S. Military and Civilian Society?" *International Security,* 23 (1998/99), 5–42; and the exchange between Holsti and Joseph Collins, "Correspondence," *International Security,* 24 (1999), 199–207.

30. Thomas Mahnken and James FitzSimonds, "Revolutionary Ambivalence," *International Security,* 28 (2003), 112–48.

31. Richard K. Betts, *Soldiers, Statesmen, and Cold War Crises* (Cambridge, Mass.: Harvard University Press, 1977), pp. 4–5.

32. Ibid., pp. 11–12.

33. Bob Woodward, *The Commanders* (New York: Simon and Schuster, 1991), p. 33.

34. Mark M. Lowenthal, *U.S. Intelligence: Evolution and Anatomy*, Washington Paper #105 (New York: Praeger, 1984), pp. 5–15.

35. James Bamford, *The Puzzle Palace: Inside the National Security Agency* (Baltimore, Md.: Penguin, 1982).

36. Lowenthal, *U.S. Intelligence*, pp. 89–92; and Stafford Thomas, *The U.S. Intelligence Community* (Latham, Md.: University of America Press, 1983), pp. 45–63.

37. See, for example, Herbert Meyer, "Reinventing the CIA," *Global Affairs*, 7 (1992), 1–13; and Marvin Ott, "Shaking Up the CIA," *Foreign Policy*, 93 (1993), 132–51.

38. See, for example, the comments made by Harold Ford and Jennifer Glaudemans in *Hearings before the Select Committee on Intelligence of the United States Senate on the Nomination of Robert M. Gates to be Director of Central Intelligence,* vol. II (Washington, D.C.: U.S. Government Printing Office, 1991).

39. Tim Weiner, "For the 'Ultimate Staff Guy,' a Time to Reap the Rewards of Being Loyal," *New York Times*, national edition, March 26, 1997, p. A14.

40. Roger Hilsman, *Strategic Intelligence and National Defense* (Glencoe, Ill.: Free Press, 1956), pp. 37–56.

41. For a discussion of these points, see Patrick J. McGarvey, *The CIA: The Myth and the Madness* (Baltimore, Md.: Penguin, 1973), pp. 148–59; and Victor Marchetti and John D. Marks, *The CIA and the Cult of Intelligence* (New York: Dell, 1974), pp. 235–77.

42. Hilsman, *Strategic Intelligence and National Defense*, pp. 199–222; and Thomas L. Hughes, *The Fate of Facts in a World of Men* (New York: Foreign Policy Association, Headline Series #233, 1976), pp. 36–60.

43. Sherman Kent, *Strategic Intelligence for American World Policy* (Princeton, N.J.: Princeton University Press, 1966); and Willmoore Kendall, "The Functions of Intelligence," *World Politics*, 2 (1949), 542–52.

44. Hughes, *Fate of Facts in a World of Men*, p. 47.

45. Thomas Hughes, "The Power to Speak and the Power to Listen: Reflections on Bureaucratic Politics and a Recommendation on Information Flows," in Thomas M. Franck and Edward Weisband (eds.), *Secrecy and Foreign Policy* (New York: Oxford University Press, 1974), p. 18.

46. Raymond Hopkins, "The International Role of 'Domestic Bureaucracies,'" *International Organization*, 30 (1976), p. 111.

47. Stephen D. Cohen, *The Making of United States International Economic Policy: Principles, Problems, and Proposals for Reform*, 2nd ed. (New York: Praeger, 1981), p. 40.

48. Ibid., p. 41.

49. Paul Bracken, "The Military after Next," *Washington Quarterly*, 16 (1993), 157 74.

50. Richard Betts, "The New Politics of Intelligence," *Foreign Affairs* 83 (2004), 2–8.

51. Richard Gardner, "The One Percent Solution," *Foreign Affairs*, 79 (2000), 2–11.

52. Quoted in Destler, *Presidents, Bureaucrats, and Foreign Policy*, p. 155.

53. Quoted in Cecil Crabb Jr., *American Foreign Policy in the Nuclear Age*, 4th ed. (New York: Harper & Row, 1983), p. 102.

54. Betts, *Soldiers, Statesmen, and Cold War Crises*, p. 11.

— *11* —

Models of Policy Making: Overview

Roger Hilsman, a former policy maker and the author of many pieces on U.S. foreign policy, states that "the business of Washington is making decisions."[1] Our purpose in this chapter is to get a better understanding of how policy makers come together to make foreign policy decisions. For a number of reasons, this is easier said than done. First, no single decision-making process exists. Decisions are arrived at in a number of ways. They may be made by an individual, a small group, an organization, or some combination of them. In each case the procedures followed and the methods used to make the decision may vary. Second, the notion of *a decision* is itself somewhat misleading. It suggests the existence of a specific point in time at which a conscious judgment is made on what to do about a problem. Reality is often far less organized. Decisions are seldom final or decisive; they tend to lack concrete beginning and end points; and they often amount to only temporary breathing spells or truces before the issue is raised again. Decisions are also often made with far less attention to their full meaning and consequences than is commonly recognized. "A government does not decide to inaugurate the nuclear age, but only to try and build the bomb before its enemy does."[2]

A final factor complicating efforts to understand how policy is made is the relationship of the policy process to policy outcomes. Our intuitive sense is that if the policy process can be made to work properly, then the policy outcome should also work. Accordingly, bad policy can be attributed, at least in part, to bad policy making. Unfortunately, the link between the two is imperfect. Good policy making does not ensure good policy. In a provocative account of the U.S. experience in Vietnam, Leslie Gelb and Richard Betts argue that the irony of Vietnam is that while U.S. policy has been roundly criticized, the policy-making system worked.[3] It achieved its basic purpose of preventing a communist victory until domestic political opinion coalesced around either a strategy of victory or withdrawal. The political system produced policies responsive to the wishes of the majority and near the political center while at the same time allowing virtually all views to be aired. The bureaucracy selected and implemented measures designed to accomplish these ends, and these policies were undertaken without illusion about their ultimate chances of success.

In an effort to make sense out of the complicated business of making decisions, models have been developed to help explain, describe, predict, and evaluate how U.S. foreign policy is made. Models are analytical tools that are designed to serve as a simplified representation of reality. As a simplification they leave out much of the detail and texture of what goes on in the policy-making process in an effort to isolate and highlight what are felt to be the most salient features. Models can be distinguished from one another in terms of how they seek to capture and depict reality. The critical task for the foreign policy analyst is deciding how to select from the range of models available and combine them in an insightful fashion.

In this chapter we survey five of the most frequently used models of U.S. foreign policy making.[4] The next chapter presents case studies that illustrate how these models can be used to gain insight into how U.S. foreign policy is made. Before turning our attention to the models, two final caveats need to be raised. First, we are not arguing that policy makers consciously choose one of these models and act accordingly. We are only arguing that these models can help us understand what is happening in the policy-making process. Policy makers are not ignorant of the existence of these models, but their actions are far more likely to be governed by the complexities, uncertainties, and time constraints inherent in the policy-making process. Second, these models should not be judged in terms of being right or wrong. A more useful standard is how helpful the model is for explaining, describing, or evaluating the workings of the foreign policy process for the policy you are studying.

The Rational Actor Model

The most frequently employed policy-making model is the rational actor model. At its core is an action-reaction process. Foreign policy is viewed as a calculated response to the actions of another actor. This action then produces a calculated response that in turn causes the state to reevaluate and readjust its own foreign policy. In carrying out these calculations, the state is seen as being unitary and rational. By unitary it is meant that the state can be viewed as calculating and responding to external events as if it were a single entity. There is no need for the analyst to delve into the intricacies of governmental organization, domestic politics, or personalities in trying to understand why a policy was selected. The state can be treated as a "black box," responding with one voice to the challenges and opportunities confronting it. We implicitly employ this model when we speak of Israeli goals, Argentine national interests, or Soviet adventurism.

The calculations by which a foreign policy is selected are assumed to be rational. The basic elements of a rational decision process are (1) goals are clearly stated and ranked in order of preference, (2) all options are considered, (3) the consequences of each option are assessed, and (4) a value-maximizing choice is made. Broadly speaking, there are two ways of carrying out a rational actor analysis of policy making. The first is inductive. It is frequently employed in diplomatic histories. The analyst tries to understand the foreign policy decision by placing himself or herself in the position of the government taking the action. The objective is to appreciate the situation as the government sees it and to understand the logic of the situation. The second approach is deductive. It is best exemplified by game theory and is frequently employed by military strategists and deterrence theorists. Here it is assumed that "a certain kind of conduct is inherent in a particular situation or relationship."[5] Rather than relying on actual events to support its analysis, the deductive approach relies on logical and mathematical formulations of how states should (rationally) behave under given conditions.

The rational actor model is attractive because it places relatively few informational demands upon the observer. It is also frequently criticized for essentially the same reason: It understates the complexity of foreign affairs and the reality of the policy process. Foreign policy is not just made in response to external events, but also is heavily influenced by domestic political calculations, personalities, and organizational factors. In addition, the rational actor model assumes that "important events have important causes." By doing so, it downgrades the importance of chance, accidents, and coincidence in foreign affairs. Critics also contend that the model's information-processing demands exceed human capabilities. Goals are seldom stated clearly or rank ordered. The full range of policy options and their consequences are rarely evaluated. And in making decisions the need for value trade-offs is denied more than it is faced up to. In place of the assumption of rationality, many critics advance a model based on an incremental decision-making process in which goals are only loosely stated, a limited range of options is examined, and the policy selected is one that "satisfies" (from *satisfactory* and *sufficient*) rather than optimizes.[6]

A final challenge to the rational actor model centers on its methodology. Carried out either inductively or deductively, the rational actor model relies heavily on intuition and personal judgment in interpreting actions or placing weights on policy payoffs. Graham Allison has captured this criticism in his "rationality theorem."[7] He states that there isn't a pattern of activity for which an imaginative analyst cannot find objectives that are maximized by a given course of action.

Bureaucratic Politics Model

Bureaucratic politics is the "process by which people inside government bargain with one another on complex public policy questions."[8] As this definition suggests, the bureaucratic politics model approaches policy making in a completely different way from the rational actor model. Policy making is seen as a political process dominated by conflict resolution and not problem solving. Politics dominates the decision-making process because no individual is in a position to decide on matters alone. Power is shared, and the individuals who share power disagree on what should be done because they are located at different places within the government and see different faces of the problem. Using military force to punish terrorists looks different to a secretary of state who must balance the diplomatic pluses and minuses of such a move than it does to the military chiefs of staff whose forces would be used or to a presidential aide who is perhaps most sensitive to the domestic implications of the success or failure of such a mission.

Not everyone in the government is a participant in a particular policy-making "game." The political bargaining process is constrained by the organizational context within which policy makers operate. Fixed organizational routines define the issue, produce the information on which policy decisions are made, link institutions and individuals together, and place limits on the types of policy options that can be implemented. Furthermore, the players in the game are not equal in their ability to influence the outcome of the bargaining process. Deadlines, the rules of the game, and action channels confer power to some and deny it to others. Rules determine what kind of behavior is permitted and by whom. Can unilateral statements be made, or must the decision be cleared by a committee? Can information be leaked? Action channels link policy makers together and determine who is in the best position to leak information, make a unilateral statement, or be included in a committee that approves action. Deadlines force issues by accelerating the tempo of the decision-making process and creating pressure for an agreement. Deadlines come in many forms: a meeting with a foreign head of state, a presidential press conference or speech, the adjournment of Congress, and the beginning of a fiscal year. Congress may also establish deadlines. It established a recurring deadline in 1977 when it required that the Secretary of State report annually to Congress on human rights conditions in every state receiving U.S. development assistance.

Rarely do policy problems enter or leave the policy process in a clearly definable manner. More frequently, they flow through it in a fragmented state and become entangled in other ongoing policy issues. The result is that policy is not formulated with respect to any underlying conception of the U.S. national interest. Instead, its content is heavily influenced by the way in which the problem first surfaces and how it interacts with the other issues on the policy agenda. A recent example is the George W. Bush administration's misstep in handling its decision to withdraw from the Kyoto Protocol. Environmental Protection Agency head Christine Whitman sought to take the lead in this policy area and assured European leaders that the administration would act to control carbon dioxide emissions. Secretary of State Colin Powell also endorsed this position. Yet Bush chose to reject their advice, responding to pressure from congressional Republicans and lobbyists from the coal and steel industries. Bush's decision placed the United States on the defensive in its meetings over the next several months with European and Japanese leaders who saw it as another troubling example of the Bush administration's penchant for unilateralism, along with the decision to go forward on a national ballistic defense system and to go slow on talks with North Korea.

In putting all of the foregoing together, advocates of the bureaucratic politics model argue that policy is not, and cannot be, a product of deliberate choice. Instead, policy is either a result of a political bargaining process or the product of organizational standard operating procedures.[9] In either case the new policy arrived at is not likely to differ greatly from the existing policy. This is because bargaining is a time-consuming and expensive process. Not only do policy makers disagree, but they are often quite deeply committed to their positions. The need for agreement pushes policy makers toward accepting a minimal decision, one that is not radically different from the existing compromise and one that will allow all sides to claim partial victory. The inflexible and blunt nature of organizational routines and procedures reinforces the tendency for policy to change only at the margins. Administrative feasibility is a constant check on the ability of policy makers to tailor policy options to meet specific problems. In sum, from the bureaucratic politics perspective, the best predictor of future policy is not the policy that maximizes U.S. national interests but that which is only incrementally different from current policy.

The bureaucratic politics model makes important contributions to understanding U.S. foreign policy by highlighting the political and organizational nature of policy making. However, it has also been the subject of extensive criticisms. First, by emphasizing compromise, bargaining, and standard operating procedures, the bureaucratic model makes it very difficult to assign responsibility for the decisions being made.[10] Second, it misrepresents the workings of the bargaining process by overstating the extent to which policy simply emerges from the policy process.[11] Third, the bureaucratic politics model is chastised for artificially separating the executive branch bargaining process from the broader social and political context. In this view Congress and domestic political forces cannot be treated as outside interlopers in the policy process. Attention must also be given to the values of policy makers and not just the policy-making games they play. Finally, it is criticized for being too complex, a virtual "analytic kitchen sink" into which almost anything can be thrown that might be related to how an issue is resolved.[12] The result is a story that may make for interesting reading but that violates one of the most fundamental rules of explanation: All things being equal, simple explanations are better than complex ones.

Small-Group Decision Making

A third policy-making model focuses on the dynamics of small group decision making. Advocates of this perspective hold that many critical foreign policy decisions are made neither by an individual policy maker nor by large bureaucratic forces. From a policy maker's perspective, small group decision making offers a number of advantages over its bureaucratic counterpart. Among its perceived advantages are the following:

> The absence of significant conflict because there will be few viewpoints to reconcile
>
> A free and open interchange of opinion among members because there will be no organizational interests to protect

Swift and decisive action

Possible innovation and experimentation

The possibility of maintaining secrecy[13]

Three different types of small groups can be identified.[14] First is the informal small group that meets regularly but lacks a formal institutional base. The Tuesday lunch group in the Johnson administration and the Friday breakfast and Thursday lunch groups of the Carter administration are prominent recent examples. Second is the ad hoc group that is created to deal with a specific problem and then ceases to function once its task is completed. In the first week of the 1950 Korean crisis, six small group meetings were held. During the Cuban missile crisis, the key decisions were made by ExCom, an ad hoc group of about fifteen individuals brought together by Kennedy specifically for the purpose of dealing with this problem. The third type of small group is permanent in nature, possesses an institutional base, and is created to perform a series of specified functions. The subcommittees of the National Security Council (NSC) fall into this category. During the Carter administration two subcommittees were established. One, the Special Coordinating Committee (SCC), was set up to deal with crisis situations when they arose. During the Iranian hostage crisis, Robert Hunter, an NSC official in the Carter administration, reported that

> Throughout the hostage crisis, the SCC met at 9:00 A.M.—at first daily and later less frequently—with an agenda coordinated with the government by the NSC staff in the early hours of the morning. Discussion was brisk, options were presented crisply, and recommendations were rapidly and concisely formulated for presidential decision. . . . The crisis team, with nearly three years' experience of working together, did its job efficiently and with dispatch. . . . Subcommittees of the SCC worked on specialized parts of the problem. The State Department Iranian Working Group worked around the clock all 444 days and fed information back and forth. . . . The results of the days' labors were reported back; new wrinkles in the crisis were assessed; and the SCC was ready to act again the next morning.[15]

Following the terrorist attacks of September 11, 2001 the George W. Bush administration established a "war cabinet" consisting of some dozen people. Almost half had played key roles in Gulf War decisions: Vice President Dick Cheney was secretary of defense, Secretary of State Colin Powell was chairman of the Joint Chiefs of Staff, Deputy Secretary of Defense Paul Wolfowitz was undersecretary of defense, Deputy Secretary of State Richard Armitage was a special envoy, and National Security Adviser Condoleezza Rice was a senior official at the National Security Council. Missing from this war cabinet was any longtime confidant of the president comparable to Secretary of State James Baker III in President George Bush's Persian Gulf War cabinet.

In spite of its advantages, small-group decision making often results in policy decisions that are anything but rational or effective. Pearl Harbor, the Bay of Pigs invasion, and key decisions in Korea and Vietnam have all been analyzed from a small group decision making perspective.[16] The Iranian hostage rescue mission and the Iran–Contra initiative can easily be added to this list.

These policy failures are held to result from the presence of strong ingroup pressures on members to concur in the group's decision. This pressure produces a "deterioration of mental efficiency, reality testing, and moral judgment" that increases the likelihood of the group's making a potentially defective decision.[17] Irving Janis coined the term *groupthink* to capture this phenomenon. He also identified eight symptoms that indicate its presence. He divides them into three categories: overestimation of the group's power and morality, closed-mindedness, and pressures toward conformity. Janis argues that the more symptoms that are present, the more likely it is that concurrence-seeking behavior will result and that defective decisions will be made. Table 11.1 presents a series of observations made by the Tower Commission report about the decision making on the Iran–Contra affair with the symptoms mentioned by Janis. While the match is not perfect (for example, illusion of unanimity is better seen as an illusion of presidential support), the parallels are striking.

Groupthink is a phenomenon that occurs irrespective of the personality traits of group members. It is not an inevitable product of a tight-knit decision group, nor is it necessarily the cause of a policy fiasco. Poor implementation, changed circumstances, or accidental factors also produce policy failures. Groupthink exists as a tendency that is made more or less likely by three sets of antecedent conditions: the coherence of the decision-making group, structural faults of the organization, and the nature of the decision context. At its core is the assumption that concurrence-seeking behavior is an attempt on the part of group members to cope with stress by developing a mutual support base. The source of the stress may be internal or external to the group. External stress is conducive to groupthink when it stems from a threat for which there appears to be little hope of finding a better solution than the one put forward by the leader. Internal stress tends to come from feelings of low self-esteem such that "participating in a unanimous consensus along with respected fellow members of a congenial group will bolster the decision maker's self-esteem."[18]

Because groupthink is a tendency and not a condition, it can be avoided. Recognizing that each proposed solution has its own drawbacks, Janis puts forward several measures that he feels would improve the quality of small-group decision making.[19] They include modifying leadership strategies so that impartial and wide-ranging discussions of alternatives will take place, establishing multiple groups for the same task, multiple advocacy, establishing a devil's advocate, and having a "second chance" meeting where decisions might be reconsidered one final time.

Three general lines of criticism have been directed at the groupthink approach to small-group decision making. First, the proposed solutions probably will not work. Consider the idea of multiple advocacy, which attempts to ensure that all views "however unpopular" will receive serious attention.[20] Two dangers exist here. In each case, they are brought on by overloading the intellectual capabilities of policy makers and by highlighting the ambiguity of the evidence before them. One outcome is that policy makers will simply choose whatever policy option is in accord with their preexisting biases. If a wide range of options are all made to appear respectable and doubts exist about the effectiveness of each, why not "let Reagan be Reagan" or "Bush be Bush" and select the one that best fits his image of the world. The other

TABLE 11.1   Groupthink and the Iran–Contra Affair

Elements of Groupthink	Findings of The Tower Commission Report
Illusion of invulnerability	The president "was all for letting the Israelis do anything they wanted at the very first briefing." McFarlane, p. 131.
Unquestioned belief in group's morality	The president distinguished between selling to someone believed able to exert influence with respect to the hostages and dealing directly with the kidnappers, p. 39.
	The administration continued to pressure U.S. allies not to sell arms to Iran and not to make concessions to terrorists, p. 65.
Collective efforts to discount warnings	"There is a high degree of risk in pursuing the course we have started, we are now so far down the road that stopping . . . could have even more serious repercussions. We all view the next step as confidence building." North, p. 167.
Stereotyping the enemy	Release of the hostages would require influence with the Hezballah, which could involve the most radical elements of the Iranian regime. The kind of strategy sought by the United States, however, involved what were regarded as more moderate elements, p. 64.
Self-censorship	Evidence suggests that he [Casey] received information about the possible divergence of funds to the Contras almost a month before the story broke. He, too, did not move promptly to raise the matter with the president, p. 81.
	Secretary Shultz and Secretary Weinberger, in particular, distanced themselves from the march of events, p. 82.
Illusion of unanimity (presidential support)	"I felt in the meeting that there were views opposed, some in favor, and the President didn't really take a position, but he seemed to, he was in favor of this project somehow or other." Shultz, p. 183.
	"As the meeting broke up, I had the idea the President had not entirely given up on encouraging the Israelis." Casey, p. 198.
Direct pressure against dissenters	"Casey's view is that Cap will continue to create roadblocks until he is told by you that the President wants this move NOW." North to Poindexter, p. 232.
Emergence of mindguards	"I don't want a meeting with RR, Shultz, and Weinberger." Poindexter, p. 45.
	North directed that dissemination be limited to Secretary Weinberger, DCI Casey, McFarlane, and himself. North said McFarlane had directed that no copy be sent to the secretary of state and that he, McFarlane, would keep Secretary Shultz advised orally on the NSC project, p. 149.

Source: President's Special Review Panel, The Tower Commission Report (New York: Bantam, 1987).

equally undesirable outcome is paralysis. Confronted with too many policy options, all of which appear to have problems, policy makers may end up doing nothing.

Second, criticism is directed at the criteria used to establish a good decision.[21] The standard used (vigilant appraisal) virtually duplicates the functional steps involved in making a rational decision that we presented in our discussion of the rational actor model. The point remains: If the rational actor model is an unrealistic benchmark against which to judge decision making, isn't the same true for groupthink? A final point is more theoretical in nature. The groupthink approach is grounded in a conflict model of individual decision making. According to this model, individuals often confront decision-making situations in which they feel "simultaneous opposing tendencies to accept and reject a given course of action."[22] Vigilant appraisal is realized when individuals successfully address this stress, and groupthink occurs when they do not. The cybernetic approach to policy making suggests an alternative starting point to understanding individual decision making. According to this perspective, individuals do not even attempt to resolve the value conflict and tensions involved in making such a decision. Instead, "the decision process is organized around the problem of controlling inherent uncertainty by means of highly focused attention and highly programmed responses."[23] Based on this line of argument, John Steinbruner suggests that in place of the calculating policy maker we focus our attention on three types of thinkers, each of whom avoids the need for making value trade-offs.[24] Any individual may exhibit these patterns of thinking or switch between them as time constraints and issues change. The uncommitted thinker has difficulty making up his or her mind on an issue and is very susceptible to the arguments and positions of others; the theoretical thinker approaches an issue from an ideological perspective; and the grooved thinker deals with a problem by placing it into a limited number of preexisting categories.

Even with these problems, recent decision making studies continue to point to importance of groupthink. One study focused on the relative importance of situational factors such as high stress and time constraints versus variation in how groups are structured and information processed.[25] Its findings suggest that situational factors have little affect on the quality of the decision compared to the other two. Another reviewed evidence regarding the effectiveness of various ways of combating groupthink's negative tendencies.[26] It found that multiple advocacy did improve the quality of the presidential policy making process but that its implementation was uneven making a full evaluation difficult.

Elite Theory and Pluralism

We have already encountered the final two perspectives on policy making that we will examine, elite theory and pluralism. During the 1960s and early 1970s, these two models served as the focal point for an intense debate that raged within political science over how best to understand the process by which public policy was made. While no longer the center of attention, elite theory and pluralism remain important approaches for understanding how U.S. foreign policy is made, and we briefly summarize the arguments that they make.

Elite theory represents a quite different perspective on foreign policy making than do the three approaches that we have examined so far. It is not concerned with the details of the action taking place inside the policy process, but it also does not ignore what goes on inside of the state. Elite theory is vitally concerned with the identity of those individuals making foreign policy and the underlying dynamics of national power, social myth, and class interests. From this perspective foreign policy is formulated as a response to demands generated by the economic and political system. But not all demands receive equal attention, and those that receive the most attention serve the interests of only a small sector of society. These special interests are transformed into national interests through the pattern of office holding and the structure of influence that exists within the United States. Those who hold office are seen as being a stable and relatively cohesive group that share common goals, interests, and values. Disagreements exist only at the margins and surface most frequently as disputes over how to implement policy and not over the ends of that policy. Those outside the elite group are held to be relatively powerless, reacting to the policy initiatives of the elite rather than prompting them. Furthermore, public reactions are often "orchestrated" by the elite rather than being expressions of independent thinking on policy matters. This explains why certain policy proposals routinely fail to attract serious attention: Ideas that do not build upon the relatively narrow range of value assumptions shared by the elite and rooted in the underlying dynamics of the socioeconomic structure will be rejected as unworkable, fundamentally flawed, or fatally naive. It also suggests that the basic directions of U.S. foreign policy will change slowly, if at all.

Within this broad consensus, elite theorists disagree on a number of points. First, disagreement exists over the constraints on elite behavior. Some see few, if any, constraints on the type of policies elites can pursue. Others see a more open policy process that is subject to periodic "short-circuiting" by the public, as perhaps was the case with the nuclear freeze movement. Disagreement also exists over how conspiratorial the elite is. Some elite theorists pay great attention to the social backgrounds and linkages between members of the elite class while others deemphasize these features in favor of an attention to the broader and more enduring forces of a capitalistic economic system that drives U.S. foreign policy to be expansionist, aggressive, and exploitive.[27]

Several recent administrations, including that of George W. Bush, have been the subject of conspiratorial-style elite analysis. In the case of the Carter administration, the object of attention was on the presence of large numbers of members of the Trilateral Commission in policy making positions. The Trilateral Commission was formed in 1973 to foster cooperation between the U.S., Western Europe, and Japan. In the Reagan administration it was on links between his appointees and the Committee on the Present Danger, a group established in the 1970s to warn against the continuing threat posed by the Soviet Union. In the George W. Bush administration, the focus is the influence that neoconservatives have on foreign policy decisions especially in the Middle East. Unlike the other two groups, neoconservatives do not have an institutional embodiment. Rather, neoconservativism refers to a broad philosophical outlook on America's role in world politics. Where conservatives are skeptical about the ability of American military and economic power to transform the world, neoconservatives are optimistic about its ability to do so and see the United States as having a responsibility to exercise that power even if other states object. With this more comprehensive sense of purpose, neoconservatives have also adopted a more all-encompassing sense of threat to the United States. The enemy is not just al-Qaeda but Hamas, Hezbollah and other terrorist groups as well as well as states such as North Korea, Iraq, Iran, and Syria. The emphasis on threats emanating from the Middle East is also consistent with the neoconservative view that Israel is among America's most valuable allies and most be protected. Key neoconservatives in the Bush administration include Deputy Secretary of Defense Paul Wolfowitz, Undersecretary of Defense for Policy Douglas Feith; Richard Pearle, who heads the Pentagon's Intelligence Advisory Board; and Lewis Libby who is Vice President Dick Cheney's chief of staff.

In sum, elite theory is a valuable source of insight into U.S. foreign policy making because it stresses the ties that bind policy makers together rather than the issues that separate them. In contrast to elite theory, pluralism is regarded as the orthodox interpretation of how the U.S. policy-making system works. Just as with elite theory, no single comprehensive statement of the argument exists. Still, six common themes can be identified:

1. Power in society is fragmented and diffused.
2. Many groups in society have power to participate in policy making.
3. No one group is powerful enough to dictate policy.
4. An equilibrium among groups is the natural state of affairs.
5. Policy is the product of bargaining between groups and reflects the interests of the dominant group(s).
6. The government acts as an umpire supervising the competition and sometimes compels a settlement.

Pluralists acknowledge that power resources are not evenly distributed throughout society. However, they hold that merely possessing the attributes of power (wealth, status, etc.) is not equal to actually possessing power itself.[28] This is because the economic and political sectors of society are held to be separate. In addition, power resources may be substituted for one another. Large numbers may offset wealth; leadership may offset large numbers; and commitment may overcome poor leadership. Pluralists would point to the grassroots movement within the United States to force South Africa to end apartheid as evidence of the validity of their case. What began as a movement on college campuses to force companies to disinvest from South Africa and later took the form of daily, peaceful demonstrations at the South African embassy gradually succeeded in sensitizing policy makers and the American public to the problem, with the result that in 1985 U.S. policy toward South Africa began to show signs of change. More recently, the change in U.S. pol-

icy on Cambodia, in which support for the rebel forces (including t
Rouge) was dropped in favor of talks with Vietnam, can also be
shifting political power of domestic political forces on this issue.

Theodore Lowi has suggested a major flaw in the pluralists' argument.[29]
Pluralists assume that competition between groups produces policy makers
who compete over the content of policy. What happens when policy makers
do not compete over policy but instead are so fragmented that they rule over
separate and self-contained policy areas? Lowi suggests that these conditions
better describe the operation of the U.S. government than does the pluralist
model and that when this happens the government is not an umpire but a
holding company. Pluralism then exists without competition as interest
groups capture different pieces of the government and shape its policies to
suit their needs. New groups or the poorly organized are effectively shut out
of the decision-making process. Just as important, interest group liberalism
reduces the capacity of the government to plan because it is unable to speak
with one voice or examine problems from a national perspective.

Summary: Integrating Models and Additional Possibilities

The scope of activity involved in making U.S. foreign policy is so vast that no
single model can hope to capture all of it, and few models try.[30] Instead,
models draw our attention to a select set of assumptions about what is central to the policy-making process. Simplifying the policy process in this way
inevitably creates problems, and, as we have seen, each model has certain inherent limitations. The task facing the student of foreign policy making is to
blend these models together to produce a picture containing the maximum
amount of insight and a minimal amount of distortion on the nature of the
policy-making process without overwhelming him or her with data demands.
Typically, there are four ways that this integration can be attempted. The
first is to shift from model to model as the focus of the analysis changes. For
example, from the rational actor perspective, the decision to send U.S.
troops to Korea in 1950 is a single decision. From the bureaucratic or small
group perspective, a number of separate decisions can be identified.[31] A distinction can also be made between the sociopolitical aspects of policy making and the intellectual task of choosing a response.[32] The pluralist and
bureaucratic politics models help us understand why policy makers act as
they do once they are "in place," but they tell us little about how they got
there or the values they bring to bear in addressing a problem. To answer
these questions, we might want to turn to insights from elite theory or the rational actor model.

A second way to integrate policy-making models is to recognize that
some models are more appropriate for analyzing some problems, or issue
areas, than they are for others. The general argument is that the more open
the policy process and the longer the issue is on the policy agenda (such as is
typically the case for structural and strategic issues), the more useful will be
the bureaucratic and pluralist models. The more closed the process and the

quicker the response, the more useful will be the rational actor, elite theory, or small group model.

A third way to integrate these models is to shift from one to another as the policy problem develops over time. Thus, the elite or rational actor model might be especially helpful for understanding how the United States got involved in Vietnam; the small group or bureaucratic politics model might be most helpful for understanding key decisions during the course of the war; and the pluralist or bureaucratic politics model might be most helpful for understanding the actual process by which the United States withdrew from Vietnam.

A final way of integrating these models is based on the values guiding one's analysis. We have already suggested that while the rational actor model may be deficient as a description of the policy-making process, it is still valuable if your purpose is to evaluate the policy process. One must be careful in using models in this way, for embedded in each are assumptions about how policy should be made that are not always readily apparent. For example, implicit in the rational actor model is a belief in the desirability of a strong president and the ability to act quickly. The model does not place great value on widespread participation in decision making or in a system of checks and balances.

The decision-making models we have examined in this chapter are not the only ones being used. We conclude by introducing two additional models that have attracted a great deal of interest of late. The first is social constructivism.[33] Instead of asking how a given outcome came to be, it seeks to understand how it was possible to imagine certain courses of action and relationships as being possible in the first place. It asks what social practices enabled people to act, frame policies as they did, and wield the power that they did. For example, shortly after following Ronald Reagan into the White House, the George H. W. Bush administration invaded Panama and overthrew the government of Manuel Noriega. The social constructivist approach would be most interested in understanding how it came to be that Noriega was redefined from being an anticommunist ally to being a drug dealer, thus making this invasion a viable option in the minds of policy makers.

The social constructivist approach is not incompatible with others discussed in this chapter. Daniel Drezner suggests that a marriage is possible with the bureaucratic politics model. He is interested in how idea-infused, or "missionary," bureaucracies survive and prosper compared to other bureaucracies.[34] His findings point to the existence of a trade-off. Missionary bureaucracies such as the Peace Corps maintain their values by becoming insulated from the influence of other bureaucracies. This comes at a cost, however. As a consequence they have a lessened influence on policy.

A second new decision-making model enjoying support today is prospect theory.[35] It takes exception to the assumptions of the rational actor model, asserting that individuals do not weight all outcomes and select the strategy that will offer them the highest expected utility. Instead, individuals tend to value what they have more than what they do not have; they stay at the status quo more often than one would predict; and they tend to be risk averse with respect to gains and risk acceptant when it comes to losses. This implies that leaders will take more risks to defend their state's international position than to enhance it and that after a loss leaders will have a tendency to take excessive risks to recover their positions.

Notes

1. Roger Hilsman, "Policy Making Is Politics," in Charles W. Kegley Jr., and Eugene R. Wittkopf (eds.), *Perspectives on American Foreign Policy: Selected Readings* (New York: St. Martin's, 1983), p. 250.

2. Ibid., p. 251.

3. Leslie H. Gelb with Richard K. Betts, *The Irony of Vietnam: The System Worked* (Washington, D.C.: Brookings, 1979).

4. A short summary of additional models can be found in Thomas L. Brewer, *American Foreign Policy: A Contemporary Introduction*, 2nd ed. (Englewood Cliffs, N.J.: Prentice-Hall, 1986), pp. 26–54.

5. Patrick Morgan, *Theories and Approaches to International Politics: What Are We to Think*, 3rd ed. (New Brunswick, N.J.: Transaction, 1981), p. 110.

6. Herbert A. Simon, *Administrative Behavior: A Study of Decision Making Processes in Administrative Organization*, 3rd ed. (New York: Free Press, 1976).

7. Graham T. Allison, *Essence of Decision: Explaining the Cuban Missile Crisis* (Boston: Little, Brown, 1971), p. 35.

8. I. M. Destler, *Presidents, Bureaucrats, and Foreign Policy: The Politics of Organizational Reform* (Princeton, N.J.: Princeton University Press, 1974), p. 52.

9. As originally presented by Allison in his *Essence of Decision*, two separate models were used to explain foreign policy making through organizational routines and governmental politics. Subsequently, Allison combined them into one model as is being done here. See Graham T. Allison and Morton H. Halperin, "Bureaucratic Politics: A Paradigm and Some Policy Implications," *World Politics*, 24 (1982), 40–79.

10. Robert L. Gallucci, *Neither Peace nor Honor: The Politics of American Military Policy in Vietnam* (Baltimore, Md.: Johns Hopkins University Press, 1975), p. 153.

11. Robert J. Art, "Bureaucratic Politics and American Foreign Policy: A Critique," in Robert J. Art and Robert Jervis (eds.), *International Politics: Anarchy, Force, Political Economy, and Decision Making*, 2nd ed. (Boston: Little, Brown, 1985), p. 471; Stephen D. Krasner, "Are Bureaucrats Important? (Or Allison Wonderland)," *Foreign Policy*, 7 (1972), 159–79; and Jerel Rosati, "Developing a Systematic Decision Making Framework: Bureaucratic Politics in Perspective," *World Politics*, 33 (1981), 234–51.

12. Jonathan Bendor and Thomas H. Hammand, "Rethinking Allison's Models," *American Political Science Review*, 86 (1992), 301–22.

13. Robert L. Wendzel, *International Politics: Policymakers & Policymaking* (New York: Wiley & Sons, 1981), p. 439.

14. Ibid., p. 438.

15. Robert E. Hunter, *Presidential Control of Foreign Policy: Management or Mishap?* Washington Paper #191 (New York: Praeger, 1982), pp. 35–46.

16. Irving L. Janis, *Groupthink: Psychological Studies of Policy Decisions and Fiascos*, 2nd ed. (Boston: Houghton Mifflin, 1982).

17. Ibid., p. 9.

18. Ibid., p. 256.

19. Ibid., pp. 172, 262–71.

20. Richard K. Betts, "Analysis, War, and Decision: Why Intelligence Failures Are Inevitable," *World Politics*, 31 (1978), 61–89.

21. Carol Barner-Barry and Robert Rosenwein, *Psychological Perspectives on Politics* (Englewood Cliffs, N.J.: Prentice-Hall, 1985), p. 247.

22. Irving L. Janis and Leon Mann, *Decision Making: A Psychological Analysis of Conflict, Choice, and Commitment* (New York: Free Press, 1977).

23. John D. Steinbruner, *The Cybernetic Theory of Decision: New Dimensions of Political Analysis* (Princeton, N.J.: Princeton University Press, 1974), pp. 66–67.

24. Ibid., pp. 125–36.

25. Mark Schafer and Scott Crichlow, "The Process-Outcome Connection in Foreign Policy Decision Making," *International Studies Quarterly,* 46 (2002), 45–68.

26. Alexander George and Erick Stern, "Harnessing Conflicts in Foreign Policy Making," *Presidential Studies Quarterly,* 32 (2002), 484–508.

27. Compare Gabriel Kolko, *The Roots of American Foreign Policy* (Boston: Beacon, 1969), with C. Wright Mills, *The Power Elite* (New York: Oxford University Press, 1956).

28. Robert A. Dahl, "A Critique of the Ruling Elite Model," in G. William Domhoff and Hoyt B. Ballard (eds.), *C. Wright Mills and the Power Elite* (Boston: Beacon, 1968), p. 31.

29. Theodore J. Lowi, *The End of Liberalism: Ideology, Policy, and the Crisis of Public Authority* (New York: Norton, 1969).

30. One model that does try is the decision-making model presented by Richard Snyder, H. W. Bruck, and Burton Sapin in "Decision Making as an Approach to the Study of International Politics," in Richard Snyder, H. W. Bruck, and Burton Sapin (eds.), *Foreign Policy Decision Making* (New York: Free Press, 1963).

31. See, for example, Glenn D. Paige, *The Korean Decision, June 24–30, 1950* (New York: Free Press, 1968).

32. Glenn H. Snyder and Paul Diesing, *Conflict among Nations: Bargaining, Decision-Making, and System Structure in International Crises* (Princeton, N.J.: Princeton University Press, 1977), p. 355.

33. Roxane Lynn Doty, "Foreign Policy as Social Construction: A Post-Positivist Analysis of U.S. Counterinsurgency Policy in the Philippines," *International Studies Quarterly,* 37 (1993), 297–320.

34. Daniel Drezner, "Ideas, Bureaucratic Politics, and the Crafting of Foreign Policy," *American Journal of Political Science,* 44 (2000), 733–49.

35. Jack Levy, "Prospect Theory, Rational Choice and International Relations," *International Studies Quarterly,* 41 (1997), 87–112.

$$-12-$$

DECISION MAKING: CASE STUDIES

In this chapter, we draw on the decision-making models in Chapter 11 in order to gain insight into how policy makers, institutions, and the American public came together to shape three important post World War II foreign policy decisions. In each case, our purpose is to illustrate the potential that different models have for helping us understand American foreign policy. We also hope to show that a full understanding of American foreign policy decision making requires using more than one model and integrating them in order to create a more complete explanation. The first is the Cuban Missile Crisis. We look at it from three perspectives: rational actor, small-group decision making, and bureaucratic politics. The second case study is U.S. intelligence policy on terrorism prior to 9/11. Again three models are used: small group decision making, bureaucratic politics, and elite theory. Our third case is NAFTA. Here, we divide the case study in two a stages, bargaining and ratification, and show how it is necessary to use different models to understand activity in each stage.

The Cuban Missile Crisis

THE CRISIS: AN OVERVIEW

Taking place over thirteen days (October 16–28, 1962), the Cuban missile crisis is widely regarded as a major turning point in the cold war.[1] Never before and never since have the United States and Soviet Union appeared to be on the brink of nuclear war. At the time of the crisis, President Kennedy estimated the odds of averting such an outcome were between one out of three and even.[2]

Soviet weapons shipments to Cuba had been taking place since the summer of 1960. A slowdown in these shipments occurred in early 1962, but the pace quickened again in late July. By September 1, the inventory of Soviet equipment in Cuba included surface-to-air missiles (SAMs), cruise missiles, patrol boats, over five thousand technicians and other military personnel, and large quantities of transportation, electrical, and construction equipment.[3] The first strategic missiles secretly arrived in Cuba on September 8. They were medium range ballistic missiles (MRBMs) possessing a range of eleven hundred nautical miles. Forty-two of these missiles would reach Cuba before the crisis was resolved. Equipment also began arriving for the construction of intermediate range ballistic missiles (IRBMs) and IRBM sites, although no IRBMs would reach Cuba. Finally, Soviet September shipments included IL-28 jet bombers, MIG-21 jet fighters, plus additional SAMs, cruise missiles, and patrol boats.

Intelligence on the exact dimensions of the Soviet buildup in Cuba came from a number of different sources: refugee reports, CIA agents operating in Cuba, analyses of Soviet shipping patterns, and U-2 overflights. Not all of the information from these sources was equally reliable, nor did it all come together at the same time and place for analysis. For example, refugees were reporting the presence of Soviet missiles in Cuba before Cuba began receiving weapons of any kind from the Soviet Union, and great care had to be taken in processing reports from agents operating inside Cuba. The United States Intelligence Board met on September 19 and approved an intelligence estimate stating that the Soviet Union would not introduce offensive missiles into Cuba.

This conclusion was not uniformly shared within the administration. In late August Director of Central Intelligence John McCone told Kennedy, Secretary of Defense Robert McNamara, and Secretary of State Dean Rusk that he believed the Soviet Union was preparing to place offensive missiles in Cuba. In late September others began to agree with McCone, and, on October 4 the Committee on Overhead Reconnaissance (COMOR) approved a U-2 overflight over western Cuba. No U-2 overflights had been authorized over this area since September 5 because of recent mishaps with U-2 overflights in Asia. Fearful that all U-2 flights might be canceled if another incident were to occur, COMOR had decided not to send any U-2s over western Cuba where SAM sites were known to be under construction. A jurisdictional dispute between the Defense Department and CIA over who would fly such a mission led to an unsuccessful flight on October 9, and it was not until October 14 that a successful U-2 flight took place. Its pictures firmly established the presence of Soviet offensive missiles in Cuba. On October 22, President Kennedy went on national television announcing their discovery.

Kennedy called together a special ad hoc advisory group known as the Executive Committee of the National Security Council (ExCom) to deal with the crisis. ExCom's initial meeting took place on October 16, and it began to identify the options open to the United States. Six major options surfaced: (1) no action, (2) diplomatic pressures either at the United Nations or at the Soviet Union, (3) a secret approach to Castro with the option of "split or fall," (4) invasion, (5) surgical air strike, and (6) a naval blockade.[4] The first option seized upon was the surgical air strike.[5] The blockade was not lobbied for strongly until the end of the day, and Kennedy's initial response to this option was one of skepticism because he was not sure how the blockade itself would get Soviet missiles out of Cuba.

By the end of the first day, Kennedy identified three options. Participant accounts suggest that attention focused primarily on two of these, the surgical air strike and the blockade. (The third option appears to have been the invasion.) In his October 22 statement, Kennedy also announced that on October 24 a naval quarantine would be imposed on Cuba and threatened future action if the missiles were not taken out. The blockade was chosen for what it did and did not do. It was a visible, forceful, military response, but it did not put the Soviet Union into a position where it had no choice but to fight. In fact, it placed responsibility for the next move back on Khrushchev. A number of additional measures were publicly taken to impress upon the Soviets the depth of U.S. resolve and to make credible Kennedy's threat of additional action: Squadrons of U.S. tactical fighters were moved to points where they could attack Cuba; an invasion force of 200,000 troops was readied in Florida; some 14,000 air force reserves were called up; and U.S. forces around the world were put on alert.[6]

The air strike remained a live option. An air strike had tentatively been scheduled for October 20 but was postponed in favor of the blockade. On October 27, one day before Krushchev offered to remove the missiles, Kennedy approved plans for an October 29 air strike on Soviet missile silos, air bases, and Cuban and Soviet antiaircraft installations. At that same meeting ExCom also concluded that an invasion would follow. McNamara held that an "invasion had become almost inevitable," and he felt that at least one missile would be successfully launched at the United States.[7]

The blockade did bring an end to Soviet military shipments to Cuba, but it did not bring a stop to the construction of Soviet missiles and missile sites in Cuba. SAM missiles became operational during the crisis and shot down a U-2 on October 23. Kennedy's original orders were that if this happened the United States would destroy the site that had launched the missile. However, when the incident occurred, Kennedy delayed retaliation in an effort to allow quiet diplomacy some additional time to bring about the withdrawal of the Soviet missiles.

Recent accounts of the Cuban missile crisis suggest that Kennedy would not have ordered an air strike had Khrushchev not responded favorably to U.S. demands, and that he was prepared to pursue additional negotiations—perhaps through the United Nations—to resolve the crisis.[8] These accounts also argue that U.S. policy makers felt a sense of urgency in their deliberations not out of a fear that Soviet missiles might soon become operational, but because the longer they remained in Cuba the more legitimate they would come to be seen by the other states.

On October 28, Khrushchev publicly agreed to remove Soviet missiles in Cuba in return for a U.S. pledge of nonintervention into Cuba. This allowed both sides to achieve their publicly stated goals. The United States got the missiles out of Cuba, and the Soviet Union could claim it had succeeded in protecting Cuba from U.S. aggression (the justification it gave for having placed the missiles in Cuba when confronted by Kennedy). Recently released documents reveal the existence of a secret agreement between Kennedy and Khrushchev with terms different from those that officially ended the crisis. In order to entice Khrushchev into removing the missiles from Cuba, Kennedy promised to remove U.S. missiles from Turkey. The secret offer was made by Robert Kennedy to Dobrynin on October 27. Dobrynin was also told that a commitment was needed from the Soviets the next day if the crisis was to be ended on these terms. For reasons of domestic politics and international prestige, Kennedy had refused to publicly accept this trade-off, which had been repeatedly called for by the Soviets and suggested to him by some members of ExCom. Implementation of the U.S. part of the agreement was made conditional on the Soviets' keeping the agreement secret.

While October 28 marks the conventional point for ending the Cuban missile crisis, it in fact continued for several more weeks as both sides struggled with the question of how to implement the agreement. Particularly troublesome issues involved defining what was meant by "offensive" weapons—the United States insisted that the IL-28s must be removed—and establishing a date for ending the blockade—the Soviets wanted the blockade ended and a no-invasion pledge issued before they took out the bombers. Within the U.S. government there occurred a repeat of the earlier debate on how to proceed: Take unilateral military action to resolve the issue, tighten the blockade, or concede the point and go on to other matters. Diplomacy again came to the rescue when on November 20 Kennedy announced that the Soviet Union had agreed to remove the IL-28s and that the blockade was being ended.

THREE VIEWS OF THE CUBAN MISSILE CRISIS

The account of the Cuban missile crisis presented above is largely consistent with a rational actor interpretation of U.S. foreign policy making. It emphasizes the thorough canvassing of alternatives once a problem has been identified and the selection of a value-maximizing choice. For U.S. policy makers the goal directing the search for policy options was clear: Get Soviet missiles out of Cuba without the appearance of having appeased the Soviets and without starting a war. A hard-line stance was in part dictated by domestic political considerations. Cuba had become an important emotional and reoccurring issue in American electoral politics since Castro had come to power in 1959, and Kennedy was vulnerable on Cuba. The Bay of Pigs fiasco had made Cuba Kennedy's political Achilles' heel, raising questions about his judgment and leadership. The Republican Senate and Congressional Campaign Committees had already identified Cuba as the major issue in the upcoming 1962 election. Inaction (a possibility suggested at one point by McNamara) and quiet diplomacy, therefore, were not policy options capable of achieving both the removal of the missiles and the demonstration of political resolve. The air strike was rejected because the Air Force could not give Kennedy a 100 percent guarantee that the missiles would be knocked out. Similar problems confronted the selection of an invasion. Coupled with highly visible signals of further military action, the blockade was selected as the option offering the greatest likelihood of getting the missiles out and demonstrating U.S. resolve without running a high risk of setting off a war between the United States and Soviet Union.

As the rational actor model would suggest, the blockade itself was structured to fit the needs of U.S. policy makers. It was not implemented until U.S. officials were sure that Soviet leaders had been able to communicate with Soviet ship captains, and the blockade was placed closer to Cuba than was militarily prudent in order to give the Soviet leadership the maximum amount of time to formulate a peaceful response. The first ship stopped was also carefully selected to minimize the possibility of a hostile Soviet response. Two ships that clearly did not carry missiles were allowed to pass through the blockade. The first ship stopped also did not carry missiles. It was a U.S.-built World War II Liberty ship, registered in Lebanon, owned by a Panamanian firm, and under lease to the Soviet Union.

A similar analysis of policy options and consequences late in the crisis would identify Kennedy's secret offer to remove U.S. missiles from Turkey as the logical follow-up move. The blockade did buy time and show U.S. resolve, but, in and of itself, it could not remove the missiles. Domestic political considerations again limited Kennedy's options as did the continued inability of the military to guarantee that the air strike/invasion would not result in one or more Soviet missiles reaching the United States. Kennedy's publicly announced deadline ensured that the military option with all of its drawbacks would be used unless Khrushchev could be convinced to take the missiles out of Cuba. The key was to find a face-saving way out for the Soviets that was also true to Kennedy's stated objectives. The combined secret agreement and public pledge of Soviet missiles out of Cuba in return for a nonintervention pledge by the United States accomplished this.

The bureaucratic perspective on decision making during the Cuban missile crisis points to a quite different picture of what transpired. Rather than emphasizing the logic of policy making, it stresses the politics and organizational context of policy making. Politics is evident first in the discovery of missiles in Cuba. Consider the following: As early as August, DCI McCone voiced concern about Soviet offensive missiles being placed in Cuba, but he was overruled by McNamara and Rusk; no U-2 flights were directed over the area most likely to have Soviet missiles from September 5 until October 14; the October 14 flight had been authorized October 4, but a jurisdictional dispute between the Defense Department and CIA over who would fly the aircraft and which aircraft would be used delayed it. (The solution agreed to was that an Air Force officer in uniform would fly a CIA plane.) Moreover, evidence now points to the fact that the United States underestimated by one-half how many troops (42,000) the Soviet Union had sent to Cuba. Had this figure been known or had the United States discovered the missiles at an earlier date, the nature of policy options considered, reading of Soviet goals, and U.S. objectives might have been quite different.

The "logic" of the blockade also suffers when the air strike option is examined in closer detail. First, the Air Force did not specifically design an option to meet ExCom's goal of removing the Soviet missiles. Instead, it merely dusted off an existing contingency plan that also called for air strikes against arms depots, airports, and artillery batteries opposite the U.S. naval base at

Guantánamo Bay. Second, Air Force calculations on its ability to destroy the Soviet missiles were based on an incorrect labeling of the missiles as mobile field type missiles when they were actually movable missiles that required six days to be switched from one location to another. Because the Air Force believed that the Soviet missiles might be moved between the time when the last reconnaissance mission was flown and the time of the air strike, it was only able to offer Kennedy a 90 percent guarantee that it could knock out all of the missiles. The limits of rational choice are also revealed in the implementation of the blockade. Like the Air Force, the Navy did not tailor its plans to meet ExCom's needs. After-the-fact reconstructions of the timing of ship stoppings show that contrary to Kennedy's orders the Navy did not move the blockade closer to Cuba but placed it where they had originally proposed.

The bureaucratic politics model would also raise a number of troubling questions about the logic of the agreement that ended the crisis. One point centers on the nature of Soviet goals. No one in ExCom gave serious consideration to the possibility that the Soviet Union was genuinely concerned with deterring a U.S. invasion of Cuba. Evidence now suggests that along with balance-of-power considerations, this was one of Khrushchev's goals. Moreover, it appears that it was not the threat of nuclear retaliation but the possibility that the United States might use the crisis as a pretext for invading Cuba that led to the decision to remove the missiles. The formal ending of the crisis on the Soviet side also raises troubling questions. Early accounts suggested that Khrushchev wasn't in full control of the Politburo and for this reason contradictory messages were being received in Washington concerning the terms for ending the crisis. Evidence now suggests that this may not have been the case but that faulty intelligence may have been responsible. The first and more conciliatory note was sent when Soviet intelligence was indicating an imminent U.S. attack on Cuba. The second and more stringent communiqué was sent once it became clear that there would not be an invasion.

Early accounts of Cuban missile crisis decision making from the small group perspective praised ExCom for not falling victim to groupthink. Janis credits ExCom with not stereotyping the Soviets but actively trying to understand what led them to try to secretly place missiles in Cuba.[9] He cites Robert Kennedy's concern about a Pearl Harbor in reverse as evidence of a sensitivity to the moral dilemmas involved in the air strike option. Janis also notes that members of ExCom frequently changed their minds and came to the conclusions that there were no good policy options at their disposal. President Kennedy is credited with having learned from the Bay of Pigs and practicing a leadership style that maximized the possibility that ExCom would produce quality decisions. To encourage free debate, he did not attend all of its meetings, and he split ExCom into smaller groups to debate the issues and reexamine the conclusions reached by other participants.

More recent accounts of ExCom's deliberations suggest that its escape from groupthink was far less complete than was originally believed.[10] At least three decision-making defects surfaced that are fully consistent with the groupthink syndrome. First, ExCom operated with a very narrow mandate: It was to consider the pros and cons of a variety of coercive measures. Kennedy had declared off limits any consideration of either acquiescence to the Soviet move or diplomacy. ExCom was true to that mandate; 90 percent of its time was spent studying alternative uses of troops, bombers, and warships. Thus, ExCom did not engage in a full search for policy options or operate as an open decision-making forum.

Second, those who sought to expand the list of options under consideration and break out of the group consensus were ostracized. U.S. Ambassador to the United Nations Adlai Stevenson initially opposed the use of force and wrote Kennedy a note cautioning him on the dangers of this option. Kennedy was annoyed by the note and blocked efforts by McNamara and Stevenson to include diplomacy on the options list. Stevenson also suggested a trade of Soviet missiles for U.S. missiles in Turkey or for the Guantánamo Bay Naval Base. For these suggestions he came under sharp personal attack by Kennedy and was frozen out of the core decision-making group.

Third, Sorensen and Robert Kennedy acted as surrogate leaders for Kennedy, reporting back to the president on the discussion and pushing group members to reach a consensus. Here too the impact was to limit the choice of policy alternatives and to stifle discussion. Stevenson observed that "we knew little brother was watching and keeping a little list where everyone stood." On Friday night, October 25, President Kennedy informed ExCom that he had chosen the blockade. The very next day the consensus within ExCom for the blockade began to unravel. At that point Kennedy told his brother to "pull the group together quickly." Sorensen would tell the group that they were "not serving the president well," and Robert Kennedy would tell them that the president could not possibly order an air strike.

Pre–9/11 Intelligence Policy on Terrorism[11]

"We were almost all wrong." This was the conclusion reached by David Kay about the assertion that Iraq possessed weapons of mass destruction. Kay was the United States' top weapons inspector in the period leading up to the Iraq War and his admission pointed to the presence of a serious intelligence failure on the part of the U.S. intelligence community. How did it happen? In this case study, we examine the performance of the intelligence community in the George W. Bush administration leading up to that fate-full day and into the immediate post attack period using three different policy models in order to provide an explanation.

THE INTELLIGENCE CYCLE[12]

Intelligence as a policy area is carried out in secret. Judging its effectiveness is not a straightforward task if for no other reason than in the final analysis policy makers are free to ignore intelligence in making their decisions. Sherman Kent, one of the founding fathers of modern intelligence analysis in the United States noted long ago "there is no universal law that obligates the use of intelligence."[13] More recently, it has been observed "policy makers sometimes use intelligence the way a drunk uses a lamppost—for support instead of illumination."[14]

We can begin to get a better understanding of how the intelligence policy area works and why failures happen by breaking it down into six steps that together form the intelligence cycle. As presented below the steps occur in sequence but in reality they are not nearly as distinct. Activity in each constantly spills into other steps and informs actions taken there.

- *Planning and Direction.* The Intelligence cycle begins with the identification of a policy problem for which intelligence is needed and the drawing up of specific intelligence collection requirements. Guidance in establishing priorities comes from two sources. The first is the professional judgments of the intelligence analysts (internal guidance). Just as importantly, guidance comes from presidents and their key advisors (external guidance).

- *Collection.* The second step in the intelligence cycle. It involves collecting the information needed to inform the policy decisions identified in the first step. Information is collected via a variety of means. Most collection is done covertly. Human intelligence is intelligence gathered from spies. Technical intelligence is intelligence gathered through electronic intercepts and satellite photography among other means. Some intelligence is collected from open sources such as newspapers and government documents. The goal is to achieve all-source coverage.

- *Processing.* Here the information gathered on a policy problem is collected into a form usable by intelligence analysts.

- *Analysis.* Intelligence is evaluated information. In this fourth stage, the analysts take the information they have been given and integrate it into a coherent whole. This process may involve the work of a single individual. It may be the result of a group effort that brings together experts from several different intelligence agencies.

- *Dissemination.* In the fifth step in the intelligence cycle, the intelligence analysis is made available to policy makers. A variety of forms exist for doing so. They include oral briefings, daily written summaries of key events, warnings of impending problems, and long range assessments of a problem area. Two key forms by which intelligence is disseminated are the President's Daily Brief, the top-secret presentation made to the president every day, and National Intelligence Estimate (NIE), which are documents that reflect the collective judgment of the intelligence community.

- *Feedback.* In this final stage, policy makers react to the intelligence they have been given: what is good; what is bad; what is missing. Their reactions help restart the cycle by providing renewed guidance on how to proceed with the production of intelligence.

INTELLIGENCE ON TERRORISM PRIOR TO 9/11

Planning and Direction. External guidance on the terrorism threat was virtually absent. It was not as high a priority for the incoming George W. Bush administration as was China, missile defense, the Persian Gulf, and the Middle East peace process. The new administration retained Clinton's key antiterrorism advisor, Richard Clarke, although they did alter its place in the national security decision-making process downward. Rather than report directly to the Principles Committee made up of the key national security secretaries and chaired by Condoleezza Rice he reported to a less important committee chaired by her deputy. Clarke objected to the move. Rice justified it as necessary to place the administration's counterterrorism efforts in broader context. One of Rice's first acts was to request her NSC staff to identify major policy reviews or initiatives. Clarke submitted a memo January 25, 2001 offering plans drawn up but not approved in December 2000 and 1998. Clarke also asked on several occasions for an early Principles Meeting where he could present information on al-Qaeda. In one early request, he stated such a meeting as "urgently" needed. No Principles Meeting was held on the subject until September 4, 2001.

Formal and informal meetings were held to discuss terrorism below this level. In March Steven Hadley met with a group to discuss action against al-Qaeda in Afghanistan and the drafting of a new presidential directive on terrorism. One point of dispute in the deliberations of the Deputies Committee chaired by Hadley, which had jurisdiction on Afghanistan, centered on the administration's desire to have a policy in place on Afghanistan and Pakistan before dealing with al-Qaeda and Clarke's desire to move forward separately on these matters. He felt linking them had slowed down the decision-making process too much. On April 30, the CIA briefed the Deputies Committee and described al-Qaeda as "the most dangerous group we are facing." One of the slides warned "there will be more attacks."

In May, Rice reported that Director of Central Intelligence George Tenet briefed the president on the terrorist threat. Bush expressed impatience with "swatting flies" and wished to go on the offensive. This led Clarke and the NSC staff to put forward a broad policy initiative to eliminate al-Qaeda. Hadley circulated it for comment as "an admittedly ambitious program." Also in May, Bush announced that Vice President Dick Cheney would lead a review of preparations for managing a possible weapons of mass destruction attack. The next few months were spent organizing the inquiry.

In early August, the CIA prepared an analysis of how terrorists might attack the U.S. for inclusion in the President's Daily Brief of August 6. This was done in response to periodic questions by the president if any of this information pointed to an attack on the United States. Rice and Hadley also reviewed a draft presidential directive on al-Qaeda. Rice felt it was "very good" and scheduled it to be discussed at the Principles Group meeting of September 4 before going forward to George W. Bush. Before that meeting took place Clarke wrote to Rice about his frustrations with the pace of decision making and urged policy makers to "imagine a day after a terrorist attack, with hundreds of Americans dead at home and abroad." Rice chaired the September 4 meeting and, according to the 9/11 Commission, the draft presidential directive that called for expanded covert operations against al-Qaeda was apparently approved. On September 10, Hadley's committee met to finalize their recommendations for a three-phase, multiyear plan to bring down the Taliban leadership.

Internal guidance with regard to the terrorist threat was minimal as well. Al-Qaeda was established in 1988, but it was not until 1999 that CIA documents began describing this organization. Until 1997, bin Laden was still being referred to as a financier of terrorism. In December 1998, following the August attacks on two U.S. embassies in Africa, DCI Tenet sent a directive to top CIA officials and his deputy for community management stating "we are at war. I want no resources spared in this effort, either inside the CIA or the Community." The memo had a negligible impact. Few received it. The head of the National Security Agency received it but thought it applied only to the

CIA. Members of the CIA who received it thought it was directed to the rest of the intelligence community since they were already heavily engaged in terrorist issues. Senior military commanders were also unaware of this directive.

Collection. The FBI's collection efforts were heavily influenced by traditional organizational practices. It took a law enforcement approach to counterterrorism where the focus was on building a legal case against the suspects. FBI offices also operated in a decentralized fashion to give local offices and agents the maximum amount of power to pursue their cases. One result was that one office frequently did not know what other offices were working on. Additionally the reward structure within the FBI was based on the number of arrests, indictments, and prosecutions. Since terrorist cases seldom produced any of these, they were not high-priority items for agents.

A major source of intelligence on terrorist activity is signals intelligence that seeks to capture communications between terrorist groups. While no one piece of information ever is likely to specify the time and place of an attack, chatter patterns can be used to track levels of activity and areas of operation. This chatter was tracked by the National Security Agency (NSA). One NSA collection problem identified by the 9/11 Commission stemmed from how it defined its intelligence role. NSA saw itself as supporting consumers who requested intelligence but not the initiator of analysis. As such key information it obtained regarding the identities of future highjackers was not exploited fully.

One key source of intelligence that was all but missing in the information gathered both prior to 9/11 and before the Iraq War was human intelligence. During the Clinton administration's hunt for bin Laden, U.S. human intelligence sources in Afghanistan usually could only pinpoint where he had been three days prior. The causes of this failing are complex. At an operational level, it is correctly pointed out that the United States began to cut back on its covert intelligence collection capabilities years before the 9/11 attack both for financial reasons and because of continuing ethnical dilemmas as to who to enlist as an agent. Additionally, the political fallout from past failed operations that had settled on the CIA had caused intelligence officials to adopt a highly cautious approach to putting forward such projects.

Processing. The processing of information was handicapped by a number of factors. First, the CIA and FBI had different classification levels that resulted in some CIA information not being given to the FBI for security reasons. Second, the CIA had concerns that information it gave the FBI might end up in court and compromise its intelligence operations. Third, organizational walls separated criminal and intelligence operations within the FBI.

In concrete terms, these and other barriers produced the following intelligence near misses. The CIA followed the movements of two of the 9/11 hijackers from Malaysia to California but did not tell the FBI or State Department to put them on watch lists. FBI agents in Minneapolis and Phoenix discovered vague information about the terrorist plots but no one in FBI headquarters followed up on them in a timely fashion. The National Security

Agency that engages in electronic surveillance uncovered links between the 9/11 hijackers but did not disseminate this information.

Processing problems also became a major concern in the Iraq War. The administration began to "stovepipe" supportive raw information up to high-level policy makers by passing established procedures for evaluating and assessing information. An Office of Special Plans was set up in the Pentagon that "cherry-picked" raw information and passed it along as intelligence to higher administration officials. In deliberations at the National Security Council the result often was conflicting intelligence analysis with one view presented by the CIA, State Department, and uniformed military and another by the Office of the Secretary of Defense and the Vice President's Office. Vice President Dick Cheney was particularly outspoken in his public comments about the need for war and the degree to which intelligence supported it, and he frequently interjected himself into the analytic process "collecting information on the threat wherever he could find it." He was also a recipient of intelligence from the Office of Special Plans.

Cheney readily defended his personal involvement in the production of intelligence on Iraq observing "this is a very important area. It is one that the President has asked me to work on. . . . In terms of asking questions, I plead guilty. I ask a hell of a lot of questions. That's my job."[15] Analysts saw a different reality. They complained of having to defend good information or provide additional information with such frequency that it prevented them from doing their work and exposing bad information. One former CIA official summed up the situation saying "the analysts at the CIA were beaten down defending their assessments."

Analysis.   Information needs to be assessed and evaluated both for its content and the reliability of its sources in order to produce intelligence. By late summer, DCI Tenet observed that the CIA's warning and indicator system used to track and combine information so as to alert policy makers to impending problems "was blinking red" indicating that significant warnings of problems were being detected. Not everyone agreed with the prospects of danger. Deputy Secretary of Defense Paul Wolfowitz commented that perhaps all bin Laden was doing was trying to study U.S. reactions to warnings. Tenet rejected this interpretation. The 9/11 Commission indicates in its report that some CIA analysts looking back at the series of warnings believe they may refer to other terrorist attacks such as the assassination of Northern Alliance leader Ahmed Shah Massoud. While this system provided warning gaps still existed. The Counter Terrorist Center, for example, did not have a warning and indicator system in place for anticipating the possibility of airplane hijackings such as occurred on 9/11. As such, this type of information was not being sought out, stored, or brought together on a systematic basis.

Far more significant problems existed in the FBI's information management system. Standard operating procedures play a major role. The FBI operates on a case basis in which a case is "owned" by agents who maintain the file on it. This information is not automatically shared with others. Within the

FBI, no one was assigned to with the job of taking this information and condensing it into meaningful intelligence that could be retrieved and disseminated. The FBI's Joint Terrorism Task Forces was the primary mechanism for sharing information with other law enforcement agencies. Thirty-five existed throughout the United States prior to 9/11, but they generally were understaffed and responded to the priorities and concerns of regional and field offices. In many cases, they lacked access to FBI information or that from their home offices if they were detailed from another agency.

Dissemination.   From April to July, the intelligence community began to process a surge in information regarding terrorist activity. On June 25, Clarke wrote to Rice that six intelligence reports showed al-Qaeda operatives warning of a pending attack. Three days later, Clarke indicated to Rice that the intelligence had reached a crescendo, and on July 2 the FBI issued a national threat advisory. A June 30 briefing paper to top intelligence officials was titled "Bin Laden Planning High-Profile attacks." On July 5, at Rice's request, Clarke briefed Attorney General John Ashcroft on the al-Qaeda threat and noted a significant terrorist attack was imminent. On July 6, the CIA told the Counterterrorism Security Group, the NSC group charged with managing the terrorist threat, the upcoming attack will be "spectacular." On July 27, Clarke told Rice and Hadley a spike in intelligence traffic indicated that the possibility of a near-term attack had passed. He urged them to keep readiness high because intelligence indicated the attack was only postponed for a few months. Along with these warnings, written reports on al-Qaeda began appearing more frequently that warned of new activity. Some of these reports were made available to President Bush in his morning meetings with DCI Tenet. None of them specifically mentioned an attack on the United States.

Between January 20 to September 10, 2001 there were more than forty intelligence articles in the President's Daily Brief (PDB) that dealt with bin Laden. The most significant of these was the August 6 PDB. In it, the CIA included a piece "Bin Laden Determined to Strike in U.S." President George W. Bush indicated to the 9/11 Commission that he considered it historical in nature.

No comprehensive national estimate was produced on terrorism prior to 9/11. There was a 1995 NIE that warned of an attack on the United States "from transient groupings of individuals." There did exist a series of reports written between 1998–2001 that highlighted the growing threat. They included "OBL [Osama bin Laden] Plans for Reprisals Against U.S. Targets, Possibly in U.S." (September 1998), "Bin Laden to Exploit Security during Holidays (December 1999), "Bin Laden's Interest in Biological and Radiological Weapons" (February 2001), and "Bin Laden Determined to Strike in U.S." (August 2001).

Feedback.   After the August 6 PDB article on the terrorist threat, the 9/11 Commission found no evidence that before September 11 the president and his advisors on the possibility of a terrorist attack in the United States. DCI Tenet briefed the president in Texas on August 17 and after his return to Washington on August 31 but does not recall any discussions on terrorism.

After the attack, the Bush administration moved quickly to focus the administration on the war against terrorism. One of the main points of controversy that arose was over the degree of Iraqi involvement. Bush asked Clarke to study the matter on September 12. On September 18, he produced a memo indicating that there was no compelling intelligence linking Iraq to the attack. On September 11, Secretary of Defense Rumsfeld indicated that both bin Laden and Iraq were possible targets of U.S. reprisals. Iraq came up for discussion again at a Camp David meeting between George W. Bush and his war cabinet on September 15. On September 17, Bush ended the policy debate stating "I believe Iraq was involved, but I'm not going to strike them now. I don't have the evidence at this point." In April, President Bush told a British reporter, "I made up my mind that Saddam Hussein needs to go."

THREE VIEWS OF AN INTELLIGENCE FAILURE

Again, the question why did intelligence not better prepare policy makers for a September 11 terrorist attack? Our decision-making models point to several factors. The small-group decision-making model directs our attention to the patterns of thought and action in the national security council system. Here we find several traits consistent with the groupthink syndrome. Recall, that model stresses consensus-seeking behavior and warns that the greater the sense of group loyalty and identification the more powerful these forces will be and that the Bush administration staff was known for its loyalty and being team players. One trait that emerged was the tendency to underestimate and stereotype the enemy. In the immediate post–9/11 meetings, Wolfowitz interrupted Clarke's presentation asserting "You give bin Laden too much credit. He could not do all these things like the 1993 attack on New York, not without a state sponsor."[16] A second was the sense that the various NSC groups were in control of events; not that events might dictate their actions. No sense of urgency existed. The speed and content of the decision-making process was determined by their priorities. They would set the timetable for action. Even as intelligence alerts mounted during the summer the pace of decision making was unaffected. Third, if we broadened our case study and moved it forward to planning for the Iraq War we would see mindguards in action. Planning for the military campaign was kept separated from planning for the reconstruction and occupation of Iraq. Moreover, within the Defense Department the official planning focus was on what could go right and not what could go wrong in combat. Planning for failure was not an option. Throughout the decision-making process, Clarke functioned as a devil's advocate. His inability to move the small-group decision-making process in this role says much about the pull of the forces identified by this model.

Finally, we can see the influence of groupthink in a failure of imagination and lack of curiosity about how terrorists might look at the world. Our values and pattern of thinking we imposed on them. Two points are telling here. First, in speaking to the commission on the 9/11 attacks. Stephen Hadley, Rice's assistant made a point repeated by many in the upper echelons of the administration on why no action was taken as alerts built: "the threat warnings did not . . . include any specific warning information to indicate attacks inside the United States." Second, it was not until after the 9/11 attacks that the CIA set up a "red cell" exercise in which analysts were tasked with assuming the worldview of the enemy and asked to outline a possible plan of action.[17]

The bureaucratic politics model also furthers our understanding of how 9/11 happened. We can see this at two levels. First, it is clear that bureaucratic structures and standard operating procedures inhibited the timely exchange of intelligence at the collection, dissemination, and processing stages. This is true both within and between intelligence organizations. By the time 9/11 occurred at least seven different memos, including one from the president, had been directed to the CIA and NSA in an attempt to define their counterterrorism responsibilities. A former chief of the DCI's Counterterrorist Center summed up the situation by asserting that from 1996–1999 of all the elements of the intelligence community only the CIA's Directorate of Operations which had responsibility for covert action was actively pursuing the war against bin Laden. His statement points to the second level at which bureaucratic politics entered the picture. The 9/11 Commission spoke to the influence of bureaucratic politics when it noted that the terrorist attack had exploited the "seams" of the institutional structures the United States used to counterterrorism. The organizational values and cultures of the intelligence organizations did not place a high value on counterterrorism intelligence work. Participants in these organizations continued to operate with a worldview that stressed the difference between foreign and domestic policy problems and that defined foreign policy problems in terms of the actions of other states. This outlook extended up to the NSC where Rice saw the role of the NSC as foreign policy coordination and not a place where terrorism issues were to be addressed.

If we look at the feedback stage and extend our analysis one last time we can profitably use elite theory to understand the George W. Bush administration's response to 9/11. Where bureaucratic politics emphasizes the role of organization values in the policy process, elite theory focuses on the possession of a shared worldview among social groups. Neoconservatives are the group most identified with Bush's foreign policy. In their view, American hegemony provides the United States with an opportunity to use its military power to transform the international system. Twin anchors to this policy are a firm alliance with Israel and the dangers posed by rogue regimes in the Middle East. Immediately after 9/11, American foreign policy began to move in this direction. Consistent with the thrust of elite theory, this was not a matter of improvisation. It was a move that reflected a deeper vision of world politics and America's role in the world.

Five years earlier, Richard Pearle, Douglas Feith, and David Wurmser produced a think piece for Israel's Prime Minister Benjamin Netanyahu.[18] One of its recommendations was the removal of Saddam Hussein from power as a necessary step in making the Middle East less hostile to Israel. In waging war against Saddam Hussein, they recommended that Israel invoke a policy of preemption, striking first in self defense. The planning document even contained recommended text for a media campaign, language that appeared in the Bush administration's public statements after 9/11. In the Bush administration, Pearle served as head of the Defense Policy Review Board, Feith served as Undersecretary of Defense for Policy, and Wursmer was Cheney's top Middle East expert. Wolfowitz is also often identified as a neoconservative.

Elite theory comes in many varieties. One does not have to adopt the more conspiratorial versions in adopting its insights. What elite theory analysis suggests here is that the guidance given in the feedback loop to the intelligence community was in large measure based less on a reading of the intelligence than it was on the underlying beliefs a group of likeminded individuals brought to their job. Following this logic, preventing future intelligence failures is not a matter of avoiding groupthink or redrawing organizational boundaries and cultures but changing the fundamental outlooks that elites bring to foreign policy making.

Negotiating the North American Free Trade Agreement (NAFTA)[19]

Traditionally, when we studied international negotiations such as those surrounding the SALT talks, GATT, or the Rio Earth Summit, our focus was on the interaction of diplomats. The study of diplomacy was what these individuals did. Only recently have we begun to appreciate the ways in which domestic politics enters into the negotiating process (and conversely, the extent to which international negotiations can shape domestic politics). Robert Putnam suggests that we can think of negotiators as simultaneously occupying positions in two linked games: one to conclude an international agreement, the other to secure domestic approval for it.[20] Success in one means little without success in the other. Thus, policy makers are forced to engage in an interactive double-edged negotiating process in which "deals at the international level change the character of domestic constraints, while the movement of domestic politics opens up new possibilities for international accords."[21] In this final case study we examine the NAFTA agreement for insight into how the two linked bargaining games that were being played out. Following Putnam, we divide the negotiation process into a bargaining phase and a ratification phase. Because our interest is in activity that bridges the two bargaining games, we will not chronicle in detail the negotiations themselves but will focus instead on the international-domestic linkages that influenced the talks.

THE BARGAINING PHASE

In the 1960s, Mexico pegged its development hopes on an import substitution strategy. Growth could come about by protecting domestic industries from foreign competition. Over time, firms now too weak to compete with foreign multinationals would become vibrant enterprises providing Mexicans with jobs and lessening its dependence on foreign states. By the 1990s, it was clear to many in Mexico that this strategy had not been able to produce sustained growth. From an economic perspective the most attractive alternative was integration into the larger markets of its industrialized trading partners. And the most logical market was that of the United States. Politically, however, this was an unattractive option given nationalistic sentiments against closer economic ties with the United States and fears that such ties would only lead to Mexican dependence on the American economy. Given these considerations, it is not surprising that Mexican President Carlos Salinas de Gortari embraced the idea of a North American free trade zone only after exploring other options. In early 1990, Salinas had tried unsuccessfully to broaden Mexico's economic ties with Japan and Western Europe. On the heels of this failure he turned his attention to securing a free trade agreement with the United States, an idea that he had virtually dismissed out of hand when inaugurated. In the United States, the idea of a continental free trade pact had emerged as early as the 1980 presidential campaign, when Ronald Reagan, Jerry Brown, and John Connally all endorsed the idea. President George Bush had embraced it in the 1988 campaign. Salinas now telephoned Bush to determine if interest still existed and the answer was positive. After months of exploratory talks, in August 1990 Salinas formally notified the United States of Mexico's interest in negotiating a bilateral free trade area.

The Bush administration was divided over the wisdom of entering into talks with Mexico. The National Security Council, the Commerce Department, and the States Department supported the idea. The Department of Agriculture and the Office of the U.S. Trade Representative (USTR) were less enthusiastic. The USTR's misgivings centered on the difficulties experienced in concluding the 1989 U.S.–Canada Free Trade Agreement (CFTA) and the fact that the Uruguay Round GATT negotiations had not yet been completed. By spring, the USTR had put these reservations behind it and joined with other agencies in recommending to Bush that the United States officially move ahead with these talks. Doing so meant informing Congress. This was done by a letter sent on September 25, 1990, to Representative Dan Rostenkowski, chair of the House Ways and Means Committee, and Senator Lloyd Bentsen, chair of the Senate Finance Committee. The letter also indicated that Canada wished to join the negotiations. In a March 1, 1991, communiqué to Congress, Bush asked for "fast track" authority to negotiate a continental free trade agreement and bring the Uruguay Round talks to a conclusion.

Fast track authority is a procedure by which Congress agrees in advance to accept or reject a trade agreement as a single package. Without fast track authority Congress would have the right to make whatever changes it feels prudent when a trade agreement is put before it for approval. The problem is that by doing so Congress might undo delicate compromises reached by negotiators and in the process raise questions about the reliability of U.S. promises. Although Senate approval of fast track authority seemed assured, it was a different matter in the House, where the administration appeared to be some 80 votes shy of the number it needed. In May, after the conclusion of the Persian Gulf War, President Bush began a fervent lobbying campaign on behalf of the fast track. He played upon his newfound popularity and defined the vote as one of free trade versus protectionism. Bush also enlisted the support of key legislators such as House Speaker Thomas Foley, House Majority

Leader Richard Gephardt, and Rostenkowski, and major business leaders and entered into agreements with labor and environmental groups. Labor Secretary Lynn Martin signed a memorandum with Mexican officials dealing with such matters as worker health and safety standards, collective bargaining, and working conditions. Efforts to placate environmental groups included the announcement of an Integrated Environmental Plan for the border, and a promise that environmental groups would serve on bodies advising U.S. Trade Representative Carla Hills. These efforts were successful, and in May both houses defeated motions denying Bush fast track authority.

NAFTA talks began in Toronto on June 12, 1991. On October 7, 1992, the 2,000-page agreement was signed in San Antonio. In between, there were countless hours of formal negotiating sessions, informal working groups, faxes, and telephone calls. Little of substance was accomplished at the first several meetings. A first attempt at producing a composite treaty was taken at the end of 1991 and amounted to nothing more than listing in sequential order the Mexican, American, and Canadian position on each topic. For some topics (agriculture, energy, textiles, automobiles, and trade remedies) it was not even possible to do this.

With this "run-on" text in place, U.S. negotiators pressed hard for concessions in early 1992 as attention turned to finding common language for each section. In part, they were motivated by the realization that at this stage the agreement was not a very good one. As one participant noted, settling for a "half-assed agreement . . . would have cost us badly needed support within the business community at a time of intense labor union opposition." Steady confirmation of the need to get real concessions from Mexico on its protectionist trade policies came in the form of a constant flow of communication from Capitol Hill.

Several factors came together to give birth to this stream of political discourse. First, angered by the Reagan administration's lack of candor in informing it about the progress of talks with Canada on the CFTA, Congress was determined to make its voice heard on NAFTA. Second, very real concerns continued to exist in many districts over the contents of any agreement, and the golden rule for most congresspeople is that "all politics is local" and foreign policy is no exception. Finally, exception was taken by some to the "five noes" put forward by Mexico's Commerce Secretary Jaime Serra Puche. Mexico would say no to diminishing its control over the exploration, development, and refinement of primary petrochemicals; guaranteeing oil supplies to other states; relinquishing its monopoly over commerce, transportation, storage, and distribution of energy; permitting high-risk contracts in exploration and production; and allowing foreign gasoline stations. In mid-March 1992, seven energy state senators proposed a set of "guiding principles" for negotiations in this area that were at odds with each of these five noes. In fact, the United States and Canada also entered the talks with their list of unnegotiable items. For the United States they included Mexican immigration to the United States; "set asides" and other preferences given to minorities, veterans, and small businesses in government contracting; and the requirement that goods shipped between U.S. ports must be carried on ships built and registered in the United States and staffed by American crews.

Progress continued to be slow, and U.S. hopes of concluding an agreement in time for congressional action before the upcoming presidential election faded. All of this changed with the February 1992 Dallas meeting. This was the first session at which all nineteen working groups were present. It also witnessed an explosion by U.S. chief negotiator Julius Katz, who charged Mexico with holding an unacceptable position on the question of trade barriers. With the Mexican negotiator acknowledging that because its economy was the most closed of the three Mexico would have to make the most concessions, the talks became energized. By late winter the twelve hundred contested or bracketed portions of the Dallas Composite Text had been reduced to a few hundred.

The endgame to the NAFTA negotiations began in July at the Watergate Hotel in Washington. The Bush administration wanted to announce that an agreement had been reached prior to the start of the Republican national convention. It looked upon the NAFTA agreement as a vehicle for generating Republican votes in Texas and California. Together these states led the United States in exports to Mexico and possessed 86 of the 270 electoral votes needed to win the presidency. Marathon sessions produced enough progress that such an announcement was made by Bush on August 12. NAFTA was mentioned frequently at the convention and USTR Carla Hills addressed the delegates extolling its virtues. The NAFTA agreement was not, however, complete. Almost round-the-clock negotiations continued for three weeks into late August as points of disagreement were resolved so that the treaty could be submitted to the Senate in September.

THE RATIFICATION PHASE

In a political sense the NAFTA ratification debate began with Bush's signing of the agreement. And the battleground was not Congress but the political campaign trail. Bush hoped that the NAFTA agreement would cement his place in the eyes of the American public as a world leader. Instead, it became a central issue in what would become a referendum on the state of the American economy. Leading the early charge against NAFTA was a one-time supporter of it, Ross Perot. Proclaiming it the product of a conspiracy among Washington insiders, foreign lobbyists, PAC-influenced congresspeople, and huge corporations, Perot asserted that NAFTA would cost American workers their jobs, homes, and savings. In mid-July, during the Democratic convention, Perot ended his presidential bid.

With that the focus of attention shifted to the views of the Democratic party and its nominee. Bill Clinton had straddled the fence on NAFTA during the primaries and would repeat this strategy during the general election. A long-standing advocate of free trade, Clinton softened his endorsement of NAFTA in order not to offend organized labor, whose voice carried a great deal of weight in many of the Democratic primaries, as it had traditionally supported Democratic candidates. After securing the nomination Clinton used the fact that all of the details of the NAFTA agreement had not been worked out as his rationale for not moving to endorse the agreement quickly. In late September the Clinton campaign team was still split on whether to back the NAFTA agreement. When Clinton finally announced his support for NAFTA in October, he conditioned it on the stipulation that the text be improved through the addition of supplemental agreements to cover "serious" omissions. Election results and exit polls showed that the Bush campaign had misread the mood of the American public. By November, only 21 percent of the voters supported NAFTA and a majority opposed it in Texas and southern California.

The three side deals required as necessary by candidate Clinton involved "surges," or the sudden inflow of large amounts of foreign goods into the U.S. market; the environment; and labor. The issues involved in the environmental side deal were sufficiently complex that it took the U.S. delegation several months to agree upon a unified position. For example, the question of whether trade sanctions should be used against polluters found the USTR, the Environmental Protection Agency (EPA), and the Treasury Department supporting the idea and the State Department opposing it. Environmental groups strongly supported the use of trade sanctions and expressed their views to a wide range of officials in the Clinton administration, including Vice President Gore's office; the White House's Office of Environmental Policy; the EPA; the National Security Council; and the offices of like-minded legislators. These multiple contact points not only reflected the reality of policy making in Washington but a decision by the Clinton administration to encourage environmental groups to submit recommendations on key issues.

As to the negotiations, it was clear that the United States was at odds with Mexico and Canada over many of the key points to be resolved. Clinton's initial response was to allow the negotiations to drift. This reflected the reality that presidents only have so much political capital to invest and that priorities must be established. Health care and the budget came far ahead of NAFTA for most in the Clinton administration. Only in later summer did the Clinton administration decide on a position with regard to sanctions. At a meeting of the National Economic Council, Clinton asked Secretary of State Warren Christopher and USTR Mickey Kantor to lay out the pros and cons of sanctions. When Secretary of the Treasury Lloyd Bentsen, a known opponent of sanctions, endorsed the concept as politically necessary for securing approval of NAFTA, Clinton came on board. Mexico continued to oppose the idea and reportedly only dropped its objections after Majority Leader Richard Gephardt informed Serra Puche that without sanctions NAFTA would not pass the House.

Formally the side deals were treated as executive agreements and not parts of the treaty to be voted on by Congress. The side deals allowed the Clinton administration to achieve three important political goals: (1) they fulfilled a campaign promise; (2) they demonstrated that the administration was capable of successfully addressing important policy problems; and (3) they laid the foundation for a pro-NAFTA lobby on Capitol Hill that would be needed for the ratification vote.

As the ratification vote neared, the Clinton administration was convinced it had won the scholarly argument over the merits of NAFTA. Support came from across the ideological spectrum. Conservatives (James Buchanan and Milton Friedman) and liberals (Paul Samuelson and James Tobin) joined with political moderates in endorsing it, as did all eight living Nobel Prize winners in economics. The problem facing the Clinton administration was that the political argument was far from won. The AFL-CIO remained steadfast in its opposition as did political figures inside and outside of Congress. Gephardt and Majority Whip David Bonior were prominent members of the first group while Ralph Nader, Ross Perot, Pat Buchanan, and Jerry Brown were vocal members of the second. Dissatisfaction with the environmental side deal negotiated by the Clinton administration led many environmental groups to continue their opposition to NAFTA. Also lobbying against NAFTA were groups that condemned ongoing electoral fraud and human rights abuses in Mexico.

Within the Clinton administration, NAFTA continued to compete with other policies, most notably health care, for the president's attention. Convinced that NAFTA would only be ratified if President Clinton actively became involved in the lobbying effort, Kantor arranged for William M. Daley to be appointed as special counselor to the president for NAFTA. His job was to raise the stakes of the NAFTA vote so high that Clinton would have no choice but to direct his energies toward securing its passage. A three-pronged effort was organized. First, Howard Pastor, the Presidential Assistant for Legislative Affairs, began building links with Capitol Hill by setting up briefing sessions and arranging for personal communications between Clinton and wavering legislators. Second, Daley mobilized the cabinet to lobby for NAFTA. Alone, the State Department produced 216 speeches and 116 media interviews on NAFTA as well as conducting sixty-three briefings for members of Congress. Laura D'Andrea Tyson, chair of the Council of Economic Advisers, called or visited almost every female legislator. Daley also arranged for major media events highlighting support for NAFTA. The first took place on September 16 when Clinton signed the three side deal agreements in the presence of former presidents Bush, Carter, and Ford.

The final element of the administration's strategy to win approval for NAFTA involved yet another round of side deals designed to gain the final votes needed. This effort was led by Kantor, who met with dozens of undecided congresspeople. Among the bargains struck: Florida legislators were assured that the administration would put in place safeguards for sugar, citrus, tomato, sweet pepper, and asparagus growers as tariffs were reduced and increasing amounts of Mexico produce entered the U.S. market; legislators from southern textile-producing states were promised that textile quotas would be phased out over fifteen years instead of ten; a Texas congressperson received an assurance that a Center for the Study of Trade in the Western Hemisphere would be located in his district; and another Texas congressperson got the administration's pledge to construct two C-17 military cargo planes. Many of these deals required Kantor to contact his Mexican counterparts and gain their approval. Reportedly, these last-minute deals angered Mexican leaders who nevertheless felt that they had no choice but to go along with them in order to get NAFTA ratified.

Congress voted on NAFTA on November 17, 1993. The Senate gave its approval by a vote of 61–38 while the House voted 234–200 in favor of it. As this case study shows, the Bush and Clinton administrations found themselves in two sets of negotiating games. The first involved getting agreement from Mexico and Canada on the details of a continental free trade pact. The second involved securing a domestic political consensus for the agreement. The two games often proceeded at the same time and agreements reached in one had major consequences for how the other was played.

Summary

In this chapter, we used policy-making models to help make sense of four complex and important sets of foreign policy decisions: the Cuban missile crisis, pre–9/11 intelligence policy on terrorism, the giving of U.S. foreign aid, and negotiating NAFTA. To repeat a point made at the end of the previous chapter, no one perspective is able to provide us with insight into all foreign policy decisions. Different models must be used at different times, and the challenge to the student of U.S. foreign policy is to decide which model(s) will be most helpful. In the next several chapters, our attention shifts from how policy is made to the range of instruments available to policy makers to achieve their goals.

The process of analyzing decisions in order to understand why American foreign policy looks like it does is never completed. New information constantly surfaces that requires us to reexamine our findings. U.S. foreign policy toward Cuba is a case in point. In March 2001, a fortieth-anniversary reunion meeting was held in Cuba that brought together both sides of the Bay of Pigs invasion. In 1999, a revised edition of *Essence of Decision* was published.[22] First published in 1977, this is the landmark work on which our discussion of the Cuban missile crisis was based. The 1999 edition qualifies and changes some of the conclusions reached by the original work. For example, it gives far less credence to the "defend Cuba argument." But even this does not end the matter as another historian has taken exception to its new conclusions.[23] Thus the debate continues, with a more recent account suggesting that the prospect theory offers important insights into the crisis that other decision-making models do not reveal.[24]

Notes

1. For discussion of Cuban missile crisis decision making, see Graham T. Allison, *The Essence of Decision: Explaining the Cuban Missile Crisis* (Boston: Little, Brown, 1971); Theodore Sorensen, *Kennedy* (New York: Harper & Row, 1965); and Richard Ned Lebow, *Between Peace and War: The Nature of International Crisis* (Baltimore, Md.: Johns Hopkins University Press, 1981).

2. James A. Nathan and James K. Oliver, *United States Foreign Policy and World Order,* 3rd ed. (Boston: Little, Brown, 1985), p. 275.

3. Allison, *The Essence of Decision,* p. 103.

4. Ibid., pp. 58–61.

5. *Washington Post,* July 25, 1985, p. A10.

6. Allison, *The Essence of Decision,* p. 64.

7. *Washington Post,* Sec. A, p. 1.

8. The most important of these is Raymond Garthoff, *Reflections on the Cuban Missile Crisis*, rev. ed. (Washington, D.C.: Brookings, 1989). The revised edition contains insights into the crisis that came out of a joint U.S.–Soviet conference on the Cuban missile crisis held in 1987.

9. Irving Janis, *Groupthink*, 2nd ed. (Boston: Houghton Mifflin, 1982), pp. 132–58.

10. Lebow, *Between Peace and War*, especially Chap. 8.

11. Unless otherwise noted the quotes and material in this section is drawn from *The 9/11 Commission Report* (New York: Norton, 2004) and *The 9/11 Investigations* (New York: Public Affairs Reports, 2004).

12. Information on the intelligence cycle can be found at the Central Intelligence Agency's website, www.cia.gov, and in Bruce Berkowitz and Allan Goodman, *Strategic Intelligence for American National Security* (Princeton, Princeton University Press, 1989), pp. 185–193.

13. Sherman Kent, Strategic *Intelligence for American World Policy* (Princeton, Princeton University Press, 1949), p. 202.

14. Pat Holt, *Strategic Intelligence and Public Policy: A Dilemma of Democracy* (Washington, D.C.: Congressional Quarterly Press, 1995), p. 80.

15. Seymour Hersh, "The Stovepipe," *The New Yorker*, 79 (October 27, 2003), 77+.

16. Richard Clarke, *Against All Enemies* (New York: Free Press, 2004), p. 231-2.

17. Bob Woodward, *Bush at War* (New York: Simon & Schuster, 2002), p. 132.

18. The study is entitled "Clean Break" and is discussed in James Bamford, *A Pretext for War* (New York: Doubleday, 2004).

19. The material in this section is taken from George W. Grayson, *The North American Free Trade Agreement: Regional Community and the New World Order*, Volume III, the Miller Center Series on a New World Order (Latham, Md.: University of America Press, 1995).

20. Robert D. Putnam, "Diplomacy and Domestic Politics: The Logic of Two-Level Games," *International Organization*, 42 (1988), 427–60.

21. Peter B. Evans, "Building an Integrative Approach to International and Domestic Politics," in Peter B. Evans, Harold K. Jacobson, and Robert D. Putnam (eds.), *Double-Edged Diplomacy: International Bargaining and Domestic Politics* (Berkeley: University of California Press, 1993), p. 397.

22. Graham Allison and Philip Zelikow, *Essence of Decision: Explaining the Cuban Missile Crisis*, 2nd ed. (New York: Addison Wesley Longman, 1999).

23. Barton Bernstein, "Understanding Decisionmaking, U.S. Foreign Policy, and the Cuban Missile Crisis," *International Security*, 25 (2000), 134–64.

24. Mark Haas, "Prospect Theory and the Cuban Missile Crisis," *International Studies Quarterly*, 45 (2001), 241–70.

— 13 —

DIPLOMACY

Selecting a Policy Instrument

Policy makers must decide not only what goals to pursue but how to pursue them. Depending on the specifics of the situation and a state's power resources, the range of instruments available to it may be large or quite restricted. The choice is an important one because an improperly chosen policy tool can do as much harm to U.S. national interests as can misguided policy objectives.[1] The most basic consideration to be kept in mind is that all choices are costly. No instrument frees policy makers from having to decide what risks they are willing to take and what values and goals they are willing to sacrifice. More problematic is how to measure these costs. The temptation is to ignore costs altogether. This danger is especially great when the options appear to be few and the need to act great. Confronted with this situation, policy makers are apt to place too great a value on the options still open to them by refusing to recognize their limitations and liabilities.

A second basic consideration is that measuring effectiveness is a complicated undertaking. Success and failure are often treated as absolute categories, yet this is seldom the case. Far more typical are situations where success and failure are both present in varying degrees. Also, a state rarely has only one goal when it undertakes a course of action, and the reality of multiple goals further complicates the calculations of costs and benefits. Estimates of success and failure also depend on one's time frame. Economic sanctions work slowly, but that does not mean that they are any less effective than fast-acting ones. They might even be preferable because they minimize the risk of miscalculation that accompanies crisis situations.

A third consideration to be kept in mind in selecting a policy instrument is the context within which it will operate. Economic strategies that worked well in an era when the United States was a hegemonic or predominant economic power may prove less useful in an era of economic decline or parity. Similarly, policy tools that were effective in a cold war international system will not necessarily be as effective in a post–cold war system. International crisis management techniques, military alliance systems, covert action, and arms transfer, to name only a few, derived their underlying rationale from the existence of global U.S.–Soviet rivalry. Today, it is argued that "soft" or intangible sources of power are fast becoming the primary means of influence that states must rely upon to achieve their goals. If this is the case, then future American foreign policy instruments will have to be based less on military power and the ability to coerce others and more on the control of information and the ability to set agendas and structure situations in such a way that others will be co-opted and accept U.S. leadership.

Our focus in this chapter is on diplomacy. As an instrument of foreign policy, diplomacy is closely identified with bargaining and negotiation. For many it remains the classic policy instrument and the one best suited to producing lasting and workable solutions to foreign policy problems. Others point out that the use of diplomacy is not without its dangers. Negotiations also hold the potential for exacerbating hostilities, strengthening an aggressor, preparing the way for an attack, and eroding the moral and legal foundations of peace.[2] They do so because in addition to solving problems, negotiations can also be used to stall for time, obtain information, and make propaganda.

HUMAN RIGHTS

The twentieth century has been a period of great change in the practice of diplomacy. Prior to World War I, diplomacy was largely European centered and dealt with a fairly restricted range of issues. Diplomacy was also the preserve of the Great Powers. Negotiations were confidential with the outcome largely rooted in a quid pro quo spirit of compromise. The diplomacy of the 1990s and beyond looks far different. It is a hybrid characterized by secret discussions and public declarations; and it is carried out in an international environment in which nonstate actors often play a prominent role.

A case in point is American human rights policy. Holly Burkhalter, the Washington director of Human Rights Watch, observes that "constructing a successful human rights policy in the 1990s is a vastly different proposition than it was in the late 1970s or early 1980s."[3] Compared to today, the issues were relatively uncomplicated and problems could be addressed by holding American policy makers responsible for the human rights violations of their client states and counseling them to "first, do no harm." Few of today's human rights problems can be directly tied to the actions of American or Russian allies, and a "do no harm" strategy offers little prospect of alleviating many of the human rights violations chronicled in the press. Human rights policy is changing in three respects. First, human rights policy has moved out of the shadows of U.S. cold war–containment thinking to focus on internal conflicts, especially in multiethnic states. In the process, human rights policy has become intertwined in U.S. support for democratization. There has been tentative movement from a strict focus on civil and political rights to one that embraces economic and social rights.

The complexity of today's human rights policy is evident at all levels of U.S. diplomacy. Since 1977, the State Department has submitted annual human rights reports to Congress. That year, eighty-two countries, all of which received American foreign aid, were reported on. In 1993, 193 reports were compiled. This figure far exceeded not only the number of states receiving foreign aid but also the total membership of the United Nations.[4] The initial drafts were prepared by U.S. embassies and then sent to Washington where they were reviewed by the Bureau of Human Rights and Humanitarian Affairs. At both stages, diplomats were in contact with officials from other parts of the State Department, nongovernmental organizations (NGOs), and international organizations (IGOs). Along with Amnesty International, the Human Rights Watch is one of the many NGOs that have come to play a prominent role in human rights foreign policy issues as agenda setters, mobilizers of public and elite opinion, and compliance monitors.[5] They target not only governments but international organizations (where they often meet in "shadow" or parallel international forums that preceed major international conferences) and multinational corporations investing in states such as South Africa or China whose human rights policies they oppose.

In addition to being carried out on a bilateral basis, American human rights policy is also conducted in multilateral settings such as in the United Nations system and at global conferences. This aspect of American foreign policy has come under heavy criticism in the 1990s. But according to Margaret Karns and Karen Mingst, on the whole multilateral institutions have not placed real constraints on U.S. strategic choices although they often have necessitated changes in strategies and tactics and influenced the makeup of the policy agenda.[6] Human rights is no exception to the rule. American involvement in UN human rights policy making went through several distinct stages during the cold war: (1) a period of limited support (1945–1953); (2) a period of neglect (1954–1974); (3) a period of renewed interest (1974–1981); and (4) a period of renewed anticommunism (1981–1990). More so than changes in the nature of human rights as a problem or the makeup of the United Nations, it was changes in the nature of American domestic politics that produced this pattern.

Implementing U.S. human rights policy raises all of the issues that we identified at the outset of this chapter.[7] A recent survey identifies seven different policy tools that have been employed most frequently. They include private diplomacy, public diplomacy, democracy promotion, cultural exchanges, and economic and political sanctions. No single policy tool will be appropriate for all situations and, like military or economic policy initiatives, human rights initiatives must be strategically timed or the impact will be minimal. Students of U.S. human rights policy add on observation that is pertinent for all policy instruments. We must be "open to the possibility of the United States being part of the problem rather than the solution."[8]

Bilateral Diplomacy

The most common form of diplomacy is bilateral diplomacy, in which two states interact directly with one another. These relations occur at varying levels from the head of government and ambassador down to the most junior foreign service officer. They also can cover a wide array of subjects ranging from sensitive security and economic issues to the routine issuing of passports. Bilateral relations are assuming a new prominence today. In part, this is attributed to the end of the cold war, the disappearance of the cold war alliance systems, and the emergence of a series of new states out of the breakup of the Soviet Union and Yugoslavia. Its increased visibility is also a product of the absence of any overarching strategic framework for guiding American foreign policy. Without it, decisions will be heavily influenced by country-specific considerations.

We can identify three different types of bilateral relationships, each of which has its own unique set of characteristics: allies, friends, adversaries. Dealings with allies are marked by high levels of commitment to the negotiation process, a recognition that a wide area of common interests exists, and a willingness to address the specific issues involved in a dispute. Relations with adversaries also are marked by a high degree of commitment and attention but lack any sense of shared interests. Instead there is an underlying sense of conflict and distrust. As a result, much of the bilateral dialogue centers on finding formula-based solutions for problems. Finally, there are bilateral relations among friends. These are relations between states that are on good terms but lack extensive dealings with one another. As a result, it is often difficult to strike a deal as each side advances its own particular interest in the absence of widely perceived common interests.

Perhaps nothing illustrates the tribulations of bilateral diplomacy more than the George W. Bush administration's attempt to construct a roadmap for peace in the Middle East. The roadmap was completed in October 2002 and consisted of a three-step plan that would produce a Palestinian state by 2005 and cement peaceful relations between Israel and the Palestinians. Technically a joint proposal developed by the United States, the European Union, Russia, and the United Nations, in practice the roadmap has been a U.S. plan assembled through bilateral negotiations with Israel and the Palestinian Authority. A string of suicide bombings, Israeli reprisals, and broken cease-fires left it in shambles, with the Bush administration conditioning its acceptance of its own plan on Yasser Arafat's removal from power and endorsing a plan by Israeli Prime Minister Ariel Sharon to withdraw from the Gaza Strip, keep some West Bank settlements, and block Palestinian refugees from settling in Israel. This last action was designed to break the deadlock but only intensified it when Sharon's own party rejected the plan and Arab states complained about the administration's actions as being tantamount to unilaterally imposing a peace agreement on the Palestinians. More broadly, critics complained that the administration's policy failed because of a pattern of bilateral diplomacy characterized by "a burst of publicity about new initiatives or special envoys, followed by policy drift and an unwillingness to push either side . . . eventually the effort goes dormant, sometimes for months, until yet another approach is crafted."[9]

It should also be recognized that bilateral diplomacy is an important factor in any multilateral diplomatic effort. This was very evident in creating and holding together the global coalition against terrorism. Pakistan at varying times warned the United States against forming an alliance with anti-Taliban forces in northern Afghanistan and opposed bombing during Ramadan. Russia made it clear that it expected to be consulted prior to any expansion of the war to Iraq, an expansion it opposed. Turkey repeatedly offered to lead an international peacekeeping operation in Afghanistan in an effort to strengthen its relationship with Europe. Coalition relations with Israel and the Arab states were complicated by the outbreak of renewed Palestinian terrorist activity and Israeli military action. The George W. Bush administration even considered recruiting Iran into the coalition. The task of coalition management was made even more complex by the need to negotiate with such non-state actors as the Northern Alliance.

INCENTIVES VERSUS SANCTIONS

One of the most difficult decisions that must be made in bilateral relations involves the choice between employing (or threatening to employ) sanctions and offering incentives. The later strategy, termed engagement, is relatively understudied compared to that of sanctions.[10] Incentives can include the removal of sanctions or the offering of additional trade and foreign aid. Diplomatic recognition, joint military training exercises, and building people-to-people contacts are also examples of incentives that can be offered. If engagement is chosen, the key decision policy makers must make is whether the strategy is conditional on the other state undertaking specific actions or if it is unconditional.

Offering incentives to a friend or ally is easily done. It becomes much more controversial when the target state is a foe. Yet, it is precisely with these states that the strategy of engagement may offer its greatest benefits because it provides an avenue for dialogue that did not previously exist. The Clinton administration's policies toward North Korea and Vietnam, for example, were based on engagement rather than sanctions. U.S. policy toward China with its emphasis on expanding trade opportunities similarly has a strong engagement element. The greatest challenge faced by architects of engagement strategies is to avoid the charge that they are appeasing dangerous states rather than providing for U.S. security. This is in large part because approached as a domestic politics problem, it is far easier to demonize the other state than engage in negotiations with it. It helps focus public attention on specific aspects of the problem, moral clarity is retained, and attention is deflected from the inconsistencies and indecisions of their policies and placed on the actions of the other.[11] The downside to a strategy of relying on sanctions and demonizing an opponent is that it limits options both for the current administration and its successors. No case better illustrates this point than Fidel Castro and American foreign policy toward Cuba.

Summit Diplomacy

The most visible of all the forms of diplomacy today is summit diplomacy in which the heads of state meet personally with one another. The most important cold war summit conferences involved meetings of U.S. and Soviet leaders. Western leaders have also begun to meet annually in summits in an effort to deal with economic problems. Summit conferences perform a number of valuable services.[12] Foremost among them is establishing a personal relationship between leaders that sensitizes each to the domestic constraints operating in the other's political system. A second valuable service performed by a summit is that it energizes the bureaucracy and sets a deadline for decision making. The benefit here is not so much the summit itself but the preparations for the summit. The SALT I negotiations and the U.S.–Japanese agreement over the status of Okinawa were both carried out under the deadline of an approaching summit conference.

Aligned against these positive virtues of summit diplomacy are a number of potentially negative consequences.[13] First, the personal contacts established may result in an inaccurate reading of the adversary's character and the constraints the adversary operates under. This appears to have happened at the 1961 Kennedy–Khrushchev summit in Vienna. Khrushchev reportedly came away from it with the impression that Kennedy could be intimidated, and many link the Soviet attempt to place missiles in Cuba to this meeting. Another prime example is Roosevelt's belief that he could establish a personal working relationship with Stalin as a result of the World War II summit conferences in Tehran and Yalta.

Energizing the bureaucracy does not necessarily guarantee the emergence of a coherent policy. It may only intensify the ongoing bureaucratic struggle so that only a lowest-common-denominator position is taken to the summit. Summit deadlines may also politicize or impede decision making. This point is most forcefully raised with reference to annual economic summitry, but as the many accounts of U.S.–Soviet arms control talks reveal, it is equally applicable to other forms of international diplomacy.[14] Other commentators suggest that periodic meetings are a questionable device for addressing a continuously evolving problem. Agreements reached in April become obsolete in November, but the next summit is still months away. Inaction rather than adaptive problem solving is likely to characterize the bureaucratic process for most of the intervening months. In addition, summit deadlines offer the recalcitrant state a golden opportunity to exploit the other's eagerness for the summit. One observer suggests that this may have happened with the Carter–Brezhnev summit. Carter's desire for a summit is seen as partly responsible for his supporting a Soviet initiative to reconvene the Geneva talks on the Middle East. The result, had this actually happened, would have been to give the Soviet Union a voice in the Middle East peace process that was denied to it as long as U.S. peace initiatives dominated the agenda.[15]

Summit conferences have also been criticized for unfairly raising public expectations about the potential for a meaningful agreement. Should no positive benefits be forthcoming, the resulting public disillusionment can greatly complicate the conduct of future diplomatic ventures. The SALT agreements were negotiated as part of the process of détente, and when détente began to unravel, arms control efforts were one of the main casualties. To deal with many of these shortcomings, President Richard Nixon advocated regular summit conferences as a way of keeping the pressure on the Soviet Union, curbing its behavior, and taking the pressure off getting a major agreement at any one summit.[16]

EAST–WEST SUPERPOWER SUMMITS[17]

East-West summit conferences were a frequent, if irregularly spaced, feature of the cold war. The first summits, from 1955-1967, dealt with European security issues. Later they would become an important mechanism for institutionalizing détente. All told they produced more than 24 agreements including SALT I and SALT II. Reagan and Gorbachev conducted a series of post-détente summit conferences. The most famous of which was the Reykjavik Summit in 1986. Here, Reagan proposed abolishing all ballistic missiles and Gorbachev countered with a proposal to eliminate all strategic arms. Nothing came of these initiatives because they would have prohibited Reagan from engaging in SDI testing outside of the laboratory, something he refused to do. With the disintegration of the Soviet Union and the end of the cold war, East-West summits declined in their overall strategic importance and increasingly focused on economic assistance instead of arms control. After 9/11 they became a vehicle for George W. Bush to enlist Russian help in the war on terrorism.

WESTERN ECONOMIC SUMMITS

Beginning in 1975, the heads of state of the major Western economies have met at an annual summit conference. With the end of the cold war, the passing of the Soviet threat, and the emergence of economic issues as paramount foreign policy concerns, economic summits have replaced "military" summits as the primary meeting place for world leaders.[18]

While economic issues dominated the discussions at the first several summits, with the passage of time other issues are now discussed at them as well. In 1996, at President Clinton's urging the summit's agenda was broadened to include terrorism and international crime. Considerable time at the 1997 summit was spent on global warming as well as the situation in Bosnia and the wisdom of the U.S. pledge to withdraw its peacekeeping forces in June 1998. At the 1998 summit, the heads of state expressed their frustration over India's detonation of a nuclear device, urged the Israelis and Palestinians to resume negotiations, and called for political and economic reform in Indonesia. The willingness to address a broad agenda has not been matched by an ability to reach a consensus on what action to take. For example, in 1996 Clinton was able to get support for a crackdown on terrorism but not for punishing firms that do business with countries that sponsor terrorism, and in 1998 the heads of state were unable to agree on whether to apply sanctions against India. The 1998 summit was significant because it marked the formal entrance of

Russia into the summit process and for its renaming from the annual meeting of the Group of Seven (G-7) to the Group of Eight (G-8).

The 2003 G-8 meeting was held in France and provided the first opportunity for George W. Bush and French President Jacques Chirac to meet since the Iraq War. Relations between the two were cool, although Bush did use the meeting to cement better relations with Russian President Vladimir Putin, who also opposed the war. In 2004, the G-8 meeting was in Savannah. Iraq dominated the meeting, with Bush pushing for but failing to get agreement for NATO troops to help govern occupied Iraq. In other matters, the G-8 leaders agreed on the need for developing an anti-AIDS vaccine and promised to do more to combat famine. Agreement was not reached on how to deal with Third World debt or on how much of Iraq's debt to forgive.

Conference Diplomacy

GATT AND WTO

In addition to summitry, the U.S. has relied heavily on international conferences to accomplish its foreign policy objectives. Particularly important for the U.S. economy have been trade talks. Historically, the most important of these have been the GATT talks. The last GATT conference ran from 1986 to 1994 and was known as the Uruguay Round. It culminated with the signing of an agreement that established the World Trade Organization (WTO) that would supervise international trade law and formally bring the GATT process to an end.

From its first meeting in Geneva in 1947, GATT had been seen as a transitional body that would deal with international trade matters only until an international trade organization (ITO) was set up. Because of political opposition within the United States to the broad powers that were to be given the ITO, President Truman never submitted the treaty creating it to Congress for approval. Similar concerns about the loss of U.S. sovereignty were expressed when the WTO was proposed. Only a last-minute compromise which reserved the right of the United States to leave the WTO should it consistently rule against the United States, cleared the way for the treaty's approval by the Senate.

Two earlier important rounds of GATT trade negotiations were the Kennedy Round (1964 to 1967) and the Tokyo Round (1973 to 1977). The Kennedy Round sought to reduce barriers to international free trade, and marked the high point of international trade cooperation. By the late 1970s tariffs averaged less than 10 percent. This compared to 25 percent in 1945 and 60 percent in 1934. The second prolonged negotiating session, the Tokyo Round, was not as successful. The new focus of concern was nontariff barriers to trade (NTBs). The Tokyo Round made some progress on NTBs. Agreements were reached on such practices as subsidies, dumping, countervailing duties, product standards, and government purchases. The principal failings of the Tokyo Round were that little headway was reached on liberalizing agricultural trade, and that questions of trade in services were not addressed.

The Uruguay Round took up these issues. Agriculture pitted the rich countries against the poor and the U.S. against Western Europe. At the heart of the problem was the need for more markets for agricultural goods, the widespread presence of subsidies and quotas that protected farmers from foreign competition, and the unwillingness of leaders to antagonize the politically powerful agricultural interests within their states. For its part, the United States was unwilling to stop subsidizing sugar growers and expose them to competition from Third World producers. But at the same time it demanded that France stop subsidizing its soybean farmers and open European markets to American soybean producers. A second area of concern to the United States was international protection for intellectual property. American firms charged that Third World states routinely disregarded copyrights and patents in the production of such items as books, compact disks, and computer software. A third area of controversy centered on the demands of the United States and Europe for setting international labor standards with regard to child labor, convict labor, minimum wages, and unions. The United States and Europe also pressed, against Third World objections, for the establishment of a body to examine the environmental impact of the GATT agreement.

In November 2001, representatives from over 140 states met in Doha, Qatar, and approved the launching of a new three-year round of global trade talks under the auspices of the recently created WTO. Among the topics highlighted for negotiation were agriculture, services, industrial tariffs, investment, and environmentally harmful fishing practices. Representatives met again in Cancun, Mexico, in September 2003 for the purpose of moving these discussions forward. Instead, they collapsed largely over Third World complaints led by China, India, and Brazil, that rich states were subsidizing agriculture at the rate of $300 billion per year resulting in overproduction that was flooding into world markets, artificially lowering the cost of food, and costing farm jobs in their countries. Whereas the Third World press hailed the failure of the WTO Cancun meeting as a "great moral victory for the world's poor," U.S. Trade Representative Robert Zoellick took a different view. He asserted failure occurred because some countries "used rhetoric as opposed to negotiation." Rich states were pressing poor states to accept new rules on foreign investment and government procurement.

ENVIRONMENTAL CONFERENCES

Conference diplomacy also has become a central vehicle for international environmental policy making. However, just as with international economic conference diplomacy, the complexity of these issues, coupled with the imperatives of American domestic politics, has made it difficult for the United States to exert leadership and has often placed it at odds with the rest of the world. This was very much the case during the first Reagan administration, which sought both to weaken domestic environmental standards and limit U.S. support for international environmental programs. The convergence of many factors brought about a policy shift in Reagan's second term as the United States assumed a leadership position in international negotiations that led to the signing of the 1987 Montreal Protocol on Substances That Deplete the Ozone Layer. Foremost among these factors were changes in personnel at the Environmental Protection Agency and the State Department; the commitment of leading American firms such as Dupont to support a ban on chlorofluorocarbon (CFC) emissions; growing global concern about the environment spurred by the Chernobyl nuclear reactor accident; and mounting scientific evidence regarding ozone depletion and global warming.[19]

The Montreal Protocol was hailed widely for the real cuts it was able to make in the production and consumption of ozone-depleting materials and for its procedural approach to the problem. Rather than seek a definitive and comprehensive statement about levels of reduction, funding, and the obligations of signatory states as had commonly been done in the past, negotiators at Montreal established a framework for addressing the problem and committed themselves to periodic review conferences where target figures and timetables could be adjusted.

The George H. W. Bush administration's principal foray into international environmental conference diplomacy was the United Nations Conference on Environment and Development. Better known as the "Earth Summit," it took place June 3 to 14, 1992, in Rio de Janeiro, Brazil. The product of almost two years of advance negotiations and attended by about 35,000 accredited delegates representing over 178 countries, the Earth Summit ended with the signing of seven major pacts and initiatives. It also found the United States on the defensive and the only major state not to sign a biodiversity treaty. The Bush administration objected to the treaty's provisions calling for all states to protect endangered animal and plant species, on the grounds that it did not provide patent protection to U.S. biotechnology firms. This was later signed by the Clinton administration. The United States was also virtually alone in its objections to a treaty for protection against global warming. It only agreed to support it after references to binding targets and timetables were dropped in favor of a more general pledge to reduce the emissions of gases that cause global warming.

One area in which very little progress was made at the Earth Summit was overpopulation. Pressure from the Vatican, conservative Catholic states, and Muslim states led to a deemphasis on population control strategies in summit documents. The Clinton administration found itself at the center of controversy on population matters with these same forces two years later at the United Nations' Third International Conference on Population and Development in Cairo. This 1994 meeting brought together representatives from 180 states and produced a 113-page "Program of Action." At issue was the conference's stand on abortion. The Vatican opposed abortion on moral grounds and successfully maneuvered to soften the language used in final conference documents. The United States' position stopped short of asserting that abortions should be an international right. Rather, it argued that abortions must be legal, safe, and voluntary and that they should be part of a wide range of health services available to women.

A major international environmental conference took place in Kyoto in 1997. It was agreed that industrial states would reduce greenhouse emissions of six gases from 1990 levels by more than 5 percent between 2008 and 2012. Kyoto was significant because it was the first legally binding environmental agreement even though no compliance mechanisms were established and

Third World states were only asked to set up voluntary targets. The United States signed the agreement but the Clinton administration indicated it had reservations and was interested in having parts changed. The George W. Bush administration took a harder stand terming the treaty "fatally flawed in fundamental ways" and withdrew the United States from it.

As these examples suggest, conference diplomacy is a time-consuming process that requires the marshaling of evidence on the severity of a problem and the creation of both a domestic and an international political consensus on how to proceed. This stands in sharp contrast to the rapid and destabilizing pace of globalization that provides the context in which many of the issues being addressed surface. Taken together these characteristics make conference diplomacy a fragile process that is easily derailed. Opposition may emerge at any point in the deliberations. For example, in 2001 the George W. Bush administration balked at participating in a global conference on racism because it objected to language equating Zionism with racism and a proposal calling for reparations for slavery. The United States refused to participate in earlier international conferences on racism in 1978 and 1983 because of concerns over language. It also announced that it would not accept a draft agreement for enforcing a 1972 treaty on germ warfare and that it would only agree to an international agreement on small arms trade if bans on civilian ownership of military weapons and trade with rebel movements was dropped.

UN Diplomacy

For months it appeared that George Bush's foreign policy consisted of little more than a failed attempt to get the United Nations to support war against Iraq. In the end, it isolated the United States from many of its long-time friends and allies and deeply divided the American public over the wisdom of acting unilaterally. American policy toward the United Nations has not always been marked by this degree of strife and discord. The United States led the push for creating the United Nations. President Franklin Roosevelt saw it as a mechanism for managing world affairs in the post–World War II era, and the Security Council veto was seen as sufficient to protect American security interests. In fact, for many years the United Nations served as a virtual extension of the U.S. State Department. All of this began to change in the 1960s as colonial areas gained their independence and sought to use the United Nations first as a tool for steering an independent course between the United States and the Soviet Union and then as an instrument for creating a new international economic order.

We can gain a greater understanding of the complexity and tensions inherent in U.S. diplomacy toward the United Nations and other international institutions by recognizing that at any one time U.S. policy represents an amalgam of four different roles.[20] First, the United States sees itself as an international reformer. Viewed from this perspective, the United Nations is an important instrument deserving U.S. support because it holds the potential to transform world politics. Second, the United States sees itself as a custodian. Here, it places itself in a position of sometimes usurping or resisting the powers of the United Nations because its agenda conflicts with the greater purposes identified and defined by the United States. The third role is that of spokesperson for the American public. The problem here, as noted in Chapter 6 on the domestic setting of American foreign policy, is that policy makers do not have a clear sense of what the public thinks. Finally, the United States finds itself in the same role as other states. It seeks to use the UN system to advance and protect American national interests by such actions as applying international sanctions against Iraq; vetoing resolutions condemning Israel; and opposing an international criminal court. The balance among these four role orientations is not fixed, and changes in U.S. policy toward the United Nations can be attributed to changes in their intensity and the manner in which they interact.

George W. Bush's UN diplomacy gives evidence of all four orientations being present. By far the most dominant has been that of international system reformer. It allowed the administration to act unilaterally and bypass the United Nations in going to war against Iraq. It displayed a similar attitude in April 2004 when Bush announced that Iran "will be dealt with, starting through the United Nations," the clear implication being that his administration would again act unilaterally if needed. The administration pursued a traditional national interest orientation in returning to the United Nations in June 2004 to gain support for its plan to formally end the occupation. That resolution passed unanimously by the Security Council approved the transfer of sovereignty to a new Iraqi government, outlined a role for the United Nations in a post-transition Iraq and authorized an American-led multinational force. It also adopted this role in continuing to demand exemptions for U.S. troops from prosecution by the International Criminal Court. The United States adopted a custodian role when in January 2004 it announced that it will demand significant changes in a World Health Organization initiative on obesity. The administration stated that the organization had gone beyond its mandate and that it preferred an approach that was based on personal responsibility rather than governmental regulation. Moreover, the administration stated its interpretation of the science in the report differed from that of the WHO. This last critique was not new as conflicts over the science on which reports were based were reoccurring points of controversy in environmental negotiations. Finally, we can see the Bush administration acting as a spokesperson for the American public in signing a treaty controlling the global marketing of tobacco. The move was supported by the American Medical Association, portions of the tobacco industry in the United States, as well as consumer groups. The agreement has only been ratified by 9 of 108 countries and there was no indication of when the Bush administration would push for a ratification vote.

Public Diplomacy

Public diplomacy consists of the statements and actions of leaders that are intended to influence public opinion in other countries. It is alien to classic diplomacy that emphasizes secrecy and confidential bargaining among government officials and, therefore, has largely been neglected and disparaged as propaganda. This is a fate that befell cold war efforts at public diplomacy such as Voice of America or Radio Free Europe that broadcast into communist-controlled areas. Renewed attention has been given to public diplomacy largely because of the revolution in communication technologies and increased role that public opinion, nonstate actors, and legislatures play in modern diplomacy. Its importance has also grown because of the increased role that ideas are seen as playing in world politics as evidenced by the debate over the merits of "soft power."

President Clinton is widely recognized as one of the most skilled practitioners of public diplomacy. He brought an American-style political campaign atmosphere to his trips abroad that sought to win foreign publics over to his cause. This stands in sharp contrast to President Reagan's forays into public diplomacy that tended to have a hit-and-run quality to them. His references to the Soviet Union as the "evil empire" played well at home but scared the public abroad. A similar problem has faced George W. Bush whose black-and-white image of the world and use of phrases associated with the American frontier has been offputting to foreign audiences.

Public diplomacy is more than just public statements. At its core are a set of institutions, programs, and practices designed to accomplish four strategic objectives:[21]

1. Inform the world accurately, clearly, and swiftly about U.S. policy
2. Represent the values and beliefs of the American people
3. Explain how democracy produces prosperity, stability, and opportunity
4. Communicate U.S. support for education

The lead organization in this endeavor is the United States Information Agency (USIA). A mainstay in the conflict with the Soviet Union, its radio broadcasts reached 50 percent of the Soviet population and as much as 80 percent of that of East Europe, it saw its size decline sharply with the end of the cold war, going from a peak of 12,000 employees in the mid-1960s to 6,715 by the end of the 1990s.[22] The war on terrorism breathed new life into America's public diplomacy. The United States now spends $5 to 10 million annually on foreign public opinion polling. It has also developed a number of initiatives that are targeted on the Middle East. One is a glossy magazine, *Hi,* funded by the State Department that is targeted at Arabs ages 15 to 35. The first issue appeared in July 2003 and is sold on newsstands. Among radio stations in operation are Radio Sawa (broadcasting in Arabic) and Radio Farda (in Farsi). Al Hurra is an Arabic-language TV station that broadcasts to the region.

The Political Use of Force

American military power serves as an instrument of diplomacy by its very existence. Without ever having to be used or even referred to, it heightens U.S. prestige and gives importance to U.S. proposals and expressions of concern.

The knowledge that it exists influences both how U.S. policy makers approach problems and the positions adopted by other states. Barry Blechman and Stephen Kaplan identified 218 incidents between 1946 and 1975 in which the United States used military forces for political purposes.[23] To qualify as a political use of force, the military action had to involve a physical change in the disposition of U.S. forces and be consciously done to achieve a political objective without going to war or trying to physically impose the U.S. position on the target state.

On average, the political use of force lasted 90 days, with U.S. military forces staying at their maximum force level for 56 days. The actions ranged from a port visit by a single warship to the deployment of major land, sea, and air units in conjunction with a strategic alert and reserve mobilizations. As many as 20 incidents and as few as 3 took place in one year with the average number of incidents being 8. The greatest number of incidents occurred between 1958 and 1965 when an average of 12 incidents per year took place. In terms of geography, the 218 incidents are spread relatively evenly across the Northern Hemisphere, although the points of emphasis changed over time. Between 1946 and 1948, Western Europe was the primary area where the United States sought to use military power for political purposes and Southeast Asia and East Asia were the predominant areas of activity between 1949 and 1955. Between 1966 and 1975, U.S. attempts to use military power for political purposes were divided relatively evenly between Southeast Asia and East Asia and the Middle East and North Africa. Only South Asia and sub-Saharan Africa have been consistently neglected.

POST–COLD WAR COERCIVE DIPLOMACY

The passing of the cold war did not end America's interest in using military power for political ends. In fact, a number of factors made the political use of force very attractive. Most prominent among them were the absence of a constraining superpower, the continued presence of serious problems, many of which had deep roots, and an expectation that as the sole remaining superpower the United States had a responsibility to act to solve world problems. Using a slightly different definition of the political use of force than did Blechman and Kaplan, a recent study examined instances of coercive diplomacy (cases where force was threatened or used in a limited fashion in order to produce a political as opposed to military resolution of the problem) and a series of conflicts with Iraq in the 1990s. These cases, ranging from Haiti to Somalia to the war on terrorism, are important because the causes that gave birth to them are likely to be present for some time to come.

The study found that of sixteen cases where military power was used to persuade rather than defeat the opponent, success was realized only five times. It clearly failed in eight cases. The limited success rate is not surprising. Studies of a smaller number of attempts at coercive diplomacy during the cold war documented an even lower success rate. Three factors seemed to contribute to what success coercive diplomacy enjoyed, although none guarantees success. First, offering positive inducements to the other state to adjust its policy was important. Second, the timing of the inducement was important. They were most effective when offered after the demonstrative use of force or after threats of using force were made. Offering inducements had little positive effect if they were offered in advance of such shows of resolve. Third, it was important to be able to clearly demonstrate to the opponent what would happen to their military forces should war occur and that their military strategy would fail. Interestingly, the type of demand made by the United States had little relation to success or failure.

Particularly important are the findings regarding the effectiveness of coercive diplomacy against terrorism. Martha Crenshaw notes that terrorism imposes unusual constraints on coercive diplomacy that may compromise its effectiveness.[24] As nonstate actors, terrorists are difficult to target. Success may require acting against multiple targets simultaneously. It is also hard to assess their motives and the intensity of their position. Lacking this information, policy makers may end up falling back on old or stereotyped assumptions. Gaining timely warning about their intentions is also problematic and can undermine the effectiveness of the political use of force. Displays of force are complicated by the fact that terrorists seek to provoke a reaction, and thus coercive diplomacy may play into their hands. Finally, the need for secrecy in combating terrorism limits the utility of coercive diplomacy. Public displays of force may have the effect of signaling intelligence breaches to the terrorists, making it more difficult to counter them in the future.

NUCLEAR DIPLOMACY

In contemplating using military power for political purposes, American policy makers have not limited themselves to thinking in terms of conventional weapons. On at least two occasions, they have threatened to use nuclear weapons.[25] Evidence suggests that Dwight Eisenhower made such a threat in 1953 as part of his plan for bringing an end to the Korean War. Richard Nixon also made such a threat in 1969 in an attempt to end the Vietnam War. Unlike the Eisenhower case where the threat of using nuclear weapons was presented as part of a deliberate U.S. strategy, Nixon cast his in quite different terms telling his chief of staff H. R. Haldeman:

> I call it the Madman Theory, Bob. I want the North Vietnamese to believe I've reached the point that I might do anything to stop the war. We'll just slip the word to them that "for God's sake, you know Nixon is obsessed about Communism. We can't restrain him when he is angry—and he has his hand on the nuclear button."— Ho Chi Minh himself will be in Paris in two days begging for peace.[26]

On October 10, 1969, U.S. nuclear forces were put on alert "to respond to possible confrontation by the Soviet Union." The actions taken were designed to be picked up by Soviet intelligence but still not be visible to the American press or public. It was Nixon's hope that this was part of a lead-up to a massive conventional offensive in Vietnam and would stampede them into a diplomatic solution to the war. In fact, Nixon had already decided against such a military operation because of the domestic opposition it would unleash in the United States and military doubts about its effectiveness. Soviet leaders do not appear to have responded to this political use of nuclear power in any meaningful way. No mention of it was made by Soviet Ambassador Dobrynin in conversations shortly after it ended. It does appear that Soviet intelligence recognized the change in nuclear readiness.

For those interested in questions of nuclear strategy, two significant points emerge from a detailed look at the history of this episode. First, the military did not automatically and uniformly implement Nixon's alert order. The Strategic Air Command balked, as did Secretary of Defense Melvin Laird, suggesting that Nixon was in far less control over the use of U.S. nuclear forces than he believed or most commentators thought. National security advisor Henry Kissinger put forward this nuclear alert with little regard for other developments in the international system. To them it was obvious this was nuclear signaling over Vietnam. However, at that very moment the Soviet Union and China were involved in an intense border dispute. Chinese leaders had been evacuated from Beijing, and its nuclear forces were on alert. From both the Chinese and Soviet perspectives, the U.S. nuclear alert could have just as easily been seen in the light of this conflict.

Arms Transfers

Arms transfers have established themselves quickly as a favorite instrument of policy makers.[27] In 1980, one observer noted that the United States annually receives nearly ten thousand requests from foreign governments for military equipment and services and over twenty thousand applications from private firms for export licenses.[28] The Arms Export Control Act of 1976 requires that all arms transfers valued at $25 million or more or those involving the transfer of significant combat equipment be reported to Congress. This same study found that over one hundred cases have been reported each year. States sell and buy weapons for a number of different reasons, and the relationship between them has been compared to a reciprocal bargaining process in which each tries to use the other to accomplish goals that are often incompatible.[29] The potential tensions are most clearly evident when each side is driven by strategic imperatives.

For arms sellers, three strategic rationales are most often advanced. First, arms transfers can provide influence and leverage abroad by serving as a symbolic statement of support for a regime and providing access to elites. Second, they can be used to protect specific security interests abroad and further regional stability. Third, they can be used as barter in acquiring access to overseas bases. None of these rationales are without their problems. Leverage tends to be a transitory phenomenon in world politics, and an arms transfer relationship can promote friction just as much as it can cement ties. It can also produce a situation of reverse leverage where the recipient state, rather than the seller, exercises the most influence. Iran provides a useful example of influence gone awry. The United States sold sophisticated weapons to the Shah of Iran in the hopes that he would use them to contain the spread of communism in the Persian Gulf, while the Shah saw these weapons as a way of realizing his dream of making Iran into a regional superpower. Not only was he quite willing to work with the Soviet Union when it suited his interests, but in the last years of his rule, the large volume of U.S. weapons in Iran created hostility among the people toward the United States. Efforts designed to improve regional stability can be easily interpreted as an attempt to alter the regional balance of power. The result can be a competitive situation that takes on all of the characteristics of an arms race such as has become commonplace in the Middle East. Like political leverage, access to bases has proven to be transitory. It can also be an increasingly costly proposition as the host state raises the economic, political, and military favors that must be granted for continued access. The Reagan administration found this to be the case in its negotiations to renew basing rights with a number of states. In 1985, Turkey publicly stated that the price for renewing U.S. basing rights would be an increase in the value of future Turkish exports to the United States from their 1984 level of $433 million to $3 billion.

There have been five major turning points in the development of U.S. arms transfer policy. The first came in the early 1960s when the Kennedy administration made a distinction between arms sales and arms transferred abroad as foreign aid. Kennedy turned to arms sales in an effort to counter the growing U.S. balance-of-payments problem that was brought about in part by the high cost of stationing U.S. troops in Europe. The second turning point came during the Nixon administration. Arms transfers now became an important instrument of foreign policy and a cornerstone of the Nixon Doctrine, which stressed the need for U.S. third world allies to assume the primary responsibility for their own defense. To that end the United States was prepared to channel aid and assistance, but it would not readily intervene into the conflict itself. Other changes also took place. Sales replaced aid as the primary vehicle for transferring arms, the Middle East became the primary area of U.S. arms transfers, and the quality of the weapons transferred increased dramatically. No longer were arms transfers dominated by obsolete weapons in the U.S. inventory. Now they regularly involved the most sophisticated weapons that it possessed. A number of statistics vividly capture these changes. Measured in constant dollars, U.S. arms transfers increased 150 percent between 1968 and 1977. In FY 1971 FMS (foreign military sales) orders were valued at $1.4 billion, in FY 1973 they reached $5.3 billion, and in FY 1975 they had jumped to $15.5 billion. In 1970 sales to Iran were valued at $13.3 million. In 1974 they were valued at $3.9 billion.

The third turning point in the evolution of U.S. arms transfer policy came with the Carter administration. It represented a turning point for what it sought to do rather than for what it accomplished. Carter sought to replace the Nixon–Ford–Kissinger view of arms transfers as a normal instrument of foreign policy with one seeing it as an "exceptional tool."[30] The Carter policy had an immediate impact. In the first 15 months after it was announced, 614 requests from 92 states for over $1 billion worth of arms were turned down.

Gradually, the Carter administration found it difficult to work within its own guidelines. The first major exception to its own rules was the sale of AWACS to Iran for $1.8 billion. The Carter administration also agreed to a $1.8 million arms package for South Korea in compensation for the reduction of U.S. ground troops to be stationed there. It soon would completely abandon all signs of restraint by approving weapons sales to Israel and Egypt as part of the Camp David Accords, and to Saudi Arabia after the Shah fell and the Soviet Union invaded Afghanistan.

The fourth turning point in U.S. arms transfer policy came with the arrival of the Reagan administration. It moved quickly to use arms transfers as a tool in its global struggle against communism. In its first three months, it offered approximately $15 billion in weapons and other forms of military assistance to other states. The George H. W. Bush administration followed suit. In 1990, it proposed making available $30 billion in arms sales. Key recipients included Egypt, Colombia, Kuwait, Spain, Japan, South Korea, and Norway. In the aftermath of the Persian Gulf War, there was a brief international movement for ending arms shipments to the Middle East. An international registrar of arms was even established to help track arms transfers. However, a reversal of direction quickly ensued and arms again began to flow into the region. In the Clinton administration, the United States became the world's leading arms supplier selling over $31 billion worth of weapons to over 140 states. George W. Bush continued along these lines. His most controversial arms sale prior to 9/11 was to Taiwan and followed on the heels of a crisis with China over the downing of a U.S. surveillance aircraft. It was the largest sale to Taiwan since 1992.

The most recent period in arms sales policy began after the 9/11 terrorist attacks. The most notable feature of this period is the embrace of arms transfers to countries once on restricted lists. Armenia, Azerbaijan, India, Pakistan, and Yugoslavia, all of which are key allies in the war against terrorism, now receive U.S. arms. In the case of India, 2002 marked the end to an almost forty-year period in which no export licenses were granted. Licenses for twenty weapons systems were granted that year. Arms trade with Pakistan also showed a considerable jump after 9/11. It, too, had been subjected to sanctions because of its nuclear weapons program. Prior to 9/11, the last time Pakistan received funds from the United States to acquire American-made weapons, services, or technology was in 1990 when it totaled $184,875,500. In 2002, this number had jumped to $690,894,000. Weapons systems of considerable value were also being supplied to other states. The top-five recipients of proposed foreign military sales agreements in 2002 were Kuwait ($2.3 billion), the United Arab Emirates ($2.1), Taiwan ($1.5), Malaysia ($1.5), and South Korea ($1.3). Overall, the United States retained its position as the world's leading arms merchant accounting for some 40 percent of all sales. It agreed to export about $13 billion in weapons and delivered arms worth about $10 billion. On the receiving end, Saudi Arabia ($64.5 billion) and Taiwan ($20.2) have been the world's largest purchasers of arms between 1995 to 2002.

Summary and the Future

Diplomacy as an instrument of foreign policy is a quite varied tool, encompassing such forms as summit and conference diplomacy, the political use of force, and arms transfers. None are without their problems. Some observers reach the conclusion that modern diplomacy, especially in its summit and conference forms, is not well suited to cope with the dilemmas of international politics. Reasons for this pessimism include the loss of flexibility and the ability to compromise, and the prominence given to the public side of international negotiations. This dissatisfaction is often accompanied by a desire to reestablish the central features of the old diplomacy. Others argue that while these problems do complicate matters, what is really needed is a change in focus. The principal problem in diplomatic negotiations has changed. It is no longer to outwit the adversaries and take more from them than they take from you, but to create a framework for resolving disputes.[31] Ideally, the framework would reduce the complexity of the issue and limit the range of variation permitted in the future so that the most undesirable developments would fall outside the range of permissible options. We have already seen movement in this direction. The SALT process and the GATT talks have been less concerned with resolving specific points of dispute than with developing a common set of perceptions and expectations on how to move forward in dealing with the problem.

As we have seen, the utility of using military power for political purposes is limited. But what does this mean? Should it be avoided? A variety of answers exist. Blechman and Kaplan, in their early study of the political use of force, present evidence that the answer may be "yes." They note that even successes may be short-lived. Often the political use of force can buy time, but that may be all it can do. Judging the value of arms transfers presents a similar problem. Are the short-term economic, political, or military benefits worth the possible negative long-term impact on regional stability or arms control efforts that might result? The later study of coercive diplomacy presents a more positive, though still cautious, view. While coercive diplomacy only had a 32 percent success rate, it is not much different from that enjoyed by economic sanctions (25 to 33 percent).[32] Leon Sigal, who has studied U.S. negotiations with North Korea, provides us with a different take on this question. He suggests that the problems with coercive diplomacy have less to do with a loss of credibility in American threats than it does with a more general unwillingness to cooperate with strangers.[33]

Notes

1. David Baldwin, *Economic Statecraft* (Princeton, N.J.: Princeton University Press, 1985), especially pp. 8–28.
2. Fred Ikle, *How Nations Negotiate* (New York: Harper & Row, 1964), p. ix.
3. Holly J. Burkhalter, "The 'Costs' of Human Rights," *The World Policy Journal*, 11 (1994), pp. 39–49.
4. "Oversight of the State Department's Country Reports on Human Rights Practices for 1993 and U.S. Human Rights Policy," *Hearings, Committee on Foreign Affairs, House of Representatives*, February 1 and May 10, 1994 (Washington, D.C.: U.S. Government Printing Office, 1994).
5. Peter J. Spiro, "New Global Communities: Nongovernmental Organizations in International Decision-Making Institutions," *Washington Quarterly*, 18 (1994), 45–56.
6. Margaret P. Karns and Karen A. Mingst (eds.), *The United States and Multilateral Institutions: Patterns of Changing Instrumentality and Influence* (Boston: Unwin Hyman, 1990).
7. Debra Liang-Fenton (ed.), *Implementing U.S. Human Rights Policy* (Washington, D.C.: United States Institute of Peace Press, 2004).
8. Jack Donnelly and Debra Liang-Fenton, "Introduction," *Ibid.*, p. 11.

9. Quoted in Glenn Kessler, "Road Map Setbacks Highlight U.S. Pattern, *The Washington Post,* October 6, 2003, p. 1.

10. Richard N. Haass and Meghan L. O'Sullivan (eds.), *Honey and Vinegar: Incentives, Sanctions, and Foreign Policy* (Washington, D.C.: Brookings, 2000).

11. Stephen Wayne, "Bad Guys and Bad Judgments," in Stanley Renshon and Debroach Welch Larson (eds.), *Good Judgment in Foreign Policy* (Lanham, MD: Rowman & Littlefield, 2003), pp. 103–26.

12. For references to the positive contributions of summitry, see Robert Putnam, "Summit Sense," *Foreign Policy,* 55 (1984), 73–91.

13. For a discussion of the negative contributions of summitry, see J. Robert Schaetzel and H. B. Malmgren, "Talking Heads," *Foreign Policy,* 39 (1980), 130–42.

14. Ibid., p. 138, for the case of economic summits; see the discussion in Strobe Talbot, *Deadly Gambits* (New York: Vintage, 1984), for examples from arms control talks.

15. Adam B. Ulam, *Dangerous Relations: The Soviet Union in World Politics, 1970–1982* (New York: Oxford University Press, 1983), p. 186.

16. Richard Nixon, "Superpower Summitry," *Foreign Affairs,* 64 (1985), 1–11.

17. For a review of U.S.-Soviet summit conferences, see the various references in James E. Dougherty and Robert L. Pfaltzgraff, *American Foreign Policy from FDR to Reagan* (New York: Harper & Row, 1985).

18. George de Menil, "The Process of Economic Summitry," in George de Menil and Anthony M. Solomon (eds.), *Economic Summitry* (New York: Council on Foreign Relations, 1983), pp. 55–63.

19. Richard Elliot Benedick, *Ozone Diplomacy: New Directions in Safeguarding the Planet* (Cambridge, Mass.: Harvard University Press, 1991).

20. This discussion is based on W. Michael Reisman, "The United States and International Institutions," *Survival,* 41 (Winter 1999–2000), 62–80, although the definition of roles is slightly different.

21. "Public Diplomacy Campaign to Rebuild U.S.-Muslim Relations," *Frontlines,* January 2003, 5.

22. Joseph Nye, Jr., "The Decline of America's Soft Power," *Foreign Affairs* 83 (2004), 16–20.

23. Barry M. Blechman and Stephen S. Kaplan, *Force without War: U.S. Armed Forces as a Political Instrument* (Washington, D.C.: Brookings, 1978).

24. Martha Crenshaw, "Coercive Diplomacy and the Response to Terrorism," *Ibid,* 305–58.

25. Scott Sagan and Jeremi Suri, "The Madman Nuclear Alert," *International Security,* 27 (2003), 150–83; and William Burr and Jeffrey Kimball, "Nixon's Nuclear Ploy," *Bulletin of the Atomic Scientists,* 59 (2003), 28–37, 72–73.

26. Sagan and Suri, p. 156.

27. For background data on arms transfers, their history, the policies of specific states, and a discussion of their rationale, see Stephanie G. Neuman and Robert E. Harkavy (eds.), *Arms Transfers in the Modern World* (New York: Praeger, 1980); Andrew J. Pierre, *The Global Politics of Arms Sales* (Princeton, N.J.: Princeton University Press, 1982); and Michael T. Klare, *American Arms Supermarket* (Austin: University of Texas Press, 1984).

28. Richard H. Wilcox, "Twixt Cup and Lip: Some Problems in Applying Arms Control," in Neuman and Harkavy, *Arms Transfers,* p. 32.

29. Edward Kolodiej, "Arms Transfers and International Politics: The Interdependence of Independence," in Newman and Harkavy, *Arms Transfer,* p. 3.

30. Klare, *American Arms Supermarket,* pp. 43–44.

31. Gilbert R. Winham, "Negotiation as a Management Process," *World Politics,* 30 (1977), 87–114.

32. Robert Art, "Coercive Diplomacy," in Art and Cronin (eds.), *The United States and Coercive Diplomacy,* pp. 359–420.

33. David Sigal, *Disarming Strangers* (Princeton: Princeton University Press, 1998), 94.

— 14 —

COVERT ACTION

Covert action seeks results by altering the internal balance of power in a foreign state. No instrument of foreign policy is more controversial or difficult to control. As the Tower Commission stated in its report, "Covert action places a great strain on the process of decision making in a free society."[1] Writing in a similar vein, two scholars who have studied the CIA extensively assert that there are only two legitimate reasons to carry out covert action: (1) when open knowledge of U.S. responsibility would make the operation infeasible and (2) to avoid retaliation or to control the potential for escalation.[2]

In popular usage covert action is all but synonymous with paramilitary undertakings. This is not the case. A number of different activities fall within its definitional boundaries. A list of key terms central to the techniques of covert action is presented in Table 14.1. Accompanying these definitions is a list of recent U.S. foreign policy initiatives in which they have been employed. In the next section we place these efforts in a broader historical context. The discussion of examples is not exhaustive but only meant to illustrate the range of situations in which covert action has been employed. Following that, congressional efforts to control the CIA are reviewed.

U.S. covert action predates the Central Intelligence Agency (CIA). The first forays into covert action were taken during World War II by the Office of Strategic Services (OSS).[3] They tended to be paramilitary in nature and were designed to bring the war to the enemy behind the front lines. After a brief interlude in which the OSS was disbanded and no central intelligence organization existed, a permanent covert action capability was created within the newly established CIA. Roughly speaking, the Eisenhower administration coincides with the heyday of the CIA.[4] The 1970s saw the CIA at perhaps its lowest point with a former chief of the Covert Action Staff lamenting that covert

TABLE 14.1   Types of Covert Action, with Recent Examples

Type of Covert Action	Recent Example
Clandestine support for individuals and organizations (training, financing, technical advice, etc.)	Anti-Khomeini exiles in France; pro-Western forces in El Salvador; training for Thai military for heroin raids
Propaganda involves making use of print media, radio, TV, news services to influence perceptions on events taking place	Misleading reports picked up in U.S. news media that Qaddafi was planning new round of terrorism and hinting at U.S. military action
Economic operations designed to disrupt economy of target state	Mining of Nicaraguan harbors
Paramilitary operations involve furnishing secret military assistance and guidance to unconventional and conventional foreign forces	Aid to Contras, Afghan rebels, pro-U.S. forces in Angola
Assassination	CIA production of psychological warfare manual in Nicaragua that contained passages that have been interpreted to call for assassination. Reported effort to target Qaddafi in Libyan bombing raid

action was becoming a "dying art form."[5] Under the Reagan administration covert action received a new lease on life but also came under intense scrutiny given the controversial nature of Reagan's foreign policy.[6] As we shall see later, covert action did not end with the cold war but has become transformed into a more visible instrument of American foreign policy.

Until recently, official histories of U.S. foreign policy largely were silent on covert action. This has begun to change. In 1994 the State Department's official history of U.S.–Indonesian relations noted how President Eisenhower approved a covert operation to support anticommunist rebels in a plan that bore similarities to the later Bay of Pigs operation against Castro. When it became clear that the anticommunist rebels would fail, Eisenhower changed direction and threw U.S. support to the Indonesian military in an effort to lessen the power of the Indonesian communist party and President Sukarno. In 1995 the CIA organized a conference at which it made public previously secret material on its role in the 1954 overthrow of the Arbenz government in Guatemala. Material released in 1997 revealed that the CIA had considered assassinating President Jacobo Arbenz. It had a "hit list" of fifty-eight targets and had trained individuals for the job. No assassinations were carried out.

Techniques of Covert Action

The most common form of covert action is the clandestine support for individuals and organizations. This support takes many forms (financial, technical, training) and can be directed at many targets (politicians, labor leaders, journalists, unions, political parties, church groups, professional associations). This form of covert action was the major focus of CIA efforts in France, Italy, and West Germany in the immediate postwar era.[7] Between 1948 and 1968, the CIA spent over $65 million in Italy on these types of programs, and in 1976 President Ford approved $6 million in secret subsidies for anticommunist forces in the upcoming election. In his 1987 book, *VEIL: The Secret Wars of the CIA, 1981–1987,* Bob Woodward reveals that DCI William Casey arranged for Saudi Arabia to supply $2 million for the May 1985 Italian election. CIA clandestine support programs were so prevalent that a former CIA station chief testified to a Senate committee that "any aspiring politician would come to the CIA to see if we could help him get elected."[8]

A widely publicized case of CIA clandestine support involved efforts to block the election of Salvador Allende.[9] These efforts succeeded in 1958 and 1964 but failed in 1970. Between 1964 and 1969 the CIA spent almost $2 million on training anticommunist organizers among Chilean peasants and slum dwellers. It spent $3 million on the 1964 election and almost $1 million on the 1970 election. Allende won a plurality of the vote in 1970, and according to Chilean law and custom, he would be selected as the next president by the Chilean Congress. The United States unsuccessfully sought to block his selection through a two-track policy. Track I was approved by the 40 Committee, the NSC committee charged with oversight of CIA covert operations. Track II was kept secret from it. In track I the CIA was ordered to engage in political, economic, and propaganda tactics to influence political events. As part of this plan, $25,000 was authorized (but never spent) to bribe members of the Chilean Congress.

Another form of clandestine support is the provision of security assistance and intelligence training to foreign governments. Third world leaders are particularly responsive to offers of training and equipment to help them combat potential coups, terrorist attacks, and assassination attempts. These operations cost between $300,000 and $1 million and are often carried out by as few as three or four people. According to Woodward's book, twelve leaders received such assistance from the CIA in 1983. Numbered among them were President Hissene Habre of Chad, President Mohammed Zia ul-Haq of Pakistan, Samuel Doe of Liberia, Philippine President Ferdinand Marcos, and President Amin Gemayel of Lebanon. Another example of covert assistance was "Project X." This was a U.S. military training program in Latin America and elsewhere that included instruction on clandestine activity against domestic political adversaries. Documents indicate that the operation was probably shut down in the early 1980s. In 1999, Clinton expressed regret for U.S. support of the Guatemalan military during that country's thirty-six year civil war, which dated back to the 1960s. An independent commission had concluded that the U.S.-backed forces were responsible for the vast majority of the human rights abuses that occurred during this war.

A second category of covert action is propaganda. The CIA has used a number of techniques for dispensing its propaganda. One of the most primitive involved using balloons.[10] In an effort to exploit dissatisfaction and increase the internal unrest in China in the early cold war era, the CIA loaded balloons with an assortment of leaflets, pamphlets, and newspapers. Reagan and Bush approved clandestine radio propaganda operations against Noriega. Neither effort was particularly successful. Press accounts characterized the former effort as "half-hearted" and the latter as "inept."

The best-known covert radio broadcasting systems were Radio Free Europe (RFE—directed at Eastern Europe) and Radio Liberty (directed at the Soviet Union). During their early years both stations took a militant, anticommunist line. The tone of their broadcasts changed after the 1956 Hungarian invasion. Critics contended that RFE broadcasts gave the distinct and misleading impression that the United States would support the efforts of the freedom fighters when no such intention existed. At its peak the CIA's propaganda assets numbered over eight hundred news and public information organizations and individuals. This number reportedly included some thirty-six American newspaper people.[11]

A third category of covert action involves economic operations. As we have already seen, economic operations were an integral part of the CIA's efforts to stop Allende. The economy was a major target of track I activity. The general goal given to the CIA's economic program was "to make the economy scream." U.S. multinational corporations were approached and asked to cut off credits and the shipment of spare parts to Chile. Covert CIA economic and political activity did not stop with Allende's inauguration.

According to one account, comparatively few economic operations have been undertaken by the CIA, and they have not been very successful.[12] The available evidence suggests that the most persistent target of CIA covert economic operations has been Castro's Cuba. One of the most famous programs that has come to light is Operation Mongoose.[13] Authorized by President Kennedy in November 1961, it was designed to "use our available assets . . . to help Cuba overthrow the communist regime." The first act of covert economic sabotage was to have been the demolition of a railroad yard and bridge that would have been made to look like an inside job. This plan was called off when the saboteurs were spotted approaching Cuba by boat. The CIA did have its successes. It succeeded in getting European shippers to turn down Cuban delivery orders and a German firm to agree to send off-center bearings to Cuba, and British buses destined for Cuba were sabotaged on the docks. In 1962 the CIA successfully contaminated a shipment of Cuban sugar destined for the Soviet Union while the ship was docked for repairs in Puerto Rico.

Operation Mongoose was canceled in January 1963, but covert economic operations against Cuba continued. For example, CIA-financed commandos set fire to an 8,000-gallon oil tank and attacked a copper mine. In June 1963 Kennedy authorized a stepped-up program of sabotage, and in October 1963 thirteen sabotage operations were approved. They too were to be carried out by CIA-financed commandos. Included in the target list were an electric power plant and a sugar mill. In 1969 and 1970, the CIA directed a program of weather modification against Cuba's sugar crop with the hope of producing rain over nonagricultural areas, leaving the cane fields parched. The CIA has also been charged with infecting Cuban pig herds with an African swine flu virus. The result was a serious shortage of pork, which is a staple in the Cuban diet. The United Nations Food and Agricultural Organization labeled the outbreak the "most alarming event of the year" and had no explanation for why it happened. Evidence has also surfaced that in 1982 Reagan approved a CIA plan to sabotage the Soviet economy by providing it with flawed software technology. In one scheme, the software would trigger an explosion in a Siberian natural gas pipeline. It was approved at a time when the United States was trying to convince its West European allies not to buy natural gas from the Soviet Union, both to prevent it from becoming dependent on Russian natural gas and to deny the Soviet Union hard currency.

The fourth category of covert action involves paramilitary undertakings. A former practitioner defines paramilitary operations as the furnishing of covert military assistance and guidance to unconventional and conventional foreign forces and organizations. He argues it represents a highly valuable "third option" between sending in the Marines and doing nothing.[14] Initially, these operations were targeted against the Soviet Union and its Eastern European satellite states.[15] Almost uniformly, they were failures. Numbered among them were efforts to support resistance fighters in the Ukraine (the program ended with their defeat by the Soviet army); an effort to establish an underground apparatus for espionage and revolution in Poland (only after several years did it become clear that the Polish secret service had co-opted the network and was using it to acquire gold and capture anticommunist Poles); and an effort to overthrow the Albanian government (virtually every mission failed, and it later became known that Kim Philby, the British intelligence officer in charge of the mission, was a Soviet agent).

As the 1950s progressed, the more significant CIA paramilitary operations were taking place in the Third World. In 1953, the United States and Great Britain undertook a joint venture, Operation AJAX, to bring down the government of Iranian Prime Minister Mohammed Mossadegh.[16] After coming into power in 1951, Mossadegh quickly established himself as the dominant figure in Iranian politics. By 1953, his power eclipsed that of the Shah, who fled into exile. The United States strongly objected to Mossadegh's antiwestern policies, and in particular it opposed the 1951 nationalization of the Anglo-Iranian Oil Company. When the Army proved unable to remove him from power, covert action was deemed necessary. The coup itself involved two stages. First, a propaganda campaign stressed the likelihood of communist takeover if Mossadegh remained in power. Second, the CIA organized pro-Shah street gangs and supported them with knives, clubs, and an occasional rifle. Mossadegh fled when his followers were unable to control the subsequent street demonstrations and rioting. With Mossadegh gone, the Shah returned, his rule more dependent than ever on U.S. support.

In 1954 the CIA helped bring down the Arbenz government in Guatemala.[17] Jacobo Arbenz took office in 1950 and set out on the path of social reform and modernization. The Truman administration's initial response was one of moderate opposition that relied heavily on economic sanctions. By the end of Truman's administration, some were convinced that covert action in collaboration with neighboring pro-U.S. dictatorships was necessary. In 1953 Eisenhower approved such a plan (PB/SUCCESS). As was the case with Iran, the paramilitary operation itself was relatively small in scale, and it was preceded by a propaganda campaign. The acknowledged key to

PB/SUCCESS was convincing Arbenz that the opposition forces would defeat his forces. Arbenz was to be frightened into accepting a *fait accompli*.

As the 1950s ended, so too did the string of CIA successes. In 1958, it supported an unsuccessful coup against President Sukarno of Indonesia. A still greater embarrassment came in 1961 with the Bay of Pigs invasion of Cuba. Originally conceived during the Eisenhower administration, the plan was approved by Kennedy in April 1961. Later that month a brigade of some 1,400 Cuban exiles was put ashore in Cuba where it was expected to link up with Cuban opposition forces and topple the Castro regime. Everything went wrong. On the first day of the invasion, two of the four supply and ammunition ships were sunk, and the other two fled. On the second day the brigade was surrounded by 20,000 well-armed and loyal Cuban soldiers. On the third day the 1,200 surviving members of the invasion force surrendered. Almost two years later most were released in exchange for $53 million in food and drugs.

The Bay of Pigs put a temporary dent into Washington's fascination with paramilitary covert action programs, but it did not put an end to them. By the mid-1970s a controversial covert paramilitary operation was under way in Angola.[18] A 1974 coup in Portugal signaled the beginning of the end of Portuguese colonial rule in Africa. In January 1975, agreement among the three rival independence movements in Angola led to the creation of a coalition transitional government that would rule Angola until elections were held in October. Angola's independence was to be officially realized in November. The United States threw its support to an alliance between the National Front for the Liberation of Angola (FNLA) under the leadership of Holden Roberto and the National Union for the Total Independence of Angola (UNITA) led by Jonas Savimbi.

Covert operations began almost immediately. Seven days after the agreement to establish a transitional government was reached, the CIA was authorized to pay $300,000 to the FNLA, traditionally the most aggressive and warlike of the independence movements. In February the FNLA was encouraged by the United States and President Mobutu of neighboring Zaire to move its forces from Zaire into Angola and attack the Popular Movement for the Liberation of Angola (MPLA). Shortly thereafter, the Soviet Union reentered the picture. It had given aid to the MPLA in the early 1970s but had stopped in 1973. Now, in March 1975, in response to Chinese and U.S. aid to the UNITA-FNLA alliance, it resumed shipments of aid to the MPLA. The CIA was informing U.S. policy makers that the MPLA would triumph unless there was a considerable escalation in the U.S. commitment. The reason for this pessimism was the arrival of a small number of Cuban advisers to aid the MPLA and the expectation that they would be followed by large numbers of well-trained Cuban regulars. As predicted, this occurred, and in November 2,800 Cubans arrived in Angola.

It was in the last stages of the fighting that the depth of the CIA's involvement became known. The CIA maintained that no U.S. personnel were directly involved in the fighting. The CIA pictured its role only as one of resupplying Mobutu and said it was he who was sending aid to the UNITA-

FNLA forces. In reality funds were being sent directly to Angolan forces, and CIA personnel were in Angola to help manage the war. Many in Congress expressed concern over the escalating U.S. involvement in Angola. Congress as a whole reacted angrily to these disclosures. In December 1975 it passed the Tunney Amendment, which forbade spending funds from the FY 1976 Defense Appropriations Bill on Angola. In 1976 it placed additional limitations on the CIA by passing the Clark Amendment, which forbade spending funds from any source "for any activities involving Angola directly or indirectly."

Pressures for a renewed U.S. involvement in Angola began to build as U.S.–Soviet relations deteriorated. For Secretary of State Alexander Haig and others in the new Reagan administration, the introduction of Cubans into Angola marked a major turning point in Soviet adventurism in the third world, and it required a U.S. response even at this late date. The first real opportunity to do so came in 1985 when Congress repealed the Clark Amendment. No immediate U.S. reinvolvement occurred because in spite of its rhetoric the Reagan administration initially was divided on how to proceed, and Congress was also unsure of what to do next.

In the 1980s, the most controversial of the CIA's paramilitary programs was its Nicaraguan operation. The impetus for CIA involvement in Nicaragua lay with evidence collected in the late 1970s that the Sandinista government was increasing its shipments of arms to El Salvadoran rebels, intensifying pressure on domestic opposition forces, and becoming the site of a substantial Cuban-backed military buildup. The Carter administration responded to these events with economic sanctions. They were continued by the Reagan administration but had little impact. In 1981, the Reagan administration authorized a $19.5 million program of covert action to stop the flow of arms to El Salvador. By November 1981 the program's goals expanded to include creating an anti-Sandinista force that might effectively challenge the "Cuban support structure in Nicaragua."[19] The CIA's paramilitary program has had its successes. It is credited with having slowed down the shipment of arms to El Salvador and with hampering Sandinista offenses in 1983 and 1984. It has also been the object of intense criticism. In particular, Congress became concerned with the scope of the CIA's program compared to the program of action that it had earlier agreed to fund. As a result, in 1982 it passed the Boland Amendment, which forbade funding the Contras for the purpose of overthrowing the Nicaraguan government. In 1984 renewed questions were raised over the mining of Nicaraguan harbors and the CIA-sponsored production of a psychological warfare manual that could be interpreted as calling for assassination. This time Congress responded by cutting off all funding for the Contras. This measure was partially lifted in 1985 when Congress voted to allow sending humanitarian aid to the Contras, but it continued to forbid the spending of CIA funds. For 1986 these restrictions were further loosened when Congress allowed the CIA to supply communication and intelligence to the Contras, but it still prohibited direct or indirect military participation in the struggle. A new twist was added to the paramilitary operation when it became known that in spite of the 1985 and 1986 congressional bans on direct military assistance, NSC staffer Lieutenant Colonel Oliver North had been deeply involved in orchestrating Contra operations and in securing foreign and private funds for them.

The largest, and in some eyes the most successful, Third World paramilitary covert operation program run by the CIA was in Afghanistan. In FY 1985 the CIA spent about $250 million, or more than 80 percent of its covert action budget, helping the Afghan guerrillas evict Soviet forces. In FY 1989, after the Soviet Union had withdrawn, the CIA was still spending $100 million on the Afghan operation. The Afghan paramilitary operation is also significant because for the first time, the CIA was authorized to send "made in America" weapons to forces it was supporting. Until then, adherence to the doctrine of "plausible denial" had blocked such transfers. This 1986 decision to send Stinger missiles to the Afghan guerrillas is widely credited with being a decisive turning point in that conflict. Those who question the wisdom of supporting the Afghan rebels point to the current problems produced by these very Stinger missile sales.[20] Concerned with the military problems these missiles create for any future deployment of U.S. forces in the Middle East, the United States has tried with little success to buy them back. An even broader problem was identified. Many of those who received U.S. arms became enemies of the United States. Some Afghan rebels joined as volunteers in other conflicts involving the Islamic cause while others became members of terrorist groups such as that led by Osama bin Laden, which was responsible for the terrorist attacks on the World Trade Center. Still others joined the ranks of the Taliban government that the George W. Bush administration later helped overthrow as part of its war against terrorism.

A final form of covert action involves the assassination of foreign leaders. The existence of a unit for the planning of "special operations" can be traced back to the earliest days of the CIA.[21] By all accounts no actual assassination operations or planning was ever done by it, but suggestions for assassination were put forward. By 1961, another CIA unit had been established for "disabling" foreign leaders, including assassination as a last resort. A former CIA official has stated that between 1959 and 1962 the White House, NSC, and CIA all talked seriously of killing foreign leaders.[22] In 1972, following the kidnapping and assassination of Chilean General Rene Schneider, DCI Richard Helms issued a directive banning assassinations. This ban has since been included in the presidential executive orders setting forth guidelines for CIA behavior.

Controversy over the meaning of the prohibition on assassination has resurfaced recently. During the Reagan administration questions were raised about CIA sponsorship of a psychological warfare manual in Nicaragua that could be read as endorsing assassination and about the real purpose of the bombing raid on Libyan leader Qaddafi's headquarters.[23] In 1990 just prior to the invasion of Panama, President George Bush authorized a $3 million covert action plan to overthrow Noriega. The plan was controversial because it acknowledged the possibility that Noriega might be killed "indirectly" because of the operation. At the time the Bush administration was under widespread criticism for its performance in a failed October coup. In defending itself, the administration argued that the existing ban on any involvement in actions that could lead to the assassination of a foreign leader had prevented it from acting in a decisive fashion.

The most thorough investigation into U.S. involvements in assassination plots was carried out by the Church Committee. It investigated five cases of alleged U.S. involvement:

Cuba	Fidel Castro
Congo (Zaire)	Patrice Lumumba
Dominican Republic	Rafael Trujillo
Chile	General Rene Schneider
South Vietnam	Ngo Dinh Diem

The committee concluded that only the Castro and Lumumba cases involved plots conceived by the United States to kill foreign leaders. In the Trujillo case the United States did not initiate the plot, but it did aid dissidents whose aims were known to include assassinating Trujillo. In the Diem case some U.S. officials sought his removal from office, but there is no indication that these officials sought his death. General Schneider's death is linked to the track II policy of the Nixon administration, which was designed to spark an anti-Allende military coup. In the Congo it appears that events overtook U.S. policy and nullified U.S. plans to assassinate Lumumba. U.S. authorities had authorized Lumumba's assassination in the fall of 1960, and CIA officers in the Congo urged his "permanent disposal." Toxic substances had been selected as the method for Lumumba's assassination. CIA planning went so far as to send vials of poison to the CIA's Léopoldville station for an assassination attempt. Led by Lumumba and Joseph Kasavubu, the Congo declared its independence from Belgium in June 1960. Shortly thereafter, Lumumba threatened to invite Soviet forces to the Congo if Belgium did not speed up its withdrawal. By mid-September Soviet troops were present in that portion of the Congo under Lumumba's control. Later that month, Lumumba was the loser in a power struggle with Kasavubu and Joseph Mobuto. In December Lumumba was captured by Mobutu's forces and placed under the custody of local authorities known to be hostile to him. Several weeks later, his death was announced. It appears that the CIA knew the likely consequences of Lumumba's capture but was not involved in the assassination.

The Church Committee found concrete evidence of at least eight CIA plots to assassinate Castro between 1960 and 1965. One former CIA official characterized these efforts as ranging from "the vague to the weird."[24] Proposed assassination devices included arranging an "accident," poison cigars, poison pills, poison pens, placing deadly bacterial powder in Castro's scuba-diving suit, and rigging a seashell to explode while Castro was scuba diving. While most of these approaches never went beyond the planning stage, some were attempted. Twice poison pills were sent to Cuba, and on another occasion weapons and other assassination devices were provided to a Cuban dissident. Following the terrorist attacks on the World Trade Center and the Pentagon, President George W. Bush raised the possibility of lifting the ban on assassinations.

POST–COLD WAR COVERT ACTION

Covert action programs have not disappeared with the end of the cold war. Two of the most "public" covert actions have taken place in Bosnia and Iraq. Bosnia constitutes a gray-area case. In 1994 and 1995, the Bosnian government survived largely due to the illegal flow of weapons from Iran. In 1992 U.S. officials learned that this was occurring in defiance of a UN embargo on weapons shipments to Bosnia and Serbia but made no effort to stop it in spite of Clinton's public support for the UN arms embargo. According to the DCI, R. James Woolsey, the CIA was ready to undertake a covert operation of its own in support of the Muslim-led Bosnian government at the time. Congressional critics of Clinton's Bosnia policy were outraged that they had not been told of the arms shipments and claimed Clinton was legally required to do so. Woolsey, speaking after resigning as DCI and in opposition to the plan, asserted that permitting the arms shipments was unwise but not illegal and that Congress did not have to be informed. It could only be seen as a U.S. covert action if American personnel had actively participated in its planning or conduct.

The CIA ran a cold war–style operation against Saddam Hussein between 1992 and 1996. The goal was to remove him from power by encouraging a military coup and reducing his control over Iraq's outlying regions such as Iraqi Kurdistan. The cost of the program is estimated to have approached $100 million. Included in the funding was support for a clandestine radio station in Jordan that blanketed Iraq with anti–Saddam Hussein propaganda. Little was achieved. In June 1996, Saddam Hussein arrested and executed more than one hundred Iraqi dissidents and military officers associated with the CIA plan. Political infighting among Kurdish leaders further crippled CIA efforts to remove him from power. A similar pattern unfolded in the Clinton administration's efforts to unseat Serb leader Slobodan Milosevic where the United States funded a divided opposition that had no specific program for reform and collaborated with plotters among his known confidants.

THE COVERT WAR AGAINST OSAMA BIN LADEN

The CIA's pre–9/11 efforts to capture bin Laden took a number of different forms.[25] Perhaps the earliest involved the recruitment of a family-based team of Afghan tribal members. Known by the code name TRODPINT, they were originally formed to capture Mir Aimal Kasi, a Pakistani national who killed two CIA employees at the CIA headquarters in 1993. Kasi was captured in Pakistan and TRODPINT was then given the task of trying to kidnap bin Laden so that he could be taken out of Afghanistan by U.S. Special Forces. The last effort before 9/11 involved the recruitment of Northern Alliance guerrilla commander Ahmed Shah Massoud in 1999 by a team of CIA operatives known as JAWBREAKER-5. Massoud had a long history of dealings with the CIA dating back to 1984, many of which were not positive. At one point, he had been given $500,000 to attack Afghan communist forces but no attack apparently ever occurred. A similar nonevent may have taken place shortly after he was recruited, this time when he claimed to have launched rocket fire on a compound where bin Laden was believed to be staying. The CIA could not confirm the attack took place. In both these cases, strong disagreements existed between CIA officials handling the cases who saw these agents as the "last best hope" for finding bin Laden in Afghanistan, where CIA resources were virtually nonexistent, and high-level figures in Washington, who saw them as "weekend warriors" who were not interested in fighting but only taking U.S. money or who were past their prime. Their plans, such as night raids on bin Laden's compound followed by holding him for thirty days in a cave until U.S. Special Forces arrived, were considered of questionable value.

In between these two operations, the CIA contacted and recruited at least three proxy forces in the region to try and capture or kill bin Laden. In 1999, Pakistan offered to create a small commando team that would kill him. The sixty-person unit was trained, supported, and equipped by the CIA. The Pakistani government made the offer as a counter to building pressure by the Clinton administration to cut its support for the Taliban. The unit was ready to act in October, but a coup brought into power a new government that refused to condone the operation. At the same time, U.S. intelligence officials had grown concerned that the operation was compromised due to security breaches within the Pakistani intelligence services. The second initiative involved covert military-to-military ties between the U.S. Central Command and Uzbekistan. Nothing came of this initiative. The third proxy group was known informally as "the tribals." They opposed both the Taliban and al Qaeda. The CIA was unable to verify that they had engaged bin Laden's forces in combat although they claimed to have done so twice. During the Clinton administration, the CIA also recruited a team of about fifteen Afghan agents to track bin Laden's whereabouts. The CIA never launched an attack on bin Laden based on their information, which was often spotty and erratic.

Formal authorization for the CIA to pursue bin Laden had been obtained in 1998 following the bombings of the American embassies in Kenya and Tanzania when President Clinton signed the first of a series of Findings consistent with the Hughes-Ryan Amendment. The original Finding emphasized the goal of capturing bin Laden but permitted the use of lethal force. The first Memorandum of Notification expanded the covert operation to include using lethal force against bin Laden and his forces even when there was little chance of capturing him. The second expansion permitted the intelligence community to target his top aides. It is believed that less than ten individuals were identified and that they were to be captured or killed. The third expansion permitted the intelligence community to shoot down a private or civilian aircraft if bin Laden was a passenger.[26]

Congress and the CIA

A discussion of covert action as an instrument of foreign policy is incomplete without examining the problem of control. In this section, we examine how Congress has interacted with the CIA. Not only do we follow the changing pattern of relations between the two institutions, but we also evaluate Congress's use of its legislative, budgetary, and oversight powers. Loch Johnson, who served as assistant to the chairperson of the Senate Intelligence Committee and as staff director of the Oversight Committee of the House Intelligence Committee, divides congressional-CIA relations into three periods.[27] From 1947 to 1974, there existed an Era of Trust. The second period, 1974 to 1976, was an Era of Skepticism. A third period, that of an Uneasy Partnership, existed from 1976 to 1989. Following that, we entered into a fourth period in which Congress was an impatient overseer. The 9/11 Commission Report called for significant congressional reform in its oversight of the intelligence community and Congress may be about to embark on another period of more centralized, intrusive, and active oversight. It calls for creating either a joint House–Senate committee or a single oversight committee in each chamber that has both appropriation and authorization powers. As our overview will highlight, calls for reform along the lines suggested by the Commission are not new. They have been a reoccurring feature of congressional–CIA relations.

ERA OF TRUST

During the Era of Trust, there was little, if any, meaningful congressional control over the CIA. Congressional reluctance to investigate the CIA had many roots. In part it was caused by the climate of the times. A national consensus existed on the need to combat communism, and the CIA was an important tool in this effort. Many also felt that command of the CIA was exclusively an executive function and that congressional oversight ran against the principle of separation of powers. Finally, there was the feeling that Congress lacked the necessary information to exercise a voice in the area of intelligence oversight and that efforts to obtain the necessary information would jeopardize the secrecy vital to the success of intelligence operations.

According to the 1947 National Security Act, which created it, the CIA is empowered to do the following:

1. Advise the National Security Council (NSC) on intelligence matters related to national security
2. Make recommendations to the NSC for coordinating the intelligence activities of government agencies and departments
3. Correlate, evaluate, and disseminate intelligence within the government
4. Perform additional services for existing intelligence agencies that the NSC believes can be done best by a central organization
5. Perform other functions and duties relating to national security intelligence as directed by the NSC

Commentators stress three points about this list of functions. First, nowhere is there a specific reference to covert action. The CIA was essentially seen as an intelligence-processing organization. Only by referring to the phrase *other functions and duties* can covert action be justified. Second, there is no reference to intelligence-collection activities, clandestine or otherwise. Third, by writing the legislation in this manner, Congress established only the broadest statement of permissible CIA activities. Statutory limits on the CIA were loosened even further with the passage of the 1949 amendments to the National Security Act. Among its provisions were exemptions from civil service regulations in the hiring and firing of personnel and permission for the director of Central Intelligence (DCI) to spend money from CIA appropriations on his own authority.

In place of detailed statutory guidelines, a body of "para laws" were developed to guide CIA activity. According to Robert Borosage, para laws are internal bureaucratic directives that give the appearance of providing legal regulations but are put into effect without the participation of Congress.[28] Collectively, these directives came to be known as the CIA's secret charter, and it was not until 1973 that Congress was given access to them. The CIA is not alone in its reliance on para laws. The National Security Agency was established and its duties laid out by a secret presidential directive, and the Defense Intelligence Agency was established on the authority of the secretary of defense.

During this period the congressional appropriations process served to protect the CIA more than restrain it. Beginning in 1949 congressional oversight committees were informed about CIA covert operations and regularly approved funding for them. The actual figures involved were not revealed to the whole Congress, and CIA funds were concealed in the budgets of other departments, especially that of the Defense Department. The fiction of congressional budgetary control came to the forefront in 1971. Senator Stuart Symington introduced an amendment placing a $4 billion limit on intelligence spending governmentwide. His proposal was defeated, but in the course of the debate, he asked Senator Alan Ellender, chairperson of the Senate Appropriations CIA subcommittee, if the committee had approved funding a 36,000-man "secret" CIA army in Laos. Ellender replied, "I did not know anything about it. . . . I never asked. . . . It never dawned on me to ask about it. I did see it published in the newspaper some time ago."[29]

Oversight of the CIA formally fell upon subcommittees of the House and Senate Appropriations and Armed Services committees. In the 1960s the Senate combined its oversight committees into one body under the chairpersonship of Senator Richard Russell. Frequently, Russell was the only legislator whom the CIA reported to on intelligence matters. Significantly, the Senate Foreign Relations Committee and the House Foreign Affairs Committee were not involved in the oversight process. When oversight did occur, it took place largely on the CIA's terms. Ray Cline, formerly a deputy director for intelligence in the CIA, notes that the very terms used to describe these meetings captured the essence of what took place.[30] They were *briefings* and not *hearings*. Congressional overseers were there to *learn*, not to *restrict* or *monitor*.

Conflicting accounts are found about the quality of CIA oversight in this period. Allen Dulles, DCI from 1953 to 1961, stated that he never cut off a question with the response that "we don't want to talk about this." Yet at the same time comments by senators suggest less than thorough oversight. Leverett Saltonstall, a supporter of the CIA, observed: "It is not a question of reluctance on the part of CIA officials to speak to us. Instead it is a question of our reluctance . . . to seek information and knowledge on subjects which I personally . . . would rather not have."[31]

Not everyone in Congress was pleased with these arrangements. Between 1947 and 1975 over 200 resolutions were introduced for the purpose of improving congressional oversight. Few ever emerged from committee. The first significant attempt to reform the structure of congressional oversight came in 1956. Senator Mike Mansfield introduced a measure calling for the establishment of a joint committee on the CIA. The committee would be kept "fully and currently informed" by the CIA and would have a mandate to investigate the activities of the CIA, look into problems related to gathering intelligence, and examine the coordination and utilization of intelligence by all government departments.[32] The bill was reported out of the Senate Foreign Relations Committee by a vote of 8 to 1 and was introduced on the floor of the Senate with 34 cosponsors. The Mansfield proposal was defeated 59 to 27, with 14 co-sponsors voting no. The Senate leadership and those serving on the existing oversight committees unanimously opposed the proposal.

The issue of congressional oversight did not become a major issue again until 1966 when Senator Eugene McCarthy introduced a resolution calling upon the Foreign Relations Committee, a committee on which he served, to undertake a "full and complete study with respect to the effects of the operations and actions of the CIA upon the foreign relations of the United States." Opposition came from members of the Senate Armed Services Committee who saw the proposal as an effort to "muscle in" on their jurisdiction. While this effort also failed, McCarthy's attempt to change the structure of CIA oversight was not without some impact. Beginning in 1967 Russell did "invite" three members of the Foreign Relations Committee to sit in on CIA oversight hearings. This practice ended, as did the oversight sessions themselves, when William Fulbright and Stuart Symington, two of the three Foreign Relations Committee members sitting in on these briefings, became outspoken in their opposition to the war in Vietnam and CIA activities.

ERA OF SKEPTICISM

Beginning in 1974 Congress's attitude toward the intelligence community began to change. One factor prompting the new outlook was a series of revelations about CIA wrongdoing and excess. The two most publicized ones implicated the CIA in a destabilization campaign directed at bringing down the Socialist government of Salvador Allende in Chile and allegations that the CIA had violated its charter by undertaking surveillance of U.S. citizens inside the United States.

The first indication of the changed congressional mood was passage of the Hughes–Ryan Amendment to the 1974 Foreign Assistance Act. It required that except under exceptional circumstances the CIA inform members of six congressional committees "in a timely fashion of the nature and scope of any CIA operation conducted for purposes other than obtaining information." According to the terms of the Hughes–Ryan Amendment, the president was also required to make a "finding" that each covert operation is important to national security. Presidential findings have included such information as the time and duration of the activity, the risks involved, funding restrictions, the relationship to prior NSC decisions, policy considerations, and the origin of the proposal.[33] This has not always meant that Congress has been well informed by the presidential finding. The presidential finding for the Iran arms transfers carried out by the NSC was signed after the operation began, and DCI Casey was instructed not to inform Congress. It is presented in Box 14.1. The 1975 presidential finding supporting U.S. activities in Angola was so vague that only Africa was identified as the location of the operation. The stated purpose was to provide "material, support, and advice to moderate nationalist movements for their use in creating a stable climate in order to allow genuine self determination."[34]

The House and Senate also created temporary select committees to investigate the intelligence community. The two committees adopted different operating styles and sets of concerns.[35] The Senate Select Committee on Intelligence was chaired by Frank Church. Its investigations focused on unmasking illegal and questionable CIA activities. Among the subjects examined were CIA mail openings, CIA activity in Chile, illegal communication intercepts by the National Security Agency, covert action, and assassination attempts. The House Select Committee on Intelligence, chaired by Otis Pike, focused its investigation on management and organizational issues. One topic it devoted considerable time to was intelligence failures. All told, the Church and Pike committees offered over one hundred recommendations, and in spite of their different approaches, they tended to agree on many points. Most significantly, neither proposed a ban on covert action, but both wanted Congress to receive prior notice on any such undertakings.

ERA OF UNEASY PARTNERSHIP

The Senate moved quickly and established a permanent bipartisan intelligence oversight committee in 1976. (The House was slower to act, creating its oversight committee in 1977.)[36] The Senate committee succeeded in establishing a working relationship with the CIA for overseeing covert action. The CIA agreed to provide it with 48 hours' notice before a plan approved by the president would be implemented. The agreement is important because while the committee cannot legally prevent a covert action plan from being executed, advance notice allows it to voice its disapproval and have input into the policy process. In summing up its first year of operations, the committee concluded that it had been "informed of every covert action requiring a presidential finding . . . and that it had formally voted on all covert action projects in the new budget." Much of the traditional congressional aversion to any detailed control over the intelligence community was still present. For while the budget subcommittee had held 45 hours of hearings, asked 500 questions for the record, and examined 2,000 pages of justification material presented by the intelligence community, only three members of the Senate took up the committee's offer to read its classified report, which spelled out the money appropriated and described the projects whose funding it had cut or eliminated.

Based on his experience as a staffer with the House Intelligence Committee, Loch Johnson made several cogent observations about the actual monitoring of CIA activities by Congress.[37] First, oversight was carried out by

Box 14.1   Presidential Finding on CIA Involvement in Arms Shipments to Iran

I hereby find that the following operation in a foreign country (including all support necessary to such operation) is important to the national security of the United States, and due to its extreme sensitivity and security risks, I determine it is essential to limit prior notice, and direct the Director of Central Intelligence to refrain from reporting this Finding to the Congress as provided in Section 501 of the National Security Act of 1947, as amended, until I otherwise direct.

Scope

Iran

Description

[Assist selected friendly foreign liaison services, third countries, which have established relationships with Iranian elements, groups, and individuals] sympathetic to U.S. Government interests and which do not conduct or support terrorist actions directed against U.S. persons, property or interests for the purpose of: (1) establishing a more moderate government in Iran, and (2) obtaining from them significant intelligence not otherwise obtainable, to determine the current Iranian Government's intentions with respect to its neighbors and with respect to terrorist acts, [and (3) furthering the release of the American hostages held in Beirut and preventing additional terrorist acts by these groups.][a] Provide funds, intelligence, counterintelligence, training, guidance and communications, and other necessary assistance to these elements, groups, individuals, liaison services and third countries in support of these activities. The USG will act to facilitate efforts by third parties and third countries to establish contact with moderate elements within and outside the Government of Iran by providing these elements with arms, equipment, and related material in order to enhance the credibility of these elements in their effort to achieve a more pro-U.S. government in Iran by demonstrating their ability to obtain requisite resources to defend their country against Iraq and intervention by the Soviet Union. This support will be discontinued if the U.S. Government learns that these elements have abandoned their goals of moderating their government and appropriated the material for purposes other than that [*sic*] provided by this Finding.

[a]Point (3) did not appear in the first draft.

Source: President's Special Review Board, *The Tower Commission Report* (New York: Bantam, 1987), pp. 217–18.

a changing combination of committee members and staffers. Often it involved only a single committee member and one or two staffers who would hear a briefing, visit a site, or write a report. Second, oversight became more intense whenever members felt that the CIA was flouting the prerogatives of Congress. Third, members made little use of congressional information resources such as the GAO (General Accounting Office) or CRS (Congressional Research Service), preferring to rely instead on their own knowledge and sources. Fourth, several minority party staffers became overseers of the majority party staff instead of the CIA. Fifth, what the committee investigated depended on the interests of its members and the nature of the subject matter. For example, it once spent two hours questioning DCI Stansfield Turner on his personnel decisions (some of those he fired came from the districts of committee members) and then touched only briefly on a technically complex, expensive, and controversial hardware issue.

During much of the Carter administration, the task of writing a charter for the CIA dominated the intelligence agenda. The first failed effort resulted in a document of over two hundred pages that spelled out detailed restrictions on CIA actions. Included in it was a provision to separate the head of the CIA from the position of overall Director of the Intelligence Community. Concern with controlling covert action gave way to concern for the CIA's failure to anticipate the fall of the Shah and the Soviet invasion of Afghanistan along with controversy over the accuracy of its estimates of Soviet missile strength. In looking at these failings, the CIA problem was one of inadequate resources and not uncontrolled behavior. As a result, when CIA oversight legislation was finally approved it took a much different form. In 1980, the Senate passed the Intelligence Oversight Act that ran only three pages. Its main feature was to reduce the reporting requirement contained in the Hughes-Ryan Act to two committees.

In the Reagan administration, relations between Congress and the CIA deteriorated markedly. The main point of contention was Nicaragua. The 1982 Boland Amendment provided the point of departure for Congress's oversight of the CIA's Nicaraguan operations.[38] The Boland Amendment grew out of congressional concern over the deepening U.S. involvement in Nicaragua and prohibited the use of CIA or Defense Department funds for purposes of overthrowing the Nicaraguan government or for provoking a war between Nicaragua and Honduras. In 1983, concerned with the level of the paramilitary program under way in Nicaragua and the clarity of U.S. goals, the Senate Intelligence Committee took the unusual step of requiring a new presidential finding before allocating any more funds to be spent in Nicaragua. After receiving the new presidential finding (which was revised to take into account the committee's views), the committee voted nearly unanimously to approve funds for the redefined program for FY 1984. The Senate passed the measure by a voice vote. Because the House had voted to terminate all funds for the program, a conference committee was established, and a compromise figure of $24 million was agreed upon.

Then according to a Senate Intelligence Committee report, "without notifying Congress as required by the Intelligence Oversight Act, major changes [were] made in the program." Included among these changes was the mining of Nicaraguan harbors. Moreover, without going to the Senate Intelligence Committee first, the Reagan administration went to the Senate Appropriations Committee for an additional $21 million for its Nicaraguan program. The first action served to undermine the "strong majority of the committee" which had suppported the funding of CIA operations in Nicaragua. The second action angered the committee to the point where Secretary of State Shultz was moved to apologize to it for violating established procedures. In the end a deadlock with the House prevented any further funds from being allocated for the Nicaraguan program, although the Senate Intelligence Committee had recommended the additional funding contingent on CIA compliance with the notification provisions of the Intelligence Oversight Act.

The involvement of the NSC in funding and running the covert action program in Nicaragua has further complicated the problem of controlling intelligence. Congressional legislation banned the spending of funds by the CIA, Defense Department, "or any other agency or entity of the United States involved in intelligence activities." Because it is not listed as a member of the intelligence community, Reagan administration officials concluded that the NSC was not prohibited from involving itself in the Nicaraguan operation by this restriction. Congress has rejected the validity of this interpretation. Also troubling to the Congress is the absence of notification by DCI Casey. Reagan directed Casey not to inform Congress, and he complied with those instructions in spite of his agreement with Congress. It should be stressed that the problem of notification is not unique to the Reagan administration. As DCI, Stansfield Turner did not inform Congress on three occasions about covert action programs approved by President Carter and being undertaken by the CIA. All of them were preparatory to the failed hostage rescue mission. In an attempt to rectify this situation, Congress considered legislation that, had it passed, would have required presidents to inform Congress within 48 hours of the start of any covert action rather than in a "timely fashion," as the law now requires. The measure was dropped in return for a pledge from President George H. W. Bush who, while maintaining that he did not have to notify Congress, promised that he would try to do so "within a few days."

CONGRESS AS IMPATIENT OVERSEER

The uneasy partnership of the third era was never placed on a firm foundation and broke down under the pressure of a series of incidents in the early years of the post–cold war era.

One point of tension involved the CIA's failure to disclose to Congress that it had paid a Guatemalan army colonel $44,000 in 1992 for information about that country's civil war, in spite of the fact that it knew him to be linked to the 1990 murder of a U.S. citizen. The incident was particularly heated because the information was made public by Representative Robert Torricelli, a Democratic member of the House Intelligence Committee. House Speaker Newt Gingrich labeled Torricelli's actions "totally unacceptable" because committee members are sworn to keep all classified information they receive secret. House Republicans demanded that Torricelli be removed from the committee, complaining that such actions made it difficult for the committee to earn the trust of the intelligence community. Torricelli defended his actions, saying he had a greater loyalty to the Constitution, and added that "I'm not going to earn their trust. . . . Their testimony is not a gift to the Congress. . . ."

Even more damaging to the health of the congressional-CIA partnership was the agency's handling of the Aldrich Ames spy affair. Ames was a thirty-one-year veteran of the CIA who worked in counterintelligence and had spied for the Soviet Union for nine years. According to an internal CIA investigation, Ames had provided the Soviet Union with information that resulted in "the loss of virtually all of the CIA's human resources reporting on its primary target in the 1980s, the Soviet Union." All of this happened in spite of his possessing what Woolsey described as a record of "alcohol abuse, sloppy operational and financial accounting, undisciplined behavior, and poor judgment." Many in Congress felt that DCI Woolsey was being overly protective of the CIA in his approach to reorganization and far too lenient in his handing out of punishment for its failure to detect Ames. While he issued eleven reprimands, no one was fired or demoted. The four most severe reprimands went to three retired CIA officials and one who was days away from retirement.

Relations between Congress and the CIA, or more accurately, the executive branch, became somewhat more strained in the period immediately following the September 11, 2001, terrorist attacks. One area of disagreement centered on George W. Bush's call for greater surveillance powers for the intelligence community. While some members of Congress welcomed these proposed moves as necessary to combat terrorism, others feared that they might lead to violations of civil liberties. Congress was more united in its opposition to another administration action. Bush ordered that briefings with sensitive information be limited to only eight members of Congress. Intelligence committee members also complained about the adequacy of the administration briefings they were receiving. The decision followed a briefing in which the administration secretly informed members of Congress that there was a 100 percent chance of further terrorist attacks and this supposedly secret information reached the press.

Intense controversy between the two branches also surrounded the establishment of an independent commission to investigate the terrorist attacks on the U.S. The Bush administration opposed the idea and agreed only reluctantly. It then sought to hold the commission to a tight deadline and again agreed only under pressure to an extension. The 9/11 Commission was not the only high-profile investigation that touched on intelligence matters. Just before its report was released, the Senate Select Committee on Intelligence issued its report on prewar intelligence assessments on Iraq. This report challenged virtually all of the Bush administration's prewar assertions regarding Iraq. Months before, in April, the Democratic members of the House Permanent Select Committee on Intelligence recommended creating the position of a director of national intelligence.

Summary and the Future

The fundamental unresolved question regarding covert action is, how useful a tool of foreign policy is it? Consider the following arguments about its use:

1. If action capabilities take time to develop, it is also important that, once in being, they be used or they will atrophy.[39]

2. The effectiveness of any intelligence service is directly proportional to the degree to which it is prepared to break the laws of its adversaries.[40]

3. Political assassination in times of peace . . . has no place in the American arsenal.[41]

We are beginning to pursue answers to these types of questions. Richard Immerman's account of U.S. involvement in Guatemala is particularly important for helping us think critically about covert action.[42] His study reveals that neither the CIA nor American policy makers held any illusions about the difficulty of the task they were attempting or the high risks it entailed. His work also reveals a capacity for clear thinking and an attention to detail on the part of U.S. officials in putting together the covert action plan. From the outset the operation was seen as psychological and political rather than military. In selecting a leader for the "revolution," an effort was made to avoid too close an identification with either the old rightist forces or the military. Efforts were carefully targeted at the group that Arbenz was most dependent on: the wealthy, urban class that made up most of the officer corps. Attention was given to establishing an international climate supportive of an anti-Arbenz coup. Finally, detailed control was exercised over all facets of the operation from gaining Eisenhower's approval for additional planes for bombing Guatemala City to the engineering of a series of juntas and resignations in order that the U.S. candidate would emerge as the victor in the wake of Arbenz's resignation.

From Immerman's account we can identify not only the reasons for success but also those for later failures. For all of their careful planning, U.S. policy makers made one fatal mistake. They confused the necessary and sufficient conditions for the success of the operation against Arbenz. The careful attention to details, the control exercised, and the appreciation of risks were necessary for the success of the plan, but they were not sufficient to guarantee its success. U.S. policy makers did not appreciate the extent to which their success was dependent on circumstances within Guatemala. In Immerman's words, the CIA "reaped the harvest" of Arbenz's failure to institute real agricultural reforms that would have cemented ties between the regime and the oppressed Indian majority.

The United States paid a high price for confusing the necessary and sufficient conditions for success with the Bay of Pigs invasion. Immerman argues that the CIA plan failed not because of its deficiencies but because of Castro's reaction to it based on his reading of events in Guatemala. Castro and Che Guevara had both concluded that Arbenz's critical mistake was in not pursuing reform forcefully enough. This left him vulnerable to outside-generated pressure because he lacked a strong base of support from which to challenge CIA-sponsored revolutionaries. With such backing they were confident that the political and psychological impact of the CIA's operation would not have been sufficient to bring down his regime. Therefore, upon seizing power Castro set out to create a strong domestic base. He pursued a radical policy of economic reform and dismantled the remnants of Fulgencio Batista's army. Later, by reacting with speed and vigor to the Bay of Pigs invasion, Castro blunted any possibility of a psychological warfare campaign against him and at the same time destroyed the CIA's image of invulnerability.

Questions about the future effectiveness of covert operations and their oversight are also raised by the trend toward overt covert operations.[43] This is most notable in the area of paramilitary operations, where the Pentagon has made a major push toward acquiring such a capability. Estimates now place the number of CIA covert operators at 600 to 700, while the Pentagon has approximately 10,000 special force combatants. Similar trends exist elsewhere. Today the National Endowment for Democracy (NED) supports political groups just as the CIA once did. NED funds went to Violetta Chamorro in her successful campaign against Daniel Ortega in Nicaragua and to anti-Milosevic groups in Yugoslavia where it was used to organize and fund the election that removed him from office. NED has also been active in Venezuela supporting the opponents of President Hugo Chavez.

In the final analysis CIA-congressional relations are congressional-executive relations. Changes in the balance of power between the two branches inevitably will become reflected in CIA oversight mechanisms. With so much of the growth in presidential power having been tied to the need for the United States to play an active role in international conflicts during the cold war, more than one observer has speculated that its end will lead to a dramatic reduction in the president's ability to gain congressional acquiescence for foreign policy initiatives. To a greater extent than in the past Congress may be positioned to play a leading role in setting America's foreign policy agenda. Should this prove to be the case, then Congress can be expected to push its views on the intelligence community with unprecedented vigor. For example, in 1995 the Clinton administration bowed to congressional pressure and approved a small-scale covert action program intended to moderate the radical Islamic regime in Iran. Working against this possibility is the increased partisanship that has come to characterize congressional decision making. The intelligence oversight committees are not immune from this problem.[44]

Notes

1. The President's Special Review Board, *The Tower Commission Report* (New York: Bantam, 1987), p. 15.

2. Bruce D. Berkowitz and Allan F. Goodman, "The Logic of Covert Action," *The National Interest,* 51 (1998), 38–46.

3. For comments on the OSS and covert action, see Victor Marchetti and John D. Marks, *The CIA and the Cult of Intelligence* (New York: Dell, 1975); and Richard Harris Smith, *OSS: The Secret History of America's First Central Intelligence Agency* (Berkeley: University of California Press, 1972).

4. The observation is made by B. Hugh Tovar in Roy Godson (ed.), *Intelligence Requirements for the 1980s: Covert Action* (Washington, D.C.: National Strategy Information Center, 1981), p. 195.

5. The observation is made by B. Hugh Tovar in Roy Godson (ed.), *Intelligence Requirements for the 1980s: Elements of Intelligence,* rev. ed. (Washington, D.C.: National Strategy Information Center, 1983), p. 71.

6. Jeffrey T. Richelson, *The U.S. Intelligence Community* (Cambridge, Mass.: Ballinger, 1985), p. 236.

7. Ibid., pp. 228–29.

8. Morton H. Halperin and others, *The Lawless State: The Crimes of the U.S. Intelligence Agencies* (New York: Penguin, 1976), p. 40.

9. Ibid., pp. 15–29.

10. Marchetti and Marks, *CIA and the Cult of Intelligence,* p. 167.

11. Richelson, *The U.S. Intelligence Community,* p. 235.

12. Marchetti and Marks, *CIA and the Cult of Intelligence,* p. 72; and Richelson, *The U.S. Intelligence Community,* pp. 230–31.

13. Warren Hinckle and William Turner, *The Fish Is Red: The Story of the Secret War against Castro* (New York: Harper & Row, 1982).

14. Theodore G. Shackley, *The Third Option: An American View of Counterinsurgency Operations* (New York: Reader's Digest Press, 1981).

15. Trevor Barnes, "The Secret Cold War: The CIA and American Foreign Policy in Europe: 1946–1956," *Historical Journal,* 24, 25 (1981, 1982), 399–415, 649–70.

16. Ray S. Cline, *Secrets, Spies and Scholars: The Essential CIA* (Washington, D.C.: Acropolis, 1970), pp. 132–33; and Barry Rubin, *Paved with Good Intentions: The American Experience and Iran* (New York: Penguin, 1981), Chap. 3.

17. Richard H. Immerman, *The CIA in Guatemala: The Foreign Policy of Intervention* (Austin: University of Texas Press, 1982).

18. John Stockwell, *In Search of Enemies: A CIA Story* (New York: Norton, 1978).

19. Christopher Dickey, "Central America: From Quagmire to Cauldron," *Foreign Affairs,* 62 (1984), 669.

20. Ted Galen Carpenter, "The Unintended Consequences of Afghanistan," *World Policy Journal,* 11 (1994), 76–87.

21. U.S. Congress, Senate Select Committee to Study Government Operations with Respect to Intelligence Activities, *Alleged Assassination Plots Involving Foreign Leaders* (Washington, D.C.: U.S. Government Printing Office, 1976).

22. Cline, *Secrets, Spies and Scholars,* p. 187; Rositzke, *The CIA's Secret Operations,* p. 196.

23. Seymour Hersh, "Target Qaddafi," *New York Times Magazine,* February 22, 1987.

24. Rositzke, Harry, *The CIA's Secret Operations: Espionage, Counterespionage, and Covert Action* (New York: Reader's Digest Press, 1977), p. 197.

25. Information in this section is drawn from various newspaper accounts. See Barton Gellman, "Broad Effort Launched after '98 Attacks," *Washington Post,* December 19, 2001, p. A1; Gellman, "Struggles inside the Government Define Campaign," *Washington Post,* December 20, 2001, p. A1; Bob Woodward and Thomas Ricks, "U.S. Was Foiled Multiple Times in Efforts to Capture bin Laden or Have Him Killed," *Washington Post,* October 3, 2001, p. A1; Bob Woodward, "CIA Paid Afghans to Track bin Laden," *Washington Post,* December 23, 2001, p. A1; and Steve Coll, *Ghost Wars* (New York: Penguin, 2004).

26. For critical accounts of the attempt to capture bin Laden see Richard Clarke, *Against All Enemies* (New York: Free Press, 2004); and Anonymous, *Imperial Hubris* (Washington, D.C.: Brassey's) 2004.

27. Loch Johnson, "Legislative Reform of Intelligence Policy," *Polity,* 17 (1985), 549–73.

28. Robert L. Borosage, "The Central Intelligence Agency: The King's Men and the Constitutional Order," in Robert L. Borosage and John D. Marks (eds.), *The CIA File* (New York: Grossman, 1976), pp. 125–41.

29. Quoted in Marchetti and Marks, *CIA and the Cult of Intelligence,* p. 324.

30. Cline, *Secrets, Spies, and Scholars,* p. 246.

31. Quoted in Harry H. Ransom, *The Intelligence Establishment* (Cambridge, Mass.: Harvard University Press, 1970), p. 169.

32. A discussion of the Mansfield and McCarthy reform proposals and how they fared in Congress can be found in Ransom, *The Intelligence Establishment,* pp. 157–79.

33. William Corson, *Armies of Ignorance: The Rise of the American Intelligence Empire* (New York: Dial, 1977), p. 472.

34. Stockwell, *In Search of Enemies,* p. 47.

35. Thomas M. Franck and Edward Weisband, *Foreign Policy by Congress* (New York: Oxford University Press, 1979), pp. 117–24.

36. Ibid., pp. 125–34.

37. Loch Johnson, "The U.S. Congress and the CIA: Monitoring the Dark Side of Government," *Legislative Studies Quarterly,* 4 (1980), 477–99.

38. For an overview of congressional oversight on the Nicaraguan program, see U.S. Senate, Select Committee on Intelligence, *Report, January 1, 1983–December 31, 1984* (Washington, D.C.: Government Printing Office, 1985), pp. 4–15.

39. Tovar in Godson (ed.), *Elements of Intelligence,* p. 87.

40. Ladislav Bittman, "Soviet Bloc 'Disinformation' and Other Active Measures," in Robert Pfaltzgraff, Uri Ra'anan, and Warren Milberg (eds.), *Intelligence Policy and National Security* (Hamden, Conn.: Anchon [*sic*], 1981), p. 214.

41. Cord Meyer, *Facing Reality: From World Federalism to the CIA* (New York: Harper & Row, 1980), p. 219.

42. Immerman, *The CIA in Guatemala.*

43. Jennifer Kibbe, "The Rise of the Shaddow Warriors," *Foreign Affairs,* 83 (2004), 102–115; and Frederick Wettering, "(C)overt Action," *International Journal of Intelligence and Counterintelligence,* 16 (2003), 561–72.

44. For contrasting views see Gregory McCarthy, "GOP Oversight of Intelligence in the Clinton Era," *International Journal of Intelligence and Counterintelligence,* 15 (2002), 26–51; and Stephen Knott, "The Great Republican Transformation on Oversight," The *International Journal of Intelligence and Counterintelligence,* 13 (2000), 49–63.

— 15 —

THE ECONOMIC INSTRUMENTS

Economic statecraft involves the deliberate manipulation of economic policy to promote the goals of the state. It is an age-old instrument of foreign policy and one that the United States has used often. Where once the cold war was the primary reference point for its use, today it is the war against terrorism. The context has also changed. For much of the post–Word War II period, we spoke of American economic domination (or, according to its critics of American foreign policy, imperialism). Today we speak of globalization. No matter the purpose for which it is used or the context in which it is used, American economic power exerts its influence by it ability to attract other countries to the U.S. economic system and then trap them in it. Walter Mead refers to it as America's "sticky power."[1]

If the web that the United State's sticky economic power weaves entraps other countries in the U.S. system, it also entraps the U.S. in global trading relations that span a wide variety of commodities and political relationships. Consider the two month period from December 2003 to January 2004. Among the issues dealt with were a Central American Free Trade Agreement, dropping steel tariffs, determining that only allies who supported the war could participate in Iraqi rebuilding, a rejection of a U.S. offer on lumber by Canada, demands by shrimpers that import tariffs be placed on six countries, the refusal of countries to take U.S. beef, and American pressure on the European Union to uphold an arms embargo against China. As mundane as some of these issues may appear, they are highly charged politically. By late February 2002, Cabinet members in the George W. Bush administration, including Vice President Dick Cheney, had met eight times to discuss what actions to take on whether to set tariffs to protect the steel industry from

European imports. Dozens of sub-cabinet meetings were also held.[2] In the end, the decision was made in March to impose tariffs of up to 30 percent. The political stakes were high.[3] Between 1994 to 2000, Pennsylvania lost an estimated 142,000 trade-related jobs. Ohio lost 135,000. North and South Carolina lost an estimated 187,000 jobs largely because of textile and furniture imports. California lost an estimated 310,000 jobs to foreign trade. After an adverse World Trade Organization ruling and the prospect of retaliation by the European Union against American exports, Bush relented in December 2003.

We begin this chapter by discussing the major strategic perspectives that govern U.S. trade and monetary policy. We then take an in-depth look at two major ways in which economic power is used in foreign policy: economic sanctions and foreign aid. As a prelude to the discussion of economic instruments of foreign policy, we define key terms in Box 15.1.

Strategic Outlooks

TRADE STRATEGIES

Free Trade.   Free trade is both an instrument of foreign policy and a strategic orientation to organizing economic power.[4] From about 1944 to 1962, access to U.S. markets was used as an inducement to get other states to adopt policies favored by the United States. Among those cold war goals were strengthening military alliances, promoting the economic recovery of Western Europe, ensuring access to strategic raw materials, and stimulating economic growth and political stability in the third world. American policy makers were also sensitive to the limits of free trade. On a selective basis, they permitted or encouraged discrimination against U.S. goods if it would further these broader U.S. foreign policy goals. At the strategic level the United States used free trade to create an international system that allowed the U.S. economy to prosper and placed it at the center of international economic trade and monetary transactions.

There is nothing inevitable or natural about free trade. International free trade systems exist because they serve the interests of the dominant power. This was true of Great Britain in the nineteenth century and the United States in the post–World War II era. Although the U.S. economy is not as dominant in the post–cold war era, the United States continues to rely on free trade to advance its interests at the bilateral, regional, and global level. The most significant use of free trade at the bilateral level has been establishing normal trade relations with China. In November 1999, after thirteen years of on-and-off negotiations, the two countries signed a trade pact wherein China agreed to significantly reduce obstacles to imported goods and foreign investment. The United States agreed to gradually eliminate quotas on Chinese textile imports, although it retained the right to take countermeasures to prevent sudden surges in Chinese imports and to penalize dumping for more than a decade. Most significantly, the United States now agreed to support Chinese membership in the World Trade Organization (WTO).

Box 15.1   Key Terms of the Economic Instrument of Foreign Policy

Boycott: A refusal to buy a product or products from another country.

Dumping: Selling a product in a foreign market below the price charged in the home country's market.

Devaluation: Lowering the value of a currency relative to those of other key currencies or gold.

Embargo: A ban on selling goods to another country.

Foreign Aid: Assistance provided to another state. It may be given bilaterally or multilaterally and for economic, diplomatic, strategic, or humanitarian purposes.

Free Trade: An international economic policy based on the open and nondiscriminatory international flow of goods and services.

Grants: Funds made available to another country that do not have to be paid back.

Loans: Funds made available to another country that do have to be paid back. The interest rate varies. Concessionary loans are made at a greatly reduced interest rate.

Nontariff Barriers (NTB): Restrictions on goods or services coming into a country other than those involving a tax.

Quota: A quantitative restriction on imports of a product or products from another country.

Revaluation: Raising the value of a currency relative to those of other key currencies or gold.

Sanctions: Penalties imposed on another state in order to coerce it into changing a policy or prevent an action from being taken.

Strategic Trade: An international economic policy that is based on an active and selective government intervention into the market place to advance state interests.

Tariff: A tax or duty placed on incoming products or services in order to raise their price relative to the cost of comparable domestic items.

The agreement required indirect approval by Congress. It would have to grant China normal trade relations status, long referred to as most favored nations (MFN) status. Congress had been granting China MFN status on an annual basis for twenty years, but the debate surrounding these votes had become increasingly acrimonious as concerns were raised about China's human rights, labor, and national security policies. In May 2000, the House approved normal trade relations status for China by a vote of 237 to 197. The margin of victory was provided by Republicans. Two out of three Democrats voted against it. The Senate gave its consent the following month.

The organizing logic of free trade has also been applied at the regional level with the establishment of the North American Free Trade Agreement (NAFTA). Negotiated by President George H. W. Bush near the end of his administration, it fell to President Bill Clinton to finalize the three-way agreement between the United States, Canada, and Mexico. From the outset NAFTA has been controversial. Hailed by its supporters as an energizing force that would provide increased investment opportunities for American capital and new jobs for American workers, it has been criticized by environmentalists and labor for taking an overly narrow view of the benefits of free trade without appreciating the costs that it entails.

George W. Bush's administration is a strong advocate of free trade. The centerpiece of its free trade strategy is the creation of a Free Trade Area of the Americas (FTAA). It had first been proposed by Clinton in 1994 but little movement toward making it a reality took place. The Bush administration energized the negotiating process but encountered firm opposition to its plans for extending NAFTA to the tip of South America. A November 2003 meeting with states from the Caribbean, Latin America, and Canada (but not Cuba) produced a vaguely worded agreement that kept this concept moving forward. Opponents led by Brazil, wanted a less inclusive agreement that would let countries pick and choose what parts of the agreement they wished to participate in. Brazil was interested in tariff reduction but not statues dealing with cross border investment and protection of copyrights.

In the absence of an FTAA agreement, the Bush administration sought to keep its free trade agenda alive by signing a series of bilateral trade agreements. In December 2003, it reached agreement with Guatemala, Nicaragua, El Salvador, and Honduras. In August 2003, the Senate approved free trade agreements with Chile and Singapore by identical votes of 66 to 31. Talks with these two states had begun in the Clinton administration and became entangled in the politics of the war with Iraq that Singapore supported and Chile did not. Negotiations for the free trade agreement with Singapore were expedited while those with Chile were put on the back burner. In February 2004, the United States and Australia announced a free trade agreement. None of the agreements are without controversy. The Central American agreements are of greater political value than they are of economic value and were opposed by representatives from textile producing states. The Singapore and Chile pacts drew complaints about immigration provisions that allow several thousand professional workers into the United States. The Australia agreement came about only after Australia agreed to provisions that closed the U.S. sugar market to their exports. Thailand, Bahrain, Morocco, the Dominican Republic, Colombia, and several southern African states are also negotiating with the Bush administration over the creation of bilateral free trade agreements.

At the global level, free trade provided the strategic foundation for the creation of the World Trade Organization (WTO). The WTO is a product of the Uruguay Round GATT talks. Its first round of WTO talks launched in Doha, Qatar, in 2001 stalled after a 2003 meeting in Cancun that left rich and poor countries in deep disagreement over free trade in agricultural products. The most significant structural innovation in the creation of the WTO is its dispute settlement procedures. Under GATT a dispute settlement panel was set up only if requested and its report was adopted only if there was a consensus in favor of it. Under the WTO a standing dispute settlement panel exists, and its report is adopted unless there is a consensus against it. This change transforms the WTO dispute settlement process into a compulsory and automatic instrument for resolving trade disputes.

The operation of the WTO dispute resolution system has become a major irritant to the United States. In general terms, fears are expressed over the loss of sovereignty and the nondemocratic nature of the decision-making procedures. In concrete terms, the United States is upset with having lost several cases before the WTO. In 2000, for example, the WTO ruled against the United States on tax breaks being given to U.S. exporters and for restrictions it placed on lamb being imported from Australia and New Zealand. The United States has also brought cases to the WTO. It charged Brazil with violating international patent laws by producing generic AIDS medicine and the European Union with unfair trade practices for its restrictions on the import of genetically modified foods from the United States. More recently, the WTO ruled twice against the United States in highly charged cases. As already noted in 2003, it ruled against the tariffs imposed on foreign steel by the Bush administration, a move that opened the way for the EU to impose retaliatory tariffs of $2.2 billion against U.S. products ranging from footwear to vegetables. The next year, in a case brought by Brazil, it ruled against U.S. cotton subsidies. Also in 2004 the EU, Canada, South Korea, and Japan led the way in challenging the Byrd Amendment. Used to protect the steel industry from foreign competition the amendment has provided some $710 million worth of protection to American industries harmed by "unfairly traded" imports.

Strategic Trade.   Competing with free trade as the strategic foundation for American international economic policy is strategic trade.[5] Its advocates argue that current U.S. trade policy cannot be sustained politically or economically because the global market is failing U.S. firms. They maintain that the comparative advantages enjoyed by states in international trade is not due to a country's resource base or historical factors but to imperfections in markets that have been deliberately created by government policy. Only by actively intervening in the international marketplace in order to create comparative advantages for selected industries can the United States hope to remain a world leader.

Strategic trade policy requires two things of the U.S. government. First, it must identify high-growth industries whose health is crucial to the overall global competitiveness of the American economy. Most frequently mentioned in this regard are industries such as computers, aerospace, semiconductors, and biotechnology. Second, the U.S. government must ensure that these firms are not shut out of foreign markets. Neither task is easy. First, identifying industries for special treatment is a politically charged decision that holds great consequences for states and localities. Just as congresspeople fight to prevent military base closures in their districts, they fight to ensure that their districts will get a fair share of research and development money. A related problem is how to address the problems faced by industries such as steel that are no longer competitive internationally but retain enormous political clout.

The second problem, ensuring access to foreign markets, is complicated by regional trade agreements that limit access by nonmember firms. An overly aggressive strategic trade policy runs the risk of spawning a trade war in which U.S. goods are singled out for retaliation. In April 2001, a long-running trade war was resolved when the European Union agreed to give greater access to the European market to U.S. companies exporting bananas. In return, the United States agreed to suspend economic sanctions it had placed on $191 million worth of European products sold in the United States.

The driving force behind strategic trade was the inability of American policy makers (and American industry) to put a dent in the U.S.–Japanese trade imbalance. In 1971 Richard Nixon was moved to act when the imbalance reached $1.3 billion. In 1991 George Bush was confronted with a $43.4 billion trade imbalance. In 1988 concern with the trade imbalance gave rise to the Omnibus Trade and Competitiveness Act. Section 301, commonly referred to as "Super 301," provides for retaliatory sanctions against states engaging in unfair trading practices against the United States. It requires that presidents identify "priority countries" and set a timetable for resolving the dispute after which time the sanctions will take effect. In his 2001 report, U.S. Trade Representative Robert Zoellick identified fifty-one trading partners that under the terms of Super 301 denied American firms adequate and effective protection of intellectual property rights, or fair access to their markets. His 2003 report singled out among others Brazil, Poland, Russia, the EU, Mexico, India, South Korea, and Taiwan for criticism. Ukraine was designated as a Priority Foreign Country for its systematic failure to act on U.S. complaints and is subject to $75 million worth of U.S. trade sanctions.

MONETARY STRATEGIES

The bulk of our discussion in this chapter focuses on trade and aid as the central economic instruments of U.S. foreign policy. It needs to be noted that financial transactions can also be used to further foreign policy goals. For example, the United States moved to freeze the assets of groups suspected of being under the control of, or aligned with, Osama bin Laden following the September 11, 2001, terrorist attacks. In a similar fashion, it moved quickly to block Saddam Hussein's ability to reach funds in Kuwaiti bank accounts following Iraq's invasion of Kuwait.

The United States played a central role in establishing the Bretton Woods system, which provided the framework for international economic transactions from the end of World War II until 1971. The two key financial institutions created were the International Monetary Fund (IMF) and the International Bank for Reconstruction and Development (IBRD or, more commonly, the World Bank). The IMF was to regulate international currencies to ensure that they did not suddenly and violently change value. The World Bank was to provide additional funds that were believed necessary for European economic recovery. Virtually from the outset the Bretton Woods system did not function as anticipated. American dollars became the international currency of choice, and American foreign economic and military aid provided the necessary funds for economic recovery.

By 1960, the situation began to change and the outflow of dollars had reached the point where U.S. officials became worried about the trade deficit. The Bretton Woods system ended in 1971 when President Nixon announced that the U.S. dollar would no longer be convertible to gold. Since then, international monetary management has taken the form of periodic exercises in crisis management rather than systemic reform. This is currently the case with respect to China. The value of the Chinese yuan has been pegged to a fixed exchange rate with the U.S. dollar. With the dollar's value falling on global markets and the Chinese economy growing at a rapid rate, an imbalance now exists between the value of the dollar and the yuan. As a result, Chinese exports have come to enjoy a significant price advantage over their domestic competitors, which in turn costs jobs. To remedy this situation, the United States is pressuring China to make a market-based adjustment of the value of the yuan.

Perhaps the most telling reason for this monetary policy of benign neglect is Susan Strange's observation that the pace and density of global financial transactions has outpaced the ability of national governments and international organizations to regulate them.[6] She likens the situation to that of a casino in which at times luck is just as important as skill in making the difference between winning and losing.

Economic Sanctions

Economic sanctions have become a popular way of exercising American economic power. By one recent count, the United States put into place thirty-three new unilateral sanctions between 1997 and 2001. According to a UN study, seventy-five countries were subject to U.S. economic sanctions in 1998.[7] What constitutes an economic sanction is highly contested. We adopt a middle of the road definition. Economic sanctions are "the deliberate withdrawal of normal trade or financial relations for foreign policy purposes."[8] Should American policy makers decide to employ U.S. economic power against another state, they have several options at their disposal.

INVENTORY OF OPTIONS

A *tariff* is a tax on foreign-made goods entering one's country. Typically, tariffs are applied in order to protect domestic industry against foreign competition or to raise revenue, but they can also be manipulated to serve foreign policy goals. Twice in the postwar era, the United States has made notable efforts to manipulate its tariff structure to accomplish foreign policy goals. First, the United States has used its tariff system as a lever in dealing with communist states. The United States excluded communist states from equal access to the U.S. market. During détente the United States sought to use access to the U.S. market and MFN status as an inducement to the Soviets for cooperation in noneconomic areas such as the SALT talks. The second attempt to use tariffs as an instrument of foreign policy came in 1971 when President Nixon placed a 10 percent "surcharge" on all imports not already under a quota. The primary objective behind this move was to force major changes in the trading practices of other states. It failed to do so and created foreign hostility toward the United States.

The primary danger inherent in the excessive use of tariffs is retaliation. The major instance of retaliation took place in the early 1930s after the United States passed the Smoot–Hawley Tariff. The highest tariff in U.S. history, the Smoot–Hawley Tariff taxed imports at an average rate of 41.5 percent of their value. Retaliation by foreign governments led to a sudden and dramatic drop in U.S. exports, which only worsened the ongoing depression, something the Smoot–Hawley Tariff was intended to help solve. In the first half of 1929, U.S. exports exceeded $2.5 billion; by the first half of 1932, they were valued at less than $1 billion. The Trade Agreements Act of 1934 broke the spiral of raising tariffs that had begun in 1879 and set off a new downward spiral. It authorized the president to lower existing tariffs by as much as 50 percent to those states that made reciprocal concessions.

Manipulating nontariff barriers (NTBs) to trade is a modern variation on this theme. Taking forms ranging from labeling requirements, health and safety standards, and license controls to taxation policy, they have become powerful tools in the hands of policy makers who want to protect local firms from foreign competition or remedy a balance-of-payments problem. U.S. use of NTBs dates at least from the 1930s when the Buy America Act required the government to purchase goods and services from U.S. suppliers if their prices were not unreasonably higher than those of foreign competitors. Another piece of legislation in the 1930s gave preferential treatment to U.S. shipping interests. It required that goods purchased overseas with U.S. loans or guaranteed funds had to be transported whenever possible in U.S. vessels.

An *embargo* is a refusal to sell a commodity to another state, and it is a third economic instrument of foreign policy. Embargoes (and the more subtle concept of export controls) have long played a prominent role in U.S. cold war foreign policy. Building upon the Trading with the Enemy Act of 1917, the United States embargoed financial and commercial transactions with North Korea (1950), the People's Republic of China (1950), Cuba (1962), and North Vietnam (1964). Trade with communist states was also controlled by the Export Control Act of 1949 and the Battle Act of 1950. The Export Control Act denied export licenses for strategic goods intended for communist bloc states. At the outset practically every commodity that might be considered to have some military or strategic value was placed on the Department of Commerce's Commodity Control List. During the Korean War the list of restricted items reached 1,000 in number.

In the post–cold war international system, embargoes have become a prominent instrument of American foreign policy. In 1994, the Clinton administration lifted the American embargo on Vietnam. That embargo was first imposed in May 1964 in response to North Vietnamese attacks on the south. Progress toward lifting the embargo was slow because of questions regarding Vietnam's cooperation in helping locate American POWs. An embargo also played a central role in American efforts to bring down the

Haitian military junta and return deposed president Jean-Bertrand Aristide to power. In June 1993, the United Nations voted to impose an oil and arms embargo on Haiti. The ease with which oil and other goods reached the military through the Dominican Republic blunted its effectiveness, and in 1993 Clinton got the United Nations to impose a near total embargo on Haiti. Only food and humanitarian supplies were exempt.

Perhaps most controversial have been two post–cold war embargoes in different parts of the world that have been linked politically in Washington. They are the arms embargo against the Bosnian Muslims and the near total embargo against Iraq. Both were instituted on a multilateral basis and pressure repeatedly surfaced that they be lifted. An embargo on trade with Iraq was put into place in April 1991. It was to be lifted only when Iraq met the United Nations' terms for dealing with its nuclear program. By 1994, France and Russia were arguing that these terms had been met because Iraq was beginning to cooperate with UN monitors. The United States considered Iraq's action insufficient and continued to view Saddam Hussein as a regional threat to be contained. It argued that Iraq still had not met all of the conditions of UN Resolution 687 regarding its invasion of Kuwait and that until it did the embargo should remain in place. About the same time that the Iraqi embargo went into effect the United Nations also put into place an arms embargo in Yugoslavia. While neutral in its language, the embargo had a far more serious impact on the military capabilities of the Bosnian Muslims than it did on the Bosnian Serbs. The Serbs were able to draw upon the military resources of the old Yugoslav army now in the possession of the neighboring Serbian government.

Since 9/11, the George W. Bush administration has also turned to sanctions, although in most cases the effect has largely been symbolic and deliberately so. One of these, the Iran–Libya Sanctions Extension Act of 2001, kept in effect sanctions approved by Congress in 1996 that were about to expire. The Act requires that the president impose at least two of six possible penalties to any firm investing over specific amounts in any one year in the energy sector of these states unless he finds it in the national interest to waive this provision. No firms have been sanctioned under its terms largely because of the strong opposition of the EU that threatened to take the issue to the WTO. In spite of his administration's hostility to Syria, in 2004 George W. Bush reluctantly imposed broad sanctions against Syria for its support of terrorism. Among other measures, the Syrian Accountability Act bars U.S. exports except for food and medicine. Bush delayed implementing the measure and immediately indicated that he would continue to permit the sale of telecommunication equipment and aircraft spare parts. The telecommunication exemption was justified on the grounds of the need to "promote the free flow of information."

A *boycott* is a refusal to buy a product(s) from another state, and it represents a fourth economic instrument available to policy makers. One case involved U.S. participation in UN-sponsored sanctions against Rhodesia (Zimbabwe).[9] Off and on, these sanctions lasted for over a decade. They were first imposed by President Johnson in a 1968 executive order, and they were finally lifted in 1979. The purpose of the sanctions was to force the Rhodesian government into accepting the principle of majority rule. The U.S. commitment to the boycott was never firm. Congress amended the boycott in 1971 to allow the import of raw chromium and other critical materials. It closed this loophole in 1977 when the same groups that lobbied for the exemption objected to the flood of low-priced Rhodesian-processed chromium into the U.S. market. Throughout 1979 the Carter administration fought a holding action against moves by the Senate to lift the boycott until such time as the British were able to mediate the changeover to majority rule.

In 1995, the Clinton administration instituted a boycott against Iran in response to evidence that it was seeking to acquire nuclear technology and expertise from Russia. Clinton publicly labeled Iran a threat to peace in the Middle East and a sponsor of terrorism. The move came on the heels of an administration ban on trade between Iran and U.S. oil companies and their subsidiaries. Political pressures played a major role in these decisions as Congress had been pressing the administration for even tougher action against Iran.

The fifth policy tool we examine in our survey is the *quota*, which is a quantitative restriction on goods coming from another state. Because of GATT, quotas have not played a large role in foreign economic policy making for most of the postwar era. This began to change as the U.S. balance-of-payments situation continued to deteriorate and as concerns grew over the international competitiveness of American-made products. One recent notable use of quotas came in 1994 when the Clinton administration threatened to limit the amount of Canadian grain entering the United States. In 2004, quotas were used in a failed attempt to ease a trade dispute with Canada. In 2002, the United States imposed tariffs on Canadian lumber entering the United States. Now it offered tariff free access to the U.S. market for Canadian lumber under a quota system.

CASE STUDIES

Removing Castro From Power: Cuba.   Castro's Cuba was a major irritant to U.S. policy makers in the 1960s, and economic pressure was only one of several policy instruments brought into play. In 1959, the year Castro came to power, Cuba was heavily dependent on the United States: 67 percent of its exports went to the United States; 70 percent of its imports came from the United States; and under the terms of legislation passed in 1934, the United States purchased the bulk of Cuban sugar at prices substantially above world market rates. Relations between the United States and Castro were tense from the very beginning. In February 1960 Castro concluded a barter deal with the Soviet Union involving an exchange of Cuban sugar for Soviet crude oil. After U.S. owned oil refineries refused to process the Soviet oil, Castro took them over. The U.S. response was to terminate all remaining foreign aid programs and to cancel all purchases of Cuban sugar for the remainder of the year. Castro retaliated with additional nationalizations of U.S. property. Next, the United States imposed an embargo on all exports to Castro except for food and medicine. With this move Cuba entered into more economic agreements with the Soviet Union, and, in turn, the United States broke diplomatic relations. Even after the Cuban missile crisis and the Bay of Pigs invasion, the United States continued to apply economic sanctions. The Foreign Aid Act of 1963 required the president to stop U.S. aid to states that refused to restrict their trade with Cuba unless he felt that it was in the U.S. national interest not to do so. The United States also succeeded in getting the Organization of American States first to expel Cuba and then to sever commercial relations with it.

Economic sanctions have remained in place ever since. Periodically, they have been tightened often as a result of electoral considerations. In 1992, Congress tightened the existing embargo by passing the Cuban Democracy Act. It placed heavy penalties on U.S. firms engaging in trade with Cuba through foreign subsidiaries. In 1996, the Helms–Burton Act threatened sanctions against countries that provided Cuba with foreign aid and allowed U.S. nationals to sue foreign firms that that now controlled properties seized during the Cuban revolution. Opposition from American allies to this last provision has been intense and both Clinton and George W. Bush waived it annually. In 2002, George W. Bush announced that Cuban Americans will only be able to visit home once every three years for no more than two weeks at a time, and they may only bring with them a limited amount of luggage and money.

Punishing Support for Terrorism: Libya.   Muammar Qaddafi came to power in Libya through a coup in 1969. His nationalization of oil fields produced only a moderate response from the United States in 1973, but relations became increasingly tense as his regime became identified with terrorist attacks and hostility toward Israel so that in 1978 the United States banned the sale of military equipment to Libya. The Reagan administration entered office determined to use its Libyan policy as a means of making a statement of America's renewed willingness to flex its power. In 1981, Reagan placed an embargo on crude oil imports from Libya and restricted the export of sophisticated gas and oil equipment to it. In 1985, the importation of refined Libyan oil products was barred. The following year, after a new wave of terrorist violence, Reagan imposed a comprehensive trade embargo that banned all imports and exports. Libyan financial assets in American banks were also frozen. Later in 1986, U.S. oil companies were forced to leave but were allowed to sign standstill agreements allowing the Libyan National Oil Company to run their affiliates until they returned. In 1993, after Libya was implicated in the explosions on Pan Am flight 103 over Lockerbie, Scotland, and a French UTA flight 772 over Niger, the UN Security Council passed resolution 883 imposing a global embargo on Libyan oil and gas products and freezing Libyan funds abroad. In 1996, the Iran–Libya Sanctions Act was passed that placed stiff penalties on companies investing more than $40 million in Libya's oil industry. In 1999, after Libya turned over two suspects in the Lockerbie bombing to the World Court, the UN suspended its sanctions. They were lifted in 2003 after Qaddafi renounced his support for terrorism. The United States and France abstained in this vote after receiving assurances from Qaddafi that Libya would increase payments to the families of those who died in these plane crashes. In December 2003, Qaddafi unexpectedly announced that Libya had attempted to develop chemical, biological, and nuclear weapons and renounced further attempts to do so. He also welcomed international inspections.

RULES OF ECONOMIC CONFLICT

Judging the successfulness of sanctions is difficult and marked by controversy. Consider our two case studies. The conventional wisdom is that sanctions against Cuba have failed. Cuba's economy and its people have suffered as a result of the sanctions, but few, if any, U.S. foreign policy goals have been realized. The sanctions have also become a source of controversy with allies. Others note that if sanctions are judged to be a failure, Soviet economic aid to Cuba must be seen as a success. Moreover, they cost the United States little and had a positive demonstration effect in Latin America about the costs of aligning with the Soviet Union. With regard to Libya, the George W. Bush administration asserts that Libya's rejection of terrorism and new openness on its nuclear capability was because of its new military strategy of preemption. Others maintain that, in fact, it was the long-term effect of over twenty years of economic sanctions plus quiet diplomacy that was responsible for the breakthrough.

We can also try and assess the effectiveness of economic sanctions by taking a more encompassing look at successes and failures. One recent study of 115 instances of economic sanctions over seventy-five years found that they succeed in accomplishing their stated objectives only 34 percent of the time.[10] The greatest success (52 percent) was enjoyed by sanctions designed to destabilize a government, while those designed to put a major dent in the target country's military capabilities were least likely to succeed (20 percent). The success rate for economic sanctions also showed a marked decrease over time. Almost one-half of those imposed prior to 1973 succeeded, and the success rate dropped to approximately 25 percent after that date. Measuring success and failure was complicated by the fact that in some cases multiple or changing goals were present. In others, the sanctions were imposed in such a way as to fail or have little impact on the target state. The study suggests that this was the case in Bush's economic sanctions imposed on China after the Tiananmen Square incident.

Overall the study concluded that economic sanctions succeeded only under a restricted set of circumstances. We can paraphrase them as follows:

1. Don't have inflated expectations about what sanctions can accomplish.
2. The more countries you need to make sanctions work, the less likely they will succeed. More is not better.
3. Countries in economic distress are far more likely to succumb to coercion than those with healthy economies.
4. Attack your allies, not your enemies. Allies are more willing to make concessions than enemies.
5. Sanctions imposed slowly or incrementally are more likely to fail than those imposed swiftly.
6. To be effective sanctions must hurt the target state.

7. Sanctions will be costly to the sender states. The greater these costs, the greater will be the domestic opposition to them.

8. Economic sanctions often work best in combination with other policy tools.

9. "Look before you leap." Sanctions, even those done for symbolic purposes, should be thought out in advance.

Even this relatively stringent set of limiting conditions is seen as overly optimistic in tone by some. A reexamination of the case studies used to generate these commandments asserted that the original study was too optimistic in classifying something as a success and did not give enough credit to the role of military force when success was achieved.[11]

SMART SANCTIONS

Dissatisfaction with the success rate of economic sanctions, and growing questions about the ethical justification for inflicting hardship and suffering on innocent people because of what their government has done, has led many to advocate abandoning conventional economic sanctions for "smart sanctions."[12] Smart sanctions differ from conventional sanctions in two respects. First, they target decision makers and political elites, not populations. Second, they protect vulnerable social groups. The first aim is achieved by focusing on arms embargoes, travel restrictions, and targeted financial sanctions. An example of such a sanction is George W. Bush's decision to freeze the assets of Zimbabwe's President Robert Mugabe and other key government officials in 2003 for undermining democracy and contributing to a "deliberate breakdown in the rule of law." The second aim is achieved by specifically exempting certain commodities such as food and medicine. The UN sanctions against Iraq were consistent with this second point. Resolution 661, approved after its invasion of Kuwait, imposed a multilateral embargo except for humanitarian goods. Resolution 705, approved in 1991 after Saddam Hussein put down a Kurdish rebellion allowed Iraq to export a limited amount of oil in order to purchase food and humanitarian supplies. Initial evaluations of smart sanctions are not encouraging.[13] They do not appear to be significantly more successful than conventional ones. The fundamental problem is the same, a lack of political will to enforce them, and no amount of technical refinement can compensate for this shortcoming.

Foreign Aid

In order to understand U.S. foreign aid it is necessary to highlight the existence of three significant structural features. First, the U.S. foreign aid budget is less than one percent of the overall U.S. budget. National Defense spending accounts for 19.7 percent. Second, a very high percentage of U.S. foreign aid funds are spent on U.S. products. The Congressional Research Service estimates that 90 percent of food aid is spent on U.S. goods and services. Third, U.S. foreign aid is not distributed evenly around the world but is concentrated on a few states. The top-ten recipients of foreign aid in 2002 are

TABLE 15.1   Leading Recipients of U.S. Foreign Aid, 2002

Country	Millions of Dollars*
Israel	2,760
Egypt	1,956
Pakistan	921
Colombia	382
Afghanistan	297
Jordan	227
Peru	196
Ukraine	160
Russia	159
Indonesia	125

*Excludes food aid.
Source: Mary H. Cooper, "Foreign Aid After September 11," The CQ Researcher, (April 26, 2002), 365.

listed in Table 15.1. Even among the leading recipients funds were concentrated on three countries: Israel, Egypt, and Pakistan.

TYPES OF FOREIGN AID

There is no standard method for categorizing the different types of U.S foreign aid programs. One approach used by the researchers with the Congressional Research Service identifies six basic categories. The overall breakdown in spending among these six categories of foreign aid for 2001 is presented in Table 15.2. Before examining the breakdown of official U.S. foreign aid it is important to note that private foreign aid, not from organizations but individuals, is now among the most important sources of funds for third world states. In 2001 remittances, money sent home by immigrants in the United States added up to $28.4 billion.

TABLE 15.2   Composition of U.S. Foreign Aid, 2001 by Type

Type of Foreign Aid	Percentage of Total	Dollar Amount
Economic Political/Security	29.7%	$4.44 billion
Military	25.1%	$3.76 billion
Bilateral Development	23.3%	$3.48 billion
Humanitarian	9.7%	$1.45 billion
Multilateral	9.5%	$1.43 billion
Non-Emergency Food	2.7%	$0.4 billion

Source: Congressional Research Service "Foreign Aid: An Introductory Overview of U.S. Programs and Policy, April 6, 2001.

The first category of official U.S. foreign aid is economic aid given for the purpose of advancing U.S. political and security objectives. This is the biggest category of foreign aid. Monies given here have supported such diverse programs the Camp David Accords negotiated by Carter, the building of democracy in the Russia and East Europe, antinarcotics efforts, antiterrorism plans, and countering weapons proliferation. George W. Bush's 2002 plan to create a U.S.–Mexico Partnership for Progress that would direct $30 billion in to Mexico in order to create jobs and discourage immigration would fall into this category of foreign aid.

The second-largest category of foreign aid is military assistance. These monies go to help allies maintain and train their armed forces, as well as buy American military equipment. Included here are Economic Support Funds. These are loans to countries not eligible for development assistance but are considered to be strategically important. Finally, the grant military assistance program provides funds to purchase American military equipment, and grant military assistance training funds.

The third category is bilateral development assistance. These aid programs are generally administered by the U.S. Agency for International Development (USAID) and have a long-term development focus on strengthening the economy, environment, health care delivery systems, and political institutions of recipient states. Funding for the Peace Corps and debt relief fall into this category. Economic development aid has become the "ideology" by which most people think foreign aid must be justified. In 1989, Alan Woods, the head of USAID, asserted that U.S. development foreign aid had lost sight of its original rationale: providing transitional help to third world states to meet their own development needs.[14] Not only had this aid become permanent, it had created a dependency on it that was stifling development. In the early. 1990s, a new consensus on how development aid should work formed. This "Washington Consensus" shifted attention away from subsidizing projects to establishing free markets.[15] By the end of the 1990s, it had also come under attack for failing to take into account the negative social impacts of free markets in the areas of income equality, abuses of labor rights, and large-scale environmental destruction.

A particularly troublesome aspect of economic aid in the 1980s and 1990s was debt relief. The sums were staggering. In 1988, Brazil's outstanding debt was $120.1 billion, Mexico's stood at $107.4 billion, and Argentina owed $59.6 billion. At first, the Reagan administration approached the problem as one that was solvable through a combination of austerity measures on the part of countries and the adoption of more prudent lending policies by banks and international organizations. This response proved inadequate and the Reagan administration sought to increase the level of funding available through the Baker Plan. With the problem continuing, George H. W. Bush devised the Brady Plan that combined a program of limited and voluntary debt forgiveness with international guarantees of the remaining loan amounts. The Brady Plan did not solve the debt problem (in 1995 Clinton found it necessary to provide Mexico with $12 billion in loans to stabilize the peso) but did seem to make it manageable compared to new debt problems that were emerging in Asia as a result of rapidly declining currency values that reverberated through global stock markets.

The fourth category of foreign aid is humanitarian economic assistance. This aid tends to be short-term and emergency-focused. Refugee assistance, emergency food aid, and disaster relief account for the bulk of the spending here. The fifth category is multilateral development assistance. It accounts for less than one-tenth of the foreign aid budget and consists of funds contributed to such international development organizations as UNICEF, the United Nations Development Plan, the World Bank, and the African Development Bank. The final category of foreign aid is non-emergency food aid. The Food for Peace program, also known as PL 480, is the primary instrument for distributing this aid. It makes surplus U.S. agricultural goods available to third world states in local currency and at concessionary prices. Critics of the Food for Peace program have noted that a tension has always existed between the humanitarian and political purposes of this aid and that the political purposes tend to triumph. In 1973, only two of the top twenty recipients of PL 480 funds were among the world's forty poorest states. Under Reagan, Egypt received the most PL 480 funds ($221 million). India was a distant second ($93.5), followed by El Salvador ($50.8) and the Sudan ($50.7).

COLD WAR FOREIGN AID

The relative importance of military and economic aid varied considerably during the cold war. The Truman administration's foreign aid program was dominated by economic development initiatives such as the Marshall Plan that made $17 billion available in loans and grants for European economic recovery and the Point Four Program whose goal it was to bring economic development and modernization to the third world through the transfer of U.S. technical assistance. In Truman's foreign aid budget, 96 percent consisted of development funds. With the outbreak of the Korean War, a change occurred. Increasingly policy makers viewed foreign aid as an instrument for furthering American national security. More than 60 percent of foreign aid now was given for military purposes. In the process, the focus of American foreign aid changed as well. Between 1949 and 1952, Europe received 86 percent of U.S. foreign aid. That fell to 25 percent between 1953 and 1957 and then 6 percent between 1958 and 1961. Correspondingly, the share of American aid to the third world increased during this time period to 68 percent.

Under Kennedy, the proportion of economic aid to military aid changed again. By the mid 1970's economic aid accounted for 75 percent of all U.S. foreign aid. Within the economic aid category, however, an important change occurred. A greater emphasis was given to loans (that had to be repaid) over grants (that did not). With the deepening American involvement in Vietnam, the balance swung back in favor of military aid. By the mid-1970s it now constituted 70 percent of U.S. foreign aid. After the war ended, economic aid reasserted itself growing to 80 percent of the total. It again faded under the Reagan administration. From 1980 to 1985, economic aid rose from about $7.5 billion to almost $10 billion, while military aid virtually tripled from $2 billion to almost $6 billion.

POST–COLD WAR FOREIGN AID

During the first decade of the post–cold war era, three controversies dominated the foreign aid agenda. The first centered on foreign aid to Russia. The United States targeted two areas for assistance. One was funding to help Russia denuclearize by providing it with funds to destroy chemical and nuclear weapons, establish safeguards against proliferation, and assess the environmental damage done with nuclear waste. Funds were provided for this purpose by the 1991 Nunn–Lugar Threat Reduction Program. The second area of funding was economic development. None argued with the need for Russia's economy to grow, but many argued that widespread corruption and government inefficiency made growth impossible.

A second area of controversy surrounded funding for combating HIV/AIDS. Donor states provided about $350 million to fight AIDS in 1999 with about half that amount coming from the United States. The American response to the AIDS crisis has been caught in a political crossfire of congressional opposition to foreign aid in general and opposition to any form of aid for family planning programs. Bureaucratic infighting has also hampered efforts to address the AIDS problem. With Congress reluctant to provide additional funds, bureaucratic rivals have sought to prevent their limited budgets from being siphoned off for this purpose. Complicating matters further are questions of protecting patents. Third world states lobbied hard to be allowed to produce generic versions of the leading AIDS drugs. In trade negotiations, the United States pressed for these states to pay full licensing fees. When South Africa passed a law permitting the government to produce drugs it considered too expensive on the world market, the United States threatened economic sanctions and placed it on a Super 301 watchlist.

The third area of controversy involved efforts to stop international drug trafficking. The most ambitious undertaking is Plan Colombia. It is a $7.5 billion aid package that hopes to advance the peace process in Colombia, strengthen its national economy, stop the production of drugs, promote justice and human rights, and foster democracy and social development. Plan Colombia has met with a mixed reception. Seventy five percent of its initial $1.5 billion in aid was military in nature and critics asserted that the plan was reminiscent of the 1980 to 1981 period when the United States became embroiled in El Salvador's civil war by an overly close identification with the military. It has also been argued that Plan Colombia was not sufficiently sensitive to the complex interactions between the drug war and the guerrilla war, whose roots date back to the 1960s.

All of these aid programs continue to be controversial, although they have been overtaken politically by new foreign aid concerns. The George W. Bush administration was not interested in continuing the Nunn–Lugar Program until after the 9/11 terrorist attack. It had ordered a review of the program upon taking office but now advocated an additional $750 million on 30 different programs in 2002. In 2004, the Bush administration rejected calls from the UN for an additional $1 billion per year in AIDS funding. At the center of this controversy are the continuing American restrictions on how AIDS funds can be spent and the administration's funding of a bilateral measure that targets fifteen countries over five years with $15 billion, $10 billion of which would be new money. In January of 2004, Secretary of State Colin Powell certified to Congress that the Colombian government and armed forces were complying with human rights standards. This finding was necessary to allow the last 12.5 percent of the Plan Colombia funds to be obligated. Human rights watch groups challenged this assessment of the situation with some asserting that the human rights situation in Colombia had worsened in parts of Colombia since Plan Colombia began.

POST–9/11 FOREIGN AID

Since 9/11, foreign aid has come to be viewed in a more positive light under the assumption that it can make a major contribution to the war against terrorism, although many are doubtful that its impact will be significant in direct and measurable ways. Interestingly, the interest in foreign aid as a tool against terrorism comes from both national security and economic development perspectives.

Almost immediately after 9/11, the George W. Bush administration sought authority from Congress to waive all existing restrictions on U.S. military assistance and weapons exports for five years to any country he determined was helping in the war on terrorism. A similar pattern existed in the area of trade. In 2002, for example, the administration proposed dropping trade restrictions on eight Central Asian countries that emerged out of the Soviet Union after its fall. All had questionable records in the areas of human rights and democratization. Only Belarus, which did not offer antiterrorism assistance, was not in line to have trade restrictions dropped. In addition to being used as a carrot, it was also used as a stick. In 2003, the administration announced that it would only allow companies from countries who supported the war against Iraq to bid on prime reconstruction contracts. Under-Secretary of Defense Paul Wolfowitz justified the decision to limit competition as necessary "for the protection of the essential security of the United States." Also that year the Bush administration announced that it was suspending military aid to some thirty-five countries because they failed to meet a congressionally imposed deadline exempting Americans from prosecution in the new UN International Criminal Court. Congress exempted twenty-seven states including NATO members, Israel, and Egypt from the loss of aid.

The signature development assistance program of the George W. Bush administration is the Millennium Challenge Account (MCA).[16] Targeted on low-income countries, it was announced in 2002, began operation in FY 2004, and will not be administered by USAID but by a new independent agency, the Millennium Challenge Corporation. One of the defining features of the MCA is to be its narrow focus. Money will be given only to countries that meet a demanding set of criteria, and its only purpose will be supporting economic growth and poverty reduction. Bush's criteria fall into three categories: 1) ruling justly, 2) investing in people, and 3) economic freedom. Preliminary calculations showed that of seventy-five low-income countries (those with a per capita income of less than $1,435 and who can draw concessionary funds from the World Bank) that would be eligible in the first year, only thirteen would qualify. Revised criteria for the second year would make only eleven countries eligible, one of which would be China. The number of potential qualifiers increases to twenty to twenty-five by the fourth or fifth year and includes Egypt and South Africa. Virtually all commentators have welcomed this initiative. Many also point out its dangers.[17] Foremost among them are the nature of the selection criteria and the small number of countries likely to be eligible for assistance, the danger of bureaucratic rivalry with USAID, the limited capacity of the targeted states to absorb foreign aid in a useful fashion, and the need to integrate MCA funds with multilateral assistance programs.

Summary and the Future

As our survey has revealed, U.S. policy makers have used a great variety of economic instruments in order to further U.S. foreign policy goals. It is less clear that any agreement exists on what mixture of economic tools is most desirable or when they will be most effective. Disagreement even exists over the very utility of economic statecraft. David Baldwin, one of its defenders, argues that four shortcomings in the standard approach to thinking about economic power tend to produce overly negative assessments of its usefulness.[18]

First, day-to-day economic exchanges are generally defined to be outside the scope of economic power. As we have already noted, free trade is typically not considered to be an economic instrument of foreign policy. Second, economic sanctions are often said to fail when they do not produce a change in policy in the target state. Underappreciated is the added cost that economic sanctions place on the target state even if it does not change its policies. This is somewhat surprising since the ability to inflict pain is generally recognized as a valuable component of military power. Part of the problem here is not recognizing that economic sanctions have political, psychological, and military consequences even when the economic impact appears to be negligible. Third, economic power has often been judged a failure because it is examined out of context. Policy makers often turn to it when no other instruments are available or to accomplish the almost impossible. Consider the following "failures" of U.S. economic statecraft:

> Getting Castro to step down
> Getting Rhodesian whites to accept majority rule
> Getting the Soviet Union to change its political system[19]

It is hard to imagine any mixture of policy instruments that would have accomplished these goals. Used more judiciously, economic statecraft is capable of producing successes. A recent study of economic sanctions against third world states suggests that when relatively subtle economic sanctions are employed (delaying the delivery of spare parts, snags in licensing technology transfers, shutting off or reducing bilateral loans and grants, refusing to refinance debts), political objectives can be realized even when there is only a moderate economic effect.[20]

Fourth, economic statecraft suffers because writers on world politics underestimate how important symbolic actions are to policy makers and to domestic pressure groups. For example, all of the Reagan administration's 1985 and 1986 uses of economic sanctions were widely acknowledged to be symbolic acts. White House–announced sanctions against South Africa were taken to head off congressionally imposed sanctions and keep policy making on South Africa in the executive branch. Included among the sanctions were bans on the sale of computers, most nuclear technology, most new loans to South African government agencies, and the sale of the Krugerrand in the United States. The U.S. sanctions also mandated that U.S. multinational corporations operating in South Africa treat black and white employees equally. These sanctions were put forward more as a statement of political necessity and/or moral outrage over apartheid than as part of a specific agenda to bring about its end.

Notes

1. Walter Russell Mead, "America's Sticky Power," *Foreign Policy*, 141 (2004), 46–53.
2. Steven Pearlstein and Mike Adams, "Bush Faces Tough Choices on Steel Imports," *The Washington Post* (February 28, 2002), A4.
3. Stephen Norton, "Net Political Gain for Bush in Dropping Steel Tariffs?" *CQ Weekly* (December 6, 2003) 2998–3001.
4. David Baldwin, *Economic Statecraft* (Princeton, N.J.: Princeton University Press, 1985), pp. 44–47, 207–09.
5. Theodore Moran, "Empirical Studies of Strategic Trade Policy," *International Organization*, 50 (1996), 175–205.
6. Susan Strange, *Casino Capitalism* (New York: Oxford University Press, 1986).
7. Mark Strauss, "Sanctions Soup," *The Chronicle of Higher Education* (June 13, 2003), B11–12.
8. Meghan O'Sullivan, *Shrewd Sanctions* (Washington, D.C.: Brookings Institution Press, 2003), p. 12.
9. Stephen R. Weissman and Johnnie Carson, "Economic Sanctions against Rhodesia," in John Spanier and Joseph Nogee (eds.), *Congress, the Presidency, and American Foreign Policy* (New York: Pergamon Press, 1981), pp. 132–60.
10. Gary Hufbauer, Jeffrey Schott, and Kimberly Ann Elliott, *Economic Sanctions Reconsidered* (Washington, D.C.: Brookings, 1990).
11. Robert A. Pope, "Why Economic Sanctions Still Do Not Work," *International Security*, 41 (1997), 90–136.
12. David Cortright and George Lopez (eds.), *Smart Sanctions* (Lanham, MD: Rowman & Littlefield, 2002).
13. Arne Tostensen and Beate Bull, "Are Smart Sanctions Feasible?" *World Politics* 54 (2002), 373–403.
14. *Development and the National Interest* (Washington, D.C.: Agency for International Development, 1988).
15. Robin Broad and John Cavanagh, "Beyond the Myths of Rio," *World Policy Journal*, 10 (1993), 65–72.
16. Steve Radelet, "Will the Millennium Challenge Account Be Different?" *The Washington Quarterly*, 26 (2003), 171–87.

17. Gene Sperling and Tom Hart, "A Better Way to Fight Global Poverty," *Foreign Affairs*, 82 (2003), 9–14; and Lael Brainard, "Compassionate Conservatism Confronts Global Poverty," *The Washington Quarterly*, 26 (2003), 149–69.

18. Baldwin, *Economic Statecraft*, makes this point throughout this work. The statement is found on p. 115.

19. Ibid., p. 133.

20. Richard Olson, "Economic Coercion in World Politics: With a Focus on North–South Relations," *World Politics*, 31 (1979), 471–94.

— *16* —

MILITARY POWER

The post–cold war era brought with it a new and different geopolitical landscape. The United States stands as the sole remaining superpower, but national security threats are not absent. The search for military policies to meet these threats has progressed through several iterations. In 1994, a Congressionally established commission recommended retaining the essentials of the two-war planning standard for the military. In 1996, Congress passed legislation requiring that the Defense Department conduct a thorough review of defense needs every four years. The first Quadrennial Defense Review (QDR) was issued in 1997. It, too, recommended continuing with the two-war planning standard. A competing congressional authorized panel disagreed with the QDR's findings asserting that it had under appreciated the extent to which the security threats facing the United States had changed.

The second QDR was issued on September 30, 2001, shortly after the terrorist attacks on the World Trade Center and Pentagon. It brought forward a mixed reaction from experts. One the one hand, it recognized the need to "deter and defeat adversaries who rely on surprise, deception, and asymmetric warfare to achieve their objectives." Yet, it did not recommend any fundamental changes in the two-war planning standard only substituting a 4-2-1 for it, in which the United States would be able to deter in four places, counterattack in two, and go to the enemy's capital in one if need be. The George W. Bush administration added to its military policy by replacing deterrence with preemption. The president foreshadowed the change in a speech at West Point in June 2002, and it became official in September 2002 with the release of its National Security Strategy. It stated we "can no longer solely rely on a reactive posture . . . we cannot let our enemies strike first . . .

nations need not suffer an attack before they can lawfully take action to defend themselves against forces that present an imminent danger of attack."

In this chapter, we will review American military power as an instrument of foreign policy. First, we will examine U.S. nuclear capabilities and strategies. We will then turn our attention to that gray area where both nuclear and conventional military power may be employed. Here we will look at deterrence, preemption, and asymmetrical conflict. Finally, we will look more closely at strictly conventional uses of military power.

Development of U.S. and Soviet Nuclear Arsenals

At 5:30 A.M. on July 16, 1945, in the New Mexican desert, the first atomic bomb was detonated. On August 6, Hiroshima was destroyed by an atomic bomb. On August 9, Nagasaki was similarly destroyed by a plutonium bomb. These two attacks effectively depleted the U.S. (and, therefore, the global) inventory of atomic weapons. The U.S. nuclear arsenal grew slowly. Only two weapons were stockpiled at the end of 1945, nine in July 1946, thirteen in July 1947, and fifty in July 1948.[1] None of these weapons were preassembled; it took 39 men over two days to put them together. The year 1949 marked the end of the U.S. nuclear monopoly as the Soviet Union detonated its first atomic bomb. Estimates suggest that by 1949 the U.S. arsenal had only 100 to 200 weapons. Part of the U.S. response was to develop a more powerful weapon, the hydrogen bomb. The United States successfully tested an H-bomb in November 1952, and the Soviet Union duplicated the feat in August 1953. Until then nuclear bombs were produced by fission. They drew their explosive power by splitting the atom, and their destruction was measured in equivalents to thousands of tons of TNT (kilotons). The bomb dropped on Hiroshima was a thirteen-kiloton weapon, and the one dropped on Nagasaki was a twenty-two-kiloton bomb. With the advent of the hydrogen bomb, a new era began. These weapons draw their power by fusing atoms together, and their destructiveness is measured in equivalents to millions of tons of TNT (megatons, or mt.). While there is an inherent upper limit to how much power can be generated by fission, no upper limit exists with fusion. It is estimated that by 1957 the United States probably had two thousand nuclear bombs and the Soviet Union possessed a few hundred.[2] Reinforcing this U.S. numerical advantage in bombs was a marked superiority in delivery systems. The Soviet bomber fleet was small and could only reach the United States on a one-way mission. The United States did not face a similar handicap because it was able to use bases in Western Europe to deliver attacks on the Soviet Union.

The year 1957 was pivotal in the development of the U.S. and Soviet nuclear arsenals. In August the Soviet Union successfully tested an intercontinental ballistic missile (ICBM), and in October it launched Sputnik into orbit. With these two actions the Soviet Union demonstrated the theoretical capability to deliver a nuclear attack on U.S. cities and its overseas military bases. Moreover, the United States was not positioned to counter these moves. Together, these concerns gave rise to the concept of a "missile gap" and the fear that the Soviet Union might attempt to exploit its advantage by boldly challenging U.S. security interests around the world. The United States took a number of measures to counter this perceived Soviet advantage. It stepped up production of its own ballistic missile force. It also constructed new early-warning radar systems and placed the Strategic Air Command (SAC) on a heightened alert status so that almost half of its planes could take off on fifteen minutes' notice.

As it turns out, no missile gap existed. While the Soviet Union gave the appearance of moving ahead with the full-scale deployment of its ICBMs, it actually deployed only about fifty of them, choosing instead to focus on research and development of a second-generation ICBM. This decision only became known to U.S. policy makers in 1961. The combined result of the Soviet decision to forgo the large-scale production of ICBMs and the U.S. decision to accelerate its ICBM program produced a situation of overwhelming U.S. nuclear superiority. At the time of the Cuban missile crisis in October 1962 the United States had an ICBM advantage of 226–75 and 144 Polaris missiles to zero submarine-launched ballistic missiles (SLBMs) for the Soviet Union. It also had a lead of 1,350 to 190 in the area of long-range bombers.

The U.S. buildup continued through the mid-1960s before leveling off in 1967. By the mid-1960s the long-predicted Soviet buildup got under way, and for several years the pace of this buildup exceeded the worst-case scenarios painted by the U.S. intelligence community. Between 1966 and 1970 the Soviet Union increased the number of its ICBMs from 292 to 1,300 with 300 more under construction. By the end of the decade, rough parity had arrived. Because of the influence of the unratified but observed SALT II Treaty, U.S. and Soviet nuclear inventories remained stable in the 1980s. In 1985 the Soviet Union possessed 1,398 ICBMs and 979 SLBMs in 77 submarines with a total of 9,207 warheads. The United States countered with 1,018 ICBMs and 616 SLBMs on thirty-seven submarines and 7,654 warheads. When long-range bombers and cruise missiles were added to these figures, the United States emerged with a small lead over the Soviet Union in the total numbers of strategic warheads: 10,174 to 9,987. The term *parity* is used because the two arsenals still did not mirror one another. Instead, they were marked by compensatory advantages. The Soviet Union's lead in ICBM launchers (1,200 to 1,054) was offset by the U.S. advantage in SLBMs and long-range bombers (380 to 1,196). Approximately 5,800 strategic nuclear warheads now existed: 4,000 for the United States and 1,800 for the Soviet Union.

In the 1970s the United States began to replace many of its single-warheaded ICBM and SLBM missiles with multiple independently targeted reentry vehicles (MIRVs). The United States pursued MIRV technology for three reasons. First, the Soviet Union was about to equal the United States in the total numbers of launchers it possessed. Second, the Soviet Union was working on an antiballistic missile system that could threaten the United States' ability to retaliate against Soviet targets. Third, it was a relatively inexpensive way to rapidly increase U.S. nuclear strength. During the 1970s the United States MIRVed 550 Minuteman III ICBMs, giving them three warheads instead of one, and the Poseidon SLBM with approximately ten warheads replaced the unMIRVed Polaris. The upshot of the United States' MIRV program was to increase the number of strategic nuclear warheads possessed by the United States from 4,000 in 1970 to 8,500 in 1977. The Soviet Union followed the U.S. lead, and by 1977 it was MIRVing its land-based launchers at a faster rate than was the United States. By 1975 it had a 1,618 to 1,054 advantage over the United States in ICBMs.

Much of the Soviet buildup in the 1970s was predictable, based on the need to modernize its nuclear forces. What became disturbing about the buildup was that once again it exceeded Western expectations. This larger-than-expected growth plus the aging of the U.S. nuclear inventory gave rise to pressures within the United States to embark upon a nuclear revitalization campaign of its own.

What Does It All Mean?

What do all of these numbers mean? The bombings of Hiroshima and Nagasaki killed an estimated 170,000 people, yet these figures do not really offer us very much insight into the amount of devastation and destruction that would follow from a nuclear war today. Today's nuclear weapons are typically three to fifty times as powerful as those dropped in 1945. We approach the question of consequences two ways. First, we outline the destructive processes that a nuclear explosion sets in motion. Second, we make use of a standard scenario for measuring the destruction produced by a nuclear weapon: the dropping of a single one-megaton bomb, a bomb eighty times more powerful than that dropped on Hiroshima. It needs to be stressed that any effort to illustrate the consequences of a nuclear attack rests on a series of arbitrary assumptions about such factors as the height of the explosion, weather conditions, wind velocity, and the nature of the target. Change the assumptions and the consequences change.

A nuclear explosion has three major components and one lesser consequence.[3] The first component is thermal radiation. Fifty percent of the energy released by a nuclear weapon is emitted as thermal radiation (heat) within ten milliseconds of the explosion. This produces flash burns caused by radiation striking directly on the skin and secondary burns caused by ignited clothing or other fires. A one-megaton blast would produce second- and third-degree burns over an area of seven to eight miles on a clear day and ignite clothing for five miles. It could cause retinal burns up to thirteen miles away on a cloudy day or fifty-three miles on a clear day. Third-degree burns over twenty-five percent of the body and second-degree burns over 30 percent of the body are generally considered to be fatal. Under certain conditions (such as those that took place at Hiroshima, Tokyo, and Dresden), individual fires might merge into large firestorms. If this happened, people in fallout shelters would be killed by heat, suffocation, or carbon monoxide poisoning.

The second major component of a nuclear explosion is a shock wave that travels at supersonic speed outward from the blast site. The Department of Defense calculates that ten seconds after a one-megaton bomb is exploded, the shock wave is three miles away. At fifty seconds, it is about twelve miles ahead and is moving at a speed slightly faster than the speed of sound at sea level. It is the overpressure produced by the blast effect that the military counts on most heavily to achieve its goals. The hardness of a target (its ability to withstand overpressure) determines the altitude at which the bomb(s) must be detonated. Destroying a hard target such as a Minuteman silo requires a near-to-the-surface blast while destroying a soft target such as an unprotected city can best be accomplished when the bomb is detonated higher in the atmosphere. A single 1 megaton weapon detonated at 6,000 feet would destroy every structure within a 2.7-mile radius. Almost no one within this circle would survive who was not in a blast shelter. From 2.7 to 4 miles from the blast site, individual residences would be destroyed and about one-half of the population killed, largely as a result of falling buildings and flying debris. Almost all who survived would be injured. From four to seven miles from the blast site, there would be widespread damage to buildings and many personal injuries. The greatest damage here would be from fires that could be expected to spread for at least twenty-four hours and consume one-half of all buildings. Finally, seven to ten miles from the blast site, there would be only light damage to commercial structures and moderate fatalities largely due to the secondary effects of the explosion. The Office of Technology Assessment (OTA) estimates that a one-megaton bomb detonated at night at a height of 6,000 feet over Detroit would produce 470,000 immediate deaths and 630,000 injuries. Flash burns and fires would result in anywhere between 1,000 and 190,000 additional fatalities depending on the physical situation at the time of the blast. A similar attack on St. Petersburg would produce some 900,000 deaths and over 1 million injuries. The OTA also made estimates of the consequences of larger nuclear exchanges between the United States and Soviet Union. These included attacks on oil refineries that were limited to 10 missiles, a counterforce attack limited to ICBM silos, and an attack on a range of military and economic targets that would involve a large fraction of each side's existing nuclear arsenal. Its findings are summarized in Table 16.1.

The third major component of a nuclear explosion is nuclear radiation. Of concern here is the damaging effect that ionization causes on cells exposed to large dosages of radiation. Severe illness sets in at about 200 rems, and a dose of 300 rems could be expected to kill about 10 percent of its victims. Exposures in the range of 600 rems within a short period of time (six to seven days) are fatal to 90 percent of those exposed. A distinction is made between prompt radiation and residual radiation, with prompt radiation being that given off within the first minute. Smaller dosages of radiation also have significant consequences for human health when measured over time. While a dose of 50 rems generally has no short-term effects, over the long run 0.4 to 2.5 percent of those persons exposed to it will die of cancer, and serious genetic effects can also be expected.

The amount of residual radiation emitted depends on the nature of the explosion. The closer the explosion is to the surface of the earth, the greater is the amount of residual radiation produced due to the large amount of debris sucked up into the atmosphere by the explosion, which returns to earth as fallout. A 1 megaton surface explosion can excavate a crater hundreds of meters in diameter and eject between 100,000 and

TABLE 16.1 OTA Nuclear War Scenarios and Their Consequences

Case	Description	Main Causes of Civilian Damage	Immediate Deaths	Middle-Term Effects	Long-Term Effects
1	Attack on single city (e.g., Detroit or Leningrad); 1 weapon or 10 small weapons.	Blast, fire, and loss of infrastructure; fallout is elsewhere.	200,000–2,000,000	Many deaths from injuries; center of city difficult to rebuild.	Relatively minor.
2	Attack on oil refineries, limited to 10 missiles.	Blast, fire, secondary fires, fallout. Extensive economic problems from loss of refined petroleum.	1,000,000–5,000,000	Many deaths from injuries: great economic hardship for some years; particular problems for Soviet agriculture and for U.S. socioeconomic organization.	Cancer deaths in millions only if attack involves surface bursts.
3	Counterforce attack; includes attack only on ICBM silos as a variant.	Some blast damage if bomber and missile submarine bases attacked.	1,000,000–20,000,000	Economic impact of deaths; possible large psychological impact.	Cancer deaths and genetic effects in millions; further millions of effects outside attacked countries.
4	Attack on range of military and economic targets using large fraction of existing arsenal.	Blast and fallout; subsequent economic disruption; possible lack of resources to support surviving population or economic recovery. Possible breakdown of social order. Possible incapacitating psychological trauma.	20,000,000–160,000,000	Enormous economic destruction and disruption. If immediate deaths are in low range, more tens of millions may die subsequently because economy is unable to support them. Major question about whether economic viability can be restored—key variables may be those of political and economic organization. Unpredictable psychological effects.	Cancer deaths and genetic damage in the millions; relatively insignificant in attacked areas, but quite significant elsewhere in the world. Possibility of ecological damage.

Source: Office of Technology Assessment, *The Effects of Nuclear War* (Montclair, NJ: Allanheld, Osmun, 1980), p. 10.

600,000 tons of soil into the atmosphere. A 1 megaton surface blast when there was a constant 15-mph wind and no precipitation would expose 1,000 square miles to a total dose of 900 rems. Approximately 4,000 square miles would receive over 100 rems. A fifteen-megaton explosion at Bikini Atoll in 1954 sent fallout with a substantial amount of contamination over an area in excess of 7,000 square miles.

A fourth component of a nuclear explosion is an electromagnetic pulse (EMP). It poses no direct threat to humans, but it is capable of destroying the communication systems that would be so important should a nuclear war ever begin. Virtually everything that relies on solid state electronics and that is not protected by an electromagnetic shield would be rendered useless. This would include automobile ignition systems, the control systems on airplanes, and the electric guidance systems of missiles. An EMP is a pulse of energy producing an electronic field up to 50,000 volts per meter. It is estimated that a 1 megaton bomb exploded 500 kilometers over Nebraska would bathe the entire continental United States in EMP sufficient to shut down the entire electrical grid. There is only one recorded case of an EMP resulting from a high-altitude explosion: an early 1960s test of a 1.4-megaton bomb exploded over Johnson Island set off burglar alarms and streetlights on Oahu, some 800 miles away.

During the cold war, the consequences of nuclear war were discussed as if they would be restricted to the main participants or at most felt on a regional basis (Europe or North America). Today, a new concern has been added: the global climatic impact of a nuclear war. The great fear is that even a limited nuclear war could trigger climatic changes due to the sunlight-blocking action of the dust particles raised by a nuclear explosion and the smoke from the urban fires it would cause. The resulting drop in temperatures could produce a "nuclear winter," threatening all survivors with cold, starvation, and a shortage of fresh water.[4] A study by the National Academy of Sciences concluded that a nuclear exchange involving only half the world's inventory of nuclear weapons would produce a temperature drop of 18 to 55 degrees Fahrenheit throughout most of North America and Eurasia, depending on whether the attack occurred in April or July. It also concluded that more than 99 percent of the sun's light would be blocked out for a period of days or weeks. If war occurred just prior to or during the growing season, virtually all land plants in the Northern Hemisphere would be killed or damaged. Continued cold weather and the loss of sunlight would seriously impair productivity and growth in the next planting season. Tropical and Southern Hemisphere food production could also be seriously reduced.

A Historical Survey of U.S. Nuclear Strategy

Once only a topic of debate among experts, the elements and assumptions of U.S. nuclear strategy have become widely debated in public circles. In the process the "nuclear priesthood" has been defrocked, and people are no longer as willing to defer to the nuclear expertise of policy makers or the professional military.[5] We make use of two concepts in organizing our discussion: declaratory policy and action policy.[6] Involved here is a distinction between what policy makers say their strategy is and what is actually called for in their plans for using nuclear weapons. The former is known as declaratory policy, and the latter is known as action policy. Analysis has shown that there have been persistent gaps between the two and that changes in declaratory policy do not necessarily lead to changes in action policy.

It is not much of an exaggeration to suggest that for the first eight years of the nuclear age there existed no such thing as nuclear strategy per se at either the declaratory or action level. The uniqueness of nuclear weapons was not yet appreciated. They were simply treated as the largest explosive device yet created, and it was expected that the next war would be fought just along the lines of World War II. Long-range bombers would deliver these weapons against Soviet cities, industries, and military support facilities. When the small stockpile of atomic bombs was exhausted, plans called for using conventional bombs and a general mobilization of U.S. forces.[7] Throughout the 1945 to 1953 period, a number of specific war plans were drawn up. The first war plan to identify atomic bomb target lists was BROILER in the fall of 1947. It called for 34 bombs to be dropped on 24 cities. TROJAN, approved in December 1948, anticipated using 133 atomic bombs on 70 Soviet cities over a 30-day period.

There was a certain degree of unreality to these war plans. We have already noted the limited nature of the U.S. stockpile. To this can be added limited delivery systems. In 1948 the SAC had only 30 modified B-29 bombers. A more fundamental critique of U.S. policy was presented by Bernard Brodie.[8] He questioned whether nuclear weapons could be used in the same way as other weapons or if deterrence rather than war fighting was not their sole credible use. Moreover, if deterrence was to be the principal purpose to which nuclear weapons were put, then some thought was necessary on how to accomplish it. Deterrence could not simply be assumed to exist.

The first formal statement of nuclear strategy was put forward by the Eisenhower administration as part of its new-look defense posture. The nuclear component of this strategy was massive retaliation. Massive retaliation was intended to deter a wide spectrum of Soviet attacks, guaranteeing not only the security of the United States but also that of its European and third world allies. It would accomplish this by threatening the Soviet Union with massive destruction in retaliation for aggressive behavior. No details were given as to what type of Soviet aggression would bring about massive retaliation or what would be attacked. All that was promised was "retaliation instantly, by means and places of our own choosing." The lack of specificity was intentional. The Eisenhower administration felt that the Truman administration's pledge of help for any country threatened by communism had given the initiative to the Soviet Union. Massive retaliation was designed to give it back to the United States.

Two recurrent lines of criticism were leveled against massive retaliation. The first concerned its credibility. Critics asserted that deterrence required more than just the capability to inflict damage. The threat also had to be credible. To threaten the Soviet Union with massive destruction for an attack on the United States was one thing, but to make the same threat for attacks on third world states was quite another. Soviet leaders would find the former credible but not the latter, and therefore, they would not be deterred. The United States would then be left with the distasteful choice of having to implement its threat or do nothing. To prevent being placed in this position, critics argued that the United States must abandon massive retaliation for a policy containing more strategic options. The second line of criticism was that massive retaliation was ill-suited to the changing nuclear relationship between the United States and Soviet Union. Massive retaliation assumed the existence of an invulnerable retaliatory force, and this was no longer the case because of the growth in the Soviet nuclear arsenal and its development of ICBM technology. The growing vulnerability of nuclear forces to attack transformed deterrence from a certainty into one based on a "delicate balance of terror."[9]

Massive retaliation was U.S. declaratory policy. Action policy was reflected in U.S. war plans. Evidence suggests that U.S. war plans were not being tailored to meet the two primary contingencies spoken of by policy makers: retaliation and preemption (striking first in self-defense). Instead, U.S. war plans had become capability plans. They were constructed in such a way as to employ all of the nuclear weapons in the U.S. inventory and provide a rationale for acquiring additional weapons.[10] The gap between what the war plans would produce and what policy makers wanted was often quite glaring. For example, in 1955 a SAC officer stated that its plan would leave the Soviet Union "a smoking, radiating, ruin at the end of two hours."[11]

Each military command developed plans for using the nuclear weapons under its control. By the end of the 1950s SAC had examined over 20,000 potential Soviet bloc targets. War games carried out by the Eisenhower administration in the late 1950s indicated that over 300 duplicate targets existed. A clearly stated and prioritized target list and war plan seemed to offer the best hope for escaping from this situation of constantly escalating target lists and larger and larger war plans. In 1960, Eisenhower took the first steps to create order out of this chaos by approving the establishment of a National Strategy Target List (NSTL) and a Single Integrated Operational Plan (SIOP) for using nuclear weapons.

The results staggered Eisenhower. Planners selected 2,600 separate installations for attack out of an overall list of 4,100 targets.[12] This translated into approximately 1,050 designated ground zeros (DGZs), 151 of which were urban-industrial targets. Plans called for launching all 3,500 nuclear warheads if sufficient warning time existed. If not, an alert force of 800 bombers and missiles would attack approximately 650 DGZs with over 1,400 weapons and a total of 2,100 megaton. According to one calculation, the SIOP assigned 300 to 500 kilowatt of weapons to accomplish the level of destruction done by a single bomb on Hiroshima. Officially known as SIOP-62, this is the war plan inherited by the Kennedy administration.

The Kennedy administration shared its predecessors' conviction that deterrence was the proper role for nuclear weapons. It differed in how to structure deterrence, and it gave attention to a problem never fully addressed in the 1950s: how to fight a nuclear war. Kennedy replaced massive retaliation with the concept of flexible response under which the United States would have a range of options to choose from in deterring and responding to Soviet aggression, running the gamut from unconventional forces (Green Berets) to conventional forces to nuclear weapons. Controlled response was the initial statement of how nuclear weapons would be employed in this strategy. It emphasized the measured and restrained use of nuclear weapons to accomplish political objectives. To that end the Kennedy administration officially incorporated three new features into U.S. nuclear thinking.

First, prominence was given to the use of tactical nuclear weapons in the hope that because of their less destructive nature they might be more manageable. Second, a new targeting policy was adopted that emphasized attacks on military forces and avoidance of population centers. In McNamara's own words, the counterforce strategy sought to use nuclear weapons "in much the same way that more conventional military operations have been regarded in the past." Third, the Kennedy administration looked into two measures that might limit the damage done to the United States in case of a nuclear war: civil defense and damage limitation.[13] Political and technical problems plagued both of these initiatives, and they were abandoned.

The value of these changes in nuclear strategy was called into question by the Cuban missile crisis. The way in which the crisis was played out suggested that "deterrence, in practice was less graduated and more absolute than had been imagined."[14] Attention now shifted back to formulating a nuclear posture built less on war fighting and more on the ability to inflict widespread devastation on the enemy. To be credible, McNamara estimated that U.S. forces must have the assured capability to destroy 25 to 30 percent of the Soviet population and 66 percent of its industrial capacity. Later he lowered these levels to 20 to 25 percent of the Soviet population and 50 percent of its industry. Assured destruction, as this policy came to be known, was not a return to massive retaliation. Massive retaliation rested on U.S. nuclear supremacy and was ambiguous as to where and when the United States would strike. Assured destruction recognized the difficulty—if not impossibility—of defending the United States against Soviet missiles and guaranteed retaliation for a Soviet attack on the United States.

Movement from massive retaliation to controlled response and then to assured destruction implied a parallel set of changes in U.S. targeting policy. Changes in the SIOP did occur, but not necessarily on the scale implied by the change in declaratory policy.[15] One observer noted that "the basic patterns of nuclear strategy it [the SIOP] embodied proved resistant to change." The SIOP remained a capabilities plan rather than an objectives plan. In spite of the change in declaratory policy, attacks on Soviet population centers remained a target of last resort.[16]

Major changes in U.S. strategic thought began to occur in the Nixon administration. And while the names given to the ideas developed here have changed and the concepts have been refined, they continued to guide U.S. thinking in the 1980s. The first change came in U.S. declaratory policy. In 1970 the Nixon administration introduced the principle of "sufficiency." Sufficiency required strategic equality between the United States and the Soviet Union rather than simply the possession of a minimum level of retaliatory threat.[17] This was seen as providing crisis stability so that neither side had an incentive to go first with its nuclear weapons in a crisis.

The Nixon administration also undertook a review of U.S. action policy. The impetus for change was strategic parity. The existence of a large Soviet nuclear force made it unwise to carry out a retaliatory attack on Soviet population centers because of the Soviet ability to retaliate against U.S. cities. Work on changing the SIOP began in 1974. The NSDM-242 authorized the drafting of a Nuclear Weapons Employment Policy (NUWEP) to establish planning assumptions, attack options, targeting objectives, and damage levels. The NUWEP emphasized the destruction of Soviet economic recovery assets as the primary objective of U.S. nuclear forces. It stipulated that under all circumstances the United States must be able to destroy 70 percent of the Soviet industrial capacity needed for postwar economic recovery. Together with NSDM-242, NUWEP laid out the foundations for SIOP-5, which officially took effect in 1976.

Neither Carter, Reagan, nor George H. W. Bush formally broke away from the concepts laid out in the Nixon years. At most, there were refinements in thinking, changes in priorities, and alterations in rhetoric. Carter's countervailing strategy called for possessing "strategic options such that at a variety of levels of exchange, aggression would either be defeated or would result in unacceptable costs that exceed gains." Along with recasting U.S. declaratory strategy, the Carter administration also undertook a restructuring of the SIOP. The document setting this reassessment in motion was Presidential Directive (PD) 59, which authorized production of a new NUWEP.

Three changes lay at the heart of the Carter administration's NUWEP.[18] First, the emphasis was shifted away from economic recovery targets to military and political targets, including the targeting of Soviet leadership. Second, the SIOP incorporated a capacity to engage in a protracted nuclear conflict, one lasting months instead of days. Third the target list grew in length. It went from 25,000 potential targets to 40,000. The list reportedly included over 20,000 military targets, 2,000 leadership and control targets and some 15,000 industrial targets.

The major notable and controversial addition by the Reagan administration to Carter's policy was the requirement that the United States be able to "prevail" and "force the Soviet Union to seek the earliest termination of hostilities on terms favorable to the U.S."

Post–Cold War Nuclear Strategy

THE U.S. STRATEGIC NUCLEAR ARSENAL

In 1998, the United States had more than 2,300 warheads on alert at any given time. Taken together they could deliver the equivalent of 44,000 Hiroshimas or about 550 megatons of TNT. They are aimed at some 3,000 targets, down from the 12,500 targets of the cold war SIOPs.

In Spring 2004, the U.S. nuclear inventory stood at some 7,000 operational nuclear warheads. Of these 5,886 were defined as strategic. The ICBM force was reduced by 17 missiles in 2003 to 592, 500 of them are Minuteman II missiles. The other 29 are MX/Peacekeepers, 23 of them will be retired in 2004–2005. There were 360 SLBMs on 15 nuclear-powered ballistic missile submarines in service in 2004. This represents about 46% of the U.S. inventory. U.S. strategic bombers are no longer maintained on day-to-day alert status. There are 72 strategic bombers whose primary mission is to deliver weapons against enemy targets.

Accompanying this reduction in the size of the U.S. strategic arsenal have been several attempts to redefine American nuclear strategy. The first presidential statement of U.S. post–cold war policy came with Clinton's 1997 Presidential Decision Directive 60 (PDD-60). This directive formally replaced PDD-13 issued by President Reagan in 1981. According to PDD-60, the U.S. military should no longer prepare to win a protracted nuclear war as was required by PDD-13. The military aim of the nuclear arsenal was defined as one of deterring the use of nuclear weapons against the United States and its allies. PDD-60 continues to call for the existence of a wide range of nuclear strike options against Russian nuclear forces and its civilian and military leadership. It also contains a requirement for planning for nuclear strikes against states that have "prospective access" to nuclear weapons or that may become hostile to the United States.

The George W. Bush administration presented its Nuclear Posture Review (NPR) to Congress in January 2002. While the report is classified, portions quickly leaked to the press. Other parts were made publicly available by the Pentagon.[19] The 2002 NPR reaffirms that nuclear weapons play a fundamental role in U.S. force projection capabilities. They are capable of providing military options that "deter a wide range of threats including WMD (weapons of mass destruction) and large-scale conventional forces. It calls for "greater flexibility" in nuclear forces and planning if credibility is to be maintained against a new generation of adversaries. The NPR specifically identifies seven states against which nuclear weapons might be used. Iran, North Korea, Iraq, Libya, and Syria were listed as rogue states that could be involved in "immediate, potential, or unexpected contingencies." The removal of Saddam Hussein from power in Iraq and Libya's renunciation of weapons of mass destruction effectively reduce this list to three states. China is identified as a potential target due to its combination of still developing strategic objectives and its ongoing modernization of its nuclear and non nuclear forces." Russia is acknowledged no longer to be an enemy but the NPR concludes a nuclear conflict remains "plausible" but "not expected." The NPR also discusses three specific nuclear strike scenarios: 1) an attack on Israel by neighboring states, 2) a North Korean attack on South Korea, and 3) a conflict with China over Taiwan.

As part of its emphasis on greater flexibility the NPR called for the development of new types of nuclear warheads. Two requirements identified for these warheads were reduced levels of collateral damage and the ability to penetrate the earth into hard and buried targets such as command and control facilities and weapons storage bunkers. Such nuclear weapons are referred to as micronukes, mininukes, and tidynukes depending upon the payload they deliver.

U.S. NUCLEAR STRATEGY

Revisions in U.S. nuclear strategy have largely been made at the margins and reflect the continued influence of cold war nuclear deterrence thinking. George W. Bush's NPR is no exception. According to Clinton administration officials, it represented only a modest shift in emphasis with that administration's nuclear thinking. Clinton's NPR envisioned two broad roles for American nuclear weapons and was widely criticized for not taking into account the shifting nature of world politics. The first role was to counter Russian strategic forces. The second was as a retaliatory strike against hostile and irresponsible states that would use nuclear weapons against the United States.

Strategic doctrines and practices developed and refined in the cold war strike many commentators as in desperate need of updating. For some, the strategic problem is one of complacency brought on by its apparent successes. Lawrence Freedman, for example, argues that the debate over nuclear deterrence has become "lazy" and that as a result the term is now "self-contradictory and confused."[20] For Paul Bracken, the strategic problem is the failure to recognize that with the emergence of Asia as the new center of military power a "second nuclear age" has begun that invalidates fundamental Western strategic assumptions.[21]

Careful thinking about nuclear weapons is especially important in two of the most controversial areas of contemporary U.S. military strategy: the rejection of deterrence and the embrace of preemption. Neither deterrence nor preemption is exclusively a nuclear or conventional military option. They serve as an uneasy bridge between the two along with the notion of asymmetrical conflict.

Bridging the Nuclear-Conventional Divide

DETERRENCE

A deterrence policy seeks to prevent something unwanted from happening. At its most basic level the United States is concerned with deterring attacks both on its own homeland and its allies. The former is known as direct deterrence and the later is extended deterrence. Up until the terrorist attacks of 9/11, it was taken for granted that direct deterrence was more easily achieved than was extended deterrence. Now both are suspect. Deterrence succeeds by threatening a would-be aggressor with an unacceptable level of damage should it engage in the unwanted behavior. It requires possessing a sufficient military power to inflict such damage, the resolve to act in the threatened manner, and the ability to communicate this policy to the enemy. We can begin to understand the problems faced in constructing a successful deterrence strategy if we look at how deterrence has failed in the past. Alexander George and Richard Smoke identify three patterns of failure.[22]

In one, deterrence fails through a *fait accompli*. Hostile policy makers detect no U.S. commitment and feel that they can control their risks. The June 1950 North Korean attack on South Korea is an example of deterrence failing through a *fait accompli*. The thirty-eighth parallel divided North and

South Korea as a result of a World War II decision to have Soviet forces accept the surrender of Japanese troops north of that point. George and Smoke argue that the *fait accompli* strategy was rational because no clear U.S. commitment existed and the risks appeared to be controllable. Public statements by leading U.S. diplomats (Secretary of State Dean Acheson) and military figures (the JCS) had placed South Korea outside of the U.S. "defense perimeter" and referred to it as a "liability" in the event of war in the Far East. Reinserting U.S. forces into Korea was not expected to be an easy task, so the most likely response to an attack would be diplomatic protest or a minimal military action.

Deterrence can also fail as a result of a limited probe where the challenging action is easily reversed or expanded depending on the nature of the U.S. response. In these cases the U.S. commitment is unclear, and the risks still seem to be controllable. The Berlin Wall crisis of 1961 illustrates how deterrence can fail through a limited probe. A succession of Berlin crises in 1948, 1958, and earlier in 1961 had demonstrated the existence of a U.S. commitment to Berlin. Yet they had also demonstrated a U.S. desire to avoid a direct military confrontation and had brought home the military reality that East Berlin was over 100 miles into communist territory, making Western military operations difficult but not impossible. From the perspective of the East German leadership, the situation in Berlin had become intolerable. An average of over 1,000 people were fleeing to West Berlin each day. Included among them were many professionals whose skills would be needed to build up the East German economy. The Soviet Union and East Germany moved at midnight on May 12 to close the border by constructing a barbed wire wall on East Berlin territory. Only when the minimal nature of the U.S. response was clear (the Western powers did not make a protest for four days) did they move to construct a more substantial and permanent wall with only a few highly guarded openings.

Finally, deterrence can fail as a result of controllable pressure where the U.S. commitment is seen as unequivocal but "soft" and where the risks are considered to be controllable. George and Smoke do not identify any situation where controlled pressure was found to operate alone. Rather, it tends to be the second phase of a deterrence failure, occurring after a *fait accompli* or limited probe has failed and when the challenging state has decided to continue to press ahead. They suggest that the second phase of the Cuban missile crisis fits this pattern. In September Kennedy made a series of public statements in which he underlined the U.S. opposition to offensive missiles in Cuba. At this point, George and Smoke argue, the U.S. commitment had to be seen as unequivocal. But rather than abandon its plans or engage in a more limited probe, the Soviet Union sought to get around the U.S. commitment or negate it by secretly placing missiles in Cuba. Khrushchev may have judged the risks to be controllable because of the secrecy of the operation and his apparent belief that Kennedy could be intimidated.

We can gain further insight into problems confronting deterrence theory if we look at two different strategies used in the past to try and prevent failure. The first is to set up a "trip wires." These were figuratively speaking lines in the sand that, if crossed, would provoke an immediate American military response. In concrete terms, the trip wires took the form of American troops stationed in Germany and South Korea who would be in the way of any enemy attack. During the cold war, the presence of American troops abroad was seen as a sign of strength and resolve. Today, the situation is different. Along with the large number of civilian contractors who now serve with them they have become targets of opportunity for terrorists and insurgents.

A second strategy was to leave the door open to a nuclear response should deterrence fail. By threatening to take a crisis to the brink of nuclear war, it was assumed that the enemy would abandon its unwanted line of action. Robert Powell points out that contrary to what appears to be the case, it is not the resolve of the "winning state" that matters in nuclear deterrence but the resolve of the state that backs down first. Deterrence works like an auction.[23] How much the winning bidder ultimately has to pay is determined by how high the second-highest bidder is willing to go. The more resolute the second-highest bidder the more dangerous the crisis becomes and the more expensive deterrence (and deterrence failure) becomes. His theoretical analysis suggests that when the balance of resolve favors the small nuclear state, it will be able to deter the United States from trying to oust the regime in power.

Problems such as these led the George W. Bush administration to move away from deterrence to preemption. Deterrence is not without its defenders. Morton Halperin asks if deterrence worked against Joseph Stalin who we knew was determined to get nuclear weapons why did we think it could not work against Saddam Hussein?[24] Ray Takeyh observes that Iran's quest for nuclear weapons is not the product of ideological zealotry but the product of national interest calculations about how to best deter the United States.[25] As such, its future nuclear decisions can be influenced by the use of carrots and sticks, one of which could be a strong deterrent posture on the part of the United States. Moreover, as we shall see below, preemption is also fraught with problems.

PREEMPTION

Preemption is striking first in self-defense when the threat is imminent. When the threat is not imminent but still held to be real, striking first in self-defense is referred to as a preventive strike. Preemption is not a new strategy. Historical examples go back at least to the Punic War fought in 264–147 B.C. It is also a strategy that the United States has employed in the past. Most recently, Ronald Reagan justified the invasion of Grenada in 1983 as a preemptive move. Lyndon Johnson acted in a similar manner sending troops to the Dominican Republic in 1965. In the more distant past, one could classify Woodrow Wilson's decision to send troops to Mexico in 1914 as consistent with the logic of preemption.

If the logic of preemption is accepted, a series of questions must be addressed.[26] First, should nuclear weapons be used? Dating back to the Carter administration, it has been U.S. policy not to be the first state to use nuclear weapons in a conflict. George H. W. Bush went so far as to refer to them as weapons of last resort. Some assert that only the specter of a nuclear attack on the homelands of America's enemies today can deter them from pursuing aggressive foreign policies. Those opposed to a first-use strategy point to the symbolic importance of making sure that the nuclear threshold is not crossed. Fear that preemption is leading in this direction led the *Bulletin of the Atomic Scientists* to move its doomsday clock forward to seven minutes before midnight in February 2002.[27] This was the third time the clock was moved forward since the end of the cold war, and it was back to the same setting the doomsday clock debuted at fifty-five years earlier. Second, should the United States act unilaterally in making the determination that a preemptive strike is necessary. Military effectiveness points to unilateral action while political legitimacy suggests a multilateral and collaborative decision-making process. Third, is preemption feasible? It demands high-quality and timely intelligence, as well as precise weapons. Finally, can the United States embrace a policy of unilateral preemption but deny it to others? Two situations are particularly troubling in this regard. One involves a conflict such as between India and Pakistan in which the United States is a third party to the dispute concerned with regional stability and the other is when it is directly involved with an adversary who, fearing an American preemptive strike, considers launching one itself.

ASYMMETRIC CONFLICTS

One of the hallmarks of the U.S.–Soviet military competition during the cold war was symmetry. Only in the early cold war years when the U.S. possessed the capacity to strike the Soviet Union with weapons and the Soviet Union could not retaliate was there a significant imbalance of forces. Both sides possessed devastating nuclear arsenals, both stationed large conventional forces in Europe, both participated in and supported guerrilla wars for control of third world states, and both engaged in covert action.

Today this has changed. It is asymmetry that presents the greatest military challenges to the United States. Where the United States relies upon precision air strikes guided by the latest technology and "shock and awe" bombing strikes, the enemy counters with suicide bombers, kidnappings and assassination, and hit-and-run attacks. More ominously, there is also fear that America's enemies will engage in acts of aggression that far exceed the level of violence employed by the United States. In particular, the concern is that terrorist groups or rogue states will employ weapons of mass destruction. Included in this category are nuclear, chemical, and biological weapons. According to one account, at least twenty-four states not counting the United States possess at least one of these types of weapons. The number of terrorist groups possessing them or seeking to acquire them is unknown. These countries are listed in Table 16.2.

What type of military force is best to use in meeting asymmetrical challenges is unclear. Traditional Western just war principles stress the proportional and discriminating use of military power. It is unclear what this means in situations where the enemy may be a stateless actor or is employing all of its resources against the United States and not abiding by these same principles.

TABLE 16.2   **Countries that Have Biochemical Weapons**

Country	Past/Present Chemical Weapons Program	Past/Present Biological Weapons Program
Canada	Yes	Yes
China	Probable	Probable
Egypt	Probable	Probable
Ethiopia	Probable	
France	Yes	Yes
Germany	Yes	Yes
India	Yes	
Iran	Yes	Probable
Iraq (pre war)	Yes	Yes
Israel	Probable	
Italy	Yes	
Japan	Yes	Yes
Libya	Yes	
Myanmar (Burma)	Probable	
North Korea	Probable	
Pakistan	Probable	
Russia	Probable	Yes
South Africa	Yes	Yes
South Korea	Yes	
Syria	Probable	
Taiwan	Probable	
United Kingdom	Yes	Yes
United States	Yes	Yes
Yugoslavia	Yes	

Source: Chemical and Biological Weapons: Possession and Programs, Past and Present," Center for Nonproliferation Studies, Monterey Institute of International Studies, www.cns.miis.edu

Strategies for the Use of Conventional Military Force

Military power can be used in a variety of ways. Below we look at three different types of situations in which conventional military power plays a central role. They are war fighting, terrorism/counterinsurgency settings, and humanitarian/peacemaking operations. Before doing so, we will introduce a number of important framing considerations that govern the use of force in any of them. The first involves the importance of alliances and coalitions. The difference between them is coalitions are informal agreements for immediate common action while alliances are more formal agreements and have a longer sense of common purpose. Controversy surrounds both of these options for multilateral action because of the conflicting imperatives of unity of command, speed, and efficiency in military operations, and the often time consuming need for consensus driven political consultation.

The most notable American alliance is the North Atlantic Treaty Organization (NATO). Long a bulk work against communist expansion into West Europe, with the end of the cold war it has now expanded to take in many of the states of East Europe. In the process, NATO has become an alliance in search of a mission. Its political and military performance in the Balkans crisis left many wondering if it could adapt to a peacekeeping role. NATO was further marginalized in the Iraq War when France and Germany took the lead in opposing the U.S. calls for action at the United Nations. The most successful coalition effort in the post–cold war era was the 1990 Persian Gulf War in which the United States led thirty-seven states in a war against Iraq. In the Iraq War, the United States put together another coalition, the Coalition of the Willing, to defeat Saddam Hussein.

A second framing consideration in the use of military power today involves health and environmental considerations that can seriously undermine the effectiveness and morale of U.S. forces. In July 2003, the United States sent twenty-two hundred troops to Liberia as part of an international peacekeeping force. They left Liberia as scheduled on October 1. In the short period of time they were there, four hundred Marines came down with malaria. That same year, an outbreak of pneumonia struck U.S. forces in the Persian Gulf and Central Asia. Nineteen needed mechanical ventilators to breathe and two died. One can add to these very real health problems potential fears about the exposure to HIV/AIDS and a reoccurrence of Gulf War Syndrome, a series of unexplained and long undiagnosed illnesses that befell many who served in the Persian Gulf War. Dealing with such health-related issues is no easy task. In the case of malaria, it was determined that the main cause of the outbreak was the failure of U.S. forces to take the prescribed once-a-week malaria-preventing drug they were given. Gulf War Syndrome has yet to be explained.

A final framing consideration involves the political conditions under which force should be used. Up until the Persian Gulf War, the debate over how and when American military forces ought to be used largely centered on the way in which they were placed into combat. On one level the debate was between those who advocated the limited use of force and supported a policy of graduated escalation (the McNamara Doctrine) versus those who argued for the decisive deployment of American military power (the Powell Doctrine). On another level it involved a disagreement over the requirements for successful military action. During much of the Reagan administration advocates of both sides of this debate were represented in the cabinet. Secretary of Defense Caspar Weinberger argued that U.S. forces should only be engaged under strictly defined circumstances that included the presence of clearly defined goals, widespread public support, and the clear intention of winning. Secretary of State George Shultz argued for a more permissive set of operating conditions. He stated that the United States must be prepared to act "even without the assurance of victory or total public support."

WAR FIGHTING

Military power can be used in three ways. It can deter (to prevent something from happening), compel (to persuade a state to change its policies), and it can fight (to impose its position on another state). War-fighting has always been ultimate measure of a state's military power. As we noted at the outset of this chapter, typically post–World War II American military policy has been cast in terms of a two-war capability. This has not always been the case. Under Richard Nixon the standard was 1.5 wars. Under Reagan it was 3.5 wars.

Specifying how many wars the United States should be prepared to fight at any one time is not the same as identifying what those wars will be. In 1991, the George H. W. Bush administration released its Military Net Assessment, which identified counterinsurgency and counternarcotics operations as the most likely conflict situations to face American forces. Among the least-likely war scenarios was a conflict in Europe. Greater specificity was added the following year when the Pentagon released its 1994 to 1999 Defense Planning Guidance Scenario Set. Without predicting that any would occur, it identified seven paths to war over this five-year period. They are listed in Table 16.3. The scenarios included an Iraq invasion of Kuwait and Saudi Arabia and a nuclear-armed North Korean attack on South Korea, as well as both invasions

TABLE 16.3   Potential Paths to War as Identified in the Pentagon's 1994 to 1999 Defense Planning Guidance Document

Path to War	Comments
Russia invades Lithuania	An expansionist and authoritarian government assumes power in Russia. Parts of Poland are also seized. NATO forces win in 89 days of combat.
Iraq invades Kuwait and Saudi Arabia	UN sanctions have slackened. Oil revenues are up and Russia has provided aircraft. U.S.-led coalition wins in 54 days of combat.
North Korea attacks South Korea	North Korea launches surprise attack during peace initiative. It possesses nuclear weapons. U.S. and South Korea win after 91 days of combat.
Iraq and North Korea invade at the same time	While the U.S. is engaged with Iraq, North Korea attacks South Korea. The U.S. tries to fight one war at a time. The U.S.-led coalition defeats Iraq in 70 days of combat. Another 157 are required to defeat North Korea.
Coup In Panama	Right-wing police alliance with Panama's military and narco-terrrorists from Colombia stage a coup. U.S. wins in 8 days.
Coup in Philippines	Opposing sides include the police and military against the New People's Army. U.S. wins in 7 days.
Reemergence of a Hostile Superpower	"A Resurgent/Emergent Global Threat" that is authoritarian and strongly antidemocratic arises that is capable of threatening U.S. interests worldwide. No outcome is presented for a global war.

Source: The Washington Post, February 20, 1992.

occurring at the same time. Absent were any scenarios involving the use of U.S. forces in conflicts in the Balkans, sub-Saharan Africa, the Indian subcontinent, the Russian near abroad, against China, or in defense of Israel.

George W. Bush has described the war on terrorism as the first war of the twenty-first century. With it has come an important change in the American way of war.[28] Dating back to the Civil War and U.S. Grant's campaign to destroy Robert E. Lee's forces the American way of war centered on a strategy of attrition in which the enemy was warn down and overcome by the sheer application of overwhelming force. World War I and World War II fit this model, as did Vietnam and Korea although with far less success. Even the Persian Gulf War was fought in line with this thinking as more than five weeks of heavy bombing preceded the ground offensive. The Iraq War, and to a lesser extent the Afghan War before it, signal a shift in thinking. It moves American war-fighting strategy away from attrition to a strategy that seeks to achieve a quick knockout with relatively few casualties. Rather than brute strength it relies on speed, deception, special operations, and psychological operations. Secretary of Defense Donald Rumsfeld is generally acknowledged to be the prime mover behind this transformation in strategy. The extent to which warfare has truly been transformed is subject to challenge. Stephen Biddle in reviewing the course of the Afghan War concludes that while changes were evident so, too, were continuities with past forms of warfare and that to focus solely on what is new increases the risk that we will lose sight of war's true nature and its place as an instrument of foreign policy.[29]

In the minds of many commentators, the course of the Iraq War highlighted several points of continuity with the past. The first is that war ultimately is designed to achieve political ends. Victory on the battlefield is not enough. In the case of Iraq, this came through in the need for a large occupying force after victory was achieved. In turn, the military and political demands of occupying Iraq brought back into focus the need for coalitions and alliances. The Coalition of the Willing numbered 45 countries when the war began. Few contributed much to the war effort but little was needed. They are listed in Table 16.4. This changed with the occupation when the United States found it necessary to return to the UN to obtain its support and participation in the occupation and reconstruction of Iraq. The tenuousness of the commitment made by coalition members to the reconstruction was highlighted first by the U.S. announcement in July 2003 that it was paying more than $200 million to support the costs of Poland's participation in peacekeeping operations and then the decision of Spain in April 2004 to pull its troops out of Iraq following the wave of kidnappings and executions of foreigners by terrorist groups in the region.

A second point of continuity, although hard to measure with great accuracy, is that war produces large numbers of deaths and casualties. Table 16.5 lists U.S. military deaths by time period. The 500th U.S. military death occurred in January 2004. By the beginning of September 2003, U.S. casualties reached twice the number they were in the Persian Gulf War. The Pentagon does not produce counts of Iraqi civilian casualties but an ongoing study relying on press accounts placed the number of Iraqi civilians killed at between 11,487 and 13,458 in early August 2004.

TABLE 16.4   **Members of the Coalition of the Willing**

Afghanistan	Netherlands
Albania	Nicaragua
Australia	Palau
Azerbaijan	Panama
Bulgaria	Philippines
Colombia	Poland
Costa Rica	Portugal
Czech Republic	Romania
Denmark	Rwanda
Dominican Republic	Singapore
El Salvador	Slovakia
Eritrea	Solomon Islands
Estonia	South Korea
Ethiopia	Spain
Georgia	Turkey
Honduras	Uganda
Hungary	United Kingdom
Iceland	United States
Italy	Uzbekistan
Japan	
Kuwait	
Latvia	
Lithuania	
Macedonia	
Marshall Islands	
Micronesia	
Mongolia	

Source: White House news release, "Operation Iraqi Freedom," March 26, 2003. Accessed January 15, 2005.

HUMANITARIAN/PEACEKEEPING OPERATIONS

Operation Restore Hope (Somalia), Operation Provide Comfort (Northern Iraq), Operation Restore Democracy (Haiti) and sending troops to Liberia are prominent examples of post–cold war U.S. military interventions that at least in part can be classified as humanitarian in nature. Similar operations are taking place in Afghanistan now that the fighting has stopped. Opposition to these undertakings has been expressed from across the political spectrum. In part, objections are directed at the multilateral nature of these operations. Deeper issues, however, have also been raised. Neo-isolationist

TABLE 16.5   U.S. Military Fatalities in Iraq

Time Period	U.S. Fatalities	Total Coalition Fatalities/Day
March 20, 2003–May 1, 2003 (start of war through declared end of major hostilities)	139	4.0
May 2, 2003–June 28, 2004 (at which point official turnover of sovereignty to Iraq occurred)	715	1.89
June 29, 2004–January 31, 2005	581	1.93
		2.91
Total	931	2.35

Source: Iraq Coalition Casualties, www.icasualties.org.oif. Accessed February 1, 2005.

commentators have questioned whether humanitarian interventions are really in the American national interest. Arguing that U.S. security interests were not involved in the Somalian operation, Ted Galen Carpenter states that "if the U.S. abandons its own security interests as the standards by which to decide whether to use military force, there is virtually no limit to the possible arenas in which American lives may be sacrificed."[30] He likens the Somalia intervention to bungee jumping: "A risky undertaking for which there is no compelling need."

During the cold war, U.S. anticommunist military interventions were consistently opposed by those on the political left on the grounds that they represented unwarranted attempts to influence the internal affairs of other states. Humanitarian interventions, on the other hand, are often embraced as justified due to the stronger moral and legal case for such interventions and the more genuinely benign goals behind them. Richard Falk argues that this view is incorrect.[31] He asserts that while nonintervention is intolerable, intervention that (1) relies on military power, (2) seeks to bring about political restructuring, and (3) takes place without consent is never good foreign policy no matter how strong the case for action may appear. After examining the Somalian, Bosnian, and Haitian operations, Falk identifies several inherent weaknesses in U.S. military humanitarian interventions. One is insufficient political will, which leads policy makers to engage in the "politics of gesture." Enough is done to reassure the public that steps are being taken to deal with the crisis but not enough is done to change the situation. A second problem is that American military interventions still take place in the shadow of Vietnam, which gives them an imperialistic tinge. They are also carried out with a concern for minimizing American casualties and operating in a quick and decisive fashion. As a result, Falk argues, rather than being the beneficiaries of the intervention they are forced to bear a disproportionate amount of the burdens imposed by peacemaking operations.

Advocates of military humanitarian interventions reject the argument that American interests are not at stake in Somalia, Bosnia, or Haiti. They contend that definitions of American national interest that focus only on the physical security of the United States or the health of its economy are anachronistic. Just as important as these traditional foreign policy goals is the creation of an overall international environment that is supportive of American values. Humanitarian interventions are an important aspect of such a strategy. At the same time, it is recognized that military humanitarian operations are complex endeavors that are fraught with danger. If they are to succeed care must be taken that the mistakes made in Bosnia, Somalia, and Haiti are not repeated. Thomas Weiss suggests that three lessons can be learned from these experiences that will make humanitarian interventions more effective in the future.[32] First, international military interventions should be timely and robust. Second, because of serious shortcomings in the UN secretary general's command and control system, U.S. forces should remain under U.S. or NATO command. And third, regional organizations are not viable alternatives to the United Nations for carrying out such missions.

Beyond the debate over the merits of such operations lie real operational concerns for the military. The foremost of these is the lack of training and expertise to deal with problems associated with restoring order to a postconflict state. What is needed according to Robert Perito is a Stability Force.[33] He notes that dealing with civil disturbances, violent demonstrations, organized crime, and armed gangs requires a military skilled not in the logic of warfare but in logic of police work, law enforcement, and jurisprudence in which the goal is using the minimum amount of force to control situations. What sets members of a Stability Force apart from members of traditional military units is that they are trained to deal with civilians. Solutions are found in political compromise and not in the use of overwhelming force. The classic examples of such constabulatory forces (police forces organized along military lines) include the Canadian Mounties and the Texas Rangers.

TERRORISM/COUNTERINSURGENCY CONFLICTS

Terrorism is not a static enemy. Al Qaeda has already transformed itself from a tightly knit highly centralized organization into a much looser union of affiliated terrorist cells operating independently of one another.[34] Further changes can be expected as terrorists will come to challenge the United States along a broader continuum of levels of violence ranging from isolated high-profile attacks, to small controlled military engagements, up to situations where they have taken control over the government and military of a state.

The evolving nature of the terrorist threat will require changes in the way in which wars are fought.[35] Ralph Peters argues that "the future of modern warfare lies in the streets, sewers, high-rise buildings, industrial parks and the sprawl of houses, shacks, and shelters that form the broken cities of our world."[36] Rather than preparing to fight in jungles, deserts, or rolling plains, he believes that the American military must be ready to fight in urban environments. Edward Luttwak sees a change not so much in the setting of future wars as in the code according to which they will be fought.[37] According to Luttwak, the culture of war that existed during the cold war demanded controlled tension, discipline, and restraint. He sees a more sinister and less restrained culture of war emerging where catastrophic destruction and widespread atrocities are commonplace. The nature of fighting in Kosovo in 1999 lends support to Luttwack's agreement. These wars also promise to be labor intensive. The historical record pegs the ratio of stability force soldiers to civilians at between 2-20: 1,0000 individuals depending upon the level of political instability. The situation is even more demanding if urban warfare breaks out. Now the requirements become roughly one company, one day, and 30 to 40 percent casualties to take a city block defended by forces one-third its strength.

Summary and the Future

During the cold war the debate over the structure and purposes of American military power were encapsulated by two terms: nuclear deterrence and containment. This is no longer the case. Both in the conventional and nuclear areas a great deal of diversity of thought exists on how to move forward. Janice Gross Stein recommends that in addition to thinking about military power in terms of deterrence and compellence we also ought to develop strategies of reassurance.[38] She notes that where deterrence tries to prevent an adversary from taking unwanted actions by threatening it with punishment or denying it any hope of victory, reassurance seeks to accomplish the same end by reducing the fears and insecurities of the would-be aggressor. Reassurance strategies are needed because deterrence is likely to succeed only against opportunistic states. For those states driven by fear it will have little impact.

The cost of the post–cold war military has become a point of growing concern, with pressures mounting for increases in defense spending. Advocates of increased defense spending argue that the frequency and duration of post–cold war peacekeeping operations have been underestimated. Not only are the costs greater than anticipated but these operations have siphoned off troops designated for meeting other contingencies, thereby reducing America's ability to fight a war if it had to. They are joined by those who point to the need for reinvesting in America's military technological base after years of budget cutting. Aligned against them are those who continue to favor cutbacks in defense spending as a means of reducing the overall level of government spending and those who see defense planners as inventing threats as a means of justifying new weapons requests.

Recently, another issue has been raised regarding the use of military power as an instrument of foreign policy. In 1999 the Army announced that as a result of the open-ended commitments in Bosnia and Kosovo two of its ten divisions were unprepared for combat. The question of defense readiness next surfaced in the 2000 presidential race when George W. Bush charged that the Clinton–Gore administration had overused and underfunded the military. While it is the second charge (inadequate funding) that has received the most attention, many defense planners assert that the key readiness issue involves the first accusation. Moreover, they assert that the issue is not so much overuse as it is identifying tasks that the military should carry out and organizing and equipping military units for that purpose. As we have seen throughout this chapter, little agreement exists on this point at either the nuclear or conventional level.

Notes

1. David Alan Rosenberg, "The Origins of Overkill: Nuclear Weapons and American Strategy, 1945–1960," *International Security,* 7 (1983), 124.

2. The Harvard Study Group, *Living with Nuclear Weapons* (New York: Bantam, 1983), p. 79.

3. Information in this section is drawn from Dietrich Schroeer, *Science, Technology, and the Nuclear Arms Race* (New York: Wiley & Sons, 1981); Office of Technology Assessment, *The Effects of Nuclear War* (Montclair, N.J.: Allanheld, Osmun, 1980); and Leo Sartori, "Effects of Nuclear Weapons," *Physics Today,* 36 (1983), 32–58.

4. For discussions of the concept of nuclear winter, see Paul R. Ehrlich and others, *The Cold and the Dark: The World After Nuclear War* (New York: Norton, 1984); Richard P. Turco and others, "The Climatic Effects of Nuclear War," *Scientific American,* 251 (1984), 33–43; and The Committee on the Atmospheric Effects of Nuclear Explosions, and others, *The Effects on the Atmosphere of a Major Nuclear Exchange* (Washington, D.C.: National Academy Press, 1985).

5. This is a theme of Michael Mandelbaum in his *The Nuclear Future* (Ithaca, N.Y.: Cornell University Press, 1983).

6. Desmond Ball, "U.S. Strategic Forces: How Would They Be Used?" *International Security,* 7 (1982/83), 32–33.

7. There are a number of excellent volumes dealing with the development of U.S. nuclear strategy. The major ones relied on in constructing this history are Rosenberg, "The Origins of Overkill"; Jerome H. Kahan, *Security in the Nuclear Age: Developing U.S. Arms Policy* (Washington, D.C.: Brookings, 1975); Michael Mandelbaum, *The Nuclear Question: The United States and Nuclear Weapons, 1946–1976* (Cambridge, Mass.: Cambridge University Press, 1979); and Richard Smoke, *National Security and the Nuclear Dilemma: An Introduction to the American Experience* (Reading, Mass.: Addison-Wesley, 1984).

8. Bernard Brodie and others, *The Ultimate Weapon* (New York: Harcourt Brace, 1946).

9. Albert Wohlstetter, "The Delicate Balance of Terror," *Foreign Affairs,* 37 (1959), 211–56.

10. See Rosenberg, "The Origins of Overkill"; and Peter Pringle and William Arkin, *S.I.O.P.: The Secret U.S. Plan for Nuclear War* (New York: Norton, 1983).

11. See David Rosenberg, "A Smoking Radiating Ruin at the End of Two Hours: Documents of American Plans for Nuclear War with the Soviet Union, 1954–1955," *International Security,* 6 (1982/83), 3–38.

12. Rosenberg, "The Origins of Overkill," pp. 116–17.

13. On the ABM decisions see Morton Halperin, *Bureaucratic Politics and Foreign Policy* (Washington, D.C.: Brookings, 1974).

14. Mandelbaum, *The Nuclear Question,* p. 134.

15. Rosenberg, "The Origins of Overkill," p. 178.

16. Ball, "U.S. Strategic Forces," p. 34.

17. Warner R. Schilling, "U.S. Strategic Nuclear Concepts in the 1970s: The Search for Sufficiently Equivalent Countervailing Parity," *International Security,* 6 (1981), 59.

18. Ball, "U.S. Strategic Forces," pp. 36–38.

19. For excerpts from the NPR see www.globalsecurity.org/wmd/library/policy/dod/npr

20. Lawrence Freedman, "Does Deterrence Have a Future?" *Arms Control Today,* 30 (October 2000), 3–8.

21. Paul Bracken. "The Second Nuclear Age," *Foreign Affairs,* 79 (2000), 146–56.

22. Alexander George and Richard Smoke, *Deterrence in American Foreign Policy: Theory and Practice* (New York: Columbia University Press, 1974).

23. Robert Powell, "Nuclear Deterrence Theory, Nuclear Proliferation, and National Missile Defense," *International Security,* 27 (2003), 86–118.

24. Morton Halperin, "Deter and Contain," *The American Prospect*, 13 (November 4, 2002), 22–25.

25. Ray Takeyh, "Iran's Nuclear Calculations," *World Policy Journal*, 19 (2003), 21–28.

26. For a variety of critiques see the various articles in the symposium, "Is Preemption Necessary?" *The Washington Quarterly*, 26 (2003), 75–145.

27. "Its Seven Minutes to Midnight," *The Bulletin of the Atomic Scientists*, 58 (March/April 2002), 4–7.

28. Max Boot, "The New American Way of War," *Foreign Affairs*, 82 (2003), 41–58.

29. Stephen Biddle, "Afghanistan and the Future of Warfare," *Foreign Affairs*, 82 (2003), 31–46.

30. Ted Galen Carpenter, "Foreign Policy Peril: Somalia Set a Dangerous Precedent," *USA Today* (May 1993), 13.

31. Richard Falk, "Hard Choices and Tragic Dilemmas," *Nation* (December 20, 1993), 755–64.

32. Thomas G. Weiss, "Triage: Humanitarian Interventions in a New Era," *World Policy Journal*, 11 (1994), 59–66.

33. Robert Perito, *Where is the Lone Ranger When We Need Him?* (Washington, D.C.: U.S Institute of Peace Press, 2004).

34. Rohan Gunaratna, "The Post-Madrid Face of Al Qaeda," *The Washington Quarterly*, 27 (2004), 91–100.

35. Robert Tomes, "Relearning Counterinsurgency Warfare," *Parameters*, 34 (2004), 16–28.

36. Ralph Peters, "Our Soldiers, Their Cities," *Parameters*, 26 (1996), 43–50.

37. Edward Luttwak, "Toward Post-Heroic Warfare," *Foreign Affairs*, 74 (1995), 109–22.

38. Janice Gross Stein, "Deterrence and Reassurance," in Philip E. Tetlock et al. (eds.), *Behavior, Society, and Nuclear War*, Vol. 2 (New York: Oxford University Press, 1991), pp. 8–72.

— 17 —

ARMS CONTROL AND MISSILE DEFENSE

Judging Success and Failure

Just as military forces and strategies that served the United States well during the cold war may now be outmoded, so too may be the strategies relied upon to stabilize military balances and prevent war. In this chapter we will examine the policy choices facing strategists and the historical context within which these choices are rooted.

During the cold war two general strategies were pursued: arms control and disarmament. Arms control seeks to place restraints on the use of weapons, while disarmament has as its ultimate goal the systematic elimination of weapons. A third strategy, defense, came into prominence late in the cold war with President Reagan's advocacy of the Strategic Defense Initiative. Today a fourth strategy, counterproliferation, is advocated by many. Gauging the potential utility of these strategies is a complex undertaking for at least two reasons. First, evaluation of the effectiveness of these policy tools differs widely and is influenced heavily by the political outlook of the observer. Second, the contemporary international system contains very different challenges then did the cold war international system when the core principles of arms control and disarmament were formulated. Even judgments about the historical record are marked by controversy.

The difficulty of coming up with a single overarching judgment about the utility of past arms control efforts is captured by Lewis A. Dunn in his detailed evaluation of the cold war nonproliferation efforts.[1] He divides the record into three categories: wins, losses, and draws. The decisions by Western European states not to acquire the nuclear weapons; the strengthening of the nonproliferation norm among third world states; the creation of a nuclear supply regime; general acceptance of the nonproliferation treaty (NPT); and institutionalizing U.S.–Soviet nonproliferation talks are cited by Dunn as wins. He cites four losses: the failure to stop China, Israel, India, and other countries from acquiring nuclear capabilities; the long-running holdout of some states against signing the NPT treaty; the widespread civilian use of plutonium; and failures of cooperation among nuclear suppliers. Finally, Dunn classifies some outcomes as draws because he judges them to have had positive and negative consequences. Here he lists the continuing openness and scope of nuclear weapons programs; the cessation of nuclear activities by some states because of U.S. pressure; the nonuse of nuclear weapons; and movement toward a nuclear free zone in Latin America.

A second factor that complicates efforts to judge the future utility of existing arms control and disarmament efforts is that they do not exist in isolation from one another. Arms control and disarmament efforts form a web of treaties, organizations, informal agreements, and principles that taken together serve to place restrictions on the behavior of states. This packaging is often referred to as a regime, and making judgments about the effectiveness of any one part of the regime in isolation from its other parts is fraught with uncertainty, as the 1995 debate over extending the NPT treaty revealed.[2] In this debate some argued that an indefinite extension of the NPT was essential if the proliferation of nuclear weapons was to be stopped, while others argued that it outlived its usefulness.

Superpower Arms Control

We can better understand the challenges of evaluating past efforts at trying to stabilize military balances and prevent war if we look at the historical evolution of cold war nuclear arms control and disarmament efforts since they continue to frame our thinking about how to accomplish these ends and served as the point of reference for introducing competing solutions to these problems. We divide this history into four periods. Activity in each is driven by a different set of priorities, guiding assumptions and sense of urgency. After providing overviews of defense and counteproliferation as means for achieving these goals we return to the problem of arms control as it exists today and the challenges of controlling the proliferation of weapons of mass destruction.

1946 TO 1957

The first period extends from 1946 to 1957. Disarmament proposals dominated the international negotiating agenda in this first period. Little by way of significance was achieved, and nuclear diplomacy was not a high-priority item. Primary attention was given to the production of nuclear weapons and the formation of nuclear strategy. As a consequence, proposals were put forward more with an eye to their propaganda and image-creating potential than to their substantive merits.

The first nuclear disarmament proposal to command global attention was the Baruch Plan. Presented by the United States at the United Nations in 1946, it sought to place all aspects of nuclear energy production and use under international control. The Soviet Union rejected the Baruch Plan. In its place the Soviet Union called for a scheme in which the United States would first disarm and then an international organization, operating under a system of vetoes, would be created to disseminate scientific expertise and establish safeguards. Negotiations between the United States and Soviet Union proved unable to resolve these differences. In fact, it is unclear whether the United States would have been willing to implement the Baruch Plan. A general reluctance existed in Congress toward sharing U.S. nuclear secrets with other states, including U.S. allies.

Proposals for lessening the danger of nuclear war were not forthcoming again until the Eisenhower administration. Its first proposal was the 1953 Atoms for Peace Plan. This was followed in 1957 by the Open Skies Proposal. The Atoms for Peace Plan was only a disarmament plan in an indirect sense. It sought to get states to cooperate on the peaceful development and use of atomic power. Eisenhower's proposal led to the creation of the International Atomic Energy Agency, but it did not produce movement in the direction of disarmament. The proposed Open Skies Treaty focused on reducing the fear of surprise attack by exchanging blueprints of military installations and allowing each side to carry out aerial surveillance of each other's territory. It too failed to serve as a first step toward disarmament. Rather than accepting the plan as a way of sidestepping the question of on site inspection, the Soviet Union interpreted it as a device of legitimizing U.S. spying.

1958 TO 1972

According to Thomas Schelling, a founding theorist on arms control, the second phase of nuclear diplomacy began in 1958 with the unsuccessful multilateral East–West negotiations on the problem of surprise attack and ended in 1972 with the ABM Treaty.[3] This period saw the emergence of arms control on the international negotiating agenda and the disappearance of disarmament proposals. The Cuban missile crisis added an element of urgency and importance to these negotiations that until then had been lacking. According to Schelling and other early arms control theorists, nuclear diplomacy was not a competitive zero-sum game in which the winnings of one side were equal to and came at the expense of the other, but one that had to be governed by the recognition of common interests and the possibility of cooperation between potential enemies. Attention needed to be directed away from a concern for reducing the destructive capacity of weapons and lowering the numbers of weapons in existence to ways of reducing the incentives to go to war and the destructiveness of war. Moreover, arms control agreements did not have to take the form of formal agreements or treaties. More flexible and informal "traffic rules" agreements were also valuable, the rationale being that the treaty itself did not produce arms control. Arms control was a product of mutual restraint, and that could be arrived at without explicit ne-gotiations or formal treaties.

The first major breakthrough came in 1963 with the signing of the Lim-ited Test Ban Treaty, which outlawed nuclear explosions (testing) in the at-mosphere, under water, and in outer space. Unlike the Baruch Plan negotiations of the first period, negotiations on the Limited Test Ban Treaty were conducted on a bilateral basis, in private, and with a sense of resignation that comprehensive institution-building solutions were not feasible in the current international system.

A second milestone was reached in 1968 with the signing of the Non-proliferation Treaty (NPT). The United States and Soviet Union had a com-mon interest in stopping the spread of nuclear weapons and in preserving their nuclear monopolies. For a long time action on this common interest was frustrated by the fact that the primary proliferation concerns of both sides were directed at Europe. In the mid-1960s, concern about European proliferation, and especially concern over a West German nuclear force, less-ened, and attention shifted to the problem of third world proliferation. The NPT represented an agreement between nuclear and nonnuclear states. Those states possessing nuclear weapons promised not to provide them to nonnuclear states and to negotiate in good faith among themselves to reduce their nuclear stockpiles. They also pledged to help nonnuclear states develop nuclear energy for peaceful purposes. In return, the nonnuclear states agreed not to try to obtain nuclear weapons.

The third major arms control agreement reached in this period was the 1972 ABM Treaty and the SALT I agreement. The ABM Treaty, which is of unlimited duration and was modified by a 1975 agreement, limits each side to one ABM deployment area, either around its national capital or an ICBM field. It also prohibits the development, testing, or deployment of ABM components, or the development of ABM components on exotic phys-ical principles that are capable of substituting for ABM launchers. The SALT I agreement on offensive forces expired in 1977. It set limits on the number of fixed launchers for ICBMs (1,054 for the United States and 1,608 for the U.S.S.R.) and prohibited the conversion of launchers used for light ICBMs into launchers for heavy ICBMs. The agreement also set numerical limits for SLBMs (656 for the United States and 740 for the Soviet Union) and permitted some additional SLBM launchers to be substituted for older ICBM launchers.

1973 TO 1988

In Schelling's eyes, the ABM Treaty marked the end point of successful arms control efforts. In the next period, he finds the United States' arms con-trol program to be lacking in "any coherent theory of what arms control is supposed to accomplish." In place of arms control, Schelling sees a public ex-change of accusations and a situation where arms control had become a dri-ving force in the arms race instead of a restraint on it. Especially disturbing to him is the shift in interest away from the characteristics of weapons to a fixa-tion with the numbers. He sees both the public and policy makers as having succumbed to this false view of what arms control is all about. Critics of arms control efforts speak of freezing the numbers while official policy in the Carter and Reagan administrations had emphasized matching numbers. One of the few exceptions to this trend was the Scowcroft Commission's endorsement of a small, single-warhead missile (the Midgetman) to replace the MIRVed MX.

A first step toward the SALT II agreement was reached in November 1974 with the signing of the Vladivostok Accords, which set ceilings on the total numbers of strategic launchers that each side could possess (2,400) and the number of vehicles that could be MIRVed (1,320). Building on the Vladivostok Accords, the SALT II agreement was to have been completed in the summer of 1973. Two new issues and a new administration caused the negotiations to drag on for almost five more years. The two new issues were the U.S. cruise missile and the Soviet Union's backfire bomber. The Soviet Union insisted that the cruise missile be counted as a strategic launch vehicle while the United States insisted that the backfire bomber be similarly counted. In the end the question of the backfire bomber was left unaddressed, and cruise missiles were only limited for a short time.

Many in the new Carter administration were sympathetic to the charges raised by critics of the Vladivostok agreement that the ceilings were set so high as not to be arms control. The Carter administration put together two options for the Soviet Union to choose from. One would leave cruise missiles and the backfire bomber out of the SALT II agreement and use the numbers from the Vladivostok Accords as the basis for an agreement. The second would include these two systems but substantially reduce the number of launchers permitted.

As it finally emerged, SALT II was a complicated multilayered document that the U.S. Senate has never given its consent to and that has now technically expired. An overall limit of 2,400 was placed on delivery vehicles. The ceiling was to be reduced to 2,250 by the end of 1981. A complex series of subceilings was also established.

In his campaign for the presidency, Reagan attacked the SALT II Treaty as fatally flawed because it placed the Soviet Union in a position of military advantage. Accordingly, the first priority of his administration was not arms control but arms modernization and expansion. Only after restoring the nuclear balance and showing evidence of a willingness to match Soviet military advances could a meaningful arms control agreement be reached. Reagan's first concrete arms control proposal was directed at the problem of nuclear weapons in Europe. In November 1981 he unveiled his "zero option." The Soviet Union would eliminate its existing intermediate range ballistic missiles (IRBMs) targeted at Europe in return for a U.S. pledge not to deploy its Pershing II and ground-launched cruise missiles (GLCMs) in Europe. This deployment was set to begin in December 1983. The Reagan administration inherited a serious political and military problem in the area of European nuclear forces. In the 1950s NATO had begun relying on nuclear weapons as a way of offsetting the Warsaw Pact's superiority in conventional forces. In the late 1970s this supremacy was seriously challenged by the Soviet Union's introduction of the mobile SS-20. In 1979, after much debate, NATO agreed on a two-track policy of response to this development. First, it pledged itself to a nuclear modernization plan. Its key elements were the Pershing II and the GLCMs. Without them NATO would not have comparable weapons to the SS-20. Second, and simultaneously, it called for talks to limit the number of nuclear weapons in Europe.

The idea of a zero option was quickly rejected by the Soviet Union. This deadlock was broken in dramatic fashion when, in September 1987, the United States and Soviet Union agreed in principle to an agreement covering intermediate range nuclear forces (INF). These are weapons with a range between 300 miles and 3,400 miles. Under terms of the proposed agreement the United States and Soviet Union would dismantle more than 1,000 weapons.

The Reagan administration's position on strategic arms control negotiations was even slower to take shape. In the same speech in which he unveiled his zero option, Reagan indicated that his administration was preparing proposals for a new round of strategic arms talks to be known as START (Strategic Arms Reduction Talks). Little visible movement was forthcoming, and public concern began to mount over the administration's commitment to arms control and its loose language about nuclear war. The nuclear freeze movement became a focal point for efforts to push the administration back to the arms control negotiating table.[4]

To blunt this criticism and regain the political initiative on arms control, the Reagan administration presented a two-step START proposal in May 1982. In the first step a reduction in the number of warheads and launchers would be negotiated. Sublimits would be placed on ICBM warheads and the numbers of ICBMs and SLBMs. No ceilings were to be placed on bombers or cruise missiles. In the second step equal limits on throw weights would be sought. The Soviet Union found the START proposal unacceptable, but it did not reject it out of hand as it had done with the Carter proposals. In 1983, Reagan changed his approach to START. He embraced the concept of a nuclear "build-down."[5] At the heart of the build-down concept is the provision that each side should reduce the size of its nuclear forces as it proceeds with its own nuclear modernization plans. The build-down approach was dismissed by the Soviet Union as "old poison in new bottles." As a result of negotiations begun in 1985, the United States and the Soviet Union were able to agree on a basic START framework by the time Reagan left office. It centered on a limit of 1,600 launchers; a limit of 6,000 warheads of certain types and sublimits on the number of permissible warheads on ballistic missiles and heavy missiles; and a reduction of about 50 percent in Soviet aggregate ballistic missile throw weight.

1989 TO 2001

The ascension into power of Gorbachev, the subsequent collapse of communism, and the end of the cold war provided the background against which the fourth and final period of cold war arms control took place. It witnessed both a broadening of the arms control agenda to include conventional forces and a flurry of unilateral arms cuts that produced unprecedented reductions in the levels of U.S. and Soviet nuclear forces.

The initial focal point for U.S.–Soviet arms control efforts in this period was the Negotiations on Conventional Armed Forces in Europe (CFE) talks begun in March 1989. In attendance were the 16 members of NATO and the 7 Warsaw Pact states. Also under way was the Negotiations on Confidence and Security Building Measures (CSBMs) talks where all 35 members of the Conference on Security and Cooperation in Europe (CSCE) were represented. Neither of these talks was without precedent.

Conventional arms control had become a familiar feature of the European political landscape. The CFE talks succeeded the Mutual and Balanced Force Reduction (MBFR) talks, which focused on the military balance of forces in Central Europe but failed to produce an agreement. Begun in 1973, they were terminated by mutual consent in 1989 so that the CFE talks could begin. The MBFR talks were never able to move beyond disagreements over such issues as the size of the two alliance armies in Central Europe, the point to which reduction should be made and how to get there, and the meaning of such key terms as *parity* and *stability*. The CSBM talks were follow-on negotiations to the Conference on Security Building Measures (CDE) talks that began in 1984 under the auspices of the CSCE (also known as the Helsinki Accords). In 1986 the CDE talks produced the first post–World War II agreement on the use of conventional arms in Europe. Among the most significant provisions of the agreement are the requirements that (1) each state must give all other signatory states two years' notice in advance of any military exercise involving over 40,000 troops; (2) a yearly calendar of all out-of-garrison military activities of formations over a certain size must be produced; and (3) all signatories must be invited to observe such exercises. In the language of arms control, the CDE agreements were in the area of traffic rules and restraints in the use of force rather than force reductions.

Movement was also forthcoming in the area of nuclear weapons. At first this movement was quite predictable, taking the form of the official signing of a START I treaty by President George H. W. Bush and President Gorbachev at a summit conference in July 1991. It then proceeded in an unexpected fashion. Rather than engaging in a new round of protracted negotiations to further reduce the size of their nuclear arsenals, the United States and the Soviet Union entered into a series of unilateral cuts. In September 1991, Bush ordered that (1) all tactical nuclear weapons except those dropped from planes be removed from the U.S. arsenal; (2) all nuclear cruise missiles and bombs be taken off naval ships, attack submarines, and land-based naval aircraft; (3) all strategic bombers be taken off high-alert status; and (4) a halt take place in the development and deployment of mobile ICBMs. Gorbachev responded by calling for the elimination of all land-based tactical nuclear weapons and the removal of all nuclear arms from ships, submarines, and land-based naval aircraft. In his State of the Union address in 1992, Bush focused on strategic weapons and offered to reduce by one-third the number of U.S. SLBM warheads in return for Russia, Ukraine, and Kazakhstan agreeing to eliminate all of their heavy multiple-warhead ICBMs. Yeltsin responded with a call for even deeper cuts that would leave each side with some 2,500 warheads. These pronouncements led to the signing of a joint understanding by George H. W. Bush and Yeltsin in June 1992 that in turn led to the January 1993 signing of START II. According to its terms both sides agreed to make deep cuts in their nuclear forces by 2003. The target figure for the United States was set at 3,500 bombs and warheads while that for the Soviet Union was 2,997. Moreover, each side agreed to eliminate all of its multiple-warhead ICBMs, and sublimits favorable to the United States were set on the numbers of submarine-launched warheads and air-launched nuclear weapons.

Before the Clinton administration could move to bring the START II Treaty to the Senate for its approval, it first had to deal with problems surrounding the ratification of START I. Here again, the problem was the breakup of the Soviet Union. Its dissolution had left four nuclear states in its wake: Russia, Ukraine, Belarus, and Kazakhstan. All expressed misgivings about giving up their nuclear weapons and sought compensation from the West in terms of security guarantees and foreign aid as a precondition for doing so. The last holdout was Ukraine, which formally did not give its approval to the START I treaty and the NPT treaty until November 1994.

2001 TO PRESENT

Arms control in the last decade of the twentieth century moved forward in an uncertain fashion. Brad Roberts describes it as having lost its political energy and having become caught in the political gridlock that gripped Washington.[6] President George W. Bush moved decisively to break that gridlock in December 2001 when he gave the required six-month notice that the United States was withdrawing from the ABM Treaty. The move was necessary from Bush's perspective in order to permit the United States to fully develop a national ballistic missile defense system. Significant work on such a system was not permitted under the ABM Treaty. For defenders of the ABM treaty this decision removed one of the cornerstones of the cold war arms control regime, and even though it may have been ancient history in terms of the security problem it was addressing, the treaty still held great symbolic value as a statement of U.S. foreign policy goals and priorities.

Russian President Vladimir Putin called the decision to withdraw from the ABM agreement a "mistake," but it did not stop him from signing a new arms control agreement with the United States in May 2002. The Strategic Offensive Reductions Treaty (SORT), also known as the Treaty of Moscow, overtakes the never-negotiated START III treaty. SORT breaks new ground in treaty language. It starts from the premise that Russia is a friend of the United States and not an enemy. The body contains only ten sentences. It lacks the appendices, caveats, statements of understanding, and covenants found in earlier arms control agreements. In essence, the treaty permits each side to do as it pleases so long as their nuclear arsenal is reduced to twenty-two hundred deployed warheads by December 31, 2012. As one senator observed, unlike in previous cases where verification was a major concern, in this treaty "there are no mileposts for performance. There is nothing really to verify except good faith." George W. Bush would have preferred no treaty in favor of a simple verbal agreement. The Russians, however, were not interested in such loose construction.

The agreement was negotiated in six months. Putin wanted a treaty that would eliminate the number of missiles, long-range bombers, and submarines because Russia could not afford to maintain its nuclear arsenal at its current size. Putin also sought to insert language that promised an American missile defense system would not be directed at Russia. The Bush administration wanted to restrict deployed warheads. The president had promised to cut the size of the U.S. nuclear weapons arsenal in his presidential campaign and sought the agreement as a means of fulfilling this promise. One issue that complicated negotiations involved information-sharing provisions as the two sides could not agree on what information to provide the other with. In the end, it was agreed that the START I Treaty inspection and notification system would be used until a new system would be agreed upon. A second problem was over how much time needed to be given if one side wanted to withdraw from the treaty. The United States wanted only forty-five days if the twenty-two hundred warhead limit was going to be exceeded. Russia felt this was too little warning. In the end, a three-month warning period for withdrawal from the treaty was set. SORT is set to expire on December 21, 2012.

Arms control scholars find both good and bad features in the SORT approach.[7] On the positive side are its simplicity and flexibility and the concern for reducing the number of operational nuclear warheads. On the negative side is the absence of a set of rules to structure the agreement and deal with the inevitable questions of interpretation and implementation that will arise. For example, the treaty contains no schedule of reductions nor does it specify the procedures by which reductions are to be achieved. Also of concern to many is the absence of provisions for the destruction of launch vehicles or limits on the size of reserve stockpiles.

Defense

THE STRATEGIC DEFENSE INITIATIVE

According to one observer, "The great missing innovation in the nuclear age is the development of means to defend against nuclear attack."[8] If this capacity is lacking, it is impossible to protect one's population and territory without the cooperation of the enemy. Both parties must agree not to attack population centers. Strategists have established that such tacit cooperation between enemies is possible and often takes place during war.[9] Still, many are troubled that the defense of the United States in the nuclear age is possible only with the cooperation of an adversary. Reagan gave voice to these concerns in a March 1983 speech when he called upon the scientific community to find a way for the United States to escape from this situation.

> What if free people could live secure in the knowledge that their security did not rest upon the threat of instant U.S. retaliation to deter a Soviet attack; that we could intercept and destroy their strategic missiles before they reached our soil or that of our allies? . . . Is it not worth every investment necessary to free the world from the threat of nuclear war?[10]

As presented by Reagan, the Strategic Defense Initiative (SDI) was a long-term research and development program designed to identify viable policy options for creating a nuclear defense system. The decisions as to which system, if any, to pursue were scheduled to be made in the 1990s. However, in early 1987 the Reagan administration began examining the possibility of an early deployment of SDI. As envisioned by most observers, Reagan's SDI system involved a series of defensive systems layered together in such a way as to create a protective shield. Each layer in this system was to perform the same tasks: It would search out and detect targets, track them, discriminate between real targets and dummy targets, and intercept and destroy the real targets. The layers in the SDI system would roughly correspond to the four major phases in the trajectory of an ICBM.[11]

During the Reagan administration the scope and funding of a "Star Wars" system was progressively cut back, although the goal was never formally abandoned. In 1989, Secretary of Defense Dick Cheney declared that SDI had been "oversold" as a leak-proof umbrella (a possibility he described as "extremely remote"). Still, the George H. W. Bush administration continued to seek funding for it under the guise of "brilliant pebbles." Under it, missiles sent into space would be sent into layered orbits and would possess the ability to detect the launch of enemy missiles at a distance of several thousand miles. Upon receiving orders to attack, the missiles would speed toward the enemy missiles and ram them at high speed, thereby destroying them.

SDI's short-lived existence formally came to an end in the Clinton administration. In May 1993, Secretary of Defense Les Aspin announced that the Strategic Defense Initiative Office was being closed. It would be replaced by a Ballistic Missile Defense Office whose mission would be to develop follow-on missiles to the Patriot system used against SCUD missiles in the Persian Gulf War. Instead of constructing a nuclear shield over the United States, the new goal would be to prevent attacks by short-range ground-launched missiles.

MISSILE DEFENSE SYSTEMS

The death of SDI in the Clinton administration did not mark the end of efforts to establish a national ballistic missile defense system.[12] In one of its few foreign policy statements, the Republican Party's Contract with America called for building a national missile defense system by 2003. Clinton vetoed legislation passed in 1995 that would have set this in motion but also proposed an alternative. The "3 + 3" program called for three years of research and development followed by a decision in 2000 on whether or not to go ahead with implementation in 2003. Surprise missile tests by Iran and North Korea in 1998 provided additional political backing for creating such a system, and in 1999 large majorities in both houses passed a bill asserting that the United States should deploy a national missile defense system as soon as it was "technologically feasible." The new target date became 2005.

Clinton's plan relied heavily upon ground-based interceptors that would be supported by a network of ground-based radars and space-based infrared sensors. Planning suggested that the first deployment of this system would be in Alaska where 20 high-speed interceptors capable of shooting down a limited number of incoming warheads would be deployed. This number was expected to expand to as many as 100 interceptors in the first phase and 250 in the second. High-resolution radars would be placed in the Aleutian Islands. Support would also come from upgraded early-warning radar stations in Greenland, Great Britain, and the United States.

Clinton's plan for a national missile defense system was thus a significant departure from SDI, which had relied much more heavily on satellite based weapons systems. The change in technological focus did not lessen the challenges involved in creating an integrated command and control system that culminated in having a missile hit a missile. The Pentagon scheduled nineteen tests to determine the technical feasibility of the proposed system. By contrast, 165 fight tests were conducted of the Safeguard missile system, 125 tests of the Polaris submarine, and 101 tests of the Minuteman missile. The first test of the system in October 1999 was successful despite the failure of the tracking system, but the second test in January 2000 and a third in July 2000 failed. Clinton then announced that he would leave the decision on whether to build a national missile defense system to his successor.

President George W. Bush campaigned as an ardent support of a national ballistic missile system, and once elected, he moved swiftly in this direction. He removed the major diplomatic and legal roadblock to the development of such a system by announcing in December 2001 that the United States was withdrawing from the 1972 ABM Treaty. In December of the following year, he signed National Security Presidential Directive (NSPD) 23 that ordered the initial deployment of a set of long-range missile interceptors in Alaska and California by September 2004. The move was billed as part of an evolutionary approach to the development of a missile defense system that will never produce a final fixed system.

The Bush system has encountered the same types of technological problems that hindered the development of earlier missile defense systems. A General Accounting Office study released in 2004 concluded that many aspects of the system had yet to be tested. Specific problems identified included the ability to discriminate between decoys and real warheads, the ability to launch multiple interceptors, and the system's ability to perform at night and under adverse weather conditions. The first attempt to launch two interceptors at two targets is not scheduled until 2007.

Beyond these operational concerns, the benefits of a national ballistic missile system continue to be debated.[13] Two issues dominate the discussion. The first is the wisdom of constructing a sufficiently robust system that it could potentially negate a Russian or Chinese nuclear capability. Should this be the case many fear that it would force these two states to undertake a large scale expansion of their nuclear programs in order to deter the United States from acting unilaterally against them. One study using documents recently declassified reveals that this is how the United States responded in 1968 to the development of a Soviet ABM system. All components of the Soviet system became high-priority nuclear targets, and the goal was to overwhelm it. The second debate is over the value of a more limited system that would be directed at protecting the United States from rogue states with smaller nuclear arsenals. Whereas some see it as a prudent investment in an age of terrorism, others prefer to rely upon diplomacy and conventional forces to protect the United States, especially given the types of technological issues raised above.

Counterproliferation

Counterproliferation is the use of military force to deter countries from acquiring and using weapons of mass destruction against the United States. Proponents of counterproliferation start from nonproliferation efforts have failed. They see the United States as operating in a postproliferated international security environment. It is one in which defense will lag behind advances in offensive nuclear, chemical, and biological warfare capabilities and in which inspections do not provide an effective long term solution to the United States' security needs. Counterproliferation is not a new strategy.

In 1993 Clinton's Secretary of Defense Les Aspin unveiled a "counterproliferation initiative." Its details were never spelled out at the time, but most who embraced the idea identified two prominent features. The first was a military capacity to operate against states that possess nuclear weapons and other WMD. The second was the construction of a defense system against ballistic missiles. Significant challenges exist on both fronts. Constructing a military capability to attack states (or terrorist groups) possessing an immature nuclear or WMD capability is quite different from constructing one to counter an adversary with a robust capability. An additional complicating factor is the timing and political context of the planned military action. Is it part of a prolonged crisis, an ongoing war, or a "bolt-from-the blue" response carried out in a time of international quiet? Only in the last case can surprise be expected. In the others, the target is likely to have advance warning and will be able to prepare for that contingency and develop retaliatory strategies. Decisions must also be made on what targets to attack. Possibilities range from the WMD themselves, infrastructure and support systems, conventional forces, and the political and military leadership of the adversary.

Few historical examples of counterproliferation exist.[14] The most frequently cited are Israel's 1981 raid on Iraq's Osiraq nuclear reactor, the bombing of Iraq's unconventional weapons during the first phase of Operation Desert Storm in 1991, and U.S. cruise missile attacks on the all Shifa pharmaceutical plant in Sudan in 1998. Contingency plans were also developed for using military force against North Korea in 1994 and China in 1963 to 1964. In each case, context-specific considerations make it difficult to develop any clearcut generalizations as to guiding principles for a counterproliferation strategy. Among the factors that have weighed heavily on engaging in counterproliferation military action are the possibility of triggering a full-scale war, uncertain intelligence, and concerns for high levels of collateral damage to people and the environment.

In its short history, counterproliferation thinking has already undergone several changes from when it was first proposed.[15] Bureaucratic infighting within the Pentagon over the costs of proliferation and the military's unease over preemptive war and opposition from arms controllers soon transformed it from an offensive policy to a largely defensive and reactive one. This orientation changed again after the terrorist attacks of 9/11. The George W. Bush administration's embrace of a national ballistic missile defense system and its rejection of deterrence in favor of preemption effectively places counterproliferation at the center of its strategy for dealing with weapons of mass destruction.

The Post-Cold War Agenda

WEAPONS OF MASS DESTRUCTION

The central preoccupation of American policy makers with regards to eliminating or containing the global nuclear weapons is no longer the Soviet strategic threat. It is proliferation. This is not entirely new ground. A number of institutions, treaties, and principles are already in place forming the basis for a nonproliferation regime. The parameters of this new proliferation agenda differ in five important respects from that which was in existence when the cold war ended. First, where as arms control was a tool for managing superpower relations, nonproliferation policy today is seen as a tool for managing North–South relations and dealing with rogue states.[16] Second, in a very real way, the nature of the weapons of concern have changed. As Richard Betts notes, proliferation concerns no longer focus on cutting-edge technologies or controlling the latest developments in the nuclear arms race.[17] They are focused on "primitive" off-the-shelf strategic technologies. Third, because these technologies are widely available, it has forced the international community to focus as much on supply-side issues as demand issues. Fourth, there has been a shift in emphasis from eliminating and stigmatizing the use of the weapons in question to stigmatizing and eliminating certain states that possess these weapons. Finally, a greater sense of pessimism surrounds today's efforts in the sense that many policy makers see some of the states that have acquired weapons of mass destruction as undeterrable. This was not the case during the cold war when, in spite of their differences, the United States and the Soviet Union were seen as having common cause in preventing the use of nuclear weapons.

As we have already discussed in this chapter these new parameters have led the George W. Bush administration to question the continued utility of the cold war proliferation policy and to favor counterproliferation and ballistic missile defense systems.[18] Within the arena of traditional nonproliferation policies this has led the administration to move away from two of the longtime anchors of the global nonproliferation regime. One anchor is the 1968 Non-Proliferation Treaty (NPT). A Review and Extension Conference took place in 1995, at which point it was agreed to extend the treaty indefinitely. The basic bargain entered into by the states signing the treaty was that nuclear weapon states agreed to work to the elimination of their nuclear arsenals in exchange for a pledge by nonnuclear states to forego efforts to obtain them. A loophole in the agreement allowed states to pursue peaceful nuclear power if they promised not to build nuclear weapons. In 2004, George W. Bush called for closing this loophole because it had been exploited by North Korea and Iran. Left unmentioned was the fact that India was the first to pursue nuclear weapons through a policy of peaceful nuclear explosions. The administration moved away from the central bargain in 2002 by announcing plans in 2002 to resume underground testing in the future. In 2003, the Senate approved low-yield testing of nuclear weapons but required that the president obtain congressional support before going ahead with the full development of a new generation of battlefield nuclear weapons.

The second nonproliferation anchor that the administration has voiced displeasure with is the manner in which inspections and verification procedures are utilized in nonproliferation agreements. In 2004, at a meeting of the United Nations–sponsored Conference on Disarmament that was working on a Fissile Material Cut-Off Treaty that would ban the production of highly enriched uranium and plutonium that is used in nuclear weapons, the administration announced that it will oppose the inclusion of an inspection and verification system in the treaty, stating an inspection regime "would have been so extensive that it could compromise key signatories' core national security interests." Critics asserted that this decision undermined ten years of diplomatic efforts to get Israel, Pakistan, and India to accept nuclear inspections.

The detonation of nuclear devices by Indian and Pakistan in 1998 and the efforts to obtain them made by North Korea, Iran, Iraq, and Libya has led some analysts to revisit the most fundamental of all questions: Why does proliferation occur? According to Albert Wholstetter, one of the first cold war nuclear theorists, the way to prevent nuclear proliferation was by providing potential nuclear states with a protective nuclear umbrella. The nuclear problem has changed in fundamental ways since the 1950s, and no single motive lies behind the decision to "go nuclear."[19] It may come about as a result of a strategic chain reaction in which the decision of one state to go nuclear prompts others to follow suit. It may come about as a result of domestic pressures in which the acquisition of a nuclear device is seen as a solution to an internal political problem. Finally, nuclear proliferation may be a result of shared international norms and beliefs about how to bolster a state's international standing and prestige.

CONVENTIONAL WEAPONS

Nuclear weapons are not the only proliferation problem facing policy makers. Proliferation in conventional weapons is also a problem, and for some it is the major problem. Traditionally, efforts to curb conventional weapons proliferation have focused on restricting the sale or transfer of major weapons systems from one state to another. For a brief period of time, it appeared that conventional arms transfers were becoming less pronounced in world politics. Between 1989 and 1991, worldwide sales fell 53 percent and U.S. sales fell almost 34 percent. This downward trend has since been reversed. Relatively little attention has been paid to the problem of curbing arms transfers. Conventional Arms Transfer Talks were held between 1977 and 1979 but ended with no agreement being reached.[20] The United States and Soviet Union entered these talks with conflicting agendas that prevented any agreement from being reached. In the aftermath of the Persian Gulf War, a new conventional arms control initiative has taken place in the form of a UN Arms Transfer Register.[21] The register identifies seven different categories of conventional weapons, and countries are requested to submit to the United Nations an annual statement of the number of these items it exported or imported during the previous year. The goal is to bring a heightened degree of transparency to the arms transfer process and thereby reduce the military advantages that arms transfers bring to states. The danger, according to one observer, is that because the system is a control mechanism, it may have the unintended effect of legitimizing those arms transfers that are registered.

Not all conventional arms controllers agree with the focus on major weapons systems. Aaron Karp argues that in the 1990s the purpose of conventional arms transfers has changed from that of maintaining or creating regional power balances to regulating the emergence of new states.[22] In his view, major weapons systems have become largely symbolic. If one looks at fighting in Bosnia, Rwanda, Liberia, and Chechnia it is small and light arms that are the weapons of choice. These are the weapons that upset strategic balances and inflict high levels of human misery.

The global scale of small arms trade is imposing.[23] The Arms Control and Disarmament Agency has estimated that some 13 percent of the global trade in conventional arms is made up of small arms and light weapons. In 1996 the State Department and Commerce Department approved the export of more than $500 million worth of small arms. One author estimates that 10 to 20 percent of the $62 billion in U.S. military grants between 1955 and 1994 consisted of these weapons. In addition to direct sales and grants, a third source of small arms is surplus sales. One source estimates that between 1990 and 1996 the United States gave away 200,000 machines through the Excess Defense Articles Program. Recipients included Mexico, Taiwan, Latvia, Bosnia, Israel, Thailand, and the Philippines. In 2001, a voluntary international agreement was reached that was designed to stop the international trade in small arms. The United States blocked efforts to include regulations on civilian ownership of military weapons and to restrict small arms trade to rebel movements.

Yet another dimension to the problem of curbing the proliferation of conventional weapons has also emerged. It involves the globalization of the arms production process. Cutbacks in defense spending and shrinking military establishments have led major arms producers to engage in a growing number of joint ventures, strategic alliances, and foreign acquisitions.[24] This is transforming the security environment facing the U.S. military by placing increasingly advanced military equipment in the hands of potential adversaries. It has also led to the development of sophisticated third world arms industries. Between 1986 and 1993, there were twenty-seven joint ventures, twenty-three strategic alliances, and 78 mergers or acquisitions among defense firms around the world. Among others, the United States has entered into coproduction agreements on the F-16 fighter with Israel, South Korea,

Singapore, Taiwan, Greece, and Indonesia. About forty third world states now possess significant defense industries; almost one hundred major conventional weapons systems have been licensed for coproduction in the third world; and seven third world states have the ability to produce land, sea, and air combat weapons.

Combining Approaches

Not surprisingly, most observers concerned with the spread of weapons of mass destruction advocate adopting a combination of the approaches we have outlined in this chapter. Also not surprisingly, the mixture varies considerably. Here we present two different approaches.

The first approach is that of the George W. Bush administration.[25] In December 2002, it presented its National Strategy to Combat Weapons of Mass Destruction. The report advocates relying on three pillars. The first pillar is counterproliferation. Several policies are advocated under this heading. One is the interdiction of materials, expertise, and technologies so that they do not reach these states. A second is deterrence via the threat to use all available options. The second pillar is strengthened nonproliferation measures to prevent rogue states and terrorists from acquiring such weapons. Included here are bilateral and multilateral diplomatic efforts, export controls, and nonproliferation sanctions. The third pillar is developing and maintaining a capability to reduce the consequences of an attack should it occur. This is the task assigned to homeland security.

The second approach is put forward by the Carnegie Endowment for International Peace.[26] Rather than organize its strategy around policy tools it focuses on objectives. Its focus is also more narrowly on nuclear weapons but the principles it espouses apply to all forms of weapons of mass destruction. The report calls for an overall policy of universal compliance. Obligations under such a system include 1) no new nuclear weapon states, 2) securing all nuclear material, 3) stopping the illegal transfer of nuclear material, technology, and expertise, 4) ending nuclear testing and reducing the importance of nuclear arsenals in their inventories, and 5) a renewed commitment to regional conflict resolution. To achieve these ends, it recommends four strategic initiatives. The first is developing a greater international consensus on threats and how to meet them. Second, strengthening the enforcement penalties for trafficking nuclear material. Third, blocking access to nuclear materials better supply side controls. Fourth, reducing the demand for nuclear weapons by a more vigorous system of rewards and punishments.

Summary and the Future

Arms control, disarmament, defense, and counterproliferation represent four attempts to escape from the dangers of nuclear war. Disarmament proposals never prospered or received serious attention. Arms control has had a checkered history. Missile defense initiatives have been put forward optimistically as a way of making nuclear weapons obsolete but have been met with great skepticism as to their technological feasibility and political merit. Counterproliferation strategies have produced fears over the lowering of the nuclear non-first-use threshold and the possibility that they may legitimate nuclear weapons by changing the focus of international concern from the existence of outlawed weapons to dangerous regimes in possession of these weapons. Beyond their individual problems all of these strategies are also challenges by the emergence of threats from chemical and biological weapons.[27] The presence of abundant dual-use technologies in these fields, the relative ease of production, the ability to hide production centers, and the multiple means of delivery present policy makers with a complex security test.

Looking back more closely at arms control two major challenges confront it. Richard Betts questions the utility of pursuing arms control agreements in an age in which there is no clearly defined enemy.[28] He argues that the fundamental purpose of arms control agreements is to stabilize military relationships between adversaries. Negotiated arms control treaties make little sense between friends because the significance of an arms control agreement depends on what we believe would happen in the absence of that agreement. Until such time as an enemy reemerges, Betts advocates the pursuit of unilateral cuts in military equipment and expenditures as the best way of reducing the likelihood of war. A second set of challenges exist at an operational level. Regardless of whether arms control is accomplished through unilateral cuts or negotiated treaties, the management of arms control arrangements has received very little attention.[29] What has received attention is the problem of compliance. Are the terms of an agreement being lived up to? Management is more than compliance. It also involves such issues as anticipating problems, planning, and searching for and exploiting possible spillover effects of an arms control agreement. Without careful attention to the management of an agreement, second- and third-order problems may not be addressed in time and may become major points of dispute.

Notes

1. Lewis A. Dunn, "Four Decades of Nuclear Nonproliferation: Some Lessons from Wins, Losses, and Draws," *Washington Quarterly,* 13 (1990), 5–18.

2. See Alexander T. Lennon, "The 1995 NPT Extension Conference," *The Washington Quarterly,* 17 (1994), 205–27; and Ted Galen Carpenter, "Closing the Nuclear Umbrella," *Foreign Affairs,* 73 (1994), 8–13.

3. Thomas C. Schelling and Morton H. Halperin, *Strategy and Arms Control* (New York: Pergamon-Brassey Classic, 1985), originally published by the Twentieth Century Fund, 1961; and Thomas C. Schelling, "What Went Wrong with Arms Control," *Foreign Affairs,* 64 (1985/86), 219–33.

4. For a statement of the nuclear freeze position, see Randall Forsberg, "Call a Halt to the Arms Race–Proposal for a Mutual U.S.–Soviet Nuclear Weapons Freeze," in Burns H. Weston (ed.), *Toward Nuclear Disarmament and Global Security: A Search for Alternatives* (Boulder, Colo.: Westview Press, 1984), pp. 384–89.

5. Alton Frye, "Strategic Build-Down: A Context for Restraint," in Charles Kegley Jr., and Eugene Wittkopf (eds.), *The Nuclear Reader: Strategy, Weapons, and War* (New York: St. Martin's, 1985), pp. 174–86.

6. Brad Roberts, "The Road Ahead for Arms Control," *Wilson Quarterly,* 23 (2000), 219–20.

7. Jack Mendlesohn, "Russia and America: Make Believe Arms Control," *Current History* (October 2002), 325–29.

8. Michael Mandelbaum, *The Nuclear Future* (Ithaca, N.Y.: Cornell University Press, 1983), p. 43.

9. Thomas C. Schelling, *The Strategy of Conflict* (New York: Oxford University Press, 1960).

10. Reagan's speech is reprinted in P. Edward Haley, David M. Kethly, and Jack Merritt (eds.), *Nuclear Strategy, Arms Control, and the Future* (Boulder, Colo.: Westview, 1985), pp. 311–12.

11. For a discussion of how a BMD system would work, see Stephen Weiner, "Systems and Technology," in Ashton Carter and David N. Schwartz (eds.), *Ballistic Missile Defense* (Washington, D.C.: Brookings, 1984), pp. 49–89; Sidney Drell, Philip J. Farley, and David Holloway, "Preserving the ABM Treaty: A Critique of the Reagan Strategic Defense Initiative," *International Security*, 9 (1984), 67–79.

12. George Lewis, Lisbeth Gronlund, and David Wright, "National Missile Defense: An Indefensible System," *Foreign Policy*, 117 (1999/2000), 120–37.

13. Stephen Glasser and Steve Fetter, "National Missile Defense and the Future of U.S. Nuclear Weapons Policy," *International Security*, 26 (2001), 40–92; and James Lindsay and Michael O'Hanlon, *Defending America*, revised and updated edition (Washington, D.C.: Brookings Institution, 2002).

14. Robert Luttwak, "Nonproliferation and the Use of Force," in Janne Nolan et al., (eds.), *Ultimate Security* (New York: The Century Foundation Press, 2003), pp. 75–106.

15. Henry Sokolski, "Mission Impossible," *Bulletin of the Atomic Scientists* (March/April 2001), 63–68.

16. Brad Roberts, "1995 and the End of the Post-Cold War Era," *Washington Quarterly*, 18 (1994), 5–25.

17. Richard Betts, "The New Threat of Mass Destruction," *America and the World* (New York: Council on Foreign Relations Press, 2002), 348–63.

18. Jason Ellis, "The Best Defense," *The Washington Quarterly*, 26 (2003), 115–33.

19. Brad Roberts, "Rethinking N+1," *National Interest*, 51 (1998), 75–80; and Scott R. Sagan, "The Causes of Nuclear Proliferation," *Current History*, 76 (April, 1997), 151–55.

20. Janne Nolan, "U.S.-Soviet Conventional Arms Transfer Negotiations," in Alexander George, Philip Farley, and Alexander Dallin (eds.), *U.S.-Soviet Security Cooperation* (New York: Oxford University Press, 1988), 27–36.

21. Edward J. Laurance, "Conventional Arms: Rationales and Prospects for Compliance and Effectiveness," *Washington Quarterly*, 16 (1993), 163–72.

22. Aaron Karp, "The Arms Trade Revolution: The Major Impact of Small Arms," *Washington Quarterly*, 17 (1994), 63–77.

23. Michael Renner, "Arms Control Orphans," *The Bulletin of the Atomic Scientists*, 55 (January/February 1999), 22–26; and Lora Lumpe, "The Leader of the Pack," *Bulletin of the Atomic Scientists*, 55 (January/February 1999), 27–33.

24. Richard A. Bitizinger, "The Globalization of the Arms Industry," *International Security*, 19 (1994), 170–98.

25. *National Strategy to Combat Weapons of Mass Destruction*. It is available at www.fas.org/irp/offdocs/nspd/nspd-17.

26. *Universal Compliance*, Carnegie Endowment for International Peace. It is available at www.ProliferationMews.org.

27. Mary Cooper, Chemical and Biological Weapons," in *Global Issues* (Washington, D.C.: CQ Press, 2001), 1–18.

28. Richard Betts, "Systems for Peace or Causes of War? Collective Security, Arms Control, and the New Europe," *International Security*, 17 (1992), 5–43. Also see the exchange between Betts and Michael Mazarr in the Winter 1992/1993 issue.

29. James Goodby, "Can Arms Control Survive Peace?" *Washington Quarterly*, 13 (1990), 93–104.

— *18* —

ALTERNATIVE FUTURES

Choices

There are always choices. In the aftermath of the September 11, 2001 terrorist attacks it may appear that the future course of U.S. foreign policy is crystal-clear and that only one path is open. In truth, the content and conduct of American foreign policy will remain contested. As we saw in Chapter 2, multiple strategies are available for meeting the terrorist challenge. There is also the need to look "beyond bin Laden" in thinking about how to reshape American foreign policy from its cold war foundations.[1] Care must be taken in doing so, for not everything has changed in world politics because of these attacks and the options to choose from may be less than we think.[2]

Those seeking change will invoke the national interest in justifying their calls for action. Yet as we saw in Chapter 2, beneath the coherence of this phrase is a complex array of individuals and institutions competing for positions of prominence in setting values and priorities. The ascendancy of one constellation of political interests does not mark their permanent triumph nor mean an end to efforts to alter the foreign policy agenda. Broad-based support for military action—even war—in the period immediately following the terrorist attack does not mean an end to the isolationist impulse or a permanent rejection of Wilsonianism.

The makers of American foreign policy are not operating in totally unprecedented territory in making these choices. Both after World War I and World War II it faced the challenge of constructing an international system in which the United States would be secure and prosper. Having emerged from the cold war as the sole remaining superpower and having defeated Saddam

Hussein in the Iraq War, the core foreign policy problem facing the United States is constructing a "victor's strategy": one that orders the world in such a way that it does not provoke a major war.[3] The great danger is that we will succumb to the "victory disease" and rely upon strategies that brought victory but are now inappropriate because of changed circumstances.

Constructing a strategy that avoids falling victim to the victory disease begins with a vision of the proper role that the United States should play in world politics. It presumes that choice exists. This choice may not be unlimited. Limitations on resources may create a frustrating gap between what U.S. foreign policy can aspire to and what it can accomplish. Choice also may be severely constrained by such factors as past foreign policy actions or inaction, the amount of time available within which to act, as well as accident and chance.

We close our treatment of U.S. foreign policy by introducing nine competing visions. The differences between them are many, but there are also points of overlap. We ask three questions of each alternative future: (1) What is the primary threat to U.S. national security? (2) What responsibility does the United States have to other states? and (3) What responsibility does the United States have to the global community? The answers given reflect different views about the degree to which the United States should be involved in world politics, how much power it possesses, and the extent to which the post–cold war world will differ from its predecessor. For each alternative future, we will also give a brief statement on its view of the war on terrorism.

Alternative Futures

THE UNITED STATES AS AN ORDINARY STATE

For some, the key to the future is realizing that foreign policy can no longer be conducted on the assumption of American uniqueness or that U.S. actions stand between anarchy and order. The American century is over, and the challenge facing policy makers is no longer that of managing alliances, deterring aggression, or ruling over the international system. It is now one of adjusting to a new role orientation, one in which the United States is an "ordinary state."[4] The change in outlook is necessary because international and domestic trends point to the declining utility of a formula-based response to foreign policy problems be they rooted in ideology, concepts of power politics, or some vision of regional orders. Governments ruling over internally divided societies and those ruling over unified populations are finding themselves forced to pursue narrowly defined national interests at the expense of international collaborative and cooperative efforts. In this altered environment, flexibility, autonomy, and impartiality are to be valued over one-sided commitments, name-calling, and efforts at the diplomatic, military, or economic isolation of states.

As an ordinary state the United States would not define its interests so rigidly that their defense would require unilateral American action. If the use of force is necessary, it should be a truly multilateral effort; and if others are unwilling to act, there is no need for the United States to assume the full burden of the commitment. Stated as a rule: "The United States should not be prepared, on its own, and supported solely by its own means, to perform tasks that most other states would not undertake."[5] Ordinariness does not, however, mean passivity, withdrawal, or a purely defensive approach to foreign policy problems. The quality of U.S. participation in truly multilateral efforts to solve international problems will be vital because the core ingredients to international influence in the future will be found in the fields where the United States is a leader: economics, diplomacy, and technology. The goal of these collaborative efforts should be to "create and maintain a world in which adversaries will remain in contact with one another and where compromises are still possible."[6] The three primary areas for such efforts (and thus for U.S. foreign policy) are to bring about a balance between Russia and the West, the Arab oil producers and the consuming states, and the rich and the poor states. To summarize, in the Ordinary State perspective:

1. The greatest threat to U.S. national security lies in trying to do too much and in having too expansive a definition of its national interest.

2. The United States' responsibility to other states must be proportionate and reciprocal to that which other states have to the United States.

3. The United States' responsibility to the global community is to be a good global citizen—nothing more and nothing less.

The imagery advanced by the Ordinary State perspective is one most Americans find troubling. Its denial of American uniqueness; its lack of optimism; its focus on restraints rather than opportunities; and its admonition to not try to do too much all run against the traditional American approach to world politics. For that reason it is a perspective that is unlikely to be endorsed (at least by this name) by politicians. At the same time, it is a perspective on the future that cannot be dismissed. Political leaders must acknowledge it because it taps into a feeling shared by many Americans that while the United States should not retreat into isolationism it should not be the first to take risks in places such as Bosnia, Somalia, and Haiti. Its admonition not to undertake herculean tasks also resonates well in some portions of the scholarly community. Ronald W. Pruessen, for example, in comparing the 1950s with the 1990s notes that one reason for the failure of American foreign policy at the earlier time was the overly optimistic "game plan" that the Eisenhower administration sought to execute.[7]

From the Ordinary State perspective, the war on terrorism happened because the United States did not follow its guidelines. Bin Laden's anger was directed at the United States above all others because it stationed troops on Saudi territory in carrying out the Persian Gulf War and was the dominant external power in the Middle East. These excesses need to be corrected in fighting the war on terrorism if future attacks are to be avoided or their likelihood minimized. Collaborative and proportionate action with others is needed regardless of whether it occurs in the context of the United Nations or in an ad hoc coalition. As in the 1950s, once again the primary danger facing the United States is the attempt to implement an overly optimistic game plan.

REFORMED AMERICA

According to proponents of the Reformed America perspective, U.S. foreign policy has traditionally been torn between pursuing democratic ideals and empire.[8] The United States wants peace—but only on its own terms; the United States supports human rights—but only if its definitions are used; the United States wants to promote third world economic growth—but only if it follows the U.S. model and does not undermine U.S. business interests abroad. Historically, the thrust toward empire (whether it is called containment, détente, or trilateralism) has won out, and democratic ideals have been sacrificed or only given lip service. Whether it is foreign aid, human rights, environmental protection, or arms control, U.S. policy makers have given highest priority to maintaining the United States' position of dominance in the international system and promoting the economic well-being of U.S. corporations.[9]

The need now exists to reverse this pattern. Democratic ideals must be given primary consideration in the formulation and execution of U.S. foreign policy. Not doing so invites future Vietnams and runs the risk of undermining the very democratic principles the United States stands for. Foreign policy and domestic policy are not seen as two separate categories. They are held to be inextricably linked together, and actions taken in one sphere have an impact on behavior and policies in the other. Bribery of foreign officials leads to bribery of U.S. officials; an unwillingness to challenge human rights violations abroad reinforces the acceptance of discrimination and violations of civil rights at home; and a lack of concern for the growing disparity in economic wealth on a global basis leads to an insensitivity to the problems of poverty in the United States.

The Reformed America perspective demands global activism from the United States. The much heralded decline in American power is not seen as being so great as to prevent the United States from exercising a predominant global influence. Moreover, the United States is held to have a moral and political responsibility to lead by virtue of its comparative wealth and power. The danger to be avoided is inaction brought on by the fear of failure. The United States cannot be permitted to crawl into a shell of isolationism or to let itself be "Europeanized" into believing that there are limits to its power and accepting the world "as it is." The power needed for success in creating what amounts to a new world order that is faithful to traditional American democratic values is not the ability to dominate others but to renew the American commitment to justice, opportunity, and liberty. In sum, the Reformed America perspective holds that:

1. The primary threat to U.S. national security is a continued fixation on military problems and an attachment to power-politics thinking.
2. The United States' responsibility to other states is great provided they are truly democratic, and the United States must seek to move those that are not in that direction.
3. The United States' responsibility to the global community is also great and centers on the creation of an international system conducive to the realization of traditional America values.

The values underlying this perspective were widely embraced in the post–cold war period as many commentators urged presidents to move more aggressively toward a neo-Wilsonian foreign policy. G. John Ikenberry, for example, asserts that a liberal grand strategy for foreign policy can be constructed around assumptions about how democracy, economic interdependence, international institutions, and political identity interact to create stable political orders.[10]

Both advocates and critics of the Reformed America perspective wrestle with the question of what specific courses of action and instruments of foreign policy further this vision of the future. Military power tends to be rejected, yet many neo-Wilsonians are adamant supporters of humanitarian interventions. Economic sanctions are a preferred option, yet they have been condemned as having "contributed to more deaths that all the weapons of mass destruction throughout history" during the post–cold war period alone.[11] Even international institutions are sometimes cited as often contributing to international problems rather than being part of the solution.

With regard to the war on terrorism, the Reformed America perspective stresses the need to place primary attention on the causes of terrorism. Victory will not be achieved solely on the battlefield. Craig Eisendrath suggests that the emphasis on military power be replaced by an agenda centered on strengthening human rights and promoting economic and social development.[12]

THE UNITED STATES AS A GLOBAL MANAGER

According to the Global Manager perspective, the key issues in world politics no longer revolve around power politics. They are rooted in dynamics growing from economic integration and globalization. When first put forward as an alternative organizing principle to power politics, interdependence tended to be treated as a positive force for international cooperation. The same was true for globalization. It would bring economic efficiency and prosperity to all corners of the globe. As we have gained experience in living with the political and economic realities of interdependence and globalization, we now recognize that neither has succeeded in bringing an end to international conflict. Responsibility for causing and fixing financial crises, trade disputes, resource shortages, environmental degradation, and the sociopolitical effects of international economic activity are now points of contention and conflict.

From the Global Manager perspective, the challenge facing the United States today is quite traditional. It has always been the task of the dominant economic power to structure and manage global economic relations. The problem today is that the depth of interdependence and pace of globalization has created an international order that frustrates both traditional unilateral exercises of economic power as well as management by committee. The need is to develop a new style of leadership.

Commentators have sought various ways to capture and express the essence of this new leadership style. One asserts that the United States must learn to lead by example and be the first to offer concessions.[13] Another speaks of the need to be an honest broker. Doing so requires not only a clear vision of the future but also earning the trust of other states through one's actions.[14] Still another speaks of the need for the United States to enter into a "constitutional bargain" with other states.[15] It can do so by joining international institutions whose rules and operating procedures place limits on its exercise of power. By accepting these constraints, the United States will lessen fears of domination and abandonment. Its use of power will become open and predictable. In sum, the Global Manager perspective holds that:

1. The primary threats to U.S. national security are economic in nature and stem from the growing pace of global interdependence.

2. The United States has a responsibility to help other states deal with their economic problems, but it cannot solve these problems for them. Its first concern must be to position itself so that others will follow its lead.

3. The United States' responsibility to the world community is great because its economic well-being is inseparable from the well-being of all states.

Glimpses of the Global Manager orientation to American foreign policy come through quite clearly in efforts to create and expand a North American Free Trade Zone and to establish the World Trade Organization and work for China's membership in that organization. It is less evident, or missing, in the continued ad hoc system of crisis management that oversees the international monetary system, in trade conflicts with Europe and Japan, and in an unwillingness to participate in the Kyoto Protocol.

The Global Manager perspective faces two primary challenges with regard to the war on terrorism. The first is to demonstrate that the Iraq War was not primarily about oil as many contend. The second is to demonstrate that globalization and its negative political and social externalities can be managed. Doing so requires moving forward with the Doha WTO Talks and incorporating into the agenda a heightened sensitivity for the concerns of Southern states that have been told the road to growth and prosperity lies with participating in the international economic system because it is from these states that many of the foot soldiers of terrorism are recruited and the charges of western imperialism find a receptive audience.

PRAGMATIC AMERICA

The Pragmatic America perspective holds that the United States can no longer afford foreign policies that are on the extreme ends of the political spectrum. Neither crusades nor isolationism serve America well. In the words of long-time strategist and policy maker James Schlesinger, what is needed in U.S. foreign policy is "selectivity."[16] The United States, he argues, must avoid impulse and image in formulating foreign policy. What is needed is a strong dose of moderation in means and ends. Above all else, the end of the cold war is seen as vindicating a policy of moderation.[17] As to ends, some world problems require U.S. attention, but not all do. The United States must recognize that the American national interest is not identical to the global interest and that not all problems lend themselves to permanent resolution. The most pressing issue on the agenda is for the United States to develop a set of criteria for identifying these problems and then acting in moderation to protect American interests.

A certain amount of overlap exists between the Global Manager and Pragmatic America perspectives. Both emphasize a utilitarian outlook on world politics and recognize the lessened ability of military force to solve foreign policy problems. They differ in their view of what needs to be managed. Instead of economics, the Pragmatic America perspective sees military problems as continuing to be the most threatening ones facing the United States. The nature of these problems is not what it used to be and thus the remedies must also differ. President Clinton's first Director of Central Intelligence R. James Woolsey pointed out that while the cold war dragon represented by the Soviet Union has been slain, the world confronting the United States is now populated by large numbers of poisonous snakes. For many who embrace this view, the most effective means of countering those snakes deemed to be threatening to the United States is through some form of collective action instead of by unilateral or bloc-based moves. One national security practitioner suggests that the ideal practical method for moving forward is the creation of international posses.[18] Just as in the old American West, when security threats present themselves the United States (the sheriff) should organize and deputize a posse of like-minded states that will end the threat. It will then disband. This is far less expensive politically and militarily than acting through standing alliances such as NATO or international organizations such as the United Nations. In sum, the Pragmatic America perspective holds that:

1. The primary threats to U.S. national security continue to be military in nature.

2. The United States has a responsibility to other states on a selective basis and only to the extent that threats to the political order of those states would lessen American security.

3. The United States' responsibility to the global community is limited. More pressing is a sense of responsibility to key partners whose cooperation is necessary to manage a threatening international environment.

President George H. W. Bush in his farewell foreign policy address argued for a position that is consistent with this view.[19] Warning against becoming isolationist, Bush asserted that the United States can influence the future but that "it need not respond to every outrage of violence." It cannot be the police officer of the world but must be prepared to act militarily. He went on to note that no formula exists that tells with precision when and where to intervene. "Each and every case is unique. To adopt rigid criteria would guarantee mistakes involving American interests and lives. . . . Similarly we cannot always decide in advance which interests will require our using military force." When force is used, Bush urged that the mission be clear and achievable, that a realistic plan exist, and that equally realistic criteria be established for withdrawing U.S. forces.

The Pragmatic America perspective is seen by some as well suited for an international system in a state of flux. Rigidly applied guiding principles such as containing communism or spreading democracy are held to be of little value in a world where change is the dominant condition. At the same time, its measured approach to solving foreign policy problems is also a fundamental weakness in the Pragmatic America perspective. Because pragmatism can be interpreted differently by different people, the policy it produces tends to move forward in a series of disjointed steps. The result is that whereas defenders see it as producing flexibility and adaptability, detractors see in it a foreign policy by lottery in which the past provides little guidance for friends or enemies as they seek to anticipate America's position.

From the Pragmatic America perspective, success in the war on terrorism demand selectivity with regard to goals, means and targets.[20] Stability is a more reasonable and achievable goal than is democratization. Multilateral action is less expensive monetarily and politically than unilateralism. Distinctions need to be made both with regard to terrorists and those who support them. Military success in Afghanistan and Iraq does not portend victory against North Korea, Syria, or Iran. For its advocates, only by moving to a post-crusading foreign policy can the United States come to enjoy true security.

NEOCONTAINMENT

The Neocontainment perspective takes issue with the assertion that a fundamental change has taken place in the nature of world politics.[21] Neither the overall stake of the United States in the makeup of the international system nor its underlying dynamics are different from those that confronted U.S. policy makers in the years immediately following World War II. World politics continues to be governed by considerations of (military) power politics. In the early post–cold war period, Russia was seen as the primary threat to national security that needed to be contained. Zbigniew Brzezinksi, President Carter's national security adviser, asserted that talk of an American-Russian partnership was premature. It was based on flawed assumptions regarding the prospects for democracy there and an incorrect reading of Russian strategic goals. From the Neocontainment perspective Russian foreign policy continued to be driven by an imperialist impulse that extended beyond the territory around its borders. A premature and overly enthusiastic embrace of Russia was held to be dangerous because it could cause the United States and its allies to squander all that has been accomplished in Europe since the end of the cold war.

Whereas for some the prospect of a resurgent Russia remains the principal national security threat to the United States, others have come to see China in this light. Just as with Russia, China possesses a strong historical sense of mission that places it at the center of regional, if not world, politics. Proponents of Neo-Containment see China's military and economic power as approaching a critical mass that will propel it into a position where its interests in regional domination will clash with the United States' interest in a balanced Asia. They note that should conflicts break out, the United States will be at a strategic disadvantage due to the great distance it must travel in projecting power and the lack of military bases and staging areas in the Pacific. For this reason, they oppose policies designed to promote U.S. investment in China and the transfer of technology to China.

Advocates of the Neocontainment perspective argue for a policy built upon the conceptual foundation that underlay the cold war doctrine of containment. Most pointedly this involves basing political relationships on power and not on notions of transnational common interests. It also involves a recognition that international stability is best assured by a foreign policy that seeks to establish a balance of power among states and to offset the military power of potentially hegemonic states. Thus, a key point of similarity between the old and new containment doctrines is the emphasis on delineating lines beyond which Russian or Chinese domination is not to extend.

In sum, Neocontainment holds that:

1. The primary threats to U.S. national security continue to emanate from quite traditional sources and call for a buildup of U.S. military power to offset that possessed by a potentially hostile superpower.
2. The United States' responsibility to other states is real but limited to its core allies.
3. The United States' responsibility to the global community is minimal. A balance-of-power system is held to exist, and the primary responsibility of the United States is to act in a manner consistent with its basic principles.

Critics of Neocontainment come from two quarters. Not unexpectedly, one set argues that Neocontainment misreads the extent to which the international system has been transformed, making balance-of-power thinking obsolete. A second group of critics agrees with the concept of containment but disagrees on the question of who is to be contained. It is not clear to all strategists that Russia is the primary threat to the United States. Colin Gray speaks of the likely need for the United States to intervene in Europe in order to support Russia and Britain against a continental bloc led by Germany.[22] Others have identified Japan as the primary future national security threat to the United States.

With regard to the war on terrorism advocates of neocontainment maintain that there is no reason to abandon this strategy in spite of what its critics say.[23] Robert Hutchings warns against falling into "we" versus "they" pattern of thinking in combating terrorism, where it is taken as a given that no shared values exist so that the application of brute force is the only policy option.[24] Just as was the case with the Soviet Union and communism, containing terrorism will be a long-term undertaking and the zealotry of the present generation of leaders will not determine the ultimate outcome. For Graham Allison and Andrei Kokshin this strategy begins with an U.S.–Russian-led alliance against nuclear terrorism.[25]

TRIUMPHANT AMERICA

Those who embrace the Triumphant America perspective on the future see the post-cold war world as a dangerous place and believe that a new strategic environment confronts the United States. But, unlike many, they see the world as having become unipolar rather than multipolar. The alternative to American unipolarity is held to be chaos, not an eighteenth-century balance of power among mature European states. The roots of today's chaos are found in the proliferation of weapons of mass destruction throughout the third world. Iraq represents the prototypical threat with North Korea and Libya not far behind.

From the Triumphant America perspective, the United States emerged from the cold war as the clear winner, and the end of the Persian Gulf War symbolized the beginning of a Pax Americana. It will take a generation before new power centers emerge that are capable of challenging the United States for preeminence. Only the United States possesses the military, economic, and diplomatic resources to intervene decisively in conflicts around the world. That the United States possesses this ability does not mean that it should involve itself in every conflict. As Charles Krauthammer, the leading exponent of this perspective, notes, primacy places great burdens on the United States. It must "make the connection between America's moral and geopolitical standing."[26] This connection is necessary because the American peace cannot rest on power alone. It must be acquiesced to by the nations of the world or the United States will find itself encountering the kind of resistance that marked the Soviet cold war rule of Eastern Europe. However, when the United States chooses to intervene it must do so in a "robust" fashion. It must act decisively and unashamedly. When possible it should act with allies in a multilateral setting, but it must not hesitate to act unilaterally if it is the right thing to do.

In sum, the Triumphant America perspective holds that:

1. The primary threats to U.S. national security stem from the proliferation of weapons of mass destruction. There are no states equal in power to the United States.
2. The United States' responsibility to other states is limited and determined by American values and interests as it defines them.
3. The United States has a responsibility to the world community that stems from its ability to lay down the rules of world order and enforce them.

Putting these principles into prescriptive policy advice, Krauthammer opposed the Clinton administration's policy in Somalia.[27] Referring to Somalia as a place for "Utopians," he argued that the United States is not in the business of nation-building. "It is bad enough playing cop to the world. Playing God is crazy." He went on to argue that with the passing of the immediate humanitarian crisis there were no U.S. interests at stake in Somalia. U.S. policy should be "to stay in Somalia just long enough to punish Aidid—preferably by killing him—to show one does not murder four American soldiers with impunity. Then get out."

In Krauthammer's view the post–9/11 era has produced the first crisis in American unilateralism, the foundation of the triumphant America perspective.[28] At the center of that crisis is how to respond to the proliferation of weapons of mass destruction. Iraq was the prototype of that threat. The status quo oriented nature of the Triumphant America perspective leads it to be deeply concerned that the war on terrorism will result in an overextension of American power that will lead to its decline and the rise of challengers. Equally troubling is the prospect of an inadequate response that will not protect American hegemony.

AMERICAN CRUSADER

At base, the Triumphant America perspective is status quo oriented. It sees the United States having won the cold war and now intent upon enjoying the fruits of its victory as the dominant global power. Threats are to be met forcefully, but there is no sense of mission or global purpose behind these actions. The concern is with protecting narrowly and self-defined American interests and prerogatives.

The American Crusader perspective starts from the same power premise as Triumphant America but rejects its relatively complacent view of the state of world politics. This perspective adds a sense of global mission and purpose to American dominance that is rooted in the perception of real and pressing security threats. Unlike the Reformed America perspective, the American Crusader perspective does not act so much out of a sense of shared humanity as out of a sense of historical mission. It builds upon an important strain in the American national style that defines security in absolute terms. The objective is "unconditional surrender." As James Chace and Caleb Carr observe, "for more than two centuries the United States has aspired to a condition of perfect safety from foreign threats" real and imagined.[29] Unlike the Reformed American perspective, the American Crusader perspective identifies military power as the instrument of choice. It is rooted firmly in that part of the American national style that rejects compromise and seeks engineering and permanent solutions to political problems.

Faint echoes of the American Crusader perspective can be found in post–World War II foreign policy. During the Eisenhower administration, some commentators called for rolling back the iron curtain, feeling that containment was too passive and accommodating a strategy. During the Persian Gulf War there was a moment when defeating Saddam Hussein had the characteristics of a crusade, at least at a rhetorical level. The American Crusader perspective burst upon the scene with full force following the terrorist attacks on the World Trade Center and the Pentagon.

In sum, the American Crusader perspective holds that:

1. The international system holds real and immediate threats to American national security that must be unconditionally defeated.
2. The United States has a responsibility to help other states that are allies in its cause because their security increases American security.
3. The United States' responsibility to the international community is great, but how that responsibility is defined is a matter for the United States to determine based on its historical traditions.

There are some who share the American Crusader's view that the international system contains immediate and serious threats to American security but question its wisdom. One concern expressed is that it overlooks the fact that superpower status does not convey total power to the United States. The challenge of bringing means and ends into balance is an ongoing one. A second concern is that by acting in this manner the United States may hasten its own decline. Rather than stay on the American "bandwagon" as an ally, second-order states may decide that since they too may become the object of an American crusade it is necessary to build up their own power and balance that of the United States.

Victories in the war on terrorism against Afghanistan and Iraq confirm the correctness of their position to supporters of American Crusader perspective. For American Crusaders the alternative to American hegemony is not multipolarity but "the anarchic nightmare of a new dark age."[30] And, American hegemony only makes sense if it is driven by transformational goals that are defined by the United States. As Michael Ledeen comments, "the only truly realistic American foreign policy is an ideological one that seeks to advance democratic revolutions wherever and whenever possible."[31] Consistent with this outlook Michael McFaul proposes a "Liberty Doctrine" that places the promotion of individual freedom as the center of America's foreign policy agenda today.[32]

AMERICA THE BALANCER

Out of a conviction that unipolarity is bound to give way to a multipolar distribution of power in the international system, some commentators argue that the prudent course of action is to adopt the role of a balancer today. The United States needs to stand apart from others yet be prepared to act in concert with them. It cannot and should not become a rogue superpower acting on its own impulses and imposing its vision on the world.

The starting point of wisdom from this perspective is that not all problems are threatening to the United States or require its involvement. It possesses a considerable amount of freedom to define its interests. In addition, the United States must recognize that one consequence of having put a global security umbrella in place is that it has discouraged other states and regional organizations from taking responsibility for preserving international stability. This must be reversed. Others must be encouraged to act in defense of their own interests. Finally, the United States must learn to live with uncertainty. Absolute security is an unattainable objective and one that only produces imperial overstretch.

In sum, the America as Balancer perspective holds that:

1. The primary national security threats to the United States are self-inflicted. They take the form of a proliferation of security commitments designed to protect America's economic interests.
2. The United States has a limited responsibility to other states because the burden for protecting a state's national interests falls upon that state.
3. The United States' responsibility to the global community is limited. American national interests and the maintenance of global order are not identical.

Christopher Layne provides a rationale for the role of balancer as part of a strategy of strategic independence.[33] He argues that a return to multipolarity is inevitable. Trying to reassert or preserve American preeminence and suppress the emergence of new powers is held to be futile. There is thus little reason for the United States to become deeply involved in the affairs of other states on a routine basis. In spite of this inevitable move toward multipolarity, Layne sees no reason to change America's long-standing foreign policy concern with the rise of a hegemony in Europe. What is needed is a hedging strategy, one that will allow the United States to realize this goal without provoking others into uniting against it or accelerating their separate pursuits of power. Blessed by its geopolitical location, Layne believes that the answer lies in adopting the position of an offshore balancer. The United States is positioned to allow global and regional power balances to ensure its strategic independence. Only when others prove incapable of acting to block the ascent of a challenging hegemony should the United States step in to affect the balance of power. Given its continued power resources, such an intervention is held likely to be decisive.

One issue that needs to be confronted by advocates of the America the Balancer perspective is how to most effectively exercise American military power. Traditionally, war was the mechanism by which a balance-of-power system preserved stability in the international system. Commentators positioned across the political spectrum have raised the question of whether wars can continue to play this role on a large scale. If they cannot, then how is the balancer to enforce its will? One possibility is that rather than using American power to deter or defeat an adversary, America the Balancer will play a central role in compelling adversaries to change their behavior. The distinction is potentially important. One commentator who has looked at compellence suggests that it is more of a police task than deterrence, which is a military task.

For Layne the war on terrorism demonstrates the failure of America's strategy of maintaining its security through the possession of an overwhelming military, political, and economic preponderance of power compared to others.[34] The attacks of 9/11 demonstrate that rather than make the United States secure, preponderance leads to insecurity. For him, the issue is not defeating the Taliban or Saddam Hussein but what comes next. The answer is to "pass the buck" and let other countries take care of themselves intervening only from a distance.

DISENGAGED AMERICA

The final alternative future put forward here calls for the United States to selectively yet thoroughly withdraw from the world.[35] The Disengaged America perspective sees retrenchment as necessary because the international system is becoming increasingly inhospitable to U.S. values and unresponsive to efforts at management or domination. Increasingly, the choices facing U.S. foreign policy will be ones of choosing what kinds of losses to avoid. Optimal solutions to foreign policy problems will no longer present themselves to policy makers, and if they do, domestic constraints will prevent policy makers from pursuing such a path. In the Disengaged America perspective, foreign policy must become less of a lance—a tool for spreading values—and more of a shield—a minimum set of conditions behind which the United States can protect its values and political processes.[36]

Becoming disengaged means that the United States will have to learn to live in a "second-best world," one that is not totally of its liking but one in which it can get by. Allies will be fewer in number, and those that remain will have to do more to protect their own security and economic well-being.

Nonintervention will be the rule for the United States and self-reliance the watchword for others. The United States must be prepared to "let" some states be dominated and to direct its efforts at placing space between the falling dominoes rather than trying to define a line of containment. In the realm of economics, the objective should be to move toward autarchy and self-sufficiency so that other states cannot manipulate or threaten the United States. If the United States cannot dominate the sources of supply, it must be prepared to "substitute, tide over, (and) ride out" efforts at resource manipulation.[37] World order concerns must also take a back seat in U.S. foreign policy. As George Kennan has said about the food–population problem, "We did not create it and it is beyond our power to solve it."[38] Kennan argues that the United States needs to divest itself of its guilt complex and accept the fact that there is really very little that the United States can do for the third world and very little that the third world can do for the United States. In sum, the Disengaged America perspective holds that:

1. The major threat to U.S. national security comes from an overactive foreign policy. Events beyond U.S. borders are not as crucial to U.S security as is commonly perceived, and moreover, the United States has little power to influence their outcome.

2. The United States' responsibility to other states is minimal. The primary responsibility of the United States is to its own economic and military security.

3. The United States' responsibility to the global community is also minimal. The issues on the global agenda, especially as they relate to the third world, are not the fault of the United States, and the United States can do little to solve them.

Consistent with the Disengaged America perspective, Earl Ravenal asserts that in a period of international nonalignment such as the one we are now in, traditional principles of defense planning are largely irrelevant.[39] Military power, for example, should no longer be employed to further human rights or economic principles beyond American borders. Rather than pursue military goals, American foreign policy must concentrate on protecting American lives and property, the territorial integrity of the United States, and the autonomy of its political system. Consistent with these priorities, American military power would only be used for three purposes: (1) to defend the approaches to U.S. territory; (2) to serve as second-chance forces to be used if deterrence fails or unexpected threats arise; and (3) to provide finite essential deterrence against the United States and its forces overseas.

Ravenal's assessment of how American foreign policy needs to be changed is shared by other analysts at the Cato Institute, a foreign policy think tank with which he is affiliated. Doug Bandow urges the United States to remain culturally, economically, and politically engaged in the world, but insists that it curtail foreign aid programs and bring its troops home.[40] Ted Galen Carpenter, its director, asserts that the primary responsibility of American foreign policy is to "guard the security and liberty of the American people. Washington has neither a constitutional nor moral writ to play Don Quixote and attempt to rectify all the ills of the world."[41] Or, in the words of Pat Buchanan, "America First—and Second, and Third."[42]

The Disengaged America perspective has few qualms with the need to defend American interests or take action unilaterally and forcefully in doing so. Preemption as a means for dealing with terrorists is not a repugnant strategy to them. What concerns them is that the war on terrorism has as its objective not simply the defeat of the enemy but their transformation. Nation-building has always been seen by supporters of the Disengaged America perspective as a fool's errand, and they look with great trepidation on the prospects of doing so in Afghanistan and Iraq. Rather than try to impose order on the Middle East or other hotbeds of terrorism, the goal of American foreign policy should be to make these areas economically and strategically irrelevant.

The Future

Agreement cannot be expected on any of these (or other) visions of American foreign policy in the near future. Deciding which among them is best suited to protect and further American interests is only one of the challenges confronting the United States today. A second and equally important challenge is obtaining the leadership resources necessary to translate a desired strategic vision into policy.[43] This challenge operates at several different levels. At a structural level, it entails acquiring the power resources necessary to lead. Whether these resources primarily are military or economic in nature will depend on the vision selected, but traditional international relations theorizing suggests that little will be accomplished unless the United States has the power to get others to follow. Realizing many of these visions will demand more than just possessing the ability to dominate others, it will also depend upon the ability to get others to follow in multilateral settings. Leadership at the institutional level will require that the United States develop a capacity for fostering cooperation among states by framing issues so that joint action is possible and providing the resources needed to implement solutions.

Finally, leadership will be necessary at the situational level. Here, the challenge will be to find creative solutions to problems, to find "good people" with insight into human nature and the dynamics of world politics so that opportunities for action are not lost.

Notes

1. Stephen Walt, "Beyond bin Laden," *International Security,* 26 (2003), 56–78.
2. Eliot Cohen, "History and Hyperpower," *Foreign Affairs,* 83 (July/August 2004), 49–63.
3. James Kurth, "The American Way of Victory," *National Interest,* 128 (2000), 5–16.
4. Richard Rosecrance, "New Directions?" in Richard Rosecrance (ed.), *America as an Ordinary Country: U.S. Foreign Policy and the Future* (Ithaca, N.Y.: Cornell University Press, 1976), pp. 245–66; and reprinted in Jeffrey Salamon, James P. O'Leary, and Richard Shultz (eds.), *Power, Principles, and Interests* (Lexington, Mass.: Ginn, 1985), pp. 433–44.
5. Salamon, O'Leary, and Shultz (eds.), *Power, Principles, and Interests,* p. 443.
6. Ibid., p. 442.
7. Ronald W. Pruessen, "Beyond the Cold War—Again: 1955 and the 1990s," *Political Science Quarterly,* 108 (1993), 59–84.

8. On this theme, see Robert A. Isaak, *American Democracy and World Power* (New York: St. Martin's, 1977); and Robert C. Johansen, *The National Interest and the Human Interest: An Analysis of U.S. Foreign Policy* (Princeton, N.J.: Princeton University Press, 1980).

9. Johansen, *The National Interest and the Human Interest.*

10. G. John Ikenberry, "Why Export Democracy?" *Wilson Quarterly,* 23 (1999), 56–65.

11. John Mueller and Karl Mueller, "Sanctions of Mass Destruction," *Foreign Affairs,* 78 (1999), 43–53.

12. Craig Eisendrath, "U.S. Foreign Policy After September 11," *USA Today Magazine* (May 2002), 12–14.

13. On this theme, see Robert O. Keohane and Joseph S. Nye, *Power and Interdependence: World Politics in Transition* (Boston: Little, Brown, 1977); and Stanley Hoffman, *Primacy or World Order: American Foreign Policy Since the Cold War* (New York: McGraw-Hill, 1978).

14. Gary Wills, "The Bully of the Free World," *Foreign Affairs,* 78 (1999), 50–59.

15. G. John Ikenberry, "Getting Hegemony Right," *National Interest,* 29 (2001), 17–24.

16. James Schlesinger, "Quest for a Post Cold War Foreign Policy," *Foreign Affairs,* 72 (1992/93), 17–28.

17. Robert W. Tucker, "1989 and All That," in Nicholas X. Rizopoulos (ed.), *Sea-Changes: American Foreign Policy in a World Transformed* (New York: Council on Foreign Relations Press, 1990), 204–37.

18. Richard Haass, "Military Force: A User's Guide," *Foreign Policy,* 96 (1994), 21–38.

19. George Bush, "Remarks at the United States Military Academy," *Public Papers of the President* (Washington, D.C.: U.S. Government Printing Office, 1993), 2230–31.

20. Robert Art, *A Grand Strategy for America* (Ithaca, NY: Cornell University Press, 2003).

21. On this theme, see Robert W. Tucker, "The Purposes of American Power," *Foreign Affairs,* 59 (1980/81), 241–74.

22. Colin Gray, "Back to the Future: Russia and the Balance of Power," *Global Affairs,* 7 (1992), 41–52.

23. Robert Lieber, "The Folly of Containment," *Commentary,* 115 (April 2003), 15–21.

24. Robert Hutchings, "X + 9/11," *Foreign Policy,* 143 (July/August 2004), 70–3.

25. Graham Allison and Andrei Kokoshin, "The New Containment," *The National Interest,* 69 (2002), 35–43.

26. Charles Krauthammer, "The Unipolar Moment," *Foreign Affairs,* 70 (1990/91), 23–33.

27. Charles Krauthammer, "Playing God in Somalia," *Washington Post,* August 13, 1993.

28. Charles Krauthammer, "The Unipolar Moment Revisted," *The National Interest,* 70 (2002/2003), 5–18.

29. James Chace and Caleb Carr, *America Invulnerable* (New York: Summit Books, 1988), 318.

30. Niall Ferguson, "A World Without Power," *Foreign Policy,* 143 (July/August 2004), 32–9.

31. See his comments in "American Power-For What?" *Commentary,* 109 (January 2000), 21–47.

32. Michael McFaul, "The Liberty Doctrine," *Policy Review,* 112 (April/May 2002), 3–22.

33. Christopher Layne, "The Unipolar Illusion: Why Great Powers Will Rise," *International Security,* 17 (1993), 5–51.

34. Benjamin Schwarz and Christopher Layne, "A New Grand Strategy," *The Atlantic Monthly,* 289 (January 2002), 36–42.

35. On this theme, see Earl C. Ravenal, *Never Again: Learning from America's Foreign Policy Failures* (Philadelphia: Temple University Press, 1978).

36. Ibid., p. 15.

37. Ibid., p. xv.

38. George Kennan, *Cloud of Danger: Current Realities of American Foreign Policy* (Boston: Little, Brown, 1977), p. 32.

39. Earl Ravenal, "The Case for Adjustment," *Foreign Policy,* 81 (1990/91), 3–19.

40. Doug Bandow, "Keeping the Troops and Money at Home," *Current History,* 579 (January 1994), 8–13.

41. Ted Galen Carpenter, "Foreign Policy Peril: Somalia Set a Dangerous Precedent," *USA Today,* 121 (May 1993), 10–13.

42. Patrick Buchanan, "America First–and Second, and Third," *National Interest,* 19 (1990), 77–82.

43. G. John Ikenberry, "The Future of International Leadership," *Political Science Quarterly,* 111 (1996), 385–402.

── INDEX ──